THE NATURE OF GERMAN IMPERIALISM

The Environment in History: International Perspectives

Series Editors: Dolly Jørgensen, *University of Stavanger*; Christof Mauch, *LMU Munich*; Kieko Matteson, *University of Hawai'i at Mānoa*; Helmuth Trischler, *Deutsches Museum, Munich*

Volume 1
Civilizing Nature: National Parks in Global Historical Perspective
Edited by Bernhard Gissibl, Sabine Höhler, and Patrick Kupper

Volume 2
Powerless Science? Science and Politics in a Toxic World
Edited by Soraya Boudia and Natalie Jas

Volume 3
Managing the Unknown: Essays on Environmental Ignorance
Edited by Frank Uekötter and Uwe Lübken

Volume 4
Creating Wilderness: A Transnational History of the Swiss National Park
Patrick Kupper
Translated by Giselle Weiss

Volume 5
Rivers, Memory, and Nation-Building: A History of the Volga and Mississippi Rivers
Dorothy Zeisler-Vralsted

Volume 6
Fault Lines: Earthquakes and Urbanism in Modern Italy
Giacomo Parrinello

Volume 7
Re/Cycling Histories: Paths to Sustainability
Edited by Ruth Oldenziel and Helmuth Trischler

Volume 8
Disrupted Landscapes: State, Peasants and the Politics of Land in Postsocialist Romania
Stefan Dorondel

Volume 9
The Nature of German Imperialism: Conservation and the Politics of Wildlife in Colonial East Africa
Bernhard Gissibl

The Nature of German Imperialism

Conservation and the Politics of Wildlife in Colonial East Africa

Bernhard Gissibl

berghahn
NEW YORK · OXFORD
www.berghahnbooks.com

First published in 2016 by
Berghahn Books
www.berghahnbooks.com

© 2016, 2019 Bernhard Gissibl
First paperback edition published in 2019

All rights reserved. Except for the quotation of short passages
for the purposes of criticism and review, no part of this book
may be reproduced in any form or by any means, electronic or
mechanical, including photocopying, recording, or any information
storage and retrieval system now known or to be invented,
without written permission of the publisher.

Library of Congress Cataloging-in-Publication Data

A C.I.P. cataloging record is available from the Library of Congress

British Library Cataloguing in Publication Data

A catalogue record for this book is available from the British Library

ISBN 978-1-78533-175-6 hardback
ISBN 978-1-78920-492-6 paperback
ISBN 978-1-78533-176-3 ebook

Contents

List of Illustrations, Figures, and Maps	vi
Acknowledgements	viii
Note on Measurements and Currencies	xi
List of Abbreviations	xii
Introduction. Doorsteps in Paradise	1

Part I. Big Men, Big Game between Precolony and Colony

Chapter 1. Tusks, Trust, and Trade	35
Chapter 2. Seeing Like a State, Acting Like a Chief	67

Part II. The Making of Tanzania's Wildlife Conservation Regime

Chapter 3. Preserving the Hunt, Provoking a War	109
Chapter 4. Colony or Zoological Garden?	141
Chapter 5. The Imperial Game	178

Part III. Spaces of Conservation between Metropole and Colony

Chapter 6. Places of Deep Time	201
Chapter 7. Rivalry and Stewardship	232
Chapter 8. A Sense of Place	268
Epilogue. Germany's African Wildlife and the Presence of the Past	299
Appendix. *Synopsis of Game Ordinances in German East Africa, 1891–1914*	317
Select Bibliography	323
Index	349

Illustrations, Figures, and Maps

ILLUSTRATIONS

0.1. Remnants of the Siedentopf farm in Ngorongoro.
Picture taken by B Gissibl (2004).   3

1.1. Nyamwezi elephant hunters (c. 1912), Bildarchiv der Deutschen Kolonialgesellschaft, Universitätsbibliothek Frankfurt.   53

2.1. An elephant shot at Lehnin farm near Rutenganio (pre-1914). Moravian Archives Herrnhut.   77

3.1. Governor Adolf von Götzen, rhinoceros. Bildarchiv der Deutschen Kolonialgesellschaft, Universitätsbibliothek Frankfurt.   116

FIGURES

2.1. Ivory exports from German East Africa, 1888–1913.   68

2.2. Number and weight of tusks exported via the German East African ports, 1892–97.   71

3.1. Weight and amount of "fiscal ivory" auctioned by the German Main Customs Office, 1898–1913.   122

4.1. Sale of hunting licenses compared with population development, 1904–13.   145

MAPS

0.1. Map of Tanzania showing regions and ethnic groups. Courtesy of Cambridge University Press.   xiv

1.1. Types of ivory and regions of the ivory trade (*Deutsche Geographische Blätter* 1889).   45

3.1. The Mahenge military district, 1905. From *Deutscher Kolonialatlas mit Jahrbuch*, edited by the Deutsche Kolonialgesellschaft, Berlin, 1905.   124

3.2. Game reserves established in the region of the Maji Maji War (Reichskolonialamt, 1913).   127

6.1. Situation and extent of game reserves in German East Africa, 1 April 1912 (Reichskolonialamt, 1913).   220

Acknowledgements

It is an extremely gratifying duty to acknowledge all the moral, intellectual, and financial support I received ever since I started inquiring into Germany's historical relationship to Africa's wildlife over a decade ago. Research for this book would not have been possible without the generous assistance of the *Bischöfliche Studienförderung Cusanuswerk* and Jacobs University Bremen who supported this study with stipends and research grants. I also would like to express my gratitude to the German Historical Institute London, which enabled research in London and Oxford through a generous travel grant, and to the Tanzanian Commission for Science and Technology (COSTECH) for research clearance in the National Archives in Dar es Salaam. The revision of the manuscript has profited enormously from a fellowship in the hospitable and stimulating environment of the Rachel Carson Center for Environment and Society in Munich.

It is impossible to thank everyone who supported this project in the numerous libraries and archives I have consulted in Germany, Belgium, Britain, Kenya, Tanzania, and the United States. I owe the greatest deal to Julia Bergmann and her team at the Interlibrary Loan Department of Jacobs University Bremen, as well as to the staff of the University Library Mannheim. My work has also been greatly aided by Lucy McCann and her colleagues at the Commonwealth and African Manuscripts Collection of the Bodlein Library, Oxford, the British Library, Hannelore Landsberg at the Museum of Natural History Berlin, the Bundesarchiv Berlin, the library of the Deutsche Institut für tropische und subtropische Landwirtschaft Witzenhausen, the Leibniz-Institut für Länderkunde Leipzig, the Public Record Office at Kew, the Archives at the St Ottilien Archabbey, the Tanzania National Archives Dar es Salaam, and the University Library Dar es Salaam. Rolf Terkatz has kindly granted me access to the collection of Carl Georg Schillings in Düren.

During the years of tracking the traces of Africa's wildlife in German colonial history, I have been privileged to work with the most inspiring academic supervisors and mentors. More than anyone else, I am indebted to Johannes Paulmann, who has fanned my interest in the topic from the outset. His confidence in the project has been challenge and confirmation throughout the years. He shaped my thinking on imperial and transnational history in countless discussions, encouraged me to be bold when I hesitated, and to think twice when things seemed all too obvious. This book would have been impossible without his continuous advice, support, patience, and encouragement. John M MacKenzie has liberally shared his tremendous knowledge about the environmental history of empires. His enthusiasm about my research was more motivation than he can possibly imagine, and I am deeply obliged to his intellectual hospitality and his willingness to serve as external examiner on my dissertation committee. Christof Mauch has given much esteemed advice on this project ever since I presented a first paper at the Young Scholar's Forum at the German Historical Institute Washington in 2004. I am very grateful to him and the series editors for including my book in the "Environment in History" series. At Berghahn, I have been in the competent hands of Chris Chappell, Jessica Murphy and Johanna Wallner, who are to be warmly acknowledged for steering me through the publication process.

My views on colonial environmental history have benefited enormously from discussions in the environment and empire seminars, which William Beinart and Lotte Hughes invited me to attend at St Antony's College Oxford. I have also been fortunate to receive critical, yet benevolent feedback from the research colloquia of Franz-Josef Brüggemeier and Jens Ivo Engels, Jürgen Osterhammel, Joachim Radkau, Wolfram Siemann, Margit Szöllösi-Janze, and Cornel Zwierlein. Conversations with Julia Angster, Caroline Authaler, Dorothee Brantz, Jane Carruthers, Steven Fabian, Larissa Förster, Dominik Geppert, Bernd-Stefan Grewe, Madeleine Herren-Oesch, Sabine Höhler, Richard Hölzl, Dominik Hünniger, Cornelia Knab, Martin Knoll, Yusufu Lawi, Thomas Lekan, Isabella Löhr, Stefanie Michels, Jamie Monson, Mieke Roscher, Corey Ross, Felix Schürmann, Benedikt Stuchtey, Emily Wakild, Roland Wenzlhuemer, Hans-Peter Ziemek, and Jürgen Zimmerer have all provided valuable food for thought at various stages of research, and I am extremely grateful for their openness to think and discuss. Felicitas Becker, Jigal Beez, Jan-Georg Deutsch, and Michelle Moyd were most helpful navigators for the novice in East African history and kindly shared knowledge and research findings. Joseph Saleko was an expert and entertaining guide to East Africa's wildlife and provided indispensable assistance in the field while doing research in Tanzania. So did Rolf Baldus, then head of the Selous Conservation Programme. His practically informed take on East African wildlife conservation was a constant and eye-opening encouragement to see things differently, and I thoroughly appreciate the critical stimulus I received from him and a lifework dedicated to the conservation of Tanzania's wildlife heritage.

Many friends and colleagues in Munich, Bremen, Mannheim, and Mainz have been generous to share their time, their knowledge, and their ideas at various stages of research, writing, and revision. Heartfelt thanks go to Nils Freytag, Elisabeth Hüls, Stefan Jordan, Wolfgang Piereth, Marcus Pyka, Wolfram Siemann, and Christiane Weinmair, whose support, ideas and suggestions have all helped the project on its way in the nascent stages at the University of Munich. Franziska Deutsch, Sonja Kinzler, Daniel Leese, and Philippa Söldenwagner have been wonderful colleagues and critical discussants of methodologies, presentations, and paper drafts during the Bremen years. So were Sebastian Schickl, Gabriel Schimmeroth, Michael Vössing, and Helge Wendt at the University of Mannheim. I have unduly stretched the friendship and kindness of Hester Barron, Ulrike Lindner, Esther Möller, Glyn Prysor, Eva Maria Verst, and Katharina Wilkens who all helped improve the argument as careful and attentive readers of the whole manuscript or individual chapters. Katharina Niederau is to be thanked for conscientious proofreading and much esteemed help with formalities and endnotes. Through their continuous support, advice, and friendship, Hans-Werner Frohn, Patrick Kupper, Karl Borromäus Murr, Anna-Maria Pedron, Patrick Ramponi, and Andrea Rehling have contributed to this book in more ways than they probably realized. A cup of coffee in Bremen's Überseemuseum has been the beginning of a decade of lively discussion and shared thinking about environmental history with Anna-Katharina Wöbse. Her inspiring enthusiasm has left a deep imprint throughout this book, beyond her meticulous reading of the whole manuscript. Raphael Muturi, who has been my spirited tandem teacher of Kiswahili at Jacobs University Bremen, passed away far too young. His dedication as *mwalimu* will never be forgotten.

My deepest appreciation goes to my family, who enabled and supported my intellectual journey between Germany and East Africa more than can be adequately expressed here. Heidi has had to live with elephants for over a decade and has done so with great understanding, amazing patience, and steady encouragement. Since 2009, Emma and Jakob slowed down the finishing of this book with innumerable small and precious moments. My parents' generous and unconditional support during the years of my studies and beyond has been invaluable, and this book is but a small return. It is dedicated to them with profound gratitude.

Measurements and Currencies

The main currency in East Africa since about the mid nineteenth century was the Indian Rupee, which was accepted as official currency in the British and German East African colonies. Currency rates fluctuated widely, but 1 rupee was roughly equivalent to 1.3 (Reichs) marks, while 1 pound sterling (£) equaled 15 rupees.

The unit of weight used to measure ivory in Zanzibar and at the East African coast was the *frasila* (frasil), which equaled about 16.2 kilograms or 35 pounds.

Abbreviations

AA KA–Auswärtiges Amt, Kolonial-Abteilung (German Foreign Office, Colonial Department; until 1907)

ADJV–Allgemeiner Deutscher Jagdschutz-Verein

AMDAE–Archives Ministère des Affaires Etrangères, du Commerce extérieur et de la Coopération au Développement, Bruxelles

BA–Bezirksamt (District station)

BAK–Bundesarchiv Koblenz

BAB–Bundesarchiv Berlin-Lichterfelde

BAM–Bundesarchiv-Militärarchiv, Freiburg

BayHStA–Bayerisches Hauptstaatsarchiv, Munich

BNS–Bezirksnebenstelle (subdistrict office)

CBRM–community-based resource management

CIC–International Council for Game and Wildlife Conservation

CITES–Convention on International Trade in Endangered Species of Wild Fauna and Flora

CO–British Colonial Office

DITSL–Deutsches Institut für tropische und subtropische Landwirtschaft, Witzenhausen

DKG–Deutsche Kolonialgesellschaft

DOA–Deutsch-Ostafrika

DOAG–Deutsch-Ostafrikanische Gesellschaft

DSWA–Deutsch-Südwestafrika

FO–British Foreign Office

FOCP–Foreign Office Confidential Print

Gov–Government

GTZ–Gesellschaft für technische Zusammenarbeit
HUB–Humboldt Universität Berlin
IBEAC–Imperial British East Africa Company
IUCN–International Union for the Conservation of Nature
IUPN–International Union for the Protection of Nature
KNA–Kenya National Archives, Nairobi
LIL–Leibniz-Institut für Länderkunde, Leipzig
MAF–Ministry of Agriculture, Fisheries and Food
MfN–Museum für Naturkunde, Berlin
MMRP–Maji Maji Research Project
NCA–Ngorongoro Conservation Area
OBL–Oxford, Bodleian Library
PRO–Public Record Office, The National Archives, London
REM–Reiss-Engelhorn Museen, Mannheim
RKA–Reichskolonialamt (Colonial Office; after 1907)
SAD–Stadtarchiv Düren
SCP–Selous Conservation Programme
SRI–Serengeti Research Institute
SPWFE–Society for the Preservation of the Wild Fauna of the Empire
StAF–Staatsarchiv Freiburg
TNA–Tanzania National Archives, Dar es Salaam
VNP–Verein Naturschutzpark
WMA–Wildlife Management Area
WWF–World Wildlife Fund
ZGF–Zoologische Gesellschaft Frankfurt

Map 0.1. Map of Tanzania showing regions and ethnic groups. Courtesy of Cambridge University Press.

Introduction
Doorsteps in Paradise

With its roughly 250 square kilometers of fertile grass, and an amazing abundance of wildlife within its forested walls, the caldera of Ngorongoro counts among Tanzania's world-renowned wilderness areas. Like the adjacent Serengeti National Park or the Selous Game Reserve, Ngorongoro features on UNESCO's World Heritage list. Hundreds of thousands of tourists annually visit the crater for the promise of a spectacular game drive in a unique geological environment. So did I, one sunny morning in November 2004. My game drive was, however, also a journey into Ngorongoro's German history.

By midday, Joseph, my guide and driver, had taken me to the gate of the Ngorongoro Conservation Area (NCA). From there, the route follows a carefully orchestrated conservationist script. After forty-five minutes of ascent along a dusty and winding track road, the visitor is finally released into the openness of the rim. Here, at Heroes Point, visitors are provided with a commanding view over the silent vastness of the crater. Tiny dots of wildlife are scattered over the verdant grassland some 600 meters below. A monument at Heroes Point, unveiled in 1981, commemorates scientists, game wardens, and rangers who lost their lives in the conservation of Tanzania's wildlife treasure. A little further along the crater rim, the motorized traveler encounters the next memorial to conservation's heroes and the first reminder of German entanglement with the fate of Ngorongoro. An epitaph indicates the site of the graves of Bernhard and Michael Grzimek, the Frankfurt Zoo Director and his son. Their films and publications catapulted Serengeti and Ngorongoro into the limelight of international conservation in the late 1950s. The memorial reminds visitors that Michael Grzimek "gave all he possessed for the wild animals of Africa, including his life." Aged only 24, he died in a plane crash near Ngorongoro in January 1959 while conducting an aerial survey of wildlife numbers and migration patterns. His father, Bernhard Grzimek, is usually credited for coining the epithet of Ngorongoro as a "wonder of the world," a standard accolade reciprocated in many East Africa travel guides.[1] More importantly,

Grzimek's book and Oscar-winning documentary film *Serengeti Shall Not Die* (1959) made him an international conservationist celebrity with enormous influence on Tanzanian wildlife politics after independence. He did not only mastermind many of the decisions taken in the management of the Serengeti National Park and the NCA since the early 1960s, but also promoted the nexus between mass wildlife tourism, development, and conservation in national parks.[2] The revenue garnered from the films and conservationist campaigns in West Germany's mass media enabled his Frankfurt Zoological Society to develop into "the single most important funding body"[3] of conservation in the Serengeti and a key stakeholder in protected area management in Tanzania.[4]

Being thus reminded to whom visitors owed the opportunity to experience wildlife in Northwestern Tanzania, Joseph and I descended into the crater to watch wildlife. However, our first encounter on the crater floor was with a Maasai herder and his cattle. Upon my inquiry about the Maasai's presence and rights in the crater, Joseph told me about the multiple land-use philosophy behind the NCA. The Maasai, I learned, "are part of the ecosystem." Occasional conflicts between the requirements of cattle and wildlife notwithstanding, Joseph emphasized the benefits the Maasai had derived from tourism and the management principles of the NCA since its inception in 1959. Talking about the crater's fauna was an altogether easier task. Having trained at the renowned Mweka College of African Wildlife Management before he entered the business of wildlife tourism as a tour guide, Joseph knew everything about the species' different uses of the available forage and how food plants contributed to the functioning of the savanna ecosystem. After I had gazed in amazement at a cheetah prowling in front of a dozen safari cars and got tired of the ubiquitous wildebeest, I asked Joseph to take me to the remnants of the German Farm in Ngorongoro. His surprise at my request confirmed anthropologist Noel Salazar's observation that driver-guides usually skip this bit of the crater in order not to spoil tourist imaginaries of pristine nature.[5] Usually, visitors are spared the reminder of what was a most contested place in colonial debates about wildlife conservation prior to World War I.

The ruins hardly constitute a visual highlight. All that is left is some rubble of the foundation walls and the still recognizable doorsteps of the farmhouse. Yet, insignificant as these stones may seem, they are vestiges of the largely forgotten German colonial empire in Eastern Africa, a stumbling block of human history in "Africa's Garden Eden." The doorsteps of the past in the wildlife paradise of the present remind everyone that, had the German colonial government had its way back in 1914, the history of Ngorongoro might have taken an entirely different course.

Illustration 0.1. Remnants of the Siedentopf farm in Ngorongoro. Picture taken by B Gissibl (2004).

The Forgotten Past of Ngorongoro

Just over a century ago, the ruins near Munge Stream in the northwest of the crater belonged to what was an impressive farm by contemporary colonial standards. It consisted of a stone-built farmhouse, shed, and stable, and was owned by a certain Adolf Siedentopf, a German from the Prussian Province of Hannover. In April 1913, Siedentopf employed four whites, fifty-eight Maasai, and several dozen Iraqw to tend to a stock of around 1,000 cattle, 2,500 sheep, 40 donkeys, and 12 horses.[6] He shared the crater with abundant wildlife—contemporary estimates reckoned as much as 20,000 wildebeest, 1,500 zebras, several thousand of Kongonis and other smaller antelopes, plus the occasional rhinoceros[7]—and, until 1907, with several hundred Maasai pastoralists.

Before coming to Ngorongoro, Siedentopf had experimented with cotton cultivation and the breeding of livestock, donkeys, and ostriches in Sukuma near Lake Victoria. He probably discovered Ngorongoro while conducting trade in livestock and elephant tusks with Maasai intermediaries. In late 1904, Siedentopf approached the colonial government in Dar es Salaam to grant him pastureland in the crater for grand-scale cattle ranching. Thanks to its altitude, Ngorongoro featured a mild climate, was free from tsetse, and remote enough from the next governmental outpost to provide leeway for an enterprising settler. A number of Afrikaner families who had come from South Africa after the Anglo-Boer War also vied for agricultural land in the crater, but German district officials preferred to support a fellow national. Under the assumption that Siedentopf was backed by substantial capital from Germany, the government condoned his mercurial character and his notorious defiance of authority. In December 1904, he was allotted 6,000 hectares of pasture in Ngorongoro with the obligation to stock the land with 2,000 heads of cattle. Depending on the development of his enterprise, Siedentopf was promised a further 3,000 hectares for every 1,000 heads of cattle, up to a total of 30,000 hectares.[8] In early 1906, Adolf was joined by his brother Friedrich Wilhelm who established a separate farm at the southeastern end of the crater near Lerai Forest.

The Siedentopfs were expected to afforest parts of the crater floor, improve its pasture, and convert sizeable chunks of it into arable land.[9] Within a few years, Adolf erected a stone farmhouse, which he baptized "Soltau," after the small town in the Lüneburg Heath north of Hannover. The brothers introduced Australian eucalyptus and alfalfa, dug irrigation canals, created tracks for ox wagons, erected kraals for livestock, and imported breeding cattle from Kenya and South Africa. But their enterprise would never have prospered without hunting. Abundant elephants and wildebeest enabled them to enter into a flourishing regional trade in ivory and wildebeest tails, the latter being a cherished exchange commodity in Sukuma where they were used as bracelets, anklets, ornaments, and fly whisks for rainmakers and prophets. Ngorongoro's wealth of wildlife helped subsidize their fledgling farms, as a considerable part of the settlers' livestock was acquired in exchange for the products of their hunting.[10]

With the next German administrative post six days away, the Siedentopf brothers occupied a lone European outpost in the heart of Maasailand. The seminomadic, pastoralist Maasai were not the only ethnic group living in the highlands and drylands comprising the Great Rift Valley in the west, most of southern Kenya and today's Maasai steppe in central and eastern Tanzania. Nor were they the ones with the most ancient claims to it. Arriving at some point in the 1700s, they displaced other pastoralists from Ngorongoro and established a regional hegemony based upon transhumant pastoralism, specialized exchange economies, and the ruthless claim to all cattle. Ngorongoro developed into a site of particular cultural and spiritual significance for the Maasai. The Lerai forest on the crater floor, for example, was not only used for rainmaking and fertility ceremonies, but also held as a sacred grove, containing the graves of a number of important and estimated Maasai elders.[11]

Many scholars have presumed that German conquest combined with *emutai,* had "removed the Masai and their cattle from the crater in the 1890s."[12] *Emutai* is the Maasai term for the "complete destruction" that struck the pastoralist communities of the crater highlands during this decade,[13] denoting the virtual annihilation of the economic basis of Maasai pastoralism through the combined onslaught of a panzootic of the previously unknown rinderpest, bovine pleuropneumonia, smallpox, and the warfare of colonial conquest. Famine followed, and contemporary estimates reckoned the death toll at about 90 percent of cattle and two thirds of the Maasai population.[14] However, various reports by district commissioners and Schutztruppe[15] officials attest not only to their continuing presence in Ngorongoro but reveal that the crater functioned as an important basis for the recovery and reorganization of the various Maasai sections during the 1890s and the early 1900s. It was the advent of the Siedentopfs that triggered their expulsion and expropriation from what they claimed as ancestral land in the crater. Siedentopf himself had represented Ngorongoro as "uninhabited" in order to make authorities regard the land as ownerless. Initially, no colonial official bothered to verify this claim. When Johannes Abel, the responsible district officer of Moshi, came to Ngorongoro in early 1905 to actually see and chart the land granted to Siedentopf a few months earlier, he found the crater inhabited by roughly 800 Maasai with approximately 500 cattle and 3,000 heads of small stock.[16] But this made no difference. "Nomads as they are," he argued, "the Maasai would never be granted land as property by any official land commission." Although colonial officials acknowledged that Ngorongoro had been "a preferred pastureland of the Maasai since time immemorial," the Ngorongoro Maasai were forcibly removed to the newly established Maasai reserve south of Kilimanjaro.[17] A land commission set up in April 1907 confirmed Siedentopf's leasehold, declared the crater as crown land, and provided an ex-post legal cover for the established fact of displacement, decreeing that "the Maasai had no more title to the land since they have been banned from Ngorongoro following their robberies and thefts."[18] By the end of 1907, only a handful of Maasai families were allowed to remain in the crater to work as herders and stable hands on Siedentopf's fledgling farm.[19]

Around 1907, the future of Ngorongoro appeared to lie in its wholesale transformation into an agriculturally productive landscape. However, Siedentopf's livestock economy neither met governmental expectations nor his own initial promise. Accusations of violence, maltreatment of workers and unpaid wages, unfulfilled leasehold obligations, wildlife damage, cattle import, and guns in the hands of African farmworkers all contributed to increasing malevolence between Siedentopf and the government. When it emerged that the presence of thousands of wildebeest constituted a constant threat of transmitting diseases to domesticated animals, colonial authorities began to consider options beyond livestock-based agriculture in Ngorongoro. A small yet vociferous wildlife conservation lobby in Germany called for the establishment of a permanent *Naturschutzpark*—the German term for a protected area inspired by the U.S. precedent of Yellowstone—in the colony. From about 1911 onward, colonial officials seriously considered preservation an attractive alternative use of the crater. "Shall this unique stock of game be exterminated just to make room for 3 or 4 farms with a few thousand cattle?", the responsible subdistrict commissioner asked the government in Dar es Salaam in April 1912. "There are plenty of areas suitable for animal husbandry, but in the whole of Africa, there will be no other patch in which so much game is concentrated on so little space."[20]

Encouraged by similar requests from the colonial office in Berlin, the government probed options to turn the caldera into a *Naturschutzpark*. However, this would have meant to remove a settler with a leasehold contract that was irredeemable by the government until 1932. Authorities were reluctant to exert too much pressure, for the Siedentopfs were connected to influential prosettlement circles in Berlin. Any policy that smacked of handicapping Germany's industrious frontiersmen for the sake of wildebeest ran the risk of public scandalization. Siedentopf rejected any compensation with farmland outside Ngorongoro, and the East African government declared itself unable to procure an estimated sum of up to 200,000 marks to buy Siedentopf out of his contract. So did the colonial office in Berlin. Also, the German Colonial Society (DKG), the country's foremost organization to support colonialism overseas, and the Verein Naturschutzpark, a preservationist organization founded in 1909 to promote the establishment of large protected areas, declined to spend considerable funds for what they regarded as, after all, only a piece of "steppe country" far away in Africa.[21]

Because the *Naturschutzpark* appeared impossible to realize, governor Heinrich Schnee announced to open the crater to private enterprise and agricultural development again. In early 1914, applicants for farmland were queuing. A safari business opened by Friedrich Wilhelm Siedentopf had already started to attract the first globetrotting German hunters to the crater, and by summer 1914, the distribution of farmland had proceeded apace. The final decision about the future utilization of the crater was still pending, but had it not been for the outbreak of World War I, Ngorongoro would have been completely divided up into agricultural estates. The war halted the sale of land, and the advance of British troops in early 1916 finally forced the brothers to leave the crater.

Germany and the Roots of Tanzania's Environmental Conservation Complex

My personal safari into the conservation history of Ngorongoro shows that there is often little "natural" about places that the hegemonic representations of wildlife tourism and conservation management entrench as timeless nature and primordial wilderness. Tourist imaginaries of the present usually elide the complex human history of iconic natural landscapes. The rubble of the German farm in Ngorongoro also reminds everyone that today's natural zoo was perceived completely different by Europeans a century ago. Until late in the first decade of the twentieth century, Europeans saw and described Ngorongoro predominantly in terms of its potential for agricultural development. It was a paradise of the farmer, while the imagery and rhetoric of a wildlife paradise only rose to prominence after the removal of the Maasai.[22]

Above all, the traces left by Siedentopf first, and the Grzimeks later, testify to the deep connections that existed between German society and the nature and wildlife of Ngorongoro over the twentieth century. Like the extensive sisal plantations at the bottom of the Pare Mountains, the remnant doorsteps in the wildlife paradise of Ngorongoro are a visible and lasting mark that German colonial rule has left on Tanzania's environment. Indeed, the ruins of Ngorongoro are a very fitting reminder, for they are easily overlooked, just as the significance of the German colonial period in the history of wildlife conservation in East Africa has so far been overlooked. But it was in the years of German colonial rule between 1885 and World War I that the legal pretext for the exclusion and alienation of the Maasai from vast tracts of their homelands was invented. Today's conflicts surrounding conservation and land use in the area started with the colonial denial of entitlements and the removal of the Maasai in 1907. Scribbled English notes on the respective files in the national archives of Dar es Salaam reveal that subsequent British authorities were aware of their content and consulted them in later quarrels over human and animal rights in Ngorongoro and Serengeti. Ngorongoro may have been poised to be developed rather than preserved in 1914, but the debates surrounding the establishment of a *Naturschutzpark* reflect the broader conflicts over hunting, access to wildlife, and land use that became a characteristic feature of colonial politics after the turn of the century. At times, these were so fierce that contemporaries employed the dramatic catchphrase of "colony or zoological garden" to capture the possible future developments of German East Africa.

The case of Ngorongoro shows that "modern" conservationist concerns as well as outside interventions on behalf of the preservation of African wildlife predate the British period. It also illustrates how much animals mattered to the course and development of colonial Tanzania. The three decades of German colonial rule in Tanzania witnessed the formation of a regime of wildlife conservation that emerged from the precolonial and colonial politics of hunting in East Africa. This was a conflict-ridden and by no means straightforward process. Yet, by the end of the German colonial period, wildlife, or at least game,[23] was routinely framed as an evolutionary heritage that was acknowledged, although not yet systematically used as a source of tourist revenue. Unlike in continental Europe, the establishment of a conservationist mode of appropriating the wildlife's value led to a regard for nature and large animals as natural capital.[24] Wild animals were not removed as an obstacle, but came to be acknowledged as the basis of an East African way into modernity that accommodated rather than exterminated wildlife.[25] The origins of Tanzania's "environmental-conservation complex,"[26] that conglomerate of a protected area estate, wildlife as a source of revenue, and transcontinental governance, date back to the years of German rule, when wildlife conservation emerged as part of the competing and often contradictory agendas of the colonial state. While Ngorongoro did not yet count among them, the British inherited fifteen game reserves and a structure of codified game laws when they took over Tanganyika as a mandated territory from the League of Nations after World War I. The East African Campaign may have been an ecologically devastating rupture, but it did not affect the legal substance and the exclusionary pattern of conservation policies as continued after 1918.

Historiographical Contexts and Analytical Perspectives

Colonial conservation and wildlife policies are such well-established themes in the environmental history of Africa and the British Empire that William Beinart, one of the foremost champions of the field, has urged scholars to move beyond the colonial paradigm a few years ago.[27] However, scholars of East Africa yet need to acknowledge the depth of German involvement in its wildlife history. The existing literature on Tanzania, most of it of Anglo-American provenance, has largely marginalized the German colonial period. Conservation policies before World War I, if registered at all, are seldom dedicated more than a few pages.[28] In Germany, the towering icon of celebrity conservationist Bernhard Grzimek and his mediatized moral campaigns since the 1950s have long handicapped rather than encouraged a deeper engagement with the fact that the country had been involved in East African wildlife conservation half a century earlier.[29] In the collective memory of German society, it is usually Grzimek who is credited to have raised people's awareness to the endangered wildlife of the African continent. However, Grzimek had a precursor more than fifty years earlier, who anticipated most of his concerns, arguments, and methods: Carl Georg Schillings, a hunter, wildlife photographer, and conservationist campaigner whose bestselling books and sold-out lantern-slide picture shows of East Africa's wildlife sensitized German audiences to the problem of wildlife destruction in the decade before the World War I. Retrieving his largely forgotten story helps restore the long-term continuities as well as the fundamental ambivalences and asymmetries inherent in Germany's cosmopolitan engagement in Africa's conservation history.

This book explores the politics of conservation and wildlife regulation in colonial Tanzania under German rule. It situates the colonial exploitation, utilization, conservation, and regulation of game in the political ecology of wildlife that evolved under the regime of the East African caravan trade over the nineteenth century. It asks how wild animals and elephants in particular have shaped the culture and geography of colonial rule, and how conservation policies evolved in a stuttering and highly uneven quest for a more sustainable utilization of the wildlife resource. The chapters that follow identify the years between 1885 and 1914 as a period of decisive transformation in the relationship between humans and wildlife. They highlight the role of wildlife as a factor in the "contested interaction between the environment, local initiative, and imperial drive"[30] that produced "Tanzania" as a political unit. A centralizing state defined a public interest in nondomesticated animals, wielded control over wildlife as a resource, and fundamentally altered the geographies of human interaction with wild animals through the establishment of game reserves. The severe restrictions placed upon the hunting rights of Africans transformed local ecologies and decisively impeded rural communities' capacities of environmental control. Colonial wildlife legislation established an ecoracist regime whose asymmetries remained in place long after formal political decolonization.

Yet, wildlife did not just play an important role in Tanzania's state-building. It was also crucial for the country's integration in transcontinental and global connections. If the ivory trade has been a driver of East Africa's connectedness across continents before the onset of colonial rule, the conservation of its wildlife acquired a similar function since 1900. Preserving elephants in particular became part of Europe's civilizing mission. Conservation engendered, at times, close cooperation among empires and became the concern of well-connected elite hunter-conservationists in Germany and Britain. Their lobbying for stricter conservation policies initiated the outside intervention on behalf of Tanzania's wildlife that is such a marked feature of the transcontinental architecture of wildlife conservation governance in East Africa to this day.³¹ In German society, the numerous representations of the colonial encounter with Africa's fauna in travelogues, photography, museums, and colonial exhibitions fostered perceptions of timeless originality that erased history and the human factor from the African landscape.

The role that the hunting and conservation of elephants attained in the context of colonialism in East Africa was unique in comparison with Germany's other colonies. It was here that wildlife products and ivory in particular had the greatest economic and political importance. The popularization of East Africa's wildlife in text and photographs held a most captivating sway on the German imperial imagination and had no parallel in any other of the German colonies. In hunting and conservation related discourses, the Maasai Steppe and Kilimanjaro plains became landscapes of desire and localizations of a wildlife paradise that helped forge the stereotypical equation of Africa with the East African savanna and its charismatic animals. East Africa is therefore a fertile ground to show what the imperial treatment of nature can disclose about the nature of imperialism. Focusing on one colony allows for an empirically grounded analysis of how the appropriation of animals has shaped the unfolding and workings of colonial rule down to the local level. While the results of this study suggest that German imperialism is more adequately understood as consisting of a variety of different colonialisms,³² this book stakes the broader claim that elsewhere, too, nature was a crucial locus of power and not merely a passive background for the human drama of colonialism. Ecology, the bodies and properties of animals, soil, natural resources, or forests, were of similar significance in other contexts of German imperial expansion.³³ Hence the title *The Nature of German Imperialism*.

By restoring the presence of animals in the colonial encounter between colonizers and colonized, this study argues for a more comprehensive understanding of empire and colonialism that includes their ecological dimensions and the multiple agencies of humans, animals, and plants. Rather than a mere "relationship of domination between an indigenous … majority and a minority of invaders,"³⁴ colonialism must be understood as a political ecology constellation that essentially pertained to the land and its properties. It did not only affect flora and fauna but worked through them. Contemporaries were well aware of the grounded and ground-taking character of the process they referred to as *Kolonisation*.³⁵ The Germans who conquered East Africa in the early 1890s tried to realize this claim to the properties of the land and especially those animals regarded as game. The appropriation of animals as well as their conservation was enmeshed in changing relationships of power, which this study engages by applying a political ecology framework. The transdisciplinary project of political ecology critically rejects unpolitical explanations of environmental change and combines, in its classic definition by Piers Blaikie and Harold Brookfield, "the concerns of ecology and a broadly defined political economy."[36] Political ecological analyses are sensitive to questions of environmental justice and situate local resource conflicts, ecological change, and nature conservation measures in broader relations of economic, political, and epistemic power. They draw awareness to the fact that concepts such as soil erosion, deforestation, wilderness, biodiversity, "threatened," or "pristine" nature are no natural phenomena, but implicated in often asymmetrical relations of power. Epistemologically, most political ecology studies subscribe to a critical realism that rejects the absolutism of discourse and representation and acknowledges the double character of nature as cultural construct and as physical materiality.[37]

In her fascinating study of early modern colonial expansion in New England, Virginia DeJohn Anderson has argued that "leaving livestock out of the story of early American history is a little like staging *Macbeth* without the scenes in which Banquo's ghost appears. The ghost has no speaking role, but it is nevertheless central to the plot."[38] The same could be said about the role of elephants or the tsetse-transmitting flies of the species *glossinae* in East African history. The following chapters seek to release these species from their confinement in apolitical natural histories and bring them back into a world they shared with humans. Although inspired by the burgeoning field of human-animal studies,[39] this study does not intend to provide an animal history or reconstruct the past ecology or ethology of certain species. Its prime interest lies with hunting and conservation as the predominant and politically relevant forms of human interaction with them. Yet, restoring the presence of animals in the contact zones of European colonialism is more than a reference to the latest academic fad.[40] The following chapters show that animals and elephants in particular were instrumental in the making of colonial rule in East Africa. Animal action and behavior influenced and determined what humans did (and vice versa). In that relational, processual, and compounded sense, animals did have agency.[41]

Furthermore, this book engages several other bodies of scholarly literature. First, it contributes to the vibrant environmental historiography of Tanzania. Thaddeus Sunseri in particular has advanced knowledge of the German period through his thorough analyses of the social conflicts surrounding the introduction of European-style rational forestry and by exposing the environmental dimensions of the Maji Maji War.[42] This study builds upon this work by analyzing the origins of statist wildlife conservation, the social conflicts that arose out of the colonial regulation of access to game, and the role elephants and ivory played in Maji Maji. By emphasizing the degree to which the political cleavages and alliances created by hunting in the precolony were continued under colonial rule, the book refines Sunseri's argument about Maji Maji. Moreover, it contributes to the longstanding controversy in Tanzanian environmental history surrounding the stability and environmental control of precolonial societies, respectively, the devastating impact and ecological destabilization wrought by colonial rule. Interpretations of a "Merry Africa" of stable communities living in harmony with nature have been contrasted by analyses that stress precolonial primitivity and poverty.[43] However, as N Thomas Håkansson has argued, both interpretations underestimate outside forces and the transformative capacities of the ever-expanding caravan trade from the middle of the nineteenth century.[44] By drawing attention to the social and political implications of elephant hunting and its enormous ramifications for the making of colonial rule, this study emphasizes the mobilizing character of the caravan trade, the dynamics of precolonial human-animal relationships, as well as important continuities between precolony and the German takeover.

Second, by analyzing the environment as a "locus of power,"[45] *The Nature of German Imperialism* seeks to restore an environmental dimension to the historiography of German colonialism. While there exists a burgeoning literature on the environmental history particularly of the British Empire,[46] the boom of German colonial studies over the last two decades has spawned comparatively little interest in the ecological entanglements between metropole and colonies.[47] The emphasis on entangled histories and the plea to analyze colony and metropole "in a single analytical field," respectively within a global framework, have been extremely stimulating for German colonial studies in general.[48] However, the reception of postcolonial methodology in German colonial studies has also been marked by a tendency to privilege discourses, fantasies, and the repercussions of the colonial encounter in the imperial "metropole" over what actually happened in the colonies.[49] In a more recent turn, the adoption of a "postcolonial perspective" on German expansionism has resulted in a wave of studies interested in continuities, parallels, and connections between colonial rule overseas and continental imperial expansion in Eastern Europe.[50] Whereas the claims about connections, impacts, and reverse flows have spawned productive controversies, for example, over military violence and genocide, the depth and character of entanglements between colony and metropole require critical qualification by thorough empirical analyses of further fields of imperial engagement. This study contributes to this literature by providing an empirically grounded analysis of the transcontinental flow of ideas and concepts in the making of colonial wildlife policies in East Africa. It is attentive to the concrete directions of these transfers and its agents. While retaining its focus on a formal protectorate as the foremost space in which German imperialism took place, it extends the analytical field of colony and metropole by situating these exchanges in a transcolonial, respectively transimperial setting. German policies in Africa were heavily influenced by concepts, models, and practices in other imperial settings, like the North American West or the British territories in Southern and Eastern Africa.[51] Finally, by analyzing the international repercussions of African wildlife conservation and by restoring the colonial dimensions of the early German *Naturschutz* movement, this book highlights the transnational dimensions of the fledgling German preservationism that has so far received but scant attention in German environmental historiography.[52] The encounter with Africa's charismatic megafauna was a source of German conservationist sensibilities in its own right.[53] Integrating the colonial experience into the history of the "new" German conservationism evolving in the last third of the nineteenth century highlights the often overlooked role of hunting as a source, as well as of hunters as advocates and promoters of conservationist sensibilities. Although their ideas about wild animals were by no means uncontested, hunters were a controversial part rather than opponents of the fledgling and amorphous German movement for nature protection around 1900.

Analyzing the politics of wildlife in East Africa between colony and metropole requires sensitivity to the spatial levels of the colonial, the transimperial, respectively international, and the "metropolitan" on which these politics unfolded and reverberated. Of course, this distinction is first and foremost analytical. The interactions, frictions, and connections between these spaces are manifold and hard to disentangle. Fear of extinction "on the spot," for example, evoked transimperial and international cooperation that impacted back upon wildlife policies in East Africa. While the interaction between these three levels is woven into the narrative that traces the unfolding of East African wildlife politics in Parts I and II of this book, the last three chapters take these spatial levels as their specific analytical starting points. Thereby, they highlight the thorough and more than ephemeral impact of German colonial policies in the field of wildlife and the evolving structural dependency of East African wildlife policies on the international and metropolitan spheres. They also draw attention to what was transferred and what was lost in translation. The development of a cosmopolitan concern in Germany with wildlife conservation far away in Africa came at the price of a narrowing of vision and a stereotypical simplification of social, political, and ecological complexity that characterizes environmental communication and perception across continents to this day.

With a view to the colony as a space of wildlife, this study is interested in the political, social, ecological, and economic conflicts caused by the establishment of colonial control over East Africa's wildlife. In his analysis of the establishment of German rule in East Africa, Michael Pesek has drawn attention to the multiple local roots of colonial rule, showing how the political and moral economies of East African caravan travel were incorporated and gradually abandoned by the traveling economy of colonial conquest.[54] His observations must be extended to the elephant hunting that supplied the ivory trade, as both the control over ivory and elephants decisively shaped the structure and the practices of colonial state-building. Therefore, it is indispensable to rehearse the importance of hunting in the precolonial ecologies of settlement and trade in order to understand the degree to which colonial rule was both a continuation and rupture of local cultures of hunting and authority.[55] In their dependence on local intermediaries and their networks, the impersonations of the colonial state at the lowest administrative level strikingly resembled the African and Swahili big men and entrepreneurs who had used hunting and ivory to accumulate wealth in people.[56] The colonial state of the 1890s continued essentially precolonial patterns of authority and used hunting less as an assertion of imperial power than as a means of establishing a working relationship with cooperating chiefs or aspirants to power. The integration of animals into the workings of colonial rule thus serves to abandon easy categorizations of collaboration versus resistance or colonizer versus colonized for more complex interrelationships in the colonial contact zones.[57]

By tracing the protracted, contested, and haphazard assertion of state control over wildlife, this study exposes both the strength and the weakness of the colonial state. With no premeditated pattern and an institutional structure that rendered every change of governor "a change of the system,"[58] the colonial administration staggered toward sustainability by exclusion. In the process, multiple lines of conflict became visible, several of them undermining the boundaries of "race". Therefore, the question of who was entitled to hunt which animals, by what means, and at what cost, is particularly well suited to reveal the inner workings and fissures of colonial society. Nevertheless, access to wildlife in 1914 was fundamentally different from 1885. From a resource exploited for their economic value as ivory, elephants had developed into an exclusive resource preserved for a handful of white hunters for the conspicuous performance of their wealth, class, race, and masculinity. The local politics of wildlife in the colony had become part of imperial and international structures of environmental governance, and the change in the economics of the hunt was mirrored by a change in ethics. The "trust in nature" that had governed hunting in the precolony had been replaced by a centralized state that held "nature in trust."

The second level on which the colonial politics of wildlife will be analyzed in this study comprises all the processes, links, and networks that transcended the boundaries of the colony and forged trans- and international, transcolonial, or transimperial connections.[59] The neighborhood of empires in Africa turned European imperialism into a culture of prestige and exposure as well as into a structure that prompted exchange and transfer. Imperialism generated its own forms of internationalism. Nature conservation came to constitute "one of the key realms of ... trans-imperial and international coordination,"[60] and colonial conservation was an important "triangulation point" for cultural transfers and contacts between Britain and Germany.[61] Highlighting the principled mutuality of these exchanges may serve as a way to deflate assumptions about British exceptionalism and put the British Empire in perspective and proportion. Rather than taking its leading role for granted, an analysis of the transimperial character of East African wildlife politics helps to analyze, in Antoinette Burton's words, "to write the British Empire into world history ... in terms of its role in the co-production of imperial globality rather than its originary character."[62]

This said, there is no denying that perceptions and exchanges between Britain and Germany in East Africa were conjunctural, asymmetrical, and often one-sided. Russell Berman has even argued that German colonial discourse was essentially derivative, as it constantly engaged with the example set by the British.[63] The prominence of Britain as rival, model, and above all, repository of imperial practices and knowledge will be approached on several levels.[64] In relative independence of the ebbs and flows of the Anglo-German antagonism in Europe, Germany's self-perception as a latecomer in colonial matters resulted in a structural propensity to learn and adopt. The political geography resulting from the scramble for Africa had a direct impact upon the phenomena under discussion in this study. Sharing borders was a structural feature of Anglo-German imperialism. German East Africa in particular bordered on British territories with similar wildlife ecologies. Consequently, the regulation of trade in animals' body parts, wildlife conservation, and its advocacy by elitist lobby groups, but especially veterinary science and the ecology of wildlife diseases, all invited exchange and cooperation across borders as much as they fanned competition. At times, they constituted "common projects" of the imperial powers,[65] at times, they merely ran parallel. Given the small circle of imperial decision-makers and the equally limited set of actors involved in veterinary science, hunting, and wildlife conservation, an actor-oriented approach is best suited to identify why some concerns transcended the realm of colony and empire and others did not. It was a result of strategic framing that the first and foremost Anglo-German concern over the depleted game stocks of East Africa lifted Africa's wildlife into the international arena and resulted in two international conferences on wildlife conservation in Africa before World War I. This study analyzes the actors and motivations behind these transimperial exchanges and connections and identifies European imperialism as an important driving force of environmental internationalism around 1900. Taking the colonies as a vantage point for transfers and exchange across several continents also draws attention to connections bypassing the metropole. While the structures of imperial governance necessitated that most colonial issues were handed back to the imperial metropole to be internationalized, the metropole was not the only reference point for the transcontinental connections forged by the politics of wildlife. Robert Koch, for example, developed his knowledge in tropical medicine in British India and Southern Africa. German veterinary scientists trained at Onderstepoort laboratory in South Africa.[66] The colonial game reserves were inspired by both the aristocratic European hunting estate and by specific, contextualized understandings of U.S. national parks. By highlighting such transcontinental exchanges, webs of meanings, globalized worldviews, and transfers between and beyond metropole and colony, this book also confronts the environmental history of hunting and conservation in East Africa with the sensibilities of multisited transnational and global histories.[67] Thereby, it adds to the recent revisionism of simple diffusionist and exceptionalist understandings of U.S. national park history.[68]

A third analytical perspective is developed upon the representations and reverberations of the colonial encounter with Africa's wildlife in Germany. The travelogues, articles, and photographs that transmitted the colonizers' experience to audiences in imperial Germany were replete with ecstatic descriptions of a radically different, "exotic," and "primeval" nature. An overwhelmed officer of the colonial military wrote his parents that the "childhood images of paradise which I keep in my head and in which thousands of animals promenade around Adam and Eve under tall trees are nothing compared to the reality I encounter here every single day." Hanns Braun, a trained historian and journalist relished in the "excitement and mystery of traveling through a continent that has not yet been shaped by man, but still remains stamped by the animal. It was a dream-like journey back to the dawn of creation."[69] Such seemingly natural renderings of African landscapes as primeval, timeless, and empty but for animals were wedded to the mental operation that characterized Europeans' ordering of the world under the impact of nineteenth-century evolutionism: the reading of geographical difference across space as historical and temporal difference over time. This process has been described as "denial of coevalness" or the "invention of anachronistic space."[70] One of the key strategies to render this assumption plausible was to "naturalize" it.

This study asks how the envisioning of African space as wilderness peopled by animals rather than humans prepared and accompanied the intervention of colonial authorities into physical environments. Often, they reified this mental separation of humans and animals on the ground. The direct colonial encounter with wildlife in the late nineteenth century also politicized and essentialized earlier discourses of evolutionism, paleontology, and zoogeography to give rise to an epistemic configuration that conflated space and species, habitat, and time in a political geography of the characteristic animal.[71] These ideologies were encapsulated in the first photographic representations of Africa's wildlife that appeared in Germany around 1900. They show that the new visuality of German colonialism in the "Magic Lantern Empire" was not only about "picturing race" or "advertising Empire,"[72] but also about the virtual authentification of wilderness that motivated cosmopolitan conservationist concern and entrenched a long lasting European stereotype of African nature. The final chapter explores the wider ramifications of this conflation of space and species for ideas about Africa, nature, *Heimat,* and the nation in Germany. It follows the textual and visual tracks left by Africa's wildlife, the representations to which they gave rise and the practical consequences these representations entailed—especially in Carl Georg Schillings's bestselling hunting tales and picture shows, in the discourses of the movement for nature conservation as well as in the German landscape. By tracing the incorporation, domestication, and restoration of the wild by various techniques of Western modernity, *The Nature of Imperialism* analyses the coconstitution of social ideas of nature and wilderness between colony and metropole "in a single analytic field."[73] Rather than a laboratory for German conservationist thinking and practices, the colonies must be understood as a source of environmental and preservationist sensibilities in their own right.

Tracking Game in the Colonial Archive

Following the tracks of hunters and wild animals between East Africa and Germany necessitates the transcontinental mining for sources. The basis of this book are records, personal papers, and manuscripts from well over twenty archives and libraries in Tanzania, Kenya, Germany, Great Britain, Belgium, and the United States.

Reconstructing the colonial politics of wildlife is impossible without resorting to material from the "colonial archive." The most substantial part of the archival material comprises official correspondence of the German imperial authorities in Berlin and in Dar es Salaam. The documents held in Berlin reveal the view from the metropole, but they also include correspondence and reports from the colony that disclose the workings of colonial rule beyond the central administration in Dar es Salaam. Because the voices from the colony that can be retrieved in Berlin are sporadic and hardly ever extend to the administrative levels below the central administration, it is imperative to complement the archive material of the colonial department (colonial office from 1907 onward) in Berlin with the surviving source material of the "German Records" in Dar es Salaam. Unfortunately, the files of the German East African colonial administration, not to mention the various district stations and outposts, are extremely patchy, because a large part of records was destroyed upon withdrawal from the advancing British forces in World War I. Records that give insight into the hunting and wildlife politics at the level of district stations have survived for the 1890s, whereas the majority of files for the years after 1900 are lost. This loss can only partially be compensated by surviving administrative correspondence and annual reports of district offices or legal cases dealing with breaches of the game regulations.[74] Beyond the memory of "official colonialism," the files contained in Germany's ethnographic and natural history museums provide another rich and hitherto hardly tapped source of information on German colonialism. For example, correspondence between hunters and museum curators has survived in the Museum of Natural History in Berlin, which held an official mandate as clearing house for all zoological material obtained on official expeditions between 1889 and 1911. Further archives have been consulted to assess the strategies of participants at the First International Conference on the Preservation of African wildlife in 1900. Given the colonial neighborhood in East Africa, the joint Anglo-German preparation of the London Conference and the overall model character of British colonial rule in terms of wildlife policies, files have been reviewed in the Kenya National Archives as well as in the Public Record Office in London to unravel processes of transfer, mutual borrowings, and observation. A final category of archival material consisted of personal papers and correspondence of leading colonial decision makers and individual hunters. Though scattered and evidently incomplete as far as the personal correspondence is concerned, the papers of Germany's eminent big game hunter of the time, Carl Georg Schillings, have allowed at least the partial reconstruction of his transnational reception as well as of his transnational conservationist contacts.

   Anthropologist Ann Laura Stoler has drawn attention to the role of the archive as the "supreme technology" of late nineteenth-century imperial governance.[75] Archives, and the colonial archives in particular, are no neutral sites of knowledge retrieval but the sedimented memory of the colonial state and thus a site where colonial knowledge was produced and the taxonomies of rule forged. It is, therefore, indispensable to read these documents as expressions of a colonial epistemology. However, although archives "see like a state," the sources they contain are polyphonous, and it is the historian's task to retrieve this polyphony by carefully contrasting "the file" with material of different provenance and other fields of knowledge. All too often, the very archive reveals the failure of imperialist aspirations. Reports and correspondence can be subjected to subversive reading "against the grain" to restore hidden meanings and the multiple agencies of "colonizers," "colonized," and also of the animals that crowded the contact zones of colonial rule.

This approach has obvious limits in the assessment of the agency of Africans whose actions are largely represented through the distortions of the colonial archive or the views of the hunter. Still, files do contain occasional reports by local African or Swahili intermediaries, and Africans also got a voice in the rare instances of bearing witness in court cases dealing with breaches of the game laws. But the extremely patchy nature of the source material disallows an observation of the localizations of hunting policies and indigenous reactions for any single area over a longer timescale. While those district officials and missionary ethnographers who produced the sources remained place-bound, hunters, together with porters, counted among the most mobile social groups in East Africa, which accounts for their overall elusive presence in the records.

The records lifted from the imperial archives are contrasted and supplemented with a variety of published material, all fraught with their own problems as historical sources. A multiplicity of travelogues, anthropological and geographical descriptions and ethnographies compiled by missionaries, colonial administrators, and early anthropologists, has been consulted to uncover the significance of hunting in the lives of African societies prior to and under colonial rule. Much of the same caution applies to these sources: travelogues based sweeping assertions upon fleeting observations, and enormous differences exist in the trustworthiness of individual observers. Hunting tales are a genre underlying their own plots of dramatization culminating in the final kill, whereas ethnographies produced by colonial officials or missionaries were implicated in the colonial project and often covered the awkward and complex negotiations with dichotomic essentializations of the colonial situation in which they were produced.[76] Still, differentiations are in place also here: there were authoritarian ethnographers who claimed to know, whereas others revealed their informants and the basis upon which they drew their conclusions. Likewise, there were hunting tales presenting an eternal contest between man and the brute, and those that proceed as detailed and localizable as a diary.

Apart from the various colonial periodicals published in Germany, the most important being the *Kolonialzeitung* and the *Kolonialblatt*, the *Deutsch-Ostafrikanische Zeitung* as the main organ of the white community and the *Usambara-Post* as the settlers' mouthpiece in the colony have been consulted as sources for the significance of hunting in colonial culture as well as for critical perspectives on official wildlife policies. Additionally, this study has for the first time made extensive use of the contemporary German hunting press, such as the periodicals *Wild und Hund* or the *Deutsche Jägerzeitung*. As staple reading for the considerable community of hunters and game lovers, these periodicals are a most rewarding source for tracking those hunters who, for various reasons, did not publish their stories in book-length volumes. Discussions in the hunting press also reveal the disputed character of big game hunting at the fringes of European expansion. Moreover, the hunting press generally discloses the degree to which a social group usually associated with provincialism actually participated in the global appropriation of the wild. Its value as a source for a social history of hunting is, however, diminished insofar as the social background of contributors is often hard to assess, especially when authors used pseudonyms or only gave their initials. Then, contemporary British and German publications on veterinary medicine have been consulted to reconstruct transimperial debates on wildlife diseases and to partially compensate for a dearth of files on the local level in Dar es Salaam. Finally, hunting and the global loss of the large mammalian fauna were topics reverberating frequently in the flurry of journals in the field of popular science, but also in the publications of the fledgling movement for nature conservation. They allow for a cautious assessment of the social reach of conservationist concern about the colonies in German society.

The book is organized into three parts. The first part consists of two chapters that analyze the political ecology of wildlife in the transition from precolony to colonial rule. They stress the continuity of a hunter principle of authority that emerged under the ivory trade and marked the years of colonial conquest. Part II charts the making of Tanzania's wildlife conservation regime in three chronologically successive chapters (3 to 5). Starting from Maji Maji as the violent end of hunting as a middle ground for political alliances, the conflicting politics of wildlife are analyzed under the conditions of an unfolding settler society and the increasing impact of hunter-conservationist networks in Germany. The first two parts together develop a narrative of how colonial wildlife regulation in Tanzania evolved from exploitation toward conservation in a haphazard manner of constant trial and error. Therefore, a synopsis of the most important game ordinances has been compiled in the appendix to provide additional orientation and helpful reference. The third part abandons the chronological organization of the previous chapters. Here, systematic perspectives on the wider ramifications of conservation between metropole and colony prevail. Drawing upon the evidence assembled in the first two parts, chapters 6 to 8 systematically entrench aspects that have received only short shrift in the chronological chapters. Chapter 6 explores the politics of reserves and protected area governance between local and global historical perspectives. The following chapter charts the transimperial and international mechanics and entanglements of wildlife conservation and reflects upon the relationship between Britain and Germany as empires among empires, both from East African and metropolitan perspectives. The final chapter, 8, focusses on the reverberations of East African wildlife conservation in Germany. By putting these themes into broader analytical contexts, the third part, together with the epilogue, highlights the lasting and broader significance of the nature of German imperialism in East Africa.

Chapter 1 sets out with the ecology of wildlife in the Tanganyikan precolony and distinguishes settlement and trade as the main regimes that governed hunting as a highly differentiated and dynamic form of African societies' interaction with nature. The incorporation of ever more societies in Tanganyika into the networks of the long-distance caravan trade toward Zanzibar brought about decisive transformations in the political, social, and moral ecology of hunting, which came to be the main economic activity by which East Africans partook in the worldwide web of trade in the nineteenth century. The rising value of wildlife commodities, especially of ivory prompted the emergence of specialized elephant hunters. The control of elephants and ivory became an important mechanism for the accumulation of wealth and authority, enabling self-made political entrepreneurs to establish themselves as big men and attract a following. When the Germans took control of East Africa in the last decade of the nineteenth century, they found a political economy benefiting a "hunter principle" of political authority as well as a marked commercialization of elephant hunting and the gradual erosion of the political, social, and cultural buffers that had served to prevent the overexploitation of elephant herds.

Chapter 2 corrects the erroneous assumption that the Tanganyikan elephant population was already too depleted to assign ivory an important role for the German colonizers. It shows how hunting and the acquisition of ivory were instrumental in the establishment of German colonial rule: ivory served as the main subsidy and currency of conquest. Until around 1900, German wildlife policies in East Africa were governed by the political ecology of the ivory trade. Chapter 3 links the themes of parts I and II by charting the transition of hunting policies from trade toward conservation. Linking the elephants of the Mahenge district in the southern highlands with the various levels of imperial governance over wildlife, the chapter interprets the Maji Maji rising in 1905 as an environmental conflict over the access to elephants and wildlife resources. The war effectively put an end to the colonial "big man" policies of hunting and ivory that had marked the years of conquest. Chapters 4 and 5 unfold the whole panorama of conflicts over the regulation of hunting after Maji Maji, when a growing number of white settlers in the colony and an emerging lobby of hunter conservationists in Germany appeared as new stakeholders on the scene. Scientific studies proved that game hosted trypanosomes that caused human and animal sleeping sickness. The controversial debate about the future of wildlife in the colony exposed the cleavages of colonial society and turned into Germany's biggest environmental scandal of the *Kaiserreich* when governor von Rechenberg attempted the creation of a cordon sanitaire devoid of game to prevent the spread of rinderpest in 1910. Moral outrage, a well-connected wildlife lobby, and the interference of German Emperor Wilhelm II resulted in a revision of the game laws largely in tune with the ideals of the conservationists. By 1912, the expropriation of Africans from the control over their wildlife was virtually complete.

Chapters 6 to 8 abandon the chronology of wildlife politics to rehearse systematically the different spatialities of the colonial encounter with the wild. Chapter 6 conceptualizes late nineteenth-century imperialism as a driving force for the globalization of environmental responsibility. It situates the establishment of game reserves in East Africa between wildlife degradation, governmental land politics, heterotopian ideals of wilderness, and the transimperial exchange of concepts that connected reserves along the Rufiji with Yellowstone in North America, the Southern Game Reserve in Kenya, and the Schorfheide outside Berlin. The introduction of game reserves entailed a shift of environmental decision-making away from the respective locality, subjecting the politics of place in East Africa to the structures and actors of imperial environmental governance. Chapter 7 explores the politics of wildlife in colony and metropole in their transimperial and international as well as in their governmental and social dimensions. It provides a synopsis of the entwined coevolution of wildlife policies in German and British East Africa and traces various forms of transimperial cooperation in wildlife-related fields. The chapter systematically assesses the conditions and factors underlying exchange and cooperation across empires and determines the relationship between imperialism and internationalism in the field of colonial conservation. Chapter 8 is concerned with the textual, visual, and conceptual reverberations and representations of the colonial encounter with the African fauna in Germany. It traces the cultural messages and environmental sensibilities conveyed through the nascent wildlife photography, and it examines how the debates about wildlife conservation in the German colonies and the global vanishing of the giant fauna nourished conservationists' anxieties about the loss of rootedness in an era of rapid industrialization and social change. The perceived originality of African nature exposed an emotional blank in

German environmental identity that motivated attempts at restoring the wild to the German landscape.

Finally, a word on words. In order to enhance legibility, I have translated all quotations from the original German into English. However, there are a few terms where the utilization of English equivalents would contort the original meaning, as in the case of *Weidgerechtigkeit,* the word German hunters used to denote the ethics and attitudes of hunting they deemed to be peculiarly German. Its closest English equivalent would be "sportsmanship." However, this term and the understanding of hunting as a "sport" in general were hotly contested by those parts of the German hunting fraternity who rejected this association with competition and records, often in nationalistic terms. *Weidgerechtigkeit* and sportsmanship constituted rivalling and ideologically charged concepts in contemporary colonial debates over wildlife regulation, and any translation would risk blurring this incommensurability. "Conservation" and "preservation" are used according to their established understanding in international environmental history, that is, with conservation denoting measures of nature protection that allowed for management and sustainable utilization to ensure the continued use of animals through humans, as opposed to preservation as noninterventionist forms of protection predicated upon assumptions of ecological integrity and natural balance.[77] However, contemporary conservationist debates were characterized by a mixture of motivations and concepts that scrambled this distinction as much as the terminology employed in German conservationist discourse: The terms *Jagdschutz* and *Wildschutz* referred to the protection of legitimate hunting and game and thus count among measures of conservation through utilization. The terms *Naturschutz* (nature protection) and the rarely deployed *Tierschutz* (animal protection) framed Africa's wildlife within the newly emerging concern over the preservation of the remnants of pristine nature in the late nineteenth century.

Writing about colonialism inevitably entails dealing with a formation of epistemic power whose language and terminology was geared to govern and render legible. Colonial rule invented and employed a system of homogenizing, derogatory, and straightforwardly racist categories with little correspondence to the self-identification of the people thus described. However, as "technical terms" of colonial rule, this terminology is often indispensable. Colonial rule and the game legislation it prompted was predicated upon a distinction between *Eingeborene* (natives) and *Nicht-Eingeborene* (nonnatives), the former including not only Africans but also Arabs, Zanzibaris, and Indians, the latter denoting any white person originating in a country counted among the "civilized" nations. Where the use of such terminology cannot be avoided, it will be placed in quotation marks.

Similarly fraught with problems are the denomination of African ethnicities. Africanist scholarship has exposed the "time-defying and history-denying" logic behind a category such as "tribe,"[78] which fails to capture complex social structures and arrested social mobility and fluid identities in archaic immobility. These ethnic referents are used nonetheless, but they are to be understood as geographical and historical references to an area and its people, not necessarily implying that they existed as a named and bounded political community during the nineteenth century. Reference to the territory under study is equally problematic: "German East Africa" was constituted as a meaningful political unit only by the end of the nineteenth century. Any application of German East Africa, Tanganyika, or Tanzania to the social, political, and economic constellations of this area earlier than the 1880s is to apply a conceptual framework that simply did not exist. As a colonial invention, German East Africa made sense for Europeans, but hardly for its inhabitants. Comprising also Rwanda and Burundi, it was neither equivalent to the Tanganyika that came to replace it as denominator, nor to the Tanzania that was formed as a union of Tanganyika and Zanzibar in 1964. Nonetheless, I use German East Africa, Tanganyika, or colonial Tanzania interchangeably as a reference for the emerging centralized territorial state that came to be the dominant framework for East Africa's politics of wildlife ever since the last decade of the nineteenth century. The colonial spelling of place names has been adapted to current usage.

Notes

1. Bernhard and Michael Grzimek, *Serengeti darf nicht sterben. 367000 Tiere suchen einen Staat* (Berlin, 1959), 306. For an early reference to Ngorongoro as a "reborn world to be glanced at as a wonder" and a "unique natural zoological garden" see, for example, Hans Reck, *Oldoway, die Schlucht des Urmenschen. Die Entdeckung des altsteinzeitlichen Menschen in Deutsch—Ostafrika* (Leipzig, 1933), 31–32.
2. Peter J Rogers, "History and Governance in the Ngorongoro Conservation Area, Tanzania, 1959-1966," *Global Environment* 4 (2009): 80, 91–92; Thomas Lekan, "Serengeti Shall Not Die: Bernhard Grzimek, Wildlife Film, and the Making of a Tourist Landscape in East Africa," *German History* 29 (2011): 224–64.
3. Anthony RE Sinclair, *The Serengeti Story. Life and Science in the World's Greatest Wildlife Region* (Oxford, 2012), xiv.
4. Katherine Scholfield and Dan Brockington, "Non-Governmental Organisations and African Wildlife Conservation. A Preliminary Analysis" (Brooks World Poverty Institute Working Paper no. 80, Manchester, 2009), 20.
5. Noel Salazar, *Envisioning Eden. Mobilizing Imaginaries in Tourism and beyond* (New York, 2011), 87.
6. Tanzania National Archives, Dar es Salaam (TNA) G 8/144, fol. 208–10: Bezirksnebenstelle (subdistrict office; BNS) Arusha to Government (Gov) Deutsch-

Ostafrika (DOA), 11 March 1913; TNA G 8/144, fol. 214: BNS Arusha to Gov DOA, 23 April 1913.
7. TNA G 8/144, fol. 178–79, Report by Lieutenant Theodor Tafel on land affairs in Ngorongoro, 4 March 1912.
8. TNA G 8/144, fol. 19: Gov DOA to Siedentopf, 7 December 1904.
9. TNA G 8/144, fol. 92, Methner to Friedrich Wilhelm Siedentopf, 6 December 1907.
10. TNA G 8/144, fol. 160–61: Moshi to Gov DOA, 13 July 1911; TNA G 31/1, unfol.: Adolf Siedentopf to Gov DOA, 22 August 1913; TNA G 31/170, unfol.: Veterinarian Braunert to Gov DOA, 23 August 1913; Reck, *Oldoway, die Schlucht des Urmenschen,* 34.
11. Oxford, Bodleian Library (OBL) Mss Afr s 1237a: H St J Grant: *Masai History and Mode of Life. A Summary Prepared for the Committee of Enquiry into the Serengeti National Park* (1957), 1–2; OBL Mss Afr s 1237b, Oltimbau ole Masiaya on behalf of the Masai of the Serengeti National Park, *Memorandum on the Serengeti National Park,* 1957; Katherine Homewood, Patti Kristjanson, and Pippa Chenevix Trench, "Changing Land Use, Livelihoods and Wildlife Conservation in Maasailand," in *Staying Maasai? Livelihoods, Conservation and Development in East African Rangelands,* ed. K Homewood, P Kristjanson, and P Chenevix Trench (New York, 2009), 5; cf. John G Galaty, "Maasai Expansion and the New East African Pastoralism," in *Being Maasai. Ethnicity and Identity in East Africa,* ed. Thomas Spear and Richard Waller (London, 1993), 74.
12. See, for example, Helge Kjekshus, *Ecology Control and Economic Development in East African History. The Case of Tanganyika 1850–1950* (London, 1977), 74; *Deutsches Kolonialblatt* 12, no. 24 (1901): 902–6.
13. Richard Waller, "Emutai: Crisis and Response in Maasailand 1883–1902," in *The Ecology of Survival. Case Studies from Northeast African History,* ed. Douglas H Johnson and David M Anderson (London, 1988), 73–112.
14. Oscar Baumann, *Durch Massailand zur Nilquelle. Reisen und Forschungen der Massai-Expedition des Deutschen Antisklaverei-Komite in den Jahren 1891–1893* (Berlin, 1894), 30–32; Moritz Merker, *Die Masai. Ethnographische Monographie eines ostafrikanischen Semitenvolkes* (Berlin, 1904), 336.
15. *Kaiserliche Schutztruppe für Deutsch-Ostafrika* was the official denomination of the military force established to conquer and secure the East African colony. It was formed in 1891 from the mercenary army that had conquered large parts of the territory under Hermann von Wissmann since 1889. Its bulk was made up from African soldiers, the so-called Askari. See Tanja Bührer, *Die Kaiserliche Schutztruppe für Deutsch-Ostafrika. Koloniale Sicherheitspolitik und transkulturelle Kriegführung 1885 bis 1918* (Munich, 2011).
16. TNA G 8/143, fol. 26: Abel to Gov DOA, 13 February 1905; cf. *Deutsch-Ostafrikanische Zeitung* 8, no. 38 (1906).
17. TNA G 8/143, fol. 26: Abel to Gov DOA, 13 February 1905; TNA G 8/143, fol. 46: Gov DOA to Moshi, undated concept; TNA G 8/143, fol. 73: Moshi to Gov DOA, 31 October 1905; TNA G 8/143, fol. 74: Gov DOA to Siedentopf, 8 February 1906.
18. TNA G 8/144, fol. 69: Protocol of the Land Commission, no. 47, Ngorongoro, 26 April 1907.
19. TNA G 8/144, fol. 198–205: Adolf Siedentopf to Gov DOA, 3 January 1912; Wilhelm Methner, *Unter drei Gouverneuren. 16 Jahre Dienst in deutschen Tropen* (Breslau, 1938), 155.

20. TNA G 8/144, fol. 178-79: Report by Lieutenant Theodor Tafel on land affairs in Ngorongoro, 4 March 1912.
21. Bundesarchiv Berlin-Lichterfelde (BAB) R 1001/6229-1, fol. 75-76: Reichskolonialamt (RKA) to Erwin Bubeck, Verein Naturschutzpark, 14 April 1914; BAB R 1001/6229-1, fol. 95: Bubeck to RKA, 26 May 1914; BAB R 1001/6229-1, fol. 98: RKA to Bubeck (draft), 29 June 1914.
22. Ironically, it was Siedentopf and one of his farm assistants who discovered, just after the Maasai had been expelled, that the history of human-wildlife coexistence in the crater had a deeper history still. While seeking stones for their farm buildings, they unearthed Neolithic burial mounds that helped trigger palaeoanthropological interest in the crater highlands. The discovery of even older hominid fossils in nearby Oldupai Gorge earned the Serengeti-Ngorongoro landscape the further epithet of a "cradle of humankind" since the 1930s, see Reck, *Oldoway, die Schlucht des Urmenschen*, 154-60; Virginia Morell, *Ancestral Passions. The Leakey Family and the Quest for Humankind's Beginnings* (New York, 1995), chapter 3.
23. Despite manifest differences between "game" and "wildlife," with the former denoting first and foremost those species suited for hunting, I use both terms interchangeably, for in the German language no such distinction existed, and contemporaries used the term *Wild* also to refer to nondomesticated animals beyond game. After 1900, the term *Tierschutz* (animal conservation) was employed occasionally to denote that *Wildschutz* (game conservation) was informed by the new sensibilities of early twentieth-century nature preservationism.
24. On conservation as a form of capitalist production see Elizabeth Garland, "The Elephant in the Room. Confronting the Colonial Character of Wildlife Conservation in Africa," *African Studies Review* 51 (2008): 51-74.
25. Jan-Georg Deutsch, Peter Probst, and Heike Schmidt, ed, *African Modernities. Entangled Meanings in Current Debate* (Portsmouth, NH, 2002).
26. Dan Brockington, "The Politics and Ethnography of Environmentalisms in Tanzania," *African Affairs* 105 (2006): 102.
27. William Beinart, "Beyond the Colonial Paradigm: African History and Environmental History in Large-Scale Perspective," in *The Environment and World History*, ed. Edmund Burke III and Kenneth Pomeranz (Berkeley, CA, 2009), 211-28.
28. See, for example, Dan Brockington, Hassan Sachedina, and Katherine Scholfield, "Preserving the New Tanzania: Conservation and Land Use Change," *International Journal of African Historical Studies* 41, no. 3 (2008): 557-79; John M MacKenzie, *The Empire of Nature. Hunting, Conservation and British Imperialism* (Manchester, 1988); Roderick P Neumann, *Imposing Wilderness. Struggles over Livelihood and Nature Preservation in Africa* (Berkeley, CA, 1998); Thomas P Ofcansky, *Paradise Lost. A History of Game Preservation in East Africa* (Morgantown, 2002), 47-63; Dan Brockington, *Fortress Conservation. The Preservation of the Mkomazi Game Reserve, Tanzania* (Oxford, 2002); David Anderson and Richard Grove, eds, *Conservation in Africa. People, Policies and Practice* (Cambridge, 1987).
29. Bernhard Gissibl and Johannes Paulmann, "Serengeti darf nicht sterben," in *Kein Platz an der Sonne. Erinnerungsorte der deutschen Kolonialgeschichte*, ed. Jürgen Zimmerer (Frankfurt, 2013), 96-108.

30. Gregory Maddox, "Networks and Frontiers in Colonial Tanzania," *Environmental History* 3 (1998): 437.
31. See Carl Death, "Environmental Mainstreaming and Post-Sovereign Governance in Tanzania," *Journal of Eastern African Studies* 7, no. 1 (2013): 1–20.
32. See George Steinmetz, *The Devil's Handwriting. Precoloniality and the German Colonial State in Qingdao, Samoa, and Southwest Africa* (Chicago, 2007), 1–3, 19–27; Trutz von Trotha, "Was war Kolonialismus? Einige zusammenfassende Befunde zur Soziologie und Geschichte des Kolonialismus und der Kolonialherrschaft," *Saeculum* 55 (2004): 53–55.
33. On Namibia, see Ute Dieckmann, *Hai//om in the Etosha Region. A History of Colonial Settlement, Ethnicity and Nature Conservation* (Basel, 2007); Manfred O Hinz, "'Waidgerechtigkeit' versus afrikanische Tradition. Deutsches Jagdrecht in Namibia?,' in *Kolonialisierung des Rechts. Zur kolonialen Rechts- und Verwaltungsordnung*, ed. Rüdiger Voigt and Peter Sack (Baden-Baden, 2001), 336–48; Bernhard Gissibl, "Paradiesvögel: Kolonialer Naturschutz und die Mode der deutschen Frau am Anfang des 20. Jahrhunderts," *Ritual-Macht-Natur. Europäisch-ozeanische Beziehungswelten in der Neuzeit*, ed. Johannes Paulmann, Daniel Leese, and Philippa Söldenwagner (Bremen, 2005), 131–54.
34. Jürgen Osterhammel, *Colonialism. A Theoretical Overview* (Princeton, NJ, 2005), 16–17.
35. See, for example, Bernhard Dernburg, *Zielpunkte des deutschen Kolonialwesens. Zwei Vorträge* (Berlin, 1907), 5.
36. Piers M Blaikie and Harold Brookfield, *Land Degradation and Society* (London, 1987), 17.
37. Paul Robbins, *Political Ecology. A Critical Introduction* (Malden, MA, 2004); Roderick P Neumann, *Making Political Ecology* (London, 2005).
38. Virginia DeJohn Anderson, *Creatures of Empire. How Domestic Animals Transformed Early America* (Oxford, 2004), 3.
39. See Brett L Walker, "Animals and the Intimacy of History," in *The Oxford Handbook of Environmental History*, ed. Andrew Isenberg (Oxford, 2014), 52–75; Bernhard Gissibl, "Das kolonisierte Tier. Zur Ökologie der Kontaktzonen des deutschen Kolonialismus," *Werkstatt Geschichte* 56 (2010): 7–28; and Gesine Krüger, "Das koloniale Tier. Natur—Kultur—Geschichte," in *Wo ist Kultur? Perspektiven der Kulturanalyse*, ed. Thomas Forrer and Angelika Linke (Zürich, 2014), 73–94.
40. The term *contact zone* denotes the "space of colonial encounters" and intersecting trajectories, defined by the interaction of individuals previously separated by geography, history, and culture, see Mary Louise Pratt, *Imperial Eyes. Travel Writing and Transculturation* (London, 1992), 6–7.
41. Chris Philo and Chris Wilbert, "Animal Spaces, Beastly Places. An Introduction," in *Animal Spaces, Beastly Places. New Geographies of Human-Animal Relations*, ed. C Philo and C Wilbert (London, 2000), 1–35.
42. See Thaddeus Sunseri, *Wielding the Ax. State Forestry and Social Conflict in Tanzania, 1820–2000* (Athens, 2009), 50–74; Thaddeus Sunseri, "Reinterpreting a Colonial Rebellion: Forestry and Social Control in German East Africa, 1874–1915," *Environmental History* 8 (2003): 430–51; Thaddeus Sunseri, "Famine and Wild Pigs: Gender Struggles and the Outbreak of the Maji-Maji War in Uzaramo," *Journal of African History* 38 (1997): 235–59; Thaddeus Sunseri, "The

War of the Hunters: Maji Maji and the Decline of the Ivory Trade," in *Maji Maji. Lifting the Fog of War,* ed. James Giblin and Jamie Monson (Leiden, 2010), 117–48; see further Christopher A Conte, *Highland Sanctuary. Environmental History in Tanzania's Usambara Mountains* (Athens, 2004).
43. See James Giblin and Gregory Maddox, "Introduction: Custodians of the Land. Ecology and Culture in the History of Tanzania," in *Custodians of the Land. Ecology and Culture in the History of Tanzania,* ed. Gregory Maddox, James Giblin, and Isaria N Kimambo (London, 1996), 1–14; Achim von Oppen, "Matuta. Landkonflikte, Ökologie und Entwicklung in der Geschichte Tanzanias," in *Tanzania. Koloniale Vergangenheit und neuer Aufbruch,* ed. Ulrich van der Heyden and Achim von Oppen (Münster, 1996), 47–84; Juhani Koponen, *People and Production in Late Precolonial Tanzania. History and Structures* (Helsinki, 1988); Kjekshus, *Ecology Control and Economic Development in East African History*; John Iliffe, *A Modern History of Tanganyika* (Cambridge, 1979); James L Giblin, *The Politics of Environmental Control in Northeastern Tanzania, 1840–1940* (Philadelphia, 1992).
44. N Thomas Håkansson, "The Human Ecology of World Systems in East Africa: The Impact of the Ivory Trade," *Human Ecology* 32 (2004): 561–91; N Thomas Håkansson, Mats Widgren, and Lowe Börjeson, "Introduction: Historical and Regional Perspectives on Landscape Transformations in Northeastern Tanzania, 1850–2000," *International Journal of African Historical Studies* 41, no. 3 (2008): 369–82.
45. Jane Carruthers, "Africa: Histories, Ecologies and Societies," *Environment and History* 10 (2004): 382.
46. See William Beinart and Lotte Hughes, *Environment and Empire* (Oxford, 2007); and James Beattie, "Recent Themes in the Environmental History of the British Empire," *History Compass* 10, no. 2 (2012): 129–39.
47. Exceptions are Philipp N Lehmann, "Between Waterberg and Sandveld: An Environmental Perspective on the German-Herero War of 1904," *German History* 32, no. 4 (2014): 533–58; Daniel Rouven Steinbach, "Carved out of Nature: Identity and Environment in German Colonial Africa," in *Cultivating the Colonies. Colonial States and Their Environmental Legacies,* ed. Christina Folke Ax, Niels Brimnes, Niklas Thode Jensen, and Karen Oslund (Athens, 2011), 47–77; Ulrike Kirchberger, "Wie entsteht eine imperiale Infrastruktur? Zum Aufbau der Naturschutzbürokratie in Deutsch-Ostafrika," *Historische Zeitschrift* 291 (2010): 41–69; H Jürgen Wächter, *Naturschutz in den deutschen Kolonien in Afrika, 1884–1918* (Münster, 2008); Birthe Kundrus, *Moderne Imperialisten. Das Kaiserreich im Spiegel seiner Kolonien* (Cologne, 2003), 138–62; Nigel Rothfels, *Savages and Beasts. The Birth of the Modern Zoo* (Baltimore, MD, 2002). A rare regional study of the environmental agency of missions in German Tanzania is provided by Robert B Munson, *The Nature of Christianity in Northern Tanzania. Environmental and Social Change, 1890–1916* (Lanham, MD, 2013).
48. See *German Colonialism in a Global Age,* ed. Bradley Naranch and Geoff Eley (Durham, 2014); Birthe Kundrus, "Von der Peripherie ins Zentrum. Zur Bedeutung des Kolonialismus für das Deutsche Kaiserreich," in *Das Deutsche Kaiserreich in der Kontroverse,* ed. Sven Oliver Müller and Cornelius Torp (Göttingen, 2009), 359–73; Dirk van Laak, "Kolonien als 'Laboratorien der Moderne?,'" in *Das Kaiserreich transnational. Deutschland in der Welt 1871–1914,* ed. Sebastian

Conrad and Jürgen Osterhammel (Göttingen, 2004), 257–79; cf. Sebastian Conrad, *Globalisation and the Nation in Imperial Germany* (Cambridge, 2010), chapter 2; Sebastian Conrad, "Globalization Effects: Mobility and Nation in Imperial Germany, 1880–1914," *Journal of Global History* 3 (2008): 43–66.

49. For surveys of the field see Sebastian Conrad, "Rethinking German Colonialism in a Global Age," *Journal of Imperial and Commonwealth History* 41(2013): 543–66; Maiken Umbach, "Forum: The German Colonial Imagination," *German History* 26 (2008): 251–71.

50. See for a survey Winson Chu, Jesse Kauffman, and Michael Meng, "A *Sonderweg* through Eastern Europe? The Varieties of German Rule in Poland during the Two World Wars," *German History* 31, no. 3 (2013): 318–44.

51. Conrad, "Rethinking German Colonialism in a Global Age"; Andrew Zimmerman, "Africa in Imperial and Transnational History: Multi-Sited Historiography and the Necessity of Theory," *Journal of African History* 54 (2013): 331–40; John M. MacKenzie, "European Imperialism: A Zone of Co-operation Rather than Competition?", in *Imperial Co-operation and Transfer, 1870-1930. Empires and Encounters*, ed. Volker Barth and Roland Cvetkovski (London, 2015): 35–53.

52. See, however, William H Rollins, "Imperial Shades of Green: Conservation and Environmental Chauvinism in the German Colonial Project," *German Studies Review* 22 (1999): 187–213; Anna-Katharina Wöbse, "Naturschutz global— oder: Hilfe von außen. Internationale Beziehungen des amtlichen Naturschutzes im 20. Jahrhundert," in *Natur und Staat. Staatlicher Naturschutz in Deutschland 1906-2006*, ed. Hans-Werner Frohn and Friedemann Schmoll (Bonn, 2006), 625–727.

53. The classic argument about the overseas colonies as the origin of European environmental sensibilities is unfolded in Richard H Grove, *Green Imperialism. Colonial Expansion, Tropical Island Edens and the Origins of Environmentalism, 1600–1860* (Cambridge, 1995). The relative insignificance of the global South for German environmentalism has recently been emphasized by Frank Uekötter, *The Greenest Nation? A New History of German Environmentalism* (London 2014), 13–14.

54. Michael Pesek, *Koloniale Herrschaft in Deutsch-Ostafrika. Expeditionen, Militär und Verwaltung seit 1880* (Frankfurt, 2005); Marcia Wright, "Local Roots of Policy in German East Africa," *Journal of African History* 9 (1968): 621–30.

55. The frictions between the bureaucratic state of the European tradition, intermediary and despotic forms of power, and African ideas of authority have been one of the core issues in the historical and political science study of the African state, see Andreas Eckert, *Herrschen und Verwalten. Afrikanische Bürokraten, staatliche Ordnung und Politik in Tanzania, 1920–1970* (Munich, 2007), 10–22, 31–38; Pesek, *Koloniale Herrschaft in Deutsch-Ostafrika*; Jeffrey Herbst, *States and Power in Africa: Comparative Lessons in Authority and Control* (Princeton, NJ, 2000).

56. Jonathon Glassman, *Feasts and Riots. Revelry, Rebellion, and Popular Consciousness on the Swahili Coast, 1856–1888* (Portsmouth, NH, 1994), 187–96.

57. Frederick Cooper, "Conflict and Connection. Rethinking Colonial African History," *American Historical Review* 99 (1994): 1527–28.

58. Speech of Bernhard Dernburg in the *Reichstag* on 18 February 1908, see *Deutsches Kolonialblatt* 19 (1908): 229.

59. This study uses "transcolonial" to refer to links across borders that took place or were relevant first and foremost in the colonies; "transnational" designates relations across national borders in Europe; "transimperial" denotes interactions between the imperial powers, which oscillated between metropole and colony.
60. Corey Ross, "Tropical Nature as Global *Patrimoine*. Imperialism and International Nature Protection in the Early Twentieth Century," *Past & Present Supplement 10* (2015): 214–39, 215.
61. David Blackbourn, "'As Dependent on Each Other as Man and Wife': Cultural Contacts and Transfers," in *Wilhelmine Germany and Edwardian Britain. Essays on Cultural Affinity*, ed. Dominik Geppert and Robert Gerwarth (Oxford, 2008), 27; John M MacKenzie, "'Mutual Goodwill and Admiration' or 'Jealous Ill-Will'? Empire and Popular Culture," in *Wilhelmine Germany and Edwardian Britain. Essays on Cultural Affinity*, ed. Dominik Geppert and Robert Gerwarth (Oxford, 2008), 91–113.
62. Antoinette Burton, "Getting Outside the Global: Re-Positioning British Imperialism in World History," in *Race, Nation and Empire. Making Histories, 1750 to the Present*, ed. Catherine Hall and Keith McClelland (Manchester, 2010), 213.
63. Russell A Berman, "Der ewige Zweite. Deutschlands Sekundärkolonialismus," in *Phantasiereiche. Zur Kulturgeschichte des deutschen Kolonialismus*, ed. Birthe Kundrus (Frankfurt, 2003), 23.
64. For the broad canvas of transimperial entanglements between Germany and Britain, see Ulrike Lindner, *Koloniale Begegnungen. Deutschland und Großbritannien als Imperialmächte in Afrika 1880–1914* (Frankfurt, 2011).
65. Ibid., 8.
66. See, for example, Karen Brown, "Tropical Medicine and Animal Diseases: Onderstepoort and the Development of Veterinary Science in South Africa 1908–1950," *Journal of Southern African Studies* 31 (2005): 513–29.
67. Conrad, "Rethinking German Colonialism in a Global Age"; Zimmerman, "Africa in Imperial and Transnational History."
68. James Morton Turner, "Rethinking American Exceptionalism. Toward a Transnational History of National Parks, Wilderness, and Protected Areas," in *The Oxford Handbook of Environmental History*, ed. Andrew Isenberg (Oxford, 2014), 282–308; Ian Tyrrell, "America's National Parks: The Transnational Creation of National Space in the Progressive Era," *Journal of American Studies* 46, no. 1 (2012): 1–21.
69. Bayerisches Hauptstaatsarchiv, Munich (BayHStA) IV, Hirsch Papers 10 35: Letter to his parents, Iraku, 3 July 1907; Hanns Braun, *Die Reise nach Ostafrika* (Berlin, 1939), 225.
70. Johannes Fabian, *Time and the Other. How Anthropology Makes Its Object* (New York, 2002), 31; Anne McClintock, *Imperial Leather. Race, Gender and Sexuality in the Colonial Contest* (New York, 1995), 40.
71. The term *characteristic animal* had been coined by Alfred Russel Wallace, *The Geographical Distribution of Animals. With a Study of the Relations of Living and Extinct Faunas as Elucidating the Past Changes of the Earth's Surface*, 2 vols. (London, 1876); cf. Charles Darwin, *The Origin of Species* (Oxford, 1996), chapters 11 and 12; Susanne Köstering, *Natur zum Anschauen. Das Naturkundemuseum des deutschen Kaiserreichs 1871–1914* (Cologne, 2003), 97–100.

72. Volker Langbehn, "Introduction. Picturing Race: Visuality and German Colonialism," in *German Colonialism, Visual Culture, and Modern Memory*, ed. Volker Langbehn (New York, 2010), 1–33; David Ciarlo, *Advertising Empire. Race and Visual Culture in Imperial Germany* (Cambridge, MA, 2011); John Philip Short, *Magic Lantern Empire. Colonialism and Society in Germany* (Ithaca, NY, 2012).
73. Ann Laura Stoler and Frederick Cooper, "Between Metropole and Colony: Rethinking a Research Agenda," in *Tensions of Empire. Colonial Cultures in a Bourgeois World*, ed. Frederick Cooper and Ann Laura Stoler (Berkeley, CA, 1997), 4.
74. Eckhart G Franz and Peter Geissler, *Das Deutsch-Ostafrika-Archiv. Inventar der Abteilung "German Records" im Nationalarchiv der Vereinigten Republik Tansania, Dar-es-Salaam*, 2 vols. (Marburg, 1973), 48–57.
75. Ann Laura Stoler, *Along the Archival Grain. Epistemic Anxieties and Colonial Common Sense* (Princeton, NJ, 2009).
76. Peter Pels, "The Anthropology of Colonialism. Culture, History, and the Emergence of Western Governmentality," in *Annual Review of Anthropology* 26 (1997): 165.
77. Libby Robin, "Conservation and Preservation," in *The Palgrave Dictionary of Transnational History*, ed. Akira Iriye and Pierre-Yves Saunier (Basingstoke, 2009), 191–94.
78. Joseph C Miller, "History and Africa/Africa and History," *American Historical Review* 104 (1999): 1–32, 16.

 PART I

Big Men, Big Game between Precolony and Colony

 CHAPTER 1

Tusks, Trust, and Trade
Ecologies of Hunting in Precolonial East Africa

> The lion is my father, and you, elephant, are my kinsman.
> —*Hunting song of the Kimbu, Western Tanzania*

Nineteenth-century East Africa was neither a paradise of peaceful coexistence between "natural" man and animal, nor a site of an eternal struggle for survival between humans and wildlife, as colonial observers would have it. Humans and wild animals coexisted in dynamic adaptation, and hunting was the main way of human interaction with them. Hunting was a highly differentiated and dynamic activity, and the growth of the caravan trade during the nineteenth century increased its economic, political, social, and symbolic significance. Ivory in particular attained an enormous commodity value, which encouraged elephant hunting and rendered it one of the most commercialized economic activities in nineteenth-century East Africa. Rather than an atavistic reminder of a waning primeval way of life, the pursuit and killing of wild animals even by hunter-gatherer societies became a modern activity. It was the main way in which East Africans participated in the networks of late nineteenth-century globalization.

This chapter maps the nineteenth-century East African hunting world at the eve of European colonial rule. It portrays hunting first as an activity that sustained an economy of subsistence in which the appropriation of animals was firmly embedded in the social and spiritual order of the respective community. This function continued to coexist with the hunting to supply the more-than-local networks of trade forged by the caravan trade. The growth of the trade in ivory provided an opportunity to procure economic and symbolical capital that was actively embraced by many East African societies. Focusing on the hunting of elephants, the chapter analyzes the social, political, and cultural consequences of increased ivory hunting. Contrary to the assumptions of earlier research that portrayed precolonial Tanzanian societies in full control of their environments, it is argued here that the ivory hunting stimulated by trade was a socially and ecologically disruptive activity that stabilized as well as destabilized political authority and enabled big men, hunter kings, and other political entrepreneurs to accumulate wealth and power. Although by no means obliterated, a relationship of trust in the wealth of nature was increasingly supplemented by more instrumental attitudes of hunters toward their prey.

Communities of Hunting—Settlement, Subsistence, and the Ecology of Wildlife Control

The expansion of trade and the ongoing human colonization of previously unsettled land were the two fundamental processes that determined East African history in the nineteenth century. Indeed, the ongoing colonization of territory by African communities was comparatively recent in most parts of the area that would later become German East Africa. Apart from the coast and the interlacustrine kingdoms, many parts still resembled a "frontier region, where society was fluid, highly adaptable, and capable of absorbing outsiders easily."[1] Historians have stressed the social capacities to exert ecological control in precolonial Tanganyika,[2] yet the vagaries of climate and drought, warfare, and the impact of the trade in slaves and ivory rendered people's control of their environment precarious and unstable.[3] Highly variable rainfall patterns, the recurrence of droughts, the changing quality of soils, and the limited availability of permanent water supplies all influenced settlement patterns and population density. In many areas, the presence of the tsetse fly and the associated risk of human and animal sleeping sickness denied settlement or disallowed the keeping of cattle. Consequently, people had to be mobile on different scales, and rather than being organized in timeless and immobile tribes, African societies and social organizations were constantly shifting and reforming.[4]

Precolonial demography is a contested terrain, and the figures delivered by colonial statistics express a desire to bureaucratic control rather than accurate numbers of inhabitants.[5] Nonetheless, the roughly five inhabitants per square kilometer suggested by the earliest German population statistics of 1902–3 suggest that areas occupied by wildlife outnumbered the pockets of cultivation[6]: in 1910, a German geographer described Tanganyika as essentially a "wilderness with islands of culture."[7] Patches of settlement were surrounded by extensive uninhabited bush and woodlands, where water was scarce and soil fertility low. German travelers and colonialists called these tracts of land *Grenzwildnisse*. They were margins where chiefly authority became elusive; they were spaces of transition crossed by links of trade and exchange; they were spiritual landscapes and locations of temporary utilization, where substances for ritual practices and medicine could be obtained. Above all, they were male domains where wild animals were stalked and trapped.

Together with poor soils, unreliable rainfall, and diseases, wild animals counted among the major threats to human livelihood. Their hunting was an ecological necessity to mitigate environmental adversities and a vital accompaniment of migration, settlement, and cultivation. Although virtually all East African societies practiced some form of wildlife control, its intensity and importance varied considerably in different environmental contexts. Wild animals were few in densely settled and cultivated areas such as the coastal belt or the slopes of Mount Kilimanjaro. Chagga farmers on Mount Kilimanjaro, for example, had a reputation for hunting very little,[8] but this did not prevent Kilimanjaro chiefs from seizing the opportunities of the ivory trade to extend or at least stabilize their position among their rivalling neighbors. Rindi of Moshi, for example, strengthened his authority by recruiting bands of specialized elephant hunters from Ukamba and Uteita. The ivory thus gained was traded, among others, for firearms with Swahili merchants from Pangani.[9] Shambaa agriculturalists in the Usambara Mountains practiced a similar cooperation with Kamba elephant hunters, who had established settlements in the Pangani Valley as early as the eighteenth century. Themselves hunting to supplement their diet, the Shambaa were not directly engaged in elephant hunting and the ivory trade, but benefited from it by the exchange of vegetables against meat with Kamba hunters.[10]

On the other end of the spectrum were foraging hunter-gatherer societies like the Hadzabe and the Sandawe who eked out their living under the inhospitable conditions of the dry *miombo* plains of central and northern Tanganyika.[11] While their foraging way of life can be regarded as adaptation to marginal environmental surroundings, the hunting and gathering of those groups in northern Tanganyika and southern Kenya, which in German and British colonial parlance were referred to as Dorobo, Ndorobo, or Wandorobbo was embedded into regional systems of exchange. Dorobo a derogatory term from the Maa language to refer to "those without cattle", denoted an occupational rather than an ethnic identity. Their hunting and gathering formed part of a regional system of trade and exchange crystallizing around Maasai pastoralism, in which the procuring of meat, hides, and tusks represented an economic specialization complementary to the surrounding agriculturalists and pastoralists.[12] Generally, hunting played a more important role in tsetse-infested areas where the danger of trypanosomiasis disallowed the breeding of cattle. This was the case in most parts of southern Tanganyika. But hunting fulfilled several vital functions also in societies whose subsistence rested to a large degree on livestock or agriculture. It was a strategy of survival during times of famine and ecological stress, and it was a means to obtain supplementary protein and important items for exchange in regional and interregional systems of trade, such as ivory, horns, and skins.

If the importance of hunting varied among different societies and in different environmental contexts, so did purpose, form, and technique. In order to catch or kill animals, East African societies had a broad range of techniques at their disposal. Groups of hunters could lurk at frequented passages or waterholes, or they could actively drive or stalk animals. The English explorer Richard Burton, traversing Tanganyika in 1857–58, asserted that at the end of the rains,

> armed with bows and arrows, and with rungu or knobkerries, the villagers have a battue of small antelopes, hares, and birds. During the hot season also, when the waters dry up, they watch by night at the tanks and pools, and they thus secure the larger kinds of game.[13]

Apart from the weaponry mentioned by Burton, the nineteenth century witnessed the increased utilization of muzzle-loading guns that were phased out in European armies and flooded East and Central Africa via the networks of the caravan trade. Moreover, East African societies had a differentiated set of traps at their disposal. European travel accounts as well as early ethnographies testify to the almost universal use of pits, traps, nets, and snares of various size and function, sometimes used in combination with fences of plaited thornbush or nets fabricated from dried bark. These passive forms of hunting only increased under colonial rule to circumvent the ever more rigid circumscription of Africans' hunting rights.

Trapping and communal game drives appear to have been the forms of hunting with the least social restrictions. Several sources testify to "whole villages" participating in game drives, which would probably have included women.[14] Hunting and stalking, on the other hand, were almost exclusively male prerogatives, as substantiated by most contemporary colonial observers and later ethnographies based on oral history. Apart from gender, expertise, also skill, and the knowledge of hunting rituals restricted access to the chase. So did the ecological and social power relations that governed the appropriation of wild animals. While all men were potential hunters, the organization of collective hunts was often the duty of the chief. Hunting animals like buffalo, hippopotamus, rhinoceros, and especially elephants, was a specialized and highly ritualized undertaking accessible only to a selected few. Their pursuit not only meant the confrontation with potentially dangerous animals, but was also connected with the invasion of the spiritually hostile environments of forest and savanna. Only few hunters and *waganga* (sg. *mganga*, healer/medicine person) knew about the necessary medicines and ritual precautions, so that the French Missionary Cado Picarda, superior of the Holy Ghost Fathers' mission at Mandera in the Wami Valley, described hunters as forming "une classe à part," distinguished by a "rituel complet de pratiques superstitieuses."[15]

These ritual practices fulfilled important social and ecological functions. By restricting access to the hunt, they guaranteed exclusiveness and functioned as a measure of conservation. But they also had an inclusive dimension, indicating as they did the general state of social and spiritual affairs of a community. The ritual requirements of a successful hunt concerned and involved the whole family, lineage, village, or chiefdom, making it an inclusive activity where the spheres of humans, animals, and ancestral spirits met.[16] Ethnographic information available from early colonial and missionary observers in German East Africa corroborates the role of hunting as an important marker of the political, moral, social, and spiritual ecology of East African societies. The German missionary Joseph Busse, who worked in Rungwe near Lake Nyassa in the 1930s, noticed that

> before the men embark upon the chase, all quarrels in the village must be settled. ... While the hunters are in the field, those remaining back in the village are neither supposed to argue nor to violate any of the traditional customs.[17]

Every hunt had to be preceded by the foregoing appeasement of the spirits in charge of the respective land. Both the hunters as well as those staying behind in the village were subject to a whole set of restrictions and prohibitions before and while the men were away. Accounts of contemporary European observers emphasize the sexual dimension of these prohibitions. Elephant hunters and their wives were supposed to refrain from sexual intercourse one or several nights before the group would take up the pursuit.[18] As in times of warfare, the absence of the men from the village was a period of potential crisis and vulnerability. The restrictions thus served to harness and control female sexuality and symbolically claimed male authority in the village while the men themselves were away. Yet, by means of ritual, the fate and well-being of the hunters was inevitably linked with the behavior of the community. Only the communal adherence to the moral order, together with the goodwill solicited from the ancestral spirits enabled the hunters' success. A safe return and a successful hunt indicated and validated the peaceful and intact social and spiritual relations in the village. Upon the hunters' return, often day-long festivities followed. In most societies, the distribution of the spoils of communal hunting appears to have followed strictly set rules that expressed a moral obligation to share and strengthened the ties between hunters and the community. Patterns of distribution usually required a symbolic tribute to the chief as the last descendant in the line of the ancestral chiefs. Personal networks of kinship, friendship, and patronage also determined who was included into the community of sharing.[19]

Hunting and meat were thus politics. The communal and spiritual embedding of the hunt reinforced the association of hunting with power on the one hand, the obligation to share on the other. The various forms of hunting, trapping, and stalking wild animals expressed, negotiated, and fostered a whole set of social, spiritual, and ecological power relations.

The World of Tusks—Trade, Consumption, and the Myth of an Ivory Frontier

Ongoing colonization and settlement was the one process that gave hunting key importance in precolonial East African societies. The other was the incorporation of inland Tanganyika into the networks of capitalist world trade via a complex system of long-distance trade routes. This globalized trade commoditized and attached new values to many East African products, and none more so than the tusks of elephants.[20] Ivory had for centuries, if not millennia, been an important good for export within the Indian Ocean ecumene, in which dhows shuttled tusks, clothing, grains, spices, timber, pottery, beads, people, knowledge, and ideas between the coasts of India, Africa, and the Arab Peninsula.[21] In this intercontinental exchange, the Swahili ports of Mombasa, Bagamoyo, and Kilwa functioned as commercial entrepôts and contact zones between the cultures and religions of the African mainland, and the trade diasporas of the Indian Ocean. Thus, the inclusion of ever more societies on the East African mainland into the world economy during the nineteenth century meant a change in volume, frequency, and direction of already existing trade flows. The commercial, political, and religious networks of the East African coast became gradually incorporated into networks of capitalist trade that were governed by the demands of the industrializing Euro-American societies.

Euro-American demand notwithstanding, the nineteenth-century ivory trade was a global phenomenon, resting upon the compound interaction of processes and people on four continents. Consumption was by no means a "Western" privilege, and trade was not a one-way street. As Jeremy Prestholdt has shown, African societies had their share in the riches of the trade, and consumer demands for industrial products in Zanzibar and East Africa, for example, for *merekani* cloths or guns, played an equal part in constituting these global trade links.[22] Enterprising Africans had forged the long-distance trade networks on the African mainland in the first place, and these networks were only gradually taken over by Swahili and Omani traders around the middle of the nineteenth century. The hunting of elephants remained the task of skilled experts in African societies, and tusks changed hands along a complex chain that involved hunters, chiefs, traders, middlemen, bankers, seamen, and finally, the craftsmen who transformed tusks into knife handles, piano keys, billiard balls, or carvings. This increasing interconnectedness between regional systems of exchange in East Africa and the centers of the Northern Hemisphere was part of the late nineteenth-century globalization of world trade. East Africa participated in this process by the reinforcement of hunting, probably the oldest economic activity of its societies. The hunting and trading of tusks thus constituted one of several strategies of "extraversion," that is, the deliberate mobilization of external resources in processes of political centralization, economic accumulation, and the social control of subordinates.[23]

While not denying the significance of hippopotami teeth, rhinoceros horns, or gazelle hides that were manufactured into gloves in Europe,[24] elephant tusks were by far the most important commodity derived from the grand-scale slaughtering of East Africa's wildlife. The nineteenth century brought about such a marked transformation in direction and scope of this trade that some scholars even spoke of an "ivory revolution."[25] Until the mid-nineteenth century, the principal market for East African ivory lay in Asia, especially in India, where locally procured ivory could not satisfy the demand for the bangles and bracelets that were used as bridal ornaments by upper-class women.[26] These older trade links persisted, but Mumbai (Bombay) increasingly came to serve as an intermediary port for tusks that were reexported to London, New York, Amsterdam, and Hamburg. In Europe, London and Antwerp were the most important harbors, with Hamburg catching up, its imports rising from 52,000 kilograms in 1840 to roughly 182,000 in 1890. During the same years, prices in Hamburg climbed by 150 percent from 10 marks to 25 marks per kilogram of "soft medium-weight East African tusks." The bulk of this ivory was imported by the trading company of Heinrich Adolf Meyer, who marketed himself proudly as "one of the largest ivory trading houses in the world."[27]

The disjointed spaces of ivory's production in Africa and consumption in Europe and North America were mediated by complex chains of transport and transaction. In Europe, established uses of ivory as an exclusive and expensive raw material for sacral and profane artworks were continued. Yet, changing patterns of production and consumption in the wake of industrialization created new and more diverse forms of utilization. These stepped up demand for raw ivory from Africa, also because similar raw materials, like baleen or whale bones, declined in the second half of the nineteenth century.[28] Its new uses made ivory partially lose its status as a luxury commodity.[29] In 1889, the abovementioned Meyer compiled a short list advertising the "thousands of things made of ivory" consumed in Europe: among these were inlets in brushes and combs, the frontispieces of prayer books, knife handles and fans, piano keys, stick handles, lids for boxes, billiard balls, and artistic carvings.[30] Furthermore, want for representation and fine education made the piano an omnipresent feature of bourgeois salons and music rooms. Between 1850 and 1914, 250 new manufacturing companies sprang up in Germany alone.[31] The use of ivory next to ebony for piano keys by Steinway, Steinweg, Ibach, Feurich, or Blüthner contributed to the East African ivory boom as well as conspicuous consumption by use of knife handles crafted from the precious material, which made Sheffields's CB Rodgers Co. Ltd. the world's leading knife maker. Elephants gave their tusks to supply gentlemen with balls to indulge in the increasingly popular game of billiards. Hardly any aristocratic and bourgeois household could do without a billiard table in a separate playing room. This boom enabled Hamburg's Meyer to sell an estimated 70,000 billiard balls per year in the late 1880s.[32]

On the other end of the commodity chain, the popularization of new uses for ivory in Europe and North America made itself felt in a spectacular increase in ivory prices on the East African coast, which mainly provided the smooth, white soft ivory derived from the tusks of the savanna elephant (*Loxodonta Africana africana*). It distinguished itself from the translucent hard ivory obtained from forest elephants by its easy workability and was used preferably for piano keys, combs, carvings, and billiard balls.[33] In 1823, one frasila—the locally applied measure for ivory comprising some 35 pounds—cost 21 dollars on the Zanzibar market. By 1853, its price had more than doubled to 45 dollars, tripling again to reach 140 dollars per frasila by the eve of colonial conquest in 1883.[34] The rising prices were related to an equal boom in the quantity of ivory exported via Zanzibar. Occasional dumps notwithstanding, the amount of tusks exported from East Africa via the island skyrocketed from 700,000 pounds in 1843 to an average of 1,240,800 pounds in the years between 1879 and 1883.[35] In 1891, some 75 percent of the world's total consumption of ivory was provided by Zanzibar alone.[36]

The ivory exported via Zanzibar was brought to the coast by caravans operating along an ever tighter grid of routes that connected the regional systems of trade in the East African interior with the international hub of commerce in Zanzibar.[37] By the middle of the nineteenth century, three major routes formed the arteries of trade. A southernmost connection linked the Indian Ocean coast with the inland regions around Lake Nyasa, starting at the Swahili ports of Kilwa and Lindi. It was mainly operated by Yao traders, but also Makua, Ngindo, and Bisa caravans used Kilwa as an outlet. This route was the earliest and most prolific channel for ivory at the beginning of the century. In 1840, it still accounted for almost one third of the total ivory exported from the East African coast before it lost importance as an outlet, probably in consequence of the disruptions and resettlements caused by the Ngoni invasions to the hinterland of the Kilwa trade.[38] Second, a northern trade route stretched from the ports of Tanga and Pangani to Moshi and Mount Kilimanjaro, continuing from there through Maasailand to Lake Victoria and the plains of southern Kenya. Here, the opportunities of long-distance trade and elephant hunting were seized predominantly by traders and entrepreneurs from Ukambani, before they faced increasing competition from Swahili caravans operating from the coast.[39] Both the northern and southern routes were, however, eclipsed in importance by the port of Bagamoyo, which rose to become the central outlet for ivory along the coast opposite of Zanzibar. A southwesterly route extended from Bagamoyo toward Uhehe, while a central route directly connected the coast with Unyamwezi and beyond Lake Tanganyika. Initially, the Nyamwezi undertook the caravan trade as a seasonal occupation at the end of the rainy season, when most fieldwork had been done and tracks and rivers allowed for passage. As the century progressed, Nyamwezi became more or less synonymous with skilled and trustworthy porter, and the caravan trade a respectable way of life. In the early 1880s, almost half of the able-bodied male population was said to be engaged in porterage.[40]

Until about the mid nineteenth century, trade on these routes rested almost entirely in the hands of Africans. Increasingly, however, caravans furnished and led by Omani and Swahili traders at the coast took over. It is probably more than mere coincidence that the presence of Zanzibari caravans increased after North American and European trade companies had established outposts at Zanzibar from the 1830s onward.[41] Thanks to the credit provided by Indian bankers and middlemen, Zanzibar traders now had privileged access to the imported commodities, especially cloth, firearms, and powder. This credit put traders under enormous pressure and may help explain some of the escalating violence connected with the trade when ivory became scarcer from the 1880s onward. The money provided by Indian bankers allowed an ever growing number of coastal caravans to gain the upper hand over their African competitors. So did a discriminatory tax regime that favored Zanzibaris, while dwindling ivory resources in Unyamwezi contributed to the decrease of independent Nyamwezi caravans. As a consequence, a growing number of young Nyamwezi adults migrated to Bagamoyo to market themselves as professional porters in the Zanzibari caravans. By 1840, the coastal traders had established a first inland outpost in Unyamwezi, which gradually developed into the town of Tabora, some 1,000 kilometers inland from the coast. Situated at the intersection of several routes, Tabora became the hub of the ivory trade in the second half of the nineteenth century and a relay station for porters and commodities.

The political, social, economic, and ecological impacts of the caravan trade in both ivory and slaves belie any assumption that precolonial East African communities led predominantly stable lives of subsistence production in harmony with their natural environments.[42] While such communities may have existed, those Tanzanian regions that were integrated into the system of world trade experienced its direct and indirect ecological effects. Indirectly, trade, transport, hunting, the wealth accumulated by extraversion, as well as the destabilization by an increasingly violent trade, affected regional systems of exchange, schemes of land utilization, settlement patterns, and local subsistence strategies. Directly, the reduction of elephant herds removed a key landscape architect and a major regulating factor of vegetation cover in regional ecosystems.[43]

Such impact of species removal upon the historical ecology of landscapes is, however, hard to assess with any precision. So is the degree to which Tanganyika's elephant herds were actually depleted by the late nineteenth century.[44] Still, available statistics and a broad sample of precolonial and early colonial sources suggest that two widespread and related assumptions about elephant ecologies in late nineteenth-century Tanganyika cannot be maintained: the idea that ivory trade and hunting advanced along a linear frontier, and the assumption that elephants in Tanzania were close to extinction by the onset of colonial rule.

Undeniably, elephant stocks in the future territory of German East Africa were seriously depleted. As early as 1872, the German explorer Georg Schweinfurth had warned that the number of elephants in Africa was rapidly deteriorating. Fantastic figures circulated about the scope of the annual elephant slaughter. Missionary David Livingstone reckoned that 44,000 elephants had to give their lives to satisfy the demands of the British ivory market in 1870 alone; in the early 1880s, German and British sources estimated the annual elephanticide as high as 65,000 animals all over Africa. With the onset of colonialism, zoo directors and zoologists, explorers, hunters, and colonialists filled the pages of German colonial, zoological, and geographical magazines with laments about the "war of extermination" (*Vernichtungskrieg*) waged against the elephant in Africa.[45] In the middle of the 1890s, the number of elephants killed for the ivory trade was estimated with absurd precision at 42,357 annually.[46] Often quoted is Scottish explorer Joseph Thomson's assessment from the middle of the 1880s that

> People talk as if the ivory of Africa were inexhaustible.... Nothing could be more absurd. Let me simply mention a fact. In my sojourn of fourteen months, during which I passed over an immense area of the Great Lakes region, I never once saw a single elephant.... The ruthless work of destruction has gone on with frightful rapidity.[47]

In the 1880s, European observers were united in the belief that the African elephant was doomed to extinction within the next fifty years if the current rate of destruction was allowed to continue unabated. Map 1.1, by the explorer Paul Reichard, combines the ecoknowledge of coastal ivory traders with the perceptions of peripatetic Europeans on East Africa's caravan routes during the 1880s. Significantly, the map leaves a suggestive blank for most of the Tanganyikan territory, and many scholars have since reciprocated the assumption that as early as the 1870s, "most of Tanganyika's ivory had been hunted down."[48]

However, the gloomy prophecies that elephants were "completely extinct"[49] in the territory claimed by Germany was often based upon generalized observations from the beaten tracks on which the European conquerors followed the caravan traders. There elephants had obviously disappeared. Assessments that tried to gauge the death toll of elephants in

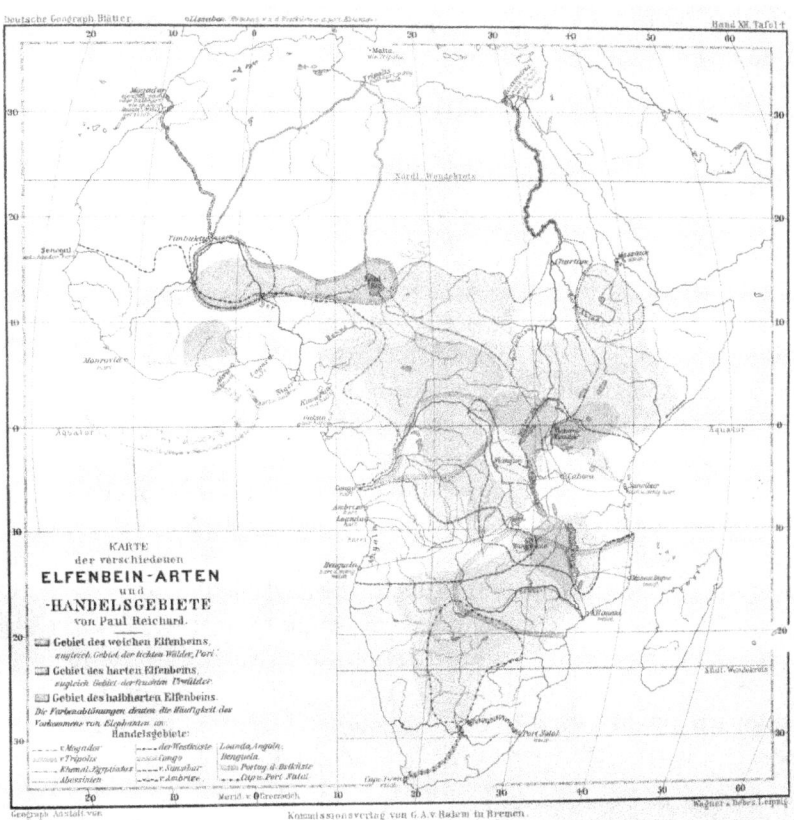

Map 1.1. Types of ivory and regions of the ivory trade (*Deutsche Geographische Blätter* 1889).

Tanganyika from the number of tusks that featured in the Zanzibari trade statistics of the 1870s and 1880s are necessarily imprecise because Zanzibar drew its ivory from a vast area, from the Zambezi in the south, to the Congo Basin in the west, and to the Banaadir ports of the southern Somali coast in the north. Further, it must be taken into account that, whenever a new region was drawn into the trade, a considerable amount of old and found ivory was fed into the market.[50] Roy Bridges's speculation that "the carnage caused by the late nineteenth-century ivory trade" was "not as serious as has often been assumed"[51] is supported by the observations of the first colonial stations and garrisons that were established over the Tanganyika territory in the 1890s. The annual report from Dar es Salaam, for example, asserted in 1897 that "none of the indigenous hunters would support the contention that elephants were on the brink of extinction. Quite the opposite: they know of uncounted herds in areas where elephants had not been known earlier." And putting the scare of extinction in the 1890s into perspective, the Schutztruppe officer Heinrich Fonck estimated in 1910 that the number of elephants was far larger than presumed about a decade ago, especially in the "endless forests of the South" and the mountains of Uhehe and Mahenge.[52]

Sources testifying to the surprisingly widespread survival of elephants also call into question the established notion that the ivory trade had penetrated Eastern Africa along an imaginary and linear "ivory frontier." This frontier allegedly followed the logic of exhaustive exploitation and was driven by the incentive of rising prices paid for ivory on the Zanzibar market. By the time the European colonizers came to East Africa in the 1880s, it had already advanced well beyond the Great Lakes and the borders of the German and British spheres of influence. As a consequence, many scholars have been led to presume that hunting and ivory were of little importance in the fledgling years of colonial rule.[53]

Undeniably, this westward shift occurred, and the Congo Basin functioned as the main area of ivory procurement by the last decades of the century. Nonetheless, the metaphor of an ivory frontier suggests a linearity that does not adequately capture the fragmented and highly uneven incorporation of many areas into the networks of the trade. There was no single but several frontiers, and East African societies participated in the ivory trade by the hunting of elephants in one area, by raiding or the levying of tolls in another, while in other regions the impact of the caravan trade was hardly felt.[54] The percolation and adaptation of coastal culture and its goods may serve as indicator for the reach of the caravan trade. When Oskar Baumann, Austrian explorer in German services, traversed the Wembere steppe and entered Sukuma in 1892, he was astonished to find people there "much more influenced by coastal culture than many tribes living close to the coast like the Wadigo, Wasch[amba] or the Wapare."[55] Some spoke Kiswahili, had traveled to the coast, possessed cotton clothes, and cultivated crops like rice and millet. The degree to which societies were affected by the trade was less determined by geographical proximity to the coast, but by the logics and geographies of hunting and trade.

The notion of an ivory frontier is especially misleading for it conflates a commercial with an ecological frontier. It does not distinguish between ivory *trade* and ivory *hunting*, and suggests that the frontier of trade followed hard on the heel of the exhaustion of elephant stocks. But the price of tusks did not rest upon a simple translation of biological scarcity into economic value. Rather, value was determined by a whole set of political, social, economic, and ecological factors. Even more than the increasing scarcity of elephants, economic rationales motivated the ever further intrusion of Zanzibari traders into the interior. As early as 1858, the British explorer John Hanning Speke noted that

> it may appear odd that men should go so far into the interior of Africa to procure ivory when undoubtedly much is to be found at places not half so distant from Zanzibar: but the reason is simple. The nearer countries have become so overstocked with beads and cloth that ivory has risen to so great a price that it does not pay to transport. Hence every succeeding year finds the Arabs penetrating further inland.[56]

Speke's observation reveals the determining role of African consumerism in the trade as well as the power Africans had in channeling the supply of ivory. They, too, determined its value and were consumers who speculated and denied trade if the goods offered by the Zanzibaris did not suit local needs and tastes. Such changing fashions made trade quite unpredictable for caravans and could lead, at least indirectly, to a release of the hunting pressure in areas closer to the coast.

Finally, elephants had agency.[57] Observations by hunters, explorers, and colonial officials suggest that elephants reacted to hunting pressure by migration and learned to be wary. Their disappearance from one area could easily lead to their reappearance in another area where trade might have already deemed to be no longer lucrative. Such was probably the case in the hinterland of Lindi between the rivers Liwale and Rovuma. An expedition setting out from Lindi in late 1891 encountered plenty of fresh spoor and the occasional herd between Masasi and the Mbwemkuru. Five years later, a German district official reported from Mikindani, that in the area up to the "middle Rovuma" elephants were encountered occasionally.[58] The German explorer and naturalist Richard Böhm, who resided near Kakoma south of Tabora for almost a year in 1880–1, confirmed other reports attesting the continued presence of elephants even in the heartlands of the ivory trade in

Unyamwezi.[59] Inaccessible swamps, dense forests, and mountainous areas provided plenty of shelter for a species that had become extremely shy.

Traditions of Power and the Power of Tradition

The insight that the elephant herds within the territory that was to become German East Africa were neither hunted out nor on the verge of extinction has important ramifications for German politics after 1885 and for understanding the importance of elephant hunting for African societies in the last third of the nineteenth century. The German colonizers entered a world in which ivory had attained an enormous symbolical, political, and economical value. So had the hunting of elephants. The successful hunter was a political figure, for he accumulated wealth that was convertible into various forms of capital, such as the maintenance or extension of client–patron relationships, or other forms of wealth like cattle, cloth, beads, or rifles. Perhaps nowhere else is the association of hunting with power and social prestige more tangibly laid down than in the oral traditions and stories that circulated in East African societies.[60] Hunters, particularly of elephants, loomed large in mythical narratives of origin, migration, and settlement. Some of them can be lifted from the lay ethnographies composed by colonial administrators or early missionaries; others have been unearthed in the context of oral history projects in various regions of Tanganyika since the 1960s. In virtually all of them, hunters were associated with wealth, protection, and authority. The mythical founders of communities and chiefdoms were either pioneer colonists who cleared the land, or strangers who came from the exterior as hunters. The Bena clan of Nyanguvila in the southern highlands of Tanzania, for example, traced its ancestry back to a famous elephant hunter named Mboga, who was said to have moved into the area generations ago.[61] The lineage of chief Mkwawa in neighboring Uhehe related its history back to a legendary hunter named Mujinga who was remembered to have come from Usagara to Uhehe for the sake of hunting.[62] In oral testimonies collected among the scattered societies of the Western Serengeti and South Mara areas in the middle of the 1990s, the founders of the Hemba, Ikoma, Ikizu, and Nata people were all remembered as hunters.[63] Most societies that had migrated into the area of Greater Unyamwezi and Ukimbu remembered wandering hunters and ivory traders as their founders.[64] But perhaps the best known example of an outside hunter as the mythical founder is enshrined in traditions of the Shambaa in the Usambara Mountains. John Prediger Farler, a missionary resident at Magila in the late 1870s, mentioned that the currently ruling dynasty had been established by a "great hunter" whose prowess so impressed the people of Usambara "that they invited him to be their king."[65] Commonly, this mythical founder of the Usambara kingdom in the nineteenth century is remembered as Mbegha, who originally came from Nguu in Uzigua and hunted wild pigs when he made contact with Shambaa people. He exchanged meat against vegetables, defended fields and settlements against the depredations of wild pigs, and distributed the spoils of his hunting among the people. When one day Mbegha killed a lion that had attacked cattle, the Shambaa imbued him with the authority of a chief, thus establishing the Wakilindi as the royal dynasty in Vuga, the Shambaa capital.[66] This mythical tradition has been recounted in several variations—historian Steven Feierman recorded no less than twenty-six versions in the late 1960s.[67]

Myths and traditions are expressions of a society's values and beliefs, charters of social and political institutions.[68] The tradition of Mbegha highlights the enormous prestige of hunters and how hunting was embedded in the social and cultural cosmos of Usambara societies. In the *Habari za Wakilindi*, a general history of the Wakilindi rulers of Vuga written between 1895 and 1907,[69] Mbegha became chief because he was a daring hunter, a powerful magician,[70] *and* a generous provider of meat and protection. Hunting and leadership were connected in a reciprocal relationship: one served as legitimization for the other. Hunting unfolded its enormous prestige and authority only in the framework of a redistributive conversion into the social capital of allegiance.

Traditions that allocated hunters a crucial role in the creation of social groups projected an ideal of chiefly authority back into a mythical time. At the same time, they reflected and incorporated recent events and responded to them. History as lived experience and tradition as the memorial preservation of a socially relevant past were enmeshed in an ongoing process of cross-fertilization. Perhaps nowhere did history come closer to an enactment of tradition than in the establishment of the short-lived Yeke kingdom, which blossomed in Katanga, southwest of Lake Tanganyika, in the second half of the nineteenth century, until it succumbed in the violent struggles for mining rights, slaves, ivory, and political power that disturbed the Eastern Congo in the early 1890s. Traditions about the founding of the kingdom, laid down in 1909, feature the stereotypical elephant hunter coming from the east. In this case, however, the migrating hunter represented actual historical events as the origin of the Yeke kingdom can be related back to a trader named M'siri, who followed elephants and the opportunities of the ivory trade to settle in Katanga shortly after 1850.[71] Within a short time, M'siri superseded the local rulers, established himself as overlord, trained people in elephant hunting, and exerted rigorous control of all trade in ivory. The name of the kingdom, *Yeke*, reflected its origins as a foundation of hunters, because elephant hunting societies in many parts of greater Unyamwezi were called *yege* or *uwuyege*.[72] The events leading to the foundation of the Nyamwezi offshoot in Katanga not only became the stuff of new traditions circulating in the area to this day. Most likely, they were reenactments of traditions themselves: hunters and ivory traders already loomed large in the cosmos of Unyamwezi and Kimbu societies from where M'siri had set out.[73] He had only followed the mythical script.

Makua, Big Men, and Hunter Kings

Oral tradition depicted hunting as an avenue to power for outsiders. M'siri was only one example for the mobilizing effect of the ivory trade that enabled "outside" hunters and traders to enter the services of powerful chiefs as clients and hunting experts, or even to attain a following themselves. Indeed, there were several instances when merchants and hunters reciprocated this pattern and used the wealth acquired by elephant hunting and the ivory trade to establish themselves as big men— self-made political entrepreneurs, whose authority relied on wealth, patronage, and coercion rather than on power derived from inheritance and tradition.[74] In order to understand this development, it must be placed within the broader context of the social and political ecology of trade-induced elephant hunting.

Many East African societies had hunted elephants before their tusks became commoditized, while others did not embrace it whole-heartedly even after ivory suddenly attained a high commercial value.[75] But the new commodity status of ivory turned elephant hunting into a promising field of enterprise and an opportunity for the socially and spatially mobile. Conjunctures of trade, scarcity of elephants, or the mobility of herds forced hunters to extend their scope of action, too. In Western Tanganyika in particular, hunters were instrumental in the process of linking regional systems of exchange with the external trade networks directed toward the coast and Zanzibar. They spread the word of ivory's commercial value and traded the knowledge of weapons, medicines, and rituals necessary for killing elephants. Not only traders, but also hunters established new links and connections between East African societies and opened them up to the outside world.[76]

If mobility and regional extension was one important characteristic of the nineteenth-century commercialization of elephant hunting, increasing specialization, professionalization, and the partial "detribalization" was another. Besides the premium placed upon tusks, the other important factor effecting these changes was the swamping of East Africa with muzzle-loading firearms outphased in Europe. In 1859, imports into Zanzibar numbered around 20,000 per year. This figure rose to an estimated 100,000 arms imported annually into East Africa via Zanzibar in 1888.[77]

Muzzle-loading rifles decisively transformed elephant hunting. Unreliable as they were, they nonetheless rendered the killing of wild animals far more effective than any method employed before. Firearms allowed for smaller groups and enhanced the hunters' mobility. It had taken twenty to thirty men to kill an elephant with spears, but as few as three to five could be sufficient when firearms were employed.[78] Undeniably, guns furthered a commercial and business-like approach to elephant hunting. Still, the newly introduced, modern weaponry did not simply displace existing, "traditional" and ritualized forms. New weapons were combined with the ritual knowledge necessary for the successful hunt of elephants, which remained a prerogative of those initiated and organized in guilds and fraternities distinguished by gender, name, and the observation of certain norms of behavior. The exclusiveness of access varied, but was usually dependent on the initiation and teaching by an experienced elder hunter. In many sources, this hunter is referred to by a variation of the Kiswahili word for a skilled master, the *fundi* (pl. *mafundi*).[79] Observations by European explorers, colonial ethnographies, and oral histories collected in the first decades after independence reveal a surprisingly uniform pattern, which emphasized the central role of "hunter magicians," that is, "skilled hunters with magic powers which give them the rights of leadership and a monopoly over resources."[80] This uniformity must in part be attributed to the fact that the spread of hunters also facilitated the circulation of knowledge about elephant hunting. If a British district officer questioning Ndamba hunters in the Ulanga Valley in the 1920s is to be believed, this exchange of knowledge extended well over Eastern and Southeastern Africa. He was told that the

> Wandamba usually averred that they learnt from the Wabena, and the Wabena from their fathers; some Wayao of Portuguese East Africa that they learnt from the Achikunda of the lower Zambezi; and Wayao of the Masaninga branch in Nyasaland, that their knowledge of hunting medicine was derived from the Wamakua of the Rovuma.[81]

If *fundi* became a kind of technical term for the leaders of hunting groups, the nineteenth-century caravan trade also witnessed the emergence of a special type of hunter-entrepreneur, which in many sources was referred to as "Makua." The development of this occupational identity testifies to the specialization of hunting as well as to its partial "detribalization."[82] While in many areas, elephant hunting continued to be undertaken as a community bound activity controlled by local chiefs, the opportunities offered by the import of firearms made hunters more flexible, mobile, and independent of established authorities. The emergence of the Makua denotes this detribalization, and it is a prime example of the scrambled identities and the circulation of knowledge in the contact zones of the caravan trade. During the second half of the nineteenth century, Makua was transformed from a term merely denoting ethnicity into an accolade of mobility, skill, and professionalism in the killing of elephants. Edward Alpers traced its origins back to itinerant hunters who constituted the vanguard of Makua migration into southern Tanzania.[83] There they formed part of an "ethnic division of labour shaped by trade" in which Makua came to denote "elephant hunter."[84] In 1877, the British explorer Frederic Elton referred to "Suleiman's Makua hunters" to identify a group of hunters rendering their services to a certain Suleiman bin Abid, a Zanzibari who operated as an ivory trader on the southern fringes of Merere's kingdom in Ussangu.[85] The association of Makua hunters with Zanzibari traders is supported by a later assessment of Oskar Baumann, who referred to the scattered settlements of Swahili traders on the mainland as centers for elephant hunting, which he called the "Makua business." This business, he explained, consisted in

> an Arab or Swahili entering into a contract with one or several elephant hunters. The first of these hunters were introduced by Sultan Seyid Said and had been Makua. The name has been assigned to all their successors, although they come from all coastal tribes and Unyamwezi. They live in small groups under the guidance of a *fundi*, a master who produces the hunting magic on which everything depends.[86]

At about the same time, another German observer realized that any attempt to localize or tribalize Makua hunters was futile. "Elephant hunters," Franz Stuhlmann stated, "are everywhere called 'Makua.'" The term referred likewise to independent African hunter-entrepreneurs, "Nyamwezi" who hunted with long muzzle-loading rifles as well as commercial hunters in the service of Arab ivory traders.[87] Makua had been transformed from a "tribal" into a traveling identity that denoted occupation rather than ethnic origin. By the 1890s, it had entered the German colonial lexicon as the technical term for elephant hunter. Itinerant hunters, too, identified themselves by the term: "I hunt, therefore I am Makua."[88]

The opportunities of the ivory trade allowed the Makua to operate as independent hunters *and* entrepreneurs. The growing number of coastal traders on the caravan routes were welcome as new partners for bartering ivory, and they also provided both African chiefs and itinerant hunters with firearms and powder. Indeed, the use of firearms appears to have become a distinguishing feature that made hunters Makua, whereas other

Illustration 1.1. Nyamwezi elephant hunters (c. 1912), Bildarchiv der Deutschen Kolonialgesellschaft, Universitätsbibliothek Frankfurt.

societies with renown for hunting, like the Kamba or Ndorobbo, retained spear, bow, and arrow as their favorite weapons.

Joining the Zanzibar merchants—as hunter, carrier, or mercenary—enabled the mobile, the ambitious, as well as the disgruntled to escape and bypass the established hierarchies of their societies. It opened up an avenue to the prestigious status of a hunter, to the symbolic capital of the Swahili culture, and to firearms and the exotic commodities available through coastal traders. In turn, many of the Arab and Swahili agents of the Zanzibari commercial empire acquired the source of their wealth not only by barter or violence, but also by attracting hunters to their following. Therefore, the ivory trade must also be seen as a competition over the access to elephants and cooperation with prodigious hunters. As if reciprocating the pattern of the oral traditions mentioned above, merchants and hunters used the wealth acquired by elephant hunting and the ivory trade to establish themselves as big men. They attracted their following by the distribution of symbolic or material capital accumulated through participation in the trade, prowess in hunting and warfare, diplomatic cunning, and patron–client relationships.[89] Likewise, traditional chiefs and rulers incorporated the control of ivory and elephant hunting into the fundaments of their authority and used the caravan trade as a "strategy of extraversion"— the marshalling of external resources for the creation or strengthening of authority within their respective polities or social settings.[90] Traditional chiefs as well as upstart leaders and big men strove to assert their control over elephant hunting and the ivory procured in their areas. The capacity to regulate elephant hunting and to enforce the claim to one or sometimes even both tusks of every elephant killed in their territories became a measure of the political strength of leaders.

In the areas affected by long-distance, caravan trade, political authority increasingly followed a cultural pattern that had striking parallels with the "hunter principle" of authoritarian rule identified by Linda Heywood in nineteenth-century Angola.[91] Elements of the hunter principle can be found in the behavior of the petty merchant whose trade-based authority vanished with the exhaustion of local ivory stocks, as well as in the strategies employed by the hunter-warlord who invested his symbolic and economic capital into a marauding army of several thousand men in arms. Precolonial Tanganyika was full of ambitious upstarts who used the increasing value of ivory as an avenue to power. They became big men, first by hunting themselves, later by the exertion of ruthless control over all elephant hunting and ivory procured in the area under their control. What they all had in common is that they resorted to the claim of one tusk of every elephant felled in their territory. Originally, there was a deeper symbolism behind this widespread and respected ritual of authority, which is often referred to as the "ground tusk principle." Oral histories from Southeastern and East Africa unanimously relate that after the successful killing of an elephant, hunters had to return that tusk to the local chief that first touched or was closer to the ground after the elephant had fallen. In doing so, hunters acknowledged the political and spiritual supremacy of the chief as the last representative in the line of the owners of the land and the animals on it.[92] Submitting the ground tusk was, thus, a gesture of respect that established peaceful relationships. Spiritually, it was supposed to reconcile the spirits of the land with the violent killing of a powerful animal. Ecologically, it was a form of control that allowed regulating the hunting of elephants in a given area, at least in theory. On a more functional level, it fulfilled purposes similar to the *hongo* tolls levied by the societies living along the caravan routes, for the visiting hunters received in turn local support in terms of food, temporary residence, or guidance. An inquiry into "native" laws and customs conducted by German missionaries and administrative personnel in 1909 and 1910 revealed that a majority of "tribes" still observed, or had practiced the principle of returning one tusk of a killed elephant to the respective chief, king, or sultan.[93] Of course, it would be wrong to assume that the handing over of tusks was always and everywhere imbued with the abovementioned meanings. What matters is that the Germans believed that claiming the ground tusk amounted up to a customary and traditional ritual of authority. They mimicked it as such a ritual, and so did the big men and traders that had preceded them.

The centralization of political power in the hands of emerging big men, trade chiefs, and hunter-entrepreneurs was accompanied by the corollary fragmentation of political authority. Such was the case in Unyamwezi, where Zanzibari traders and rising local warlords diminished the political influence of the established *butemi*. The splintering of authority seems to have been a widespread consequence of the interregional caravan trade. In the mountainous region of South Pare in northeastern Tanzania, for example, the number of politically independent chiefdoms rose from around five in the eighteenth century to twenty-two by the end of the nineteenth century.[94] The new challengers filled the interstices of the political fabric of precolonial East Africa and brought about a shift in local power geometries, however incomplete. Existing chiefdoms seldom disappeared entirely, but diminished in size and following, while in other areas, authority rested almost entirely with big men. In southeastern Tanganyika, for example, a "string of big men" strove for power through patronage, coercion, and trade in rubber, slaves, and ivory, among them a certain Abdallah Mapanda who gained reputation as elephant hunter in the Liwale area.[95] Further inland, the southern caravan route in Ungoni, the Ngoni leader Mharule strove to attract traders to his territory and allowed an Arab merchant named Rashid bin Masoud to settle at Songea in the early 1880s. A notorious figure in the trades in ivory, rubber, and possibly slaves, he was also alleged to command a force of 400 guns to hunt elephants in the late 1890s. For the Germans, he became an indispensable local ally in the extension of colonial rule to the area.[96] The lands surrounding the carrefour of the ivory trade routes in central Tanganyika probably witnessed the most marked transformation of political authority through the access and command over the resources of the ivory trade. Here, dwindling local ivory resources and increasing numbers of caravans led to frenzied competition over the control of trade routes and commodities and favored the rise of East Africa's famous entrepreneurial kings between the 1860s and 1880s: Mirambo and Isike in Unyamwezi, Nyungu-ya-Mawe in Ukimbu, and to a lesser degree, Simba of Ukonongo and Mkwawa in Uhehe. Elephant hunting was an important factor contributing to their rise. Mirambo, for example, claimed the complete monopoly over all ivory procured in his territories.[97] So did other chiefs and big men who were in power when Germany's expeditionary forces strove to impose European ideas of statehood upon Eastern Africa. The struggle over power after the middle of the 1880s, long held to be a struggle between a modern bureaucratic state and traditional tribal chiefs, essentially played out as a struggle over ivory.

But what did the ivory trade and the entrepreneurial take on elephant hunting mean for the moral ecology of hunting in precolonial Tanzania? Undeniably, hunting lost some of its spiritual and integrative social significance through its adoption by trade-minded big men. Nonetheless, the widespread practice of the ground tusk principle suggests that wild animals were still regarded as part of a spiritual and moral universe that imposed certain restrictions and codes of conduct upon the individual's interaction with the environment. Acknowledging the spiritual webs of meaning that surrounded the hunting relationship between African societies and animals is important not only because these cultural patterns should matter in the colonial politics of wildlife. They also serve to qualify the verdict that, once elephant hunting had turned into a commercial business under the corruptive outside influence of Western capitalism, Africans had allegedly exposed a "complete lack of a sense of conserving animals for future exploitation or for a more general aesthetic or moral purpose."[98]

The commoditization of ivory and the mass import of firearms hardly rendered East African elephant hunters "ecologically noble savages." But did the onslaught of trade and guns really erode any sense of conservationism? Any assessment of what "conservation" might have meant in precolonial East Africa requires a close look at the context, practices, and rituals surrounding hunting and the appropriation of wild animals. Sources as diverse as oral histories collected by scholars at various times in different areas affected by the ivory trade, contemporary travelogues, and ethnographies, but also scholarly descriptions of East and South African practices of elephant hunting show a considerable degree of similarity. "The elephant hunt," noted Richard Burton, "is with the African a solemn and serious undertaking" for which he "fortifies himself with periapts and prophylactics given by the mganga who also trains him to the use of his weapon."⁹⁹ The role ascribed in Burton's account to the *mganga,* a spiritual priest, is in most other accounts taken by an experienced, skilled, and knowledgeable elder hunter, the *fundi.* He led the hunt, and, most importantly, he was responsible for the necessary medicines, the *dawa.*¹⁰⁰ The *fundi* initiated younger hunters, he negotiated with traders and local chiefs once the hunters had left their home territory, and he procured the ground tusk. The *fundi* also presided over the ritual preparations that were indispensable before a group of hunters would take up the pursuit of elephants. These could start as early as a week before the hunt with the gathering of the necessary barks, roots, herbs, and ingredients for the various hunting medicines. German observers stated unanimously that no African would ever hunt without the previous inoculation of these potions.¹⁰¹ Usually, these medicines were rubbed into the skin after the scarification of hands, forearms, and near the temples in order to sharpen eyesight, provide strength, and diminish the scent of the hunters. Rituals were flexible enough to accommodate new weaponry, which was often adorned with amulets. The German ethnographer Karl Weule, referring to a Makua informant who had allegedly been a renowned hunter himself, reported that also the gun was daily treated with medicines.¹⁰² Other preparations included the bathing in medicines in order to attain spiritual protection during the hunt, and ceremonial offerings to propitiate the ancestral spirits to grant protection.

The actual hunt was equally governed by a number of rules. It was vital for itinerant hunters to observe practices such as the ground tusk principle, which ensured the hospitable reception and support by local chiefs. However, under the circumstances of increased competition between traders and a growing scarcity of elephants, this rule lost in liability, and the violent appropriation of ivory contributed to the escalating circle of violence reported by many European explorers who ventured into the East African interior in the early 1880s. Other rules affected the relationship between hunter and prey. Once the hunters had come across an elephant's spoor, measures were taken to connect with the animal's spirit. According to German missionary Wilhelm Blohm, who claims to have accompanied Nyamwezi hunters several times, the hunters turned to a spirit called *Livwelelo,* who was believed to influence and guide the animals' movements. Success in hunting was therefore as much due to the hunter's skill as to the spirit's guarding of the animal, which was taken to fall prey to the hunter thanks to the intervention of *Livwelelo.*¹⁰³ Finally, various rituals of reconciliation were performed to placate the animals' spirit and guard the hunters against retaliation after an animal, especially an elephant, had been felled.

What do these practices, sanctions, and rituals amount to? If stripped from the evolutionism read into them by colonial and some latter-day observers and taken as expressions of an alternative human–animal relationship—different but contemporaneous—the question of a conservationist attitude appears to be wrongly put. Conservation presupposes an instrumental relationship toward nature as something out there that can be managed. It is predicated upon a dualistic separation of humans from the physical world around them. Animals are reduced to a resource, and the hunter's position is conceived as one of domination and opposition toward his prey. Nature is something acted *upon*, albeit with responsibility, not a framework acted within. The abovementioned rituals, however, suggest that the hunting of elephants took place *within* a cosmos of nature as an animated lifeworld "saturated with powers of agency and intentionality."[104] Despite all the commercial ends the ivory was finally put to (and of which many African hunters were probably quite unaware), much of the elephant hunting to supply the trade can be understood within a paradigm of human–animal relationships, which anthropologist Tim Ingold has, in another context, identified as trust.[105] Trust does not locate agency merely on the side of the hunter. Rather, it is based upon the assumption of mutual bonds between hunters and their social environments as well as between hunters and their prey. Rituals of trust take responsibility and agency from the hunter and share it among all faculties involved—the village, the ancestral spirits, the hunter, and the hunted animal. If the relationship between the spirits guarding the prey and the hunter could be influenced and restored by ritual, then successful hunting was an effect of trust: the skill of the hunter is matched by the animal presenting itself to be hunted. Traces of that trust not only informed rituals of hunting, but were also enshrined in tales and stories. The missionary Alfons Adams relates an alleged Yao tale of origin, where man finds himself cast alone in the wilderness. He is rescued by an elephant who placed the man on his back to show him the forests, savannas, and all animals that lived in them. The elephant also fed the man with wild honey and the fruits of the forest. One day, they finally encountered a woman on their way. The elephant placed the man next to her, and the two built a hut, procreated, and peopled the wilderness with their offspring. Such, Adams concluded, was the origin of the Yao.[106]

Hunting understood and perceived as a spiritually embedded, horizontal activity in a lifeworld hardly required a reflected ethic of conservation, for the rules and rituals that governed it ensured that nothing was taken that should not be taken. If elephant herds disappeared locally, there was always a horizon, a river, a forest, or savanna beyond which the animals could still be believed to roam.

Notes

1. Richard Waller, "Ecology, Migration, and Expansion in East Africa," *African Affairs* 84 (1985): 348.
2. Kjekshus, *Ecology Control and Economic Development in East African History*, 5; Giblin, *The Politics of Environmental Control in Tanzania*.
3. Iliffe, *A Modern History of Tanganyika*, 13; Håkansson, *The Human Ecology of World Systems in East Africa*.
4. Igor Kopytoff, "The Internal African Frontier. The Making of African Political Culture," in *The African Frontier. The Reproduction of Traditional African Societies,* ed. I Kopytoff (Bloomington, IN, 1987), 3–84.
5. Karin Pallaver, "Labor Relations and Population Developments in Tanzania: Sources, Shifts, and Continuities from 1800 to 2000," *History in Africa* 41 (2014): 307–35.
6. Kjekshus, *Ecology Control and Economic Development in East African History*, 24.
7. Fritz Jaeger, "Der Gegensatz von Kulturland und Wildnis und die allgemeinen Züge ihrer Verteilung in Ost-Afrika. Eine anthropogeographische Skizze," *Geographische Zeitschrift* 16 (1910): 130.
8. Ludger Wimmelbücker, *Kilimanjaro—A Regional History. Vol. 1: Production and Living Conditions, c. 1800–1920* (Münster, 2003), 129; A Widenmann, *Die Kilimandscharo-Bevölkerung. Anthropologisches und Ethnographisches aus dem Dschaggalande* (Gotha, 1899), 80–81.
9. Gabriel Ekemode, "German Rule in North-East Tanzania, 1885–1914" (PhD diss., University of London, 1973), 37; Sally Falk Moore, *Social Facts and Fabrications. "Customary" Law on Kilimanjaro, 1880–1980* (Cambridge, 1986), 28–29; Iliffe, *A Modern History of Tanganyika*, 59–61; James Cox, "Nineteenth Century Diplomacy on Mt. Kilimanjaro: Rindi of Moshi Reconsidered," in *Personality and Political Culture in Modern Africa. Studies Presented to Professor Harold G Marcus*, ed. Melvin E Page et al. (Boston, 1998), 111. Rindi was also known as Mandara in contemporary European parlance.
10. Steven Feierman, *The Shambaa Kingdom. A History* (Madison, WI, 1974), 125–27.
11. Erich Obst, "Von Mkalama ins Land der Wakindiga (Deutsch-Ostafrika). Vorläufiger Bericht der Ostafrika-Expedition der Hamburger Geographischen Gesellschaft," *Mitteilungen der geographischen Gesellschaft in Hamburg* 26 (1912): 1–45; Martin Porr, *Hadzapi, Hadza, Hatza, Hadzabe, Wahadzabe, Wakindiga, WaTindiga, Tindiga, Kindiga, Hadzapi? Eine Wildbeuter-Kultur in Ostafrika* (Tübingen, 1997).
12. Roderic H Blackburn, "In the Land of Milk and Honey: Okiek Adaptations to Their Forests and Neighbours," in *Politics and History in Band Societies*, ed. Eleanor Leacock and Richard Lee (Cambridge, 1982), 283–305.
13. Richard F Burton, "The Lake Regions of Central Equatorial Africa, with Notices of the Lunar Mountains of the White Nile; Being the Results of an Expedition Undertaken under the Patronage of Her Majesty's Government and the Royal Geographical Society of London, in the Years 1857–1859," *Journal of the Royal Geographical Society of London* 29 (1859): 373. The *rungu* is a kind of baton or throwing stick, usually with a knob head.

14. See, for example, Franz Stuhlmann, *Mit Emin Pascha ins Herz von Afrika* (Berlin, 1894), 86–89.
15. Cado Picarda, "Autour de Mandéra. Notes sur l'Ouzigoua, l'Oukwéré et l'Oudoé," *Les Missions catholiques. Bulletin hebdomadaire illustre de l'oeuvre de la propagation de la foi* 18 (1886): 258.
16. Mary Douglas, *Implicit Meanings* (London, 1975), 35–36; see also Brian Morris, *Animals and Ancestors. An Ethnography* (Oxford, 2000), 221-54.
17. Joseph Busse, *Die Nyakyusa. Wirtschaft und Gesellschaft* (Münster, 1995), 68.
18. Restrictions of female behavior during the absence of their husbands on the hunt are mentioned in Karl Weule, *Negerleben in Ostafrika. Ergebnisse einer ethnologischen Forschungsreise* (Leipzig, 1908), 39; Godfrey Dale, "An Account of the Principal Customs and Habits of the Natives Inhabiting the Bondei Country," *The Journal of the Anthropological Institute of Great Britain and Ireland* 25 (1896): 207; Ernst Nigmann, *Die Wahehe. Ihre Geschichte, Kult-, Rechts-, Kriegs- und Jagdgebräuche* (Berlin, 1908), 120; Paul Reichard, *Deutsch-Ostafrika. Das Land und seine Bewohner, seine politische und wirtschaftliche Entwickelung* (Leipzig, 1892), 427; A Karasek, "Beiträge zur Kenntnis der Waschambaa," *Baessler-Archiv* 3 (1913): 88; Allen F Isaacman and Barbara S Isaacman, *Slavery and Beyond. The Making of Men and Chikunda Ethnic Identities in the Unstable World of South-Central Africa, 1750-1920* (Portsmouth, NH, 2005), 90; Brian Morris, *The Power of Animals. An Ethnography* (Oxford, 1998), 97, 100.
19. Dale, "An Account of the Principal Customs and Habits of the Natives Inhabiting the Bondei Country," 207–08; Picarda, "Autour de Mandéra," 259; Audrey I Richards, *Land, Labour and Diet in Northern Rhodesia. An Economic Study of the Bemba Tribe* (Oxford, 1939), 345; Burton, "The Lake Regions of Central Equatorial Africa," 374; Busse, *Die Nyakyusa*, 70; Elise Kootz-Kretschmer, *Die Safwa. Ein ostafrikanischer Volksstamm in seinem Leben und Denken*, vol. 1 (Berlin, 1926), 139; Wilhelm Blohm, *Die Nyamwezi. Land und Wirtschaft*, vol. 3 (Hamburg, 1931), 110–11; Morris, *The Power of Animals*, 67–68, 93; Stuart Marks, *Large Mammals and a Brave People. Subsistence Hunters in Zambia* (New Brunswick, 2005), 121–25.
20. Concise surveys of the East African ivory trade are provided by Jonas Kranzer, "Tickling and Clicking the Ivories: The Metamorphosis of a Global Commodity in the Nineteenth Century," in *Luxury in Global Perspective. Objects and Practices, 1600-2000*, eds. Bernd-Stefan Grewe and Karin Hofmeester (Cambridge, 2016), 240-260; and Edward A Alpers, "The Ivory Trade in Africa. An Historical Overview," in *Elephant. The Animal and Its Ivory in African Culture*, ed. Doran H Ross (Los Angeles, 1992), 349–63. See also Abdul Sheriff, *Slaves, Spices and Ivory in Zanzibar. Integration of an East African Commercial Empire into the World Economy, 1770–1873* (London, 1987).
21. Edward A Alpers, *The Indian Ocean in World History* (Oxford, 2014); Abdul Sheriff, *Dhow Cultures of the Indian Ocean. Cosmopolitanism, Commerce and Islam* (New York, 2010); John Middleton, *The World of the Swahili. An African Mercantile Civilization* (New Haven, CT, 1992), especially chapter 1.
22. Jeremy Prestholdt, *Domesticating the World. African Consumerism and the Genealogies of Globalization* (Berkeley, CA, 2008), especially chapter 3; Jeremy Prestholdt, "On the Global Repercussions of East African Consumerism," *American Historical Review* 109 (2004): 755–81.

23. Jean-François Bayart, "Africa in the World. A History of Extraversion," *African Affairs* 99 (2000): 218–19, 222.
24. See, for example, Staatsarchiv Hamburg 621-1: Papers Wm. O'Swald & Co., 3/47, fol. 91: O'Swald Office Hamburg to Zanzibar branch, 25 March 1897.
25. Isaacman and Isaacman, *Slavery and Beyond*, 85.
26. Abdul Sheriff, "Ivory and Commercial Expansion in East Africa in the Nineteenth Century," in *Figuring African Trade. Proceedings of the Symposium on the Quantification and Structure of the Import and Export and Long Distance Trade of Africa in the Nineteenth Century (c. 1800–1913)*, ed. Gerhard Liesegang et al. (Berlin, 1986), 417.
27. Paul Reichard, "Das afrikanische Elfenbein und sein Handel," *Deutsche geographische Blätter* 12 (1889): 167–68; Sheriff, *Slaves, Spices and Ivory in Zanzibar*, 86; Heinrich Adolf Meyer, *Erinnerungen an Heinrich Christian Meyer—Stockmeyer* (Hamburg, 1900), IX. However, in 1886, the scope of Meyer's trade in Zanzibar was estimated at merely a quarter of the ivory that the Salem-based trading companies exported to the United States, see Norman Robert Bennett, *The Zanzibar Letters of Edward D Ropes, Jr* (Boston, 1973), 54.
28. John F Richards, *The Unending Frontier. An Environmental History of the Early Modern World* (Berkeley, CA, 2003), 610.
29. Raymond W Beachey, "The East African Ivory Trade in the Nineteenth Century," *Journal of African History* 8 (1967): 288.
30. "Über Elfenbein," *Illustrirte Jagd-Zeitung* 17 (1889–90): 129; Wilhelm Westendarp, "Das Gebiet der Elephanten und der Elfenbein-Reichthum Indiens und Afrikas," *Mitteilungen der geographischen Gesellschaft in Hamburg* 3 (1878–79): 201–13.
31. Hagen W Lippe-Weißenfeld, "Das Klavier als Mittel politischer Distinktion im Zusammenhang mit der Entwicklung des Klavierbaus in London und Berlin an den Beispielen Broadwood und Bechstein" (PhD diss., FU Berlin, 2006), 70–144.
32. David H Shayt, "The Material Culture of Ivory Outside Africa," in *Elephant. The Animal and Its Ivory in African Culture*, ed. Doran H Ross (Los Angeles, 1992), 366–81; George Frederick Kunz, *Ivory and the Elephant in Art, in Archaeology, and in Science* (Garden City, NJ, 1916); Beachey, "The East African Ivory Trade in the Nineteenth Century," 288–89.
33. Paul Reichard, "Das afrikanische Elfenbein und sein Handel", *Deutsche geographische Blätter* 12 (1889): 132–168; Franz Stuhlmann, "Elfenbein," in *Deutsches Kolonial-Lexikon*, vol. 1 (Leipzig, 1920), 556–59.
34. Iris Hahner-Herzog, *Tippu Tip und der Elfenbeinhandel in Ost- und Zentralafrika im 19. Jahrhundert* (Munich, 1990), 344.
35. Wilhelm Westendarp, "Der Elfenbein-Reichtum Afrikas," in *Verhandlungen des fünften deutschen Geographentages zu Hamburg*, ed. Heinrich Michow (Berlin, 1885), 85; Stuhlmann, "Elfenbein," 558.
36. Beachey, "The East African Ivory Trade in the Nineteenth Century," 289; see further CS Nicholls, *The Swahili Coast. Politics, Diplomacy and Trade on the East African Littoral 1798–1856* (London, 1971); Norman Robert Bennett and George E Brooks, eds, *New England Merchants in Africa. A History through Documents 1802 to 1865* (Boston, 1965).

37. For a concise survey, see Stephen J Rockel, "Decentering Exploration in East Africa," in *Reinterpreting Exploration. The West in the World*, ed. Dane Kennedy (Oxford, 2014), 172–94.
38. Cf. Sheriff, *Slaves, Spices and Ivory in Zanzibar*, 158–64.
39. Ibid., 155–83; Edward I Steinhart, *Black Poachers, White Hunters. A Social History of Hunting in Colonial Kenya* (Oxford, 2006), 47–51.
40. Jan-Georg Deutsch, *Emancipation without Abolition in German East Africa c. 1884–1914* (Oxford, 2006), 18–26; Stephen J Rockel, *Carriers of Culture. Labor on the Road in Nineteenth Century East Africa* (Portsmouth, NH, 2006).
41. Karl Evers, "Das Hamburger Zanzibarhandelshaus Wm. O'swald & Co. 1847–1890. Zur Geschichte des Hamburger Handels mit Ostafrika" (PhD diss., University of Hamburg, 1986), 92.
42. See Kjekshus, *Ecology Control and Economic Development in East African History*, 182.
43. Håkansson, "The Human Ecology of World Systems in East Africa"; Håkansson, Widgren, and Börjeson, "Introduction." On the role of elephants as ecosystem engineers see, for example, Robert Guldemond and Rudi van Aarde, "A Meta-Analysis of the Impact of African Elephants on Savanna Vegetation," *Journal of Wildlife Management* 72, no. 4 (2008): 892–99.
44. See Roy Bridges, "Elephants, Ivory and the History of the Ivory Trade in East Africa," in *The Exploitation of Animals in Africa. Proceedings of a Colloquium at the University of Aberdeen, March 1987*, ed. Jeffrey C Stone (Aberdeen, 1988), 197.
45. See Westendarp, "Der Elfenbein-Reichtum Afrikas," 85; Heinrich Bolau, *Der Elephant in Krieg und Frieden und seine Verwendung in unsern Afrikanischen Kolonien* (Hamburg, 1887); Reichard, "Das afrikanische Elfenbein und sein Handel," 168; Gerhard Rohlfs, "Zur Elefantenfrage in Africa," in *Kölnische Zeitung*, 10 January 1892.
46. Beachey, "The East African Ivory Trade in the Nineteenth Century," 287; Westendarp, "Der Elfenbein-Reichtum Afrikas," 91; Bolau, *Der Elephant in Krieg und Frieden und seine Verwendung in unsern Afrikanischen Kolonien*, 27; Reichard, "Das afrikanische Elfenbein und sein Handel," 168; Karl Möbius, "Elfenbein-Ausfuhr aus Afrika und Zahl der Elefanten," *Sitzungsberichte der Gesellschaft naturforschender Freunde zu Berlin* (1896): 23–24.
47. As quoted in Martin Meredith, *Africa's Elephant. A Biography* (London, 2001), 86.
48. See for example, Deutsch, *Emancipation without Abolition in German East Africa*, 36.
49. See, for example, Gustav Fischer, *Mehr Licht im dunklen Weltteil. Betrachtungen über die Kolonisation des tropischen Afrika unter besonderer Berücksichtigung des Sansibar-Gebiets* (Hamburg, 1885), 8.
50. The vast amount of "dead ivory" procured from areas where the commercial value of ivory was hitherto unknown is emphasized by Frederick Dealtry Lugard, "Nyassa-Land and Its Commercial Possibilities," *Proceedings of the Royal Geographical Society* 11 (1889): 690. For a detailed discussion see Bridges, "Elephants, Ivory and the History of the Ivory Trade in East Africa."
51. Bridges, "Elephants, Ivory and the History of the Ivory Trade in East Africa," 211.

52. TNA G 8/55, fol. 127: Annual Report District Station Dar es Salaam, undated [1897]; Heinrich Fonck, *Deutsch-Ostafrika. Eine Schilderung deutscher Tropen nach 10 Wanderjahren* (Berlin, 1910), 406.
53. See, for example, Sheriff, *Slaves, Spices and Ivory in Zanzibar,* 183–90; Iliffe, *A Modern History of Tanganyika,* 48–49; Juhani Koponen, *Development for Exploitation. German Colonial Policies in Mainland Tanzania, 1884—1914* (Helsinki, 1995), 201; Gregory H Maddox, *Sub-Saharan Africa. An Environmental History* (Santa Barbara, CA, 2006), 109.
54. Ruth Rempel, "Trade and Transformation: Participation in the Ivory Trade in Late Nineteenth Century East and Central Africa," *Canadian Journal of Development Studies* 19 (1998): 529–52.
55. TNA G 1/30, fol. 5-12: Baumann to Antisklaverei-Lotterie, 21 July 1892.
56. John Hanning Speke, *What Led to the Discovery of the Source of the Nile* (Edinburgh, 1864), 240–41.
57. For recent assessments of elephants' cognitive and social capacities, see Cynthia J Moss, Harvey Croze, and Phylis C Lee, eds, *The Amboseli Elephants. A Long-Term Perspective on a Long-Lived Mammal* (Chicago, 2011); Joyce H Poole and Cynthia Moss, "Elephant Sociality and Complexity. The Scientific Evidence," in *Elephants and Ethics. Towards a Morality of Coexistence,* ed. Christen Wemmer and Catherine A Christen (Baltimore, MD, 2008), 69–98.
58. Hugold von Behr, "Die Wakua-Steppe," *Mittheilungen von Forschungsreisenden und Gelehrten aus den Deutschen Schutzgebieten* 6 (1893): 42–60; TNA G 8/55, fol. 77: BA Mikindani to Gov DOA, 12 December 1896; TNA G 8/55, fol. 80: BA Lindi to Gov DOA, 17 May 1897; Sergeant Bergmann, "Bezirksnebenstelle Liwale," *Berichte über Land- und Forstwirtschaft in Deutsch-Ostafrika* 1 (1903): 101; Karl Ewerbeck, "Bezirksamt Lindi," *Berichte über Land- und Forstwirtschaft in Deutsch-Ostafrika* 1 (1903):109; "Vom Rovuma", in: *Deutsch-Ostafrikanische Zeitung* 4, no. 39 (1902): 27 September.
59. Richard Böhm, *Von Sansibar zum Tanganjika. Briefe aus Ostafrika,* ed. Herman Schalow (Leipzig, 1888), 84; Leue, "Ueber die Zustände im Bezirk Tabora," *Deutsches Kolonialblatt* 7 (1896): 184–86.
60. Eugenia W Herbert, *Iron, Gender, and Power: Rituals of Transformation in African Societies* (Bloomington, IN, 1993), 164–88.
61. Seth Ismael Nyagava, "A History of the Bena to 1908" (PhD diss., University of Dar es Salaam, 1988), 74.
62. Nigmann, *Die Wahehe,* 109.
63. Jan Bender Shetler, *Telling Our Own Stories. Local Histories from South Mara, Tanzania* (Leiden, 2003), 165, 246, 256, 260, 268.
64. Aylward Shorter, *Chiefship in Western Tanzania. A Political History of the Kimbu* (Oxford, 1972), 40; Ray G Abrahams, *The Political Organization of Unyamwezi* (Cambridge, 1967), 31–32.
65. JP Farler, "The Usambara Country in East Africa," *Proceedings of the Royal Geographical Society* 1 (1879): 84.
66. Feierman, *The Shambaa Kingdom,* 40–69; Abdallah bin Hemedi bin Ali Liajjemi, "The Story of Mbega," *Tanganyika Notes and Records* no. 1 (1936): 38–51 and *Tanganyika Notes and Records* no. 2 (1936): 80–91.
67. Feierman, *The Shambaa Kingdom,* 43.

68. See the classic functionalist interpretation of myth by Bronislaw Malinowski, "Myth in Primitive Society," in *Magic, Science, and Religion and Other Essays*, ed. Bronislaw Malinowski (Boston, 1948), 79, 122.
69. On the *Habari za Wakilindi* and its author, see Katrin Bromber and Jürgen Becher, "Abdallah bin Hemedi—ein Vertreter der administrativen Elite im Transformationsprozeß zwischen Busaidi-Herrschaft und deutscher Kolonialadministration," in *Alles unter Kontrolle. Disziplinierungsprozesse im kolonialen Tanzania (ca. 1850-1960)*, ed. Albert Wirz et al. (Cologne, 2003), 54-70.
70. Where the term "magic" is applied, it is used deliberately as an intellectually disturbing category to refer to alternative ontologies of the naturalization of human actions in a nonevolutionary sense, see Randall G Styers, *Making Magic: Religion, Magic and Science in the Modern World* (Oxford, 2004), 7, 19-20.
71. Hugues Legros, *Chasseurs d'Ivoire. Une histoire du royaume yeke du Shaba (Zaire)* (Bruxelles, 1996).
72. Legros, *Chasseurs d'Ivoire*, 35; Frank Gunderson, *Sukuma Labor Songs from Western Tanzania. "We Never Sleep, We Dream of Farming"* (Boston, 2010), chapter 2.
73. Shorter, *Chiefship in Western Tanzania*, 40.
74. On the concept of big man, see Marshall D Sahlins, "Poor Man, Rich Man, Big-Man, Chief: Political Types in Melanesia and Polynesia," *Comparative Studies in Society and History* 5 (1963): 285-303; for its application to Africa see Jean-François Médard, "Le 'Big Man' en Afrique: Esquisse d'Analyse du Politicien Entrepreneur", *L'Année sociologique* 49 (1992):167-92.
75. See, for example, Burton, "The Lake Regions of Central Equatorial Africa," 441.
76. Gerald W Hartwig, *The Art of Survival in East Africa. The Kerebe and Long-Distance Trade, 1800-1895* (New York, 1976), 65-71.
77. Evers, "Das Hamburger Zanzibarhandelshaus Wm. O'swald & Co. 1847-1890," 99-100; Raymond W Beachey, "The Arms Trade in East Africa," *Journal of African History* 3 (1962): 453.
78. Cf. Reichard, *Deutsch-Ostafrika*, 429-30.
79. See for example Picarda, "Autour de Mandéra," 258; Reichard, "Das afrikanische Elfenbein und sein Handel," 139; Baumann, *Durch Massailand zur Nilquelle*, 243-44; AGO Hodgson, "Some Notes on the Hunting Customs of the Wandamba of the Ulanga Valley, Tanganyika Territory, and Other East African Tribes," *The Journal of the Royal Anthropological Institute of Great Britain and Ireland* 56 (1926): 60; Kootz-Kretschmer, *Die Safwa*, 141; Blohm, *Die Nyamwezi*, 97, 99.
80. Richards, *Land, Labour and Diet in Northern Rhodesia*, 342; see also Morris, *The Power of Animals*, 65.
81. Hodgson, "Some Notes on the Hunting Customs of the Wandamba of the Ulanga Valley, Tanganyika Territory, and Other East African Tribes," 60. Cf. Arthur Theodore and Geraldine Mary Culwick, *Ubena of the Rivers* (London, 1935), 168, 172.
82. For parallels with the Chikunda in South Central Africa, see Isaacman and Isaacman, *Slavery and Beyond*, chapter 3.
83. Edward Alpers, *Ivory and Slaves. Changing Patterns of International Trade in East Central Africa to the Later Nineteenth Century* (Berkeley, CA, 1975), 11-12.

84. Felicitas Becker, *Becoming Muslim in Mainland Tanzania 1890-2000* (Oxford, 2008), 32.
85. Frederic J Elton, *Travels and Researches among the Lakes and Mountains of Eastern and Central Africa* (London, 1879), 344, 353, 355, 358, 362; Kootz-Kretschmer, *Die Safwa*, 1.
86. Baumann, *Durch Massailand zur Nilquelle*, 243.
87. Stuhlmann, *Mit Emin Pascha ins Herz von Afrika*, 804.
88. Felicitas Becker, "A Social History of Southeast Tanzania, ca. 1890-1950" (PhD diss., University of Cambridge, 2001), 45.
89. Jan Vansina, *Paths in the Rainforest. Toward a History of Political Tradition in Equatorial Africa* (Madison, WI, 1990), 73-74; Becker, "A Social History of Southeast Tanzania," 46; Jane I Guyer, "Wealth in People, Wealth in Things—Introduction," *Journal of African History* 36 (1995): 83-90; Rita Smith Kipp and Edward M Shortman, "The Political Impact of Trade in Chiefdoms," *American Anthropologist* 91 (1989): 372.
90. Bayart, "Africa in the World," 222.
91. Linda Heywood, "Towards an Understanding of Modern Political Ideology in Africa: The Case of the Ovimbundu in Angola," *The Journal of Modern African Studies* 36 (1998): especially 151-54.
92. Isaacman and Isaacman, *Slavery and Beyond*, 94.
93. BAB R 1001/4999, various reports. The "custom" that at least one tusk had to be returned to the political authority that claimed supremacy over the respective territory is testified in the reports for the areas of Arusha, Ubena, Udjiji, Uhehe, Ussangu, Ukimbu, Ungoni, and Unyamwezi.
94. N Thomas Håkansson, "Rulers and Rainmakers in Precolonial South Pare, Tanzania: Exchange and Ritual Experts in Political Centralization," *Ethnology* 37 (1998): 269-72; Isaria N Kimambo, *Penetration and Protest in Tanzania. The Impact of the World Economy on the Pare 1860-1960* (London, 1991), 1; Giblin, *The Politics of Environmental Control in Tanzania*, 10, 45.
95. Becker, "A Social History of Southeast Tanzania," 46, 59.
96. BAB R 1001/698, fol. 155-64: Tom von Prince: Geschichte der Wagwangwara; BAB R 1001/278, fol. 8-27: Ewerbeck to Gov DOA, 30 November 1899.
97. Norman Robert Bennett, *Mirambo of Tanzania 1840?-1884* (New York, 1971), 73.
98. Steinhart, *Black Poachers, White Hunters*, 3-4; see also Roy Willis, *Man and Beast* (London, 1974), 47.
99. Burton, "The Lake Regions of Central Equatorial Africa," 374.
100. Cf. M Singleton, "*Dawa*: Beyond Science and Superstition," *Anthropos* 74 (1979): 821, 835-36.
101. Reichard, *Deutsch-Ostafrika*, 426; August Knochenhauer, "Jagdlicher Aberglaube und Geheimmittel der afrikanischen Eingeborenen," *Deutsche Jägerzeitung* 26 (1895-96): 505-06; Karl Weule, *Wissenschaftliche Ergebnisse meiner ethnographischen Forschungsreise in den Südosten Deutsch-Ostafrikas* (Berlin, 1908), 38; Blohm, *Die Nyamwezi*, 97.
102. Weule, *Wissenschaftliche Ergebnisse meiner ethnographischen Forschungsreise in den Südosten Deutsch-Ostafrikas*, 37-38; see also Dale, "An Account of the Principal Customs and Habits of the Natives Inhabiting the Bondei Country," 207.

103. Blohm, *Die Nyamwezi*, 98.
104. Tim Ingold, *The Perception of the Environment. Essays on Livelihood, Dwelling and Skill* (Abingdon, 2000), 14.
105. Tim Ingold, "From Trust to Domination. An Alternative History of Human-Animal Relations," in *Animals and Human History. Changing Perspectives*, ed. Aubrey Manning (London, 1994), 1–22.
106. Alfons Adams, *Lindi und sein Hinterland* (Berlin, 1903), 55–56.

 CHAPTER 2

Seeing Like a State, Acting Like a Chief
The Colonial Politics of Ivory, 1890–1903

> You whites, you hate the elephant, you want his demise.
> Constantly you are thinking about shooting elephants
> —*Song of Safwa elephant hunters, Western Tanzania*[1]

Neither the riches derived from the flourishing ivory trade nor the destruction of elephants had gone unnoticed in Germany. East Africa's "white gold" had aroused the interest of overseas traders and colonial enthusiasts well before the scramble for Africa in the middle of the 1880s. Hanseatic trading companies like Hansing, O'Swald, and Meyer had a stake in the Zanzibar-based ivory trade since the 1840s and operated through permanent representatives on the island.[2] Travelogues written by the German missionaries Johann Ludwig Krapf and Johannes Rebmann, the explorers Carl Claus von der Decken, Richard Böhm, and Paul Reichard, but also the translated editions of David Livingstone, Henry Morton Stanley, and Richard Burton all elicited fantasies of immense riches in the African interior. Ivory was one of the incentives of imperialist imaginations. When the German Reichstag debated a more active German colonial policy in 1878, Hermann von Hohenlohe-Langenburg, the later head of the Deutsche Kolonialgesellschaft, quoted extensively from Stanley to urge for Germany's increased engagement in the opening up of Central Africa. There, he fantasized, "entire villages" were built from ivory.[3] Germans may not have colonized East Africa for its ivory, but elephants and their tusks decisively shaped the making and the course of German colonialism in East Africa.

This chapter first adopts the perspective of the customs house to assess the economic importance of elephants for the fledgling colonial state. Critically examinig the surviving ivory statistics also allows for some cautious speculation about the ecologies of hunting during the 1890s. Shifting the perspective to the imperial hunting culture imported by the Germans into East Africa, the next section analyzes how hunting became a middle ground of conflicting interaction and asymmetrical accomodation between European and African actors. The chapter then goes on to contrast the first legal attempts to check excessive elephant hunting with the politics of elephant hunting and ivory practiced by the local stations in the middle ground. Such a political ecology perspective scrambles the stark dichotomies of precolonial and colonial by interpreting the making of colonial rule as the incorporation of and engagement with determining political, economic, and ecological patterns of the precolony. The politics and culture of hunting that had evolved under the regime of the East African ivory trade shaped the making of colonial rule in East Africa. Seen through the lens of hunting and the politics of ivory, the colonial state in the making appears as a polycentric and hybrid mixture of the rational, administrative, and fiscal state of the European tradition and the local cultural pattern of the "hunter king."

Seeing Elephants Like the Customs House

Existing analyses of colonial Tanganyika have not given sufficient credit to hunting and ivory as factors in the making of colonial rule. The main reason for this was the erroneous equation of an economic frontier with an ecological one. As argued in the previous chapter, the westward advance of the "ivory frontier" was interpreted not only as a frontier of trade governed by the exchange and market value of a commodity but also as a frontier of hunting behind which elephants were assumed to have been more or less "hunted out." Gloomy predictions of the conquering vanguard of German colonialism further nourished the assumption that elephant hunting was no longer a relevant political and economic activity,[4] and so did the relative decline of the ivory trade volume during the years of German colonial

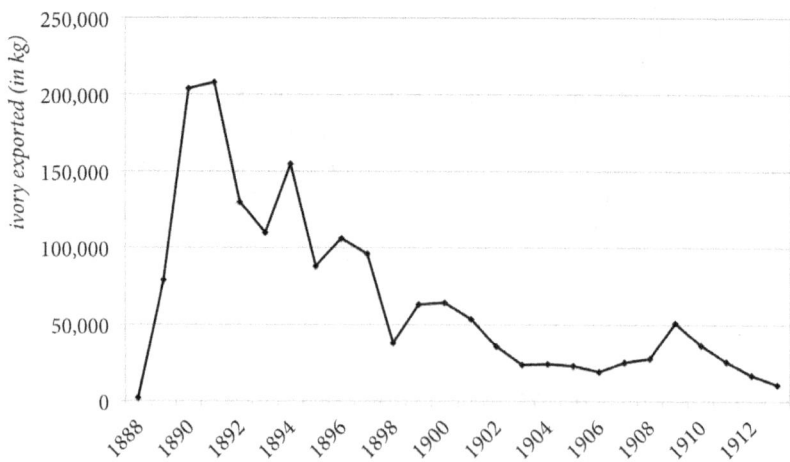

Figure 2.1. Ivory exports from German East Africa, 1888–1913.[5]

rule. However, while the records of the colonial customs house document the declining volume of the trade, they cast doubt on the conclusion that this also meant a decline of ivory procurement within the German colony. Rather, the surviving ivory statistics of German colonial provenance testify to the continuing political and economic significance of ivory and elephant hunting within the German sphere of influence, and they even allow cautious guesses about the ecological consequences of hunting.

Figure 2.1 depicts the ivory volumes exported from the German colony. The comprehensiveness of these figures is hard to assess. They cover mainly the exports via the Swahili seaports, and in their suggestive exactness, they are quite probably wrong. Yet they illustrate some general trends. For once, they show that the onset of German colonial rule in East Africa coincided with the demise of the caravan-based ivory trade via the Swahili port towns. With few exceptions, the total volume of ivory exported from German East Africa declined steadily. Already Carl Peters's Deutsch-Ostafrikanische Gesellschaft (DOAG), the chartered company that set out to administer the colony after the granting of state protection in 1885, had been desperate to tap the networks of the ivory trade. In 1887, the DOAG founded stations in Mpwapwa, Moshi, and Arusha with the prime purpose to buy up ivory cheaper by bypassing the established Swahili and Indian middlemen in the port towns. The endeavor soon turned into a financial and political fiasco, and the company's blunt and violent attempts at participating in the trade contributed to the outbreak of the coastal rebellion in 1888.[6] The rebellion disabled most of the ivory trade from the mainland, and exports plummeted markedly in 1888–89. After a mercenary army sent by the German Parliament under the command of Hermann von Wissmann had ruthlessly quelled all opposition, export figures witnessed a steep rise. In the following two years, caravans that had been locked up in the interior now found an outlet for their loads. In 1892, for example, some 4,000 frasila of ivory waited in Tabora to be transported to the coast. In turn, some 10,000 guns and around 30,000 pounds of powder came up from the coast. Export volumes from the Swahili ports rose considerably to reach, for a last time, the volumes of the late 1870s.[7]

Between 1893 and 1896, the statistics mirror chief events of colonial conquest. Particularly large stocks of ivory fell into German hands when the mercenary army, now turned into the colony's official military force, raided the capital of the Nyamwezi chief Isike in December 1892 and the capital of the Hehe, Iringa, in 1894. Extraordinary numbers of tusks found their way to the coast and into the statistics, where they glossed over the fact that the general trade volumes already deflated.[8] The relative peaks in 1894 and 1896 were also caused by ivory brought to the coast by Arab and Swahili traders whom the war in the Congo Free State forced out of business. The propagandistically embroidered war waged by conglomerate European forces against the "Arab slave traders" was a decisive factor that curbed the established flow of the ivory trade toward Zanzibar. So were heavy export duties and brute force on the part of the Belgian authorities.[9] Smuggling and efforts to attract ivory from Belgian and British territories remained a defining phenomenon of border regions until World War I.[10] But this could not prevent the enormous slump in the ivory exports via the German East African coast effected by the gradual enforcement of the colonial borders and the consequential redirection of trade routes from the mid 1890s onward.

German authorities did everything to safeguard the little trade that was left, including the deliberate counteracting against the rhetoric of antislavery internationalism. Although officially subscribing to Europe's imperial humanitarian cause to battle the "Arab slave traders", the military expeditions sent to the Great Lakes to control the main caravan routes tolerated and even cooperated with the Arab and Swahili traders operating from Ujiji. Mohamed bin Halfan, for example, a slave and ivory trader also known as Rumaliza shifted his loyalties according to opportunities. He acted as *liwali*[11] on behalf of the Germans at Ujiji in 1893. At the same time, he deployed a force of 3,000 *ruga-ruga* mercenaries against the Congo Free State, who were allies at least on paper in the pan-European effort to combat the slave trade.[12] Desperate to halt the dwindling ivory trade, the German administration at times even reimbursed traders part of their customs expenses and stepped up the sale of powder and weapons as the indispensable exchange commodities for elephant hunters.[13] However, all these measures could only defer the reorganization of trade routes. While in 1897, some 4,672 kilograms (10,313 pounds) of ivory still left Ujiji for the coast, the volume was reduced to a trifling 366 kilograms (865 pounds) by 1899.[14] In 1902, a frustrated government in Dar es Salaam had to acknowledge that the "whole Arab trade that had been oriented towards our protectorate has been stamped out by the politics of the Free State."[15]

The fact that East Africa's ivory trade toward Zanzibar was in decline during the 1890s made hunting and the acquisition of ivory in the territory of German East Africa itself even more important. The ivory statistics above also allow for a different reading if put into the context of the colonial economy in general. Then, the 209,000 kilograms of tusks that left the colony via the ports under German control in 1890 represented 61 percent of the total export value of German East Africa in that year. Apart from rubber, elephants and their ivory were the only obvious and readily extractable resources the colony had to offer. Even in decline, elephant tusks continued to dominate the export statistics as the colonies' biggest source of revenue until about the turn of the century.[16]

The fledgling colonial state capitalized on the killing of elephants indirectly by the levying of tolls on exported tusks,[17] and directly by the sale of hunting licenses and the acquisition of so-called fiscal ivory, that is, tusks received by the stations or military expeditions as tribute, payment, or by confiscation, looting, and extortion.[18] The scope and some ecological implications of the colonial state's claim to ivory can at least be adumbrated if we take into consideration a second set of figures lifted from the colonial archive. Figure 2.2 charts the number of tusks exported via the port towns of the German East African coast, together with the average weight of tusks derived from the volumes given in the statistics. Unfortunately, figures have only survived for the years between 1892 and 1897, and they should not be taken at face value but merely as suggestive of some trends. The figures confirm that the amount of tusks arriving at the coastal ports declined, falling from roughly 16,500 tusks in 1892–93 to 12,240 in 1895–96 to rise again to slightly over 15,000 in 1896–97. If we presume that most of this was fresh ivory and that both tusks of each slain elephant were immediately traded on, this would have meant the killing of around 7,500 to 8,250 elephants annually. However, the figures only roughly represent the annual cropping of elephants because fluctuations in the export volume were also influenced by price development and traders' calculation. In 1897, for example, the district administration in Dar es Salaam observed that the chiefs dominating the ivory export would strategically retain their tusks to wait for more advantageous prices.[20]

Another development illustrated by these figures is a decline of the average weight of tusks. With the exception of 1895–96, not only were there

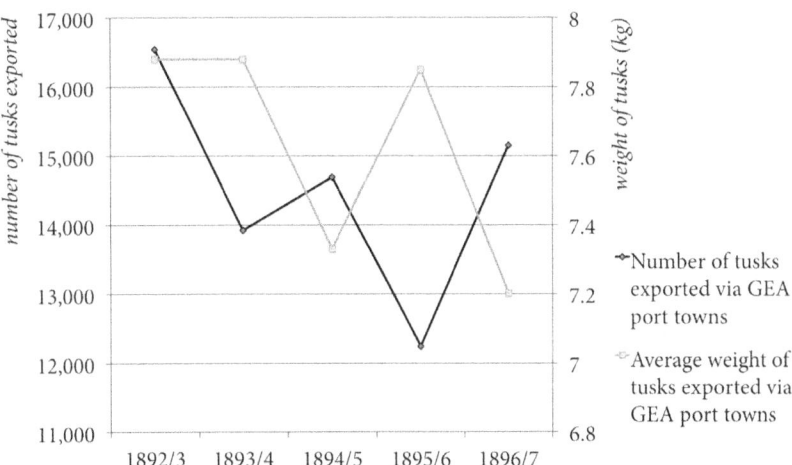

Figure 2.2. Number and weight of tusks exported via the German East African ports, 1892–97.[19]

fewer tusks fed into the trade, but these tusks also became smaller in size and weight. The decreasing tusk size was not only a relative effect due to the breakaway of trade in large tusks from the Congo. Rather, small tusks increased in absolute figures. This development must have been so noticeable that from 1895 onward, the amount of tusks lighter than 6 pounds (approximately 2.72 kilograms) was explicitly noted in the records. In 1895–96, some 924 tusks were lighter than 6 pounds, one year later the number of underweight tusks had risen to 5,304. The decrease in tusk sizes was one of the reasons that motivated the German governor Hermann von Wissmann to issue the first comprehensive game ordinance for the colony in May 1896, which foresaw a ban on the hunting of elephants with a tusk weight lower than 3 kilograms. All trophies acquired in contravention to this ordinance were liable to confiscation. Presumably, the decrease in the weight of tusks for the years 1896–97 and the rising number of exported tusks were effects of the ordinance, as it probably made ivory merchants throw their underweight tusks on the market to prevent their possible confiscation.

Because only sizeable tusks paid off the long and risky transport from the far interior, the increase in small tusks also suggests that hunting intensified in the German East African territory itself. Presumably, hunters increasingly went after females and younger elephants with smaller tusks[21] for quick profit, but also because there were fewer sizeable "tuskers" left. One German Schutztruppe member claimed that among the hundreds of elephants he had seen during his six years of service in the colony, only five or six would have born tusks heavier than 15 kilograms.[22] Of course, this is an erratic observation, but it could well hint at the possibility that small tusks or even tusklessness increased as a consequence of unconscious selection through hunting. By 1900, Tanzania's elephant herds had been exposed to at least half a century of intense and constant predation. For elephants, bearing tusks had turned from an asset into a liability.[23] Decades of ivory hunting also meant that remaining herds were comparatively shy and young, while the remaining big tuskers were few, experienced, and wary.[24] One of the small number of white commercial ivory hunters operating in German East Africa in the 1890s, August Knochenhauer, not only complained in 1897 that sizeable tuskers were extremely hard to be found, but delivered another explanation for the increase of small tusks at the customs stations. African hunting groups would wait until matriarchal herds congregated and male elephants joined them for mating. The tuskers would, from "decades of experience", always escape the attack of the hunters, who then resorted to the indiscriminate slaughter of the maternal herds.[25] His portrayal, although blinkered by the racial bias that underlay his description of African hunting, may well have been plausible. The average weight of tusks returned as fiscal ivory decreased from almost 10 kilograms in

1900 to an all-time low of 5.5 kilograms in 1904, just to rise again to around 8 kilograms afterward.[26]

The surviving ivory statistics also testify to the degree to which elephants became subject to the basic administrative and economic rationales of colonial rule. Like other raw materials and commodities with an extractable value, elephants were seen "like a state"[27] and treated as an economic and fiscal asset to capitalize on. In their suggestive exactness, the statistics of the customs house rendered the complex world of tusks legible by reducing them to mere figures expressive of size, weight, and value. As an expression of the "modern" side of the fledgling bureaucratic state in Tanganyika, the statistics expressed the administrative view from coast and capital. But the attempt to read elephants into these ivory statistics revealed not only that ivory retained its precolonial economic significance also in the first decades of German colonial rule. The statistics also infer the intensification of hunting in German East African territory, and they hint at least at evolutionary effects and behavioral adaptation of elephants after decades of intense, selective hunting.

Above all, the invention of the technical category of fiscal ivory shows that, since the early 1890s, the agents of the colonial state themselves evolved into the single most important traders in ivory. Tusks served as an almost universal currency in the making of the colonial state. In the remainder of this chapter, the insights gleaned from the coastal statistics will be complemented with the perspective from the stations beyond the coast as well as with the practical politics of hunting and ivory during the years of conquest. The economic and ecological implications of the ivory statistics only become fully understandable if put into the overall social, cultural, and ideological context of hunting in the making of colonial rule.

Imperial Man the Hunter: Ideologies and Practices in the Middle Ground

"It is strange," mused Julius Stentzler, a German military officer, in his memories of his service in the German East African Schutztruppe, that "every European who steps on East African soil turns into a passionate hunter, at least during his first days on the continent, even if he had never laid hand to a rifle as long as he was at home." The pursuit and killing of wild animals was such an ubiquitous phenomenon in the colony that he did not feel the need to provide any explanation for the remarkable change of Europeans' occupational preferences once they had entered the African continent.[28]

Stentzler's allegation is indicative of hunting's wider allure and significance to the culture of imperialism. The hunting of so-called big game was a multidimensional and multifunctional, ritualized performance of power over nature. Almost any travelogue, diary, or article published by Germans who came to East Africa as military or administrative officials, settlers, or visiting travelers, contains lengthy descriptions of encounters with African wildlife. Obviously, exotic species in an exotic environment were an enormous thrill for men who had so far encountered mainly roe or wild pigs in well-managed forest estates, if they had been hunters at all. There were just no contemporary central European equivalents to intimidatingly large species like elephants or buffalo, or dangerous predators like lions or leopards. Hunters engaged in endless debates about which game species afforded the most courage and bestowed the most prestige. Elephants, rhinoceroses, lions, and buffalo usually scored highest, and several sources understood these species as necessary educators whose hunting would restore a natural manhood that had allegedly been civilized away in Europe.[29] The encounter with them was often portrayed as a chivalrous duel in which a dangerous animal opponent was invested with all the desired qualities of masculinity—strength, intentionality, consciousness, strategy, at times even reason. Occasional reports of European hunters seriously wounded or even killed in the encounter with elephants or rhinoceroses lent plausibility to the hunters' claim of the danger involved in their pursuit.

But of course, the presence of potential prey, however charismatic the species may have been, did not yet make hunting. Germans aspired to big game hunting also because the British had firmly established the role model of imperial man the hunter in frontier settings from India over North America to Southern Africa.[30] The big game hunter as the archetype of imperial man was taken up and popularized in Germany from the middle of the nineteenth century. Novelist Theodor Fontane, for example, translated Roualeyn Gordon Cumming's lion-hunting tales for an educated readership as early as 1853, and the big game hunting theme loomed large in translated travelogues of European explorers, in hunting periodicals, as well as in illustrated magazines that reached broader audiences.[31] Precolonial German explorers, like Carl Claus von der Decken, complied with the pattern of heroic exploration that essentially included hunting. With the onset of colonial rule in the middle of the 1880s, the close connection between African exploration and travel, heroic masculinity, and the hunting of big game was forged further, for example, in the transitory communities of talk between German and British imperialists aboard the steamships to East Africa. During the three-week journey, hunting was a foremost theme of male display and conversation, and the fact if one was an old hand or a newcomer in big game hunting often proved more important than a hunter's country of origin.

If big game hunting appeared as something that the men who ventured to the fringes of European expansion simply did, their cultural background certainly enhanced the prestige of hunting further. The German minority that set out to establish colonial rule over East Africa came from a society in which hunting had for centuries been associated with power and aristocratic privilege.[32] This association had weakened since the middle of the nineteenth century, when the right to hunt became tied to property in land. However, the aura of privilege and exclusiveness had remained largely intact, and access to game in Germany continued to be restricted to a selected few because the exertion of hunting rights was still tied to exclusive property qualifications. German aristocrats who came to East Africa in the colonial service or as visiting hunters imported the habitus of privilege and social distinction afforded by hunting.[33] At the same time, the colony enabled even the subaltern clerk and the settler of modest means who could never afford the lease of a hunting estate back in Germany to share into a ritual that was laden with a long heritage of privilege in Europe. Essentially, Germans brought three notions of their central European hunting culture with them to East Africa: The first was a notion of territoriality and the idea that game could and should be managed in bounded space. The second was a set of norms and practices that constituted the German hunting ethic of *Weidgerechtigkeit*. It comprised, among others, an ethical responsibility and an attitude of respect of the hunter toward the game, the exertion of hunting with restraint, and the observation of a number of rules such as the sparing of feeding females, the quick and painless infliction of death and the avoidance of unnecessary suffering, and the overall responsibility for the sustainable management of game.[34] In the colonial context, *Weidgerechtigkeit* was relevant not so much as an actual practice but as a language of distinction that could be invoked and mobilized against those that should, for various reasons, be excluded from the Hunt. The third notion that Germans imported into East Africa was an experience of radical contrast. Indeed, the most widespread and recurrent theme in hunters' narratives was an exhilaration of "the feeling of the unrestrained, free hunter, whom no game law, no border restricts in his pursuit of the chosen game. It is the knowledge to be the uninhibited master of creation that makes the African Hunt so enormously appealing."[35] Karl Rehfus, a manufacturer of hats in the Baden-town of Kehl, visited East Africa in 1900 to strike the same chord of masculine conquest when he praised the "feeling to be the ruler of a kingdom whose borders are determined only by personal strength and endurance and whose laws are established solely by the hunter's will."[36] An East-Elbian aristocrat addressing the readership of *Wild und Hund* after World War I claimed it was the "direct contact with wilderness, the originality of all action untainted by civilization, the freedom and the boundless possibilities that enable the European a whole new existence beyond the regulations, limits, customs, prejudices and conventions that constrain him at home. Only gradually can he accustom himself to that feeling of mastery that he has lost almost completely at home."[37] These assessments stem from hunters with varying social backgrounds who describe their experience of hunting in Africa in differing sources and various decades. They all contrasted an experience of authenticity, freedom, and individuality in Africa with an artificial and emasculating civilization in Europe. If we accept Georg Simmel's definition of adventure as "exterritoriality vis à vis the continuum of ordinary life,"[38] stalking and killing animals in East Africa was adventure in a very literal sense. Big game hunting was the one activity that allowed Germans most radically to experience Africa as a countersite to European modernity, a space of individuality and primal masculinity where the bearers of the imperial civilizing mission could themselves shake off the shackles of civilization.

The experience of at least relative freedom and mastery over an exotic environment coupled with the multiplicity of functions that hunting attained in the colonial situation. It procured meat and knowledge, it prepared and accompanied settlement, and it offered distraction in the boredom of imperial outposts. The collecting frenzy of natural history museums in North America and Europe allowed self-made explorers and colonial officials to hunt in the name of science and capitalize on their imperial worldliness by donating furs, hides, horns, and tusks to collections back home.[39] But hunting in the outposts of empire did not only supply the raw material for the visual representation of taxonomy, evolution, and zoogeography in dioramas that conjured up "fictions of liveness."[40] It was also a means of procuring "scientific" knowledge in other disciplines, such as early ecology, veterinary science, or tropical medicine. In any case, Europeans' hunting in the colony, be it for commerce, science, subsistence, or sport, was politically and ideologically charged. When European hunters shot game to distribute the spoil among porters and villagers; when district commissioners staged the killing of predators as "spectacles of responsible force"[41] in front of the colonized; or when sporting gentlemen mimicked official colonial expeditions with the military demeanor of their entourage, hunting was not just a symbol or metaphor of colonial rule.[42] It was one of its constitutive practices and "an actual exercise in sovereignty."[43] At times, hunting was identical with colonization itself.

Like the protagonists of European expansion in India, North America, and South Africa,[44] also the Germans who came to colonize East Africa understood the hunting of charismatic, dangerous, and larger-than-human species of big game as a ritual that epitomized their superiority and claim to domination over land, people, and wildlife. They contributed their share

Seeing Like a State, Acting Like a Chief 77

Illustration 2.1. An elephant shot at Lehnin farm near Rutenganio (pre-1914). Moravian Archives Herrnhut.[46]

to the thousands of pictures showing white hunters brimming with pride and achievement perched atop the dead bodies of elephants or rhinoceroses. This iconography is deeply engrained in the visual and mental archive of European imperialism.[45] Enshrined in photographs, it conveyed, above all, an *imagined* freedom, superiority, mastery, and masculinity that was used for personal memory or to communicate with audiences at home. However, trophy pictures also encapsulate concrete moments situated in space and time. When contextualized, individual photographs can transcend mere symbolism and imperial ideology to allow at least a glimpse at how the imperial politics and performances of hunting resonated with African ideas, practices, and expectations on the ground. Illustration 2.1 shows an elephant shot in the vicinity of the farm Lehnin near the Moravian missionary station of Rutenganyo, situated in the area of Mbeya in southwestern Tanganyika.

The picture is one of several trophy pictures the Moravian missionary Adolf Ferdinand Stolz had taken of this particular elephant hunt. Stolz's presence at the mission in Rutenganyo allows the picture to be dated between 1903 and 1914. The hunter is probably a certain Schale who is identified as the owner of a farm near the mission in the caption of one of the pictures from that series. The picture arranges the white hunter at the center of the scene and visualizes his claim to the slain elephant. Often, such trophy pictures feature the white hunter alone with his prey, framing the Hunt as an archaic contest between man and wild nature. This picture, however, shows that the white hunter hardly ever was alone in his pursuit. Trackers, gun bearers, and a remarkably large number of African onlookers are all visible. Among them are women and children from nearby villages congregating, according to information provided by Stolz, in the expectation to receive some meat from the slain elephant. Their presence not only enabled the hunter to stage his mastery but also pressurized him to share the spoil of the hunt. Although the picture clearly visualizes the European ideology of big game hunting, it also encapsulates definite signs of African meanings imported into the hunt. One may speculate if the person to the right is merely holding the gun or actually pointing it—to the elephant, or even to the hunter? The knot in the elephant's trunk is clearly discernible; so is the person to the right lifting the elephant's tail. Both practices are in accordance with ethnographic descriptions about African customs of elephant hunting.[47] The knot in the trunk appears to have served the purpose to prevent the animal's spirit from leaving the corpse and seize the hunter.[48] Other ethnographies describe the cutting of the trunk's tip as a means to curb the power of the elephant, while the tail was usually cut by the successful hunter to stake his claim to the killing of the elephant. Hans Schomburgk, the later wildlife filmer who came to East Africa as a big game hunter after 1900, relates the customary practice of one of his accompanying hunters "to lift the tail of the elephant and spit into the animal's anus. After that he cut off the tail, solemnly strode around the elephant beating it with its own tail before placing it upon the bottom of the animal."[49] Count Bernhard zur Lippe states that the first thing his African hunter and guide did after the killing of an elephant was to cut off the tip of his trunk and the tail of which he made an arm ring for the white hunter.[50] The making of arm rings from the tail's hair was a visible sign of hunting prowess and also served as *dawa* to guarantee further successful hunting. Several accounts of German hunters relate their African guides and trackers' application of what appeared to be magic practices to influence the animal's behavior, protect the hunters, and provide for successful hunt and safe return.[51]

Apparently, the microcosmos of the hunting expedition constituted an arena where African and European ideas and values associated with the killing of animals coexisted alongside each other. Europeans and Africans may have stalked the same species, but the appropriated animals were often imbued with fundamentally differing meanings. While the one may have hunted a Pleistocene remnant of nature's brute force, the other saw himself confronted with a spirited being that was intimately tied to the lifeworld of his community. But although European hunters and their African companions hunted in differing cultural environments, they shared some general ideas about hunting as an expression of masculinity and power. The fact that European hunters usually described their activity in racialized terms did not automatically imply that African participation in hunting consisted merely in antagonistic responses. What ultimately mattered is that they acted together at all. In doing so, they created a makeshift working relationship and what Frederick Cooper has, in another context, referred to as a "limited space of mutual intelligibility and interaction."[52]

Such observations from the nucleus of the hunting expedition defy simple generalization, but they should caution against interpreting the contact zone of imperial hunting merely in terms of a clash of cultures. There is no denying that Germans understood hunting as an expression of racial mastery, claimed their *weidgerecht* hunting ethics as superior, despised African hunting as primitive and cruel, and strove to introduce game laws that excluded Africans, at least in the long run. But during the years of conquest, their position was far too weak to achieve all that. Therefore, the late nineteenth-century world of trade and hunting in East Africa is better understood as a brief period of what Richard White in his analysis of colonial encounters in the Great Lakes region of North America has characterized as middle ground, not in a geographical but in a metaphorical sense. A place between European conquest and the defeat of local populations, a place in between cultures marked by accommodation and the making of a "common, mutually comprehensible world" through processes of "creative, and often expedient, misunderstandings."[53] And even when the introduction of ever more exclusive game laws indicated that the stronger party no longer needed such accommodation, elements of the middle ground survived, for example, in the dependent mastery that characterized the transcultural cosmos of the hunting safari.

Hunting provided the performative language and the symbolism to constitute such a middle ground, especially until Maji Maji. Occasional excesses of individuals notwithstanding, European hunters were few and remained comparatively insignificant in Tanganyika throughout the 1890s. German authorities' main target was to accommodate and control African and Swahili elephant hunters. In order to achieve this aim, it proved unintentionally supportive that both African and European cultures associated the hunter with authority and political leadership. The colonizers' obsession with hunting met with a political ecology in which the command over access to elephants constituted an established means to attract a following and forge alliances. Rather than a clash between colonizer and colonized, hunting often eluded this binary and allowed to forge the cross-cultural connections, alliances, and networks upon which German colonial rule was built.

Hunting the Subsidies of Conquest

Hunting was a means to establish local alliances, but this was not its only political expediency. It also gave the colonizers access to vital subsidies of colonial conquest like local knowledge, meat, and ivory. The appropriation of animals, thus, formed part of the many institutions, practices, and bodies of knowledge that linked the military and hunting expeditions of the colonizers with the precolonial cultures of travel, hunting, and the regime of the caravan trade. This is perhaps best illustrated by the colonial career of the Kiswahili term *safari*. Itself an import from the Arabic that originally denoted "travel" or "journey," both the British and the Germans incorporated the word into their vocabulary as a technical term. They extended its meaning to refer also to the social collective of the caravan before it narrowed down gradually to denote a journey undertaken afoot in the company of porters with the prime purpose of hunting.[54]

Beyond terminology, the imperial expeditions tapped "the enormous reservoir of specialist knowledge about the logistics and culture of travel"[55] accumulated by hunters and traders. Like the Swahili trade caravans of earlier decades, European expeditions acknowledged the key position of the *mnyampara*, the headman and leader of porters in trade caravans..[56] Usually, these indispensable experts of travel were contracted in the coastal ports, and identical names in different expeditions suggest that reliable headmen were recommended and employed over and over again, regardless if the purpose of expeditions was "official" or "private."[57] The same holds true for the innumerable guides, trackers, assistants, and local residents who steered the movement of Germany military and hunting expeditions through completely unknown environments. Any expedition that traversed greater areas had to engage local guides. They were sometimes coerced, but more often provided by village elders and chiefs or, later, those *majumbe* or *maakida* who had been installed by the Germans.[58] Chiefs who provided porters and information expected trade goods or parts of the hunting spoils in return, often the meat of the slain animal. Even smaller hunting expeditions had to make sure they took enough "change" cargo with them, and the rules of exchange and hospitality that had marked the caravan trade remained relevant for travel under colonial rule, at least partially. Many of the early guides for German caravans were Makua who had acquired their familiarity with the respective locales by elephant hunting or the trading of ivory. Several German hunters asserted that their guides had previously been elephant hunters themselves. Sometimes they also referred to them as *fundi*.[59] Dorobo hunters were widely acknowledged as the best available guidance in the Maasai steppe, and almost any region that became popular among German hunters featured its recommended and reliable local guide. In the Ulanga Valley, for example, this was the "experienced and intrepid" *jumbe* Makua.[60] A certain Mussa achieved similar fame in the hinterland of Lindi and Kilwa during the 1890s and early 1900s. His origin at the Western shore of Lake Nyassa, his embrace of Islam, and his occupation identify him as part of the caravan trade along the Southern route. Versed in the local Mwera language, Mussa not only negotiated with chiefs but actually commanded the conduct and itinerary of the European hunters who hired his services. One colonial official noted admiringly how much he had learned "from the stories of this man. Every evening we sat by the fire, chatting over a cup of tea, and I listened to the stories of this old fundi."[61] While some German travelogues are rather outspoken in their acknowledgement of local support, more often this indigenous knowledge was silently incorporated into the colonial archive.[62] Because hunting helped district commissioners as well as settlers familiarize with the land, its topography, botany, and wildlife well beyond the years of initial conquest, the continued dependency of imperial hunters on local knowledge created considerable space for indigenous agendas and everyday resistance. Accounts of hunting contain many examples of villagers denying support or information about hunting opportunities; they tell of porters failing to trace a wounded animal to allow local villagers to appropriate meat and trophies, and they report of guides and trackers abandoning European hunters as a consequence of the latter's disrespect for the moral economy of travel.[63]

Apart from local knowledge, hunting procured meat as another indispensable subsidy to colonial conquest. As John MacKenzie was right to emphasize, game meat was the "great concealed subsidy of the European advance."[64] Indeed, hunting was often indispensable to secure the bare survival of a caravan stranded in uncharted territory, and the itineraries of many Schutztruppe columns were determined as much by the necessity of provisioning the caravan with game meat as by the military aims of the campaign. Hunting for meat by Askari was a regular practice to feed expeditions undertaken by military stations,[65] and article 5 of the first comprehensive game ordinance issued in 1896 explicitly decreed that no license was necessary to provide for a caravan by hunting.[66] This necessity to hunt waned the more the colonizers familiarized themselves with the territory and the more they developed their own reliable logistics. Yet, it never entirely vanished. Schutztruppe columns, commissioners touring their district, scientific expeditions, private hunting safaris, and cinematographic expeditions supplemented their food logistics with game, not to mention the enormous resurgence of military subsistence hunting during the East Africa campaign of World War I.[67]

Hunting for meat is a particularly revealing example for how a thoroughly practical purpose could be portrayed as a performance of male imperial power in the colonial context. Game meat, in Europe a distinguishing privilege of wealth and status, experienced an inverse valuation in the colonial context. Those Europeans who occasionally consumed game meat themselves depicted it either as adventurous curiosity or as a last heroic resort in order to secure survival. Otherwise, game meat was the food of porters and Askari, provided by the European hunter. Yet, the mechanisms of power between providers and consumers were far from unanimous. There were practices and customs associated with meat that a caravan leader had to respect. Several accounts mention that Muslim porters despised pig meat and rejected meat from animals that had not been slaughtered *halāl*.[68] Also the songs sung by carriers show that the rules of the expedition were as much dictated by the porters as by the caravan leader. Lyrics like "The master is shooting stones, the meat is ready," or: "If our *bwana* only shot a giraffe, a giraffe has a lot of meat" show how porters communicated their expectations and ridiculed the colonizers at the same time.[69] Some white hunters solemnly spoke of a "grave sense of responsibility imposed upon the European shouldn't he be able to provide the desired game meat."[70] In doing so, they exposed not only paternalism. They also admitted to their dependence on the porters' cooperation and contentment, and to the pressure exerted by the self-imposed obligation to perform in front of an African audience. All these power plays notwithstanding, the distribution of meat undoubtedly contributed to the fostering of bonds between the hunting leader and his following. Rather than reducing it to mere ideology, the paternalist hunter as benign provider can also be understood as another working relationship on the East African middle ground. As has been shown above, the obligation of the successful hunter to share in his spoil had been a central element of African hunting cultures, and entire villages congregating to celebrate the success of a European hunter are mentioned so frequently in hunting narratives that they could hardly have been mere inventions of the imperial imagination.

Finally, there was the politics of ivory. If meat helped to bolster authority in times of hardship, ivory was important as an almost universal currency. Military expeditions firmly reckoned with the acquisition of ivory to make the campaign financially self-supporting. Wissmann's punitive expedition to Kilimanjaro in 1891 settled virtually all expenses by looted or tributed ivory. District commissioners and military stations reported proudly to Dar es Salaam whenever a punitive expedition was self-financing thanks to the cattle or ivory received or extorted as tribute or punishment.[71] Ivory could finance the conquest of the colony for it was easily convertible into monetary value. Yet, its symbolic value made it even more important for the extension of German rule beyond the coastal belt. Looting and extorting ivory were easy to interpret as actions claiming hegemony and overlordship, especially as the acquisition of ivory by coercion and submission had already been characteristic for the violent political landscape produced by the frenzied competition for ivory and slaves in late precolonial Tanganyika.[72] The expectation was common that minor chiefdoms had to acknowledge newly installed paramounts with gifts like ivory, slaves, or cloth. The handover of tusks, for example, served as a signal to initiate negotiations and the end of warfare.[73] Under colonial rule, the submission of ivory—and to a lesser degree of cattle—became the single most important procedure representing the political relations between colonizers and colonized. Tusks were used to indicate hospitality, mark the end of hostilities, and establish peaceful relations, at least temporarily and superficially. Wilhelm Langheld, for example, accepted tusks as sign of peaceful reception and did not finish warfare in any of his "pacification" campaigns in Unyamwezi unless his opponents had symbolically surrendered by handing over ivory. Theodor Bumiller's unpublished diary of the Wissmann expedition to Kilimanjaro in early 1891 leaves little doubt that the Germans impressed their understanding of the submission of tusks upon their opponents. Having defeated Sina of Kibosho, Wissmann made the chief's emissaries "go down on their knees and eat dirt as a sign of submission" before he accepted an enormous tusk worth about 1,000 marks "as salaam." When chief Merere of Ussangu, another trade chief in southwestern Tanzania who had laid a strict claim on every tusk of ivory in his country, died in 1893, his elected successor had to pay the district officer in the recently erected station of Langenburg 100 pounds of ivory as tribute.[74]

The symbolism of ivory was not restricted to assigning real or alleged chiefs their rank in the new colonial order. It permeated the day-to-day politics of the stations, and it was open to the expedient misunderstandings characteristic of the middle ground. Africans used the symbolism of tusks to pursue their own agendas. Touring his district in early 1898, the Schutztruppe officer Prittwitz von Gaffron mentions one local who presented him two tusks. Interpreting the ivory as "a sure sign of his friendly attitude towards the Germans," Prittwitz allowed him to settle as trader in Iringa.[75] Examples like the latter indicate that the asymmetrical symbolism the Germans ascribed to the submission of ivory was not always as straightforward as they wanted it to be. Indeed, there are cases when the presentation of tusks was intended to establish friendly relations with the Germans and use them as an ally in local conflicts and power plays. A passage in Paul Reichard's comprehensive manual on East African affairs shows that the colonizers were aware to the ambivalence and interpretive openness of such exchanges. "One always has to make sure to return less than one has received," he advised his readers. "Otherwise the black chieftain would automatically deem himself equally powerful and deny that any form of subordination had taken place."[76]

The exchange of ivory was inexorably entwined with what Jamie Monson has characterized as "the politics of alliance and authority."[77] So was hunting as the practice of ivory "production." The German colonizers tried to use the right to hunt elephants to reward and secure the allegiance of African collaborators. Wherever they had succeeded in founding a station, elephant hunting served as a tool to foster alliances, achieve control over the local ivory trade, and establish the colonizers as new authority. Mtinginya of Usongo, a Nyamwezi chief grown powerful by controlling the caravan route between Tabora and Karagwe, counted among the main allies of the Germans in central Tanzania in the 1890s. German district commissioners regarded him as a "great elephant hunter," rewarded his cooperation with exclusive rifles, and had Mtinginya collect ivory tribute from minor chiefs in Unyanyembe.[78] The best documented example for the local politics of hunting is found on Mount Kilimanjaro. After the restoration of German authority in February 1891, Wissmann, recently appointed the colony's first governor, introduced a system of hunting licenses for the district supervised from Moshi. This regulation stipulated fees for European sport hunters, and for each elephant and rhinoceros killed. It also tried to appropriate a central right of the local Chagga chiefs, as it made "professional" elephant hunting dependent on the payment of a fee of 500 rupees to the German station at Moshi.[79] Because the fee could be returned in tusks, it was in fact an adaptation of the ground tusk principle. Only the leading hunter-entrepreneur (*fundi*) had to pay the fee. After payment, he was allotted a certain area for hunting and received permission to provide his hunters with muzzle-loading guns and powder. In turn, they had to hand over one tusk of each killed elephant to the *fundi*, while the other tusk remained theirs as remuneration.

The rationale behind this "divide and rule" approach to elephant hunting was to secure the cooperation of influential local intermediaries and to use their networks to curb the smuggling of ivory into British territory. The right to hunt elephants was soon to become a central element of the station's own politics of alliance and authority. Its main beneficiary was the ivory and slave trader Fundi, a big man thanks to trade and a prime example for the fluidity of social and cultural categories along the caravan routes.[80] Native from Kavirondo near Lake Victoria, himself at times enslaved and a convert to Islam later, Fundi dealt first in slaves, later in ivory. Operating between Pangani and Kilimanjaro, his widespread connections made him "the greatest of all the traders"[81] in European eyes, and he soon became indispensable to the Germans as universal political agent and utility man. Fundi helped with the acquisition of porters, guided military expeditions, and acted as Kiswahili interpreter and political mediator. Wissmann installed him as the German station's intermediary to Sina of Kibosho in 1891. When Kurt Johannes took over at Moshi in September 1892, Fundi rose further to become the most important ally, informer, and agent of the Germans in the complicated power plays on the mountain.[82] In order to secure his cooperation, the station more or less outsourced elephant hunting in the Kilimanjaro area to Fundi. Johannes also hoped that the licensing system would enhance control and mistrust among the hunter-entrepreneurs. Those who had paid the fee were expected to watch jealously over their acquired privilege and report anyone hunting without a license to the station.

Undeniably, the system encouraged and intensified elephant hunting. It was both in the interest of the hunters and of the enterprising *fundi* to shoot as many elephants as possible, especially as the latter had to amortize the 500 rupees. Fundi did not fail to exploit the patronage granted by the German station to his own ends. His privileged position gave him the upper hand over rivalling traders and allowed him to use elephant hunting as a tool to attract and cater for his own clientele. While the German station at Moshi claimed authority over the land, Fundi actually exerted it over people and elephants. In 1897, the district official of neighboring Pangani complained that Fundi had virtually turned into the sole "Lord of the Hunt" (*Jagdherr*) in the Kilimanjaro area.[83] This assertion was hardly exaggerated. Between 1895 and 1897, the station at Moshi earned just 1,000 rupees from hunting licenses, which means that only two entrepreneurs were officially "accredited" by the station.[84] Allegations that Fundi had up to 400 hunters under arms may even have been too moderate. The district commissioner of Pangani complained in December 1897 that his station would issue virtually no license for elephant hunting, because up to 600 men from Uzigua would seasonally relocate to Kilimanjaro where Fundi permitted them to hunt elephants under his license.[85] Indeed, it was one of Fundi's Chagga hunters who killed the elephant that provided the largest tusks ever sold on the Zanzibar market in 1898. These so-called Kilimanjaro tusks weighed both well over 200 pounds. Today, they are stored in the collection of the Natural History Museum London.[86]

Introducing Conservation: The Game Ordinance of 1896

The degree to which the German Kilimanjaro station handed over the control of hunting and ivory to an African intermediary remained unnoticed in Dar es Salaam. When Hermann von Wissmann returned to East Africa as Imperial Governor in 1895–96, he deemed the system on Kilimanjaro so successful that he extended it to the whole colony in a game ordinance introduced to regulate hunting all over German East Africa in May 1896. In his opinion, experiences on Kilimanjaro had shown that "a considerable number of native hunters have paid the comparatively high fees for licenses to shoot elephants."[87] Therefore, the ordinance subjected all professional elephant hunters to the previous payment of an annual fee of 500 rupees. Moreover, the government claimed shooting fees for each elephant killed—100 rupees for the first, 250 rupees for every further elephant—and forbade the hunting of elephant calves with tusks weighing less than 3 kilograms.[88] The same obligations applied to expeditions hunting merely for sport.

Beyond elephant hunting, the ordinance made all other hunting dependent on the previous issue of a license. In order to include any potential hunter, the ordinance reduced the social complexity of the societies in the interior, the cosmopolitan Swahili port cities, the mobile traders, and the trade-associated hunter-entrepreneurs and the incoming personnel of German colonialism to the three categories of Europeans, nonindigenous, and indigenous, that is African hunters. Europeans had to pay 20, Africans 5 rupees for a license; the category of nonindigenous hunters was only relevant for professional elephant hunting and denoted, de facto, hunter entrepreneurs with a Swahili or Arab background. District stations were encouraged to control hunting by allowing them to retain half of the proceeds from the sale of hunting licenses. The other half had to be submitted to the government; stations in the interior could keep the whole sum and were supposed to invest this revenue into development measures like roadworks or the introduction of new crops.[89] The ordinance linked the hunting of animals with colonial notions of development also by forbidding the hunt of species deemed suitable for domestication, such as zebra, eland, and ostrich.

The game ordinance of 1896 was conceived entirely on the spot in Dar es Salaam. The foreign office in Berlin was informed, but did not alter or influence the ordinance's content. Just like the system introduced on Mount Kilimanjaro in 1891, the ordinance gazetted in 1896 grew out of the perception of local practices and necessities, and it drew upon Wissmann's previous experience in African exploration. In a later elaboration on the guiding principles of his ordinance, Wissmann linked his approach to the practices of the trade chiefs and big men created by the ivory trade:

> When, in 1887, I made my third journey through the districts between Lomani and the Upper Congo (Lualaba), … it transpired that these districts belonged to the sphere under the control of Tippu Tipp, and that he

had only accorded special permission to shoot elephants under the condition that half of the ivory should be surrendered to him. Why should we not then directly prohibit elephant hunting on the part of a whole tribe, and make this tribe (of course through its Chiefs) responsible for the prevention of elephant hunting in the tribal district by any outsider? It would be possible to compensate this tribe for the prohibition of hunting by some special privilege, or else allow a certain number of hunters a certain number of elephants.[90]

Wissmann's considerations are remarkable for they reveal that indirectly, Tippu Tip, the much maligned slave trader of German imperial propaganda, had delivered the model on which Wissmann crafted his hunting laws. The fledgling colonial state mimicked the practices of precolonial ivory hunting and transferred hunting into patron–client relationships. If this made hunting and wildlife regulation another field in which German colonial policies had deep "local roots,"[91] Wissmann's game ordinance also contained European elements that became important in the long run. By establishing two game reserves west of Mount Kilimanjaro and along the Upper Rufiji River, it was the first game law to introduce spatial concepts of conservation into East Africa. Obviously, the ordinance ordered and categorized the African fauna according to European values and perceptions. Although usually entitled *Jagdverordnung,* such regulations effectively did more than just regulate hunting. They are biopolitical classifications that define human–animal relationships and determine how wild animals can and should be treated. Entitlement to hunting was redistributed and new taxonomies were introduced that ruled out or enabled specific forms of violence against specific animals in specified places by specific persons. The ordinance reified colonial social categories like European or indigenous, and imbued them with practical relevance by allotting or denying them certain rights or access to weapons. With a view to animals, some species were singled out as game; access to others was regulated or restricted according to their economic importance or their presumed potential for domestication. Beasts of prey, monkeys, wild pigs, and other pests to livestock and agricultural production were declared as exterminable vermin. At times, the shooting of so-called *Raubzeug,* that is, all the feline predators, crocodiles, wild dogs, and baboons, was encouraged by bounties for each killed specimen.

The values guiding these ordinances, as well as the social and biopolitical categories introduced by them, changed over time. The idea that wild animals and their habitats required order, management, and partial protection did not. The complex African world of spiritual and magical relationships between humans and animals came to coexist alongside Western utilitarian and conservationist values, and it mixed with them. For the first time, animals were subjected to the rationale of a central state, which defined interests within the spatial category of German East Africa that had heretofore no social, ecological, economic, or political relevance at all. If the practice deployed to translate the state's claim into action was modelled on patterns reminiscent of local big man policies, in theory, wild animals were subject to an abstract and uniform rule of codified law in the form of ordinances, bureaucratic administration, and police sanction. Norm-setting ordinances put wild animals under state custody and framed them as a common in the public interest. As a consequence, local interests and values were colonized by the overarching motivations of a state-defined public interest that was not only defined in Dar es Salaam, but increasingly influenced by imperial and international debates and developments.

The game ordinance of May 1896 was the remarkable personal initiative of a controversial governor. Born in Frankfurt/Oder in 1853, Wissmann had entered a career as officer in the Prussian military. The acquaintance with the explorer Paul Pogge offered him the opportunity to join the latter's Central African expedition in 1880. After Pogge abandoned the expedition, Wissmann continued to attain the fame of the first European to cross Central Africa from West to East. In the years after, he made himself a name as the German equivalent of Henry Morton Stanley, conducting two further expeditions into the Congo sponsored by the Belgian King Leopold II.[92] Between 1888 and 1891, Wissmann was acting imperial commissioner with the order to conquer and pacify the territory claimed by the German East African Society (DOAG). After a spell in Germany, he returned to East Africa as imperial governor in 1895–96. German imperial propaganda lionized him as "Germany's greatest African" and the redeemer of East Africa from the slave trade. His followers admired his energy and charm; critics accused him of ruthlessness, megalomania, and a propensity to "hang everyone" who got in the way of German conquest.[93]

Wissmann's dedication to hunting has often been reduced to a mere biographical anecdote. Yet, it was not only a private passion that took him across the globe to Central Asia, India, and South West Africa.[94] On the one hand, the autocratic mastery of the hunter as arbiter over life and death as well as over acceptable forms and objects of killing and violence perfectly fit the imperial mindset. On the other, Wissmann was committed to the German ethics of hunting and game management. On his expeditions, Wissmann claimed, he had "too often seen how every European who possesses a gun … fires in the most reckless fashion …, without having any regard as to whether or not he can possess himself of the animal when killed."[95] This assessment as well as his correspondence and publications reveal his thinking in terms of *Weidgerechtigkeit,* the set of norms and practices that constituted the German ethics of hunting and game management. His commitment to negotiate between the colonialist imperative of resource exploitation and the emerging concern about the destruction of game species worldwide was also motivated by an ethical imperative that hunting had to be exerted with respect and restraint, and that game could and should be managed sustainably.

Wissmann's 1896 game law also tried to reconcile the fiscal interests of the colonial state with the will to preserve wildlife from extinction and its hunting for future generations. Personal and structural factors combined in the ordinance's making. There was the obvious necessity to secure future income from a declining ivory resource by a more sustainable regulation of its hunting. The unbridled hunting of officials and soldiers as well as a handful of professional ivory hunters and a daring vanguard of travelling hunters called for regulation, too. So far, they had enjoyed hunting unrestrained by any law or regulation and their impact, although few in numbers, was devastating thanks to the high-precision weaponry they employed.[96] Rinderpest was another factor. The great panzootic of the early 1890s, which long remained undiscerned as identical with the rinderpest already known from Europe, had not only exerted a ruinous impact upon cattle, but also upon ungulate populations such as buffalo, zebra, and antelopes. Wissmann was an eyewitness to this devastation during the military campaigns around Kilimanjaro in 1891. The north of the colony in particular was struck further by droughts and locusts, which culminated in crop failure and famine. The concomitant collapse of livestock-based human ecologies resulted in increased hunting to secure bare survival, which in turn increased European perceptions of social and ecological turmoil that seemed to require and justify military and administrative intervention.[97] Finally, Wissmann perceived developments in East Africa within the framework of the global deterioration of the larger fauna in the wake of European expansion: the extension of white settlement in North America and South Africa had swept away almost all larger game and left a devastating record that dominated debates about hunting and conservation in East Africa. Regulating the hunt in East Africa was also an attempt to learn from the previous experience of European imperial expansion.

These factors notwithstanding, the ordinance would not have been enacted had it not been for Wissmann and the circumstance that the responsible governor was also a passionate hunter who could draw upon a rich experience of African exploration. As the first attempt to introduce conservation on a Tanganyikan scale, the ordinance combined local and global, parochial and universal considerations with moral, economical, ecological, and political concerns. Wissmann was a vanguard witness of how wildlife vanished with the extension of commercial and colonial frontiers. Unlike his immediate predecessors and followers in the office of governor, he was not willing to accept the alleged fatality of this development and wielded his official powers for the conservation of wild animals.

Colonial Rule According to the Hunter Principle

Judged merely by the series of enacted game laws, the German colonizers seemed to have subscribed to ever stricter conservation from 1896 onwards. Yet, surviving archival records of the government in Dar es Salaam for the years up to 1900 reveal that the intended conservation turned out quite differently when translated into practical politics. Local necessities and circumstances took the edge off many provisions. In the surroundings of Mikindani, for example, the frequent occurrence of depredations by lions made it impossible for the station to enforce the ban on game drives. After several women had been attacked during fieldwork by lions, the station rather handed out guns, powder, and ammunition to enable villagers to defend themselves.[98] The district commissioner in nearby Lindi objected to enforce the compulsory purchase of a license in order to hunt elephants. There were, he argued, "several hundreds" of elephants still shot annually between the rivers Rovuma and Mbwemkuru. The introduction of a license would not only result in the smuggling of their ivory into Portuguese territory, but it would also choke the considerable influx of tusks across the Southern border, which made up the bulk of the ivory trade conducted via Lindi. The powerful local ally to appease in that area was a caravan trader referred to in the German sources as "Abdallah Damlah", whose commercial links across the Rovuma were apparently instrumental in supplying the trade via Lindi.[99]

The administrators of border districts in particular struggled with the problem that charging hunters resulted in smuggling and the occultation of ivory hunting. But inland districts had their problems with borders, too. After Mpwapwa station had announced the introduction of fees for elephant hunting, many hunters left for Kilimanjaro to join the ranks of Fundi or have their fee paid by European settlers or traders.[100] Migration and mobility of both game and hunters turned out to be an enormous challenge for the fledgling colonial administration. The spatial units of administrative and military districts existed only in the colonizers' maps, and given the difficult circumstances of communication between the various stations in the interior, hunters could quite effectively evade identification and taxation by simply crossing district boundaries. The rivalries between Moshi and Pangani over the status of Fundi testify to the frictions arising from the fact that district stations directly profited from the sale of hunting licenses, especially when hunters had or claimed to have paid their license at one station, but shot their elephants in the territory of another.

Stations in the interior faced the problem that they could not "sell" licenses because money had not yet been introduced. This favored flexible local arrangements, for the power politics of the stations usually functioned in-kind anyway. Some stations, as a visitor to Muanza observed, even deferred the introduction of hard currency, as stations were permitted to retain payment in-kind while cash had to be delivered to Dar es Salaam.[101] But the one stipulation of the game ordinance that caused most confusion was the licensing of professional elephant hunting. In the months following the ordinance's publication, many stations turned to the government for an authoritative interpretation of the term professional. In areas, where elephants had already become scarce, one only encountered occasional elephant hunting, while in areas where elephant hunting was still frequent, the introduction of fees had quite varied effects: some stations complained it would drive elephant hunting into secrecy, others feared it would be curbed altogether if every single hunter was forced to pay 500 rupees. In Ujiji, the introduction of the license fee appeared to have partially resulted in the unintended effect that *mafundi* who paid the fee increased the number of hunters they took with them. In this case, the regulation achieved quite the opposite of the intended conservation.

The divergent ways in which the ordinance was put into practice show that by no means all district administrators regarded elephant conservation a pressing issue. Nor did Wissmann's successor in office, Eduard von Liebert, who decided to mitigate the measures introduced by his predecessor. In a first circular in November 1896, just half a year after Wissmann's ordinance had been proclaimed, he decreed that district officers should dispense African elephant hunters from taking out a license beforehand and oblige them to return one tusk of each killed elephant to the station instead. In early 1897, the central administration in Dar es Salaam calculated on the basis of its statistics that the charging of shooting fees for every elephant killed threatened to render hunting no longer profitable.[102] Consequently, a revision of the game ordinance in January 1898 brought further alleviation.[103] While the revised ordinance retained the main conservationist instruments—licenses and reserves—it revoked many of the provisions that had turned out to be impracticable. While the hunting of all larger game remained liable to the purchase of a license, fees were reduced by 50 percent for nonprofessional indigenous (5 rupees) and European hunters (10 rupees) alike. A bounty was placed upon the shooting of lions and leopards, but the most important element were the stipulations concerning professional elephant hunting. The fees for each elephant killed were reduced from 250 to 100 rupees, or the return of one tusk, respectively.

This obligation ceased once the value of returned tusks had equaled the 500 rupees of the license fee—an open invitation to excessive hunting. In areas where big chiefs "traditionally" laid a claim on one tusk of each elephant, the station should claim every second tusk only.

Effectively, the government put the regulation of elephant hunting back into the hands of the district stations, which were recommended to use the hunting of elephants as a reward for political allegiance. Preference should be given to "reliable and trustworthy" persons, who were to be equipped with guns and powder by the station. Although Liebert advised stations to ban hunting entirely if this seemed necessary for the preservation of elephants, in practice the ordinance encouraged their hunting. Therefore, conservation-minded observers criticized Liebert's measures as essentially a return to the "status quo ante" before Wissmann.[104] Liebert was well aware of the practical consequences of his ordinance, for he ordered stations that *mafundi* should be allowed an entourage of no more than 30 hunters, and that any hunting of elephant calves and within the two game reserves should be prevented—"by all means."[105] In the overall architecture of Liebert's game ordinance, the reserves were hardly more than conservationist fig leaves with paradoxical effects: simply by existing as areas colored green on the map, they could be taken as a justification to exploit wildlife even more recklessly in the rest of the colony.

The years between 1897 and 1900 were marked by the balancing of exploitation and conservation according to the local political and ecological situation in individual districts. Coastal districts around Bagamoyo or Dar es Salaam did not have to bother as elephants had long ceased to occur even seasonally. Other stations, like Kilimatinde in Central Tanganyika, had little reliable information about the elephant herds in their district. Here, the commissioner adopted a policy of issuing as many licenses as possible to attract hunters and create revenue for the station. Langenburg station again reported that the new regulations were introduced and announced in public, but largely ignored by local hunters. Half a year later, only one elephant hunter had applied for a license. The district commissioner of Bukoba refrained from claiming a tusk because hunters were "traditionally obliged" to return a tusk to the chief. Neither could district commissioners in Ujiji insert themselves into the networks of the ivory business. Although there was a considerable amount of *mafundi* operating in the district on behalf of Arab traders, hardly a tusk found its way to the station. After a search of one of the traders procured a large number of underweight tusks, the station introduced a complete ban on elephant hunting in September 1898.[106] The same had been done a year before in Kilossa, where the district commissioner wanted to prevent the complete extermination of elephants in the district. In Mpwapwa, sources suggest that around 1897, the station maintained differentiated relations of influence and authority with various groups of hunters. A group of Makua hunters attached to the *liwali* of Mkondoa was only supposed to return every fourth tusk to the station, probably because the station did not want to alienate the influential *liwali*. Things were different with a group of Hehe hunters who had settled in the district in late 1895. Here, the station occupied the place of a chief or hunter-entrepreneur as it supplied the hunters with guns and received every second tusk in turn. Then, the district commissioners of Mpwapwa admitted, there was also a number of Gogo hunters who stood in client–patron relationships with Nyamwezi traders and, thus, remained beyond the reach of the station.[107]

Finally, there were districts where conquest and warfare continued until about the turn of the century. This was the case in parts of Uhehe and Songea in South Central and South Eastern Tanzania, but also in the hinterland of Lindi. Here, the passing of colonial game laws hardly affected local practices. After the putting down of Ngoni resistance, the station in Lindi appears to have secured the cooperation of several elephant hunters situated along the Rovuma River up to Sassawara. In early 1900, the station claimed one tusk until the value of 500 rupees was reached, provided the hunters with powder and ammunition, and used a "well-known and shrewd elephant hunter" to have an eye on any contraventions.[108] In Songea, the colonizers' claim to regulate access to elephants was not made public until January 1899, but this hardly impeded the operations of powerful Ngoni chiefs, nor of the already mentioned hunter-entrepreneur Rashid bin Masoud. The latter had been appointed as *akida*[109] by a German military expedition in 1894 in order to secure his cooperation against the Ngoni. Rashid established himself at Kikole at the eastern fringes of the Ngoni sphere of influence where, in late 1899, he still commanded a force of some 400 elephant hunters. Being one of the most important middlemen and informants of the German station, Rashid remained an influential big man who commanded elephant hunting in the area. Governing one of the districts with large stocks of elephants left, the station prided itself of punishing any contravention against the game regulations in the most severe manner. In 1901, the revenue from tusks and licenses amounted up to 13,000 rupees.[110]

In those southwestern regions subjected to military government from Iringa, cooperative local "sultans" initially retained their rights to control elephant hunting, like Kiwanga in the Kilombero Valley or Merere in Ussangu. In the Hehe kingdom of Mkwawa, however, the Schutztruppe officer Tom von Prince could capitalize on the fact that the forested highlands around Iringa were the habitat of perhaps the most sizeable elephant population still left in the colony. This enabled him to stabilize German rule after conquest by adopting the hunter principle. The chief he ousted,

Mkwawa, had all qualifications of a hunter king, with a large military following and a loose network of local representatives and agents, the so-called *wazagila*.[111] All over his territory, Mkwawa had claimed every tusk, which provided von Prince with the opportunity to grant previously excluded groups access to elephant hunting. In 1898, he operated a system in which the station, the hunter, and the newly installed local *majumbe*[112] each received one tusk.[113] Von Prince was convinced that this system would support the political reorganization of the region and strengthen the authority of the new *majumbe* who replaced Mkwawa's *wazagila*. Therefore, he refused to introduce the regulations stipulated by the 1898 game ordinance. His system, he boasted proudly in January 1899, had "excellently functioned and resulted in the return of *all* [!] ivory to the station, a situation which has probably been achieved by Iringa only." Indeed, the statistics feature Iringa as prime supplier of fiscal ivory from 1898 onward, and an independent witness, the Schutztruppe lieutenant Harald Pfeiffer, stated that the station had earned an impressive 20,000 rupees from hunting licenses in 1899 alone. The respective annual report for 1899–1900 recorded 50 licenses for elephant hunting and a return of 2,675 kilograms of ivory to the station, which allegedly amounted up to 500 elephants killed.[114]

What does this survey of local hunting politics in the second half of the 1890s tell about the making of the colonial state in German East Africa? On the one hand, it reveals that the rhetoric of conservation that permeated the 1896 game ordinance was first and foremost a discursive construct that bore only limited meaning for the actual practice of hunting politics in the late 1890s. Wissmann's attempted transfer of German sensibilities for sustainable hunting was overruled by the political realities and fiscal necessities of the early colonial state. The history of colonial wildlife regulation in the 1890s, it could be argued, consisted mainly of local circumvention and strategic obfuscation that frequently defied the colonizers' plans. The politics of hunting, thus, disclose the limits and weaknesses of the colonial state's claim to authority and control.

On the other hand, African chiefs, Swahili traders, and hunter-entrepreneurs actively seized the opportunities offered by the German takeover of the ivory trade. The colonial politics of hunting also constituted a middle ground of negotiation, strategic interaction, and pragmatic working relationships that produced instances of "mimicry in the contact zone."[115] In its initial conceptualization by Homi Bhabha, mimicry has been understood as "one of the most elusive and effective strategies of colonial power and knowledge,"[116] a tool of imperial education and regulation, a form of resistance, as well as an ambivalent and destabilizing effect of colonial discourse that produced ambivalence and menace. Bhabha was interested, above all, in the subversive potential that mimicry opened up for colonial subjects and the intermediaries of empire. Yet, as a phenomenon produced by the encounter and interaction at the cultural boundaries of European expansion, mimicry can also be understood as a form of camouflage. Historian Michael Pesek has described the performances of European travelers as forced and involuntary mimetic adaptations of local rules and practices,[117] while the practice of *shauri* meetings between German district officials and African elites has led Jan-Georg Deutsch to ask "whether German district officers consciously tried to emulate the way in which they thought African chiefs behaved."[118] These analyses shift the focus from the sly deception suggested by the term mimicry to the mimetic appropriation and incorporation of elements perceived to belong to local political culture.

In their respective ways, both deception and appropriation are weapons of the weak. The regulation of access to wildlife resources was another instance where the colonizers had no choice but to adopt patterns they understood as "traditional", "African" or at least a common practice within the framework of the caravan trade. Like von Prince in Uhehe or Johannes on Kilimanjaro, district commissioners claimed the right to hunt elephants as an asset of power, just like the big men and trade chiefs had done before them. This mimetic practice found its most significant expression in the colonial adaptation of the ground tusk principle.[119] When the Schutztruppe officer Georg Prittwitz von Gaffron encountered an alleged sultan in Ufipa in 1899, he staged a pompous ceremony of the sultan's inauguration and investiture with the insignia of German power. Having thus associated the chief's authority with the overlordship of the white colonizer, Prittwitz claimed the ground tusk that hitherto was to be handed to the chief. In the future, the hunter and the colonial state would share in the tusks of every elephant felled in the area, bypassing the sultan.[120] The idea of mimicking and replacing traditional authorities found its most obvious expression in article 11 of the 1898 game ordinance, which ruled that in areas, where big chiefs traditionally claimed one tusk, the station should lay a claim on every second tusk only.[121] The deeper spiritual significance of this practice escaped the German colonizers, but already the trade chiefs they mimicked had appropriated the form rather than the content of this ritual. The German posts practiced a commercialized version of providing guns and powder in exchange against tusks, a means to bind hunters to the station or recruit new indigenous hunting elites. Unsurprisingly, colonial officials based in Iringa were most explicit in describing German rule in terms of an actualization of "indigenous" patterns of authority. The abovementioned Harald Pfeiffer, for example, found himself treated "less as a representative of the government, but as their sultan according to the laws of conquest. They regard taxes as a kind of tribute to me."[122]

Such statements were, of course, self-justifying persuasions about the legitimacy of colonial rule. There are no other sources than the colonizers' interpretations to assess how these performances were seen from the other side. Hunters who entered into relations of cooperation and patronage with the new rulers did not necessarily have to believe in the legitimacy of the new authority to accept it as a matter-of-fact and use it for their own ends. The important point about the colonial adaptation of the ground tusk is not so much that German big men and African hunters interpreted their interaction in similar terms but that they interacted at all. Undoubtedly, the representatives of the early colonial state shared many qualities with the hunter kings and big men of the nineteenth-century world of the ivory trade: authoritarian and autocratic, ruthless and violent, often keen hunters themselves, and appropriating the symbolism of ivory and other commodities of the trade to forge their own alliances. The setup of the colonial state favored such appropriation of indigenous patterns of authority, because at its lowest level, it functioned not as an abstract bureaucratic institution but was an effect of the personal rule of its district officials. Political entrepreneurs themselves, they could not help but govern through the personal relationships forged, among others, by hunting. The localization of the colonial state appears as a hybrid mixture of the rational administrative state and indigenous cultural patterns: the German colonizers saw like a state, but acted like big men. Essentially, the colonizers themselves effected the indigenization of the rational, bureaucratic state by incorporating African patterns of authority.

Notes

1. Song sung by Safwa elephant hunters; interpreting translation by Kootz-Kretschmer, *Die Safwa,* 130–31.
2. Felix Brahm, "Handel und Sklaverei am 'Tor zu Ostafrika.' Hamburger Kaufleute auf Sansibar, 1844–1890," in *Hamburg—Sansibar. Sansibar—Hamburg. Hamburgs Verbindungen zu Ostafrika seit Mitte des 19. Jahrhunderts,* ed. Rita Bake (Hamburg, 2009), 45–67.
3. *Stenographische Berichte über die Verhandlungen des Deutschen Reichstags* 51 (29 March 1878), 616; for the opposing view, see Westendarp, "Das Gebiet der Elephanten und der Elfenbein-Reichthum Indiens und Afrikas".
4. See for example Baumann, *Durch Massailand zur Nilquelle,* 245–46; Gustav Adolf Graf von Götzen, *Durch Afrika von Ost nach West. Resultate und Begebenheiten einer Reise von der Deutsch-Ostafrikanischen Küste bis zur Kongomündung in den Jahren 1893/94* (Berlin, 1895), 320.
5. The statistics are compiled from Reichskolonialamt, *Jagd und Wildschutz in den deutschen Kolonien* (Jena, 1913), 38; Stuhlmann, "Elfenbein," 558; Public Record Office, The National Archives, London (PRO) British Foreign Office (FO) 881/7395 D, Appendix 2: Return showing approximately the amount of ivory

exported from Africa from 1891 to 1899, 18; and Kunz, *Ivory and the Elephant in Art, in Archaeology, and in Science,* 462.
6. Glassman, *Feasts and Riot,* 177–248.
7. According to Indian merchants, "more ivory than ever before" was stored in Bagamoyo in July 1892, see TNA G 3/54, fol. 116–17: Customs Officer Schmidt to Gov DOA, 17 July 1892; *Deutsches Kolonialblatt* 3 (1892): 164–66.
8. Cf. BAB R 1001/7802-1, fol. 49–50: Über die Elfenbein-Ausfuhr in Deutsch-Ostafrika; *Deutsch-Ostafrikanische Zeitung* 2, no. 10 (1900): 17 March; "Der Elfenbeinhandel während der letzten 10 Jahre," *Deutsches Kolonialblatt* 11 (1900): 180; BAB R 1001/7778, fol. 298: Emil Jaenke to RKA, 8 January 1912.
9. BAB R 1001/9077, fol. 8: Mankiewitz to Gov DOA, 13 March 1895; BAB R 1001/9077, fol. 34: Langheld to Gov DOA, 1 June 1895; BAB R 1001/698, fol. 141: Testimony by Hamed bin Mohamed (Tippu Tip), Dar es Salaam, 4 July 1893; BAB R 1001/644/1, fol. 18: Gov DOA to AA KA, 3 July 1893; BAB R 1001/9057, fol. 124–26: Gov DOA to AA KA, 27 March 1896; Hahner-Herzog, *Tippu Tip und der Elfenbeinhandel in Ost- und Zentralafrika,* 324–28.
10. See for example Kenya National Archives, Nairobi (KNA) PC 1/6/136, Game rangers' monthly reports to the Game Warden, Taveta, 28 April 1912; 27 December 1912. Foreign Office Confidential Print (FOCP) Vol. 6557, Further Correspondence respecting East Africa, April to June 1894, no. 126: FO to IBEAC, 3 May 1894.
11. The office of a *liwali* was introduced by the Sultan of Zanzibar to govern the coastal towns and trading places in the interior. The Germans, as well as the British after 1918, adopted the system.
12. *Ruga-ruga* were troops built up by the Unyamwezi trade chiefs Mirambo and Nyungu-ya-Mawe from the 1860s to the 1880s. Consisting of deserted porters, former slaves, war captives, and social outcasts, they were organized according to military principles and developed a particular reputation for raiding, see Michael Pesek, "Ruga-ruga. The History of an African Profession, 1820–1918," in *German Colonialism Revisited. African, Asian, and Oceanic Experiences,* ed. Nina Berman, Klaus Mühlhahn, and Patrice Nganang (Ann Arbor, MI, 2014), 85–100.
13. BAB R 1001/644/1, fol. 54–55: Circular, Acting Governor von Trotha, 14 July 1895.
14. TNA G 1/8, unfol.: BA Ujiji to Gov DOA, 22 July–19 August 1900; TNA G 1/8, fol. 122: BA Ujiji to Gov DOA, 16 June 1900.
15. BAB R 1001/9065, fol. 59–60: Gov DOA to AA KA, 17 October 1902; BAB R 1001/9065, fol. 92–95: Johann Albrecht zu Mecklenburg to AA KA, 16 July 1903.
16. Rainer Tetzlaff, *Koloniale Entwicklung und Ausbeutung. Wirtschafts- und Sozialgeschichte Deutsch-Ostafrikas 1885–1914* (Berlin, 1970), 71–72.
17. See TNA G 3/54, fol. 218: Customs regulations for German East Africa, 23 March 1893. The toll comprised 16.5 percent of the value of the tusk.
18. The tusks thus acquired were auctioned off up to three or four times a year in the early 1890s, then only once or twice a year at the Main Customs Office in Bagamoyo, from 1899 onward in Dar es Salaam.
19. This data is compiled from statistics in BAB R 1001/644/1, unfol. and fol. 70 (export figures 1892–93; 1896–97) and BAB R 1001/6467, fol. 12 and 14 (1893–94; 1895–96).

20. TNA G 8/55, fol. 127-28: Annual report, district administration Dar es Salaam, undated [December 1897].
21. TNA G 8/55, fol. 131-32a: Knochenhauer to [Lindi station] (copy), 1 December 1897.
22. BAB R 1001/7778, fol. 298: Emil Jaenke to RKA, 8 January 1912.
23. Edmund Russell, *Evolutionary History. Uniting History and Biology to Understand Life on Earth* (Cambridge, 2011), 17-19; see also H Jachmann, PSM Berry, and H Imae, "Tusklessness in African Elephants: A Future Trend," *African Journal of Ecology* 33 (1995): 230-35.
24. Cf. EJ Milner-Gulland and Ruth Mace, "The Impact of the Ivory Trade on the African Elephant *Loxodonta Africana* Population as Assessed by Data from the Trade," *Biological Conservation* 55 (1991): 221-22.
25. TNA G 8/55, fol. 131-32a: Knochenhauer to [Lindi station] (copy), 1 December 1897; TNA G 8/55, fol. 152-56: Knochenhauer to Lindi station, 26 February 1898. See also Raman Sukumar, *The Living Elephants. Evolutionary Ecology, Behavior, and Conservation* (Oxford, 2003), 175-84.
26. See the relevant statistics in TNA G 59/2.
27. James C Scott, *Seeing Like a State. How Certain Schemes to Improve the Human Condition Have Failed* (New Haven, CT, 1998).
28. J Stentzler: *Deutsch-Ostafrika. Kriegs- und Friedensbilder*, 2nd ed. (Berlin, 1910), 77-78.
29. See for example Fritz Bley, "Ein deutscher Naturschutzpark," in *Tägliche Rundschau*, 10 January 1910, 26-27; Hans Paasche, *Im Morgenlicht. Kriegs-, Jagd- und Reiseerlebnisse in Ostafrika* (Berlin, 1907), 230; Theodor Zell, *Riesen der Tierwelt. Jagdabenteuer und Lebensbilder* (Berlin, 1911), 172-78 ("The Brute as Educator").
30. John M MacKenzie, "The Imperial Pioneer and Hunter and the British Masculine Stereotype in Late Victorian and Edwardian Times," in *Manliness and Morality. Middle-Class Masculinity in Britain and America, 1800-1940*, ed. JA Mangan and James Walvin (New York, 1987), 176-98.
31. See for example Helen Chambers, "Th. Fontane, Albert Smith und Gordon Cumming," in *Theodor Fontane im literarischen Leben seiner Zeit*, ed. Theodor-Fontane-Archiv (Berlin, 1987), 268-302; Wilhelm von Freeden, *Reise- und Jagdbilder aus Afrika. Nach den neuesten Reiseschilderungen zusammengestellt* (Leipzig, 1888).
32. See Thomas T Allsen, *The Royal Hunt in Eurasian History* (Philadelphia, PA, 2006) on the stunning universality of the association of hunting with power; further Wolfram G Theilemann, *Adel im grünen Rock. Adliges Jägertum, Großprivatwaldbesitz und die preußische Forstbeamtenschaft 1866-1914* (Berlin, 2004).
33. For analogies in the British imperial experience, see Roderick P Neumann, "Dukes, Earls and Ersatz Edens: Aristocratic Nature Preservationists in Colonial Africa," *Environment and Planning D: Society and Space* 14 (1996): 79-98.
34. Hubertus Hiller, *Jäger und Jagd. Zur Entwicklung des Jagdwesens in Deutschland zwischen 1848 und 1914* (Münster, 2003), 122-59.
35. Hermann von Wissmann, "Afrikanische Jagd," *Militär-Wochenblatt* no. 99 (1894): 2629-30.
36. Oberländer [i.e. Karl Rehfus], *Eine Jagdfahrt nach Ostafrika. Mit dem Tagebuch eines Elefantenjägers* (Berlin, 1903), 199.

37. R Freiherr von L, "Plaudereien über meine jagdlichen Erlebnisse," *Wild und Hund* 28 (1922): 715.
38. Georg Simmel, "Das Abenteuer," in *Philosophische Kultur. Über das Abenteuer, die Geschlechter und die Krise der Moderne* (Berlin, 1998 [1923]), 28.
39. John M MacKenzie, *Museums and Empire. Natural History, Human Cultures and Colonial Identities* (Manchester, 2009); Lynn K Nyhart, *Modern Nature. The Rise of the Biological Perspective in Germany* (Chicago, 2009), chapters 6 and 7; Köstering, *Natur zum Anschauen*.
40. Jane Desmond, "Displaying Death, Animating Life: Changing Fictions of 'Liveness' from Taxidermy to Animatronics," in *Representing Animals*, ed. Nigel Rothfels (Bloomington, IN, 2002), 159–79.
41. Anand S Pandian, "Predatory Care: The Imperial Hunt in Mughal and British India," *Journal of Historical Sociology* 14 (2001): 79.
42. See for example Matt Cartmill, *A View to a Death in the Morning: Hunting and Nature through History* (Cambridge, MA, 1993), 134; Tina Loo, "Of Moose and Men. Hunting for Masculinities in British Columbia, 1880–1939," *Western Historical Quarterly* 32 (2001): 299; Joseph Sramek, "'Face Him Like a Briton': Tiger Hunting, Imperialism, and British Masculinity in Colonial India, 1800–1875," *Victorian Studies* 48 (2006): 659–80.
43. Allsen, *The Royal Hunt in Eurasian History*, 18.
44. MacKenzie, *The Empire of Nature*; Mahesh Rangarajan, *India's Wildlife History: An Introduction* (Delhi, 2001), chapter 5; EJ Carruthers, *Game Protection in the Transvaal 1846 to 1926* (Pretoria, 1995), chapter 2; Greg Gillespie, *Hunting for Empire. Narratives of Sport in Rupert's Land, 1840–1870* (Vancouver, 2007); Daniel Justin Herman, *Hunting and the American Imagination* (Washington, 2001).
45. James R Ryan, *Picturing Empire. Photography and the Visualization of the British Empire* (Chicago, 1997); Finis Dunaway, "Hunting with the Camera: Nature Photography, Manliness, and Modern Memory, 1890–1930," *Journal of American Studies* 34 (2000): 207–30; Karen Wonders, "Hunting Narratives of the Age of Empire: A Gender Reading of their Iconography," *Environment and History* 11 (2005): 269–91.
46. Taken from: International Mission Photography Archive, ca.1860–1960, Photographs of the Moravian Church, Herrnhut, Germany, ca.1890–1940, Box Nyassa 1, 03640. The picture was used in two different slide series used for advertising the missionary enterprise in East Africa, first in a series entitled "Into Kondeland by Railway and Caravan" used during World War I. In the 1930s, the pictures from Konde were rearranged under the title "Nyassa. Under the Spell of East Africa's Creation." I am grateful to Rüdiger Kröger from the Moravian Archives for sharing this information.
47. See Sture Lagercrantz, "Hunting Trophies and Hunting Magic," *Anthropos* 49 (1954), 164–68, 170–71.
48. This practice is described in an ethnography roughly from the area where the picture was taken, see Kootz-Kretschmer, *Die Safwa*, 143–44. Kootz-Kretschmer has, in fact, been married for several years to Stolz, the photographer of the picture.
49. Hans Schomburgk, *Wild und Wilde im Herzen Afrikas. Zwölf Jahre Jagd- und Forschungsreisen* (Berlin, 1926), 208; see also Reichard, "Das afrikanische Elfen-

bein und sein Handel," 144–45; Paul Reichard, "Die Wanjamuesi," *Zeitschrift der Gesellschaft für Erdkunde zu Berlin* 24 (1889): 311; Reichard, *Deutsch-Ostafrika*, 416, 431; Stuhlmann, *Mit Emin Pascha ins Herz von Afrika*, 87; Nigmann, *Die Wahehe*, 116; Martha Kattwinkel, "Am Natronsee," *Wild und Hund* 26 (1920): 826; Buschläufer [Pseud], "Elefantenjagd," *Wild und Hund* 27 (1921): 200; David Neckschies, *Safarizauber. Jagdabenteuer in afrikanischer Wildnis* (Braunschweig, 1923), 89; Hodgson, "Some Notes on the Hunting Customs of the Wandamba of the Ulanga Valley, Tanganyika Territory, and Other East African Tribes," 63.

50. Bernhard Graf zur Lippe, *In den Jagdgründen Deutsch-Ostafrikas. Erinnerungen aus meinem Tagebuch mit einem kurzen Vorwort über das ostafrikanische Schutzgebiet* (Berlin, 1904), 131.

51. See for example August Knochenhauer, "Jagdlicher Aberglaube und Geheimmittel der afrikanischen Eingeborenen," *Deutsche Jägerzeitung* 26 (1895–96): 505–06; Carl Georg Schillings, *With Flashlight and Rifle: A Record of Hunting Adventures and of Studies in Wild Life in Equatorial East Africa* (London, 1906), 298; Weule, *Wissenschaftliche Ergebnisse meiner ethnographischen Forschungsreise in den Südosten Deutsch-Ostafrikas*, 40.

52. Frederick Cooper, *Decolonization and African Society. The Labor Question in French and British Africa* (Cambridge, 1996), xii.

53. Richard White, *The Middle Ground. Indians, Empires, and Republics in the Great Lakes Region, 1650–1815* (Cambridge, 1991), ix–xi.

54. Safari as "expedition" is mentioned for example in *Deutsch-Ostafrikanische Zeitung* 3, no. 38 (1901): 28 September; Lippe, *In den Jagdgründen Deutsch-Ostafrikas*, 85; Adolf Friedrich Herzog zu Mecklenburg, *Ins innerste Afrika. Bericht über den Verlauf der Deutschen Wissenschaftlichen Zentral-Afrika-Expedition 1907–1908* (Leipzig, 1909), 26; Oskar Erich Meyer, *Afrikanische Briefe. Erinnerungen an Deutsch-Ost-Afrika* (Munich, 1923), 23; the term *Jagdsafari* can be found, for example, in Lippe, *In den Jagdgründen Deutsch-Ostafrikas*, 143; *Deutsch-Ostafrikanische Zeitung* 11, no. 18 (1909): 6 March; *Deutsch-Ostafrikanische Zeitung* 11, no. 25 (1909): 31 March; *Deutsch-Ostafrikanische Zeitung* 13, no. 61 (1911): 2 August; *Deutsch-Ostafrikanische Zeitung* 14, no. 67 (1912): 21 August. Safari as synonymous with hunting expedition: *Deutsch-Ostafrikanische Zeitung* 9, no. 1 (1907): 5 January; Arthur Berger, *In Afrikas Wildkammern als Forscher und Jäger* (Berlin, 1910), 24; Oskar Karstedt, *Deutsch-Ostafrika und seine Nachbargebiete. Ein Handbuch für Reisende* (Berlin, 1914), 9–10; Müller, "Jagdtage in der Serengeti," *Wild und Hund* 21 (1915): 7; Neckschies, *Safarizauber*, 118.

55. Rockel, "Decentering Exploration in East Africa," 172.

56. Pesek, *Koloniale Herrschaft in Deutsch-Ostafrika*, 65–66; Rockel, *Carriers of Culture*, 92.

57. See for example Götzen, *Durch Afrika von Ost nach West*, 3; Max Schoeller, *Mitteilungen über meine Reise nach Äquatorial-Ost-Afrika und Uganda 1896–1897*, vol. 1 (Berlin, 1901), 31; Hauptschule Düren-Gürzenich, Schillings Papers: Lohnbuch für Träger 1902/03, Entry 14 June 1902; Martha Kattwinkel, "Am Natronsee," *Wild und Hund* 26 (1920): 809.

58. See for example Götzen, *Durch Afrika von Ost nach West*, 23, 32; Waldemar Werther, *Die mittleren Hochländer des nördlichen Deutsch-Ost-Afrika. Wissenschaftliche Ergebnisse der Irangi-Expedition 1896–1897* (Berlin, 1898), 51; Lippe, *In den Jagdgründen Deutsch-Ostafrikas*, 106.

59. Waldemar Werther, "Thierwelt und Jagderlebnisse in Deutsch-Ostafrika," *Der Weidmann* 27 (1896): 222; Carl Georg Schillings, *Mit Blitzlicht und Büchse. Neue Beobachtungen und Erlebnisse in der Wildnis inmitten der Tierwelt von Äquatorial-Ostafrika* (Leipzig, 1905), 23; BayHStA Papers von Hirsch 11, Diary entry 28 August 1907; Weule, *Wissenschaftliche Ergebnisse meiner ethnographischen Forschungsreise in den Südosten Deutsch-Ostafrikas,* 86–87; Wilhelm Langheld, *Zwanzig Jahre in deutschen Kolonien* (Berlin, 1909), 131; Hans Besser, *Raubwild und Dickhäuter in Deutsch-Ostafrika* (Stuttgart, 1915), 53; Schomburgk, *Wild und Wilde im Herzen Afrikas,* 208–09.
60. Fonck, *Deutsch-Ostafrika,* 469; Angelika Grettmann-Werner, *Wilhelm Kuhnert (1865–1926). Tierdarstellung zwischen Wissenschaft und Kunst* (Hamburg, 1981), 40.
61. August Knochenhauer, "Aus dem Tagebuch eines Elefantenjägers," in *Eine Jagdfahrt nach Ostafrika. Mit dem Tagebuch eines Elefantenjägers,* ed. Oberländer [i.e. Karl Rehfus] (Berlin, 1903), 267, 272–73, 275, 284–85, 305; Deutsches Institut für tropische und subtropische Landwirtschaft (DITSL), Theodor von Hassel, *Ein Tagebuch aus Ostafrika* (Unpublished and undated typescript), 13–20; see also Stentzler, *Deutsch-Ostafrika,* 82–83.
62. Alexander Becker, *Aus Deutsch-Ostafrikas Sturm- und Drangperiode. Erinnerungen eines Alten Afrikaners* (Halle, 1911), 131; Baumann, *Durch Massailand zur Nilquelle,* 65–66; Werther, *Die mittleren Hochländer des nördlichen Deutsch-Ost-Afrika,* 21, 51.
63. Schoeller, *Mitteilungen über meine Reise nach Äquatorial-Ost-Afrika und Uganda,* vol. 1, 68, 82; Lippe, *In den Jagdgründen Deutsch-Ostafrikas,* 77–78; Schomburgk, *Wild und Wilde im Herzen Afrikas,* 286–87.
64. MacKenzie, *The Empire of Nature,* 130–32, 155–58.
65. See for example TNA G 8/99, fol. 70: Moshi station to Gov DOA, 15 January 1897; BAB R 1001/288, fol. 193–98: Moshi to Gov DOA, 18 August 1897; Hermann Wissmann, *Afrika. Schilderungen und Rathschläge zur Vorbereitung für den Aufenthalt und Dienst in den Deutschen Schutzgebieten* (Berlin, 1894), 101–2.
66. "Circular concerning the Conservation of Wildlife in German East Africa," *Deutsches Kolonialblatt* 7 (1896): 340, § 5.
67. TNA G 21/539: Trial of Hans Otto Mosler for shooting an antelope to feed his porters; Eckard Michels, *"Der Held von Deutsch-Ostafrika": Paul von Lettow-Vorbeck. Ein preußischer Kolonialoffizier* (Paderborn, 2008), 234–42.
68. See for example Reichard, *Deutsch-Ostafrika,* 416; Behr, "Die Wakua-Steppe," *Mittheilungen von Forschungsreisenden und Gelehrten aus den Deutschen Schutzgebieten* 6 (1893): 49; Wissmann, *Afrika,* 101; Bay HStA Papers von Hirsch, no. 11: Diary entry 13 August 1907; Humboldt Universität Berlin (HUB) Museum für Naturkunde (MfN), Zool. Museum S III Fromm, Hunting Diary, Entry 8 July 1908 (33), 5 September 1908 (61).
69. Friedrich Fülleborn, *Das Deutsche Njassa- und Ruwuma-Gebiet, Land und Leute, nebst Bemerkungen über die Schire-Länder* (Berlin, 1906), 20; Meyer, *Afrikanische Briefe,* 18–19. See further Pesek, *Koloniale Herrschaft in Deutsch-Ostafrika,* 236; Leibniz-Institut für Länderkunde, Leipzig (LIL) Prittwitz Papers, Box 245/1: Mohoro/Uhehe Diary, 89 (September 1897).
70. Schulz, *Jagd- und Filmabenteuer in Afrika. Streifzüge in das Innere des dunkeln Erdteils* (Dresden, 1922), 139.

71. See for example BAB R 1001/9055, fol. 59-60: BA Tabora, Sigl to Gov DOA, 30 September 1893; BAB R 1001/287, fol. 7: Moshi to Gov DOA, 19 October 1895; Reichard, *Deutsch-Ostafrika*, 279-80; Wilhelm Wolfrum, *Briefe und Tagebuchblätter aus Ostafrika* (Munich, 1893), 83; H Hermann Graf von Schweinitz, *Deutsch-Ost-Afrika in Krieg und Frieden* (Berlin, 1894), 179.
72. Alpers, "The Ivory Trade in Africa," 356; Pesek, *Koloniale Herrschaft in Deutsch-Ostafrika*, 210.
73. Shorter, *Chiefship in Western Tanzania*, 130.
74. Langheld, *Zwanzig Jahre in deutschen Kolonien*, 171, 251; Achim Gottberg, ed., *Unyamwesi. Quellensammlung und Geschichte* (Berlin, 1971), 316, 345, 346; Reiss-Engelhorn Museen, Mannheim (REM): Bumiller Papers, Diary of the Kilimanjaro Expedition 1891, 18 February 1891; BAB R 1001/286, fol. 163: Kilossa station to Gov DOA, 18 November 1895.
75. LIL Prittwitz Papers Box 245/1: Mohoro/Uhehe Diary, entry 25 February 1898.
76. Reichard, *Deutsch-Ostafrika*, 282-83; see also Andrew Zimmerman, *Anthropology and Antihumanism in Imperial Germany* (Chicago, 2001), 150-52.
77. Jamie Monson, "Relocating Maji Maji: The Politics of Alliance and Authority in the Southern Highlands of Tanzania, 1870-1918," *Journal of African History* 39 (1998): 95-120.
78. TNA G 8/55, fol. 175-76: Bagamoyo to Gov DOA, 21 July 1898; Report by Chief Mtinginya and Moses Willing, trans. Charles Stokes, 27 May 1892, printed in Gottberg, ed., *Unyamwesi*, 345-46. Cf. BAB R 1001/9055, fol. 33-60: Tabora to Gov DOA, 30 September 1893, especially fols. 42, 50, 54v.
79. Cf. Reichard, *Deutsch-Ostafrika*, 283; "Jagdgesetzliche Bestimmungen im deutschen Gebiete von Ostafrika," *Der Weidmann* 22 (1891): 277.
80. German and British sources usually refer to him as "Schundi," or "Shundi." Several authors claim Fundi to be identical with the "Fundi Hadji" mentioned by Carl Claus von der Decken as apprentice in the entourage of the elephant hunter and ivory trader Msuskuma, cf. Gabriel Ekemode, "Fundi: Trader and Akida in Kilimanjaro, c. 1860-1898," *Tanzania Notes and Records* 77/78 (1976): 95-101.
81. WDM Bell, *The Wanderings of an Elephant Hunter* (London, 1923), 39.
82. Cf. TNA G 8/99, fol. 102-3: Moshi station to Gov DOA, 19 March 1897; TNA G 8/55, fol. 119: Moshi station to government, 14 September 1897; REM Mannheim: Bumiller Papers, Kilimanjaro Diary 1891, Entries 18 and 19 February 1891; Ekemode, "German Rule in North-East Tanzania," 100-1, 138, 149-51.
83. TNA G 8/55, fol. 119: Moshi station to government, 14 September 1897; TNA G 8/55, fol. 123: Pangani station to Gov DOA, 16 December 1897.
84. TNA G 8/55, fol. 119: Moshi station to government, 14 September 1897.
85. TNA G 8/55, fol. 123: Pangani station to Gov DOA, 16 December 1897.
86. Bell, *The Wanderings of an Elephant Hunter*, 39; John Frederick Walker, *Ivory's Ghosts. The White Gold of History and the Fate of Elephants* (New York, 2009), 1-3.
87. BAB R 1001/7766, fol. 39-43: Wissmann to Colonial Department, 2 April 1897.
88. "Circular concerning the Conservation of Wildlife in German East Africa," *Deutsches Kolonialblatt* 7 (1896): 340.
89. Ibid., § 2; TNA G 8/55, fol. 40: Circular Gov DOA, 11 August 1896; TNA G 8/55, fol. 72: Circular Gov DOA, 14 April 1897; TNA G 8/55, fol. 116, Circular

2 February 1898 (unsent draft); TNA G 8/55, fol. 116: Ordinance concerning the Conservation of Wildlife in German East Africa, 17 January 1898, § 12.
90. PRO FO 403/302, no. 22, attachment 2: Wissmann to AA KA, 2 April 1897 (English translation). The German original is documented in BAB R 1001/7766, fol. 39–43. Allegedly, Wissmann proposed the establishment of an elephant reserve in the Kasai to the Belgian King Leopold as early as 1888, see Jean-Paul Harroy, "Contribution à l'histoire jusque 1934 de la creation de l'Institut des Parcs Nationaux du Congo Belge," *Civilisations* 41, no. 1/2 (1993): 428.
91. Wright, "Local Roots of Policy in German East Africa."
92. Hermann Wissmann et al., *Im Innern Afrikas. Die Erforschung des Kassai während der Jahre 1883, 1884 und 1885*, 3rd ed. (Leipzig, 1891); Hermann Wissmann, *Unter deutscher Flagge quer durch Afrika von West nach Ost. Von 1880 bis 1883 ausgeführt von Paul Pogge und Hermann Wissmann* (Berlin, 1889).
93. See Thomas Morlang, "'Finde ich keinen Weg, so bahne ich mir einen.' Der umstrittene 'Kolonialheld' Hermann von Wissmann," in *Macht und Anteil an der Weltherrschaft. Berlin und der deutsche Kolonialismus*, ed. Ulrich van der Heyden and Joachim Zeller (Münster, 2005), 37–43; Alexander Becker et al., *Hermann von Wissmann. Deutschlands größter Afrikaner* (Berlin, 1914); BAB R 1001/740, fol. 3–12, Konteradmiral Deinhard to Imperial Naval Office, 13 May 1889 (quote).
94. Hermann von Wissmann, *In den Wildnissen Afrikas und Asiens. Jagderlebnisse* (Berlin, 1901).
95. *Correspondence relating to the Preservation of Wild Animals in Africa*, London 1906 (= Parliamentary Papers, vol. lxxix, 25), enclosure in no. 10: Wissmann to Baron Richthofen, 2 April 1897.
96. *Illustrirte Jagd-Zeitung* 17, no. 32 (1889/90): 385; BAB R 1001/7776, fol. 2: Wissmann to the Colonial Department in the German Foreign Office, 28 April 1890; TNA G 1/10, fol. 153–54: Gov DOA to Count von Götzen, 14 July 1893.
97. Kjekshus, *Ecology Control and Economic Development in East African History*, 126–32; Clive A Spinage, *Cattle Plague. A History* (New York, 2003), 497–524.
98. TNA G 8/55, fol. 9–10: Mikindani to Gov DOA, 3 March 1896; TNA G 8/55, fol. 11: Mikindani to Gov DOA, 6 May 1896; TNA G 8/55, fol. 137: Mikindani to Gov DOA, 3 January 1898; TNA G 8/55, fol. 138: Gov DOA to Mikindani, 28 January 1898.
99. TNA G 8/55, fol. 87: Lindi to Gov DOA, 8 August 1897; TNA G 8/55, fol. 94–95: Lindi to Gov DOA, 8 September 1897; BAB R 1001/288, fol. 103–12: Lindi to Gov DOA, 14 March 1897; BAB R 1001/288, fol. 202: Songea to Gov DOA, 2 August 1897.
100. TNA G 8/55, fol. 83: Mpwapwa to Gov DOA, 14 May 1897.
101. LIL Leipzig Uhlig Papers, Box 188/22, Diary April/May 1904, 10.
102. This conclusion was reached after comparing the relationship between the average weight of tusks and their average price over the last four years, see TNA G 8/55, unfol.: Gov DOA to Ujiji, 15 February 1897 [draft; calculation in the margin].
103. TNA G 8/55, fol. 116–18, Ordinance dated 17 January 1898.
104. Fritz Bronsart von Schellendorff, *Thierbeobachtungen und Jagdgeschichten aus Ostafrika* (Berlin, 1900), 125.
105. TNA G 8/55, fol. 75: Circular dated 18 November 1896; TNA G 8/55, unfol.: Gov DOA to Ujiji, 15 February 1897 (draft); TNA G 8/55, fol. 116: Verordnung betreffend die Schonung des Wildstandes in Deutsch-Ostafrika, 17 January 1898.

106. TNA G 8/55, fol. 92: Kilimatinde to Gov DOA, 13 July 1897; TNA G 8/55, fol. 102: Kilimatinde to Gov DOA, 13 October 1897; TNA G 8/55, fol. 162: Kilimatinde to Gov DOA, 9 March 1898; TNA G 8/55, fol. 89: Langenburg to Gov DOA, 10 July 1897; TNA G 8/55, fol. 200: Bukoba to Gov DOA, 1 September 1898; TNA G 8/55, fol. 201a: Usumbura to Gov DOA, 10 September 1898.
107. TNA G 8/55, fol. 85: Kilossa to Gov DOA, 27 May 1897; Gov DOA to Kilossa (draft), 11 June 1897; TNA G 8/55, fol. 83: Mpwapwa to Gov DOA, 14 May 1897.
108. *Deutsch-Ostafrikanische Zeitung* 2, no. 6 (1900): 10 February.
109. *Akida* denoted a nonindigenous intermediary, usually of coastal or Zanzibari origin, who was employed by the government at the level of district administration, usually for tax collection and overseeing the *majumbe*.
110. TNA G8/99, fol. 215: Songea to Gov DOA, 20 January 1899; BAB R 1001/234, fol. 7: Bericht über eine Dienstreise im Bezirk Songea, 15 November 1904; BAB R 1001/700, fol. 204–20: Report of the battalion Johannes, 18 November 1905 to 10 March 1906; *Deutsch-Ostafrikanische Zeitung* 3, no. 50 (1901): 21 December.
111. Alison Redmayne, "Mkwawa and the Hehe Wars," *Journal of African History* 9 (1968): 409–36.
112. *Jumbe* (pl. *majumbe*) was the Swahili expression for small chiefs, village elders, and headmen. The German colonial administration used the *majumbe* as local intermediaries and the lowest level of the administrative hierarchy.
113. This practice was possible thanks to the large stores of ivory that had been in Mkwawa's possession, so that the station could exchange two tusks into three of the same overall weight.
114. TNA G 8/55, fol. 100: Iringa to Gov DOA, 21 September 1897; TNA G 8/55, fol. 168: Iringa to Gov DOA, 16 April 1898; TNA G 8/55, fol. 169: Gov DOA to Iringa, 17 May 1898; TNA G 8/55, fol. 215: Songea to Gov DOA, 20 January 1899; TNA G 8/55, fol. 218–20: Iringa to Gov DOA, 9 January 1899; TNA G 59/2, unfol.: Deliveries from Iringa to the Customs House Dar es Salaam 18 tusks on 11 June 1898, 78 (25 July 1898), 130 (10 August 1899), 65 (30 April 1900), and 320 (12 August 1901); *Deutsches Kolonialblatt* 12 (1901): 516–18; BAM N 85/3; Oskar Pusch, *Ostafrikanische Briefe des Leutnants der Kaiserlichen Schutztruppe Harald Pfeiffer und sein mysteriöser Tod* (Oberhausen, 1962), 37.
115. Pesek, *Koloniale Herrschaft in Deutsch-Ostafrika*, 140–46, 207–18.
116. Homi K. Bhabha, *The Location of Culture* (London, 2004), 121–31.
117. Pesek, *Koloniale Herrschaft in Deutsch-Ostafrika*.
118. Jan-Georg Deutsch, "Celebrating Power in Everyday Life: The Administration of Law and the Public Sphere in Colonial Tanzania, 1890–1914," *Journal of African Cultural Studies* 15 (2002): 101; Michael Pesek, "Cued Speeches. The Emergence of Shauri as Colonial Praxis in German East Africa, 1850–1903," *History in Africa* 33 (2006): 395–412.
119. TNA G 8/55, fol. 78: Saadani to Gov DOA, 5 January 1897; similarly TNA G 8/55, fol. 83: Mpwapwa to Gov DOA, 14 May 1897; TNA G 8/55, fol. 85: Kilossa to Gov DOA, 27 May 1897; TNA G 8/55, fol. 89: Langenburg to Gov DOA, 10 July 1897; TNA G 8/55, fol. 97: Kilwa to Gov DOA, 16 September 1897; TNA G 8/55, fol. 104: Tabora to Gov DOA, 5 October 1897; TNA G 8/55, fol. 162: Kilimatinde to Gov DOA, 9 March 1898.
120. LIL Prittwitz Papers, box 246/1: Diary Udjiji/Ufipa/Ukonongo, 18 March 1899, 63.

121. BAB R 1001/7776, fol. 56–57: Verordnung betreffend die Schonung des Wildstandes in Deutsch-Ostafrika, 17 January 1898, § 11.
122. BAM N 85/3: Pusch, Ostafrikanische Briefe, 68; see also Ernst Nigmann, *Geschichte der kaiserlichen Schutztruppe für Deutsch-Ostafrika* (Berlin, 1911), 78.

 PART II

The Making of Tanzania's Wildlife Conservation Regime

 CHAPTER 3

Preserving the Hunt, Provoking a War
Wildlife Politics and Maji Maji

> What we call Man's power over Nature turns out to be a power
> exercised by some men over other men with Nature as its instrument.
> —Clive S Lewis, *The Abolition of Man* (1947)

Shooting an Elephant, or:
How Theodor von Hassel Became Mangula

In December 1904, Theodor von Hassel assumed the command over the German Schutztruppe forces stationed in Mahenge. Situated on a plateau overlooking the Kilombero Valley in Tanganyika's southern highlands, Mahenge had been established as the center of a military district in 1899.[1] Thirty-six years of age, von Hassel not only commanded the local military forces, but also held the post of a district official (*Bezirksamtmann*). His responsibility was to assert German authority over 33,000 largely forested square kilometers of enormous geographical and ethnical diversity.[2] If we believe his diary, this was best done by shooting elephants.

Shortly after von Hassel arrived in Mahenge, a *jumbe* named Likoko called on the district official in the urgent matter of an elephant that had taken to ravage his village and the surrounding fields. Only recently, the rampaging animal had killed two women and destroyed several huts. Von Hassel should come to redeem the haunted village from "Mangmula" or "Mangula," as the elephant had been named.[3] "As long as the elders could think," the *jumbe* reported, Mangula displayed the same strategy when pursued, taking a rest hidden in the bush beside his track to surprise hunters with a sudden attack. None of the African soldiers of the Schutztruppe garrisoned in Mahenge displayed much enthusiasm to join von Hassel in the hunt. Judging from his malicious behavior, they believed the elephant to be possessed by an evil spirit (*shetani*). All these warnings only fanned von Hassel's ambition. He was determined to take up the fight alone, like a duel, leaving all the men behind me and in shelter. I did not want to shoot the elephant for his ivory, but wanted to put him to death like one puts to death a villain and mass murderer. The number of his victims was frightening, a minimum of 25 to 30 people a year.[4]

Theodor von Hassel took up the pursuit of Mangula in February 1905, accompanied by two "boys", *jumbe* Likoko, two Askari, and a gunbearer. The party soon got the scent of Mangula and another elephant. After a day-long chase, von Hassel killed both with well-placed shots in the heart. If his own words are to be trusted, his return to Mahenge was triumphant:

> The whole village of Mahenge came to meet me halfway, among them many Wabunga, most of them elephant hunters, but also sultans and *majumbe*. … They put on a *ngoma* [dance, BG] for several days, and always and again I was asked to show myself on the parade-ground where thousands were dancing *ngoma* for me. … Already on my way back, people greeted me as *Bwana Mangmula*. They had given me the name of the one I had defeated.[5]

Von Hassel relates the story in an unpublished typescript entitled *Ein Tagebuch aus Ostafrika*—An East-African Diary. Containing reminiscences of his years as a military officer in Lindi and Mahenge between 1903 and 1906, it remains unclear when exactly von Hassel had written these memories and whether he ever intended to publish them.[6] Therefore, it is questionable which elements of von Hassel's story can be qualified as past reality, and which must be credited to the reordering forces of memory or the imperative of a heroic narrative emplotment. Von Hassel's account of his acquisition of the name Mangula oscillates between myth and history and can be read in two ways. First, it provides a symbolic interpretation of imperial colonialism and how Theodor von Hassel perceived and invented his role in it. The narrative of his shooting of Mangula bears striking similarities to George Orwell's famous essay *Shooting an Elephant*, published in 1936. In Orwell's story, the main character, a British subdivisional police officer in Burma, feels compelled to shoot an escaped work elephant in the presence of hundreds of villagers in order to comply with their presumed expectation of what a representative of empire allegedly had to do.[7] Despite Orwell's critical and von Hassel's celebratory emplotment, both stories present the shooting of an elephant as a highly relevant, ideologically charged imperial activity. For Orwell, the shooting of an elephant disclosed "the real nature of imperialism,"[8] as it was a palpable display of colonial power and the exertion of what its agents imagine as an indispensable obligation of the colonizer. In von Hassel's typescript, the incident of the killing of Mangula is but one of several stories where von Hassel claims to have gained the acknowledgement of Africans by hunting and delivering villages from crop predators and field-raiding elephants. His whole diary is concerned with portraying himself as a hunter, who defends the indigenous communities of his district. Shooting elephants serves as a metaphor to frame colonialism as "predatory care" and the paternalistic redemption of "natives" from a hostile nature they seem incapable to manage.[9]

However, the incident of killing Mangula was more than mere symbolism. It was a past event and an imperial performance that took place near Mahenge in February 1905. It can be corroborated by other sources, and its word spread in German colonial circles. Heinrich Fonck, for example, mentions Mangula as a well-known vicious elephant in the district of Mahenge, who was alleged to have killed several people before he met his fate in the person of von Hassel.[10] Some ninety years later in 1994, von Hassel's daughter explained her father's acquisition of the name Mangula the following way:

> Then there were no wildlife reserves yet in Africa, and the elephant herds were roaming freely in the area. Quite often they intruded the plantations of the blacks and raided them. ... The natives then possessed only spears, bow and arrow as weapons, which were useless against the pachyderms. In their plight they came to the officers and asked them to shoot the respective elephants. My father was known among the natives as a good shot and owner of an elephant rifle. During his first years in Africa, he was asked seventeen times to kill dangerous elephants. ... From then onwards the blacks called my father "Bwana Mamula."[11]

Gertrud von Hassel regarded the devastations wrought by elephants as an effect of the *absence* of wildlife reserves, which she portrayed as a colonial invention in order to keep wild animals at bay. Yet, archival evidence paints a different picture. The colonial invention of reserves in fact contributed to the devastations wrought by elephants, which von Hassel was called to counteract. The allegedly normal and natural state of affairs—villagers unable to defend their fields and homesteads against raiding elephants—was rather the unnatural result of colonial intervention. Theodor von Hassel's transformation into Bwana Mangula must, therefore, be put in the context of the gradual fostering of game conservation after 1900. Colonial conservationist interventions called forth the unnatural upsetting of the local ecologies of hunting and wildlife control in the Mahenge district. They also played an important role in the making of Maji Maji, which erupted just a few months after von Hassel's successful hunt and developed into the biggest armed conflict under German colonial rule in East Africa. Warfare and scorched earth policies resulted in a catastrophic loss of life in the Southern districts of the colony, followed by famine and starvation for years after the fighting ended in 1907. Conservative estimates figure the African death toll around 180,000; some historians have gauged the losses closer to 300,000.[12]

The war not only constituted a decisive turning point for German colonial policies in German East Africa, but has long held a pivotal place as "a charter event in national history" and the first instance of African anticolonialist resistance.[13] Recent research has rejected these earlier renderings of Maji Maji as a monolithic, anticolonial movement to emphasize the complexity of causes and alliances.[14] Thaddeus Sunseri in particular has interpreted Maji Maji as essentially an environmental conflict fought over forest and resource use, the control of predators and crop pests, as well as over access to elephants and ivory.[15] This chapter, too, adopts a political ecology perspective on the conflict to refine previous interpretations of the role that hunting and colonial schemes of wildlife conservation played in it. It charts the development of game policies in German East Africa between colony and metropole and brings together the framing of African wildlife conservation as an imperial and international obligation in Europe and the local repercussions of these policies in the southern highlands of Tanganyika, one of the heartlands of Maji Maji. The woodlands and mountains of southern central and southwestern Tanzania were not only among the last areas to be subjected under German rule, but they were also the regions still hosting the largest stocks of elephants. The international framing of game conservation as part of the imperial mission, a shift from exploitation to conservation on the level of colonial governance and the continuing importance of local big man policies of patronage intersected to make conflicts over environmental control and access to resources a critical component of the war. In what follows, the story of Theodor von Hassel's transformation into Mangula will be woven into the making of Maji Maji as a conflict over elephants, fought along the networks of alliance and patronage that had coalesced around the access to ivory.

The Local Politics of Conservationist Internationalism in German East Africa

In order to understand what happened in Mahenge in early 1905, it is necessary to rehearse what happened in London five years earlier. In May 1900, representatives of all European governments with colonial possessions in sub-Saharan Africa came together for the first International Conference on the Preservation of Wild Animals, Birds, and Fish in Africa. The meeting had been envisioned by Hermann von Wissmann as early as 1896. He perceived the situation of the mammalian fauna in East Africa in the broader context of wildlife deterioration in the wake of European expansion and urged to have his East African game ordinance complemented by similar measures in neighboring colonies in order to be truly effective. Wissmann, however, the driving force behind the conference on the German side, retired from active colonial service in 1896, so that the preparation of the conference between up to 1900 had little recourse to the actual developments of game policies in German East Africa. Rather, it was the result of a remarkable Anglo-German transimperial cooperation between hunting-minded individuals in the European centers of imperial decision-making.

As one of the first instances of imperial environmental internationalism, the making and the mechanics of the conference are discussed in due detail in a later chapter.[16] The conference established wildlife preservation as one of the moral principles of colonial rule in sub-Saharan Africa. Although its convention was never ratified by all signatory powers, its main provisions had tangible reverberations in colonial policies on the ground. The conference stipulated a ban on the export of elephant tusks below a weight of 5 kilograms. Animals were classified into five groups according to the desirability of their protection, which should be achieved through the regulation of hunting and the establishment of extensive game reserves. Certain African techniques of hunting were to be prohibited, and the convention envisaged a ban on the hunting of female and nursing elephants. For the development of Tanganyikan game laws, it was important that German East African authorities immediately decreed that the trade and export of tusks below 5 kilograms was banned to discourage the hunting of elephant cows and calves.[17] The conference also ushered in a prolonged debate in the colonial department in Berlin which elements of the convention should be implemented in the German colonies. East Africa stood out as the one colony where the immediate introduction of conservation measures was deemed to be most pressing, and for the first time, metropolitan decision-makers interfered decisively with the exploitative practices of hunting in the East African colony. Von Wissmann and Carl Georg Schillings, who had been members of Germany's delegation to the conference, submitted extensive memoranda. Both were hunters and both were judged experts for their personal acquaintance with the wildlife situation in East Africa. Schillings, an estate owner and gentleman rider from Düren, had undertaken two hunting expeditions to the Maasai steppe and Kilimanjaro, the first accompanying the industrialist and self-made explorer Max Schoeller in 1896–97, the second in 1899–1900 with support from various natural history museums in Germany. Both Wissmann and Schillings shared the conviction that the "giants of the continent: the rhinoceros, the hippopotamus and above all, the elephant" were threatened with extermination without due protection.[18] Yet, they submitted quite differing suggestions about how to arrive at more sustainable forms of hunting in East Africa.

The former governor and hunter-turned-conservationist Hermann von Wissmann, who had not returned to East Africa since he left office in 1896, suggested to set up the game regulations as similar as possible to those of British East Africa. The draft ordinance he submitted in October 1900 consisted of some 300 pages, and his proposal largely followed the London Convention.[19] While Wissmann left the control of indigenous hunting to the superior knowledge of the local administrations, his proposal foresaw a differentiated system of licenses for Europeans. He also borrowed from the game law in neighboring Kenya the restriction of the number of animals that could be hunted under each license. Effectively, no hunter would have been allowed to shoot more than two elephants within one year.[20] Wissmann's focus on regulating the white hunter drew on his own experience, but he was also influenced by the self-accusatory tone of British imperial debates about species extinction. There, the devastating record of white frontier hunting in North America and South Africa was a core argument for conservation as a means of self-civilizing big game hunters.

Schillings, on the other hand, based his suggestions on his eyewitnessing during his expeditions through the north of the German colony. On his first hunting trip to Kilimanjaro in 1896–97, he had witnessed the "Fundi system" operated by the Kilimanjaro station in full swing. Schillings went away not only with the conviction that the "Swahili caravans equipped with German Mauser breech-loading rifles" were the actual "curse of the game," but that the incentive of firearms had turned agriculturalists back into hunters. The "commercial black elephant hunters (Makuas)" assumed "the main role in the wildlife destruction going on in East Africa." Schillings was especially infuriated about one caravan of African hunters, which he encountered in early 1897. It comprised "several hundred men" following a "professional Swahili hunter," furnished with powder, breech-loaders, and an authorizing license by a German station. Having been obliged to pay 500 rupees for his own license, Schillings was irate about a double-edged governmental policy that used game conservation as a pretext to milk the European hunter while at the same time it actively promoted indigenous hunting through the sale of powder and rifles.[21]

Considering Schillings's ardent commitment to the preservation of Africa's wildlife just a few years later, his recommendations in 1901 are astonishingly stern and utilitarian. There is no talk yet of imminent extinction, no mention of the cultural meaning of unique species, and no appeal to the government to preserve an imperial heritage. Instead, Schillings pointed to the sustainable management of game in Germany. The prime target of the colonial government should be to organize hunting "properly" to realize "an extraordinary source of revenue." Schillings's outspoken criticism of administrative practices in the colony was not restricted to the stations' role in encouraging commercial hunting. Another important factor that contributed to the devastation among the East African game were the Askari of the German Schutztruppe. Their shooting of an exorbitant amount of game was often justified with the argument that soldiers had to practice their aim on "living targets."[22] Apart from the ban on trading underweight ivory, Schillings demanded, first, to prohibit the furnishing of indigenous hunters with firearms by Europeans; second, an end of the practice to collect tusks as fine, duty, or as an equivalent to a hunting license, and, third, an end to hunting undertaken by the Askari. Wissmann's plan to restrict the number of animals to be shot under one license failed to gain the support of Schillings, who deemed it uncontrollable and likely to result in a vast number of animals that were merely left wounded. Instead of gazetting vast stretches of land as game reserves without having the means to adequately patrol them, Schillings suggested to declare the lands between Mounts Kilimanjaro and Meru as an elephant reserve and add further reserves later. Finally, Schillings differentiated between four types of nonindigenous hunters: the settlers and planters, who had to hunt in the vicinity of their farms and plantations to prevent damage to crops and livestock; the scientific hunter, who shot specimens for natural history museums and gathered zoological knowledge about little known species; the wealthy tourist hunter who brought revenue to the colony; and the commercial hunter, who posed the greatest threat to wildlife. The government, Schillings recommended, should realize the economic potential of wildlife as a resource not by exploitation, but by attracting wealthy globe-trotting hunters.[23]

Both memoranda formed the basis of deliberations at an in-house summit on wildlife conservation in the colonial department in Berlin in April 1901. The meeting convened administrative heads of various departments in the foreign office and representatives of the local administrations in the colonies. Compared with Wissmann and Schillings's extensive agendas, the outcome of this consultation was disappointing. The introduction of reserves in East Africa was strongly recommended, but otherwise the matter was put back into the hands of the governors. They should translate those stipulations of the London Convention into administrative practice they deemed feasible.[24]

Thus, it was of fundamental importance to the further administrative take on hunting and wildlife conservation in East Africa that the deliberations at the foreign office coincided with a change in the governorship of the colony. Just in April 1901, Adolf Graf von Götzen took over from Eduard von Liebert. Born of Silesian nobility in 1866, von Götzen had grown up in

Illustration 3.1. Governor Adolf von Götzen (left), rhinoceros. Bildarchiv der Deutschen Kolonialgesellschaft, Universitätsbibliothek Frankfurt.

a world of landed estates and hunting. His aristocratic upbringing paved the way for a career in military and diplomatic service, but more important was von Götzen's prehistory as a big game hunting traveler and explorer of private means. In 1891, he first set foot to the German East African colony on a brief hunting trip to Usambara and Ugweno, followed by a major expedition that made him the thirteenth European to cross the African continent, and the first German to do so from East to West.[25]

Von Götzen's penchant for hunting combined with the power of office and an autocratic understanding of governorship.[26] Like Schillings, he realized the potential of wildlife as one of the colony's foremost economic assets, and he was also aware about the virtual extinction of elephants in most of Southern Africa.[27] Von Götzen was determined to "grant our wildlife better protection" by coming down on the "native" as "the actual destroyer" of the game.[28] Before proclaiming the new ordinance, he sought

Schillings's advice, and the general thrust against African hunting was prominently expressed in the game ordinance that was gazetted in June 1903.[29] Already the title of a *Jagdschutzverordnung* indicated that its aim was not only the regulation of hunting, but the promotion of what was regarded to be its legitimate form, including the protection of game from poaching.[30] Given von Götzen's determination, it is somewhat surprising that it took altogether three years between the conference in London and the passing of a new game ordinance in German East Africa. Diplomatic tactics played their part, as none of the parties wanted to commit itself entirely to the London Convention unless the others had ratified it. Von Götzen appears to have discussed matters with the commissioner of British East Africa, who was allegedly skeptical about the feasibility of many stipulations contained in the London Convention. Therefore, the *Deutsch-Ostafrikanische Zeitung* is probably right with the suspicion that the proclamation of the ordinance was delayed to wait for the first experiences made with the game regulations introduced in Uganda and British East Africa.[31]

The ultimate version of the German East African game ordinance took up suggestions from Wissmann's and Schillings's memoranda and presented several clauses of the London convention in a modified form. This was most discernible in the ban of all hunting and trading of tusks below 5 kilograms in weight, as well as in the considerable extension of game reserves. According to von Götzen, the two reserves established in 1896 had fulfilled their purpose in increasing wildlife numbers, so that the ordinance decreed eleven further reserves in almost all inland districts.[32] Any contravention against the strict prohibition of hunting in the reserves was liable to a fine of 3,000 rupees, or imprisonment of three months. Additionally, the government enacted temporary bans on the hunting of single species. Elephant hunting, for example, was completely banned around Kilimanjaro between 1903 and 1908, which virtually choked the remnant ivory trade along the northern route.[33]

If von Götzen took up Wissmann's recommendation to establish reserves, he agreed with Schillings that a restriction of the number of animals to be shot under one license was impracticable. Instead, the ordinance introduced a basic hunting license of 10 rupees, payable by all nonindigenous hunters and those indigenous hunters who hunted with muzzle-loading rifles. With a view to nonindigenous hunters, the ordinance heeded the principle that who shot more should pay more. Fees had to be paid for each specimen of elephant, rhinoceros, buffalo, wildebeest, and all antelopes. All hunters were supposed to conduct shooting lists and pay according to the amount of animals they had killed. The basic fee pertaining to all white hunters alike may look democratic at first sight. However, critics were quick to spot the privileging of wealth and fiscal interest behind it, for it also meant that who could afford to pay more, could shoot more. The *Deutsch-Ostafrikanische Zeitung*, therefore, rose to defend the interests of the colonizing frontiersman struggling for a living on his farm or plantation in the interior, who now had to pay for every antelope he shot to feed himself and his laborers. Instead of granting protection to wildlife, the new ordinance appeared to be yet another "source of revenue to increase the meagre earnings of the colony" to the detriment of settlers who were themselves needy of every possible support.[34]

Von Götzen's conviction that the "mass murder of wildlife is wrought by those indigenous hunting communities furnished with firearms"[35] made itself felt in a special section dealing with African hunting. The prohibition of hunting with nets, fire, and pitfalls was emphasized anew. Above all, elephant hunting was severely curbed. The obligation to obtain a special permission from the district station was maintained, and it should only be granted to "trusted and reliable" persons. While this enabled the continuation of the hunting politics of alliance and authority, other checks cut to the heart of established hunting practices. The 1898 ordinance had, for political reasons, still acknowledged the right to the ground tusk at least to the more powerful chiefs. The new ordinance did away with it, thus depriving chiefs of a major source of income and symbolic capital. Indigenous elephant hunters were also forbidden to hunt with breech-loading rifles and poisoned arrows, the latter a preferred technique of hunter-gatherer societies.[36] Moreover, hunting parties were now restricted to six persons only. Given the unreliability of muzzle-loading rifles and the practice of encircling elephants and shoot in volleys, the small group size rendered the hunt an even more dangerous affair. Finally, the ordinance impeded mobility as the prime feature of elephant hunting. The enterprising Kamba, Nyamwezi, and Makua elephant hunters of the precolony had roamed far and wide to follow their prey. Now the ordinance obliged the "accredited" indigenous elephant hunters to operate only in their respective districts of residence. As the movement of elephant herds hardly followed the political geographies of administrative and military districts, this was a peculiarly harsh blow. Technically, the hunting of all other game with a muzzle-loading rifle was still accessible to the African hunter at the cost of 10 rupees. Still, this meant a doubling in price compared with 1896 and 1898. Regulations like this were presumably of limited relevance with increasing distance from the stations, but its overall effect was to curb African hunting and drive it into secrecy and obfuscation. In the district of Dar es Salaam, the number of licenses taken out by indigenous hunters decreased from "at least 50–60" before the 1903 ordinance to " two to three" afterward.[37]

The general thrust of the game ordinance becomes apparent when taking into account that just a few months before, another government circular had banned the sale of firearms and ammunition to Africans.[38] Their import had been the corollary to the export of ivory and was essentially kept up to continue ivory hunting and enable communities to defend themselves against predators. But concerns about decreasing game numbers coupled with a growing uneasiness about "natives in arms." Since December 1903, stations were advised to register all firearms in the possession of Africans. Anxieties increased further after the outbreak of war in Germany's South-West-African colony. In November 1904, the government declared all unregistered arms as liable to confiscation and destruction from June 1905 onward.[39]

Seen alongside the attempts to check indigenous ownership of firearms, the government's aim was no longer to regulate African hunting in a way that it served the colonial interest in the ivory trade. It was an integral part of a policy to render African hunters sedentary, controllable, and "native". The game ordinance pursued a vision of tolerated "native hunting" by colonial definition. Only the hunting with spear, bow, and arrow was tolerated and explicitly declared free; other customary methods like bushfires, game drives, and pitfalls became outlawed. The model behind the 1903 game ordinance was, in the words of von Götzen, the "primitive hunter," who had for millennia roamed the steppe in coexistence with wild animals and who was not yet corrupted by a culture unsuited for "natives", of which firearms were deemed the most visible expression.[40] This "primitive hunter" existed, however, only in the imperial imagination.

Beyond Conquest: From Exploitation to Conservation

The 1903 game ordinance marked a shift from the big man politics of the 1890s toward a political ecology of conservation distinguished by more rigid mechanisms of inclusion and exclusion. As such, it was part of a comprehensive set of colonial measures that sought to gear the extractive economies of the decade of conquest toward more productive and sustainable forms of creating value. These measures amounted up to a "modernization program"[41] geared toward tightening the grip especially on the male African population in order to push them into a colonial economy. Africans' control of land and resources was constrained under the pretext that indigenous forms of utilization were intrinsically destructive and unsustainable. The implementation and exaction of the hut tax, albeit highly uneven, furthered monetization and obliged agricultural producers to sell surplus crops or force them into relations of at least casual wage labor on nearby plantations or missionary stations. Tax defaulters were obliged to engage in "tax labor" for the district station, or were made to work on

European-owned plantations.[42] Other measures, such as the labor card systems operated in several districts should also help create an indigenous labor force. The reorganization of economic and social geographies according to colonial needs included the usurpation of trade networks other than ivory, especially of wild rubber and the promotion of rubber cultivation.[43] Still more important than rubber was, however, cotton, which was envisioned as *the* future cash crop to be cultivated by African labor.[44] In 1902, a scheme was introduced that coerced all villages under a *jumbe* to grow cotton on so-called communal shambas. In the district of Dar es Salaam, for example, thousands of people were forced to work these fields, which resulted in the unsettling of agricultural systems based upon subsistence, autonomy, and regional resilience.[45]

If the cultivation of cotton and rubber meant the mise-en-valeur of agricultural landscapes by the production of cash crops, the declaration of extensive game reserves in most administrative districts followed a similar logic. The setting aside of seemingly "wild" and unoccupied areas integrated them into the political economy of the colony as specific landscapes of production. By providing a sanctuary for wild animals, they should produce "game." At the beginning of this colonial reorganization of space stood the Crown Land Declaration of November 1895, which had imposed the state's claim to all "ownerless land," that is, land that was not "effectively" occupied or cultivated.[46] The foremost aim of the crown land ordinance was the controlled alienation of land for European plantations, settlement, or the "rational" utilization of forests, and in June 1900, stations were once more advised to "principally leave natives only as much land as is absolutely necessary for the village community under the circumstances of the current exchange economy."[47]

The crown land ordinance was coupled with a decree that all wood cut in so-called state forests on crown land was liable to a 30 percent tax if not used for the construction or reparation of huts. Furthermore, any use of fire for swidden cultivation on crown land was forbidden. The motivations behind the transfer of rational forestry to the tropics were similar to the motivations at the beginnings of scientific forestry at the end of the eighteenth century.[48] The fiscal interest of the state and the economic need for timber and fuel combined with the perception of rapid deforestation, which was deemed even more dramatic in the tropics given the forests' ecological role in regulating microclimates and local rainfall. Regional ordinances pertaining to the utilization of forests in the Usambara mountains and the Rufiji basin started as early as 1894 and were incorporated into more systematic reglementation under von Götzen in 1904. After a trained official forester was installed in 1903, the declaration of a forest conservation ordinance resulted in the conversion of the first patches of crown land into forest reserves one year later. Although still limited in scope before Maji Maji, the establishment of forest reserves was in some cases combined with the forced resettlement of the local population from these areas, as in the case of the Mwera-Rondo Plateau west of Lindi.[49] By 1913, an area of 750,000 million hectares had been turned into forest reserves.[50]

The revised game ordinance of 1903 also reflected the waning importance of ivory as an export commodity and fiscal subsidy of the colonial state. In 1898, the overall volume of ivory exported from the colony plummeted for the first time below 50,000 kilograms per year, just to remain around this mark after the turn of the century. This was a mere quarter of the trade's volume in 1890. By 1903, the worth of ivory had dropped to little more than 6 percent of the colony's overall export trade.[51] The revenue secured from tusks took a back seat to other trade items, such as rubber, copal, coffee, and increasingly, hides and furs. This relative waning of ivory's significance made elephant conservation both possible and necessary. Yet, ivory's decline as an export commodity should not gloss over considerable differences between various districts. Elephant herds on and around Mount Kilimanjaro had been exposed to the combined onslaught of European and African hunters since the middle of the 1880s. Here, the heyday of ivory and hunting-based big man politics was in the first half of the 1890s, while comparatively little ivory was procured from this area after 1900. In the southern highlands, however, the incorporation of elephant hunting into the big man politics of German stations had only started in the second half of the 1890s. There, political alignments continued to crystallize around the politics of hunting and ivory. Hunters as well as district commissioners reported a noticeable retreat of elephant herds to the less accessible woodlands and forests of the south.[52] This uneven wildlife geography is confirmed by the surviving statistics of the Customs House. Figure 3.1 shows the development of the average weight and amount of "fiscal ivory" as auctioned off by the German Customs Office between 1898 and 1913.

Fiscal ivory comprised all the ivory that the government and the various stations collected by confiscation, in return of hunting licenses, as payment of other dues and taxes in kind, or as tribute and gifts from local chiefs. The annual organization of the data is slightly deceptive, for auctions were not held regularly.[54] Nevertheless, it is noticeable that until about 1902, stations collected comparatively few but sizeable tusks of an average weight generally heavier than 8 kilograms. While the rising numbers between 1900 and 1901 can be attributed to substantial deliveries from the stations in the "elephant districts" of the southern highlands, that is, Iringa, Songea, Mahenge, and Kilimatinde, the overall low number was due to the fact that the stations accepted only sizeable tusks worth more than 100 rupees as a

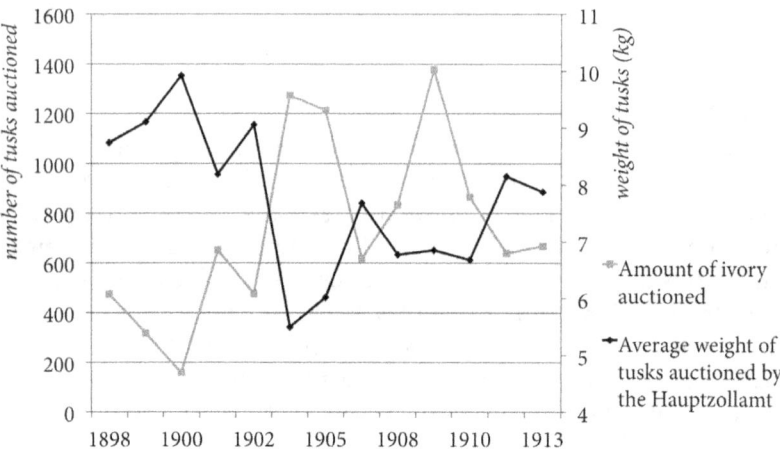

Figure 3.1. Weight and amount of "fiscal ivory" auctioned by the German Main Customs Office, 1898–1913.[53]

tribute from elephant hunters. One can only speculate if the comparatively low number of tusks must be read as a sign of failed enforcement or the opposite, for elephant hunting was to be restricted to a small number of "trusted" *mafundi*, which would also have resulted in the return of comparatively few tusks.

The rise between 1902 and 1904 is partially misleading, as no fiscal ivory was auctioned in 1903. Therefore, the amount of tusks sold in 1904 was considerably higher. Regarding the weight of tusks, however, a marked decrease for the years 1903–4 until 1907 can be registered. Such a sharp reduction can only be explained by the enhanced confiscation of underweight ivory that followed the enforcement of the trade ban in 1903.[55] Because the records kept by the Customs Office registered the volume as well as the origin of tusks, they confirm that the majority of fiscal ivory was derived from stations situated in the southern part of the colony, especially in the southern highlands. Iringa, Mahenge, and Songea, to a lesser degree also Lindi and Kilimatinde, were the foremost suppliers of fiscal ivory after 1900. For all these stations, the statistics reveal a considerable increase in the amount of tusks twinned with an equally marked decrease in their weight. The colonial administration did indeed enforce the ban on underweight ivory as envisioned by the London Convention. In order to assess the effects of the new game ordinance on the ground, it is necessary to return to the southern highlands and revisit Theodor von Hassel's acquisition of the title Mangula.

How Theodor von Hassel became Mangula—Continued

Geography and vegetation of the Mahenge district had been favorable to both elephants and cultivation. The area's characteristic features were rugged highlands interrupted by a system of rivers tributary to the Great Ruaha and Rufiji. Its lifeline of cultivation and communication was the Kilombero Valley, where the meandering branches of the Ulanga River created a seasonally inundated floodplain of some 250 kilometers length.[56] Contemporary European travelers were impressed by the region's luxuriant fecundity and its abundance in wildlife.[57] With its surrounding highlands and mountains, the area provided an ideal habitat and plenty of natural shelter for elephants. However, the Scottish explorer Joseph Thomson, who traversed the area in 1879, marveled at the animals' absence:

> On our way to Mahenge we had heard strange stories about the extraordinary abundance of elephants in that country. They were said to be looked upon with such reverence that they were never molested. … A certain chief of Mahenge had had such a regard for these noble animals, that no one was permitted to disturb them. However, much to our chagrin, we found that even here, during the last generation, evil days had befallen the elephant after their patron died, and now not one is to be seen over the wide jungles which surround Mahenge.[58]

Thomson's story probably condensed the transformation wrought by the advent of ivory hunters and traders to the area. The inhabitants of the valley, especially the Bena, entertained a lively ivory trade with Arab and Swahili traders operating from Kilwa.[59] A German Schutztruppe officer, who was stationed on the northern escarpment of Kilombero Valley in late 1897 and early 1898, repeatedly noticed tracks of elephants, but only managed to see and shoot an elephant after nine months of service in the area.[60] Another described the animals as "extremely shy,"[61] probably a consequence of intensive hunting. In an area where structures of authority were instable, the access to lucrative trade goods such as ivory, rubber, and slaves, as well as the supply of services and food to the trading parties provided new avenues to wealth and authority for local political entrepreneurs.[62] Political leaders in the area competed to secure a following, and the control of elephant hunting and the supply of ivory to the trade achieved pivotal place in this. Tusks formerly used for ceremonial purposes and ornaments turned into a valued commodity, and elephant hunting became the monopoly of specialized guilds that were believed to be in possession of a powerful medicine, which made them invisible to the animals.[63]

The advent of German colonialism in the southern highlands of Tanganyika meant that German missionaries as well as colonial authorities had to enter into the local politics of alliance and authority of which elephant hunting was such a vital part. In the protracted war of conquest and revenge against the Hehe leader Mkwawa, for example, the Germans drew on the support of Merere from Ussangu and *mtwa* Kiwanga of the Kilombero Valley. Since 1890, Kiwanga had used the military collaboration of the Germans to extend the position of the lowland Bena in the valley against the attacks from their Ngoni and Hehe neighbors.[64] The German colonizers, in turn, probably benefited from Kiwanga trading his ivory directly at the coast with German stations, bypassing the Swahili and Zanzibari traders in the interior.[65] The Germans removed Kiwanga's political rivals and provided him with means and opportunities to enhance his political standing to a degree that the German Schutztruppe officer von Prittwitz und Gaffron even counted Kiwanga among the most powerful "sultans" of the colony.[66] Among the strategies of extraversion adopted by Kiwanga was the appropriation of German dress and symbols that allowed his self-fashioning as a *mzungu* [European], but also the embrace of Swahili culture imported by the caravan trade. But taking the side of the Germans paid especially because the colonizers assigned the right to hunt elephants to

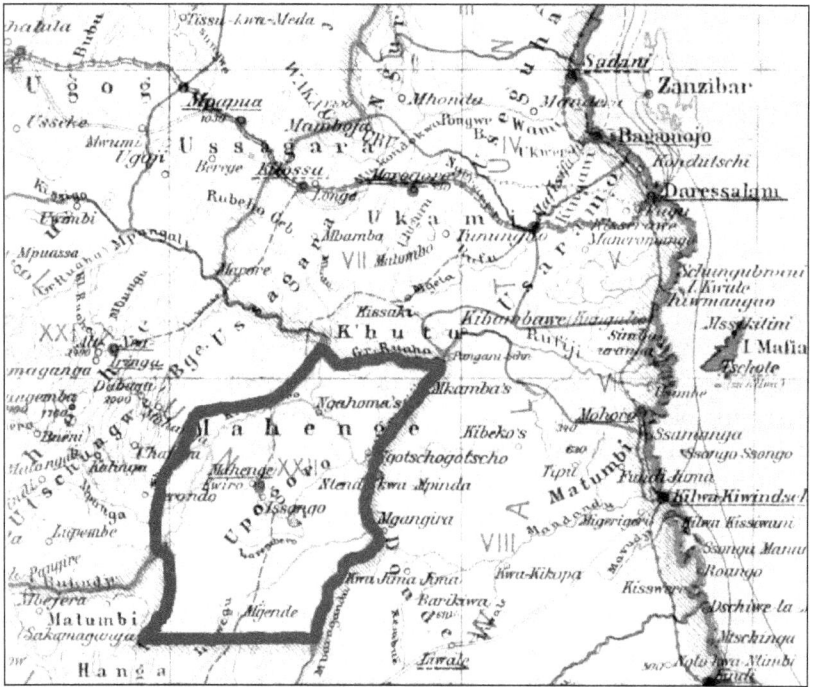

Map 3.1. The Mahenge military district, 1905. From *Deutscher Kolonialatlas mit Jahrbuch*, edited by the Deutsche Kolonialgesellschaft, Berlin, 1905.

those they trusted. In late 1903, von Hassel's precursor in Mahenge, Gideon von Grawert noted that Kiwanga had attracted a large following of Pogoro, Mbunga, and Ndamba people,[67] and von Hassel's diary refers to support from Kiwanga's elephant hunters, who surely counted among the "trustworthy" hunters and traders affiliated with the station.

Between 1902 and early 1905, Mahenge was one of the main suppliers of ivory to the government auctions,[68] which indicates that the station increasingly managed to enforce its claim to the wealth derived from elephant hunting. The considerable returns from Mahenge also confirmed the impression in Dar es Salaam that the southern highlands were one of the last areas of the colony that still featured a considerable elephant population.[69] Consequently, the government enacted bans to preserve what was believed to be the last sizeable stocks. Between November 1901 and September 1903, the issue of licenses for elephant hunting was forbidden in the districts of Kilwa and Songea in order "to safeguard the elephants." Both bordered the Mahenge district in the east and south. Von Hassel's diary features repeated calls by villages situated at the rivers Luwegu and Mbarangandu, where elephants demolished fields of maize and millet.[70] Between July 1902 and June 1903, von Götzen even enacted a complete ban of hunting "to prevent the extermination of elephants" in the lands of Kiwanga,[71] only to be replaced by the revised game ordinance, that scheduled the establishment of two game reserves in the district of Mahenge. One was situated to the northeast of the government station, bordered by the rivers Ulanga, Ruaha, and Rufiji. Covering an area of some 4,500 square kilometers, it was the largest game reserve established in German East Africa at the time. The other sanctuary comprised about two thirds of the size of the Ruaha reserve and was established southwest of Mahenge in the area of Lupembe, probably incorporating the western swathe of Kiwanga's territory. Locals referred to it as *Kisiwani*, as it was situated on the "island" between the rivers Mnyera and Ruhudje.[72] The gazetted game and forest reserves were so extensive that they could never be effectively policed with the personnel at hand. Still, the government found reason in November 1903 to remind district stations again that both European and indigenous people living within the borders of such a reserve should not be prevented from protecting their settlements against predators, wild pigs, and other "vermin."[73] Later correspondence concerning conflicts about the Liwale Reserve reveals that hardly all colonial officials knew about this alleviation, so that some continued to proclaim that all hunting in reserves was forbidden.[74] No mercy whatsoever was allowed in the case of elephant hunting, and just a few months after the proclamation of the ordinance, the Zanzibar-based ivory traders Hansing and the DOAG voiced their protest to the government. They complained that the "sharp implementation of the provisions concerning elephant hunting" had intimidated African hunters to a degree that all ivory trade was jeopardized. The complaint explicitly mentioned von Hassel's district of Mahenge, where hunters would rather hide or bury their ivory than deliver it to the coast.[75]

By September 1903, large tracts of the district had been turned into elephant reserves. No penal records have survived, but stations were advised to instruct the population of their districts "repeatedly and thoroughly" about the borders of the reserves and the prohibition of hunting. District officials and locally appointed game wardens, usually *majumbe* of villages in the vicinity of the reserves, were ordered to guarantee compliance with the game ordinance.[76] Hence, when Theodor von Hassel came to the area in late 1904, colonial interference had already significantly impeded Africans' control over elephants. En route in the vicinity of the Ruaha reserve, von Hassel noted in his diary that wild animals and elephants acted as if aware "that no shot was allowed" in that area.[77] The German wildlife painter Wilhelm Kuhnert, who was hunting for motives and elephants in the region of the Rufiji and Ruaha reserves in July 1905, was but one of several European eyewitnesses who found "unbelievable" devastations caused by the pachyderms in the area.[78] An incident of villagers defending themselves against crop-raiding elephants is related by Hans Paasche, who was deployed against Maji Maji rebels along the Rufiji River. He marveled in the romantic primitivism of "half-wild humans wrestling for their subsistence with antediluvian animals," without considering that colonial politics had contributed a fair share to this supposedly natural contest.[79]

Thus, the seventeen elephants claimed by Gertrud von Hassel as the bag of her father were probably even underestimated. Kuhnert, who met von Hassel in Mahenge in August 1905, noted admiringly in his diary that "von Hassel alone has shot nineteen elephants, besides plenty of other game." Several photographs in the 1906 issue of *Ostafrikanisches Weidwerk,* a supplement to the *Deutsch-Ostafrikanische Zeitung* dedicated exclusively to hunting, show elephants felled by von Hassel.[80] What appeared as a natural hunting dorado for the bored colonial official was in fact the consequence of the local loss of wildlife control following colonial game legislation. Only a few months after von Hassel had killed Mangula in February 1905, the majority of the Pogoro and Mbunga people in the district stood up against the German *boma* at Mahenge. The first action of the Maji Maji warriors was an attack on a caravan of 100 porters, who carried loads for the Mahenge station and were accompanied by four soldiers and "six elephant hunters"—the very symbol of the expropriated wealth of hunting.[81] In August and September 1905, the garrison of Mahenge was beleaguered for six weeks, until another Schutztruppe company came to the rescue. Like many of his German contemporaries, von Hassel regarded Maji Maji as a rising born out of magic and superstition. He admiringly registered "hundreds of elephant hunters" among the attackers, many of whom had celebrated him just half a year earlier, but he did not establish a connection between colonial measures of elephant control, wildlife conservation, and Maji Maji.[82]

A War over Elephants: Maji Maji as Environmental Conflict

There is substantial evidence to suggest that ecological conflicts over access to elephants and ivory, the control of pests and predators, and the circumscription of local resource use through forest and game reserves were all critical for the outbreak and spread of Maji Maji. The various measures to halt Africans' mobility; control their access to forests, guns, and game;

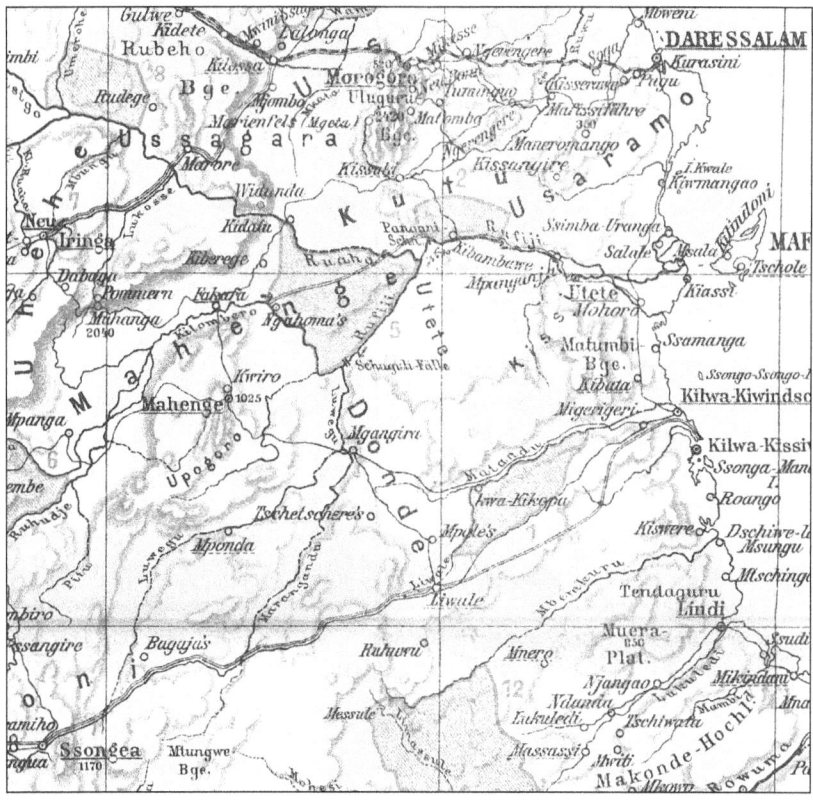

Map 3.2. Game reserves established in the region of the Maji Maji War (Reichskolonialamt, 1913).[83]

and to redirect their agricultural practices had compounded effects. The ban of bushfires, the hunting with nets and game drives together with the introduction of game reserves seriously affected communities' control over their environment.

Map 3.2 shows that the region south of the Rufiji River as well as the Matumbi Mountains were surrounded by three extensive game reserves where all hunting was forbidden. It was in these regions that Maji Maji originated to spread west and southwards. The millenarian prophecies associated with Maji Maji abounded with "metaphors of life-endangering predatory creatures"[84] that reflected the enhanced vulnerability of many villages to wildlife predation. Reports about lion attacks on humans preceded the rebellion. If the *Deutsch-Ostafrikanische Zeitung* is to be believed, the hot spots of such attacks were in the districts of Rufiji, Kilossa, and, again, Uzaramo.[85]

In February and April 1905, just a few months before the outbreak of hostilities, man-eating lions were again reported from Uzaramo.[86] With very few exceptions, the victims of these attacks were Africans, and their number was estimated at several hundreds. Obviously, not all reports about predating lions must be ascribed to colonial interventions or increased preying on humans. Conflicts between people and wildlife continued to happen naturally, and village headmen often used the claim to be haunted by wild pigs or other predators to elicit guns and powder from stations.[87] But it was probably more than mere coincidence that Kissaki, a place regularly mentioned in reports about lions predating on humans in the months before Maji Maji, was situated right on the northwestern corner of the Rufiji Game Reserve. Also, it is not unlikely that the increasing numbers of wild pigs and lions were interrelated phenomena. Recent research by wildlife biologists in Tanzania has ascertained that the presence of bush pigs near villages attracted lions and resulted in a noticeable increase of lion attacks on humans.[88] The constellation in areas such as Uzaramo and the Rufiji could well have been similar.

The connections between the colonial measures at environmental regulation, Maji Maji, and local vulnerability to wildlife predation had not escaped the attention of colonial decision makers. Only a few months after the first news of warfare in the south of the colony had reached Dar es Salaam, governor von Götzen appointed a commission to examine the motivations behind the rebellion. As the fighting was still going on, the commission's investigations were restricted to an analysis of station records and interviews with local *majumbe*, mainly in the Uzaramo region in the southern part of the Dar-es-Salaam district. The commission's findings singled out the various colonial interventions in local economies and ecologies as the major factors that had triggered the rebellion. Two members of the commission came to the conclusion that devastations wrought by wild pigs had been an "important moment" in the making of the rebellion. Interviews with local *majumbe* had brought to light that the prohibition of hunting with nets had resulted in increased devastations of fields by wild pigs.[89] Such damage was hardly restricted to the outbreak region of Maji Maji. However, the districts of Lindi as well as Uzaramo seem to have been affected particularly badly. The recollections gathered by the Maji Maji Research project in the late 1960s contain many testimonies recalling Maji Maji as a "time of very many wild pigs in this country."[90] Already in February 1905, when reports about the plague of bush pigs in Uzaramo reached Dar es Salaam, it was suspected that the pest was connected with the curbed sale of powder and guns and the ban of indigenous hunting techniques.[91] The report of the commission, therefore, came to the conclusion that of all restrictions placed upon indigenous hunting, the renewed ban of hunting with nets affected the widest range of people. Future wildlife policies should therefore provide that Africans were not deprived of their capacity to "struggle with nature."[92]

The revionist scholarship of Maji Maji has emphasized the "multitude of social meanings"[93] the maji medicine could attain as a means of mobilization. It was not only a war medicine supposed to grant invulnerability and turn bullets into water. Similar medicines were used to legitimate the power of big men, to heal the land, relieve agricultural grievances, and to grant protection from wild animals. "It is noteworthy," the abovementioned report concluded, "that the sorcery that was later used against the Germans was first directed towards protections against pigs."[94] Oral testimonies collected in Uhehe during the 1960s recalled a group of hunters who went to Udzungwa "with the hope of getting medicine for more expert hunting of elephants," but received the *maji* instead.[95]

Indeed, the ritual preparations of Maji Maji warriors and that of professional elephant hunters shared many similarities. German militaries noted on several instances the prominent participation of elephant hunters, whose skills and knowledge of the terrain commended them for leading the rebellion.[96] The abovementioned commission of inquiry observed, too, that "the striving of the government to protect the precious ivory was one of the causes of dissatisfaction; for among the leaders of the rebellion has been an exceptionally large number of elephant hunters who are now handicapped in the exercise of the hunt."[97] The commission's judgement is lent further support by military reports, ethnographies, and written as well as oral traditions.[98] North of the Rufiji river, the ban on hunting in the reserve meant a serious impediment to elephant hunting among the Zaramo, whose traditions of migration and settlement featured several prominent elephant hunters. The best-known Zaramo participant in Maji Maji was a certain Kibasira, himself the latest descendant of a lineage famed for elephant hunting.⁹⁹ In the area between Lindi and the Mbwemkuru River, two key figures in the rebellion had been adversely affected by colonial hunting regulations. The homestead of Omari Kinjala, a *jumbe* and leader of anti-German resistance in the hinterland of Liwale, was situated close to the newly established Matandu game reserve, which severely curbed his ability to hunt.¹⁰⁰ Omari Kinjala joined forces with the already mentioned elephant hunter Abdallah Mapanda, who has been singled out as the "moving spirit of the rebellion" in the area of Liwale.¹⁰¹ Mapanda's village was directly affected by the policies of wildlife conservation for it came to be situated right on the fringes of the newly gazetted Matandu river game reserve (marked by No. 1 in the map above).¹⁰² German reports of the fighting in the district of Songea in early 1906 suggest that elephant hunting was an important factor in the choosing of sides among the warring parties. The station at Songea had halted the sale of licenses for elephant hunting in the district between 1901 and 1903. This and the government's more ruthless claim to monopolize the procurement of tusks adversely affected chiefs whose authority had rested upon the profits from trade in ivory and slaves. German officers noticed that resistance was organized largely around the hunters of the Ngoni chiefs, "numerous elephant hunters based in the forests along the Rovuma River," and the "notorious elephant hunter Kopa-Kopa." In March 1906, a German column met a force of "300 elephant hunters and Ngoni" under the command of an elephant hunter named Magewa.¹⁰³ On the other side, the Germans were lent major support in their operations against the Maji Maji warriors by the abovementioned Kiwanga or the trader and elephant hunter Rashid bin Masoud. He assisted the Germans with his hunters and especially his knowledge of the area. As a reward, he was granted the privilege to continue elephant hunting after the war, and he was one of the few non-European hunters still supplied with rifles and ammunition by the German stations after Maji Maji. In the second half of 1909, the cash books of Songea station confirm the sale of more than 200 pounds of gunpowder to 46 of Rashid's elephant hunters. Rashid bin Masoud was one of the last "trustworthy" hunters still granted that privilege, and he made ample use of it: the majority of the 78 elephants killed in Songea in the second half of 1909 were to his name.¹⁰⁴ The government safeguarded the "politically important" opportunity to reward powerful chiefs and big men with the prestige of a breech-loading rifle and associated hunting rights.¹⁰⁵ As late as 1911, it defied demands of the colonial office in Berlin to ban indigenous elephant hunting completely as it would negatively affect "several elephant hunters, with Rashid bin Masoud as the best known, who had fought bravely on the German side during the uprising in 1905–6."¹⁰⁶

Ecological conflicts and access to elephants were thus critical factors that motivated people's participation in the Maji Maji movement. While Thaddeus Sunseri has been right to emphasize that the war was "propagated and fought in large part through ivory trading and hunting networks" that predated the onset of German colonial rule,[107] the material presented here casts doubt on his reading of Maji Maji as, above all, "a symbolic clash of hunting cultures."[108] Although von Götzen's wildlife policies decreed from Dar es Salaam aimed at the conservation of a species regarded as threatened, it was neither a conflict between conservation imposed from above and traditional rights asserted from below, nor a monolithic clash between a *weidgerecht* German hunting culture and African understandings of legitimate access to wild animals. Instead, the conflict was fought along the untidy networks of trade and hunting—which included the Germans through the connections their district commissioners had forged with their big men politics of privilege and alienation. The southern highlands constituted a special case insofar as conquest had set in comparatively late. Hunting still constituted a middle ground, and the politics of local alliances in Songea and Mahenge were still in full swing when the governmental concern over elephant conservation materialized in the 1903 game ordinance. While elephant hunters, many of them ousted by the ever more exclusive German hunting policies, constituted the backbone of the rebellion, there were also chiefs and traders well-known for their involvement in the hunting and trade of ivory, like Kiwanga or Rashid bin Masoud in Songea, who sided with the colonizers. Maji Maji did not follow a neat division of "colonizers" on the one side and "colonized" on the other. The alliances forged over hunting and ivory cut across this divide.

This said, Maji Maji definitely changed the colonial middle ground of hunting. With the establishment of colonial rule, the big man politics of hunting and ivory lost their importance, yet, other contact zones of hunting retained or increased their relevance. Among these were the growing number of white settlers or trading companies who hired African hunters, but especially the everyday situation of the safari, where different assumptions, expectations, and practices of hunting met. Maji Maji also marked a drastic rupture in the networks of the ivory trade. During the war or in its aftermath, indigenous elephant hunting was virtually extinguished: hunters died fighting, were executed, or fled into Portuguese territory. When the Schutztruppe officer Paul Fromm traversed the Mahenge district in June 1908, he noticed the presence of "formidable herds of elephants," now more numerous still, for the "many native hunters of the area" had "all joined the rising against us and were consequently hanged or shot."[109] The compulsory submission of weapons and penal labor in the rebel regions, combined with an even stricter surveillance of indigenous possession of rifles should severely hamper the ability of survivors to keep hunting elephants. The woodlands of the Lindi, Kilwa, Songea, Mahenge, and Iringa districts remained the main areas of ivory procurement. Because Maji Maji had removed most indigenous competition, white commercial ivory hunters took over the business of shooting elephants after the war. Exterminatory methods of warfare and a brutal policy of scorched earth entailed widespread famine after the actual fighting was ended, which resulted in the further depopulation of the already sparsely settled lands. Governmental attempts to alleviate some of the restrictive hunting and forest regulations were, therefore, of little avail.[110] Formerly cultivated lands returned to wilderness and became infested with lions and wild pigs. Depopulation, destroyed homesteads and people sleeping in the open, weakened resistance due to harsh famine, but, above all, the ubiquitous availability of rotting corpses resulted in hundreds of casualties from lion attacks. By 1909, the problem of "maneaters" had become an endemic notoriety in the southern districts.[111]

Maji Maji was thus not only a battle lost politically, but a major factor in the long-term marginalization of Southeast Tanzania.[112] In many formerly cultivated areas, bush spread and tsetse followed in its wake. The German government took the opportunity to extend areas reserved for forest and wildlife preservation: In June 1907, the upper Rufiji reserve, the core area of today's Selous Game Reserve, was extended to approximately double its previous size.[113] Although the German administration never planned to resettle villages to guarantee the functioning of game reserves, nature itself appeared to evict people from the reserves in the Maji Maji heartlands. In 1909, the *Deutsch-Ostafrikanische Zeitung* informed its readers that vast stretches of land between Ruaha and Rufiji, the site of the Mahenge reserve, were inhabited by a "few dozen" people only. According to identical information from several informants, "residents have left their homesteads due to the massive increase of elephants and hippopotami and moved north towards Kissaki and Maneromango." Similarly, a German planter taken to court in early 1912 for illegally hunting elephants in the Rufiji Reserve reported about plenty of villages deserted by their inhabitants: people, he was told in the village of Mkalinzo, would abandon the area because of the damage done by elephants from the nearby sanctuary.[114] The villagers' plight was the hunters' paradise: elephants crossing out of the reserves and over the Rufiji and Ruaha rivers made the region south of Kissaki a preferred haunt of ivory hunters.[115]

How Theodor von Hassel Became Mangula—An Open End

Still, there is the Mangula puzzle. The vivid depictions of elephants haunting fields and villages in von Hassel's diary undeniably represented actual past events. His inheritance of name and spirit of Mangula is corroborated by surviving memories and oral traditions collected during the 1960s. They repeatedly mention Mang'ula or Mangula as von Hassel's name.[116] Most informants simply called von Hassel Mangula, suggesting that he *was* Mangula rather than had only been named after him, and that the ferocious spirit displayed by the animal had been conferred to its hunter. When advancing to the *boma,* the Maji Maji warriors had chanted "their famous song 'Ponga Mangula ponga.'" The words meant "Mr. Vonhassel [!] should be calm so that they may take him prisoner."[117] Apparently, the song's intention was to placate the fierce spirit of Mangula.

What did it mean that von Hassel became Mangula? In his memories, von Hassel mentions the *ngoma* celebrations, in which people imitated the charging and his shooting of the elephants. These dances were a mimetic depiction of the event, a kind of performative ethnography that filled the colonizer's action with indigenous meanings. Undeniably, the killing of an elephant bestowed enormous prestige on the successful hunter, especially of an elephant who had for some reason been singled out with a name. Then again, people refused to eat meat of the slain elephant, allegedly because they believed the animal to be possessed by an evil spirit.[118] Anthropologist Axel Köhler relates the belief among the Baka in the Congo that certain humans have the capacities to transform into elephants. Only initiated persons are able to distinguish these *mòkìlà* elephants from real ones, and no hunter would want to kill a *mòkìlà* elephant for this would mean murder and incur revenge.[119] In many East African myths, the borders between humans and animals were permeable: spirits could possess both men and animals, deceased chiefs were believed capable to transform into animal shape, but shape-shifting could also be associated with witchcraft and predatory intentions.[120] Various reports of travelers, missionaries, and early ethnographers testify that the possibility of humans or spirits transforming into animals was widely believed.[121] Indeed, such assumptions were a constitutive part of Maji Maji prophecy.

During the 1890s, the Germans had encountered particularly fierce resistance in the Mahenge area by a chief referred to in the sources as "Magnula." This hints as much at hidden layers of meaning—had the chief's spirit returned in the elephant?—as the occurrence of other fierce pachyderms in the area which were equally honored with a name, at about the same time as Mangula.[122] Sources are too few to allow for a thick description of the political anthropology of wildlife as part of Maji Maji, but in any case, Theodor von Hassel was entangled in more complicated webs of meaning than he realized.

Two years after von Hassel had put down the Maji Maji rising in his district, the fathers of the nearby Kwiro mission compiled a dictionary of the local idiom spoken around Mahenge. It featured an entry for "Magnulla," which translated as "Mordgeselle" and "Totschläger"—a killer and murderer.[123] Whoever Theodor von Hassel may have shot the day he killed Mangula, this meaning of the name was telling in its ambiguity.

Notes

1. Lorne E Larson, "A History of the Mahenge (Ulanga) District, ca. 1860–1957" (Unpublished PhD diss., University of Dar es Salaam, 1976), 1–10; "Circular by governor von Liebert," *Deutsches Kolonialblatt* 10 (1899): 652.
2. Theodor von Hassel was born on 29 September 1868 in Trier and died 29 November 1935 in Mahenge. He entered the service of the German East African Schutztruppe in April 1903 and served as *Kompaniechef* in Dar es Salaam, Lindi, and Mahenge.
3. DITSL, von Hassel, *Ein Tagebuch aus Ostafrika*, 42.
4. Ibid., 43.
5. Ibid., 53 [my italics]. The name appears in different varieties in the sources, including Mangmula, Mangula, Mang'ula, Mamula, Mangmulla, or Magnula.
6. DITSL, von Hassel, *Ein Tagebuch aus Ostafrika*, 12, 32. It is likely that he compiled the manuscript at about the same time when he wrote down his memories of the Maji Maji War in the late 1920s, inspired by the *genius loci* after he had returned to the Mahenge area to start a coffee plantation in 1926. The copy held by the library of the former German Colonial Academy in Witzenhausen was not typed by von Hassel himself. Additional pictures and translations of some Kiswahili expressions, which were amended in brackets, indicate later editorial intervention, probably by his son Kai Uwe von Hassel. See also Archiv der Erzabtei St. Ottilien: Theodor von Hassel, *Der Militairbezirk Mahenge im Aufstand 1905* (Unpublished manuscript, Mahenge, 1929).
7. George Orwell, "Shooting an Elephant," in *The Collected Essays, Journalism and Letters of George Orwell. Vol. 1: An Age Like This, 1920–1940*, ed. Sara Orwell and Ian Angus (Harmondsworth, 1970), 265–72.
8. Orwell, "Shooting an Elephant," 266.
9. Pandian, "Predatory Care".
10. Fonck, *Deutsch-Ostafrika*, 413.
11. Gertrud von Hassel, *Meine Kindheit in Afrika* (Heide, 1994), 6–7.
12. Ludger Wimmelbücker, "Verbrannte Erde. Zu den Bevölkerungsverlusten als Folge des Maji-Maji-Kriegs," in *Der Maji-Maji-Krieg in Deutsch-Ostafrika 1905–1907*, ed. Felicitas Becker and Jigal Beez (Berlin, 2005), 93–94.
13. Marcia Wright, "Maji Maji: Prophecy and Historiography," in *Revealing Prophets. Prophecy in Eastern African History*, ed. David Anderson and Douglas H Johnson (London, 1995), 125; cf. Donald Denoon and Adam Kuper, "National-

ist Historians in Search of a Nation. The 'New Historiography' in Dar es Salaam," *African Affairs* 69 (1970): 329-49.
14. James Giblin and Jamie Monson, eds, *Maji Maji. Lifting the Fog of War* (Leiden, 2010); Becker, "A Social History of Southeast Tanzania"; Monson, "Relocating Maji Maji."
15. Sunseri, "Reinterpreting a Colonial Rebellion"; Sunseri, "The War of the Hunters."
16. See chapter 7 below.
17. BAB R 1001/7776, fol. 119: Ordinance dated 23 November 1900—gazetted in *Amtlicher Anzeiger für Deutsch-Ostafrika* 1, no. 34 (1900), 22 November. The ban was finally put into practice in German East Africa in April 1901, cf. *Amtlicher Anzeiger für Deutsch-Ostafrika* 1, no. 36 (1900), 13 December.
18. BAB R 1001/7768, fol. 48-312: Entwürfe und Denkschrift zu einer Jagdverordnung gemäß den Beschlüssen der Londoner Konferenz, October 1900, fol. 134.
19. BAB R 1001/7768, fol. 40-41: Wissmann to AA KA, 7 September 1900; and fol. 46-47: Wissmann to AA KA, 13 October 1900.
20. BAB R 1001/7768, fol. 48-312: Entwürfe und Denkschrift zu einer Jagdverordnung gemäß den Beschlüssen der Londoner Konferenz, October 1900, fols. 106, 109, 128-141.
21. HUB MfN, Zool. Museum S III Schillings, fol. 3-5: Schillings to Matschie, February 1897.
22. See for example BAB R 1001/7770, fol. 215: Circular Rechenberg to all stations, 20 October 1908; Ernst Nigmann, *Felddienstübungen für farbige (ostafrikanische) Truppen* (Dar es Salaam, 1910), 48.
23. BAB R 1001/7769, fol. 43: Schillings to AA KA, 21 March 1901, enclosure: Carl Georg Schillings: Ausführungen zum Wildschutzgesetz für die deutschen Kolonien in Afrika (not dated, probably Jan-March 1901).
24. BAB R 1001/7770, fol. 11: internal memorandum on the creation of game reserves [undated]; BAB R 1001/7770, fol. 13: AA KA to Gov DOA (draft), undated (March 1901); BAB R 1001/7770, R 1001/7769, fol. 49-54: Protocol of the internal meeting in the colonial department, 13 April 1901.
25. "Der Afrikareisende Adolf Graf von Götzen," *Deutsche Rundschau für Geographie und Statistik* 17 (1895): 470-71.
26. Von Götzen used the colony as a hunting estate to entertain visiting German aristocrats, such as the Duke Adolf Friedrich von Mecklenburg in 1902, see *Deutsche Jägerzeitung* 39, no. 23 (1902), 19 June: 365.
27. BAB R 1001/7770, fol. 7: von Götzen to AA KA, 6 September 1901. Schillings and von Götzen appear to have been exchanging views on the matter, cf. Schillings, *Mit Blitzlicht und Büchse*, 504.
28. BAB R 1001/7776, fol. 134: Gov DOA to AA KA, 15 July 1902; cf. *Deutsch-Ostafrikanische Zeitung* 5, no. 12 (1903), 21 March.
29. The *Jagdschutzverordnung* was gazetted in *Amtlicher Anzeiger für Deutsch-Ostafrika* 4, no. 14 (1903), 13 June. Various stages of the draft and the final version can be found in BAB R 1001/7776, fol. 156-59: Gov DOA to AA KA, 1 January 1903; and fol. 192-94.
30. On contemporary definitions of *Jagdschutz*, that is, the policing of any contravention against the lawful order governing the hunt, see for example Adam Schwappach, *Forstpolitik, Jagd- und Fischereipolitik* (Leipzig, 1894), 323-26.

31. *Deutsch-Ostafrikanische Zeitung* 5, no. 22 (1903), 30 May 1905.
32. BAB R 1001/7776, fol. 156–59: Gov DOA to AA KA, 1 January 1903.
33. Archive Tierpark Hagenbeck Hamburg, Folder Kilimanjaro Handels- und Landwirtschaftsgesellschaft: Annual report, 10 November 1902.
34. Unsere neue Jagdschutzverordnung, *Deutsch-Ostafrikanische Zeitung* 5, no. 32 (1903): 8 August.
35. BAB R 1001/7776, fol. 156–59: Gov DOA to AA KA, 1 January 1903.
36. BAB R 1001/244, fol. 7: Reisebericht über Dienstreise durch den nördlichen Teil des Bezirks; Richtung Kidete, Kilossa, 3 April 1901; cf. Edward Steinhart, "Elephant Hunting in 19th-Century Kenya: Kamba Society and Ecology in Transformation," *International Journal of African Historical Studies* 33 (2001): 335–49.
37. BAB R 1001/726, fol. 109: Report on the causes of the Maji Maji rebellion in the district of Dar es Salaam, 17 January 1906, enclosure 8: Westhaus report, 21 December 1905.
38. BAB R 1001/7770, fol. 162: AA KA to Wissmann (draft), 31 August 1903.
39. *Deutsch-Ostafrikanische Zeitung* 5, no. 32 (1903), 8 August; *Deutsch-Ostafrikanische Zeitung* 5, no. 50 (1903), 12 December; *Deutsch-Ostafrikanische Zeitung* 7, no. 3 (1905), 21 January; *Deutsch-Ostafrikanische Zeitung* 7, no. 9 (1905), 4 March.
40. BAB R1001/7776, fol. 156–59: Gov DOA to AA KA, 1 January 1903.
41. The genesis of modernizing colonial policies on the colonial periphery has been stressed by Wright, "Local Roots of Policy in German East Africa," John Iliffe, *Tanganyika under German Rule 1905–1912* (Cambridge, 1969), and recently Pesek, *Koloniale Herrschaft in Deutsch-Ostafrika*. An excellent case study analyzing the colonial introduction of market labor relations is provided by Thaddeus Sunseri, *Vilimani. Labor Migration and Rural Change in Early Colonial Tanzania* (Portsmouth, NH, 2002).
42. The hut tax was proclaimed in November 1897, but went in force five months later. See Iliffe, *A Modern History of Tanganyika*, 132–34.
43. Koponen, *Development for Exploitation*, 237–40.
44. See Thaddeus Sunseri, "The *Baumwollfrage*. Cotton Colonialism in German East Africa," *Central European History* 34 (2001): 31–51.
45. Sunseri, "Famine and Wild Pigs," 247–49.
46. Harald Sippel, "Aspects of Colonial Land Law in German East Africa: German East Africa Company, Crown Land Ordinance, European Plantations and Reserved Areas for Africans," in *Land Law and Land Ownership in Africa. Case Studies from Colonial and Contemporary Cameroon and Tanzania*, ed. Robert Debusmann and Stefan Arnold (Bayreuth, 1996), 17–28.
47. Cf. *Amtlicher Anzeiger für Deutsch-Ostafrika* 1, no. 12 (1900), 2 June.
48. See Sunseri, *Wielding the Ax*; Richard Hölzl, *Umkämpfte Wälder. Die Geschichte einer ökologischen Reform in Deutschland 1760–1860* (Frankfurt, 2010).
49. BAB R 1001/726, fol. 91: Report of the Commission on the causes of the rebellion, 4 December 1905, 17.
50. Hans G Schabel, "Tanganyika Forestry under German Colonial Administration, 1891–1919," *Forest & Conservation History* 34 (1990): 133.
51. In 1902, ivory had made up 11.9 percent of the trade value via the coastal ports; in 1903 and 1904, its value had dropped to 6.4 percent and 5.6 percent, respectively; cf. Karl Most, *Die wirtschaftliche Entwicklung Deutsch-Ostafrikas 1885–1905* (Berlin, 1906), 2.

52. Oberländer, *Eine Jagdfahrt nach Ostafrika*, 260; *Denkschrift über die Entwickelung der Schutzgebiete in Afrika und der Südsee im Jahre 1906/07.* Teil B: *Deutsch-Ostafrika* (Berlin, 1907), 37; Fonck, *Deutsch-Ostafrika*, 406.
53. The figures are compiled from the records of the single auctions in TNA G 59/2: Utilisation and treatment of fiscal ivory, 1898–1915.
54. Cf. for example *Deutsch-Ostafrikanische Zeitung* 2, no. 32 (1900), 18 August; TNA G 3/39, unfol.: Note Main Customs Office Dar es Salaam, 2 January 1907; TNA G 3/39, unfol.: Gov DOA to Main Customs Office, 14 February 1907.
55. The amount of confiscated underweight ivory was also noted by contemporary observers, see for example *Deutsch-Ostafrikanische Zeitung* 6, no. 4 (1904), 23 January; and *Deutsch-Ostafrikanische Zeitung* 7, no. 14 (1905), 8 April.
56. German colonizers usually referred to today's Kilombero Valley as Ulanga Valley.
57. Cf. *Deutsch-Ostafrikanische Zeitung* 10, no. 3 (1908), 11 January; BAB R 1001/278, fol. 66–88: Heinrich Fonck: Report on the Rufiji-Ulanga-Expedition 1907, 15 January 1908; Joachim Graf Pfeil, "Die Erforschung des Ulanga-Gebietes," *Petermanns geographische Mitteilungen* 32 (1886): 358–62.
58. Joseph Thomson, *To the Central African Lakes and Back. The Narrative of the Royal Geographical Society's East Central African Expedition, 1878–80,* vol. 1 (London, 1881), 176–77.
59. Thomson, *To the Central African Lakes and Back,* 179; Nyagava, "A History of the Bena to 1908," 181–84.
60. LIL Prittwitz Papers, Box 245/1: Diary June 1897 to August 1898, 175, 214. Georg Robert Wilhelm von Prittwitz und Gaffron (1861–1936) was stationed at the military post Muhanga during the campaigns against the Hehe chief Mkwawa.
61. BAM N 85/3: Pusch, *Ostafrikanische Briefe*, 63 (8 August 1900). See also W Marwitz, "Aus meinem Tagebuch in Uhähä [!]," *Das Waidwerk in Wort und Bild* 8 (1899): 289–95.
62. Monson, "Relocating Maji Maji," 99–105.
63. Nyagava, "A History of the Bena to 1908," 181–84.
64. On Kiwanga, see Seth I Nyagava, "Were the Bena Traitors? Maji Maji in Njombe and the Context of Local Alliances Made by the Germans," in *Maji Maji. Lifting the Fog of War,* ed. James Giblin and Jamie Monson (Leiden, 2010), 244–45. Cf. BAB R 1001/288, fol. 181: Proclamation by Governor Liebert, 11 July 1897.
65. Eduard von Liebert, *Neunzig Tage im Zelt. Meine Reise nach Uhehe, Juni bis September 1897* (Berlin, 1898), 37–38.
66. LIL Prittwitz Papers: Box 245/1, typescript diary June 1897 to 11 August 1898, 166.
67. Gideon von Grawert, "Bericht des Oberleutnants v. Grawert (Gideon) über die Bereisung des Bezirks Mahenge vom 17. November bis 18. Dezember 1903," *Deutsches Kolonialblatt* 15 (1904): 479.
68. TNA G 59/2: Fiscal ivory statistics: Returns between 24/25 November 1902 and 20 January 1904: Return from Mahenge, 8 December 1903.
69. BAB R 1001/278, fol. 66–88, fol. 85: Heinrich Fonck: Report on the Rufiji-Ulanga-Expedition 1907, 15 January 1908.
70. DITSL, von Hassel, *Ein Tagebuch aus Ostafrika*, 65–76.
71. *Amtlicher Anzeiger für Deutsch-Ostafrika* 2, no. 34 (1901), 14 November; *Amtlicher Anzeiger für Deutsch-Ostafrika* 4, no. 16 (1903), 11 July; *Amtlicher Anzeiger für Deutsch-Ostafrika* 4, no. 14 (1903), 13 June.

72. "Jagdschutzverordnung für das Deutsch-Ostafrikanische Schutzgebiet," *Amtlicher Anzeiger für Deutsch-Ostafrika* 4, no. 14 (1903), 13 June; TNA G 8/910: List of Wildlife Reserves, Nos. 5 and 6; the name *Kisiwani* is mentioned in BAB R 1001/278, fol. 66–88, fol. 85: Heinrich Fonck: Report on the Rufiji-Ulanga-Expedition 1907, 15 January 1908.
73. *Amtlicher Anzeiger für Deutsch-Ostafrika* 4, no. 28 (1903), 21 November.
74. BAB R 1001/814, fol. 191: Gov DOA to RKA, 9 October 1909.
75. BAB R 1001/644/1, fol. 87: Hansing and DOAG to Gov DOA, Zanzibar, 8 September 1903; cf. BAB R 1001/7770, fol. 172, Gov DOA to AA KA, 1 July 1904.
76. BAB R 1001/7776, fol. 198: Circular no. 31 to all district and military stations, Dar es Salaam, 1 June 1903. Cf. TNA G 21/148, fol. 8: Hearing of the game warden Amdallah, Mahenge, 6 September 1907.
77. DITSL, von Hassel, *Ein Tagebuch aus Ostafrika*, 116–17; *Deutsches Kolonialblatt* 15 (1904): 479.
78. Private Collections Angelika Grettmann-Werner, Bremen: Papers Wilhelm Kuhnert, Diary of his second East African expedition 1905/06, 3 July 1905.
79. Paasche, *Im Morgenlicht*, 229–30; DITSL, von Hassel, *Ein Tagebuch aus Ostafrika*, 56–57, 65–73, 114.
80. Private Collections Angelika Grettmann-Werner, Bremen: Papers Wilhelm Kuhnert, Diary entry 10 August 1905; *Ostafrikanisches Weidwerk* 1906, no. 11.
81. *Missionsblätter* 15 (1911), 88.
82. DITSL, von Hassel, *Ein Tagebuch aus Ostafrika*, 30–31, 53–54.
83. Detail from a map showing the game reserves established in German East Africa (1912); taken from: Reichskolonialamt, *Jagd und Wildschutz in den deutschen Kolonien*, appendix.
84. Wright, "Maji Maji," 129.
85. *Deutsch-Ostafrikanische Zeitung* 3, no. 26 (1901), 6 July; *Deutsch-Ostafrikanische Zeitung* 4, no. 40 (1902), 4 October; *Deutsch-Ostafrikanische Zeitung* 4, no. 50 (1902), 20 December; *Deutsch-Ostafrikanische Zeitung* 5, no. 18 (1903), 2 May; *Deutsch-Ostafrikanische Zeitung* 5, no. 20 (1903), 16 May; *Deutsch-Ostafrikanische Zeitung* 5, no. 35 (1903), 29 August; "Jagdunfälle in Deutsch-Ostafrika," *Wild und Hund* 9 (1903): 621.
86. *Deutsch-Ostafrikanische Zeitung* 7, no. 5 (1905), 3 February; *Deutsch-Ostafrikanische Zeitung* 7, no. 13 (1905), 1 April; cf. *Deutsch-Ostafrikanische Zeitung* 8, no. 5 (1906), 3 February.
87. Cf. *Deutsch-Ostafrikanische Zeitung* 3, no. 43 (1901), 2 November; *Deutsch-Ostafrikanische Zeitung* 7, no. 5 (1905), 3 February.
88. Paasche, *Im Morgenlicht*, 48; Craig Packer et al., "Lion Attacks on Humans in Tanzania," *Nature* 436 (2005), 18 August: 927–28.
89. *Berichte über Land- und Forstwirtschaft in Deutsch-Ostafrika* 2 (1904–06): 57; cf. Sunseri, *Vilimani*, 90–91.
90. See for example the testimony by Mzee Ndundule Mangaya of Kipatimu, interviewed 2–10 September 1967, in *Records of the Maji Maji-Rising*, ed. GCK Gwassa and John Iliffe (Dar es Salaam, 1967), 4.
91. *Deutsch-Ostafrikanische Zeitung* 7, no. 5 (1905), 3 February.
92. BAB R 1001/726, fol. 103–8: Report by Wilhelm Schultz and John Booth, Dar es Salaam, 11 December 1905; Sunseri, *Vilimani*, 78–80.

93. Felicitas Becker, "Traders, 'Big Men' and Prophets: Political Continuity and Crisis in the Maji Maji Rebellion in Southeast Tanzania," *Journal of African History* 45 (2004): 20.
94. BAB R 1001/726, fol. 103–8: Report by Wilhelm Schultz and John Booth, Dar es Salaam, 11 December 1905.
95. "Interview with Mzee Lusulo Mwamkemwa, Ilula," in Maji Maji Research Project (MMRP), *Collected Papers*, Department of History, University College of Dar es Salaam 1968, no. 3/68/1/3/5, 10 April 1968.
96. DITSL, von Hassel, *Ein Tagebuch aus Ostafrika*, 22–23, 30, 54; Paasche, *Im Morgenlicht*, 107–8; BAB R 1001/700, fol. 260: Bericht über die Tätigkeit des Expeditions-Korps Major Johannes in der Zeit vom 3. Mai bis 31. Juli 1906.
97. BAB R 1001/726, Denkschrift über die Ursachen des Aufstandes in Deutsch-Ostafrika 1905, 8. For alleviations of the forest ordinances see *Amtlicher Anzeiger für Deutsch-Ostafrika* 7, no. 12 (1906), 7 April.
98. The following section draws extensively upon Sunseri, "The War of the Hunters."
99. *Deutsch-Ostafrikanische Zeitung* 7, no. 39 (1905), 29 September.
100. *Deutsch-Ostafrikanische Zeitung* 8, no. 40 (1906), 6 October; Lorne Larson, "The Ngindo: Exploring the Center of the Maji Maji Rebellion," in *Maji Maji. Lifting the Fog of War*, ed. James Giblin and Jamie Monson (Leiden, 2010), 108–10; Sunseri, "The War of the Hunters," 140–41.
101. RM Bell, "The Maji Maji Rebellion in Liwale District," *Tanganyika Notes and Records* 28 (1950): 44.
102. Ibid., 55; RW Crosse-Upcott, "The Origin of the Maji Maji Revolt," *Man* 60 (1960): 73; Gilbert Clement Kamana Gwassa, *The Outbreak and Development of the Maji Maji War 1905–1907* (Cologne, 2005), 153–54.
103. BAB R 1001/700, fol. 204–20: Tätigkeitsbericht des Detachements Johannes vom 18. November 1905 bis 10. März 1906; BAB R 1001/700, fol. 247–54: Bericht über die Tätigkeit des Expeditions-Korps Major Johannes in der Zeit vom 11. März bis 3. Mai 1906.
104. BAB R 1001/7777, fol. 337–38: RKA to Gov DOA, 13 September 1911; BAB R 1001/7778, unfol. Extract of the cash books of Songea for the second half of 1909, dated Dar es Salaam, 16 June 1911.
105. The "political importance" of this concession to "a few especially renowned and influential coloureds" is emphasized in TNA G8/54, unfol.: Gov DOA to BA Tabora, 7 June 1909. The extreme rarity of awarding a breech-loading rifle to indigenous chiefs is emphasized in TNA G 8/908, unfol.: Gov DOA to Kommando Schutztruppe, 3 June 1909 (draft).
106. BAB R 1001/7778, fol. 196: Gov DOA to RKA, 11 November 1911; cf. *Deutsch-Ostafrikanische Zeitung* 8, no. 7 (1906), 17 February; further Archiv der Erzabtei St. Ottilien: von Hassel, *Der Militairbezirk Mahenge im Aufstand 1905*, 30, 65.
107. Sunseri, "The War of the Hunters," 141.
108. Ibid., 119.
109. HUB MfN, Zool. Museum S III Fromm, Hunting Diary, Entry 26 June 1908.
110. Already in November 1905, Governor von Götzen decreed that any tusk obtained remained the property of the finder, see BAB R 1001/7776, fol. 238: Circular, 11 November 1905. The alleviation was heavily criticized, cf. "Sonderbare Finanzpolitik," *Deutsch-Ostafrikanische Zeitung* 9, no. 4 (1907), 26 January.

111. Oral testimony by Mzee Camelius Kiango of Nandete, interviewed 5 September 1967, in *Records of the Maji Maji-Rising*, ed. GCK Gwassa and John Iliffe (Dar es Salaam, 1967), 27-28; BAB R 1001/812, unfol.: Sixth session of the governor's council, 18/19 May 1906; "Nachrichten aus der Mission," *Missionsblätter* 11 (1906-7): 82 (Kwiro near Mahenge); *Deutsch-Ostafrikanische Zeitung* 9, no. 21 (1907), 25 May; *Deutsch-Ostafrikanische Zeitung* 10, no. 27 (1908), 16 April; *Deutsch-Ostafrikanische Zeitung* 10, no. 35 (1908), 13 May (Morogoro); BAB R 1001/814, fol. 168: Liwale to Gov DOA, 28 March 1909.
112. Felicitas Becker, "Sudden Disaster and Slow Change: Maji Maji and the Long-Term History of Southeast Tanzania," in *Maji Maji. Lifting the Fog of War*, ed. James Giblin and Jamie Monson (Leiden, 2010), 295-321.
113. *Amtlicher Anzeiger für Deutsch-Ostafrika* 8, no. 11 (1907), 1 June. Surviving statistics measure the reserve at 1,500 square kilometers, cf. TNA G 8/910, unfol.: List of wildlife reserves.
114. *Deutsch-Ostafrikanische Zeitung* 11, no. 13 (1909), 17 February; Fonck, *Deutsch-Ostafrika*, 514; Besser, *Raubwild und Dickhäuter in Deutsch-Ostafrika*, 64-65; TNA G 21/411, fol. 2: Wilhelm Grolp to Gov DOA, 7 January 1912; see also Neckschies: *Safarizauber*, 77; Christoph Schulz, *Auf Großtierfang für Hagenbeck. Selbsterlebtes aus afrikanischer Wildnis* (Dresden, 1921), 53-54.
115. Besser, *Raubwild und Dickhäuter in Deutsch-Ostafrika*, 48; Neckschies, *Safarizauber*, 75, 77; Schomburgk, *Wild und Wilde im Herzen Afrikas*, 317-61.
116. MMRP, *Collected Papers*, Department of History, University College of Dar es Salaam 1968, no. 8/68/1/1: EE Kazimoto: The Assault on Mahenge Boma.
117. MMRP, *Collected Papers*, Department of History, University College of Dar es Salaam 1968, no. 9/68/1/4/19, Martin Mlagani, interviewed 7 May 1968 in Fimbo.
118. DITSL, von Hassel, *Ein Tagebuch aus Ostafrika*, 51. Von Hassel uses the expression *shetani*. On the *shetani* cult cf. Linda L Giles, "Spirit Possession and the Symbolic Construction of Swahili Society," in *Spirit Possession, Modernity, and Power*, ed. Heike Behrend and Ute Luig (London, 1999), 142-64.
119. Axel Köhler, "Half-Man, Half-Elephant. Shapeshifting among the Baka of Congo," in *Natural Enemies. People-Wildlife Conflicts in Anthropological Perspective*, ed. John Knight (London, 2000), 50-77.
120. Cf. Iliffe, *A Modern History of Tanganyika*, 11; on the possibility of crossing the boundaries between humans and animals see Alice Werner, *Myths and Legends of the Bantu* (London, 1968), 24, 83, 93; Marks, *Large Mammals and a Brave People*, 38.
121. Morris, *Animals and Ancestors*, 234-35; James Sutherland, *The Adventures of an Elephant Hunter* (Long Beach, 2002 [¹1912]), 70; Innozenz Hendle, "Erinnerungen aus meinem Missionsleben in Deutsch-Ostafrika," *Missionsblätter* 7 (1903): 25.
122. *Deutsches Kolonialblatt* 3 (1892): 562; cf. Larson, "A History of the Mahenge (Ulanga) District," 46-47; Sutherland, *The Adventures of an Elephant Hunter*, 41-42, 53-54.
123. Innozenz Hendle, *Die Sprache der Wapogoro (Deutsch-Ostafrika) nebst einem deutsch-chipogoro und chipogoro-deutschen Wörterbuche* (Berlin, 1907), 106, 152.

 CHAPTER 4

Colony or Zoological Garden?
Settlers, Science, and the State

> Whether it is not in the character of the German to convert theory into practice, or to grasp the fact that without common sense it is of little value; whether members of a nation still deeply stamped with the impress of a century's red-tapism and militarism find it difficult to shake off such characteristics when out in the Colonies, and thus start at a disadvantage, need not be considered here.
> —Louis Hamilton, "Colonial Education in Germany," *United Empire* 2 (1911): 27–28.

A few months after his return from action as military officer in the Maji Maji campaign in German East Africa, Hans Paasche, then twenty-five years of age, published an article in the *Deutsch-Ostafrikanische Zeitung* entitled "Kolonie oder Zoologischer Garten." Paasche had been deployed in the quelling of Maji Maji in the Rufiji district and used the opportunity for a few months of hunting in the Maasai Steppe at the end of his official duties.[1] Thus familiarized with the state of game in the north and south of the German colony, Paasche rose to criticize the widely held conviction that progress and development were incompatible with the presence of larger game. Instead, he argued that, the problems of crop devastations and disease transmission from game to livestock notwithstanding, the colony's wildlife could be beneficial for colonial development if the administration followed the Kenyan example of opening the country to wealthy tourist hunters. Railways, a tourist infrastructure, and reasonable game laws with expensive licenses would help to preserve East Africa's "living monuments" for posterity. The question of "colony or zoological garden," Paasche concluded, was wrongly put. Game was no obstacle, but could be an integral part of colonial development.[2]

Paasche's article was part of an ongoing controversy after Maji Maji on how wildlife could be reconciled with agricultural development in a colony that was increasingly turning into a settler society. "Colony or zoological garden" became an oft-quoted catchword of contemporary debates, and the stark alternative it encapsulated makes the years after Maji Maji a decisive period for the future of Tanganyika's wildlife. Problems and developments previously overshadowed by the war came to the fore and caused such conflicts that in May 1907, a German newspaper counted the game ordinance among those governmental measures whose overall utility was fundamentally at odds with the bad blood it caused among both Africans and European colonists.³ This chapter traces these discussions and places the regulation of hunting in the colony at the intersection of four partially conflicting developments: the growth of white settlement and the increased presence of white commercial ivory hunters; the discovery of the wildlife's ecology of disease; the emergence of a small, but well-connected lobby of wildlife conservationists in Germany; and the imperative of colonial reform under the governorship of Albrecht von Rechenberg. The debate pitted settlers "on the spot" against visiting hunter-conservationists and exposed the cleavages within the white settler society. It contrasted the embarrassment of German malpractice with an idolized model of tourist game utilization in British Kenya, and it subjected animals to the conflicting authorities of a development-oriented veterinary science and a conservationist-minded zoology. If in 1903, merely the "expertise" of hunters like Wissmann or Schillings had shaped colonial politics of wildlife, now conflicting "scientific" authorities tried to bring their influence to bear on the revision of the game laws.

The Settler's Game

Maji Maji represented a watershed in the politics of wildlife in German East Africa. It marked the extension of colonial control over the ivory trade also in the less accessible southern districts, and imperial decision makers came away with the insight that the access to wild animals was a highly political and sensitive issue that had contributed to the outbreak of the war. This belief prevented the government from further circumscribing Africans' hunting, at least for a few years. The fact that the game laws had counted among the grievances that unleashed Maji Maji was, however, not the only issue that made a reform of the game laws an urgent necessity. The politics of wildlife were enmeshed in the broader reform-oriented realignment of colonial policies in the aftermath of the war and must be situated at the intersection of several overarching developments that spanned colony, metropole, and other empires, especially the British. These included the increase of white settlement, changing perceptions of the disease ecology of wildlife, the growth of an influential wildlife conservation lobby in Germany, and the colonial reform policies associated with the names of colonial secretary Bernhard Dernburg and governor Albrecht von Rechenberg.

The growth of white settlement after the turn of the century marked the beginnings of an actual colonial society in German East Africa. This changed the climate of political debates. A new interest group appeared on the scene and staked its claims to participate in decision making of colonial politics. The nature of colonialism in German East Africa shifted markedly toward "settler colonialism,"[4] which was characterized by a multipolar structure of negotiation between imperial metropole, local administration, indigenous population, the settler community, and the colony's wildlife. Its other distinguishing features were a "structure of privilege" and the principle to organize and distribute resources, rights, and political and economic participation along the racial divide.[5] Settlers came to claim wildlife as "their game" and this agenda constituted a serious challenge to governmental wildlife policies after Maji Maji.

White settlement in the colony was gradual, uneven, and largely concentrated in "hotspots" like the Usambara Mountains or the plains around Mounts Kilimanjaro and Meru. First attempts date back to the late 1890s and entered an "experimental phase" around 1900. Doubts about the economic viability of white settlement and Europeans' capability to acclimatize to the tropical climate were widespread, so that preference was given to applicants whom the government deemed to be already "acclimatized" or who had otherwise proven their capacity to persevere under frontier conditions. A few German expatriates, often former members of the Schutztruppe, Greeks, "Palestinian," and "Russian" settlers of German origin, and especially South African Boers were admitted to test the suitability of the country for white colonization. Their numbers remained quite small—in January 1906, some 397 Afrikaners occupied 126 homesteads on the foothill of Mount Meru.[6] It was not until after Maji Maji that the "main phase"[7] of European settlement began. The wars in Germany's two biggest and most important colonies, the prominence of colonial politics in the so-called Hottentot elections in 1907, and vigorous propaganda by the colonial organizations in the *Kaiserreich* had all drawn attention to the overseas colonies. Together with the government's colonial *Reformpolitk*, these developments coalesced to attract a relative, yet significant increase of German settlers: in 1898, the European population of the colony classified as settlers, planters, and farmers (i.e., not including the administrative, military, commercial, or missionary personnel) had amounted to a mere 57. Their number increased almost six-fold to 315 in 1906, and by 1912, some 758 of a white male population numbering 3,200 tried to wrench a living from a farm or plantation.[8]

The significance of hunting for the white settler community can be gleaned from the lists of European license holders that were compiled on the basis of obligatory reports required from the stations since 1903.[9]

Published in the official gazette, these lists rendered legitimate hunters visible and controllable for district stations. However, they soon attained a function beyond a mere legal technicality as being listed became a form of social display, distinguishing those who afforded to hunt and shared in the ritual domestication of land and nature. At the same time, the lists are a valuable source for probing the widespread rhetoric that every European coming to East Africa automatically turned a hunter. They reflect how wildlife policies became ever more restrictive and refined, and how these policies shaped and determined the social composition of hunters by introducing distinctions of race, wealth, and class. In short, they reveal the internal tensions of the settler community.

Significantly, neither nationality nor gender were mentioned in the lists, as hunters were self-evidently taken to be white and male. The number of women who took out a license was so infinitesimal that the occasion was marked in the statistics by either adding the first name or "Frau."[10] With the introduction of *große* and *kleine Jagdscheine* from 1909 onward, the list took on an additional function of social differentiation within colonial society. It distinguished those hunters who had the means to pay the 750 rupees for a *große Jagdschein* from those who only afforded the *kleine Jagdschein* for 50 rupees. Settlers who hunted on cheap district licenses were not mentioned at all. Starting with the last quarter of 1911, license holders were further divided into residents and visitors, and the introduction of an additional permission for the hunting of up to two elephants in 1912 added a further element of distinction: any reader perusing the *Amtliche Anzeiger* could see who afforded the luxury of shooting elephants. Figure 4.1 gives a rough idea of how the sale of hunting licenses fared in relation to the overall development of the white population in German East Africa.

Again, sources are unreliable and hardly comprehensive, yet sufficient to illustrate general trends. The figures between 1904 and 1909 indicate that the sale of hunting licenses increased in pace with the male population. Colonial society was a masculine society in which hunting played an important role to assert and define imperial manhood. "He must not be a man," stated the *Deutsch-Ostafrikanische Zeitung* in 1901, "who comes out here and does not have the sacred wish to pit his courage and pluck with the primeval strength of lions and buffaloes."[12] Those who hunted regarded it as defining their imperial selves; those who did not hunt still talked about it. Yet, the statistics are insensitive to the geography of white males' residence. While the administrative staff and merchants based in Dar es Salaam would afford a license only when traveling into any of the game-rich areas, the percentage of men in possession of a license was, for example, considerably higher in the settlement areas in Usambara or around Kilimanjaro.[13] Finally, the graph indicates a noticeable drop in

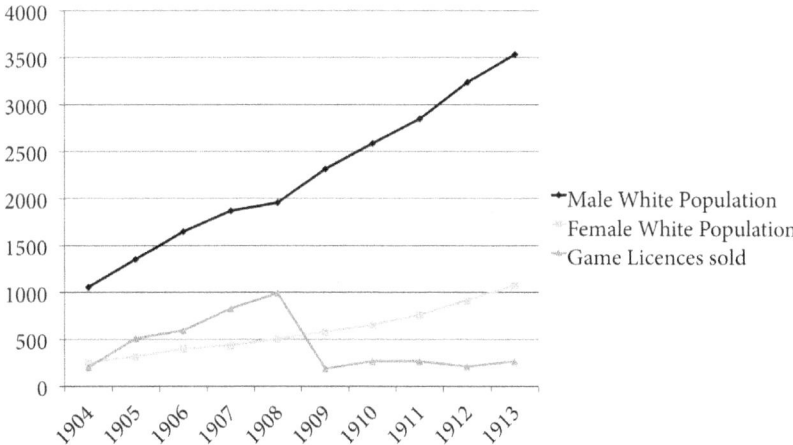

Figure 4.1. Sale of hunting licenses compared with population development, 1904–13.[11]

the sale of hunting licenses from 1909 onward, marking the impact of the reformed game ordinances of 1909 and 1911, respectively. Both entailed a drastic increase of the license fees and put the more prestigious species of game beyond the reach of the average hunter.

Official game policies forced the internal social differentiation of white hunting from 1909 onward. This becomes more palpable once the total number of sold licenses is unpacked to distinguish *große Jagdscheine* from *kleine Jagdscheine*. In 1909, some seventy-three hunters still afforded a *großer Jagdschein*. Afterward, the high price of this license and the ceiling on the numbers of game to be shot under one license resulted in a noticeable decrease. The administrative intention to render big game hunting a matter of plutocratic exclusivity was indeed put into practice. Names indicating Afrikaner origin, or those bearing the attribute of a *Jäger* or *Elefantenjäger* as their prime occupation vanished from the lists. The number of *kleine Jagdscheine* bought by residents of the colony increased; the sale of the specific elephant licenses introduced by the revised ordinance in late 1911 remained low: in 1912, there were thirty, one year later twenty-one hunters applying for permission to shoot one or two elephants. These developments do not mean that white colonists hunted less—not featured in the statistics is, for example, a new one-day license that was introduced in 1908. It allowed the shooting of most antelopes and gazelles for the small fee of 5 rupees. But the statistics mirror how the fiscal needs of the state, conservationist pressure, agriculturalists' interests, and hopes to encourage tourist hunting combined to make hunting a socially differentiated performance, with the prestigious species reserved for prestigious hunters. The few lists that register the occupations of license holders illustrate the increasing social exclusivity of big game hunting in German East Africa. The holders of *große Jagdscheine* and elephant licenses were almost exclusively hunters with an aristocratic or military background.

The growth of white settlement in the colony influenced the politics of wildlife in at least three ways. The practice of hunting became an arena for negotiating settler identities; the claim to hunting constituted a vehicle of staking broader claims against the government; and the extension of white ranching and farming made wildlife and wildlife-transmitted diseases the subject of fierce political and scientific controversies.

Hunting became an arena in which conflicting identity politics were played out. With the growth of white settlement, reference to the German hunting ethic of *Weidgerechtigkeit* became more widespread. Already in Germany, recourse to *Weidgerechtigkeit* had gained salience after 1849 when game laws granted an increasing number of people access to wild animals. *Weidgerechtigkeit* came to be invoked as a category to distinguish "proper" hunters from *Schießer, Aasjäger, Sonntagsjäger,* or *Jagdprotzen*—derogatory terms to denigrate all those who allegedly lacked ethical attitude, merely butchered game, shot indiscriminately, or hunted for self-presentation, as an occasional pastime or the pursuit of records. The *weidgerecht* hunter, on the other hand, claimed to be qualified by character, attitude, and respect toward the game, which obliged him, among others, to hunt with restraint, avoid suffering, observe the mating seasons, or spare foals and females.

The importance of *Weidgerechtigkeit* in the colonial context was not that hunters actually complied with its pretensions—sources on colonial hunting abound with examples to the opposite—but that it provided a convenient language of inclusion and exclusion. The most prominent attempt to foster the ties between the dispersed settlements of the white German community in the colony through the communication of a German hunting ethos was the *Ostafrikanische Weidwerk*. Published as a monthly supplement to the *Deutsch-Ostafrikanische Zeitung* between 1905 and 1907, it provided a forum, however short-lived, for anecdotes, self-congratulatory distinction or criticism of visiting hunters who traded themselves as wildlife experts home in Germany. Above all, the invocation of *Weidgerechtigkeit*, in this publication as in general, was a means to vilify the hunting of others as wanton and indiscriminate shooting. Although sportsmanship and *Weidgerechtigkeit* in fact shared many values, British sportsmanship was portrayed as fundamentally opposed to German hunting by reducing it to the mere striving for records. The experiment of Boer settlement on Mount Meru was a particularly convenient target for the identity formation of German colonists because a considerable number of these

Afrikaners made their living from hunting and the exchange of wildlife products against grain and vegetables with local Dorobo and Chagga traders.[14] Behind the harsh bashing of the Boers as innate game butchers were anxieties over the respectability of the white settler community and the superiority of *weidgerecht* German attitudes toward the game. Yet, *Weidgerechtigkeit* was not only a language to express environmental chauvinism and prescribe certain codes of behavior to potentially subversive whites. Hunting also provided an idiom in which more material interests could be framed and negotiated. Critique of Boer hunting and depredations among the game was often associated with implicit and explicit criticism of a governmental policy accused of discouraging German settlers at the same time it alienated valuable farming and pastoral lands to individuals who were regarded as belonging to an "inferior race."[15]

The same mechanism of stabilizing the colonial self, criticizing governmental policies, and marginalizing an unwanted social group in the colony was at work in German settler's vilification of white commercial ivory hunters of non-German origin. For all its emphasis on conservation and the extension of reserves, the 1903 game ordinance had also made commercial elephant hunting extremely attractive to nonindigenous hunters. Contrary to Kenya and the other surrounding British colonies, German East Africa continued to allow unlimited shooting. Anyone who paid the 10 rupees for a license could go after the pachyderms, the sole further obligation being the payment of 100 rupees or the return of one tusk of each elephant killed to the next government station. The appeal of unlimited shooting turned the elephant districts of German East Africa into a haven for adventurers, fortune makers, and a rough and rugged lot of white professional ivory hunters. A considerable number of these commercial hunters were of British imperial and often South African origin. But subaltern employees and struggling settlers, too, turned at least temporarily to elephant hunting for a living. The government was hesitant to come down on these ivory harvesters because of the support granted by some of them during Maji Maji. Yet, the practice faced mounting criticism from both the German colonists in East Africa and the emerging wildlife lobby in Germany. Both protested against the butchering of a "national" economic asset by foreign freebooters and desperados, exploiting the fact that the most notorious of commercial ivory hunters were "other whites" of non-German origin. This, together with their itinerant lifestyle and the exploitative nature of their business, made them a preferred target for accusations of becoming *washenzi Uleya*, the East African variety of "going native" and the equivalent of the "low and licentious" white subalterns in other European empires.[16] Criticism of commercial ivory hunting thus formed part of a broader debate about the German character of the colony, the maintenance of colonial prestige, the stabilization of racial boundaries, and the sustainable development of the colony.

The increase of German colonists resulted further in the monitoring and criticism of the government's actions from within. Wissmann and Liebert had been able to draft and enact their game ordinances in 1896 and 1898 more or less independently, and in exchange with district officials and colonial department only. Game legislation after Maji Maji took place in an imperial public sphere that consisted of wildlife lobbyists at home and German settlers in the colony. The community of European colonists was small, heterogeneous, and vociferous. They founded associations, utilized their connections to the prosettlement factions in German colonial circles, and voiced their opinion in newspapers like the *Deutsch-Ostafrikanische Zeitung* in Dar es Salaam or the *Usambara-Post* in Tanga.[17] Already the 1903 game regulations had met the settlers' fierce criticism for they felt it discriminated the German frontiersman against Africans. The Usambara Planters' Union (*Pflanzerverein Westusambara*), for example, responded with a draft ordinance that generously privileged resident colonists and administrative personnel over visiting sportsmen and indigenous hunters, and granted the settlers the right to hunt on their property. It was, however, halted in the governor's council in May 1905.[18]

From 1906 onward, the campaign for settler-friendly game regulations formed part of the general opposition against the postwar policy of reconstruction and reform under von Rechenberg, who succeeded von Götzen as governor. This opposition was framed in an overtly nationalist and racialist rhetoric, and it emphasized the heroism of white frontiersmen, the harshness of settler life, the lack of other spare time distractions, and the need to provide farmworkers with the occasional game meat in the settler's daily "struggle for life." Politics of distinction against the allegedly indiscriminate slaughtering of game by British, Boer, and African hunters predominated, but the colonists' pivotal demand was the entitlement to hunt on one's own landed property without the need to take out a license.

The relationship between hunting and property rights in land was awkwardly poised between contradictory legal practices in colony and metropole. A policy that dissociated property in land from the right to appropriate the game living on it smacked of the aristocratic prerogative that had governed German hunting laws prior to 1848–49.[19] The colonial game laws were predicated upon the assumption that the appropriation of wild animals in the precolony had been free to anyone.[20] Treating wild animals as *res nullius* was the logical prerequisite for the imposition of state custody and the transformation of wildlife into public property. With the introduction of the first codified game laws, the right to hunt, capture, or breed all species declared as game had to be granted by the state in the form of a license. While in Germany, the right of killing and capturing game (*Jagdrecht*) had become tied to the possession of landed property and was thus one of the few revolutionary rights that was retained after the revolution of 1848–49,[21] the colonial administration acted like an early modern European territorial ruler. It never positively acknowledged the right to hunt as a part of the property in land for essentially two reasons. On the one hand, the disputed character, if not outright denial, of indigenous property rights would have resulted in endless conflicts about the allotment of hunting entitlements. On the other hand, the dissociation of hunting rights from landed property meant to retain state control over the private utilization of wildlife.[22] Individual landowners could thus be prevented from managing wildlife on their land for their own use or as an estate for tourist hunters. Landowners were only entitled to shoot game damaging fields or plantations, and they could prevent other hunters from trespassing on cultivated land. These were, however, concessions by the state, not rights. By claiming mere stewardship over a public property, but not ownership of wild animals, the state also shed off any responsibility for wildlife damage.

However, the growth of white settlement made wildlife control in the vicinity of farms and plantations an ever more urgent issue. Game damage jeopardized agricultural development. Faced with colonial authorities who defied remuneration for wildlife damage, but obliged every settler to take out a license in order to exert wildlife control, settlers were increasingly enraged and bitter about governmental hunting policies.[23] In November 1904, a furious settler scathed the game ordinance for granting undue protection to zebras and buffalo, in his eyes the foremost transmitters of diseases to healthy livestock. His protest culminated in the demand to turn "our East Africa into a colony, not a zoological garden." The wildlife debates that followed had their catchy slogan.[24]

The Game of Science—Wildlife Ecology and Diseases

The relationship between wildlife conservation and agricultural development was the foremost issue dominating the wildlife debates from 1905 onward. The question of the overall compatibility of wildlife conservation and livestock cultivation was not only linked with the growth of European settlement, but also with the government's intentions to improve indigenous agricultural production. A report by the government's medical department in 1906 emphasized the importance of a healthy livestock to the development of the colony: "all economic enterprises" would depend on cattle in one form or another. Hides constituted a considerable export commodity; small-scale settlement was almost impossible without cattle-breeding; cotton plantations needed oxen for ploughing the ground, while other forms of cultivation depended on livestock for additional income and valuable manure.[25] Like African labor, livestock was considered a locally available productive resource that required conservation and rational utilization.

The heightened awareness to livestock diseases fits in with the more "scientific" approach to colonialism that is usually associated with the governorship of Albrecht von Rechenberg and the introduction of Bernhard Dernburg as colonial secretary in 1906–7. But the issue had come to the fore well before both took office. From the turn of the century onward, livestock had recovered enough from the rinderpest pandemic of the early 1890s to become a noteworthy economic factor again. Especially in the areas of white settlement in the northern part of the colony, the trade in cattle gradually replaced ivory as the prime commercial commodity. The recrudescence of various epizootics, including an outbreak of sleeping sickness in Uganda that spread into German territory in 1902, forced the colonial government to promote scientific investigation into the ecology of these diseases. Establishing the exact role of various wildlife species in the transmission of rinderpest, east coast fever, and, especially, human and animal trypanosomiasis, became a vital question on which the agricultural productivity of the colony appeared to hinge. The debates that followed brought about a decisive shift in the rationales that governed hunting and wildlife legislation in general. If heretofore, it had been mainly the political economy and ecology of ivory that mattered, the economics of wildlife and its appropriation was now equally governed by a more general ecology of wildlife and disease that pertained to game animals beyond elephants.

Historical research on tropical medicine in German East Africa has so far mainly focused on the research and medication of human sleeping sickness and its questionable scientific and administrative practices.[26] More recently, the European and transimperial character of the scientific utilization of Africa as a "living laboratory" has been stressed, again with human sleeping sickness as its focus.[27] However, wildlife-related diseases were equally transcending colonial and imperial boundaries, necessitated scientific cooperation, and evoked measures at the control of African environments and the movement of human and animal bodies.[28] Arguably, nagana, the animal variety of trypanosomiasis was no less important, for both diseases were intimately related. Research into the etiology, ecology, and medication of nagana actually predated research in human sleeping sickness. Contemporary scientists regarded the study of human sleeping sickness as a subfield of the trypanosomiasis problem in general.[29] Furthermore, measures developed to control and eradicate nagana were afterward transferred to the colonial treatment of sleeping sickness a few years later. Attempts to inoculate and then isolate the bodies of infected hosts from the vector were first made in the realm of animals.

Of all the major animal-related diseases the Germans encountered in East Africa, only the virus-borne rinderpest was already familiar from Europe, although the disease was long not recognized by veterinarians as the same disease but referred to as *Rinderseuche* or with the Swahili term *sadoka*.[30] The etiologies of both east coast fever (a form of theileriosis) and trypanosomiasis were largely unknown at the time. Both are vector-borne diseases in which the protozoan parasite causing the infection is transmitted by an invertebrate vector. The vectors are ticks of the genus *Rhipicephalus* in the case of east coast fever, and tsetse flies of the genus *Glossina* in the case of human and animal trypanosomiasis. The protozoa are ingested by the vector when it feeds on the blood of an infected host, which are primarily wildlife, livestock, and, in the case of sleeping sickness, humans. Therefore, both diseases are distinguished by the complex and still not fully understood interaction between landscape, vegetation, wild and domestic animals, insects, protozoa, and humans.[31] Around 1900, scientists yet had to disentangle that wildlife served as a host for trypanosomes causing both human sleeping sickness and nagana. Equally, they were just about to establish that there existed different varieties and subspecies of *glossinae*, not all of which carry trypanosomes. Trypanosomes, however, are dependent on tsetse flies (and ticks in the case of east coast fever) for transmission, so that the range and distribution of tsetse fly directly govern the spread of sleeping sickness.

The problem of a disease-transmitting fly called tsetse had not escaped the attention of precolonial European explorers. Burton and his followers noticed that most domestic animals, but hardly any game species were susceptible to tsetse. Yet, the nature and transmission of the disease remained unknown. As late as the early 1900s, colonial newspapers and publications spread the opinion that animals were killed by some kind of poison transmitted by the fly.[32] According to ecologist John Ford and historian James Giblin, the virulent recrudescence of east coast fever and trypanosomiases after 1900 was a side effect of the devastating sweep of the great rinderpest panzootic.[33] The combined impact of the catastrophes of the 1890s—rinderpest, colonial conquest, famine, and smallpox—had resulted in the "breakdown" of a long-established ecological balance" between East African societies and their natural environment.[34] The temporary disappearance of tsetse flies after the death of their cattle and wildlife hosts initiated the collapse of a fragile and dynamic coexistence maintained by practices of management, which, according to Ford and Giblin, did not rest upon the separation from humans and animals from tsetse, but upon carefully balanced forms of "limited exposure." Rather than trying to eradicate tsetse populations, precolonial livestock management consisted of occasional but continuous, light exposure to infection that allowed cattle populations to acquire trypanotolerance. Ford and Giblin base their arguments upon evidence from Uzigua and Sukuma, but other pastoralist or agropastoralist societies might equally have fitted into that pattern.[35] These precolonial forms of environmental management and disease control succumbed under the combined onslaught of rinderpest and the afflictions of colonial warfare, famine, and smallpox. On the one hand, tsetse flybelts receded with the disappearance of their preferred animal hosts, with the consequence of a local disappearance of tsetse infections as well. On the other hand, depopulation and the disappearance of cattle prevented vegetation control through grazing, clearance, and burning. Pastures turned to bush and provided an ideal habitat when tsetse flies returned together with trypanosome hosts like the ubiquitous bush pigs. The above discussed colonial interventions, such as the ban of fires and certain techniques of hunting, also had negative effects upon the local control of hosts and vector.[36] The almost complete eradication of cattle in areas affected by the rinderpest confronted societies with the necessity to rebuild stocks from cattle hitherto not exposed to trypanosome diseases. This made stocks especially vulnerable when trypanosome diseases reappeared early in the twentieth century, first among cattle introduced into Moshi in 1902.[37] The spread of east coast fever and nagana after the turn of the century thus was a prime example that natural hazards like pandemics were no "natural" and inevitable scourges of certain environments, but a product of political constellations and human as well as nonhuman agency.

The eradication of cattle and many ungulate species by the rinderpest panzootic meant that for a few years, the problem of disease transmission from wildlife to livestock virtually vanished from sight. Although colonial observers had noticed during *sadoka* or the *Rinderseuche* that the proximity of wild animals presented a danger to livestock through the transmission of viral diseases, little was done to investigate these interrelationships throughout most of the 1890s.[38] In 1902, the government afforded two veterinarians for hundreds of thousands of heads of cattle in an area of almost one million square kilometers.[39] When the protozoal livestock diseases reappeared in the settlement-prone northeast of German East Africa in 1902, the government was struck completely unprepared. Measures at their containment were developed only slowly.[40]

In the years that followed, colonialism came to replace the indigenous ecology of experience in dealing with livestock diseases with the authority of state and science.[41] The combined eruption and spread of human and animal trypanosomiases as well as east coast fever galvanized the colonial state into action. On the news of the outbreak of east coast fever and tsetse in early 1903, stations were advised to report on livestock diseases in their districts, collect specimens of flies, and curb all traffic and trade in animals from affected herds or regions.[42] In its actions, the government followed largely the recommendations of noted bacteriologist Robert Koch, the head of the Prussian Institute for Infectious Diseases (Preußisches Institut für Infektionskrankheiten) since 1891. Koch had for years been part of the imperial and transnational scientific networks that dealt with tropical diseases,[43] and his imperial careering exemplifies how the production of knowledge by the application of "science" constituted a powerful tool in the colonization of tropical environments. Since the early 1890s, he had investigated plague and various livestock diseases in India and Southern Africa, where his suggestions for prophylactic vaccination of especially settler-owned cattle against rinderpest contributed to prevent mortality rates of East African dimensions.[44] The German imperial administration both in Berlin and in the various African colonies relied upon Koch as official adviser whenever they were confronted with unknown tropical diseases. As early as 1895, infected horses sent to Berlin from Togo provided Koch with an opportunity to study tsetse and to dispute the transmission by poison.[45] Two years later in 1897, a first expedition to German East Africa enabled him to study several tropical diseases "on the spot." While the main focus of his work appears to have been on malaria prophylaxis and the question of the suitability of German East Africa for white settlement,[46] he also investigated into livestock diseases. Among them were cases of tsetse, which he initially took for an East African variety of surra, a protozoal disease of cattle he was familiar with from his research in India. Koch identified blood parasites of the genus *trypanosoma* as the cause of tsetse, confirming the discovery of the British entomologist David Bruce two years earlier in Rhodesia.[47] Already at this point, Koch was aware of the connection the British researchers in South Africa suspected between the spread of trypanosomes and the habitat of antelopes and buffalo. But the observation of immunity in wildlife in regions where tsetse flies prevailed first convinced Koch that artificial immunization was possible. As in the case of rinderpest before, Koch gave preference to the development of a reliable method to vaccinate livestock against nagana by inoculating virulent trypanosomes into cattle after the protozoa had passed through other species before. Indeed, his experiments resulted in immunized individuals, and further tests conducted by veterinary surgeons in the colony produced equally positive results.[48] For a while, it looked as if science would lead colonizers the African way, with limited exposure replaced by artificial inoculation.

By 1904, however, Koch regarded immunization no longer as a practicable option. British researchers had confirmed that also human sleeping sickness was caused by a blood-borne trypanosome and transferred by a fly of the *Glossina* type, suggesting that a comprehensive method was needed that tackled both forms of trypanosomiasis. More importantly, experiments during another expedition to Rhodesia in 1903 had revealed that animals apparently immune to nagana did still host infectious trypanosomes. "If we were to attempt to make whole herds of cattle immune in this way," Koch concluded in 1904, "we would produce more permanent sources of infection, and tsetse disease ... would in this way be permanently retained."[49]

The discovery of pathological protozoa in phenomenologically healthy animals made wildlife appear in a different light: every specimen was suddenly suspicious as a possible carrier of trypanosomes. Indeed, research by a British commission revealed that species like wildebeest, kudu, and buffalo acted as a reservoir for the disease.[50] In a lecture to the medical society of Berlin in October 1904, Koch joined the "judgement of all experienced experts" that the large game was the main reservoir for tsetse infection. Experience, Koch contended, had shown that in areas where the larger game was hunted out, also the tsetse fly and sleeping sickness disappeared. Therefore, he shifted the focus away from immunization as the leading paradigm to the isolation of the actual and potential hosts and herds of infection: decision makers should clarify if they preferred a good stock of wildlife or a good stock of livestock. "Both cannot live together on African soil."[51]

It remains a curious fact that, although Koch disputed the further coexistence of game and livestock, his assertion elicited but little response, possibly due to the ongoing colonial wars. Two further expeditions to East Africa served to refine his knowledge about trypanosome transmission. In 1906–7, experiments conducted around Lake Victoria led to the insight that game appeared not only as a threat to the livestock, but also jeopardized the health of the indigenous population—the indispensable labor force of the colony. In February 1908, Koch reiterated his accusation of the game in the plenary session of the German Agricultural Commission (Deutscher Landwirtschaftsrat) in Berlin. Under the eyes of Emperor Wilhelm II, Koch recommended to take South Africa as a role model (*Lehrmeister*) for the roll back of sleeping sickness and coast fever. South African authorities had allegedly made the experience that nagana had disappeared wherever the so-called big game—antelopes, buffalo, and so on—had been exterminated. Koch's advice was straightforward: "Wherever tsetse prevails, the so called large game (antelopes, buffaloes) as well as wild pigs" were to be exterminated.[52] In the discussion that followed, former governor von Götzen rose to the game's defense and proposed to restrict the large game's extermination to areas of human settlement, whereas in unpopulated areas, reserves should guarantee the preservation of wildlife. Koch accepted this reconciliation of the interests of settlers and wildlife conservationists and suggested to start with a local attempt at game extermination in the tsetse-infested areas at the bottom of the Usambara Mountains.[53] The effects of this experiment on the distribution of tsetse and the occurrence of nagana should then form the basis for the further strategy to tackle the tsetse.

Despite the compromise reached in the Landwirtschaftsrat, Koch's proposal provoked an enormous outcry and heated discussions within a few weeks of its publication in a German newspaper. In the colony, he earned applause from settlers and the more development-minded among colonial officials like Hans Zache, who reciprocated Koch's assertion that

> game and livestock are at constant war with each other, for the first is the most dangerous host of infections. As hard as it is for animal lovers and hunters, the alternative of zoological garden or livestock pasture must be for the latter. Our officials and colonists must stop to think and feel huntsmanlike but become determined, if not reckless economic politicians. The maxim "exterminate the game where we want to cultivate" can be mitigated into "conserve the game where we do not want to cultivate." But that's all.[54]

Opposition against Koch's proposition formed first and foremost among a small, but vocal and well-connected lobby of wildlife conservationists in Germany. For them, the word *Ausrottung*—extermination—was anathema, and they envisioned a different way how to reconcile wildlife, livestock keeping, and colonial development.

Gathering the Hunters—The Commission for Improvement of Game Conservation

The emergence of an influential wildlife lobby in the imperial metropole was the third critical factor that had a bearing upon the development of wildlife regulations in German East Africa after Maji Maji. Already in the late 1880s and 1890s, fears about the imminent extinction of the African elephant had spawned the formation of a Komitee zur Zähmung des Afrikanischen Elefanten (Committee for the Taming of the African Elephant) in 1895. It assembled a number of noted geographers, explorers, aristocrats, and zoo directors, including the Hamburg-based animal trader Carl Hagenbeck and Ludwig Heck, the director of the Berlin Zoo. The committee campaigned for the pachyderm's taming to achieve both the aims of its conservation and its utilization as a working animal that was adapted to the East African climate.[55] However, their campaign foundered within years for want of funds and viable perspectives.

The interest in imperial game conservation did not find another institutionalized form until the formation of a nongovernmental "commission for the improvement of game conservation in Germany's African colonies" in 1907.[56] Several factors were instrumental in this formation of a colonial wildlife lobby. A growing number of Germans had been to the colonies and digested their experience and especially their encounter with African wildlife in articles, best-selling books, and lantern-slide lectures.[57] Improved infrastructure and transport systems enabled more travelers and globetrotting big game hunters, like Prince Bernhard zur Lippe, to include German East Africa in their itineraries. Others again contributed their experience garnered on safari in neighboring colonies.[58] They all stood up in opposition to Koch's proposal and in favor of game conservation, but it was Carl Georg Schillings who rose to prominence as Germany's most influential campaigner for wildlife conservation in the African colonies. Having participated as German delegate to the London conference in 1900, he returned to East Africa twice on further expeditions dedicated to hunting, the collection of specimen for German museums and the live photography of Africa's wildlife. All of his trips had taken Schillings to the Maasai Steppe and Kilimanjaro, and on every return, he found the plains more depleted of game. In 1905 and 1906, he digested the compounded experience of his four expeditions in both British and German territory in two voluminous and best-selling books. Framing his personal experience in the image of a lost paradise of wildlife, Schillings predicted the imminent extinction of Africa's giant fauna if not strict measures were taken to ensure its sustainable utilization. Hence, he especially urged Germany's *weidgerechte* hunters to ensure the preservation of "natural monuments" (Naturdenkmäler) also in the German lands overseas.[59] Schillings became the mouthpiece and moving spirit of the colonial wildlife conservation lobby, which formed a distinct branch of the fledgling movement for nature protection in Germany.[60]

This growing social concern for the protection of nature was another crucial factor for the formation of the colonial wildlife lobby. As the example of Schillings demonstrates, the debates about *Naturschutz* in Germany provided the colonial hunting lobby with preservationist concepts and a language that allowed them to make their rather singular experiences understandable to a wider audience. The wildlife conservation lobby took over these concepts to refashion the established principle of sustainable resource management by exclusion. The language of German hunters that operated with concepts of *Hege* (conservation) and *Weidgerechtigkeit* was supplemented with terms like natural monument or *Naturschutz*, the protection of nature for nonutilitarian reasons. If these concepts were deemed thoroughly German, lobbying for colonial wildlife conservation was not. Critical impulses came from abroad, especially from the model provided by the British Society for the Preservation of the Wild Fauna of the Empire, which had founded in 1903 in the wake of the London Conference. Its German counterpart formed as the abovementioned commission in spring 1907. The Allgemeine Deutsche Jagdschutz-Verein (ADJV) and the Verein Hirschmann, two influential hunting associations, helped the commission on its way, and Duke Victor II of Ratibor became its first president. Despite the commission's comprehensive name that claimed to care for the improvement of game conservation in all German colonies, its foremost concern lay with East Africa. Little is known about its exact membership, but allegedly, it assembled "the most resonant names of the German hunting world."[61] Fritz Bley, one of the vanguard colonial officials in East Africa during the late 1880s and a member of the Pan-German League and the ADJV, had been among the foremost campaigners for the commission's establishment.[62] Other participants included the Schutztruppe lieutenant Max Weiß, a member of Duke Adolf of Mecklenburg's Congo expedition, the Pomeranian forester Hans Müller, botanist and zoologist in Wissmann's Congo-expedition in 1883–85, Prince Friedrich zu Solms-Baruth, a millionaire and large-scale estate owner in Brandenburg, the East-Elbian count Finck von Finckenstein, the Dukes of Mecklenburg and the hunter-naturalist Carl Georg Schillings.[63] Apart from a shared background of elite hunting, most members had an aristocratic or upper middle-class background, and their personal contacts were forged and fostered through the sociability of distinguished pastimes, such as gentleman riding or automobilism. The Duke of Ratibor, for example, a Silesian magnate with an estimated wealth of over 20 million marks in 1912, was not only a member of the Reichstag, the first chamber of the Prussian diet, and the exclusive circle constituted through the hunting invitations entertained by the Kaiser.[64] He was also president of the ADJV and a leading figure in the Kaiserliche Automobil-Club, as well as the Berlin Union-Klub, an exclusive association of gentleman riders drawn largely from the ranks of aristocracy and the military. Schillings and the Duke Adolf of Mecklenburg regularly called at the Union-Klub's premises in central Berlin.[65]

The tsetse controversy was a galvanizing moment for the commission and its conservationist cause. Just two days after Robert Koch had exposed his plans of local game extermination in the Landwirtschaftsrat, the commission petitioned the colonial office to remind them of their obligation to ratify and adhere to the provisions of the London Convention. Under the perhaps deliberate exaggeration that Koch had argued for the wholesale extermination of *all* African big game, the commission convoked a meeting in Berlin in April 1908 to organize opposition against Koch's proposal. Allegedly, the gathering was "very well visited." Apart from Fritz Bley, lectures were given by Karl Ludwig Sander, a tropical disease specialist who had himself investigated the tsetse problem on Kilimanjaro in 1902, and by the zoologist Paul Matschie. The latter was curator of the mammalian department at the Berlin Museum of Natural History, a personal friend of Schillings and the author of the standard volume on the German East African fauna at the time.[66] Sander and Matschie challenged the scientific validity of Koch's recommendation.[67] Sander deemed it more reasonable to tackle the vector rather than the reservoir and recommended to reduce the fly's preferred habitat of dense bush and undergrowth. Matschie disputed the close relationship between game and tsetse by drawing upon evidence derived from travelogues, existing British and German research, and a British Blue Book on wildlife conservation in the African colonies that had been published in 1906.[68] A memorandum submitted by the commission to the colonial office by the end of March 1908 reiterated the same point, stressing that the fly existed in areas without game and vice versa. As long as there existed no irrefutable proof for the connection between game and fly, game could advance the development of the colony by its conservation rather than its extermination. As nations all over the world were embarking upon the preservation of the remnants of their fauna, the preservation of the singular wildlife entrusted to Germany in her African colonies was not only an economic, but also an ethical imperative for a society that regarded itself as *Kulturvolk*.[69] The protests achieved their target: upon return from a journey to the United States and Japan, Koch was astonished by the fierce reactions and portrayed his argument as grossly misrepresented.[70] Consequently, the Reichskolonialamt refrained from taking up Koch's proposition, at least for the moment, and resorted to local attempts to eradicate the fly by destroying its habitat.

The wildlife lobbyists turned the territories of the German Empire into a moral space distinguished by certain ethical standards of human behavior toward wildlife. Few were as radical as Curt Hennings, lecturer in zoology at the Technical University in Karlsruhe, who questioned the ethical entitlement of humans to exterminate animals that presented no damage to life and limb.[71] For the majority of conservationists, it was no question that wild animals could and should be killed, but it mattered how, why, and by whom. The conservationist argument combined ethics, economics, and the colonial politics of race, class, and gender. Opposing Koch's view of wildlife as an impediment to development, conservationists framed wildlife as a valuable economic capital. The moral imperative of preservation, the German hunting ethos of *Weidgerechtigkeit,* and the economics of exploitation were combined in the argument for elite and tourist hunting as a source of income as demonstrated by the British in Kenya. Hunting as a form of "conspicuous consumption" for *weidgerecht* hunters and sportsmen from Europe and North America's leisured classes justified conservation and created additional revenue for the colony. It was also portrayed as a more sustainable utilization of the colonies' wild animals compared with the ongoing unfettered exploitation by commercial hunters. The wildlife lobby believed that restricting the number of animals allowed for one hunter would automatically curb indiscriminate shooting and educate the hunter to select his prey carefully. The hierarchies of the game should correspond with the hierarchy of licenses, which would, finally, reflect the hierarchies of race and class in the colonial situation. As argued above, the application of *Weidgerechtigkeit* as ethical yardstick to the colonies was not intended to inculcate German ideas of sustainable game management and parsimonious attitudes toward the hunted creature into Africans. It was a discourse of self-civilization and an assertion of imperial respectability supposed to stabilize the fragile boundaries between colonizers and colonized, and exclude those destabilizing elements like poor whites and commercial hunters deemed on the verge of "going native."

Wildlife and the Postwar Agenda of Colonial Reform

With its ethical implications and the rhetoric of "nature in trust," the debates about wildlife conservation were tied in with the broader agenda of colonial reforms that are usually associated with the "Dernburg era" in colonial policy between 1906 and 1910. This reform-oriented thrust of imperial policies in Berlin and Dar es Salaam is the last determining factor of wildlife policies after Maji Maji that requires consideration. The comprehensive crisis of the two wars in Germany's largest African colonies and a series of colonial scandals had resulted in a double change in political responsibilities both in metropole and colony. In April 1906, Governor von Götzen was replaced by the reform-oriented Albrecht Freiherr von Rechenberg, an East Prussian Catholic who had served as district official in Tanga and Dar es Salaam between 1893 and 1895 and as diplomat in Zanzibar between 1896 and 1900. In Berlin, Chancellor Bernhard von Bülow installed the liberal banker Bernhard Dernburg as head of the colonial department in September 1906. A few months later in May 1907, colonial affairs became institutionally independent from the foreign office with the establishment of the Reichskolonialamt. Dernburg consequently became the first secretary of state responsible for the colonies.[72]

Rechenberg in Dar es Salaam and Dernburg in Berlin initiated a policy of reform and reconstruction that strove to replace the oppressive and exploitative practices believed to have caused Maji Maji with a scientific, technocratic, and humanitarian form of colonization. Their approach acknowledged Africans as autonomous economic agents and envisioned indigenous peasant production as an indispensable pillar of the colonial economy. Colonialism was conceptualized as development that rested essentially upon the commercial stimulation of indigenous forms of production. This was to be achieved by an infrastructure that integrated coast and interior through the construction of railway lines, and by the introduction of German scientific expertise to direct and control development.[73] Dernburg and Rechenberg are usually portrayed as having pursued a rather consistent line of policy based upon shared convictions and ideas on "development."[74]

The issue of wildlife conservation, however, has so far been missing from these analyses and sheds some doubt on the uniformity of this reform agenda. Rechenberg took little interest in the ritualized or commercial killing of game and shared few of the sentimentalities that European big game hunters held toward African wildlife.[75] His take on hunting was pragmatic, and the regulation of wildlife interfaced with his ideas of the future development of the colony in two important ways. On the one hand, hunting inhibited the creation of a free market of indigenous wage laborers. As long as commercial hunting, be it for ivory, rhinoceros horns, or the sale of meat, hides, or trophies, remained accessible for indigenous hunters, the pursuit of game presented an economic alternative to agricultural cultivation or wage labor on European plantations. However, after the experiences of Maji Maji, Rechenberg clearly prioritized not to interfere too heavily with indigenous hunting, and he left it to the planters to create sufficient incentives for Africans to make wage labor attractive.[76] On the other hand, the fostering of indigenous cultivation was doomed to fail if hunting regulations impeded the defense of livestock and cultivations against depredations from or diseases transmitted by wildlife. Rechenberg's correspondence with the authorities in Berlin left little doubt about his conviction that the oppressive character of the existing hunting regulations had not only contributed to the outbreak of Maji Maji, but seriously impeded indigenous cultivation and environmental control. He criticized his predecessor's will to incorporate the provisions of the London Convention into the local regulations, which he regarded as biased one-sidedly to the interest of hunters.[77] Although Rechenberg's general ideas about colonial development earned him the deep enmity of the German settlers, their development-oriented attitudes toward the regulation of game shared some commonalities. Both were convinced that local interests, experience, and expertise should govern the regulation of wildlife, not the sensibilities of elite hunters far away in Europe.

Rechenberg saw himself confronted with the triple challenge of preventing further unrest after Maji Maji, appeasing a growing number of white settlers, and protecting livestock from diseases. Only in the last aspect, his ideas were congruent with that of the new secretary of state for the colonies Dernburg, whose notions about wildlife and the potential of its conservation were essentially shaped by the "wilderness experience" during his East African study trip between July and October 1907. This journey did not turn Dernburg into an ardent conservationist, but he encountered the arrangements for safari hunting in Kenya and he himself was eyewitness to the spectacular masses of plains game along the Uganda Railway. Both experiences taught him that Schillings and the wildlife lobbyists had a point about the economic potential of hunting tourism.[78] A few months after his return, Dernburg promised a reform of the existing East African Game Law that would acknowledge wildlife as a "considerable and advertising capital." The new ordinance should grant enhanced protection for the big game by introducing "rather expensive licenses" and a significantly increased shooting fee for elephants.[79] The solution to the conflict between "colony and zoological garden" lay in a spatialization of landscape use: while in areas of settlement and cultivation, game was to be driven out, reserves in largely uninhabited and uncultivated regions should secure the conservation of the wildlife.

Following his announcement to base his colonial policy upon "expert" knowledge by harnessing the sciences to the colonial project,[80] Dernburg delegated wildlife matters in the colonial office to no other than Carl Georg Schillings. Sources are silent how exactly Schillings was recruited, but Dernburg probably reacted to the combined challenge of lobbyist pressure from the commission and renewed diplomatic attempts from Britain to make Germany ratify the London Convention. At the time, Schillings enjoyed widespread admiration and the status of the foremost authority on African wildlife matters. In summer 1907, Emperor Wilhelm II had granted him the title of a professor in honor of his research on East African wildlife.[81]

Schillings produced yet another extensive report in which he commented on the future organization of hunting and wildlife conservation in East Africa. This time, he chose *Tierschutz* (animal protection) as his vantage point,[82] a vivid expression of his metamorphosis from gentleman hunter into a committed, if not fanatical conservationist. Many of his suggestions, like the introduction of a professional game department, were a result of transimperial learning. The British Blue Book of 1906 confirmed Schillings's earlier conviction that development and wildlife conservation could be reconciled if German East Africa followed the Kenyan example of encouraging tourist hunting. The cornerstone of his proposal was to turn big game hunting, especially the shooting of prestigious species like elephants, into the prerogative of a privileged few who could afford expensive hunting licenses. Species he believed to be threatened with extinction, like zebra, buffalo, and giraffe, were to be protected. However, Schillings departed from his earlier convictions in two significant ways. Now he adopted a global perspective on wildlife decline in East Africa. His argument was rife with the key words of preservationist discourse that had been missing in his earlier memorandum. And while in 1901, Schillings had cautioned against incorporating too many provisions of the London Convention, he now championed the international agreement and urged the colonial office to ratify it with slight modifications. Schillings's internationalism was in part strategic, for he hoped that the binding nature of an international agreement would curb the strong position of the governors in the colonies. The disciplining effect of the convention should guarantee a consistent policy of wildlife conservation independent of the personal attitudes and convictions of the respective governor.

Schillings's report was directed straight against Rechenberg and indeed, the revision of the game ordinance developed into an extended battle of drafts between the international-minded conservationist and the governor. After a flurry of draft ordinances, Rechenberg objected to any further discussion in late 1908 by circulating his final proposal to all district stations, arguing that continued exchange with Berlin would defer the reform of the hunting regulations for another year. Thereby, he forced Dernburg into accepting the ordinance. Schillings was ultimately sidelined and released from his duties soon after the ordinance was gazetted.[83]

"A Bad Game Law"

Although some commentators regarded it as a "weak compromise between Schillings's and Rechenberg's ideas" on wildlife policy,[84] the revised game ordinance was to a remarkable degree stamped by the governor's convictions. Significantly, when it was gazetted in November 1908, *Jagdschutz* was dropped from its title. Unlike previous regulations, the game ordinance did not draw a distinction between *Eingeborenenjagd* and "nonnative" hunting. The structuring principle of the ordinance was the employed weaponry. This virtually introduced the same distinction along "racial" lines. Because breech-loading rifles were prohibited for Africans, and no European settler would have hunted with an outmoded muzzle-loader, the cheapest license introduced by the new game ordinance was effectively a "native license."

With a price of 3 rupees, it cost less than a third of the previous standard license, and it allowed the hunting of all species including elephants, however with a muzzle-loading rifle only. The fact that stations were again ordered to hand out the 3-rupees license only to a few known and "trustworthy" *majumbe* or *maakida* who could also receive ammunition and muzzle-loaders shows that indigenous ivory hunting should still not be curbed entirely. The main rationale behind this license was, however, the prevention of damage to fields and villages.[85]

The other four licenses were intended to reflect the differentiated needs of settlers and visiting hunters. A new one-day license for 5 rupees that enabled the hunting of all antelopes and gazelles on a single day should allow flying visitors a cheap stint of hunting without the need to afford a full-scale safari.[86] A new annual district license of 25 rupees restricted hunting to the more common plains game (classified in category I) within the license holder's district of settlement, while the so-called *kleine Jagdschein* at 50 rupees enabled the hunting of the same species in the entire colony. Only the *große Jagdschein* allowed for the hunting of animals classified in category II. It comprised all animals estimated for their economic value, their rarity, or the prestige they bestowed upon their hunter: elephant, eland, giraffe, rhinoceros, and zebra. Its expensive price of 750 rupees or roughly 1,000 marks was a concession to the conservation lobby. In effect, the ordinance, with its two categories of game and the distinction between *kleine* and *große Jagdscheine,* introduced a colonial adaptation of the German distinction between *niedere* and *hohe Jagd*—the hunting of smaller, "ordinary" game, and of the prestigious, "noble" game. The *große Jagdschein* should attract high-profile hunting tourists and discourage commercial elephant hunters who had so far been charged the comparative trifle of 10 rupees.[87] In turn, the shooting fees for all big game were dropped, apart from the extra charge for each bagged elephant. Hunters were now liable to pay 150 rupees or return one tusk, provided it had a minimum weight of at least 10 kilograms.

Although Dernburg had appeased the wildlife lobbyists that the new ordinance would include the extension of existing reserves, Rechenberg's ordinance actually entailed the latter's considerable reduction. It confirmed the earlier abolishment of the reserve in the Tabora district and decreed the removal of sanctuaries in the districts of Moshi, Kilimatinde, and Mwanza (the latter on Ukerewe Island was reestablished just a few months later). A general ban on elephant hunting, in force in the district of Moshi since 1903, was lifted, for the Kilimanjaro area was the most likely to attract tourist hunters. Among the nine reserves that were retained, only the abovementioned Upper Rufiji reserve was increased in size, benefiting from human depopulation after Maji Maji.[88] Drastic fines should sanction any infringement of the regulations. Hunting in reserves, or the shooting of animals classified in category II without the appropriate license incurred a sentence of three months or the payment of up to 5,000 rupees. Indigenous perpetrators were liable to corporal punishment or forced labor in chains.

As far as the other contested issues were concerned, the ordinance tried to appeal to both indigenous and settler agricultural development by the payment of bounties for the killing of "vermin" and by admitting any hunting to prevent damage from cultivated land. Trespassing of hunters on private or cultivated land was forbidden, yet there was no positive admission that landed property also entitled to the lawful appropriation of its game. And because the ordinance neither foresaw the creation of a game department nor a restriction of the number of animals to be shot under one license, core demands of the conservation lobby remained unaddressed.

If Rechenberg had ever expected his ordinance would exert a check on commercial ivory hunters, any such hope was dashed within weeks after its gazetting in early November 1908. Ironically, the first effect produced by the ordinance was a resurgence of ivory hunting in areas renowned for their remnant elephant herds. Facing a 75-fold increase in the fee for elephant hunting from 1909 onward, hunters made the most of their old licenses before they lost validity by the end of the year. In November and December 1908, Boer and German colonists alike raided the elephant haunts between the game reserves north and south of the Rufiji. In mid-December, some 26 shooting parties were camping in distances of about two hours from each other.[89] When the ordinance entered into effect in January 1909, further transintentional effects became apparent. The suspension of the ban on elephant hunting in the district of Moshi turned out as an invitation to the district's white settlement community to compensate the expensive license by rapacious elephant hunting. Ten days into the new year, the station had already sold 15 *große Jagdscheine,* most of them to Boer settlers and only one to the desired aristocratic sports hunter.[90] Instead of attracting Europe's hunting aristocracy, elephant hunting around Kilimanjaro was now in the hand of resident Greek traders, who hired penniless Boers as elephant hunters and paid the license fee for them. By March 1909, the elephants killed in the district of Moshi amounted between 60 and 80 so that the government declared the forests of Kilimanjaro a game reserve again to prevent the pachyderms' wholesale destruction.[91] District commissioners in other "elephant districts" criticized the revised ordinance as willfully sacrificing elephants to "professional butchers" trying to amortize their license fee as quickly as possible by indiscriminate shooting. Small tusks or those not valuable enough to warrant the payment of 150 rupees would simply vanish or were bartered against foodstuff with locals, who then brought in the tusks as "found ivory."[92] Only the district commissioner of Morogoro was pleased to announce that the station's revenue from hunting had increased considerably after the onslaught of white hunters on the elephant-rich woodlands between Kissaki and the Ruaha River.[93] The attempt to render elephant hunting exclusive turned out as completely futile as long as the number of elephants to be shot was not limited, too.

Confronted with the consequences of the ordinance on the ground, the government saw itself forced to modify its hunting regulations within weeks after their going into force. In order to avoid the impression of administrative incompetence,[94] Rechenberg objected to any changes in the substance of the ordinance and advised changes in the administrative practice instead. As early as the end of January 1909, he decreed that no station was entitled to issue more than three elephant licenses annually, with any further requests to be reported to and confirmed by the government. Not the amount of elephants to be shot by one hunter was restricted, but the amount of hunters. The first-come-first-serve principle introduced by this restriction triggered another wave of protest: commissioners in the elephant districts criticized that it did nothing to prevent itinerant commercial hunters to purchase their licenses elsewhere and then flock to the elephant districts. Hunters who were denied a license blamed the stations of unjust treatment of applications. The advocates of the rational *mise-en-valeur* of the colony's large game complained that restricting the sale of expensive licenses ran counter to the intention of increasing the fiscal revenue, while the champions of conservation and limited tourist hunting scathed the restriction's deterring effect upon globetrotting visiting hunters, who would hardly stand a chance to obtain one of the few licenses.[95] Yet, the restriction to three *große Jagdscheine* per district was maintained in 1910, with absolute preference to be given to residents of the district. One year later, the government even made the issuing of these licenses dependent on its previous consent: stations had to give reference about an applicant's "trustworthiness and reliability."[96] The central administration started to set up lists of "trustworthy" hunters as well as another register of those hunters who should be denied a license in the future. This so-called black list was the consequence of Rechenberg's encouraging the district station to resort to paragraph 7 of the game ordinance to address the misuse of the *große Jagdschein* by ivory harvesters. The paragraph allowed stations to deny hunting licenses to persons who had been sentenced for contraventions against property or the hunting regulations during the last five years, or if the applicant could "potentially jeopardize the public order." It also enabled stations to cancel the issuing of licenses if hunting by further license holders could "potentially endanger" the game stock of the district. Such loose definitions left ample room for administrative arbitrariness. Unsurprisingly, the black list featured most of the notorious commercial elephant hunters and reveals that the Boers around Kilimanjaro and Meru were strategically turned down by their respective district offices. In the German East Africa of 1910, access to the "royal game" of elephants and rhinoceroses was not an entitlement that could be claimed according to transparent principles, but a privilege arbitrarily bestowed by the government. Hans Paasche, therefore, criticized Rechenberg's ordinance not only as "a bad game law" but also a very German law in its obsession with order and principle: it was "identified as bad even by the government, but was nonetheless retained, for officials argued it would damage the reputation of the government to immediately alter a given law. Apparently, the law as such is more important than its purpose."[97]

The observation that the game law achieved its purpose very inadequately is corroborated by a set of further circulars issued by Rechenberg in early 1909. One interdicted the passing-on of breech-loading rifles to African hunters, another prohibited Europeans to hire indigenous hunters. Both suggest that those who could not afford to pay the expensive license had found strategies of evasion which, again, opened new opportunities for African hunters. In the face of the marked rise of hunting fees, white settlers and planters bought the cheap license for their African laborers and sent them hunting.[98] For the colonial administration, it was difficult, if not impossible to distinguish the furnishing of laborers with muzzle-loaders from the "hiring" of African hunters and "regular" relations of trade and exchange that included wildlife products. Hunter-gatherers like the Dorobo and Tindiga were particularly attractive as partners, for their use of spears and arrows was not covered by the game laws. Such exchange relations were common between traders of European or Indian origin, Maasai, Dorobo hunters, and the white settlers on Kilimanjaro and Meru, but also among the American, European, and Indian trading companies in Mwanza and Shirati who cooperated with Western Serengeti people in the procurement of a wide range of wildlife products.[99]

The few surviving annual reports of district stations unanimously state a relative rise in the sale of the cheapest license for 3 rupees, signifying a slight revival of African hunting. This scant evidence indicates that commercial hunting became attractive to new social groups such as former German Askari, who used the cheap license to supply a flourishing trade in horns and trophies.[100] In any case, Africans continued to hunt beyond the radar of the colonizers, refining their own "arts of resistance" (James C Scott), such as increased use of more passive and anonymous forms like pits and traps. Remaining pockets beyond the German radar still offered opportunities for elephant hunting by scattered groups of Makua and Dorobo hunters, for example around Kondoa-Irangi.[101] However, after Maji Maji, most indigenous hunting had been driven into obfuscation, and the majority of stations strictly observed the banned sale of gunpowder to Africans beyond the trusted *maakida* and *majumbe*. In fact, there is evidence to suggest that the recovery of game stocks and an increase in wildlife damage to cultivations reported by "almost all stations" was linked with the severe restrictions upon the sale of rifles and powder to Africans.[102] The continuing exclusion of Africans from the use of firearms promoted the erosion of local environmental control, which conflicted heavily with Rechenberg's aim to encourage indigenous agricultural production. Spear, bow, and arrow were hardly weapons suitable to ward off lions or to defend a field against crop-raiding elephants. Undoubtedly, the banned sale of powder was an important factor that increased local susceptibility to wildlife damage, especially when it hit societies already destabilized and depopulated by recurrent intensive colonial warfare or large-scale labor migration. Source material is very scarce and unevenly distributed, but suggests that the Western Plateau of Unyamwezi and the Maji Maji regions were particularly exposed. A vivid description of local environmental vulnerability as a consequence of colonial interventions is delivered by Edwin Hennig, who gained a deeper knowledge of the southeastern districts as a member of the German paleontological Tendaguru expedition between 1909 and 1911. Hennig found villagers along the Rovuma and Mbwemkuru Rivers exposed to damage by wild pigs, hippopotami, buffalo, eland antelopes, and elephants wandering in from Portuguese territory. In the immediate hinterland of Kilwa, he witnessed "mtama fields completely ravaged by criss-crossing elephant tracks" with villagers standing by "unable to do anything to defend their daily bread." Elsewhere,

> antelopes of all kinds intruded upon the new seedlings and trample what they do not feed. … Yet, it is not in the hands of the owners to protect themselves against so many enemies. It is not courage they are lacking. But the natives had to be deprived of their firearms after the last rebellion, and only very few are handed out for hunting purposes.

Hennig reported that even spear, bow, and arrow were forbidden to Africans.[103] Damage to fields by wildlife was a similarly serious problem in Unyamwezi. The very report that stated an "increased request of hunting licences" in Tabora had to admit that only 18 "native licences" were actually sold. Indeed, obtaining a license was quite futile when, as the district commissioner criticized, the "complete restriction of the sale of gunpowder" had made it impossible to African cultivators to prevent the "damage to their fields caused especially by roan antelopes and wild pigs." With devastations of cultivated land increasing, many of these agriculturists "had already been forced to leave their homesteads and settle elsewhere."[104] In Unyamwezi, another important factor contributed to the loss of environmental control: the absence of male adults.[105] Oskar Karstedt, who passed through central and northern Unyamwezi in 1910, unveiled the political ecology of colonial labor migration in Unyamwezi and identified the increased vulnerability to wildlife devastations as an often underestimated push factor that made people abandon their homesteads: of course, Karstedt argued, people have always been exposed to damage by wildlife.

> But then, they were in a position to defend themselves. Pitfalls, nets and large bags thanks to the possibility to purchase gunpowder enabled them to defend themselves and protect their property. Today, this is impossible; hunting with nets is prohibited and hardly an exception is made; and especially in the interior, the purchase of gunpowder is virtually impossible.[106]

Karstedt's observations show that the representatives of colonial rule were not merely agents of oppression but, at times, also advocated the interest of the African communities they administered. Karstedt or Prittwitz von Gaffron, the district official of Tabora in 1908-9, for example, argued in the name of local interests and human requirements in the discussion about wildlife preservation, which met the approval of Rechenberg. The reports from the lower ranks of the white colonial hierarchy also indicate that vulnerability to wildlife damage may well have been more widespread under the radar of German posts where the restriction of the sale of arms and powder could be enforced more rigidly. In any case, there is strong evidence that in many regions, African farmers did not experience the years of colonial reform under Rechenberg as an "age of improvement."[107] When the government collected material for an official memorandum on hunting and game preservation in 1912, the returned reports contained information on structural and reiterated wildlife damage in almost all districts. Additional sources from areas as diverse as Unyamwezi, Mahenge, Morogoro, Mkomazi, Dar es Salaam, Lindi, and Kilwa show that especially wild pigs had increased in phenomenal numbers, probably due to reasons similar to the spread of tsetse flies, that is, the conversion of once cultivated lands into thickets and coppice in the wake of warfare and population decline. Repeated government circulars reminded stations to temporarily lift the ban on game drives in order to get a grip on the recurring ravaging of indigenous plantations by wild pigs. These circulars once more reiterated the conviction that loss of wildlife control was a consequence of the bans of indigenous hunting techniques and the sale of gunpowder. As much as the enhanced vulnerability to wildlife damage were local and seasonal phenomena, colonial rule added a structural dimension to them by intentionally incapacitating Africans to exert control over their environments.[108]

Notes

1. The experience of Maji Maji played a considerable role in Paasche's (1881-1920) metamorphosis into an ardent pacifist and vegetarian. He later became a key figure of the alternative German youth movement. For an emphatic biography, see Werner Lange, *Hans Paasches Forschungsreise ins innerste Deutschland. Eine Biographie* (Bremen, 1995).
2. Hans Paasche, "Kolonie oder Zoologischer Garten," *Deutsch-Ostafrikanische Zeitung* 9, no. 10 (1907), 9 March.
3. "Licht und Schattenseiten des Wildschutzes in Ostafrika," *Tägliche Rundschau* no. 24, 30 May 1907.
4. The authoritative study on the growth of the German settler community in East Africa is Philippa Söldenwagner, *Spaces of Negotiation. European Settlement and Settlers in German East Africa, 1900–1914* (Munich, 2006).
5. Caroline Elkins and Susan Pedersen, "Introduction: Settler Colonialism: A Concept and Its Uses," in *Settler Colonialism in the Twentieth Century. Projects, Practices, Legacies,* ed. Caroline Elkins and Susan Pedersen (New York, 2005), 2–4.
6. BAB R 1001/700, fol. 189: Gov DOA to AA KA, 23 January 1906; *Deutsch-Ostafrikanische Zeitung* 7, no. 38 (1905), 23 September; Söldenwagner, *Spaces of Negotiation,* 58–70.
7. Söldenwagner, *Spaces of Negotiation,* 70.
8. Ibid., 54–83.
9. These lists were first compiled annually, from 1907 onward, about every three months and publicized in the official gazette (*Amtlicher Anzeiger*). Sometimes, first names or the places of residence were added, more often they were not, and in some years, names appear twice.
10. Also the lists of reserved hunting licenses in TNA G 8/909 contain not a single female name.
11. The figures of hunting licenses have been compiled from a count of the names as published in the *Amtliche Anzeiger für Deutsch-Ostafrika,* cf. *Amtlicher Anzeiger für Deutsch-Ostafrika* 5, no. 17 (1904), 2 July; *Amtlicher Anzeiger für Deutsch-Ostafrika* 6, no. 16 (1905), 1 July; *Amtlicher Anzeiger für Deutsch-Ostafrika* 7, no. 31 (1906), 22 September; *Amtlicher Anzeiger für Deutsch-Ostafrika* 8, no. 1 (1907), 12 January; *Amtlicher Anzeiger für Deutsch-Ostafrika* 8, no. 9 (1907), 27 April; *Amtlicher Anzeiger für Deutsch-Ostafrika* 8, no. 15 (1907), 13 July; *Amtlicher Anzeiger für Deutsch-Ostafrika* 8, no. 23, (1907), 5 October; *Amtlicher Anzeiger für Deutsch-Ostafrika* 9, no. 4 (1908), 15 February; *Amtlicher Anzeiger für Deutsch-Ostafrika* 9, no. 18 (1908), 12 September; *Amtlicher Anzeiger für Deutsch-Ostafrika* 9, no. 22 (1908), 4 November; *Amtlicher Anzeiger für Deutsch-Ostafrika* 10, no. 1 (1909), 13 January; *Amtlicher Anzeiger für Deutsch-Ostafrika* 11, no. 5 (1910), 29 January; *Amtlicher Anzeiger für Deutsch-Ostafrika* 11, no. 30 (1910), 10 September; *Amtlicher Anzeiger für Deutsch-Ostafrika* 12, no. 9 (1911), 22 February; *Amtlicher Anzeiger für Deutsch-Ostafrika* 12, no. 26 (1911), 15 June; *Amtlicher Anzeiger für Deutsch-Ostafrika* 12, no. 48 (1911), 15 November; *Amtlicher Anzeiger für Deutsch-Ostafrika* 13, no. 14 (1912), 16 March; *Amtlicher Anzeiger für Deutsch-Ostafrika* 13, no. 32 (1912), 26 June; *Amtlicher Anzeiger für Deutsch-Ostafrika* 13, no. 56 (1912), 28 September; *Gesetz und Recht für Deutsch-Ostafrika* 1, no. 22 (1912), 6 July; *Amtlicher Anzeiger für Deutsch-Ostafrika* 14,

no. 1 (1913), 4 January; *Amtlicher Anzeiger für Deutsch-Ostafrika* 14, no. 20 (1913), 16 April; *Amtlicher Anzeiger für Deutsch-Ostafrika* 14, no. 27 (1913), 21 May; *Amtlicher Anzeiger für Deutsch-Ostafrika* 14, no. 51 (1913), 17 September; *Amtlicher Anzeiger für Deutsch-Ostafrika* 14, no. 75 (1913), 31 December; *Amtlicher Anzeiger für Deutsch-Ostafrika* 15, no. 31 (1914), 22 April; *Amtlicher Anzeiger für Deutsch-Ostafrika* 15, no. 48 (1914), 27 June. The population figures are taken from *Die deutschen Schutzgebiete in Afrika und der Südsee 1910/11*, Statistik, 5; respectively, *Die deutschen Schutzgebiete in Afrika und der Südsee* 1912–13, 9.
12. *Deutsch-Ostafrikanische Zeitung* 3, no. 38 (1901), 28 September.
13. See for example TNA G 1/5, Annual Report for Mwanza 1908/09, Appendix 3.
14. For an exceptionally insightful contemporary analysis of the political ecology behind Boer hunting see BAB R 1001/238, fol. 151–99, Travel report by Hans Paasche [1906].
15. Cf. *Deutsch-Ostafrikanische Zeitung* 7, no. 23 (1905), 10 June; *Deutsch-Ostafrikanische Zeitung* 7, no. 30 (1905), 29 July.
16. See Harald Fischer-Tiné, *Low and Licentious Europeans. Race, Class and "White Subalternity" in Colonial India* (New Delhi, 2009).
17. Cf. Söldenwagner, *Spaces of Negotiation*, 215–22.
18. Cf. BAB R 1001/812, fol. 55–58: 3rd session of the Governor's Council, 15/16 May 1905.
19. The question if the colonial state had in fact established such a prerogative over hunting was controversially debated by legal commentators, see Ewald Lüders, *Das Jagdrecht der deutschen Schutzgebiete* (Hamburg, 1913), 8–23; Louis Pink and Georg Hirschberg, *Das Liegenschaftsrecht in den deutschen Schutzgebieten*, vol. 1 (Berlin, 1912), 161. On the early modern aristocratic *Jagdregal* in Europe, see Werner Rösener, *Die Geschichte der Jagd. Kultur, Gesellschaft und Jagdwesen im Wandel der Zeit* (Düsseldorf, 2004), 254–77, 348–71, and, for similar practices in England, Emma Griffin, *Blood Sport. Hunting in Britain since 1066* (Yale, 2007), 111–12.
20. For contemporary legal commentators confirming this assumption see Lüders, *Das Jagdrecht der deutschen Schutzgebiete*, 14; Hermann Edler von Hoffmann, *Einführung in das deutsche Kolonialrecht* (Leipzig, 1911), 118; Werner Stahl, "Zum kolonialen Jagdrecht," *Zeitschrift für Kolonialrecht* 13 (1913): 79.
21. Hiller, *Jäger und Jagd*, 37–56.
22. For the more liberal take on the matter by the British in South Africa, see MacKenzie, *The Empire of Nature*, 203, and Lance van Sittert, "Bringing in the Wild: The Commodification of Wild Animals in the Cape Colony/Province c. 1850–1950," *Journal of African History* 46 (2005): 269–91.
23. TNA G 8/54, unfol.: Siedentopf to Gov DOA, 27 March 1908; cf. Heinrich Pfeiffer, "Die Ostafrikanische Jagd- und Wildschutzverordnung," *Deutsch-Ostafrikanische Zeitung* 10, no. 34 (1908), 9 May; BAB R 1001/7776, fol. 152: Stuhlmann to AA KA, 22 November 1902.
24. *Deutsch-Ostafrikanische Zeitung* 6, no. 48 (1904), 26 November; EJ, "Nochmal Kolonie oder Zoologischer Garten," *Ostafrikanisches Weidwerk* no. 4 (1907); Hans Paasche, "Deutsch-Afrikanische Naturschutzparke," *Der Tag*, no. 198 (1911), 24 August.
25. BAB R 1001/6070, fol. 99: Report on the distribution of east coast fever by Surgeon Hoesemann, 26 September 1906.

26. See for example Mari Webel, "Ziba Politics and the German Sleeping Sickness Camp at Kigarama, Tanzania, 1907–14," *International Journal of African Historical Studies* 47, no. 3 (2014): 399–423; Christoph Gradmann, *Krankheit im Labor. Robert Koch und die medizinische Bakteriologie* (Göttingen, 2005), 229–52, 297–336; Wolfgang U Eckart, *Medizin und Kolonialimperialismus. Deutschland 1884–1945* (Paderborn, 1997), 340–49. For the British colonies in Africa see Helen Tilley, *Africa as a Living Laboratory. Empire, Development and the Problem of Scientific Knowledge 1870–1950* (Chicago, 2011), chapter 4; Kirk Arden Hoppe, *Lords of the Fly. Sleeping Sickness Control in British East Africa, 1900–1960* (London, 2003).
27. Sarah Ehlers, "Europeanising Impacts from the Colonies: European Campaigns against Sleeping Sickness 1900–1914," in *Pour une lecture historique de l'europeanisation au XXe siecle [Europeanisation in the 20th Century: The Historical Lens]*, ed. Matthieu Osmont et al. (Brussels, 2012), 111–26; Deborah J Neill, *Networks in Tropical Medicine. Internationalism, Colonialism, and the Rise of a Medical Specialty, 1890–1930* (Stanford, CA, 2012); Tilley, *Africa as a Living Laboratory*.
28. See Sunseri, "The Entangled History of *Sadoka* (Rinderpest) and Veterinary Science in Tanzania and the Wider World, 1891–1901," *Bulletin of the History of Medicine* 89, no. 1 (2015), 92–121; Clive A Spinage, *African Ecology. Benchmark and Historical Perspectives* (Berlin, 2012), part IV; Karen Brown and Daniel Gilfoyle, eds, *Healing the Herds. Disease, Livestock Economies, and the Globalization of Veterinary Medicine* (Athens, OH, 2010).
29. Robert Koch in a letter to Georg Gaffky, 31 August 1905, in Bernhard Möllers, *Robert Koch. Persönlichkeit und Lebenswerk 1843–1910* (Hannover, 1950), 303.
30. Sunseri, "The Entangled History of *Sadoka* (Rinderpest) and Veterinary Science in Tanzania and the Wider World."
31. On the epizootiology of east coast fever, see James L Giblin, "East Coast Fever in Socio-Historical Context: A Case Study from Tanzania," *International Journal of African Historical Studies* 23 (1990): 403–9. The ecology of sleeping sickness is treated, among others, in Spinage, *African Ecology*, 915–48; John Ford, *The Role of the Trypanosomiases in African Ecology* (Oxford, 1971), 1–12; Hoppe, *Lords of the Fly*, 5–9; James Giblin, "Trypanosomiasis Control in African History. An Evaded Issue?," *Journal of African History* 31 (1990): 59–65.
32. Burton, "The Lake Regions of Central Equatorial Africa, with Notices of the Lunar Mountains of the White Nile," 158; cf. Carl Claus von der Decken, *Baron Carl Claus von der Decken's Reisen in Ost-Afrika in den Jahren 1862 bis 1865. Nebst Darstellung von R Brenner's und Th Kinzelbach's Reisen zur Feststellung des Schicksals der Verschollenen*, ed. Otto Kersten (Leipzig, 1871), 37; Reichard, *Deutsch-Ostafrika*, 515–17; and Ernest Edward Austen, *A Monograph of the Tsetse-flies (Genus Glossina, Westwood) Based on the Collection in the British Museum* (London, 1903).
33. Ford, *The Role of the Trypanosomiases in African Ecology*, 86–90; Giblin, "East Coast Fever in Socio-Historical Context"; Giblin, "Trypanosomiasis Control in African History."
34. Kjekshus, *Ecology Control and Economic Development in East African History*, 126; Iliffe, *A Modern History of Tanganyika*, 163–65.
35. Examples of cattle keeping in tsetse-infested areas are provided by Kjekshus, *Ecology Control and Economic Development in East African History*, 53–54; Georg

Lichtenheld, "Beobachtungen über Nagana und Glossinen in Deutsch-Ostafrika," *Archiv für wissenschaftliche und praktische Tierheilkunde* 36 (1910): 272; BAB R 1001/6068, fol. 129: Grothusen to Gov DOA, 22 March 1903; cf. Robert von Ostertag, "Über Rinderpest. Ein Beitrag zum Stande und zur Bekämpfung der Tierseuchen in Deutsch-Ostafrika," *Zeitschrift für Infektionskrankheiten, parasitäre Krankheiten und Hygiene der Haustiere* 18 (1916): 43.

36. The effect of colonial interventions such as the ban of grassfires on the spread of *glossinae* near Saadani and Tabora was already acknowledged by some colonial veterinarians, for example, Lichtenheld, "Beobachtungen über Nagana und Glossinen in Deutsch-Ostafrika," 278–79; Walter Busse, "Die periodischen Grasbrände im tropischen Afrika, ihr Einfluß auf die Vegetation und ihre Bedeutung für die Landeskultur," *Mitteilungen aus den deutschen Schutzgebieten* 21 (1908): 136.

37. BAB R 1001/6068, fol. 9: Gov DOA to AA KA, 25 March 1902; BAB R 1001/6068, fol. 129: Grothusen to Gov DOA, 22 March 1903. The recrudescence of east coast fever was witnessed in the hinterland of Saadani and parts of Usambara in January 1903, cf. BAB R 1001/6068, fol. 68: Gov DOA to AA KA, 21 January 1903.

38. *Deutsches Kolonialblatt* 2 (1891), 28 March: 205–6; Karl Ludwig Sander, "Die Viehseuchen in Afrika und Mittel zu ihrer Bekämpfung," *Verhandlungen der Gesellschaft deutscher Naturforscher und Ärzte* 65 (1893): 515–26; Robert Koch, "Reiseberichte über Rinderpest usw. in Indien und Afrika, Report dated Dar es Salaam, 27 October 1897," in *Gesammelte Werke,* ed. J Schwalbe, G Gaffky, and E Pfuhl, vol. 2, part 2 (Leipzig, 1912), 723; see also Sunseri, "The Entangled History of *Sadoka* (Rinderpest) and Veterinary Science in Tanzania and the Wider World," 111–12.

39. BAB R 1001/6068, fol. 52: Brauer and Ochmann to AA KA, 11 December 1902. The stock of cattle in the colony was estimated at 574,000 heads in 1904, decreasing to 523,000 due to disease in 1905; cf. BAB R 1001/6070, fol. 99: Report on the distribution of east coast fever by Stabsarzt Hoesemann, 26 September 1906.

40. BAB R 1001/6069, fol. 88: Gov DOA to AA KA, 5 July 1904.

41. For the parallel development in Kenya, see Richard Waller, "'Clean' and 'Dirty': Cattle Disease and Control Policy in Colonial Kenya, 1900–1940," *Journal of African History* 45 (2004): 45–80.

42. BAB R 1001/6068, fol. 68: Gov DOA to AA KA, 21 January 1903; BAB R 1001/6068, fol. 119, Gov DOA to AA KA, 6 April 1903; BAB R 1001/6068, fol. 129: Bericht über das Vorkommen der Tsetse (Surra) Krankheit im Bezirk Moschi, 22 March 1903; BAB R 1001/6068, fol. 137: Gov DOA to AA KA, 9 June 1903; Gerhard Grothusen, "Das Vorkommen der Tsetse-(Surra) Krankheit beim Zebra," *Archiv für Schiffs- und Tropen-Hygiene* 7 (1903): 387–88.

43. Neill, *Networks in Tropical Medicine,* chapter 1; Gradmann, *Krankheit im Labor,* 253–67.

44. Koch's findings were, however, highly controversial, cf. Daniel Gilfoyle, "Veterinary Research and the African Rinderpest Epizootic: The Cape Colony 1896–1898," *Journal of Southern African Studies* 29 (2003): 141–44, 153; Karen Brown, "Political Entomology: The Insectile Challenge to Agricultural Development in the Cape Colony, 1895–1910," *Journal of Southern African Studies* 29 (2003): 545.

45. Robert Koch, "Report to the Ministerium der geistlichen, Unterrichts- und Medizinalangelegenheiten, Berlin, 25 August 1895," in *Gesammelte Werke,* ed. J Schwalbe, G Gaffky, and E Pfuhl, vol. 2, part 2 (Leipzig, 1912), 922–23.
46. Robert Koch, "Berichte des Geheimen Medizinalrats Professor Dr. R. Koch über die Ergebnisse seiner Forschungen in Deutsch-Ostafrika," in *Gesammelte Werke,* ed. J Schwalbe, G Gaffky, and E Pfuhl, vol. 2, part 1 (Leipzig, 1912), 307–25.
47. Robert Koch, "Ueber die Viehseuchen in Deutsch-Ostafrika," *Deutsches Kolonialblatt* 8 (1897): 719–21. Koch knew that Bruce had identified a *Trypanosoma brucei* as the cause, and *Glossina morsitans* as the main vector transmitting nagana, see Robert Koch, "Reiseberichte über Rinderpest usw. in Indien und Afrika: Report dated Dar-es-Salaam, 27 October 1897," in *Gesammelte Werke,* ed. J Schwalbe, G Gaffky, and E Pfuhl, vol. 2, part 2 (Leipzig, 1912), 722.
48. BAB R 1001/6068, fol. 116: Gov DOA to AA KA, 24 April 1903; BAB R 1001/6068, fol. 119: Gov DOA to AA KA, 6 April 1903; Robert Koch, "Ein Versuch zur Immunisierung von Rindern gegen Tsetsekrankheit (Surra)," in *Gesammelte Werke,* ed. J Schwalbe, G Gaffky, and E Pfuhl, vol. 2, part 2 (Leipzig, 1912), 743–47.
49. Robert Koch, "Remarks on Trypanosome Diseases," *British Medical Journal,* no. 26, (1904), 19 November: 1449. The article was published simultaneously in English and German medical journals, see Robert Koch, "Ueber die Trypanosomenkrankheiten," *Deutsche medizinische Wochenschrift* 30, no. 47 (1904): 1705–11.
50. David Bruce, "The Advance in Our Knowledge of the Causation and Methods of Prevention of Stock Diseases in South Africa During the Last Ten Years," *Science* 22 (1905): 297.
51. Koch, "Remarks on Trypanosome Diseases," 1449.
52. "Bericht über die Verhandlungen der 36. Plenarversammlung des Deutschen Landwirtschaftsrats vom 10. bis 13. Februar 1908," *Archiv des Deutschen Landwirtschaftsrats* 32 (1908): 105.
53. Ibid., 109–10, 112–13.
54. Hans Zache, "Koloniale Aphorismen," *Deutsch-Ostafrikanische Zeitung* 11, no. 1 (1909), 6 January.
55. Members included, among others, the zoo directors of Hamburg, Leipzig, Breslau, Frankfurt, and Cologne, and the director of the Berlin Museum of Natural History, Karl Möbius. The Belgian King Leopold II and the President of the German Colonial Society, Duke Johann Albrecht of Mecklenburg-Schwerin, were recruited as honorary members. See BAB R 1001/8540: fol. 19–20 and fol. 35–36.
56. BAB R 1001/7770, fol. 212: Commission to RKA, Berlin, 15 February 1908. Its German name was Kommission zur Besserung des Wildschutzes in Deutsch-Afrika.
57. See for example Paasche, *Im Morgenlicht*; *Deutsch-Ostafrikanische Zeitung* 9, no. 12 (1907), 23 March.
58. Lippe, *In den Jagdgründen Deutsch-Ostafrikas*; Paul Niedieck, *Mit der Büchse in fünf Weltteilen* (Berlin, 1905), 423; Louis von Brandis, *Deutsche Jagd am Victoria Nyanza* (Berlin, 1907).
59. Schillings, *Mit Blitzlicht und Büchse*; Schillings, *Der Zauber des Elelescho* (Leipzig, 1906), 492–93; BAB R 1001/7777, fol. 90–113: Gutachten des Prof. Schillings über den Entwurf einer Jagdverordnung für Deutsch-Ost-Afrika vom Gesichtspunkte des Tierschutzes, 2 April 1908.

60. On the conservation movement in Germany, see Friedemann Schmoll, *Erinnerung an die Natur. Die Geschichte des Naturschutzes im deutschen Kaiserreich* (Frankfurt, 2004); Thomas Lekan, *Imagining the Nation in Nature: Landscape Preservation and German Identity, 1885-1945* (Cambridge, MA, 2004); Raymond Dominick, *The Environmental Movement in Germany. Prophets & Pioneers, 1871-1971* (Bloomington, IN, 1992).
61. Fritz Behn, "Naturerhaltung und Wildmord in Deutsch-Ostafrika—ein Kulturskandal," *Naturwissenschaftliche Wochenschrift* 10 (1911): 807.
62. Fritz Bley, *Deutsche Pionierarbeit in Ostafrika* (Berlin, 1891); Bley, "Besseren Wildschutz in unseren Kolonien!", *Monatshefte des Allgemeinen Deutschen Jagdschutzvereins und der Deutschen Versuchsanstalt für Handfeuerwaffen* 12 (1907), 119-22, 132-36.
63. Cf. Johannes Müller-Liebenwalde, "Wildschutz in Deutsch-Ostafrika," *Deutsche Jägerzeitung* 51 (1908): 165-70; Wilhelm Puchmüller, ed., *Verein Hirschmann. Chronik 1894-1980* (Springe, 1982), 21, 253; BAB R 1001/7770, fol. 215-16: Duke Victor of Ratibor to RKA, 21 February 1908; H Roland, "Wildschutz in Deutschafrika," *Zeitschrift des Allgemeinen Deutschen Jagdschutzvereins* 16, no. 34 (1911), 25 October: 408-9; Max Weiss, "Eine Löwenjagd am Kilimandscharo," *Kolonie und Heimat* no. 3 (1907), 27 October.
64. Viktor von Ratibor (1847-1923) was also a nephew of Chancellor von Hohenlohe-Schillingsfürst and president of the Silesian Provincial Diet between 1897 and 1921, see Hartwin Spenkuch, "Viktor von Ratibor," *Neue Deutsche Biographie*, vol. 21 (Berlin, 2003), 181-82.
65. Generalsekretariat des Union-Klubs, ed., *Der klassische Sport. Ein Beitrag zur Geschichte des Rennsports und der Vollblutzucht anläßlich des 75jährigen Bestehens des Union-Klubs* (Berlin, 1942), 69, 183, 189, 248; BAB R 1001/266, fol. 16-17: Von Podbielski to District Government Aachen, 10 March 1898.
66. Paul Matschie, *Die Säugethiere Deutsch-Ostafrikas* (Berlin, 1895). Matschie (1861-1926) was the foremost zoologist to digest the zoological specimens, observations, and descriptions from Germany's African colonies into taxonomic knowledge. Convinced about the existence of small-scale zoogeographic units, Matschie undeniably fanned hunters' zeal to identify yet unknown species and acquired, in the words of biologist George B Schaller, a reputation for creating "species and subspecies with wild abandon, often on the basis of one skull alone," see George B Schaller, *The Year of the Gorilla* (Chicago, 1964), 8.
67. The involvement of Sander and Matschie suggests that the German variety of the tsetse controversy cannot be reduced to a conflict merely between big game hunters and bacteriologists. For such an interpretation of the British debate, see Clapperton Mavhunga, "Big Game Hunters, Bacteriologists, and Tsetse Fly Entomology in Colonial South-East Africa: The Selous-Austen Debate Revisited, 1905-1940," *Icon* 12 (2006), 75-117.
68. A detailed report of the meeting in the Berlin *Kontinental-Hotel* is provided by Johannes Müller-Liebenwalde, "Wildschutz in Deutsch-Ostafrika," *Deutsche Jägerzeitung* 51 (1908): 165-70. Müller-Liebenwalde was the first director of the Zoological Garden of Halle.
69. BAB R 1001/7770, fol. 212: Commission to RKA, 15 February 1908; BAB R 1001/7770, fol. 221-27: Memorandum by the Kommission für Besserung des

Wildschutzes in Deutsch-Afrika, submitted 31 March 1908; "Die Bekämpfung der Tsetse-Fliege," *Deutsch-Ostafrikanische Zeitung* 10, no. 38 (1908), 23 May.
70. Cf. Johannes Müller-Liebenwalde, "Ostafrikanisches Großwild," *Deutsche Jägerzeitung* 52 (1908–9): 263–65; Johannes Müller-Liebenwalde, "Exzellenz Koch und das Großwild in Deutsch-Afrika," *Deutsche Jägerzeitung* 52 (1908–9): 493–95; Möllers, *Robert Koch*, 351–53.
71. Curt Hennings, "Heimatschutz und Naturdenkmalpflege," *Verhandlungen des Naturwissenschaftlichen Vereins Karlsruhe* 22 (1908–9): 105.
72. On Dernburg and Rechenberg's reform policy and the controversies surrounding them, see Bradley D Naranch, "'Colonized Body,' 'Oriental Machine': Debating Race, Railroads, and the Politics of Reconstruction in Germany and East Africa, 1906–1910," *Central European History* 33 (2000): 299–338; Dirk van Laak, *Imperiale Infrastruktur. Deutsche Planungen für eine Erschließung Afrikas 1880 bis 1960* (Paderborn, 2004), 130–46; Werner Schiefel, *Bernhard Dernburg, 1865–1937: Kolonialpolitiker und Bankier im wilhelminischen Deutschland* (Zürich, 1974), 55–142.
73. Van Laak, *Imperiale Infrastruktur,* 130–46; Naranch, "'Colonized Body,'" 305.
74. See for example Wächter, *Naturschutz in den deutschen Kolonien in Afrika,* 83.
75. *Deutsch-Ostafrikanische Zeitung* 11, no. 2 (1909), 9 January; F Metzke, "Die Jagdverordnung für Deutsch-Ostafrika in der Praxis," *Deutsche Jägerzeitung* 57 (1911): 515; HUB MfN, Zool. Museum S III Schillings, fol. 250–51: Schillings to Matschie, 24 October 1907.
76. *Amtlicher Anzeiger für Deutsch-Ostafrika* 9, no. 23 (1908), 7 November: German East African game ordinance; cf. Sunseri, *Vilimani,* xxiii; Söldenwagner, *Spaces of Negotiation,* 147–48.
77. BAB R 1001/7770, fol. 202: Gov DOA to RKA, 22 June 1907.
78. BAB R 1001/300, fol. 34*ff*.: Bericht über eine vom 13. Juli bis 30. Oktober 1907 nach Ostafrika ausgeführte Dienstreise (geheim), 38; Oskar Bongard, *Die Studienreise des Staatssekretärs Dernburg nach Deutsch-Ostafrika* (Berlin, 1908), 16–17, 19, 27–28.
79. BAB R 1001/7777, fol. 122–23: Ostafrikanische Fragen. Eine Unterhaltung mit dem Staatssekretär des Reichs-Kolonialamts [undated note, May 1908]; *Deutsch-Ostafrikanische Zeitung* 10, no. 43 (1908), 10 June.
80. Dernburg, *Zielpunkte des deutschen Kolonialwesens.*
81. C.G. Schillings zum Professor ernannt," *Dürener Volkszeitung* no. 142 (1907), 24 June; BAB R 1001/7777, fol. 28: Dernburg to Gov DOA, 30 April 1907. Dernburg and Schillings knew each other as members of a *Kolonialpolitisches Aktionskomitee* that had formed among learned and scientific elites in January 1907 to support von Bülow's election campaign, cf. Kolonialpolitisches Aktionskomitée, ed., *Schmoller Dernburg Delbrück, Schäfer Sering Schillings Brunner Jastrow Pemnck Kahl über Reichstagsauflösung und Kolonialpolitik.* Offizieller stenographischer Bericht über die Versammlung in der Berliner Hochschule für Musik am 8. Januar 1907 (Berlin, 1907).
82. BAB R 1001/7777, fol. 90: Gutachten des Prof. Schillings über den Entwurf einer Jagdverordnung für Deutsch-Ost-Afrika vom Gesichtspunkte des Tierschutzes, 2 April 1908.

83. Schillings left the RKA on 27 November 1908, see BAB R 1001/7770, fol. 233, margin.
84. *Deutsch-Ostafrikanische Zeitung* 12, no. 93 (1910), 23 November.
85. BAB R 1001/7777, fol. 216–18: Circular concerning the enactment of the game ordinance, 5 November 1908. See also *Deutsch-Ostafrikanische Zeitung* 10, no. 57 (1908), 29 July; for the critique of the Colonial Office see BAB R 1001/7777, fol. 179–92: Memorandum: Welche Änderungen hat der durch die alte ostafrik. Jagdv. v. 1. Juni 1903 gewährte Thierschutz durch die neue Jagdv. v. 8. Nov. 1908 erfahren? [12 February 1909].
86. The immediate trigger for the inclusion of this license were the flying visits of the Prussian Princes Friedrich Heinrich and Joachim Albrecht in 1907, see BAB R 1001/7777, fol. 142: Gov DOA to RKA, 30 July 1908; BAB R 1001/292, fol. 5: Gov DOA to RKA, 24 May 1907; BAB R 1001/292, fol. 9: Gov DOA to RKA, 30 July 1907; "Prinz Friedrich Heinrich in Moschi," *Usambara Post* 6, no. 7 (1907), 13 July; "Prinzentage in Daressalam," *Deutsch-Ostafrikanische Zeitung* 9, no. 32 (1907), 13 July.
87. BAB R 1001/812, fol. 223: Rechenberg on the 8th meeting of the governor's council, 20/22 July 1908.
88. *Amtlicher Anzeiger für Deutsch-Ostafrika* 9, no. 23 (1908), 7 November, Art. 3 der Ausführungsbestimmungen zur Jagdverordnung vom 5. November 1908; TNA G 8/54, unfol.: BA Moshi to Gov DOA, 23 April 1908.
89. *Denkschrift über die Entwickelung der Schutzgebiete in Afrika und der Südsee im Jahre 1908/09*, 40; *Deutsch-Ostafrikanische Zeitung* 10, no. 100 (1908), 31 December.
90. See for example TNA G 31/5, unfol. Arusha to Moshi, 10 January 1909.
91. TNA G 8/908, unfol.: Moshi to Gov DOA, 10 January 1909; Moshi to Gov DOA, 14 January 1909; Moshi to Gov DOA, 7 April 1909; Carl Müller, "Afrikanische Jagden," *Wild und Hund* 15 (1909): 321–22; "Ostafrikanische Jagdgesetze," *Deutsche Jägerzeitung* 55 (1910): 462; *Amtlicher Anzeiger für Deutsch-Ostafrika* 10, no. 5 (1909), 22 February; *Deutsch-Ostafrikanische Zeitung* 11, no. 25 (1909), 31 March.
92. TNA G 8/908, unfol.: Kilwa to Gov DOA, 19 March 1909; Iringa to Gov DOA, 29 March 1909; *Deutsch-Ostafrikanische Zeitung* 11, no. 15 (1909), 24 February; Fonck, *Deutsch-Ostafrika*, 414–15.
93. TNA G 1/5: Annual report from Morogoro, undated [received by Gov DOA 2 July 1909].
94. BAB R 1001/7777, fol. 204: RKA to Prince Bernhard zur Lippe, 18 March 1909 [concept]; fol. 224: Circular to all stations, 1 March 1909; TNA G 8/908, unfol. Gov DOA to Kilwa, 22 April 1909.
95. TNA G 8/908, unfol.: Circular to all stations, 28 January 1909 and 18 February 1909; BA Kilwa to Gov DOA, 19 March 1909; BA Moshi to Gov DOA, 7 April 1909; Residency Kigali to Gov DOA, 15 April 1909; Gov DOA to BA Moshi, 16 May 1909; BAB R 1001/7777, fol. 196: Prince Bernhard zur Lippe to RKA, 30/31 December 1908; fol. 264: Commission for the Improvement of Game Preservation in German Africa to RKA, 31 January 1910; Franz Kolbe, "Schutz dem Großwilde in unseren afrikanischen Kolonien," *Deutsche Jägerzeitung* 54 (1909–10): 428–29; Fritz Bley, "Schutz unseres afrikanischen Großwildes!," *Deutsche Jägerzeitung* 54 (1909–10): 745–46.

96. BAB R 1001/7777, fol. 290: Circular to all stations, 21 January 1910; fol. 332: Circular to all stations, 19 November 1910.
97. Paasche, "Protest in elfter Stunde," *Der Vortrupp* 1 (1912): 6–9.
98. See for example BAB R 1001/701, fol. 40: Gov DOA to RKA, 25 December 1907; Müller, "Afrikanische Jagden," 321–22; TNA G 8/143, fol. 26: Abel to Gov DOA, 13 February 1905; *Deutsch-Ostafrikanische Zeitung* 14, no. 22 (1912), 16 March; TNA G 55/27, fol. 54: Adolf Siedentopf to BNS Umbulu, 13 March 1912.
99. Methner, *Unter drei Gouverneuren*, 177–78; TNA G 1/5: Annual Report for Mwanza and Shirati, undated [received by Gov DOA on 1 July 1909]; Jan Bender Shetler, *Imagining Serengeti. A History of Landscape Memory in Tanzania from Earliest Times to the Present* (Athens, 2007), 187.
100. TNA G 1/5: Undated annual report from Morogoro [received by Gov DOA 2 July 1909]; TNA G 1/5: Annual Report from Mpwapwa to Gov DOA, 15 June 1909; TNA G 1/6: Annual Report from Tabora to Gov DOA, 18 June 1909; Werner von Wiese und Kaiserswaldau, "Die schwarzen Jäger," *Tägliche Rundschau*, no. 234 (1910), 23 May.
101. See for example BAB R 1001/222, fol. 5–6: Methner to Gov DOA, 27 June 1907; BAB R 1001/238, fol. 151–99: Travel report by Hans Paasche [1906], fol. 163; LIL Prittwitz Papers, Box 248/1: Diary entry 23 July 1906.
102. BAB R 1001/7777, fol. 171: Rechenberg to RKA, 14 November 1908.
103. Edwin Hennig, *Am Tendaguru. Leben und Wirken einer deutschen Forschungs-Expedition zur Ausgrabung vorweltlicher Riesensaurier in Deutsch-Ostafrika* (Stuttgart, 1912), 67, 122–25.
104. TNA G 1/6: Annual Report from Tabora, 18 June 1909.
105. Sunseri, *Vilimani*, 171–78.
106. Oskar Karstedt, "Betrachtungen zur Sozialpolitik in Ostafrika," *Koloniale Rundschau* 12 (1914): 138. Cf. PRO British Colonial Office (CO) 691/16, fol. 156–64: Report Byatt to CO, 5 October 1918.
107. Iliffe, *Tanganyika under German Rule*, 166.
108. BAB R 1001/7778, fol. 124: Circular to all stations, 30 June 1911; for the persistence of damage see also BAB R 1001/7779, fol. 3: Acting Governor Methner to Gov DOA, 31 December 1911.

 CHAPTER 5

The Imperial Game
Rinderpest, Wildmord, and the Emperor's Breakfast, 1910–14

The last five years before the outbreak of World War I witnessed the firm establishment of African wildlife conservation on the imperial agenda in Germany. The issue gathered momentum and wider social acceptance through both its integration into a broader discourse of *Weltnaturschutz* (global protection of nature) and the scandalization of colonial wildlife policies in German East Africa. Both developments were decisively shaped by the attempted clearing of game along the Anglo-German border to prevent the spread of rinderpest in 1910. The moral outrage that followed resulted in the compromise between an imperial view of conservation advocated by elite hunters and conservationists in Germany and a wildlife policy sensitive to colonial development and the economic requirements of white settlers in East Africa. The imperial view of hunting and wildlife conservation was encapsulated in two further revisions of the game ordinance in December 1911 and July 1913, which were both crafted according to the model of the game regulations in force in the neighboring British colonies. Elephant hunting was finally turned into a prerogative of wealthy imperial elites.

This chapter discusses first the rationalities behind the rinderpest scare that motivated the massive shooting of ungulates along the northern border of the colony in August 1910. The scandalization of this action by conservationists in Germany will be portrayed in the second section. Decrying Rechenberg's shooting order as *Wildmord* (murder of wildlife), the public scandalization of Rechenberg's policies prompted another revision of the game law, which is discussed in the third section. Thanks to the mobilization of exclusive social networks, including the hunting-minded Emperor Wilhelm II and colonial secretary Wilhelm Solf, the conservationists managed to include central, though by far not all demands in a game ordinance that was drafted in Berlin and finally resembled the stipulations in force in neighboring Kenya. Yet, as the last paragraph will show, attempts to promote German East Africa as an alternative destination for hunting tourism were nipped in the bud by World War I.

The Rationality of Game Slaughter: Livestock Economy and the Threat of Rinderpest

By the end of 1909, it had become clear that Rechenberg's efforts to reconcile a "native-friendly" policy after Maji Maji with the fiscal interests of the state and the demands of white colonists and wildlife lobbyists had largely failed. Schillings kept pestering imperial authorities to "finally, finally arrange wildlife preservation according to the established and well-proven British pattern." The wildlife commission debunked the ordinance as simply "untenable."[1] The colonial office in Berlin officially defended the game law, yet internally, Dernburg made it unmistakably clear that he expected Rechenberg "to seriously consider at least a limitation of the number of elephants" allowed under the *große Jagdschein*.[2]

However, any steps toward another reform of the game law had to be postponed for the problem of the disease ecology of game and livestock had returned with a vengeance since October 1909. Then, news had broken about a mysterious disease among the cattle in Ukerewe on the eastern shore of Lake Victoria. Alarmed by Koch's verdict of the impossible coexistence of wildlife and livestock on African soil, Rechenberg immediately ordered an inquiry. No enhanced mortality of the game could be observed. But as there was no information yet from the British authorities in Nairobi, the government remained skeptical. "If against all expectations the diagnosis of rinderpest was confirmed," acting governor Methner wrote to Berlin, "only the most comprehensive and expensive vaccination measures could prevent the livestock of the colony from a catastrophe likely to spread quicker than in 1891–93 due to the improved conditions of transport."[3]

The colonial office, similarly nervous, once more turned to the expertise of Robert Koch.[4] The bacteriologist sent a catalog of symptoms that the veterinary surgeons on the spot should check in order to determine the nature of the disease. Three of the four official veterinaries of the colony were deployed to examine and isolate diseased cattle in Ukerewe and surroundings. Yet, the disease remained a puzzle and cattle kept dying. By the end of November, 800 cattle were dead, but no species of the larger wild fauna appeared to be affected.[5]

It was in this tense atmosphere that a telegraph from the German Consulate in Mombasa reported the outbreak of rinderpest just beyond the border in Kenya in August 1910. The Rift Valley south of Nairobi and the Southern Maasai reserve were allegedly affected, and Rechenberg immediately dispatched two veterinary surgeons. One was sent to Kenya to study the British response to the outbreak, another to Moshi to take measures against the spread of the disease into German territory. All import of cattle and other domestic animals, game, meat, and hides from British territory was prohibited. As a further protective measure, Rechenberg resorted to the large-scale killing of game along the Anglo-German border. All available Askari from the police and military forces stationed in the districts of Tanga, Wilhelmstal (Lushoto), Moshi, and Mwanza were deployed to police the border, aided by further 400 men of "supportive native personnel." In order to "minimize the danger of wild animals spreading the epidemic," Rechenberg declared a stretch of 50 kilometers along the entire Anglo-German border from the ocean toward Lake Victoria open to shooting. The order went into effect on 14 August, all game was allowed apart from elephants, rhinos, colobus monkeys, zebras, chimpanzees, vultures, and small owls. Additionally, the Askari companies received explicit order to create a buffer zone devoid of game along the border. Hunting was partially restricted again on 9 September, when Georg Lichtenheld, the veterinarian dispatched to Nairobi, telegraphed that preventive measures were unnecessary in the northeastern sections of the border. The disease in question was probably a new plague or a virulent form of catarrhal fever. Another month later, Lichtenheld confirmed further that neither cattle nor game in the Southern Maasai reserve showed any symptoms of rinderpest. Consequently, Rechenberg revoked all given orders on the same day, the shooting of game included.[6]

The official correspondence reveals that Rechenberg's prime aim was to defer the spread of the disease as long as possible in order to produce serum and vaccinate as many cattle as possible. His actions remain ill understood without taking into account the economic situation in northern Tanzania at the time. The outbreaks in Kenya were only about a hundred kilometers from the districts of Mwanza, Moshi, and Arusha, which were, apart from Rwanda, the areas best stocked with cattle in the colony.[7] Indigenous pastoralists, especially the Maasai, had achieved a remarkable recovery of stocks after the panzootic of the 1890s, while a growing number of white farmers were attracted by the fertile pastureland between Mounts Kilimanjaro and Meru. Because the area was one of the few regions in the colony that was largely free from tsetse, cattle rearing counted among their foremost economic activities. In 1911, the districts of Moshi and Arusha registered some 214 cattle farms. The growth of the settlers' livestock economy occurred at the cost of the Maasai's forced concentration in a reserve south of Kilimanjaro in 1906. Moving the Maasai should render mobile pastoralists controllable and open "several hundreds of thousands of hectares of best pasture" to white settlement. Moreover, at a time when coast fever was rife, it was hoped that once removed from contact with possibly infected cattle, the Maasai's livestock would turn into a valuable reservoir of cattle for the whole colony.[8] The reserve should spur the transition from the mere pastoralist use of cattle, which the colonizers regarded as largely unproductive, toward a more intensive utilization of cattle through breeding and ranching. These expectations were never met, but with thousands of cattle concentrated in the reserve, stocks would have been quickly eradicated in case the rinderpest struck with a similar vengeance as two decades earlier.

The memory of the devastating impact of the *Rinderseuche* in the early 1890s was one reason that spurred authorities into frantic action. But the government also knew that it was ill-prepared to deal with a large-scale epizootic. The number of government veterinarians had doubled by 1908, but this still meant that no more than four veterinarians were responsible for over 1 million heads of cattle. The efforts to eradicate the tsetse fly put additional strain on already limited financial and institutional resources. The prophylactic inoculation of cattle, for example, was neglected unless there was immediate necessity to do so. The government had neither the personnel nor the means to implement a premeditated veterinary policy. By 1913, there still existed no separate veterinary department within the colonial administration. When the government finally decided to build up a stock of vaccine and invest into the necessary equipment for the production of anti-rinderpest serum, it had to rely upon transimperial networks: the first doses had to be purchased from the British in Kenya and the Egyptian State Institute of Hygiene in Cairo, directed by the German Heinrich Bitter.[9]

Therefore, the extermination of those species that could serve as a possible vector was not only a radical and desperately simple means to halt or slow down the spread of the disease. It was also the comparatively cheapest measure. Neither the problem nor the practices chosen for its solution were new, nor were they unique to German colonialism. British authorities planned and carried out similar action in the context of the tsetse-game controversy in their Southern African colonies. Since 1901, the British South African company frequently resorted to the temporary suspension of game laws to erase nagana in districts infested by tsetse in southern Rhodesia. In Malawi, local medical staff and the legislative council advocated to throw open "the whole of the Angoniland Districts to free shooting for the purpose of exterminating the game in that neighbourhood." The government refused "to commit itself on hypothetical grounds to measures of such an extreme character," but decided to create a "natural laboratory" of ten square miles in 1911—just like Koch had proposed for German East Africa in 1908. Within this area, all game was to be exterminated to gather "material testimony" for the relationship between wild animals and *glossinae*.[10] Even the short German history of colonial rule in Africa featured precedents, albeit on a reduced scale compared with the measures in East Africa in 1910. During the first rinderpest epizootic in 1896–97, its spread into German South-West Africa should be slowed down, if not prevented by a picket fence of patrolling soldiers who had the concrete order to exterminate any living creature entering the prospected *cordon sanitaire*.[11] Reports testify to selective vaccination to safeguard as much of the colonizers' livestock, whereas German authorities welcomed a mortality among Herero cattle of up to 95 percent as it would erase the "root of their power" and cast them on the labor market.[12] Contrary to the context of conquest in Namibia, the Maasai cattle were considered far too important for the colonial economy to be deliberately sacrificed on political grounds. Yet a possible epizootic would have struck similarly unequal: in the case of an emergency inoculation campaign the stations' and the white settlers' cattle would have been clearly prioritized. There are no hints in the records that any of the earlier experiences in Namibia directly influenced the steps taken more than a decade later in German East Africa. But Dernburg's successor as secretary of the Reichskolonialamt, Friedrich von Lindequist, had been actively involved as acting governor in South-West Africa back in the 1890s. Unsurprisingly, he gave his full consent to Rechenberg's decision.[13]

It is hard to assess how many wild animals were killed under the assumption that the colony's livestock was threatened by an epizootic. A report submitted by the East African government in November 1911 suggested that altogether 341 Askari spent 41,130 bullets to shoot 4,981 specimens of game. However, figures from one military station were missing; no estimates as to the numbers of game killed by hunters outside the police and military were included, not to mention animals that escaped wounded. Moreover, these statistics were only compiled after a storm of public protest in Germany had pressurized the colonial office to inquire into the details of the matter. Therefore, the officially admitted figures were presumably kept deliberately low.[14] While the overall tally was probably nowhere near the number of 30,000 killed animals that later circulated in the German public, the official figure of 4,981 gazelles and antelopes was surely well below the actual total of animal casualties. Rechenberg himself admitted that the effort to create a *cordon sanitaire* devoid of game had failed. Only in areas where wildlife had been sparse anyway did the game temporarily vanish. In any case, the stress caused among the remaining wildlife populations must have been immense. Two years later, British game wardens still found the animals all "along the German border … excessively wild and few in numbers."[15]

The Scandal of Game Slaughter and Preservationist Mobilization in the Metropole

Adopting a panoptic view on events in German East Africa and Germany in June 1911, one can discern a deep divergence in the perception of Africa's wild fauna by those dissociated in space and time from the realities of life and settlement on the ground, and those who had to live in immediate interaction and coexistence with it. In June 1911, Rechenberg deployed Askaris again to survey game and cattle movement in another scare of rinderpest, this time along the Ugandan border.[16] Early in the same month, the official gazette proclaimed that the "Kisiwani" game reserve in Lupembe, coadministered by the military districts of Mahenge and Iringa, would be opened to shooting for the first time in eight years. The measure was justified by the enormous damage to fields and plantations wrought by an ever-increasing number of elephants migrating in and out of the reserve. A few days later, the semi-official Deutsch-Ostafrikanische Rundschau explicitly drew the hunters' attention to this "rare opportunity" to make a good bag. Hunters raided the reserve and wiped out elephant stocks within weeks.[17] During these very days, anxieties over wildlife extermination in East Africa reached a new peak thousands of kilometers further north in Stuttgart, where the German Colonial Society (Deutsche Kolonialgesellschaft, DKG) gathered for its annual meeting on 9 and 10 June 1911. The meeting unanimously passed a motion to establish a commission for wildlife conservation under the auspices of the DKG to replace the existing commission and urge the colonial office to gazette large-scale sanctuaries. The elite hunters, colonial activists, and scientists congregating in Stuttgart saw developments in German East Africa in a global and declensionist perspective and framed Africa's megafauna as an evolutionary heritage that only immediate action was able to safeguard.[18] In East Africa, the colonial government deployed soldiers to kill that very game, receiving the support of white settlers who were convinced that livestock and livelihoods in the colony were threatened with eradication when wild animals were left unchecked. To be sure, there were sympathizers of the conservationist view in the colony, and critical questions were raised in Stuttgart if large sanctuaries were not an impediment to the development and rational mise-en-valeur of the colony. Nonetheless, the conflict between "colony" and "zoological garden" was essentially organized around the spatial and political divide between imperial metropole and colony.

Although completely overlooked by the existing literature on the origins of German nature protection, the East African game slaughter of 1910–11 counted among the biggest conservationist controversies in imperial Germany. Many of the early conflicts over conservation in Germany, for example, over the Laufenburg rapids, the canalization of the Isar river, and even the Lüneburg heath, were enmeshed in local and regional conflicts. Protecting the charismatic wildlife of Africa, however, became a national affair and a question of imperial honor. The discursive hegemony gained by the wildlife conservationists in 1911 can be traced back to at least five factors and developments. First, the purchase of their argument benefited from a time-lag of more than half a year between the game clearing in the colony and the first news about it in Germany. This meant that the threat of rinderpest had already been exposed as nonexistent when the first details of the action became known in Germany in May 1911. The restrictive information policy of colonial authorities both in East Africa and Berlin allowed information about the game slaughter to leak only gradually. Rumor and exaggeration flourished and made conservationists' reactions even more anxious and intense. The underlying problem of the possibly conflicting ecologies of wildlife and livestock hardly mattered. Instead, Schillings, Paasche, and the other advocates of wildlife preservation presented the attempted creation of a buffer zone as a colossal carnage. Some asserted that 16,000 buffalo had been killed within four weeks. Other sources spoke of 600,000 bullets spent to kill around 30,000 specimens of noble *Hochwild*, the German term to refer to the prestigious game that used to be reserved for the hunting aristocracy.[19] The time lag allowed the conservationists to turn a localized act of administrative rationality into a pointless and intentional "mass murder of innocent animals,"[20] sanctioned officially by a government unchecked in its administrative absolutism. Second, the scandalization of game slaughter could reach fever pitch because it occurred in the general climate of what the Center party's foremost investigator of colonial scandals, Matthias Erzberger, termed a veritable *Rechenbergkoller* (Rechenberg frenzy).[21] Although the conservationists' intervention was concerned predominantly with the preservation of game, their cause was aided by the parallel scandalization of Rechenberg for the alleged entertaining of homosexual relationships with one of his male servants.[22] If Rechenberg already faced fierce opposition from settlers, missions, the military, and colonial circles in Berlin for his "native-friendly" policies, his extermination of the white colonists' foremost toy only added to the agitated and hostile climate against him as a political person. By 1911, Rechenberg simply had not much credit left that any of his actions and decisions would find acceptance.

Third, the East African savanna and its megafauna lent themselves to be charged with a whole set of cultural meanings that reflected the needs and desires of a society undergoing rapid modernization. Charismatic species like elephants, zebras, or rhinoceroses had enormous emotional appeal.[23] Contemporary conservation activists presented the East African fauna as embodiments of innocent nature and victimized them as sentient beings that were "murdered." Such rhetoric strategies appealed to the "humaneness" of the object of advocacy and stood in a tradition of humanitarian engagement for other "voiceless" groups such as slaves or the poor. Rechenberg, on the other hand, was ascribed all the attributes usually applied to African and Boer hunters: indiscriminate, wanton, and cruel. Rechenberg had acted like a barbarian, while the conservationists symbolically adopted the game under their stewardship. Appeals to posterity, the anathema of extinction, and the moral obligations of empire were complemented with other justifications for game conservation. Early advocates of "biodiversity" emphasized the East African savanna as a "hotspot" featuring 160 different mammalian species, with 24 of them being outstanding species of wildlife. Scientists like the Munich paleontologist Ernst Stromer von Reichenbach underscored the necessity for preservation with the evolutionary information embodied in the East African fauna, which would enable analogies with a similar mammalian fauna once prevalent also in Europe.[24] Wilderness and East Africa's wildness were essentially mediated by the presence of large animals, whose European equivalents had long given way to progress. All of these arguments were permeated by psycho-spiritual values: the megafauna of the East African savanna provided an ideal canvas for exoticist imaginations of a primeval and wild paradise that could be charged with a rich heritage of European cultural meaning. Images of a lost paradise and garden Eden loomed large. Hans Paasche, for example, depicted the Maasai Steppe as a virgin paradise of harmonious wildlife and assigned it a special place in the German colonial imaginary, eternalized as it already was in the paintings of Wilhelm Kuhnert or Schillings's narrative and photographic images of the African wildlife.[25] The Munich sculptor Fritz Behn deployed an equally powerful rhetoric of cultural criticism when he envisioned the East African savanna as a place where civilized humanity could get "back to nature." Therefore, it should be preserved for posterity in the form of a *Naturschutzpark*.[26] Such reading of the savanna as paradise, Eden, and wilderness inscribed a timeless primeval originality into African space, which not only erased any previous human history of these places, but also current human ecologies. After all, the whole rationale behind the creation of a *cordon sanitaire* had been to safeguard the presence of human farmers and domestic livestock in these areas. But once declared as the spatial and temporal opposite of Europe—pristine, wild, uncultivated, and devoid of people—conservationists disposed with East African lands at their will. Contrary to the German *Heimat,* where private property rights impeded many local efforts at nature preservation, the colonial state in East Africa had millions of hectares of allegedly "undeveloped land" to create the *Naturschutzpark* that was so hard to realize at home.[27] Despite all moral and idealist rhetoric, an economic line of reasoning characterized almost any contribution to the debate: conservation and agricultural development could be combined; game was no impediment but "walking capital" that could be sustainably exploited by tourist hunting.[28] Conserving game also meant conserving the pleasures of the hunt for future generations, and there were already arguments for visual consumption as a less violent and more democratic form of game utilization. Whereas a hunted specimen of wildlife, Schillings argued, could be consumed by only one person, the living creature could serve as a pleasure for thousands of viewers.[29]

Fourth, the imperial conservationists resorted to strategic campaigning as well as to the conscious and public scandalization of Rechenberg's failure at conservation in East Africa. Extending the mere petitioning of previous years, they now made broad use of the media and of the various colonial, hunting, and conservationist public spheres. The protests were triggered by an article entitled *Der Massenmord in Ostafrika* by Hans Paasche, which was quickly reprinted by several other newspapers and taken up in a lecture delivered by the Swiss conservationist Paul Sarasin to an audience of bird conservationists in Stuttgart in May 1911.[30] There, it was picked up by Schillings who then spread the message in colonial circles. Just a month later, petitions by the DKG-branches of Magdeburg and Lyck (East Prussia) brought colonial wildlife conservation and the creation of a *Naturschutzpark* in German East Africa onto the agenda of the colonial society's general assembly in Stuttgart.[31] Scores of articles appeared in daily newspapers as well as in periodicals dedicated to colonial matters, hunting, nature preservation, and the popularization of natural science. The mere number of articles could easily obscure the fact that their authors were actually but a few hunters and natural scientists. The articles ruminated and brokered the same scarce bits of information about the shooting order, framed its effects within a global conservationist perspective of wildlife destruction, and placed these texts strategically in various contexts. Schillings's speech to the general assembly of the Deutsche Kolonialgesellschaft, for example, was published with only slight modifications in the printed proceedings of the assembly, in the *Naturwissenschaftliche Wochenschrift*, the *Blätter für Naturschutz*, and the periodical of the Allgemeine Deutsche Jagdschutzverein. Thereby he addressed all relevant social target groups sensitive to colonialism, nature conservation, natural science, and hunting.[32]

Finally, the advocacy for wildlife conservation in Germany's colonial Empire had experienced a considerable expansion of its social constituency by 1911. The Koch-controversy in 1908 and the *Kulturskandal* of the state-administered killing of thousands of game animals in German East Africa lifted the issue of colonial conservation beyond its original adherents in the colonial and hunting communities. Paul Sarasin's speech at the meeting of Germany's bird conservationists in 1911 shows that conservation in the

African colonies also benefited from the attention aroused for other moralized environmental causes, such as the campaign against the trade and conspicuous consumption of plumage, which was related to the conservation of birds of paradise in Germany's Pacific colonies.[33] The supporting constituencies of both campaigns were largely divided along gender lines, yet key activists were identical: Schillings and Paul Sarasin, the first president of the Swiss Commission for the Protection of Nature, integrated East Africa's wildlife and the tropical avifauna into a comprehensive agenda of global nature protection.[34]

The issue of colonial conservation cut across the social and political alignments of Wilhelmine Germany. The Social Democrats took the matter up in Parliament in June 1910, raising the question if the wildlife in Germany's colonies was adequately protected against large-scale hunting expeditions and foreign adventurers. They found the colonial wildlife question expedient for they could extend their campaign for a more humanitarian colonial policy to the realm of animals and combine it with a mild objection of hunting as a ritual assertion of class. At the same time, the issue also resonated with both wings of the Lebensreform movement in German society: Schillings found a forum in the conservative-nationalist Dürerbund and the *Süddeutsche Monatshefte*, while Hans Paasche used the liberal-reformist *Vortrupp* to present wildlife conservation as a necessary step of self-civilization toward an idealist refinement of "Germanness."[35]

Two qualifications have to be made with regard to the extension of colonial conservation as a social concern. First, it would be misleading to describe the extension of the social constituency of colonial conservation merely within the framework of the nation-state. In a debate where the conservationists pitted wildlife destruction on a global scale against narrow, local interests of development, the recruitment of evidence, concepts, and expertise supporting the global perspective was imperative. If the call for colonial wildlife conservation was increasingly marked by powerful nationalist appeals and language, this was to a considerable degree effected by imperial transnationalism. The national park to be adopted was American, the game law to be emulated was British, and it was the Swiss Paul Sarasin who demanded to make the governor of the German East African colony accountable for his "mad deeds."[36] Second, the broader social constituency may have granted the issue greater public resonance. But ultimately, it was not strength in numbers that brought about a change in conservationist policies, but privileged access to colonial decision makers. Like in Britain, constant lobbying by a closely knit male network organized around hunting ultimately did the trick. Public scandalization may have paved the way, but it was at the emperor's breakfast table that East African wildlife policies ultimately turned toward sustainability.

Serving Wildlife—A Breakfast at Emperor's

Voices from the colony featured only marginally in the controversy about the "mass murder" of game in East Africa. In the light of later outbreaks of rinderpest, white settlers vindicated Rechenberg's order as the "sole measure promising some success in preventing the spread of the plague." The *Usambara-Post*, a settler organ otherwise distinguished through a decidedly oppositional stand toward Rechenberg's policies, refuted the rhetoric of imminent extinction as grossly exaggerated and accused the "apostles of conservation" of outright hypocrisy. Schillings was alleged to have breached the Kenyan Game Laws on his expeditions,[37] and the colonial administration in Dar es Salaam did not refrain from providing the colonial office with confidential information to undermine the moral high ground of the conservationists. Their target was Hans Paasche, who was not only accused of shooting ivory worth thousands of marks during his first stay in East Africa in 1906, but was also found to defy the payment of outstanding shooting fees for elephants killed during his second East African journey in 1909–10. The moralists, was their message, had themselves never practiced what they preached.[38] Rechenberg also underlined that the attempted creation of a buffer zone devoid of game had actually been a means of applied game protection, for a rinderpest panzootic would have killed livestock and wildlife. Moreover, he emphasized that the existing game reserves were actually *Naturschutzparke* without bearing the name.[39] Yet, the double pressure of the colonial office and the Deutsche Kolonialgesellschaft's commission for wildlife conservation made clear that the patience with his deference of reform was over. The colonial office had used the emotionalized atmosphere in 1911 to analyze all its available information on the current administration of game conservation in East Africa. Moreover, Lindequist systematically compared Rechenberg's ordinance with the regulations in force in the surrounding British colonies to find that German East Africa fared quite unfavorably. In all British colonies, for example, female and cow elephants were exempt from hunting, the number of elephants to be shot under one license was restricted to two or four specimens only, and the minimum weight of ivory for legal export was considerably higher, at least in Kenya. Obviously, a stricter handling of elephant hunting was practicable, and in September 1911, Lindequist ordered the central administration in Dar es Salaam to take the Kenya and Malawi game ordinances as models for an immediate reform.[40]

Rechenberg was extremely quick to revise the ordinance to prevent interference by the wildlife commission. The new game law was published only two months later. In order to maintain an impression of administrative consequence and continuity, the new regulations were only gazetted as amendment to the previous ordinance. The revision was one of the last official duties before Rechenberg was granted leave for Europe in October 1911. He was not to return to his office again, and his resignation is often explained with weariness after years of hostilities. However, his later correspondence reveals a considerable disappointment with being out of office, and the timing of his demisson suggests that it may have been quite literally "game over" for Rechenberg. His revised ordinance was once more found insufficient and modified immediately after he had left. Theodor Gunzert, a long-standing district official and surely an insider of East African politics, probably had a point when he claimed later that the shooting order, "this piece of foolishness," had been instrumental in Rechenberg's downfall.[41]

In the last weeks of 1911, the wildlife commission used its exclusive social connections to make sure that Rechenberg's ordinance was not enacted without substantial modifications by the conservation lobby. Carl Hagenbeck, one of the commission's members, had visited Emperor Wilhelm II at his estate in Cadinen in September 1911 to discuss plans for a "zoological paradise" in the northern districts of Berlin, similar in kind to his premises in Stellingen. Hagenbeck skillfully combined his private business interests in live animal trade, ostrich farming, and the breeding of hybrid cattle for the colonies with the general problem of wildlife destruction. He presented the hazardous policies of Rechenberg as jeopardizing both his enterprises and the game stock of the colony. Schillings had provided Hagenbeck with additional supportive material, including a letter from Theodore Roosevelt that expressed the former U.S. President's conviction that steps were necessary to enhance the protection of East Africa's wildlife.[42] The combination of Hagenbeck and Roosevelt did not fail to impress the Kaiser who requested the colonial office to report on the state of affairs in German East Africa immediately after the meeting. Wilhelm found the amendments introduced by Rechenberg's revision in November by far not restrictive enough and demanded a considerable increase of the fees, the further circumscription of indigenous hunting, and the extension of reserved areas in which absolute protection was granted to all game. Wilhelm II clearly echoed Schillings when he reprimanded the colonial office that his majesty was "unable to understand how in our colonies regulations could not be enacted which the English have successfully enacted in theirs."[43]

Just a few days before Christmas on 21 December, Wilhelm II invited Schillings, the Duke Adolf Friedrich von Mecklenburg and Wilhelm Solf, the new secretary of states for the colonies, to an exclusive breakfast of conservation-minded hunters at the emperor's.[44] Little is known about the event, but as Schillings intimated afterward, it made "a strong and powerful hand intervene on behalf of German East Africa in December 1911."[45] Undeniably, Wilhelm II, Schillings, and Adolf Friedrich von Mecklenburg impressed their wishes for further restrictions of the East African game law upon the new colonial secretary. Just one day after the breakfast, Solf communicated the gentlemen hunters' wishes to the government in Dar es Salaam. It took acting-governor Methner several nightshifts to produce another revised ordinance, which was issued in the nick of time on 30 December, without any previous consultation of the local governor's council.[46]

What did the intervention of the strong hand finally achieve? First and foremost, the conservationists effected the extension of enhanced protection to the larger game species, including elephants. Only two elephants were allowed under a special license accessible only to holders of a *große Jagdschein*, and shooting an elephant in German East Africa now cost the payment of 750 rupees for the license and the additional previous payment of 150 rupees for the first, 450 rupees for the second elephant.[47] The minimum weight of "legitimate" ivory was raised from 5 kilograms to 15 kilograms, making the German East African regulations match the ones in force in Kenya. Also the number of specimens of buffalo, rhinos, giraffes, and elands was reduced to two under the *große Jagdschein*. Only four specimens of zebra and several other antelopes were allowed under any license, and the Kaiser's intervention regaled further, that the fee for the small settlers' license was considerably reduced. As far as reserves were concerned, already Rechenberg's revision had commanded the reintroduction of the suspended Lupembe reserve, which was now listed under "Iringa I." To this was added a number of new reserves. Despite demands from the side of the elite hunter-conservationists, Rechenberg had not followed the Kenyan example of excluding Africans entirely from the hunting with firearms. Once more, it was justified with the traumatizing experience of Maji Maji, but it was also an expression of economic calculations, for a *große Eingeborenen-Jagdschein* was introduced to enable the continued engagement of African hunters as suppliers to the trade with trophies, antelope skins, and rhino horns. African hunting remained, however, circumscribed by the administrative boundaries of the colonial districts. Elephants were now entirely prohibited as prey for the rifle-bearing African hunter,[48] and upon the Kaiser's intervention, the fee for the cheapest "native" license was raised from 3 to 10 rupees.

Apart from an amendment in July 1913, which shuffled the categories of game to include several further species among those whose hunting was restricted, the game ordinance that entered into force in January 1912 was not substantially altered for the rest of German colonial rule in East Africa. Some criticism in detail notwithstanding, it was considered a "great step forward" by the settlers' organs in East Africa, whereas the Colonial Society's wildlife commission still found severe shortcomings in comparison to the Kenyan ordinance. Their demands for the complete protection for any species threatened with extinction, the establishment of further large-scale wildlife reserves, the complete exclusion of native hunters from firearms, the hiring of a sufficient number of wardens, and finally, the establishment of a separate department for wildlife conservation in the colonial office remained, however, unfulfilled until World War I reached the African colonies.[49]

The Undiscovered Paradise—The Failure of Tourist Hunting in German East Africa

By 1912, the elephant had been transformed from a species slaughtered for its ivory to a species conserved for the exertion of ritual white domination by a privileged few. Exploitation had finally made way for the sustainable utilization of African game by privileged hunters, ongoing circumventions, and breeches of the ordinance notwithstanding. The stage was set to attract globetrotting hunters who could afford the high fees for exclusive thrill and social distinction.

Nonetheless, the German East African colony never developed into a destination on a par with the neighboring Kenya colony, although suggestions and efforts in that direction have been made at least since Schillings recommended tourist hunting as a promising source of income in 1901. While the economic demands of time and finance to organize a hunting safari in East Africa were so high to restrict this form of leisure travel to aristocrats and the new industrial wealth, the growth of tourist hunting in German East Africa was encumbered by a lack of infrastructure combined with red tape and Kenyan competition. Hunting regulations, at least until 1911, granted visiting hunters little privilege, and game laws that did not tie the right to hunt to landed property were hardly encouraging for safari enterprises that might otherwise have been established on vast estates. Marketing was surely not invented in German East Africa, as is documented by a comprehensive hunting manual compiled in 1912 to attract tourist hunters. Whereas steamship companies, the Uganda Railway, and the Safari enterprises located in Mombasa and Nairobi marketed the distinctiveness of "Safaris de luxe" in Kenya, the German East African *Jagdhandbuch* promoted hunting in the spirit of bureaucracy: the first seventy pages of the booklet detailed all the administrative regulations touching upon hunting in the colony. Veterinary regulations and the "do's and don'ts" in the government's protected forests completed the picture that hunting in the colony was not adventure but administrative hassle. Indeed, the book did its best to repel anyone who was potentially interested.[50]

Commercial structures supporting more than the occasional hunting expedition emerged only gradually after Maji Maji. The few entrepreneurial-minded hunters who tried faced the overwhelming competition of the British safari enterprises in Kenya, where the business already flourished since the turn of the century. Big game hunting in Kenya could draw upon a British cult of sport-hunting that had evolved in India, North America, and South Africa over the nineteenth century. Its adherents discovered the plains north of Kilimanjaro as the latest fashionable outlet after the turn of the century. Geography favored British East Africa, too, for the journey to Mombasa was slightly shorter from Europe, and the game-rich plains were more easily accessible from the coast than comparable areas in the German colony. The blossoming safari business in Kenya handicapped a like development in German East Africa also because the boom enabled entrepreneurs to pay such high wages that it attracted labor migration from German East Africa. Younger males from the Western provinces of Unyamwezi and Sukuma went to Mombasa and Nairobi for seasonal work as safari porters. In doing so, they added to the shortages on the German East African labor market and continued the long tradition of labor migration already encountered in the caravan trade. British colonial authorities had the will to utilize game through hunting tourism, they provided the necessary infrastructure, and unlike the Germans at the time, they did not refrain from a business-like approach to wildlife. After its completion in 1901, the Uganda Railway prompted the development of a comprehensive infrastructure for tourist hunting in both Mombasa and Nairobi and conveniently carried visiting hunters disembarking at Mombasa to the capital, providing the spectacle of "Nature's Zoo" along the way.[51] Advertising campaigns quickly popularized "Safari" in its new colonial meaning as a temporary, well-organized, and ritualized confrontation with wildlife and wild nature. Kenya was marketed as an escape for the "Piccadilly swell," from the "wearisome demands of Society existence," where evening dress was dispensable and a shave no necessity. The

> fascination of Africa with all its alluring mystery comes upon the traveller; ... the feeling that civilization with all its burdens is far behind, the perennial attraction of sport—the pursuit of the lion, the leopard, the buffalo, the rhinoceros, the hartebeeste, or the smaller gazelles—all these things produce an exhilaration of spirits, a *joie de vivre*, which fashionable life at home can never furnish. The delights of "Safari" in the British East African Highlands make glad the heart and strengthen the body of the traveller.[52]

It was in the first decade of the twentieth century that the myth of wild Africa was commercialized by a tourist industry that has not ceased to exploit and extend that myth ever since. As early as 1907, the British colonial office had to sooth conservationists concerned about the East African safari boom that no more than 500 sportsmen licenses would be issued annually to prevent "many of the rarer varieties of game" in the colony from extermination.[53] Among the globetrotting hunters who flocked to Kenya were many Germans who, like the Frankfurt-based banker and millionaire Rudolf von Goldschmidt-Rothschild, preferred the "comfort and ease" of arrangements in Kenya over the neighboring German colony.[54] He and other distinguished German and Austrian big game hunters, such as Prince Schaumburg-Lippe or the Austrian Count Richard Coudenhove, lent their name for the advertising campaigns of the Uganda Railway, which also cooperated with the state-subsidized German East Africa Line Steamship Company. Both enterprises together offered a comprehensive transport package from Hamburg right to the encounter with "prehistoric" wilderness in Kenya, which they advertised in a jointly edited brochure in German in 1905.[55] A handful of Africa-experienced Germans sensed the potential for profit in Kenya's safari boom and established themselves as safari entrepreneurs in the neighboring colony. From 1903 onward, German big game hunters could use the facilities of Richard Huebner, a globetrotting jack-of-all-trades who ran a rather shanty hostel for visiting hunters close to the Uganda Railway at Kibwezi. When he retired in 1908, his enterprise was taken up by Konrad Schauer, who opened a safari hotel at Kijabe Hill in Kikuyuland. There, he accommodated a great number of German traveling hunters, including the Wittelsbach Highnesses Princes Georg and Konrad of Bavaria.[56]

Apparently, Germany's globetrotting hunters did not need their own colonies as a stage, as much as colonial propagandists might have demanded so. Although a special edition of the *African World* on occasion of the twenty-fifth anniversary of the colony promoted German East Africa as a hunting destination among its British readership,[57] Tanganyika remained a territory yet to be discovered by the cosmopolitan constituency of big game hunting.[58] By the outbreak of World War I, only Friedrich Wilhelm Siedentopf in the Ngorongoro Crater appears to have offered the kind of professionalized local guidance and organization similar to the "white hunters" of the Kenyan Safari.[59] Not only the marketing and commodification of Africa's wildlife for tourist hunting had its roots in the first decade of the twentieth century, but also the comparative structural disadvantage of Tanzania vis-à-vis to Kenya, which has remained the more popular destination of international wildlife tourism for most of the twentieth century.

Notes

1. BAB R 1001/7777, fol. 224: Circular to all stations, 1 March 1909; Carl Georg Schillings, "In Afrikas Wildkammern als Forscher und Jäger. Ein Geleitwort zu dem gleichnamigen Buche Dr. Bergers," *Wild und Hund* 15 (1909): 854; Fritz Bley, "Schutz unseres afrikanischen Großwildes!," *Deutsche Jägerzeitung* 54 (1909–10): 745.
2. BAB R 1001/7777, fol. 252: RKA to Gov DOA, 10 January 1910; fol. 295: Circular to all stations, 12 March 1910.
3. BAB R 1001/6070, fol. 156–57: Gov DOA to RKA, 27 October 1909.
4. BAB R 1001/6070, fol. 156–57: telegraph RKA to Gov DOA, 27 1909; BAB R 1001/6070, fol. 186: Koch to RKA, 8 March 1910.
5. *Norddeutsche Allgemeine Zeitung* no. 285 (1909), 4 December; BAB R 1001/6070, fol. 175: Gov DOA to RKA, 8 January 1910; BAB R 1001/6070, fol. 186: Koch to RKA, 8 March 1910; BAB R 1001/6070, fol. 188: Gov DOA to RKA, 26 April 1910; BAB R 1001/6070, fol. 188, enclosure: Report by veterinary official Probst, 20 March 1910; BAB R 1001/6070, fol. 203–10: RE Montgomery: Report on a visit to investigate an outbreak of cattle disease in German East Africa; BAB R 1001/6070, fol. 225: Gov DOA to RKA, 30 November 1910.
6. BAB R 1001/6070, fol. 212: Telegraph Gov DOA to RKA, 11 August 1910; fol. 213: Gov DOA to RKA, 13 August 1910 (quote); *Amtlicher Anzeiger für Deutsch-Ostafrika* 11, no. 27 (1910), 14 August; *Amtlicher Anzeiger für Deutsch-Ostafrika* 11, no. 34, (1910), 8 October; BAB R 1001/7777, fol. 325: Telegram Gov DOA to RKA, 8 October 1910; BAB R 1001/6070, fol. 225: Gov DOA to RKA, 30 November 1910.
7. In 1910, the number of cattle in the colony was roughly estimated at 1,500,000, the majority of which were concentrated in Rwanda, see *Die deutschen Schutzgebiete in Afrika und der Südsee 1910/11*, 26.
8. BAB R 1001/768, fol. 44: Von Prittwitz to Gov DOA, 27 December 1906 (excerpt); fol. 151: Gov DOA to RKA, 18 September 1909, quote). Cf. Lotte Hughes, *Moving the Maasai. A Colonial Misadventure* (Houndmills, 2006).
9. *Kilimandjaro- und Meru-Zeitung* 1, no. 12 (1913), 21 June; BAB R 1001/6071, fol. 11–12: Gov DOA to RKA, 16 May 1911.
10. *Further Correspondence relating to the Preservation of Wild Animals in Africa* (London 1911), no. 19: Acting Governor HR Wallis to CO, 21 January 1911; PRO CO 885/22/287, no. 10: Royal Society to CO, 4 March 1913; no. 21: Royal Society to CO, 15 April 1913; MacKenzie, *The Empire of Nature*, 237–38.
11. See Giorgio Miescher, *Namibia's Red Line. The History of a Veterinary and Settlement Border* (Basingstoke, 2012), chapter 1; Lehmann, "Between Waterberg and Sandveld," 544–45.
12. BAB R 1001/6062, fol. 157–58: Gov Deutsch-Südwestafrika (DSWA) to District Offices, 13 January 1897; fol. 168: Count von Hageneck to acting governor Lindequist, 14 December 1896; BAB R 1001/6063, fol. 31: Gov DSWA to AA KA, 17 May 1897.
13. BAB R 1001/6070, fol. 215: RKA to Gov DOA, 14 September 1910; cf. BAB R 1001/7778, fol. 120: RKA to Emperor Wilhelm II, 25 October 1911.
14. The data from Moshi, for example, states that a quarry of 1,000 heads of game was made with 1,600 bullets only. See BAB R 1001/7778, fol. 258–59: Gov DOA to RKA, 24 November 1911.

15. KNA, PC Coast 1/1/286, Journey Report of Captain Luckman, July, 16–19 1912; KNA, PC 1/6/136: Report by Assistant Game Warden CW Woodhouse, 27 December 1912.
16. BAB R 1001/7778, fol. 6: Gov DOA to RKA, 16 May 1911; fol. 10: Gov DOA to RKA, 7 June 1911; fol. 63: Proceedings concerning the Shooting of Game in German East Africa 1910, telegraph dated 31 August 1911; fol. 120: RKA to Emperor Wilhelm II, 25 October 1911; fol. 127: Steudel to Gov DOA, 4 September 1911.
17. *Amtlicher Anzeiger für Deutsch-Ostafrika* 12, no. 24 (1911), 4 June; BAB R 1001/7778, fol. 311: Mahenge to Gov DOA, 26 November 1911; *Deutsch-Ostafrikanische Zeitung* 13, no. 48 (1911), 17 June; no. 98, 9 December 1911; BAB R 1001/7802-1, enclosure, 27; "Wildvernichtung in Deutsch-Ostafrika," *Wild und Hund* 15 (1911), 539.
18. For the broader context, see Peter Coates, "Creatures Enshrined: Wild Animals as Bearers of Heritage," *Past & Present, Supplement 10* (2015): 272–98.
19. BAB R 8923/2236, fol. 23: Bericht über die Hauptversammlung der Deutschen Kolonialgesellschaft im Oberen Museum zu Stuttgart am 9. und 10. Juni 1911, 53, 67; Fritz Behn, "Naturerhaltung und Wildmord in Deutsch-Ostafrika—ein Kulturskandal," *Naturwissenschaftliche Wochenschrift* 10 (1911): 805.
20. Hans Paasche, "Der Massenmord in Ostafrika," *Deutsch-Ostafrikanische Zeitung* 13, no. 38 (1911), 13 May; Paul Sarasin, *Über nationalen und internationalen Vogelschutz, sowie einige anschliessende Fragen des Weltnaturschutzes. Vortrag, gehalten am 12. Mai 1911 am zweiten deutschen Vogelschutztag in Stuttgart und in dessen Auftrag in Druck gegeben* (Basel, 1911), 24.
21. BAB R 1001/7778, fol. 19: Erzberger to Rechenberg, 20 June 1911; BAB R 1001/7778, fol. 20: Rechenberg to Erzberger, 4 August 1911.
22. See Heike I Schmidt, "Colonial Intimacy. The Rechenberg Scandal and Homosexuality in German East Africa," *Journal of the History of Sexuality* 17 (2008): 25–59; Frank Bösch, *Öffentliche Geheimnisse. Skandale, Politik und Medien in Deutschland und Großbritannien 1880–1914* (Munich, 2009), 288–309.
23. See Jamie Lorimer, "Nonhuman Charisma," *Environment & Planning D: Society and Space* 25 (2007): 911–32.
24. Carl Georg Schillings, "Zur Frage des Naturschutzes in den deutschen Kolonien, namentlich in Deutsch-Ostafrika," *Naturwissenschaftliche Wochenschrift* 10 (1911): 807–14; Ernst Stromer von Reichenbach, "Die einstige Verbreitung afrikanischer Säugetiere," *Naturwissenschaftliche Wochenschrift* 10 (1911): 814–16.
25. Paasche, "Der Massenmord in Ostafrika;" Paasche, "Deutsch-afrikanische Naturschutzparke."
26. Behn, "Naturerhaltung und Wildmord in Deutsch-Ostafrika," 801, 807. Fritz Behn (1878–1970) had been hunting in East Africa and counts among the best-known artists in the field of animal sculptures in Germany in the twentieth century. He is perhaps most famous for the enormous red-brick elephant erected as a monument to Germany's lost colonies in Bremen in 1932.
27. BAB R 8023/1000, fol. 79: Report on a Committee Meeting of the Deutsche Kolonialgesellschaft, Berlin, 15 May 1911, 13; Schillings, "Zur Frage des Naturschutzes in den deutschen Kolonien," 810, 813.
28. The term "wandelnde Kapitalien" was coined by Georg Richelmann, "Über Tierschutz in den Kolonien," *Deutsche Kolonialzeitung* 29, no. 17 (1912): 271.
29. Schillings, "Zur Frage des Naturschutzes in den deutschen Kolonien," 813–14.

30. Paasche, "Der Massenmord in Ostafrika"; Sarasin, *Über nationalen und internationalen Vogelschutz*; "Der zweite Vogelschutztag," *Berliner Tagblatt*, no. 247 (1911), 16 May.
31. BAB R 8923/2236, fol. 23: Bericht über die Hauptversammlung der DKG; cf. *Deutsche Kolonialzeitung* 28 (1911): 401–3.
32. See for example BAB R 8923/2236, fol. 23: Bericht über die Hauptversammlung der DKG; "Auszug aus der Rede von Prof. CG Schillings auf der Hauptversammlung der Deutschen Kolonialgesellschaft am 10. Juni 1911 in Stuttgart," *Zeitschrift des Allgemeinen Deutschen Jagdschutzvereins* 16 (1911): 361–64, 375–78; Schillings, "Wildgemetzel in Deutsch-Ostafrika," *Blätter für Naturschutz* 2, no. 6 (1911): 4–11; no. 7: 4–6; no. 8: 2–4; no. 9: 1–2; Friedrich Regensberg and Carl Georg Schillings, "Naturschutzparke in den Kolonien," in *Naturschutzparke in Deutschland und Österreich. Ein Mahnwort an das deutsche und österreichische Volk*, 2nd ed., ed. Verein Naturschutzpark (Stuttgart, 1911), 54–57.
33. Gissibl, "Paradiesvögel"; cf. Barbara T Gates, *Kindred Nature. Victorian and Edwardian Women Embrace the Living World* (Chicago, 1998).
34. Paul Sarasin, *Weltnaturschutz. Global Protection of Nature* (Bern, 1910); Paul Sarasin, *Ueber die Aufgaben des Weltnaturschutzes. Denkschrift gelesen an der Delegiertenversammlung zur Weltnaturschutzkommission in Bern am 18. November 1913* (Basel, 1914); Carl Georg Schillings, "Die Arche Noah," *Süddeutsche Monatshefte* 11/2 (1914): 147–54.
35. Carl Georg Schillings, "Hagenbeck als Erzieher," *Süddeutsche Monatshefte* 8 (1911): 275–90; Carl Georg Schillings, "Die Tragödie des Paradiesvogels und des Edelreihers," *Süddeutsche Monatshefte* 8 (1911): 789–96; Carl Georg Schillings, "Giraffenschlachten in Deutschostafrika," *Süddeutsche Monatshefte* 10 (1912–13): 151–56; Hans Paasche, "Protest in elfter Stunde," *Der Vortrupp* 1, no. 1 (1912), 1 January; Hans Paasche, "Deutscher Naturschutz," *Der Vortrupp* 1, no. 1 (1912): 609–17, 641–45. Cf. Rüdiger vom Bruch, "Kunstwart und Dürerbund," in *Das konservative Intellektuellen-Milieu in Deutschland, seine Presse und seine Netzwerke (1890–1960)*, ed. Michel Grunewald and Uwe Puschner (Frankfurt, 2003), 353–75; Ulrich Linse, "Der Vortrupp (1912–21). Ein lebensreformerisches Organ des fortschrittlich-liberalen Konservatismus," in *Das konservative Intellektuellen-Milieu in Deutschland, seine Presse und seine Netzwerke (1890–1960)*, ed. Michel Grunewald and Uwe Puschner (Frankfurt, 2003), 377–406.
36. Sarasin, *Über nationalen und internationalen Vogelschutz*, 24.
37. "In elfter Stunde," *Usambara-Post* 11, no. 13 (1912), 13 April; BAB R 1001/813, Meeting of the governor's council, 21–28 June 1913, 14; Agricola, "Wild und Vieh," *Usambara-Post* 12, no. 38 (1913), 20 September.
38. BAB R 1001/7778, fol. 66: Paasche to RKA, 1 September 1911; BAB R 1001/7779, fol. 118: Gov DOA to RKA, 17 January 1912; BAB R 1001/7779, fol. 123: RKA to Paasche, 7 March 1912; fol. 142: note confirming the payment of 800 marks by Hans Paasche, 26 May 1912; BAB R 1001/7780, fol. 4: Gov DOA to RKA, 5 September 1913; BAB R 1001/7780, fol. 45: Gov DOA to Paasche, 27 November 1913.
39. BAB R 1001/7778, fol. 120: Gov DOA to RKA, 25 October 1911.
40. BAB R 1001/7777, fol. 336: Comparison between Game Ordinance for Nyasaland (1911) and Game Ordinance German East Africa (1908; undated draft); BAB R 1001/7777, fol. 337–39: RKA to Gov DOA, 13 September 1911. A detailed

analysis of the Kenyan game ordinance gazetted in December 1909, including a comparison with the German East African game laws, was already provided by the consulate in Mombasa in March 1910, cf. BAB R 1001/7797, fol. 87: Brode to RKA, 17 March 1910.
41. Bundesarchiv Koblenz (BAK) N 1053/33, Vol. 1, fol. 60: Rechenberg to Hanna Solf, 9 October 1913; BAK N 1053/33, Vol. 1, fol. 193: Rechenberg to Hanna Solf, 27 February 1913; OBL Micr. Afr. 446: Theodor Gunzert, Service in German East Africa & German Foreign Service, 1902–33 [undated], 30. Cf. Wächter, *Naturschutz in den deutschen Kolonien in Afrika*, 76–80.
42. BAB R 1001/7778, fol. 75: Kaiserliches Zivilkabinett to RKA, 20 September 1911; BAB R 1001/7778, fol. 101: Hagenbeck to Wilhelm II, 29 September 1911, enclosure; BAB R 1001/7778, fol. 107: Roosevelt to Schillings, 5 September 1911. The meeting took place on 18 September 1911, BAB R 1001/8390, fol. 21: Hagenbeck to Gov DOA, 17 November 1911.
43. BAB R 1001/7778, fol. 193: RKA to Gov DOA, 8 December 1911, enclosure: Zivilkabinett to RKA, 21 November 1911.
44. "Neues von der kolonialen Rechtsunsicherheit," *Frankfurter Zeitung*, 9 April 1912.
45. Schillings, "Giraffenschlachten in Deutschostafrika," 156–57.
46. BAB R 1001/7778, fol. 261: Telegram RKA to Gov DOA, 22 December 1911 (draft); BAB R 1001/7778, fol. 266: Gov DOA to RKA, 23 December 1911; BAB R 1001/7778, fol. 269: RKA to Gov DOA, 28 December 1911; *Gesetz und Recht für Deutsch-Ostafrika* 1, no. 1 (1912), 3 January; *Amtlicher Anzeiger für Deutsch-Ostafrika* 13, no. 3 (1912), 17 January; Methner, *Unter drei Gouverneuren*, 272–74.
47. Permanent residents in the colony paid only 450 rupees instead of the 750 charged from visiting hunters for the *große Jagdschein*.
48. *Amtlicher Anzeiger für Deutsch-Ostafrika* 12, no. 37 (1911), 3 September; *Amtlicher Anzeiger für Deutsch-Ostafrika* 12, no. 46 (1911), 5 November; *Amtlicher Anzeiger für Deutsch-Ostafrika* 12, no. 49 (1911), 19 November; BAB R 1001/7778, fol. 196: Gov DOA to RKA, 11 November 1911; "Zu den neuen Jagdbestimmungen," *Usambara-Post* 10, no. 46 (1911), 18 November.
49. *Bericht über die Arbeiten der Wildschutz-Kommission der Deutschen Kolonialgesellschaft* (Berlin, 1912), 20–21.
50. *Jagdhandbuch für Deutsch-Ostafrika. Auf Grund amtlicher Quellen bearbeitet* (Dar es Saalam, 1912), 1–71. See also Edward Stewart White, *The Rediscovered Country* (London, 1915), 9–10, who claimed to have waited for a year to obtain the permission to enter German territory from Kenya for hunting.
51. The hunting literature abounds with enthusiastic descriptions of the railway journey. See for example Berger, *In Afrikas Wildkammern als Forscher und Jäger*, 6–7; Emil Ludwig, *Die Reise nach Afrika*, 2nd ed. (Berlin, 1913), 53–55.
52. All quotes from the brochures entitled *For Real Sport Take a 303 or a 450 Express over the Uganda Railway* by the Uganda Railway Company, issued probably 1909, and *African Travel De Luxe*, issued in 1909 by the travel agency Way & Co. Ltd. Exemplars of both brochures can be found in Staatsarchiv Freiburg (StAF) U 101/1: Ruprecht Böcklin von Böcklinsau Papers, no. 11.
53. *Further Correspondence relating to the Preservation of Wild Animals in Africa* (London, 1909), no. 23: Colonial Office to SPWFE and the editor of *The Field*, 22 May 1907.

54. Rudolf von Goldschmidt-Rothschild, "Aus dem britischen Massailand," *Wild und Hund* 20 (1914): 421–25.
55. Deutsche Ost-Afrika-Linie, in Verbindung mit der Eisenbahn von Uganda, Britisch Ost-Afrika, ed., *Die Uganda-Eisenbahn, Britisch-Ostafrika. Von Mombassa bis zum Viktoria-See und Rundfahrt per Dampfer auf dem großen See*. s.l. [1905], 27.
56. Konrad Schauer, *Höhenkurort "Kijabe-Hill." Handbuch für Jagd- und wissenschaftliche Expeditionen sowie Vergnügungsreisen nach Ost-Afrika*, Kijabe-Hill s.a., 19, 59–61. A copy of the brochure is available at the library of the DITSL in Witzenhausen.
57. See Lindner, *Koloniale Begegnungen*, 179–80.
58. See for example White, *The Rediscovered Country*, 8–9.
59. Wilhelm Siedentopf, "Auf Löwen in Deutsch-Ostafrika," *Deutsche Jägerzeitung* 59 (1912): 196–200; Wilhelm Siedentopf, "Jagd und Jagdexpeditionen in Deutsch-Ostafrika," *Deutsche Jägerzeitung* 64 (1914–15): 82–83.

 PART III

Spaces of Conservation between Metropole and Colony

 CHAPTER 6

Places of Deep Time
The Political Geography of Colonial Wildlife Conservation

In 1896, governor Hermann von Wissmann set aside large tracts of land between Mounts Kilimanjaro and Meru as well as along the northern bank of the Rufiji River for purposes of game conservation. This was the beginning of what was to become a standard practice in the field of wildlife preservation in colonial and independent Tanzania throughout the twentieth century: the demarcation and bounding of space for the preservation of wild nature in the form of game reserves, national parks, and other forms of protected areas. The reserves gazetted in German East Africa gave a novel preservationist twist to the centuries old idea of the bounded game reserve. They laid the basis for Tanzania's world-renowned environmental-conservation complex, and they pioneered the establishment of game reserves all over East Africa. Albeit hesitantly, all British colonies bordering German East Africa followed the example set by Wissmann and established sanctuaries between 1896 and 1899.[1] The area reserved specifically for the preservation of wildlife in German East Africa grew steadily: in early 1911, there existed twelve reserves with 29,900 square kilometers; by 1914, a further three had been added to make it 36,900 square kilometers. They comprised about 3.7 percent of the colony's land mass and covered an area larger than Belgium.[2]

This chapter deals with the spaces of conservation that were created through German colonial rule in East Africa. It analyzes the emergence of game reserves as localizations of Western understandings of human relationships toward nature. The chapter opens with an assessment of the connection between perceptions of wildlife degradation and their translation into policies of conservation. The second paragraph explores the political expediency of game reserves and interprets them as a means of asserting the state's authority over the natural resources of the colony. Then, the creation of game reserves in German East Africa is analyzed in its entanglements with the geopolitics of conservation in Europe, North America, and the neighboring British East African colony. The fourth section interprets game reserves as European heterotopias and the result of a particular way of seeing Africa as a timeless wilderness animated by big game, while the final section of this chapter explores the consequences of reserves on the ground. How was the colonial state's claim to preservation within their boundaries translated into practice?

Wildlife Degradation and the Politics of Reserves

The establishment of game reserves in German East Africa resulted from the perception of a profound environmental crisis in the 1890s. Its causes have been explored in previous chapters and need only be briefly reiterated here: excessive hunting for ivory, the increasing presence of white hunters with high-precision rifles, and a series of natural hazards and manmade catastrophes like the rinderpest epizootic. From a global perspective, events in East Africa form part of the late nineteenth-century closure of what John F Richards has termed the seemingly "unending frontier" of wildlife.[3] In East Africa, just as in North America and Southern Africa at about the same time, the perpetrators of destruction themselves sounded the alarm bell: besides professional naturalists, it was a tiny elite of big game hunters who demanded the preservation of wildlife, or at least its more sustainable management as a critical resource.

Yet, the scope and degree of wildlife decline was a contested issue. Fleeting and local observations were generalized. Combined with a lack of knowledge about the zoogeography of the colonial territory, the destruction of its mammalian fauna appeared more dramatic than it probably was. The fate of the bison (*Bison bonasus*) in North America and the extinction of bluebuck (*Hippotragus leucophaeus*) and quagga (*Equus quagga*) in Southern Africa were known and only encouraged expectations that species extermination was imminent also in East Africa. It is easy to prove all the predictions about the elephant's extinction wrong in hindsight, but it is hard to assess the elephants' fate had political decision makers not reacted to the alarm of hunter-conservationists. Both doomsayers and appeasers had their point and were hard to disprove: Schillings witnessed the vanishing of game from the Maasai Steppe on his repeated visits and argued that it was high time to act. His critics among the settlers opposed the establishment of reserves since the extensive and largely unsettled savanna landscapes of the colony still featured large numbers of wildlife.[4] There existed neither means to anchor "degradation" in ecological models nor ideas about minimum viable populations of a certain species in a given area. District commissioners sometimes included observations about the fluctuations of certain species of wildlife. Time and again, also the government encouraged stations to count or estimate the presence of species, their numbers, and their mating periods in their districts.⁵ But these evaluations were based upon random observations and hearsay. Few of them survived in the colonial archive, and they did not result in game legislation being put on a more "biological" basis. The most thorough and systematic wildlife assessment was ordered in 1911 when the colonial office was once more accused of disinterest in wildlife conservation.⁶ In order to prove the government's dedication to the cause, all stations (and all other German colonies as well) were presented a detailed questionnaire. The results were published under the title *Jagd und Wildschutz in den deutschen Kolonien* in 1913. However, the volume fulfilled first and foremost the purpose to soothe public opinion, and it confirmed that administrative questionnaires yielded little reliable information about wildlife, let alone its geography, ecology, or behavior. It contained a list of all species regarded as "game" in German East Africa, their occurrence in the various districts being described in vague terms such as "rare," "frequent," and "at times."⁷ The systematic and scientific study of wildlife should be enabled by reserves. It was not their prerequisite.

The general decrease of wildlife numbers was undeniably an important motif for conservation, but neither the establishment nor the siting of reserves automatically followed from the diagnosis of degradation. As in wildlife policies in general, much depended on the degree to which political decision makers on the local, colonial, and imperial levels were sensitized to conservation as a political responsibility. The most important stage of administrative action was the lowest echelon of military posts and district stations. They not only singled out suitable areas but were also responsible for enforcing the prohibition of hunting within the reserves, either by their own control or via game wardens or local *majumbe*. Unfortunately, the dearth of sources makes it almost impossible to assess their actions. Because of their relative absolutism within the architecture of colonial governance, the attitude and interest of individual governors was *the* decisive factor.⁸ Hunters like Wissmann and von Götzen were both convinced about the necessity of reserves in economic as well as in moral terms. Initially hesitant about the practicability of reserves, Wissmann personally singled out areas vaguely familiar to him from his own expeditions. Nine years later in 1903, von Götzen found that the reserves proclaimed under Wissmann had served their purpose. Claiming that the wildlife numbers within them had "increased considerably,"⁹ the governor supplemented the two existing reserves by a further eleven. Others, like von Liebert and Rechenberg, acknowledged in principle that wildlife should be preserved, but for various reasons objected to the gazetting of further reserves. Von Liebert let himself be convinced by the doubts voiced by district commissioners who argued that reserves were hard, if not impossible to patrol with the personnel at hand.¹⁰ He did not abandon the reserves established by his predecessor, but ignored Wissmann's proposition for their considerable extension.[11] The only reserve newly decreed under his governorship resulted from a proposition of a local district commissioner and was created to protect a small herd of elephants on Ukerewe Island in Lake Victoria.[12] As a consequence, the existence of reserves almost disappeared from the institutional memory of the colonial department in Berlin until the issue was brought back on the agenda by the London Conference.[13] Under the impression of Maji Maji and the tsetse controversy, Rechenberg was particularly unwilling to let wildlife preservation interfere with overall concerns of security and the economic and agricultural development of the colony. His reduction of reserves in size and number resulted in fierce clashes with the conservation lobby in Germany, especially when Rechenberg temporarily suspended the Mahenge reserve to sacrifice its considerable elephant stocks to the rifles of commercial ivory harvesters. Sensitized to the issue by Rechenberg's fate, Methner as acting governor and Heinrich Schnee took conservation seriously as a political task. Both increased the number of reserves to sixteen by September 1913, so that by the eve of World War I, altogether fifteen reserves were distributed over the administrative districts of the colony.

It becomes apparent from the development of reserves that their increase in number and extent in 1903 and after 1911 was closely associated to external interference by actors on the third, metropolitan level of imperial governance. In 1903, it was the London Convention and its recommendation to achieve wildlife preservation by the establishment of reserves. Under Rechenberg's successors, the siting of reserves was strongly influenced by the conservationist lobby in Germany, including Wilhelm II himself. But again, there was no automatic translation of metropolitan demands into local policies: in 1903, it was von Götzen's decision to put part of the recommendations of the London Convention into practice after the colonial department in Berlin had given him a free hand to deal with the convention as he saw fit. After 1911, when Colonial Secretary Solf urged all governors to comply with the justified demands of the "conservationist movement that has recently held so much sway in Germany and other European countries,"[14] Schnee was willing to set aside suitable areas of the colony as *Naturschutzgebiete*. However, district stations displayed little enthusiasm, and the Ngorongoro caldera as the one area that was singled out became a fiercely contested site.

Natural Resources and the State—The Political Expediency of Reserves

Degradation and the embrace of conservationist attitudes on the various levels of political decision-making were thus crucial elements in the establishment of reserves. Still, none of them would have come into being if reserves had not been politically expedient. Establishing sanctuaries for wildlife was not just the last resort to preserve the remnants of wild nature. Rather, reserves were also a legitimate form of land use in their own right. The decision about how land was to be used and who was to settle it was at the heart of colonial rule. Although later advocates of conservation often tend to portray protected areas as a good idea established in an objectionable political context,[15] the deliberate setting aside of land—"Nature"—for nonutilization cannot be severed from the general mechanisms of disposal over land under conditions of colonial rule. It was an integral part of colonialism's political culture, not its opposite.

The creation of game reserves was firmly tied in with the gradual fostering of state authority over the natural resources of the colony. Claims to the moral responsibility toward a unique animal fauna and the preservation of aesthetically pleasing landscapes were undeniably genuine. Yet, ecological degradation also provided the colonial state with a powerful tool to assert its claim over the allocation of resources and the disciplinary power associated with their control. Declaring reserves in areas deemed useless for other economic enterprises was a powerful expression that not even "uninhabited" and seemingly "worthless" lands were exempt from the aspirations of the colonial state.[16] Moreover, they have to be seen within the overall economic geography of colonial rule. The establishment of game reserve also had the side effect to drastically impede, if not extinguish commercial or subsistence hunting of the area's inhabitants. Therefore, they also had the side effect of pushing Africans into other economic activities such as wage labor or cultivation. At the same time, reserves could severely jeopardize goals of agricultural development: the rearing of livestock as well as crop cultivation in their vicinity meant a serious risk of disease transmission and crop damage by animals migrating out of the reserves.

Wissmann's high-handed initiative to declare wild and allegedly uninhabited stretches of land as "government property" and administer them as game reserve in the interest of the state had been prepared by the Crown Land Declaration of November 1895.[17] The ordinance had asserted the state's entitlement to all land that was not "effectively" occupied or cultivated, that is, "ownerless" (*herrenlos*) in the logic of colonial law. It has been argued that the Crown Land Ordinance only asserted a formal claim to the land. Before the state could appropriate territory and hand it out again, a land commission had to identify existing property rights.[18] However, differing understandings of "effective" land use practices bore enormous potential for conflict. Nomadic pastoralism, shifting cultivation, or the itinerant lifestyles of hunter-gatherer societies hardly fulfilled the colonizers' criteria of "rational" land utilization, and Europeans often discerned nothing but wilderness where they were actually confronted with living, cultural landscapes. In the majority of cases, it was enough that the respective district commissioner communicated to Dar es Salaam that the land was not or only sparsely peopled to effect an area's declaration as a game reserve. The extension of reserves in the north, for example—in late 1913, the reserves on Kilimanjaro and Meru had been supplemented by a large reserve around Lake Natron and an elephant reserve near Umbulu—was a corollary to the Maasai herders' concentration in the Maasai reserve from 1906 onward.[19] Moreover, the procedure of negotiating land ownership could only be applied after peaceful conditions had been established. In many areas, however, the violence of colonial conquest had effected the dispersal or relocation of resident populations. The Upper Rufiji and the land between Mounts Kilimanjaro and Meru were both declared as game reserves in the wake of warfare and "punitive" expeditions in 1896. Driving Meru farmers "into virtual hiding on the mountain" was a prerequisite to creating the empty landscape of the reserve.[20]

The spatial circumscription of access to natural resources by enclosure had for centuries been an accompaniment of top-down processes of state formation both in Europe and its colonies. The fiscal necessities of state resource management were a powerful driving force in the development of conservationist principles like the sustainable management of forests as timber.[21] This sustainability was as much based upon power, exclusion, and conflict as in the case of game management. Hunting reserves and parks stood in a long tradition as "symbols of sovereignty" in European societies who themselves adopted this practice from the ancient Empires of Asia and the Middle East. Here, wild animals were managed sustainably less for economic or fiscal capital but for the symbolic assertion of power and for the capital of royal and aristocratic pageant that surrounded their ritualized hunting.[22] The game reserves in German East Africa drew upon this European tradition of the managed game estate, but extended its rationale gradually beyond game toward species preservation. Of course, the areas declared as reserves in German East Africa were far too extensive to allow for anything that resembled the management of game estates in Europe. Also, it was neither within the means of the colonial state to tie hunting to the possession of landed property or to introduce a system of compartmentalized estates with allocated hunting rights, as practiced in the majority of German states. Nor was it in its interest: individuals demanded frequently that the state would lease out large areas to private persons for hunting purposes, but authorities in Dar es Salaam objected to sharing the state's claim to the revenue to be realized from the killing of game.[23] Still, Wissmann's ordinance of 1896, and the ordinances that followed, can be read as attempts at adapting German hunting institutions to East African ecologies. The reserves proclaimed in German East Africa tried to solve the impossibility of controlled game management by casting sustainability into African space. As was the case in the hunting estates existing in Germany, animals qualified for special conservation within reserves because they were "game." Indeed, the definition of game reserves that was included in the London Convention of 1900 upon suggestion of the German delegation was informed by the European experience of the manageable game estate with its clearly definable and identifiable breeding seasons. It decreed that reserves should comprise "sufficiently large tracts of land which have all the qualifications necessary as regards food, water, and, if possible, salt" to afford the animals within them the "necessary quiet during the breeding time."[24] The sanctuaries were also to serve the very practical purpose of producing overflow populations of game to allow for the harvesting of the animals that "spilt" over their confines.

The bounding of reserves in East Africa also contained elements of the feudal practice to enclose common land as game estate and hunting reserve.[25] The feudal subtext of setting aside space for game conservation became most palpable in Wissmann's initial proposition to lift the hunting ban in reserves for dignitaries visiting East Africa for hunting purposes, as well as in his plan to reserve all animals kept therein to the emperor by labeling them "imperial game" (*kaiserliches Wild*). Apparently, Wissmann, elevated to nobility since 1890, aspired to aristocracy also in his lifestyle and imagined an East African equivalent of the representative hunting estates of Wilhelm II in Rominten and Schorfheide. Thus, the governor as the highest representative of the state could act out his aristocratic aspirations, direct any important visitor to one of the reserves, and showcase "his" colony as an exotic and primeval wilderness.[26] An undated reference by an officer serving under Wissmann indicates that the upper Rufiji area may occasionally have served as a destination for hunting-minded Europeans.[27] However, this initial rationale remained most noticeable in the denomination of reserves. Despite the fact that all hunting within them was strictly forbidden, they were for years referred to as *Jagdreservate* (hunting reserves). It was not until 1908 that another revision of the game ordinance replaced the term by the more appropriate *Wildreservate* (game reserves). Even then, boundaries of reserves mattered little when aristocratic visitors were to be accommodated, like the Wittelsbach Princes Leopold and Konrad in early 1914. Although the whole country around Lake

Natron had been set aside as reserve the year before, the Highnesses were allowed to hunt in the hope that their precedent would make the colony a fashionable destination for the German aristocracy.[28]

The shifting denomination—from hunting to wildlife reserves to the *Naturschutzpark* that was discussed, but not realized before the war—indicates that reserves were politically expedient in yet another way. The purposes ascribed to them were anything but static, and they were supposed to fulfill various functions over time. For years, the "production" of game was their foremost task. Government and planters alike hoped that a complete ban of hunting over large areas would frustrate native hunting and force Africans onto the labor market. When reserves came under attack during the tsetse controversy, its champions promoted them as a possible compromise of development by conservation in order to attract wildlife tourism. Indeed, tourist utilization had been a central motive in the attempts to emulate the success of Kenya's Southern Reserve along the Uganda Railway. Here, the habituation of animals to the trains was a desired effect in order to stage the plains as a natural zoo for visual consumption from the carriage window. Enterprising farmers on Mount Kilimanjaro petitioned the government in 1912 to introduce game reserves along the planned extension of the Northern Railway toward Lake Victoria. These should be buffered by extensive hunting zones to attract tourist hunters.[29] The transferability of the Uganda Railway experience to Tanganyika was, however, subject to dispute, and colonial authorities argued that the model of the Uganda Railway was not applicable as the Northern Railway did not cut across miles and miles of barren country unsuitable for agriculture.[30] Still, there were attempts to mimic the Uganda Railway experience on a smaller scale when a reserve was established at the bottom of the Pare Mountains that skirted the Northern Railway for some 70 kilometers. The effort, however, appears to have largely failed. Only one report from November 1913 mentions that passengers actually spotted some ostriches, zebras, and antelopes from the train.[31] Further efforts were considered along the newly erected Central Railway, but plans for a reserve along the railway line in the animal-rich and marshy Mkata Plain never materialized, probably because of the proximity of white plantations on its southern border and other interests in the development of the Mkata. The *Kolonialwirtschaftliche Komitee* was for years prospecting the area with the aim to introduce large-scale cash crop plantations of cotton or tobacco.[32]

Since the *Wildmord* debates of 1911, the advocates of wildlife conservation in the colonies applied another key term from the language of conservationist discourse in Germany to their cause: the *Naturschutzpark*. Africa's vanishing wildlife should be safe from administrative whims in at least one permanent sanctuary, and again, preservation was twinned with hopes for profit by attracting wealthy travelers to the colony. If landscapes earlier qualified through the presence of game, a potential *Naturschutzpark* should ideally feature also "natural beauty." One serious candidate, the Mahenge Reserve, qualified not only for its dense game population but also because it would have been possible to include natural monuments like the Rufiji Falls at Shuguli or the so-called Pangani Rapids (near Mpanga) into a possible park. The colonial office in Berlin advised Dar es Salaam to suggest suitable *Naturschutzparke* in the colony in early 1912, and in Berlin, it was already discussed if such a park was to preserve the typical or the outstanding—a savanna landscape or the Ngorongoro Crater.[33] As discussed in the introduction, the latter was the prime candidate, especially after the Maasai had been relocated from Ngorongoro to the Maasai reserve.

In the eyes of conservationists, the permanent setting aside of nature in a *Naturschutzpark* would have testified to Germany's modernity and its dedication to the idealist cause of nature preservation in comparison with the other European empires. The fact that the project did not materialize despite year-long debates surrounding Ngorongoro points to the limits of the reserves' political expediency. Game reserves, as opposed to a park, could be abolished by the stroke of a pen if other utilizations of the respective landscape deemed more profitable. Their preliminary character was better suited to the piecemeal and makeshift character of colonial policies in general. Most conveniently, reserves already served a political purpose as soon as they existed on paper. Reference to patches of land colored in green on a map was often enough to soothe public opinion at home and shake off conservationists' requests. Such was the main function of the Reichskolonialamt's publication on hunting and wildlife conservation in 1913, which featured the game reserves in all German colonies colored in a reassuring green.[34]

An internal memorandum on wildlife conservation compiled in the Reichskolonialamt in 1909 reveals the sterner political realities of conservation. Its author was convinced about the inevitability of the march of progress that could only be slowed down, but not halted by the establishment of reserves. Conservation's minimum target was, therefore, to retain "at least one reserve, even if the advance of culture demanded its removal."[35] The plans to introduce a permanent *Naturschutzpark* would have fulfilled this requirement, but it would have been little more than an island of preservation in a sea of accepted transformation and exploitation of nature around it. In a long-term perspective, this was perhaps the most important aspect of why regimes of spatial conservation were politically expedient: setting aside reserves as spatial repositories of nature was a powerful apology for the unbridled exploitation of nature at will outside of them. The spatial segregation of landscape utilization encouraged a spatial bifurcation of responsibilities that could already be witnessed in the case of the early game reserves: an ethics of preservation, care, and responsibility was developed only for animals within the confines of reserves. Outside, hunting and exploitation continued more or less unabated. Sustainability was relegated into space, not incorporated into ethics and action, so that even from a preservationist perspective, reserves were a very ambivalent achievement.

The Global Geopolitics of Conservation in East Africa

Wildlife conservation in German East Africa was part of the global geopolitics of wildlife preservation and the assertion of European mastery and stewardship over wild nature. The blueprint of the European game estate behind the early game reserves has shown that the mindset Europeans brought with them undoubtedly played a commanding role. But ideas about nature, its exploitation, management, and preservation were not only negotiated between imperial metropole and colonial periphery.[36] Other spaces equally mattered. In the late 1880s, the aristocratic landowner Friedrich Falz-Fein had started to set aside five hundred hectares of steppe just north of the Crimea at the mouth of the Dnepr in Southern Ukraine. The estate, called "Askania Nova," consisted of a zoo, stables for breeding and acclimatization, a botanical garden, and a vast enclosure of steppe land. Askania Nova constituted a nucleus of conservation in Russia,[37] and it was widely hailed as an "animal paradise" by contemporaries. The steppe enclosure plus the more than 50 mammalian species held at the estate, including African animals such as zebras and eland, attracted visits and inspired conservationists abroad. Among them were key protagonists of colonial conservation in Germany such as Ludwig Heck, Fritz Bronsart von Schellendorff, Carl Hagenbeck, or Paul Matschie, many of whom stood in close contact with Schillings and Wissmann.[38] In the controversial debates following Rechenberg's shooting order in 1911, the Swiss national park in the Lower Engadine was invoked as an example of pristine nature used for scientific study,[39] and even the botanical gardens in Buitenzorg and Peradeniya served as sources of inspiration for game preservation in German East Africa. During an expedition in 1905–6, the Munich-based zoologist Franz Doflein had visited the Peradeniya Botanical Gardens in Ceylon and identified the combination of scientific research with a large-scale natural estate as transferable to the German colonies. His proposal to establish at least one tropical forest reserve and another in a savanna landscape in East Africa linked up with ongoing discussions about the necessity of a permanent research station for colonial zoology.[40] Both should be associated with a scientific institute and a game department to combine preservation with the scientific study of animals, animal diseases, and anthropoids. As a kind of zoological garden on the spot, these reserves should preserve threatened and scientifically interesting species.[41] These examples show how global Germany's imperial conservationists cast their gaze in search for inspiring conservationist models, and they reveal the degree to which utilization and preservation, acclimatization, and zoological study of wild animals were still thought together.

Yet, the most important point of reference by far was the U.S. national park. Wissmann made explicit use of the term in 1896 to explain to Chancellor Chlodwig zu Hohenlohe-Schillingsfürst what he had in mind: "I beg your Excellency's permission to turn some of the particularly game-rich areas of German East Africa into, let me say, a national park" in order to reserve "partially very scenic landscapes, of course only when unpopulated and teeming with game ... as government property and prohibit all kind of hunting within them."[42] In a more detailed memorandum on game preservation composed in March 1898, Wissmann referred to the Yellowstone Park as the precedent to set aside "vast, unpeopled areas with a healthy stock of wildlife," if possible including beautiful scenery and formations of scientific interest.[43]

The "national park," as well as other conservationist ideas and concepts such as sustainable forestry, was part of the broader intercultural transfer of concepts, ideas, models, and policies from Europe to the United States and vice versa between the 1870s and World War II.[44] Wissmann's import of the national park idea into East Africa shows that these crossings were at times triangulations, as they included the transfer of ideas between the fringes of American and German Empires. Indeed, in the course of conservationist discussions in East Africa, the precedent set by Yellowstone would influence German East Africa indirectly even via the British in Kenya, who equally regarded the U.S. national park as "the forerunner of true Game Reserves" from which "useful lessons" could be derived for British policies in Africa.[45]

By the late nineteenth century, Yellowstone and the other national parks established in the United States since 1872 had become reference points for nature conservationists worldwide.[46] Yet, at the time Wissmann appropriated the term, it was still far from clear what "national park" actually meant. Yellowstone was itself still an experimental landscape for conservation,[47] and when colonial conservationists in Germany referred to Yellowstone, they singled out those features of the national park that appeared to correspond with the problems perceived in their colony. In a context of imperial competition, a key function of transimperial references was to shame German authorities into action by portraying conservation as a cause to which other "civilized" nations already aspired.⁴⁸ Seen from East Africa, Yellowstone meant the state taking over responsibility for the preservation of charismatic fauna in an inviolable sanctuary of large and seemingly uninhabited stretches of wilderness. It was of minor importance if the qualities projected onto Yellowstone were actually congruent with the realities in the American Northwest: at the time Wissmann referred to Yellowstone as a model game sanctuary in 1896, for example, its management by the U.S. Army was still subject to dispute, and the bison herd within the park seriously depleted by market hunters.

Processes of transfer and appropriation were rife with projection, misperception, selection, and modification. Most obviously, this happened at the level of translating categories. Wissmann soon abandoned the terminology of "national park" for what he deemed to be equivalent German expressions for the purpose, and the later utilization of the term *Naturschutzpark* as the German adaptation of the national park was motivated by a widespread anti-Americanism among conservationists eager to indigenize a concept borrowed from abroad. But the most important aspect of Yellowstone's reception among European imperialists was its perception through the peculiar lens of European traditions of wildlife management. Wissmann, like many other German and British hunters, explorers, and colonial officials, understood Yellowstone not as a "democratization" of awe-inspiring nature for all, that is, white Americans, but as a game reserve for the American bison. German hunting periodicals, illustrated magazines, Karl May's popular adventure novels, public lectures by big game hunters who had visited the American West, but also William Hornaday's 1889 publication on the extermination of the American bison all impressed upon their readership that Yellowstone was essentially established as a sanctuary for the characteristic fauna of the American West—"a vast national hunting estate" in Roosevelt's parlance.⁴⁹ The hunters' view of the American West stamped the impression that national parks stood firmly in the European tradition of exclusive wildlife preserves. Consequently, Wissmann defined the "national parks" to be established in the German East African context as "particularly game rich and sizeable areas."⁵⁰ The reading of Yellowstone as a game sanctuary not only made it a suitable solution to the degradation of wildlife encountered in East Africa. With "sublime" nature largely absent and no nation to appeal to, the presence of charismatic fauna was the main aspect in which the North American West and colonial East Africa intersected.

If Wissmann referred to Yellowstone to make his reserves in East Africa internationally meaningful, respectable, and modern, the conservation advocates used the very argument after the turn of the century to remind the government that its conservation policies after Maji Maji were insufficient. The Kenyan reserve and the North American national parks gained particular salience as examples of how "civilized" nations treated their wildlife, in comparison to Rechenberg's game slaughter in late 1910. The reframing of the *Wildreservate* as *Naturschutzparks* under the influence of the *Naturschutzbewegung* in Germany was paralleled by a shift in the features that were identified as exemplary and worthy of emulation in German East Africa: "Yellowstone" was now used to rationalize spatial preservation on political, scientific, and ecological grounds.[51] On the one hand, Yellowstone was praised for its permanence beyond administrative arbitrariness. In contrast to arbitrary degazetting, for example, of the Mahenge reserve in East Africa, Yellowstone was seen as signifying the victory of preservationist idealism over blunt materialism, ironically exposed by a society widely associated with unbridled capitalism among European intellectuals. On the other hand, the narrow interest of hunters and the sole focus on game were transcended to embrace environmental justifications. The tsetse controversy, above all, shifted the question of wildlife conservation into the realm of ecology. Reserves were now portrayed as ecological laboratories necessary for scientists to find out about the intricate interrelationships among species.[52] These needed to be permanent because too little was known, for example, about "the connections between the realm of animals and the realm of plants." Science was not yet "in a position to say which of them are indispensable to the survival of another species."[53] There was no straightforward mention of "ecology" or, as contemporaries used to call it, "biocoenosis"; but the nature to be preserved in a park was understood as a complex and interrelated system of flora and fauna—to the exclusion of humans. Schillings portrayed East Africa as even more suitable for a large-scale reserve thanks to the *Weltwunder* of its enormous species diversity. Whereas Yellowstone would feature only a few species, a park in the steppes of East Africa could preserve an approximate number of 160 mammalian species.[54] And also colonial secretary Wilhelm Solf used Yellowstone as a prescription to identify the ideal landscape for the *Naturschutzpark* that was never established in East Africa: the "whole character" inclusive of flora and fauna should be preserved "in pristine originality for decades and more."[55]

The Political Geography of Wildlife—Reserves as European Heterotopias

The idea of nature as "pristine originality" was perhaps the most significant aspect of Yellowstone as a model for conservation in East Africa. The representation of Yellowstone's nature as wilderness in "pristine originality" was predicated on the mental and political erasure of the previous human occupation and utilization by Indians.[56] The conservationist discourse on German East Africa was marked by a like mental erasure of existing human ecologies in landscapes deemed as wild.

The "pristine originality" to be preserved in a German East African *Naturschutzpark* shifts attention to the politics and ideology of wilderness as a further critical factor involved in the creation of reserves. The questions of where reserves were to be localized and what kind of nature was to be preserved within them were inextricably entwined with the mental geographies and the images and imaginations Europeans projected onto African landscapes. Translated into political practice, this was often associated with the erasure and denial of previous human ecologies and the misreading of cultural landscapes as wilderness.

Environmental historians as well as political ecologists have identified the quest for Edenic paradises as a powerful incentive for policies of colonial conservation.[57] Conservation policies in German East Africa formed no exception. Indeed, it took few elements to make landscapes appear wild, primeval, and original in the colonial eye: the lush vegetation of the *pori*, the acacia trees, baobabs and brachystegia of the savanna, and large mammals in abundant numbers. This understanding of African landscapes was closely linked with the mental operation that characterized Europeans' ordering of the world under the impact of nineteenth-century evolutionism: the reading of geographical difference across space as historical and temporal difference over time. The plausibility of this assumption was, above all, read out of and into nature. Reading nature as wilderness and cultural backwardness was, however, more than just "denial of coevalness."[58] It was also the mental prerequisite of political practice like the Crown Land Ordinance, which took a phenomenology of wilderness as argument against the humans that had shaped the history of these landscapes.

The presence of wild animals turned savannas otherwise described as barren deserts into pristine wilderness, paradise, garden Eden, primeval nature, "proper" Africa, locating it outside or at the beginning of historical time. Bronsart von Schellendorff, a former Schutztruppe member who attempted to breed zebras and ostriches south of Kilimanjaro, deemed the landscape around him the only "place in the whole world where the beauty of landscape, fresh climate and plenty of wild animals are united in organic wholeness. And this wonderful piece of land is German. We possess it in pristine originality." Amid his exploits of warfare and hunting during Maji Maji, Hans Paasche waxed enthusiastic about the Rufiji landscape: "Is there a greater wilderness than the one surrounding me here with such wonderful charms? The biggest living pachyderm, the strong and cunning cat, the wild bull: where this trefoil is still to be found must be paradise." Carl Georg Schillings, finally, anticipated yet another of the arguments forwarded by celebrity conservationist Bernhard Grzimek half a century later, when he saw the East African savanna as confirmation of the "truth underlying the myth of a Paradise, in which the animal world lived all together in harmony. ... Enormous herds of harmless animals, as well as beasts of prey, forming one general community."[59]

Wilderness was embodied by charismatic megafauna. It was in such landscapes that the game reserves were established, and hunters played a pivotal role in this. Thanks to their occupation and itinerant lifestyle, they were not only perpetrators but also the first witnesses of game destruction. They identified game-rich areas and thus established the topography of wilderness in the colony. Many of the areas recommended by the hunting manual for German East Africa as prime hunting grounds were located in the vicinity of game reserves.[60] The language deployed to describe these areas abounds in cultural imagery of natural originality, paradise, Eden, and the sacredness of the pristine. Wilderness and the cultural practice of its conservation were charged with religious values, and it comes as no surprise that reserves were often called sanctuaries or *heilige Freistatt*. These religious references imbued wilderness with moral and spiritual meaning, but they did not preclude contesting visions and other utilizations of the same landscape: seeing and fantasizing Africa as wilderness was also the mental prerequisite for transformation and development. The Wembere Steppe, repeatedly hailed as one of the hunting doradoes of the colony and gazetted as a reserve between 1903 and 1905, was discussed to be inundated for a large-scale irrigation project to grow cotton. A gigantic system of dams, canals, and power stations should tap Lake Victoria to direct water to the arid Mbala and Wembere steppes.[61] Other development projects included the *mise-en-valeur* of the Ulanga Valley by rice cultivation, the irrigation of the Mkata Plain for growing cotton and tobacco, and the conversion of Ngorongoro into pastoral farmland.[62] The psychospiritual functions of wilderness were hardly top notch on an agenda dominated by economic imperatives. Yet, also in the colonial situation, "wilderness" increased in value the more it appeared to vanish, and the relegation of wild nature to specific areas came to fulfill a deeper and ever more important function. Its champions explained the value of the wild as a product and consequence of industrialization, progress, and civilization: "Mankind," Carl Georg Schillings opined, "needs the 'wild' and pristine nature as arcane spaces of relaxation and as an antipode to the speed of evolution."[63] The more colonial territory was measured, developed, and distributed, the more did reserves come to function as such antipodes that enshrined the essential otherness of Africa. They were heterotopias, serving as countersites that reflected the modernity, civilization, and masculinity of the colonial conquerors.[64]

"Wilderness" is a complex set of negotiations between the material and the discursive, the images and knowledge about Africa Germans brought with them, and the nature they encountered. It is located at the intersection of history, representations, desires, political power, and the physical materiality of nature. Scholars have identified a specific European "landscape way of seeing" behind the ideal of preserving nature untrammeled by human interference. The idea of a pictorialized sublime nature, the denial or erasure of human labor, the detachment of the observer from the land, and the spatial division of production and consumption in the landscape were all crucial elements of an emergent Euro-American aesthetics of nature that found its spatial realization in national parks.[65] Much of this applies equally to the colonial gaze on East African landscapes. Yet, more than landscape aesthetics, it was the presence of game that animated landscapes as wild, original, ideologically significant, and worthy of protection. The magnetism of wild animals pertained to hunters and colonialists "on the spot" as well as to people who had never been to East Africa themselves: "Anyone can see beautiful landscapes easier and with less hassle elsewhere," the Stuttgart-based naturalist Kurt Floericke argued. "Also the vegetation is usually of secondary interest to the traveller, whereas everybody yearns to watch big game roam freely over the steppe, at least once in a lifetime."[66] Game communicated the difference and quintessential otherness of the African continent that was to be relegated and preserved within the confines of the reserves and *Naturschutzparks*.

However, there was an unresolved tension and ambivalence underlying European notions of wilderness in the colonial situation. Colonialism, after all, was about the mastery and domestication of wilderness as an obstacle to civilization. At the same time, wilderness mirrored Europe's own civility and modernity, it was a residue of unspoilt originality and a remnant of humankind's evolutionary past. From the outset, the colonial encounter was characterized by the awkward ambivalence of destruction and desire that made wilderness so essential to colonialism: it was the brute and backward "other" to civilize, subdue, and conquer, but it was also the primal and original source of strength, an antidote to civilization, and a reminder of the colonizers' own roots. Darwinist readings of the savanna as a site of an ongoing struggle for life stood alongside the original harmony of humans with nature in the Garden of Eden.[67] In a radical inversion of the Biblical Eden, where the garden was fenced off against a threatening wilderness, the wild was now located inside Eden, enclosed by the virtual fences of a game reserve.

Describing the homelands of others as wilderness was, therefore, a powerful epistemic accompaniment of colonization. The cultural imagery to describe African landscapes—wilderness, paradise, Eden, a Pleistocene fauna—turned African nature into a prehistory of Europe, a landscape of deep time, where the presence of a unique fauna allowed European visitors a glimpse into the planet's evolutionary past, or a landscape entirely outside history. Such imagery established an asymmetrical topography of wild versus civilized that constructed Africa as the other of civilization and legitimized colonial rule as a civilizing enterprise. Wildlife conservation rested upon these representations that often meant to obfuscate the presence of humans or of human activity in favor of an overwhelming nature. Even without the forceful evacuation of residents, the setting aside of such spaces deliberately to retain "wild animals for many decades, even centuries in their African originality"[68] was an enterprise that encapsulated core colonial values that cannot easily be disentangled from the "noble" cause of preserving certain animals from extinction.

Conservation in Practice—Residents, Reserves, and Environmental Control

The policy of wildlife reserves under German colonial rule has so far been described as a high-handed state practice of assigning use and meaning to landscapes imagined to be empty spaces that were animated and peopled only by game. Much of the above dealt with aspirations, discussions, and imaginations. But any discussion of colonial conservation remains incomplete without at least an attempt to assess the practical politics of reserves on the ground. Yet, such an assessment is plagued by the distortions of the colonial archive and the general dearth of sources at the level of the district administrations. No records have survived that would allow an in-depth exemplary assessment of one reserve over an extended period of time. What is available is scrap information and occasional references to the making and the policing of different reserves, among others from court records. The picture thus gained is necessarily incomplete. Yet, together with the evidence provided above on Ngorongoro and the impact of the reserves established in the heartland of Maji Maji, the source material is sufficient to show that reserves had a practical reality beyond administrative declaration.

The hunting and wildlife reserves established before World War I were certainly not the conservation fortresses that were erected on their basis later on in the twentieth century. They were as makeshift as colonial policies in general, often invisible on the ground, hard to police, and hardly policed. Their supervision and administration by a specialized game department remained an unfulfilled dream of conservationists.[69] In many respects, the reserves were more akin to the regional hunting bans enacted by district stations to prevent the shooting of certain species.[70] There were no controls to pass upon entry and usually no signs demarcating their borders. Significant landmarks like roads, rivers, or mountain ranges had to do. Only from 1900 onward—probably as a first reaction to the conference discussions going on at London—stations were ordered to mark the lay of reserves and the most important restrictions on hunting upon the licenses of hunters venturing into the interior.[71] The legal existence, but practical invisibility of reserves on the ground created a situation of legal insecurity on their purported fringes, much to the annoyance of Europeans hunting in the vicinity.[72] The deplorable record-keeping on the part of some military and district commissioners often meant that a change in administrative personnel could include considerable administrative amnesia. New personnel sometimes had to inquire at the central government or learn from local *majumbe* and intermediaries about the lay of reserves.[73]

Slender evidence has survived about how the respective sites were identified and what role the "silent knowledge" of local intermediaries might have played in the process. The first reserves were "game-rich" landscapes that had featured on Wissmann's itineraries. In 1896, stations were required to suggest further areas suitable as game reserves, but the feedback was feeble since few of the commissioners were familiar with the landscapes they were supposed to govern.[74] The federal distribution of reserves over the various military and administrative districts since 1903 mirrors the political structure of the colony. In some cases, such as the Upper Rufiji or the bottom of the Pare Mountains, the borders of reserves were partially identical with the district borders. By 1913, only three reserves transcended district or, in the case of the sanctuary around Lake Natron, colonial boundaries. An exchange of notes between the central administration in Dar es Salaam and the military station Kilimatinde in early 1903 suggests that the government continued to ask stations to identify unpopulated or no more than sparsely populated areas with a considerable game population as potential sites for a reserve. Together with a doodle map of the region under discussion, the station suggested the eastern part of the Wembere steppe between the Wembere River and the Iramba Plateau. Unlike the well-watered and densely populated western part of the steppe, the eastern chunk was allegedly devoid of people apart from three *majumbe* resident at its fringes. While the appointment of wardens was considered too dangerous given the overall "hostility of the people," the station was confident that the reserve could be effectively supervised by weekly Askari patrols deployed from nearby Mkalama, a military post established just a few months ago after Schutztruppe detachments had put down several "risings" in northern Turu in 1902. The reserve was indeed gazetted, just to be suspended again two years later. The exact reasons are hard to gauge, but quite probably control was impossible to put into practice in an area where resistance against taxation and other colonial impositions remained a structural feature throughout the first decade of the twentieth century.[75] When in 1911, a Schutztruppe officer suggested the establishment of a reserve in parts of the Wembere Steppe to wean the Tindiga off their hunter-gathering ways, the motion was abandoned, for its effective policing would have required so many wardens that the expected benefits stood in no relation to the costs.[76] The exchange of notes between the station at Kilimatinde and the government in Dar es Salaam shows that the government put a marked emphasis on the fact that potential reserves should be very sparsely populated, if at all. Yet, the case of the Upper Rufiji and several others prove the opposite,[77] and von Götzen himself had to admit later that the siting of reserves had more often than not paid little attention to settlements. It is likely that the prevention of conflicts between wildlife and agricultural development was a major rationale behind Rechenberg's partial reshuffle of reserves after Maji Maji, just as damage to indigenous cultivations and villages was the main justification for the temporary suspension of the hunting ban in the Mahenge reserve in 1911.[78]

The files in the Tanzania National Archives contain undated draft maps of every game reserve with the exact perimeter and acreage. Many of the drawings feature exact figures of how many kilometers of the perimeter were to be "left open," indicating that there existed plans to fence the reserves toward the end of the German rule, possibly to contain the spread of diseases from wildlife to livestock.[79] Generally, political rationales dominated over ecological considerations when it came to the siting of reserves. A glance at the lie of reserves in 1912 reveals that in most cases, the drawing of boundaries followed pragmatic reasons: often, they were identical with administrative boundaries between districts, or they followed roads, natural, or geographic features like rivers or mountain ranges to allow for their identification in the landscape. The extension of reserves under von Götzen in 1903 was also an expression of the heightened belief in the administrative capacities of the district and military stations. In early 1899, when the conquest of Uhehe was still under way, von Prince objected in plain terms to establish a reserve in the Udzungwa mountains (the northwestern escarpment of the Kilombero Valley), because enforcing a ban in this inaccessible area would require "hundreds of forest wardens" and "continued executions."[80] While this was also a pretext to ward off interference from Dar es Salaam with the big man politics of the station, the very military station gazetted even two reserves four years later, probably in reaction to the ongoing depletion of elephants in the district, but also because the station had become an established authority.

Map 6.1. Situation and extent of game reserves in German East Africa, 1 April 1912 (Reichskolonialamt, 1913).[81]

Some areas with plenty of game were not explicitly demarcated as they were regarded as "natural" reserves. Their remoteness and allegedly sparse population made them both impossible and unnecessary to patrol. Such was the case with the Serengeti plains in northwestern Tanganyika, a landscape whose complexity was thoroughly misunderstood by the colonizers. Completely unaware of the social, political, and ecological changes introduced by the disasters of the 1890s,[82] the Serengeti was generalized as a vast, monotonous, waterless, and therefore empty wilderness "fabulously plentiful of game," but to be avoided by travelers for lack of water and provision. Although indispensable for every German caravan traversing the Serengeti for their knowledge of water and provision, its few human inhabitants were completely marginalized: "Only he who has seen the masses of game in these plains has an idea of how abundant a country can be with game.

The absence of people accounts for these countless numbers," Count von Schleinitz wrote in 1904.[83] Until the outbreak of World War I, the Serengeti remained "one of the last blank spaces on the map of German East Africa," a mythical place surrounded by the "lure of the unknown."[84]

Elsewhere, reserves were established and retained despite the fact that over the years they turned out to be ill-suited for the purpose. Often, wildlife occupied reserves only seasonally, or disappeared in the wake of increased settlement or the construction of a railway line, as was probably the case with the reserve along the bottom of the Pare Mountains by 1908.[85] In the joint reserve of the Bagamoyo and Morogoro districts, colonial decision-makers had to learn that the "wilderness" they had sought to preserve ceased to exist without human management. A forester named Redslob who inspected the reserve in 1912 reported that there was hardly any game in it. In his view, this was due to the fact that locals, for fear of punishment, would abstain from the controlled burning of the savanna after the rains, a widely observed practice to destroy insects, fertilize the soil with ashes, encourage new growth, and thus attract game for hunting. Because the fires were abandoned, the number of antelopes and other herbivores had decreased. Additionally, predators contributed to their decrease because the high grass would provide better shelter for stalking their prey than previously.[86] There are, however, no hints that this observation about the human ecology of wildlife had any impact on the future "management" of reserves in general.

The archival record also provides scant information about how the hunting ban in the reserves was enforced, especially in the years before Maji Maji. Neither do the respective game regulations. Wissmann had charged the posts and stations closest to the reserves with their supervision, and he was confident that the usual tactics of setting up a drastic example would suffice to impress: if only "the first few offenders [were] duly punished, it will be quite possible to ensure a considerable amount of respect for the game reserves."[87] Indeed, game ordinances threatened with drastic fines to deter hunters from breaching the ban in the reserves. Over the years, charges rose from between 50 and 1,000 rupees in 1896 to a maximum of 5,000 rupees in 1908, or alternatively, imprisonment of up to three months.

Given the overall duties of the district officials, the supervision of game reserves was clearly at the bottom of the local administrative agenda. The few surviving annual reports only contain brief assessments of hunting policies but do not make particular mention of the reserves. Announcing a hunting ban within a certain area was an issue dealt with in the *shauri* meetings at the district station or when commissioners and officers toured their districts. Surviving files suggest that the day-to-day policing of reserves was among the tasks of military outposts, German foresters, and African forest wardens, occasional Askari patrols and sometimes even missionary stations.[88] But above all, stations appear to have delegated the supervision of reserves to various local intermediaries. Stations' feedback to a government circular in late 1911 revealed that they made widespread use of local chiefs, *majumbe,* tax collectors, and between one and three informally contracted residents in or near the reserves who acted as game wardens. In the district of Kilwa, a local *jumbe* was paid 12 rupees a month for acting as game warden in 1905, and reference to the dismissal of two game wardens after the abandonment of the Tabora reserve in October 1906 lends plausibility to the assumption that the hiring of local game wardens was practiced in most of the reserves established in 1903.[89]

Enforcing the hunting ban thus fell within the duties of the lowest echelons of the colonial administration, the African intermediaries who have aptly been referred to as the actual but "hidden linchpins of colonial rule."[90] Unfortunately, the murky terrain where the dichotomies of "colonizers" and "colonized" blurred and the pretensions to colonial rule interfaced with the claims, authority, and interests of local intermediaries is hardly accessible with the sources at hand. Several district commissioners claimed that their "coloured wardens" had proven their worth and that the borders of the reserves were duly respected by white settlers and Africans alike. However, one would hardly expect them to say otherwise in a report that was bound for inclusion in a publication aiming to convince the Reichstag and the German public that sufficient care was taken of the colony's wildlife. Undeniably, the position of a game warden enabled individuals to increase their personal wealth and status, not only because they could exploit their post to hunt themselves. The wardens and *majumbe* supervising the Iringa reserves, for example, were promised rewards for each poacher they reported—a continuation of the divide-and-rule policy introduced under von Prince in the late 1890s. Their duty to survey the integrity of the reserves located them precariously at the intersection of "colonizers" and "colonized," and Thaddeus Sunseri has drawn attention to the disruptive consequences of turning the *majumbe* from protectors from nature into protectors of nature.[91] If earlier they had been responsible for organizing communal hunts and protection from pests, their task was now to prohibit people's utilization of game and forest resources. Often, the result was an awkward position of weakening influence and authority among their people on the one hand, and punishment for any infringement of the reserves from the side of the Germans. From the perspective of the colonizers, using Africans to police the border of reserves destabilized the feeble border of the "racial" color line. Official considerations in 1914 to invest all white personnel of the Schutztruppe with the power to supervise the hunting regulations are ill understood without taking the problem of African personnel policing a key ritual of white superiority into account.

The necessities of colonial governance undermined the racial foundations of colonial rule.[92] Several convictions of white hunters' illegal chase in game reserves drew upon evidence produced by African wardens who also appeared in court to reiterate their allegations.[93] It is hard to assess the number of such cases as only parts of the original records have survived, yet, even if accusations of white hunters by black wardens were the exception rather than the rule, they bore a considerable potential for conflict. Alarmed that the station at Moshi planned to have the reserve around Lake Natron supervised by a handful of "colored game wardens," the short-lived mouthpiece of the German settlers in the north, the *Kilimandjaro- und Meru-Zeitung,* saw the whole racial order undermined if blacks could simply accuse whites of poaching.[94]

Local intermediaries did also report African hunters' trespassing the borders of game reserves, but such indigenous breaches of the hunting ban are hardly traceable in the sources. Accountable as "native law," they fell into the legal competence of the district and military commissioners. Any such case would have been dealt with in the highly formalized *shauri* meetings of whose proceedings the district officers did not have to keep detailed records.[95] Surviving penal records are too few to allow for any balanced judgement if and how many fines, floggings, and imprisonments were imposed for African contraventions of the game laws. The penal book registering the sentences imposed by Tabora station between July 1902 and April 1904 does not record any contraventions against the reserve, which has only been established in September 1903. However, the six weeks in chains administered in October 1902 to a certain Sultan Mchamba for instigating his following to hunt elephants without permit and three other hunting parties convicted of "poaching" in the few months after the ordinance had been enacted show that stations were serious about enforcing the hunting regulations. A forest commissioner who proposed the introduction of closed seasons for certain species of game in 1912 hastened to add that "contraventions against them should not immediately be punished with imprisonment or other heavy sentences, as in other breaches of the game law."[96]

The absence of substantial written evidence that African infringements on the game reserves were indeed persecuted should, therefore, not lead to presume that reserves had but little impact on the ground. Surely, hunting within the reserves continued under the radar of the colonial administration and its local aides, especially when hunters turned to more hidden and passive techniques such as pitfalls or trapping. The supervision of reserves suffered from financial and personal constraints, was notoriously ephemeral, and incomplete. Yet, the impact of reserves on livelihoods based on hunting could be considerable, as their contribution to the making of Maji Maji has shown.[97] Moreover, one should not underestimate the psychological effect of such a ban in combination with the experience of the earlier terror of conquest or Maji Maji. The establishment of reserves was no isolated attempt to preserve the colony's wildlife. Even if reserves could not be effectively policed, the combined effect of the governmental hunting regulations brought about a decrease in indigenous hunting. Local names ascertain that reserves were incorporated into villagers' day-to-day realities. The Lupembe reserve in Iringa, for example, was referred to as *kisiwani*—"between the rivers"—while Redslob, the aforementioned forester in Morogoro, found in 1912 that locals spoke of game reserves generally as "*shamba ya bibi*."[98] The term is something of a puzzle. In Kiswahili, *shamba* denotes a field or farm, whereas *bibi* means grandmother or madam and is usually a term of respect. After World War I and to this day, the term appears to have been applied to various protected areas and is sometimes translated as the "Queen's Game Reserve," sometimes as "grandmother's field."[99] Allegedly, the term originated in the 1890s when the Upper Rufiji Reserve was declared a hunting reserve dedicated to the Kaiser's wife, but I have found no contemporary evidence to substantiate this origin. It can at least be speculated if the term may not have indicated a bifurcation of activities along gender lines to denote an area where the male activity of hunting was forbidden. In any case, alternative contemporary references to reserves as *shamba ya serikali*, which still echo today in references to protected areas and the game within them as "government's property," lend plausibility to the association of space and authority. While any definite answer to this question must be left to linguists and anthropologists, the story of Mangula and the political geography of wildlife conservation in the Maji Maji regions discussed above have provided incisive examples for the enhanced vulnerability of local communities to wildlife damage, within and on the fringes of reserves. Stations were well aware to the problem of crop devastations. The military station at Iringa, for example, shifted the borders of the Kisiwani Reserve to mitigate the devastations of fields and huts by elephants. Other stations did nothing and accepted the situation as "natural."[100]

For villagers, the introduction of reserves under colonial rule meant that, simply by continuing to do what they always had done, they now committed acts that were illegal. They bore the brunt of colonial ideologies of wilderness and wildlife conservation. With a view to the latter, the reserves definitely fulfilled their purpose. "More than any game law it is space that protects animals best in Africa," noted one district commissioner after more than a decade of service in the colony.[101] Even if hunting was not entirely suppressed within them, reserves provided such space. Observers emphasized that "these smart animals" would intentionally withdraw to the reserves, and occasionally, hunters believed to discern the behavioral adaptations to the reserves that later were referred to as "national park effect," that is, a certain habituation to human presence and a considerable decrease in the usual flight distance of single species. Intentional or not, with the exception of the Bagamoyo/Morogoro reserve, almost all stations reported an increase of wildlife numbers within the sanctuaries. In Mahenge, Iringa, and the Mbwemkuru and Upper Rufiji reserves, elephant herds were witnessed to have increased markedly, while on Kilimanjaro, the reserve was gauged to function effectively as numbers had stabilized and herds included "several strong specimens."[102] After World War I, the British retained most areas designated to game protection. According to Chief Game Warden Swynnerton, the "Germans appear to have been actuated by very sound reasons in the choice of many of their reserves."[103]

Notes

1. *Correspondence relating to the Preservation of Wild Animals in Africa* (1906), no. 7: Sharpe to Salisbury, 9 September 1896 (Game Regulations British Central Africa), no. 9: Berkeley to Salisbury, 25 November 1896 (Game Regulations Uganda), no. 36: Craufurd to Salisbury, 11 August 1899 (Game Regulation East Africa Protectorate); MacKenzie, *The Empire of Nature*, 205–7.
2. *Die deutschen Schutzgebiete in Afrika und der Südsee 1910/11. Amtliche Jahresberichte, Statistischer Teil*, 71; TNA G 8/912, List of Reserves; Reichskolonialamt, *Jagd und Wildschutz in den deutschen Kolonien*, 35, 62–65. Several previous works contain erroneous information regarding the dates and the number of reserves established in Tanganyika under German Rule, probably following wrong dates contained in an official statement on the Wildlife Policy of Tanzania issued by the Ministry of Natural Resources and Tourism in 1998, cf. Maddox, *Sub-Saharan Africa*, 146, 251–54; Neumann, *Imposing Wilderness*, 99; Roderick P Neumann, "Africa's Last Wilderness. Reordering Space for Political and Economic Control in Colonial Tanzania," *Africa* 71 (2001): 644.
3. Richards, *The Unending Frontier*.
4. For settlers' criticism of the constant alarm sounded by the wildlife preservationists, see *Kilimandjaro- und Meru-Zeitung no. 2* (1913), 25 January.
5. Cf. *Amtlicher Anzeiger für Deutsch-Ostafrika* 1, no. 16 (1900), Circular 12 June; TNA G 55/8, unfol.: Report on the economic development of the Kilimatinde district, 27 February 1903; BAB R 1001/7776, fol. 72: Circular Gov DOA to all stations, 8 June 1899; TNA G 58/41, fol. 2: Circular Gov DOA to all stations, 31 January 1913.
6. BAB R 1001/7802-1, fol. 3: RKA to all colonial governments, 4 December 1911.
7. Reichskolonialamt, *Jagd und Wildschutz in den deutschen Kolonien*, 1–35.
8. For a similar observation concerning other German colonies, see Wächter, *Naturschutz in den deutschen Kolonien in Afrika*, 82–83.

9. BAB R 1001/7776, fol. 134, Gov DOA to AA KA, 15 July 1902.
10. TNA G 8/55, fol. 44, Bukoba to Gov DOA, 1 August 1896; fol. 92, Kilimatinde to Gov DOA, 13 July 1897.
11. TNA G 8/55, fol. 85: Gov DOA to Kilossa, 11 June 1897; TNA G 8/55, fol. 85: Gov DOA to BA Dar es Salaam, [11 June 1897]; BAB R 1001/7766, fol. 56–63: Wissmann to AA KA, 20 March 1898.
12. TNA G 8/55, fol. 189: Mwanza to Gov DOA, 27 April 1898; cf. Gaston Schlobach, "Die Volksstämme der deutschen Ostküste des Victoria-Nyansa," *Mitteilungen von Forschungsreisenden und Gelehrten aus den Deutschen Schutzgebieten* 14 (1901): 192–93.
13. BAB R 1001/7770, fol. 17: AA KA to Gov DOA, 18 April 1902; cf. BAB R 1001/7770, fol. 11: internal memorandum on the creation of game reserves, not dated [1901].
14. BAB R 1001/6229-1, fol. 16–17.: RKA to Gov DOA, 24 February 1912.
15. See for example Paul Jepson and Robert J Whittaker, "Histories of Protected Areas: Internationalisation of Conservationist Values and Their Adoption in the Netherlands Indies (Indonesia)," *Environment and History* 8 (2002): 129–72; Rolf Baldus, *Wildlife Conservation in Tanganyika under German Rule*, http://www.wildlife-baldus.com/download/colonial.pdf.
16. C Michael Hall and John Shultis, "Railways, Tourism and Worthless Lands: The Establishment of National Parks in Australia, Canada, New Zealand and the United States," *Australian-Canadian Studies* 8, no. 2 (1991): 57–74; Alfred Runte, *National Parks. The American Experience* (Lincoln, NE, 1979), 48–49.
17. Von Oppen, "Matuta," 52–59; Sippel, "Aspects of Colonial Land Law in German East Africa," 3–38.
18. Söldenwagner, *Spaces of Negotiation*, 85–123; Sippel, "Aspects of Colonial Land Law in German East Africa," 29–30.
19. "Noch mehr Wildreservate!," *Kilimandjaro- und Meru-Zeitung* 1, no. 22 (1913), 8 November.
20. Neumann, *Imposing Wilderness*, 60–61; Thomas Spear, *Mountain Farmers. Moral Economies of Land & Agricultural Development in Arusha & Meru* (Oxford, 1997), 76–77.
21. See for example Joachim Radkau, *Nature and Power. A Global History of the Environment* (Cambridge, 2008), 136–42; Scott, *Seeing Like a State*, 11–22; Paul Warde, *Ecology, Economy and State Formation in Early Modern Germany* (Cambridge, 2006).
22. Allsen, *The Royal Hunt in Eurasian History*, 34–51, 46 (quote), chapters 7–9; Griffin, *Blood Sport*, chapter 2.
23. See for example TNA G 8/99, fol. 204: Bronsart to Gov DOA, 12 May 1898; BAB R 1001/8390, fol. 19: Gov DOA to RKA, 4 January 1912; TNA G 8/193, fol. 21–45: Moshi to Gov DOA, 22 July 1912; TNA G 8/193, fol. 50: Gov DOA to Gustav Adolf Rose, 14 May 1913; TNA G 31/32, unfol.: Arusha to Gov DOA, 15 April 1913; Friedrich Wilhelm Siedentopf to Gov DOA, 2 August 1913.
24. "Convention for the Preservation of Wild Animals, Birds and Fish in Africa, 19th May 1900," *Correspondence relating to the Preservation of Wild Animals in Africa* (1906), no. 55, Article II, § 5; PRO FO 881/7395 B: Protocols of the 3rd session, 27 April 1900.

25. For similar transfers in the British case, see Roderick P Neumann, "Dukes, Earls and Ersatz Edens: Aristocratic Nature Preservationists in Colonial Africa," *Environment and Planning D: Society and Space* 14 (1996): 79–98; Steinhart, *Black Poachers*, 177–79.
26. See also BAB R 1001/7766, fol. 56–63: Memorandum of Wissmann, 20 March 1898.
27. Stentzler, *Deutsch-Ostafrika*, 85–87.
28. *Deutsch-Ostafrikanische Zeitung* 16, no. 14 (1914), 14 February; BAB R 1001/240, fol. 68: Gov DOA to Prince Leopold of Bavaria, 10 July 1913.
29. "Ein phantastisches Projekt," *Deutsch-Ostafrikanische Zeitung* 12, no. 93 (1910), 23 November; BAK N 1053 33, fol. 252–55: Denkschrift des Wirtschaftlichen Verbandes vom Kilimanjaro, August 1912.
30. Schillings, *Mit Blitzlicht und Büchse*, 356–57; BAB R 1001/7777, fol. 179ff.: Internal memorandum on game conservation, 12 February 1909; cf. R 1001/7778, fol. 276: Solf to Schillings, 14 January 1912.
31. *Deutsch-Ostafrikanische Zeitung* 16, no. 2 (1914), 7 January.
32. TNA G 58/40, unfol.: Gov DOA to Morogoro, 16 March 1912; Redslob to Morogoro, 5 August 1912; Morogoro to Gov DOA, 5 August 1912; Otto Stollowsky, "Die wirtschaftliche Bedeutung Kilossas und der Makattasteppe," *Deutsch-Ostafrikanische Zeitung* 11, no. 34 (1909), 1 May; no. 35 (1909), 5 May; no. 36 (1909), 8 May; Paul Vageler, *Die Mkattasteppe. Beiträge zur Kenntnis der ostafrikanischen Alluvialböden und ihrer Vegetation* (Berlin, 1910).
33. BAB R 1001/6229–1, fol. 21: Gov DOA to RKA, 2 October 1912; BAB R 1001/6229–1, fol. 56: RKA to Gov DOA, 25 July 1913 (concept; marginal notes).
34. Reichskolonialamt, *Jagd und Wildschutz in den deutschen Kolonien*, attachments.
35. BAB R 1001/7777, fol. 179–80: Internal memorandum on game conservation, 12 February 1909.
36. Kirchberger, "Wie entsteht eine imperiale Infrastruktur?"
37. Willard Sunderland, *Taming the Wild Field. Colonization and Empire on the Russian Steppe* (Ithaca, NY, 2004), 204.
38. See for example Bronsart von Schellendorff, *Thierbeobachtungen und Jagdgeschichten aus Ostafrika*, 131; Woldemar von Falz-Fein, *Askania Nova. Das Tierparadies. Ein Buch des Gedenkens und der Gedanken* (Neudamm, 1930), V, 83. Bronsart von Schellendorff named an outpost of his ostrich and zebra breeding enterprise south of Kilimanjaro after Askania Nova, see Munson, *The Nature of Christianity in Northern Tanzania*, 57.
39. Patrick Kupper, *Creating Wilderness. A Transnational History of the Swiss National Park* (Oxford, 2014), chapter 5.
40. August Brauer, "Ueber die Notwendigkeit einer Sammel- und Auskunftsstelle für medizinisch-, forst- und landwirtschaftlich wichtige Tiere in unseren Kolonien," *Verhandlungen des Deutschen Kolonialkongresses 1910*: 76–83. For the broader picture of contemporary field research see Raf de Bont, *Stations in the Field. A History of Place-Based Animal Research, 1870–1930* (Chicago, 2015).
41. Franz Doflein, "Wildschutz und Wissenschaft in den deutschen Kolonien," *Naturwissenschaftliche Wochenschrift* (1911): 817–20; see also Franz Doflein, *Ostasienfahrt. Erlebnisse und Beobachtungen eines Naturforschers in China, Japan und Ceylon* (Leipzig, 1906), chapter 22; and Alexander Sokolowsky, *Gesammelte*

Aufsätze zoologischen Inhalts. Für Zoologen, Landwirte, Tierzüchter und Kolonialfreunde (Leipzig, 1909), 76–80.
42. BAB R 1001/237-1, fol. 55: AA KA to Gov DOA, 23 April 1896.
43. BAB R 1001/7776, fol. 56: Memorandum on Game Preservation by Hermann von Wissmann, 20 March 1898.
44. Daniel T Rodgers, *Atlantic Crossings. Social Politics in a Progressive Age* (Cambridge, MA, 1998).
45. *Journal of the Society for the Preservation of the Wild Fauna of the Empire* 2 (1905): 7; see also *Journal of the Society for the Preservation of the Wild Fauna of the Empire* 3 (1907): 27.
46. See Karen Jones, "Unpacking Yellowstone. The American National Park in Global Perspective," in *Civilizing Nature. National Parks in Global Historical Perspective*, ed. Bernhard Gissibl, Sabine Höhler, and Patrick Kupper (Oxford, 2012), 31–49; Tyrrell, "America's National Parks"; John Sheail, *Nature's Spectacle. The World's First National Parks and Protected Areas* (London, 2010).
47. See Bernhard Gissibl, Sabine Höhler, and Patrick Kupper, "Introduction: Towards a Global History of National Parks," in *Civilizing Nature. National Parks in Global Historical Perspective*, ed. Bernhard Gissibl, Sabine Höhler, and Patrick Kupper (Oxford, 2012), 1-27.
48. See for example Fritz Bley, "Wildschutz in Afrika," *Der Weidmann* 31 (1900): 669–70.
49. Theodore Roosevelt, *Jagden in amerikanischer Wildnis. Eine Schilderung des Wildes der Vereinigten Staaten und seiner Jagd* (Berlin, 1905), 13; William Temple Hornaday, *The Extermination of the American Bison, with a Sketch of Its Discovery and Life History* (Washington, 1889), 527; similarly Arnold Hague, "The Yellowstone Park as a Game Reservation," in *American Big Game Hunting. The Book of the Boone & Crockett Club*, ed. Theodore Roosevelt and George Bird Grinnell (New York, 1893), 240–70. See also Hanns Maria von Kadich, "Der nordamerikanische Bison in der Vergangenheit und Gegenwart," *Das Waidwerk in Wort und Bild* 9 (1899–1900): 4–8, 30–34, 45–49, 53–58, 65–68, 77–81, 89–95, 101–3, 133–37, 157–61; Wolfgang von Garvens-Garvensburg, "Wild im Yellowstonepark," in *Naturschutzparke in Deutschland und Österreich*, 43–46.
50. BAB R 1001/7766, fol. 56–63: Memorandum of Wissmann, 20 March 1898; see also BAB R 8923/2236, fol. 23: Bericht über die Hauptversammlung, 52–54.
51. See for example Sarasin, *Ueber die Aufgaben des Weltnaturschutzes*, 29–31.
52. See for example Doflein, "Wildschutz und Wissenschaft in den deutschen Kolonien."
53. BAB R 8023/1000, fol. 59: Bericht über die Hauptversammlung, 56–58.
54. Ibid., 69–70.
55. BAB R 1001/6229-1, fol. 16–17: RKA to all governors, 24 February 1912.
56. From a rich literature see Mark David Spence, *Dispossessing the Wilderness. Indian Removal and the Making of the National Parks* (New York, 1999), and, for the broader context, Raf de Bont, "'Primitives' and Protected Areas: International Conservation and the 'Naturalization' of Indigenous People, ca. 1910–1975," *Journal of the History of Ideas* 76, no. 2 (2015): 215–36.
57. Anderson and Grove, "Introduction: The Scramble for Eden: Past, Present and Future in African Conservation," in *Conservation in Africa*, 1–12; Jonathan S Adams and Thomas O McShane, *The Myth of Wild Africa. Conservation without*

Illusion (Berkeley, CA, 1992); Grove, *Green Imperialism*; Neumann, *Imposing Wilderness*; William M Adams, "Nature and the Colonial Mind," in *Decolonizing Nature. Strategies for Conservation in a Post-colonial Era*, ed. William M Adams and Martin Mulligan (London, 2003), 16–50.
58. Fabian, *Time and the Other*, 31.
59. Bronsart von Schellendorff, *Thierbeobachtungen und Jagdgeschichten aus Ostafrika*, 127; Paasche, *Im Morgenlicht*, 228; Schillings, *With Flashlight and Rife*, 9–10.
60. Cf. *Jagdhandbuch für Deutsch-Ostafrika*, 92–97.
61. "Wassertechnische Vorarbeiten in der Mkattasteppe, am Viktoriasee, am oberen Pangani und am unteren Ruvu in Deutsch-Ostafrika," *Verhandlungen der Kolonial-technischen Kommission des Kolonial-Wirtschaftlichen Komitees* no. 1 (1910), 21 November: 54–60; "Ausarbeitung des Bewässerungsprojektes im Südosten des Victoriasees," *Verhandlungen der Kolonial-technischen Kommission des Kolonial-Wirtschaftlichen Komitees* no. 1 (1913), 17 November: 39–50.
62. BAB R 1001/278, fol. 66–88, fol. 85: Heinrich Fonck, Report on the Rufiji-Ulanga-Expedition 1907, 15 January 1908; BAB R 1001/238, fol. 151*ff*.: Reisebericht des Leutnants Paasche [received 19th February 1907].
63. Carl Georg Schillings, "Die Arche Noah," *Süddeutsche Monatshefte* 11/2 (1914): 148.
64. Michel Foucault, "Of Other Spaces," *Diacritics* (1986, Spring): 22–27.
65. Neumann, *Imposing Wilderness*, 15–25; WJT Mitchell, "Imperial Landscape," in *Landscape and Power*, ed. WJT Mitchell (Chicago, 2002), 5–34.
66. BAB R 8023/1000, fol. 59: Bericht über die Hauptversammlung, 70.
67. On the historical association of the Persian *paridaida*, denoting "enclosure" with royal hunting grounds in the Middle East see Allsen, *The Royal Hunt in Eurasian History*, 34–35. Similarly, the etymological roots of the word *Eden* in the Babylonian *eindu* and the Hebrew *Ēdhen* respectively denoted, among others, hunting grounds, see Max Oelschlaeger, *The Idea of Wilderness. From Prehistory to the Age of Ecology* (New Haven, CT, 1991), 31.
68. Reichskolonialamt, *Jagd und Wildschutz in den deutschen Kolonien*, 35.
69. Hauptschule Gürzenich Düren, Schillings Papers Album I, fol. 34: Solf to Schillings, 14 January 1912.
70. These areas were registered as reserves for individual species, cf. TNA G 8/910.
71. *Amtlicher Anzeiger für Deutsch-Ostafrika* 1, no. 17 (1900), Circular 28 June.
72. *Kilimandjaro- und Meru-Zeitung* 1, no. 14 (1913), 19 July; TNA G 21/411, fol. 23–24: Hearing of Wihelm Grolp, Morogoro, 6 April 1912; TNA G 58/40, unfol.: Morogoro to Gov DOA, 5 August 1912.
73. TNA G 58/41, unfol.: Report forestry station Morogoro, 31 August 1913; On the lack of record keeping see RHO Micr. Afr. 446: Theodor Gunzert: Service in German East Africa & German Foreign Service, 1902–33 [undated], 29–30; cf. TNA G 21/148, fol. 8: Statement of the *jumbe* Kapila, 6 September 1907.
74. TNA G8/55, fol. 41: Tabora to Gov DOA, 14 July 1896; TNA G8/55, fol. 44: Bukoba to Gov DOA, 1 August 1896; TNA G8/55, fol. 92: Kilimatinde to Gov DOA, 13 July 1897; TNA G8/55, fol. 218–20: Iringa to Gov DOA, 9 January 1899.
75. TNA G 55/8, unfol.: Gov DOA to Kilimatinde, 2 April 1903; Kilimatinde to Gov DOA, 15 May 1903. The reserve was abolished again by governmental decree

in November 1905, cf. *Amtlicher Anzeiger für Deutsch-Ostafrika* 6, no. 30 (1905), 25 November; Eberhard von Sick, "Die Waniaturu (Walimi). Ethnographische Skizze eines Bantu-Stammes," *Baessler-Archiv* 5 (1916): 60.
76. BAB R 1001/7777, fol. 333: Gov DOA to RKA, 29 March 1911.
77. See for example Becker, *Aus Deutsch-Ostafrikas Sturm- und Drangperiode,* 74-75, 79-81.
78. "Bericht über die Verhandlungen der 36. Plenarversammlung des Deutschen Landwirtschaftsrats vom 10. bis 13. Februar 1908," *Archiv des deutschen Landwirtschaftsrates* 32 (1908): 109-10; TNA G 21/148, fol. 11: Hearing of Gustav Johannes Willi Pietsch, Lindi, 4 November 1907; TNA G 8/912, unfol.: List of requests for shooting permissions to prevent wildlife damage, Lindi [1911]; TNA G 58/40, unfol. BA Morogoro to Gov DOA, 5 August 1912; *Amtlicher Anzeiger für Deutsch-Ostafrika* 12, no. 24 (1911), 4 June; "Weitere Wildverwüstungen in Deutsch-Ostafrika," *Deutsche Jägerzeitung* 57, no. 41 (1911): 651-52.
79. TNA G 8/910, enclosed drafts.
80. TNA G 8/55, fol. 218-20: Iringa to Gov DOA, 9 January 1899.
81. The map can be found as an attachment to Reichskolonialamt, *Jagd und Wildschutz in den deutschen Kolonien.*
82. See the detailed discussion in Shetler, *Imagining Serengeti*, 135-68. For the opposing view of the biologist see Sinclair, *The Serengeti Story*, especially 51-56.
83. BAB R 1001/238, fol. 94: Reisebericht des Hauptmanns Freiherr von Schleinitz durch das Massaigebiet von Ikoma bis zum Ostafrikanischen Graben, March 1904; Karl Müller, "Jagdtage in der Serengeti," *Wild und Hund* 21 (1915): 6-9; Joseph Deeg, "Wildschutz," *Kilimandjaro- und Meru-Zeitung* 1, no. 2 (1913), 25 January; "Das Massaigebiet, eine Wildkammer in Deutsch-Ostafrika," *Wild und Hund* 10 (1904): 668-69.
84. Paul Vageler, *Afrikanisches Mosaik. Fünfundzwanzig Jahre Wanderungen durch die afrikanische Wirklichkeit* (Berlin, 1941), 41.
85. "Zur neuen Jagdverordnung," *Usambara-Post* 7, no. 49 (1908), 12 December. The reserve was, however, retained and taken over by the British under the name "Northern Railway Reserve," see TNA TT AB 729, Draft Game Ordinance, 1921; TNA TT AB 150, fol. 45: Swynnerton to Central Admin, 17 March 1920.
86. TNA G 58/40, unfol.: Morogoro to Gov DOA, 5 August 1912; see also TNA G 58/41, fol. 3: Forestry station Manjangu to Forestry Department Dar es Salaam, 29 February 1913; BAB R 1001/7802-1, fol. 113: Gov DOA to RKA, 19 September 1912, attachment: Material concerning the memorandum on Hunting and Game Conservation in German East Africa, Question no. 13, Bagamoyo, Morogoro; cf. Busse, *Die periodischen Grasbrände,* 136.
87. PRO FO 403/302, no. 4: Head of the Colonial Department Paul Kayser to Martin Gosselin, 15 July 1896, enclosure in: Gosselin to FO, 15 July 1896.
88. See also Munson, *The Nature of Christianity in Northern Tanzania,* 150-54.
89. BAB R 1001/7802-1, fol. 113: Gov DOA to RKA, 19 September 1912, attachment: Material concerning the memorandum on Hunting and Game Conservation in German East Africa, Question no. 14: Answers Iringa, Bagamoyo, Kilwa, Mpwapwa, Lindi, Moshi, Mahenge, Mohoro, Morogoro, Neulangenburg, Udjidji, Wilhelmstal; TNA G 8/912, List of Game Reserves, no. 2 (Mohoro), no. 6 (Mahenge), no. 11 (Tabora), no. 13 (Langenburg); TNA G 21/148, fol. 8: Statement of the Game warden Amdallah [!], 6 September 1907; Eduard Elven,

"Wildreservate und Jagdgesetz in Deutsch-Ostafrika," *Wild und Hund* 20 (1914): 281–82; Sunseri, *Vilimani,* 90.
90. Benjamin N Lawrance, Emily Lynn Osborn, and Richard L Roberts, "Introduction. African Intermediaries and the 'Bargain' of Collaboration," in *Intermediaries, Interpreters and Clerks. African Employees and the Making of Colonial Africa,* ed. Benjamin N Lawrance, Emily Lynn Osborn, and Richard L Roberts (Madison, WI, 2006), 4.
91. Sunseri, *Vilimani,* 89, 96–97.
92. TNA G 50/12, unfol.: Circular Gov DOA, 5 March 1914.
93. TNA G 21/148, fol. 8: Statement of the Game warden Amdallah [!], 6 September 1907; TNA G 21/247, unfol.: Testimony of the Game Warden Ruaha Reserve, 14 November 1909; TNA G 8/912, List of Contraventions against the Game Laws: Frank Moore Craig, Sentence of 1,000 rupees for illegal hunting in a game reserve, District Court Tanga, 1909; TNA G 21/411, fol. 26–27: Conviction of Willy Grolp for illegal hunting in the Upper Rufiji Reserve, Dar es Salaam, 3 May 1912.
94. *Kilimandjaro- und Meru-Zeitung* 1, no.10 (1913), 24 May.
95. Deutsch, "Celebrating Power in Everyday Life," 96, 100–2.
96. TNA G 50/9 Strafbuch Militär-Station Tabora, July 1902 to April 1904; TNA G 58/40, unfol.: BA Morogoro to Gov DOA, 5 August 1912.
97. See chapter 3.
98. TNA G 58/40, unfol.: Morogoro to Gov DOA, 5 August 1912. The singular form "shamba la bibi" is more widespread.
99. Shetler, *Imagining Serengeti,* 182, 202; Eleanor Fisher, "What Future for the Shamba la Bibi? Livelihoods and Local Resource Use in a Tanzanian Game Reserve" (PhD diss., University of Hull, 1997), 3.
100. BAB R 1001/7802-1, fol. 113: Gov DOA to RKA, 19 September 1912, attachment: Material concerning the memorandum on Hunting and Game Conservation in German East Africa, Question no. 7, Iringa; TNA G 58/40, unfol.: Morogoro to Gov DOA, 5 August 1912.
101. Fonck, *Deutsch-Ostafrika,* 364.
102. BAB R 1001/7802-1, fol. 113: Gov DOA to RKA, 19 September 1912, attachment: Material concerning the memorandum on Hunting and Game Conservation in German East Africa, Question no. 13: Iringa, Lindi, Mahenge, Mohoro, Neulangenburg; for Kilimanjaro, see Munson, *The Nature of Christianity in Northern Tanzania,* 154.
103. TNA TT AB 145, fol. 26: Circular AC Hollis, 4 August 1921, attachment: Memorandum on Game Preservation and Tsetse Control by CFM Swynnerton [undated].

 CHAPTER 7

Rivalry and Stewardship
The Anglo-German Origins of International Wildlife Conservation in Africa

> Then the conscience of Europe awoke! That tender conscience that always awakes when this continent has directly or indirectly caused a major catastrophe. Everywhere it was to be heard: "Preservation of Africa's Wildlife!"
> —Hans Schomburgk, *Von Mensch und Tier und etwas von mir* (Berlin, 1947), 129.

"What Have You Done in East Africa?" or: All Maasailand a Reserve

In March 1901, the superintendent of the African Protectorates in the British Foreign Office, Sir Clement Hill sent a letter to Hermann von Wissmann, the retired governor of the German East African colony. Enclosed in his letter were the game regulations of the British East and Central African colonies, and Hill was curious to learn about the action taken by the German authorities on behalf of game preservation in East Africa. "You will see," he wrote, that "I have taken a large area west of the R[ai]lway as a reserve—and one near L[ake] Rudolf—What have you done in East Africa?"[1]

Hill's question referred back to a private meeting with Wissmann a few months earlier in September 1900, when they had discussed the implementation of the provisions of the International Conference for the Preservation of Wild Animals, Birds and Fish, held in London in May 1900. Being the leading delegates of their respective governments at the conference, both had decided to coordinate the conservationist efforts in their East African colonies as far as possible. Three months after Wissmann had been entrusted by the German Foreign Office to elaborate game regulations for all German colonies in accordance with the London Convention,[2] he met Hill to compare their draft regulations. Together, they envisioned an enormous transboundary game reserve including almost all of Ukamba and Maasailand, from Mount Kilimanjaro in the east to Lake Victoria in the west, Lakes Manyara and Eyasi in the south and the Uganda Railway in the north.[3] Hill immediately embarked upon a tour to East Africa in order to extend the Athi or Southern Game Reserve in British East Africa.[4] Wissmann, however, no longer held an official function in the colonial service and was unable to act accordingly on the German side. When the colonial department in Berlin discussed the future of game conservation in German East Africa in April 1901, the transboundary accord in wildlife matters carved out by Wissmann and Hill was discarded as impracticable.[5]

The establishment of a transboundary game reserve in Maasailand was, however, only deferred for a few years. Encouraged by the prosettlement attitude of Commissioner Sir Charles Eliot, the first decade of the twentieth century witnessed the constant influx of a small but wealthy and predominantly aristocratic class of settlers in Kenya, who established grand estates in the southern highlands and soon got in conflict with the Southern Game Reserve. During the dry season, especially at the turn of 1910–11, a lack of rainfall caused the wildlife to migrate beyond the reserve's borders in search of food and pasture. Soon, "ravages of game and vermin" were reported "to constitute a serious handicap to agricultural progress" in the neighboring Ukamba Province. Also the twenty or so settlers in the Ulu area declared farming virtually impossible "so long as the game continues to exist," impressing the view upon Governor Percy Girouard that it was "quite impossible to carry on farming operations with the presence of this game reserve." In January 1911, he was willing to surrender to the settlers' pressure, suggesting to the colonial office "that the present Southern Masai Reserve should be thrown open to shooting."[6]

The future for game and reserve looked bleak when the game warden of the Kenya colony, Richard B Woosnam, happened to meet two German aristocrats in the last days of January 1911. Baron Ruprecht Böcklin von Böcklinsau, a peer of the Baden Parliament, and Count Hans von Königsmarck, an Anglophile military officer with a particular admiration for the Indian *shikar,* had just been passing through Nairobi, one finishing, the other just embarking upon safari. In the course of their conversation, Woosnam expressed his hopes that the authorities of German East Africa "may be induced to close as a game reserve a large tract of land corresponding to our reserve and bordering on it." Such a "joint reserve" would double the size of the Southern Reserve and thus be "of far greater value and of international interest."[7] If we are to trust Woosnam's account, the German aristocrats "promised to use their influence to promote the scheme privately until the time should be ripe for official negotiations." Indeed, Böcklin went to see the governor before embarking upon his return journey and appears to have left him "strongly in favour" of the project.[8] The Rechenberg controversy probably halted the project for several months, but in April 1912, a wildlife sanctuary was established between Lake Natron and Kilimanjaro, abutting the British reserve on the German side of the border.

Lifting these early efforts at establishing a joint reserve from the amnesia of the colonial archive is important for it highlights the degree of transimperial cooperation and mutual exchange in the early stages of African conservation. This is important because so far, the story of wildlife conservation in Africa has been told mainly from a British perspective that was both imperial and parochial because it took little notice of what was going on beyond the empire.[9] However, although the British had their own "imperial archive" of conservation in South Africa and India, there was a world of other empires beyond their borders that impacted upon policies in the British colonies. "What have you done in East Africa?"—Clement Hill's question expresses a haughty awareness to the colonial neighbor, while Woosnam used conservation policies in German East Africa to enhance his leverage in debates about conservation in Kenya. In both cases, wildlife policies in the East African colonies were no self-contained phenomena, but interacted.

The repeated attempts at connecting and aligning conservation measures across borders suggest that the "rise of the Anglo-German antagonism" (Paul Kennedy) in Europe before the Great War was not necessarily matched by a similar decline of Anglo-German relations overseas.[10] The scramble for Africa undeniably thrived upon nationalist rivalries among the European powers. But at the same time, imperialism was a globalizing force. It did not only export European notions of territoriality, but, by doing so, also created new spaces and arenas for transnational cooperation. Wissmann and Hill met at an international conference that convened to coordinate imperial policies in wildlife matters; Böcklin and Königsmarck used hunting tourism as a new arena for transnational aristocratic encounters opened up by colonial rule. The very way the imperial powers distributed Africa among themselves is suggestive. In order to draw the colonial borders on the ground, the colonial powers had to cooperate by setting up a joint boundary commission. Cutting across existing links in geography, ecology, and diseases, as well as connections of trade and the routes of migratory animals, the new colonial borders not only divided but also generated new opportunities and necessities for Europeans and Africans alike. The borders became spaces of trespassing and smuggle, migration, and contagion, as well as exchange and cooperation.

The efforts at coordinating game conservation in British and German East Africa show that Europe's overseas colonies, as much as they were fraught with nationalist expectations, were spaces of inter- and transnational exposure and competition as well as cooperation, exchange, and learning.[11] This chapter is concerned with this ambivalent nature of imperial colonialism. It takes imperialism as both enabling and limiting structure for internationalism and analyzes the transimperial dimensions of wildlife conservation in East Africa before World War I. First, the parallel and at times entangled evolution of German and British wildlife policies in East Africa will be analyzed in order to expose the colonies' role as sites of transimperial encounters and cooperation. Then, the chapter traces the mechanics of international wildlife conservation in Africa as an example of governmental internationalism effected by the "New Imperialism" of the late nineteenth century. The final paragraph of this chapter remains in Europe to distinguish two strands of advocacy for the conservation of Africa's wildlife that emerged from the alleged failure to implement the London Convention. One remained closely tied to the institutions of empire, as exemplified by the British Society for the Preservation of the Wild Fauna of the Empire (SPWFE) and the two German Commissions for the Improvement of Game Preservation in the German colonies. The other transcended imperial responsibilities and the hunters' concern with "game" to understand Africa's wild fauna as part of a broader agenda of *Weltnaturschutz*—the global protection of nature. Although attempts at implementing elements of *Weltnaturschutz* into environmental diplomacy failed before World War I, it continued to constitute a rivalling claim to the imperial responsibility for Africa's wildlife until the imperial and global strands of stewardship collapsed into the establishment of international environmental organizations after World War II.

"A Great Solidarity of Interests"?
German and British Wildlife Policies in East Africa

German and British wildlife policies in East Africa evolved in parallel and were at times entwined. Three stages of contact and exchange can be identified. In the formative years up to the London Conference on Wildlife Conservation in 1900, game legislation in the German and British East African possessions was closely intertwined. In the first decade of the 1900s, Kenya developed safari tourism and became a model for German East Africa. From 1912 onward, wildlife policies in both colonies had been brought into line, with German East Africa trying to catch up in terms of safari tourism.

The last decade of the nineteenth century was marked by competition over the tapping of the ivory routes from the Congo Basin, but also intense exchange between German and British authorities. As shown in the first two chapters, the flows of the ivory trade were heavily in favor of the Germans. The main caravan routes connecting the Swahili Coast with the Great Lakes and beyond ended up in the port towns along the German stretch of the coast, while Mombasa was largely bypassed by the trade and only served as a minor outlet. The surviving export figures of the 1890s indicate the disproportionate participation in the trade: in 1894, British East Africa procured ivory worth £20,975, compared with ivory worth £121,567 exported from German territory via Zanzibar. Despite decreasing volumes, the revenue the Germans garnered from ivory was still more than three times higher than in neighboring British East Africa in 1896 and 1897.[12] This disproportionate participation in trade flows was an important motif for the construction of the Uganda Railway to connect the coast with the main areas of ivory production west of the Great Lakes.[13]

The channeling of the trade flows from the inland to the coast constituted an obvious cause for rivalry and encouraged smuggling in the border regions. The agents of the fledging colonial states on both sides used ivory as a subsidy for their expeditions and for colonial state-building. However, German East Africa did initially not attract or produce the profligate breed of "pioneer hunters" and freebooting ivory harvesters who were such a marked feature of British conquest in Africa.[14] There was no German equivalent to the frontier ideology that attracted British hunters to East Africa as the most recent and fashionable hunting opportunity within their Empire. Moreover, as a consequence of the firm integration of Tanganyikan territory into the caravan trade, the networks of trade and hunting remained to a large degree in the hands of African and Swahili entrepreneurs. Finally, official German authorities tended to regard third parties, such as private expeditions or companies, as unwelcome witnesses and a challenge to their authority. Therefore, they tried to reduce their interference to a minimum, especially during the years of conquest in the 1890s.[15]

The second half of the 1890s developed into a period of intense cooperation between German and British authorities. Both powers were equally affected by the closure of the ivory trade from the Congo Basin, and both registered rapidly decreasing elephant populations within their territories. Imperial elites on both sides of the channel interpreted events in East Africa in the light of the previous record of game extermination in South Africa and North America.[16] In translating perception into action, the individual role of Wissmann as imperial internationalist, erstwhile explorer, and hunter can hardly be overestimated. Archival sources reveal how thoroughly impressed he was by an article in the British *Gazette for Zanzibar and East Africa,* whose anonymous author compared the devastation of big game in Africa by "the rifle-bearing hunter, professional, and amateur" to the destruction of the North American bison.[17] The article was a direct inspiration for Wissmann's game ordinance of 1896, which in turn galvanized the authorities in British East Africa into action. Discussions about bringing the "excessive destruction ... of the larger wild animals" in Africa to a halt were already well under way when the translation of Wissmann's game ordinance arrived at the British Foreign Office by the end of June

1896. A few weeks earlier, Lord Salisbury, the British prime minister and foreign secretary, had recommended the introduction of reserved districts and the limitation of the number of game to be shot to the commissioners in British East Africa and Uganda, demanding some kind of legislation in that matter.[18] But, as John MacKenzie has stated, it is a "curious fact" that the responsible British authorities had not tapped the experiences and practices of British conservation in South Africa as a model for East Africa.[19] Part of the explanation lies in the institutional setup of the metropolitan administration of the British Empire. Because Kenya had the status of a protectorate, the monitoring of the activities of the Imperial British East Africa Company (IBEAC) in the 1890s counted among the responsibilities of the Department for the African Protectorates in the British Foreign Office, whereas South African affairs were a matter of the colonial office. Apparently, the institutional entropy of British imperial administration had prevented the exchange of such information until the arrival of the German ordinance instigated correspondence between the departments. In the following months, the British Foreign Office accumulated all available knowledge on game conservation, including the game laws from Zululand, Natal, Bechuanaland, the Cape Colony, and several memoranda from forest conservators as well as the forest regulations, which incorporated the wildlife conservation measures taken in British India.[20] Between 1896 and 1899, all British colonies bordering on German East Africa, sometimes hesitantly, established sanctuaries.[21] To coordinate conservationist efforts and to discourage the smuggling of ivory, British authorities agreed to make their hunting regulations match those of German East Africa, however, with one important difference. While Wissmann's successor as governor denied foreign sporting expeditions access to the hunting grounds in the interior of German East Africa,[22] his British counterpart, Commissioner Sir Arthur Hardinge, established as a principle to

> keep as close as possible to the German Regulations, but make our own slightly more favourable to wealthy sportsmen who bring money into the territory, and who, so long as their destruction of its game can be kept ... within safe limits, should be encouraged rather than otherwise to visit it.[23]

The period of active exchange and transfer between German and British authorities lasted as long as Hermann von Wissmann shaped wildlife policies in German East Africa—as governor in 1895–96 and as "elder statesman" and informal counsellor to the colonial department in the German Foreign Office after his retirement. It was also Wissmann who, in October 1895, had first suggested making game preservation in Africa a matter of international responsibility and coordination. Together with the British

Foreign Office, he prepared the agenda for the International Conference in London in 1900, undoubtedly the pinnacle of Anglo-German cooperation. While parts of the resolutions arrived at the conference were put into practice, the rejection of Wissmann and Hill's vision of large-scale transcolonial game preservation marked the growing divergence in German and British wildlife policies in the first decade of the 1900s. The colonial governments kept on exchanging their ordinances via the usual diplomatic channels and collected the game legislation of the other European colonial powers for information and analysis.[24] However, after the ordinances of Uganda and British East Africa had been drafted, now including all the available experience from South Africa, the commissioners of the British East and Central African colonies could not find any more provisions in the German game laws that "could with advantage be incorporated."[25]

The pivotal difference between the governance of hunting in German and British East Africa in the first decade of the twentieth century was the embrace of the economic value of wildlife for hunting tourism by the British administration. They promoted the necessary infrastructure and issued game ordinances that rendered commercial hunting impossible and made elephant hunting distinctive. Kenya, Uganda, and Southern Rhodesia had all restricted the amount of elephants to be shot under one license in 1899.[26] The colonial administration in Dar es Salaam continued to admit commercial ivory hunting, which made the geography of comparatively unbridled hunting shift: German East Africa became attractive for British imperial or South African ivory harvesters whose business had ceased to be profitable in the British territories of Equatorial East Africa. Wealthy German aristocrats and trophy hunters, on the other hand, appreciated the amenities offered by the fledgling tourist infrastructure in Kenya. This development was one of the complaints raised by the wildlife conservation lobby in Germany, whose core demand was the alignment of game policies in German East Africa with those practiced in Kenya. In several respects, the organization of their campaign was inspired by British examples. The German Commission for the Improvement of Game Conservation that formed in 1907 took the British SPWFE as its model. In numerous articles and speeches, Germany's wildlife lobbyists presented the British game legislation as an orientation for the colonial newcomer, based as it seemingly was upon "centuries of colonial experience."[27] Economic arguments as well as idealist motivations for game conservation were all rationalized with a view to British practices in Kenya. What had already been achieved in a similar setting, the conservationists argued, could not be impossible in German East Africa.

The sustained lobbying and campaigning by hunters and preservationists in Germany effected that the administration in Dar es Salaam gradually aligned its wildlife policies with British East Africa. By 1911, the German consul at Mombasa could conclude that the present "German and British game regulations" were "more or less similar."[28] The attempts to establish game reserves along the Central and Usambara Railways in German East Africa show that the transfer of practices from Kenya anything but ceased afterward, and the fledgling safari entrepreneurism in German East Africa borrowed heavily from the business arrangements established by the British competitors in Kenya. A renewed effort to coordinate the minimum weight of traded ivory was made in 1914, and the imperative to reconcile wildlife preservation with agricultural development forced both governments to refine their conservation measures. Joining protected areas across borders was part of that refinement and illustrates that transcolonial cooperation was not a strategy of the latecomer only.

The Anglo-German exchange concerning hunting-related wildlife policies was characterized by an undeniable asymmetry. If we extend the focus to the veterinary aspects of wildlife policies, a slightly different picture emerges. Cooperation and exchange were based on a more equal footing in the case of combating the spread of diseases like trypanosomiasis, rinderpest, or east coast fever. The virtual impossibility to control animal movements meant that the border linked rather than separated the two colonies. Research on the role of wild animals in the spread of bovine diseases and especially of human and animal trypanosomiasis was a transimperial project in which scientists defined diseases as their "common enemy"[29] and themselves as "conquerors venturing out to subdue with their weapons those corners of the earth that could not be conquered by blood and iron."[30] They exchanged publications, drew upon each other's research findings, and used the colonies as field laboratories irrespective of colonial borders.

Cooperation in the field of bacteriology and medicine had a prehistory beyond East Africa, starting as early as Robert Koch's expedition to Egypt and India in 1884–85 to study the bacterium that caused cholera.[31] British authorities continued to invite Koch to investigate unknown diseases. His studies of cattle diseases in East Africa in 1897–98 commended him to the British as a leading expert in the field. Consequently, Koch was asked again to study an outbreak of east coast fever in Southern Rhodesia in 1903.[32] Also in 1907, the bacteriologist received "gratifying support from the British authorities" during his sleeping sickness expedition in German and British territories on Lake Victoria.[33]

As in matters of game conservation, South Africa was a pivotal source of knowledge and experience to be transferred to East Africa. Shortly after veterinary science had become institutionalized in the Onderstepoort Veterinary Institute outside Pretoria in 1908, its leading researcher, the Swiss-born Arnold Theiler, was invited as veterinary adviser to British and German East African authorities. Theiler found that veterinarians in both colonies had adopted some practices lately developed in South Africa, such as the method to clear grazing grounds for at least one year to prevent the ticks causing east coast fever from feeding on cattle.[34] Similar to the Javanese Buitenzorg in the field of botany, Onderstepoort became a "model institute for bacteriological research" and veterinary science that elicited not only admiration in Germany but also became a site for imperial research cooperation.[35] These transfers between South and East Africa, but also plans to send a veterinarian from Dar es Salaam to study the treatment of cattle diseases in British India suggest that also in matters of science, colonial policies were enmeshed in networks of knowledge that extended beyond the confines of metropole and colony and across empires.[36] As Karen Brown has observed, the European "metropole" was no longer the sole and authoritative point of reference: the colonies themselves started to play "a significant role in the expansion of an imperial, and indeed an increasingly global, scientific culture."[37]

Still, the established arenas of scientific internationalism in Europe remained core zones for the making of a European scientific community across imperial borders. Above all, this was true for congresses and conferences. An international conference convened in London in June 1907 promoted the exchange of information on sleeping sickness.[38] Sidestepping French efforts to institutionalize research on the disease at the recently founded Office International d'Hygiène Publique (the forerunner of the World Health Organization) in Paris, German and British experts met again in London in October 1908 for a confidential discussion of "scientific questions with a view to seeing if ... it would not be possible for Great Britain and Germany to draw up some joint Regulations for local application in the neighbourhood of Uganda."[39] The informal meeting also had the purpose to allow Koch's participation right after his return from East Africa. Concerting measures against sleeping sickness in East Africa ranked high on the agenda, and determining the exact relationship between migratory animals and the various species of *glossinae* was a key scientific target. "In all infected districts," the participating scientists agreed, "steps shall be taken to ascertain what migratory animals there are whose blood could provide nourishment for the *glossina palpalis*; in accordance with the result of this investigation, local measures will be decided on for the extermination of the animals, or for their removal from the infected district."[40] As a consequence of the agreement reached in London, German and British officials stationed along the border between German East Africa and Uganda were allowed to directly communicate about developments regarding sleeping sickness,[41] while British and German scientists, according to one German surgeon, "supported each other wherever they had the opportunity."[42] However, the evidence produced by bacteriologist research was interpreted differently according to dissimilar political and social contexts in the East African colonies. After the game slaughter of 1910 and its consequences, German scientists were cautious and questioned too close a relationship between game and the spread of tsetse, whereas British scientists were more inclined to venture experimental game extermination.[43]

As this survey has shown, wildlife policies in British and German East Africa up to World War I are best understood as entwined coevolution. Arguably, both colonies were more important for the development of each other's wildlife policies than the policies of hunting and wildlife anywhere else in the German and British Empires, including the imperial metropoles. Conjunctures and asymmetries notwithstanding, exchange and learning across colonial borders in Africa was an important and often overlooked source of knowledge and policy formation. In the case of hunting, but also the associated veterinary policies, these exchanges were characterized by rivalry, cooperation, and the commonality of European stewardship for wildlife conservation and the eradication of disease on the continent. The development of wildlife policies in East Africa did not mirror the rapprochements and antagonisms in the imperial metropole. They were neither marked by a "principled rivalry," nor by the simple mechanism of pioneer and latecomer, nor by a linear development from confrontation to coexistence. The most important element to prompt transfer and cooperation were local structures and shared problems of colonial governance.[44] The control of the ivory trade, the sustainable hunting of elephants, and the prevention of contagious diseases were all cases that made coordination across borders imperative because they could not be contained by the instruments available within the bounded territory of the colonial state. The deficits of the fledgling colonial states were another commonality that motivated transfer and learning. The availability of an institutional "colonial archive" in the British case helps explain why transcolonial learning, borrowing, and observation were so asymmetrical. As soon as British authorities had tapped the available knowledge about how the appropriation of wild animals was organized in other parts of the empire in the second half of the 1890s, the perceived necessity to draw upon experiences made by the colonial neighbor vanished. Germans were more receptive to what the British did than vice versa. According to the German Consul in Zanzibar and Mombasa, Heinrich Brode, the reason was "obvious":

> The English are a nation of long colonial experience. For experiments in a new colony they easily find models in one of their old possessions; they do not need to go to school to such a colonial parvenu as their German neighbour appears to them to be. We, on the contrary, are glad to learn wherever we can, being novices in all colonial questions.[45]

Observation, learning, and transfer were all means for the latecomer to tap the European archive of colonial governance. This observation should caution against taking contemporary assessments of the "success" of other nations' colonial policies and achievements at face value. Transimperial reference was seldom a representation of colonial realities. First and foremost, it was a language of interest, activism, and motivation that was strategically used to gain leverage in domestic discussions. A second observation is closely related. Transimperial encounters and transfers were often affected by the very structures and spaces that imperialism created. The increasingly global infrastructure of steamships and railways were not only the lifelines of global economy but also contact zones for the agents of empire. However, cooperation did not follow inevitably from these structures. Colonial borders also cut through arteries of trade and routes of wildlife migration along the borders that German East Africa shared with the Congo Free State and Portuguese East Africa. Nonetheless, a special relationship of cooperation, rivalry, and transfer only developed between the Germans and the British. Structural predispositions like trade routes may have commended transboundary coordination, but they did not automatically produce political action. The same holds true for the prestige of the white "race,"[46] which was constantly invoked when nationalist reservations were to be bridged. Such rhetoric functioned as an important discursive legitimation for transimperial cooperation.[47] The self-assumed "trusteeship by the European nations over an inferior race," as Colonial Secretary Dernburg called it, legitimized concerted measures, and it also constituted the boundaries of the community of imperial conservationists and scientists. Their conferences, meetings, and networks were for whites only. Yet, two qualifications about "race" and transimperial connections have to be made. On the one hand, the discursive bonds forged along the lines of "race" were only partially an effect of the colonial color line. The imperial hunting discourse also provides instances of the construction of racialized differentiation within a shared whiteness, for example, when German and British hunters invoked a shared "Anglo-Saxon" passion for hunting and a love for game and the wild which not only Africans, but also the "effeminate" French and "Latins" were allegedly missing. Such racialized self-perceptions and projections constituted a further fault line within the manifold tensions and differentiations of European imperial whiteness. On the other hand, the rhetoric of "race" did not automatically produce consistent policies oriented along the lines of "race." The protection of game may have been a matter of great Anglo-German concern, but it was also a field where more parochial fiscal and economic objectives were pursued, both by individuals and the agents of the colonial state. The solidarity of the white "race" mattered little with a view to the proliferation of firearms and powder in the 1890s or the secret support lent by German authorities to the Zanzibari traders on Lake Tanganyika. The British used Maasai scouts to report intrusions into the Southern Game Reserve by Boer settlers from the German side, while British and German stations on Mount Kilimanjaro strategically turned a blind eye on tusks illegally crossing the border as long as this happened in the right direction.[48] Authorities on both sides exposed an astonishing creativity when it came to circumnavigate the minimum weight of traded ivory and encourage the cross-border smuggling of small tusks. One reason for the widespread rhetoric of maintaining the prestige of the white "race" was that it was constantly undermined in practice.

The third characteristic of transfer and cooperation in the colonies was that it was unthinkable without imperial cosmopolitans. Making conservation a topic of transimperial concern depended on moral entrepreneurs like Wissmann, Schillings, or Clement Hill who deemed the conservation of wildlife an issue significant enough for political regulation. The agents of cross-border cooperation were first and foremost social groups with cosmopolitan affinities: aristocrats, scientists, and the higher echelons of the administrative hierarchy in the colonial service.[49] These groups had the time or the means to travel, or they were mobile anyway thanks to their professional occupations. Language skills were another important prerequisite: the lingua franca of imperial exchange was English, in tropical medicine as well as in conservation. Social and professional hierarchies mattered: hunting and game conservation did engender transnational cooperation because its practitioners and advocates shared a common background of aristocratic cosmopolitanism, military masculinity, or an interest in natural history that helped to bridge national differences. Shared interests, values, similar codes of conduct, and ideals of social exclusivity all rationalized the moral entrepreneurship of hunters irrespective of nationality. When these imperial internationalists were part of the hierarchies of the colonial state, as in the case of Wissmann and Hill, intergovernmental cooperation was eased. When they were denied access to the institutional channels of decision-making, as in the case of Carl Georg Schillings, the calculated transfer of information and strategic personal networking across the borders of empire was a viable strategy to compensate the blocked institutional access and gain political leverage by public campaigning and the import of authority from abroad.

This highlights a fourth characteristic aspect of the Anglo-German connections established in the field of colonial wildlife policies: issues needed to be *framed* as matters of transimperial concern, imperial obligation, and a civilizing mission, both inside and outside of the political institutions of empire. Awareness to how problems were framed as relevant discloses the strategic character of crossing the borders of empire: rather than being a somehow "natural" accompaniment of imperialism, transcending the borders of empire was a strategic, political tool. It was deliberately chosen by nonstate actors to exert pressure upon political decision makers both in Europe and the colony. Colonial authorities could use it to share financial burdens or secure earnings in the face of tight budgets. Declaring the combat against tropical diseases a matter of international concern motivated other colonial powers to mobilize research and resources as well, while internationalizing game conservation was supposed to discourage the smuggling of tusks and thus prevent a decrease in fiscal revenue.

Finally, imperialism did generate internationalism, understood here as the conscious extension of political, cultural, social, and economic practices beyond the realm of the nation-state and the deliberate creation of international movements with the aim to reform societies and politics by transnational cooperation.[50] Both were important structural dimensions of late nineteenth-century globalization, and at first sight, they appear to be fundamentally different. Imperialism included the establishment and extension of political and economic control over space and territory, especially overseas. It was essentially concerned with drawing boundaries, whereas internationalism was characterized by the deliberate attempt to cross such boundaries. One established structures of dominance, the other strove for understanding. However, imperialism and internationalism not only thrived upon the same structural conditions such as the globalization of transport, communication, and information that marked the nineteenth century. They also shared key mechanisms of inclusion and exclusion, such as "race," a culture of experts, and epistemic communities.

Some scholars of internationalism have drawn a sharp distinction between imperialism and internationalism. Akira Iriye, for example, claims that imperialism never spawned internationalism in the sense of a "global community in which all nations and people shared certain interests and commitments."[51] Such a normative understanding of internationalism, however, underestimates imperialism as a structuring principle of international affairs before World War I. It also neglects that universalist aspirations could easily be deployed as rhetoric strategy and were always associated with friction and exclusion in practice, and it takes insufficient account of the universalist aspirations of the imperial mind.[52] Problems resulting from the imperialist partition of the world not only forged links across individual colonies, but spanned metropole and colony to engender international cooperation back in Europe. Tropical medicine and agriculture, veterinary science, or the preservation of wildlife and tropical birds were all issues that generated trans- or international linkages in the form of treaties, congresses, movements, or exchange of information. All of these issues have in common that their internationalism was inextricably bound up with the functioning of empire and colonial rule. Hunters were convinced that the exclusive and restrictive wildlife policies they advocated were in the interest of the whole of mankind. At the same time, conserving elephants for more sustainable harvesting of ivory generated state earnings that enabled the running of an oppressive colonial state. The scientists who met on international conferences to discuss methods to eradicate tropical diseases dangerous to men and animals were inspired by benign ideas of healing the sick and furthering the good of mankind. Nonetheless, they acted within the framework of European empires and undertook their research with the support of colonial governments. Their methods included the application of dubious and partially dangerous medicine, while their policy recommendations entailed segregation and resettlement, and were supposed to further the development of the colonies' resources. What Frederick Cooper has stated with a view to the rhetoric of late nineteenth-century abolitionism that justified imperial domination, also holds true for conservation and medicine: "A globalizing language stood alongside a structure of domination and exploitation that was lumpy to an extreme."[53]

Imperialism was tied to internationalism in complex ways. Both enabled and limited each other at the same time. If there was one instance where internationalism, the universalist rhetoric of a "benefit to mankind,"[54] and the asymmetrical power relations of imperialism intersected, then it was the International Conference on the Preservation of Wild Animals, Birds, and Fish in Africa held in London in April and May 1900.

London 1900—Imperial Internationalism and the Transcontinental Governance of Game

In 1900, two international congresses met in London to discuss matters concerning the African continent. One of them was the Pan-African Congress in July, which gathered forty men and women from the United States, South Africa, the Caribbean as well as Abyssinia and Liberia at Westminster Town Hall. "For the first time in the history of the world," the slave-born American Bishop Alexander Walters pointed out in his opening address, "black men had gathered together from all parts of the globe with the object of discussing and improving the condition of the black race."[55] The Congress is especially remembered for WEB Du Bois's speech "To the Nations of the World," in which the civil rights activist identified the "color line" as the "problem of the twentieth century."[56] Du Bois's assessment would have found its confirmation by another conference held in London a few weeks earlier. Diplomats, hunters, and wildlife experts from several

European countries convened in London to discuss the conservation of Africa's mammalian fauna. This conference was perhaps of even more tangible importance for Africans, for it actively drew the global color line. The environmental imperialism that followed from its resolutions should affect people's livelihoods in colonial territories throughout the continent.

The First International Conference on the Preservation of Wild Animals, Birds, and Fish in Africa was a product of internationalized and moral imperialism extended to wild animals. The desirability to protect especially the elephant by means of an international agreement among all colonial powers had been expressed since the late 1880s, and in at least two respects, this concern can be interpreted as the animal-related complement of the antislavery internationalism related to East Africa.[57] On the one hand, European observers regarded the slave and ivory trades as intricately entwined; on the other, there were individuals actively engaged in both campaigns, like Hermann von Wissmann. However, while the transimperial antislavery campaigns aimed at "civilizing" the "Arab" slave traders, the wildlife-related internationalism sought to civilize not only the African but also the European big game hunter. "Humanitarian" sensibilities toward elephants did play a role and optimistic observers ventilated hopes that the conference would terminate the "age of extermination" and usher in a "century ... of mercy to the beasts."[58] The sense of obligation arising from such a moral and self-civilizing rhetoric should not be underestimated, but the necessity at transimperial coordination arose, above all, from the very fear of trade decline and species extinction that had motivated hunting legislation in German and British East Africa in the 1890s.

The title of the conference was a misnomer in almost any respect. "International Conference on the Preservation of Wild Animals, Birds, and Fish in Africa" suggests a rather comprehensive concern with Africa's wildlife. But the one animal that dominated negotiations was the elephant, and the final convention only aimed at the "preservation ... of the various forms of animal life existing in a wild state which are either useful to man or are harmless."[59] Its internationalism was restricted to the imperial powers holding territory in Africa, and instead of the whole of Africa, the conference was only concerned with the area between the twentieth parallel north, thereby following a demarcation adopted by earlier imperial conferences, and the twentieth parallel south, the latter to exclude the warring parties of the Anglo-Boer War (1899–1902). Finally, the title trumpets the preservation of wild animals as the key concern. Its conveners, however, were at least as much interested in preserving the ivory trade.

The first concrete steps toward the transimperial coordination of game conservation seem to have been taken in October 1895, when Wissmann first impressed upon the German Foreign Office the necessity of an international agreement concerning the ivory trade. His argument centered on introducing a minimum weight for exported ivory throughout sub-Saharan Africa. If this minimum weight was not acknowledged by all colonies, stricter regulations in one territory would only have the effect to redirect trade to other countries.[60] In Britain, too, the initiative to internationalize the protection of elephants came from the colonial periphery. Here, it was Alfred Sharpe, a profligate turned penitent ivory harvester and acting commissioner of the British Central Africa Protectorate, who demanded "that all the Powers who hold territory in Africa should agree to prohibit the export of tusks of less weight than, say 15 lbs. each."[61] The proposal to internationalize wildlife conservation and control of the ivory trade by the "men on the spot" was translated into the institutional mechanics of European diplomacy. As the colonies were dependent territories, issues concerning their "foreign" policy automatically became matters of the diplomatic institutions in the imperial centers. Taking up Wissmann's initiative, the director of the German Colonial Department, Paul Kayser, approached the British Ambassador in Berlin in July 1896—just months after Wilhelm II had alienated Britain with the Kruger dispatch—to inquire about the attitude of the British government toward an international conference on the protection of African wildlife. Convinced that "British and German authorities would heartily co-operate in the effort to protect elephants and other big game from extermination," Kayser hinted, however, at the problem that other territories like the Congo Free State or Portuguese East Africa might seek to benefit from protection measures merely in the British and German protectorates by providing an alternative market for underweight ivory.[62]

The proposals of Wissmann and Kayser in 1895 and 1896 show that initially, German officials were the more active part in initiating transimperial cooperation.[63] The agenda for an international conference, which Wissmann, by then retired as governor of German East Africa, sketched out in April 1897 extended concern beyond the question of ivory. It foresaw the powers holding territory in Sub-Saharan Africa as possible participants and suggested large-scale reserves, the domestication of potentially useful game such as zebra and eland, as well as the regulation of indigenous hunting as further points to be covered by the conference. With an optimism yet untainted by later revelations about the atrocious regime of ivory extraction in the Congo, Wissmann expected both the Belgian and the French Congo to "show the utmost readiness to take measures to preserve its natural wealth, ivory."[64] His suggestion of Brussels as the most suitable conference venue stood in the continuity of the Belgian capital as a foremost site of imperial internationalism,[65] but the British Foreign Office pressed to host the conference in London, arguing with the availability of issue-related knowledge in the heart of the British Empire.⁶⁶ Indeed, the British authorities took care that the conference was convened after the hunting season in East Africa was over so that all "experts" had returned to Britain. The change of location was indicative of a larger shift in initiative: Wissmann and the German Foreign Office were still in the boat as co-conveners, but the British took over the agenda-setting. From the London Conference until the end of direct European colonial rule, the British regarded wildlife conservation in Africa as essentially their domain, and British institutional memory was quick to erase the transimperial origins of conservation before 1900.⁶⁷

The knowledge of "experts" remained a characteristic feature in the preparations and at the conference itself. Indeed, the congress and its organization were occasions when expertise was defined and created. Those whose advice was sought and who were invited to participate as additional plenipotentiaries were assigned the status of experts. Before drafting the agenda for the conference, Lord Salisbury, prime minister and secretary of state for foreign affairs, approached hunters, zoologists, and officials with African experience to hear their opinion. Drawing on Wissmann's suggestions and the advice of these authorities, six points were singled out for discussion at the conference: the prohibition of the export of elephant tusks below a certain weight; the creation of reserves; closed seasons and the prohibition of the hunting of females; a system of licenses for both "native" and European hunters; the enforcement of the provisions of the Brussels Act in regard to the supply of arms and ammunition to "natives"; and the complete protection of the animals and birds deemed to be useful.⁶⁸ In successive drafts, the grand aim of achieving uniform regulations throughout the continent made way for the more limited objective to arrive at cooperation between the territories of mainland Sub-Saharan Africa north of the Zambesi and German South-West Africa, excluding the warring self-governing colonies of South Africa and the Boer Republics. The zone finally demarcated still included the independent African states of Liberia and Abyssinia, who had not been admitted to the imperialists' conference. They were, however, expected to accede to the regulations afterward.⁶⁹

The conference finally took place at the foreign office between 24 April and 19 May 1900. The British Foreign Office had invited representatives from France, Germany, Italy, Portugal, Spain, and the Congo Free State. The composition of their delegations already indicated the varying degree of interest the governments took in the matter. Only the Germans added technical delegates with consultative functions to their delegations. Germany's four plenipotentiaries included government officials as well as Hermann von Wissmann and Carl Georg Schillings—a choice of experts praised by the German hunting press.⁷⁰ The British party nominally consisted of the Earl of Hopetoun, who also presided over the conference; Sir Clement Hill and the Director of the London Natural History Museum, Edwin Ray Lankester. Italy and Portugal sent only one representative from their embassies, while the Congo Free State was represented by a colonial official who had at least worked in the Congo. The French interest, finally, was advocated by a diplomat from the London Embassy and Louis Gustave Binger, an erstwhile explorer and governor of the Ivory Coast colony, who had been appointed director of African affairs in the French Colonial Department in 1896.[71] Only the German and British delegations involved representatives who contemporarily counted as experts on the matter, whereas the others treated the subject largely as diplomatic business. The *Morning Post,* a London daily, found it; therefore, "a little difficult to discover on what principle certain of the governments had chosen their representatives to take part in a discussion for which special knowledge would appear to be an essential qualification."[72]

The disproportionate interest in the associated questions of trade regulation and game conservation was clearly discernible in the strategies of negotiation at the conference. Portugal feared that the commerce in ivory might suffer in Mozambique as long as most of South Africa was not included within the convention. France and the Congo Free State emphasized the character of the Congo Basin as an internationally acknowledged zone of free trade. In the French Congo, the government had just started to split up the territory among some forty-two companies who were granted a thirty-year monopoly to extract natural products, and ivory exports were yet to reach peak value in 1905. The Belgian Foreign Office was unwilling to accept restrictions on the trade in skins, hides, horns, plumes, and immature ivory, and advised its representative not to sign any stipulations that were contrary to the Congo Free State's *liberté commerciale absolue.*[73]

The conference was thus split into an Anglo-German bloc for whom conservation was already vital to retain a minimum of trade in ivory, and the other colonial powers who were eager to retain the trade as unbridled as possible. This division dovetailed with the geographies of ivory exhaustion that most affected the two colonial powers in East Africa. Moreover, participants and observers alike interpreted the Anglo-German cooperation as expression of a culture of hunting peculiar to the "Germanic races." Schillings, for example, understood the Anglo-German concern about wild nature in terms similar to the conservative *Morning Post,* which opined that "the Latin peoples do not view the question of the preservation of big game from the same point of view as the Teutonic races. But if the interests of sport make no appeal to our French and Belgian friends, they can at least appreciate the commercial value of animals whose tusks and skins play an appreciable part in the exports of the Continent."[74]

The conference easily agreed on general measures of protection. The game animals of sub-Saharan Africa were classified into five categories according to the degree of protection they were to be afforded. Out of a list of 148 species of "great and small game," approximately fifty were singled out as affording special attention.[75] A first group of animals whose preservation was desired either "on account of their usefulness," their rarity, or their threatened extermination contained eleven species, among them vulture, giraffe, the larger anthropoid apes, or the mountain zebra. For its obvious economic importance, the elephant was not classified in the first category but included in three other schedules. One of them comprised those animals of which the killing of foals should be prohibited, another of which the killing of females when accompanied by young was to be prevented, and the third those animals of which only limited numbers should be killed. A last group contained all animals whose numbers were to be reduced "within sufficient limits": predators, baboons, crocodiles, poisonous snakes, and wild (hunting) dogs. Banning African techniques of hunting by the restriction of the use of nets or pitfalls gained general approval, as did closed seasons or the protection of animals classified as useful. Constraints on the trade both in arms and in animal products, were, however, subject to heated debate. Particularly the Anglo-German proposition to prevent the killing of young elephants by prohibiting the export of tusks below a weight of 10 pounds, and simultaneously raising the custom duty for those weighing between 10 and 30 pounds, was met with staunch opposition by the representatives of France, Portugal, and Belgium. The final convention did not forbid the export, but only rendered all elephant tusks smaller than 5 kilograms (approximately 10 pounds) liable to confiscation, combined with a general prohibition of the hunting of young elephants.[76]

The final wording of the convention contained a host of vaguely phrased provisions. Expressions like "to a certain extent" or "as far as it is possible" reduced many paragraphs to mere recommendations.[77] For years, British efforts to achieve the ratification by all parties were thwarted by individual states for fears to be disadvantaged by the possible "free-riding" of neighbors. Ironically, when in early 1912, all states were finally agreed to ratify, it was Britain that objected, claiming that the new insights gained into the relationship between game and sleeping sickness would require significant modification of the convention.[78]

In several respects, the convention that sprang from the deliberations in London in 1900 was a hunting treaty rather than a conservation treaty.[79] Turn-of-the-century conservationists were not concerned with biodiversity or ecosystems, but with game species that were charismatic, cherished for their trophies, and, above all, economically important. Hunting, not habitat loss, was the main threat to game populations, and the concepts to render hunting sustainable were derived from the practices and experiences in Europe and the United States. The schedule into which animals were classified followed the logic of hunting and colonial development. Such classifying of animals according to the degree they are threatened with extinction seems an obvious and logical principle, but it had severe biopolitical implications. Being on the list influenced human relations with the respective species (and those not on the list). It impacted upon hunting regulations and thus decided over life and death of the individuals of a species. Over the decades, it has become a standard tool of conservation biology, for example in the form of the Red Lists issued by the International Union for the Conservation of Nature (IUCN) over half a century later.

As much as the London Convention of 1900 can be regarded as the "first elephant treaty,"[80] it was not a conference concerned with *migratory* animals.[81] The spread of rinderpest had surely sensitized colonial authorities to the role of game in the cross-border spread of diseases.[82] Some commentators also advanced the argument that the mobility of wildlife did not respect borders and therefore necessitated coordinated transboundary conservation. Yet, this aspect hardly mattered at the conference, and there was no clause in the convention that addressed the transborder migration of animals. Situating reserves along the border would have been akin to an invitation for poaching from the other side, so that the system of reserves envisioned in the convention was no connected network but territorialized islands within the sovereignty of the respective colonial state. The conservation of African game was not internationalized because animals crossed borders, but because commercially relevant body parts did. Hopetoun's opening speech left no doubt that trade reigned supreme: "Quand l'éléphant aura été détruit, il faudra bien que le commerce cesse; s'il est préservé et si la chasse est réglementée, on pourra continuier à obtenir de l'ivoire, en quantité moindre, il est vrai, mais encore considérable."[83] It was the movement of tusks, not of tuskers, that was to be checked,[84] and the conference was about the political economy of game, not its ecology.

The priority of this concern is best illustrated by a second international conference dedicated to the protection of African elephant and rhinoceros held in London in May 1914.[85] Again, the main concern was to achieve uniform standards of minimum weights in tusks legitimately entering the trade, especially with a view to West Africa, where ivory still played a more vital part in colonial economies by that time than it did in Eastern Africa. The minimum weight of 10 kilograms adopted at the conference never mattered in practice; Germany, once a motor of internationalizing conservation, blocked the proceedings by tying regulations in the trade of ivory to regulations of the arms trade. The conference is virtually unknown in the literature because its findings became irrelevant with the changes of Africa's political landscape following the Great War. Yet, like the London Convention fourteen years earlier, it represented another early attempt to achieve the conservation of an endangered species by trying to regulate the trade that endangered it. Both conferences anticipated elements of the later Convention on International Trade in Endangered Species of Wild Fauna and Flora (CITES) signed in Washington in 1973.

The fact that the 1900 game convention was never ratified by all signatory powers has led to judgements about its relative insignificance in practice in parts of the historiography of international environmentalism. Triumphant accolades of "the first ever 'international' environmental conference,"[86] the "world's first international environmental agreement," and its celebration as an epitome of "trans-imperial concern about environmental degradation"[87] are usually followed by disappointed conclusions about the convention's limited effects and sometimes straightforwardly erroneous interpretations that attributed the convention's failed ratification to the distinction established between "magnificent and noxious species."[88]

Such verdicts inadequately capture the significance of the conference, which established enduring regulatory and disciplining principles for wildlife conservation across the African continent. Licenses, restrictions of indigenous hunting, animal-related trade regulation, and protected areas all dominated conservationist thinking and practice in the twentieth century. Already in London, it was discussed if reserves were of a temporary nature or "absolues et perpétuelles,"[89] and many of the reserves created or extended in its wake became conservation fortresses later in the twentieth century. Of equal significance was the conference's combination of diplomacy and environmental expertise, at least according to contemporary understandings. Those who debated the future fate of Africa's wildlife were official governmental functionaries and a handful of experts drawn from the ranks of hunters and natural history. These experts classified animals in a combination of contemporary biological taxonomies and the values of game, gain, and usefulness. This was "scientific conservation" according to turn-of-the-century standards, not yet informed by ecology and conservation biology as half a century later,[90] but drawing upon the knowledge and interests of natural history, biogeography, and taxonomy. By allowing only imperial diplomats, hunters, and naturalists to the conference table, the London meeting introduced "conservation without representation" on the international level.[91] "It rests with the great European nations to combine to preserve a sample of a remarkable and almost unique development of living nature,"[92] wrote *The Times* on occasion of the conference's opening. This transcontinental architecture of wildlife conservation as a European and later Western civilizing mission in Africa should survive formal decolonization to remain relevant well into the present.[93]

Even without ratification, the London Convention motivated and justified game legislation that translated some of its core elements into the practice of several colonies.[94] When some thirty years later in April 1932, the British Economic Advisory Council discussed the preparation of a new International Conference on the Protection of Nature in Africa, it was emphasized "that although the Convention of 1900 had never been ratified, it had been very largely followed in practice by this country and ... other European countries were also gradually coming more into line."[95] In Tanganyika, Wissmann's grand design of a joint Anglo-German reserve may not have materialized, but the conservation policies after London 1900 seriously impeded Africans' access to wild animals and affected the livelihoods of thousands of rural Africans who happened to live in or next to the colonial game reserves. British colonies in West and East Africa implemented parts of the convention, such as a minimum weight for traded ivory and the establishment or extension of game reserves, especially in Central and East Africa. The stipulations of the London Convention also encouraged the further extension of existing game reserves when the Boer Republic of the Transvaal was integrated into the British Empire after 1902.[96] Even the Congo Free State felt compelled to introduce a first game ordinance in April 1901, which entered into effect from 1902 onward. It took over the schedule of animals and the different levels of protection accorded to them, adapted the London Convention to the trade interests in the Congo, and lowered the minimum weight for legitimate ivory to 2 kilograms. Moreover, the ordinance envisioned to introduce a reserve comprising the whole river basin of the Aruwimi and mandated a closed season for hunting between 15 October and 15 May. A later ordinance in 1905 reiterated these stipulations and extended the reserved area.[97] Doubts remain if these ordinances had any practical relevance. Yet, even if they existed merely on paper, they are proof that Belgium felt the need to comply at least symbolically with conservation as a new transimperial norm established by the conference. Herein lies the foremost significance of the London convention. It established as an international norm that wildlife was, in principle, to be preserved and the extinction of certain animals averted. This alone makes the conference a milestone in international environmentalism.

Holding Empires Accountable—African Wildlife in the Campaign for Weltnaturschutz

Finally, framing the conservation of wild animals as an imperial obligation in an official document meant that governments could be monitored and held accountable to their pledge by others. As Corey Ross has recently stated, the lack of ratification or implementation may actually have provided "the greatest impulse to the cause of global nature preservation," for it provided advocates with additional leverage.[98] Such politics of accountability were not restricted to the realm of diplomacy and the states represented at the conference. They were also seized as a strategy by conservationists. Discontent with the inadequacies of putting the conference's findings into practice spawned the formation of influential pressure groups for wildlife conservation in both Great Britain and the German Empire.[99] In both cases, the emergence of these pressure groups was related to the London Convention. The British SPWFE formed in 1903 after news transpired that authorities in Sudan planned to abandon a recently created game reserve along the Nile River. It was the society's declared aim to encourage "the protection of the wild fauna in all British possessions," create a sound public opinion on the matter, "further the formation of game reserves or sanctuaries," contribute to "the enforcing of suitable game laws and regulations," and generally monitor the governmental implementation of the London Convention.[100] Accordingly, the first issue of the society's journal published the complete text of the convention. The society was small and well-connected. Thanks to its membership from the highest social ranks, it had privileged access to the nodes of imperial decision-making so that lobbying and networking rather than campaigning and public scandalizing were its main strategies.

Germany witnessed the formation of a similar pressure group a few years later in 1907. Involuntarily, the restrictive information policies of Germany's colonial authorities promoted the formation of the Kommission zur Besserung des Wildschutzes in Deutsch-Afrika, because the stipulations of the London Convention were never officially gazetted, and any inquiries related to it were frustrated or treated dilatorily by the colonial department. But wildlife politics took place in a transimperial public sphere. Interested German hunter-conservationists resorted to the British Blue Book published in 1906 to obtain the information denied by the German colonial department. The almost 400 pages of "Correspondence relating to the Preservation of Wild Animals in Africa" provided German conservationists with the power of information they were denied at home. Here, readers could learn what the effective lobbying and the manipulation of social connections as exemplified by the British SPWFE could achieve. Schillings's library contained a thoroughly perused copy with many comments in the margin; Fritz Bley directly quoted the British SPWFE as a model for the effective lobbying of target political actors when he called for a like German "commission of experts" to take on the task of analyzing all the zoological, biological, and bacteriological questions relevant for the regulation of hunting and wildlife.[101] The German Commission was rooted in the exclusive circles of hunting associations, the *Deutsche Kolonialgesellschaft,* and the institutions of upper-class sociability in Berlin. Like its British counterpart, it was not supposed to attract a broad social constituency: its membership probably never encompassed more than the forty-one princes and aristocrats, naturalists, zoologists and animal traders, hunters, and colonial officials that made up its successor organization, the wildlife commission established by the *Deutsche Kolonialgesellschaft* in June 1911.[102]

Conservation lobbyists on both sides of the channel framed the reform of wildlife policies in a nationalist language of imperial obligation. In Britain, conservation was portrayed as a matter of imperial leadership, in Germany as an example of imperial backwardness used for the mobilization of shame.[103] Both the British SPWFE and the successive German wildlife commissions had, however, in common that they approached conservation through the lens and logic of hunting and empire. Apart from exceptional situations like Rechenberg's *Wildmord,* they saw their role as consultants of their governments rather than in an oppositional stance or public criticism. But discontent with the nonratification and only gradual implementation of the London Convention also spawned reactions that championed preservationism and strove to transcend imperial borders in order to pressurize governments by alliances beyond empire. In the wildlife debates before World War I, probably the most comprehensive agenda to understand African wildlife conservation as part of global conservation policies was developed by the Swiss naturalist, explorer, and conservationist Paul Sarasin.[104] Born 1856 in Basel, Sarasin had studied zoology in Würzburg. In the 1880s, 1890s, and early 1900s, he undertook several anthropological, zoological, and archaeological expeditions to Ceylon and Celebes with his cousin Fritz Sarasin. These expeditions turned them into eyewitnesses of the profound transformation of the indigenous flora and fauna by the advance of European rule.[105] Similar to Schillings and Paasche in Africa, this was as profoundly disturbing an experience for Sarasin as was the observation of the impact of "advancing civilization" upon so-called *Naturvölker* like the Vedda people of Sri Lanka. Sarasin became the moving spirit behind the Swiss League for nature protection and actively intervened in German debates over the conservation of wildlife and birds of paradise in Germany's African and Pacific colonies. Himself a key protagonist in the vociferous protests against Rechenberg, the German colonial *Wildmord*-scandal confirmed Sarasin's conviction that wildlife could not be entrusted to the imperial powers alone. This was a key driving force behind his campaign for *Weltnaturschutz*—the global protection of nature—which started in August 1910 when Sarasin addressed the International Congress of Zoologists in Graz. In order to monitor the environmental dealings of empires, Sarasin demanded the establishment of an international commission to extend the protection of nature over the whole planet.[106] The commission's task was to gather information, supervise the national efforts undertaken at the preservation of nature, and monitor protection particularly in stateless areas such as the polar worlds or Spitzbergen. The development of protective measures for threatened species was as much a task of the commission as the annual publication of a "Bluebook of the protection of nature throughout the world," apparently an idea lifted from British parliamentary and administrative practice. Sarasin's vision drew heavily upon national experiences in nature protection, first and foremost of his native Switzerland. He recommended his home country's organization and laws of conservation, as well as its "League for Nature Protection" and the project of a "total reservation" in the form of a national park for emulation elsewhere. The mandatory national chapters for nature preservation would report annually to the international commission and raise the money for the creation and maintenance of "a scarcely interrupted tract of free land stretching across the whole of Europe, even over the globe."[107] Unaware of the transboundary reserve created in East Africa, Sarasin demanded the establishment of joint "total reserves" of the size of European states. These should be left completely to nature so that they could revert into the state that existed before the advent of the white man.[108] Science was to play a pivotal role, as preservation was to be prepared and supported by the thorough study of the relationship between plants and animals. Within the total reserves, all plants and animals were to be protected "to bring a partly impoverished life back to its original state." Sarasin's *Weltnaturschutz* was not only about protection, but, if possible, about restoration of a somehow more authentic "natural" state, and this included "the preservation of the last rests of those interesting varieties of the species Homo which we call 'races in the state of nature.'"[109]

Sarasin's conservation of "nature's anthropological monuments"[110] was fraught with paternalist and Eurocentric notions of "race" and civilization, history and "naturalness," and a Darwinist reading of the social world as engaged in an inevitable struggle for survival. It denied agency and cultural sovereignty to those he wanted to see preserved, and it rested upon questionable European definitions of indigeneity and authenticity. Yet, in Sarasin's view, there was only the choice between preservation and extinction. More than any other of the nature conservationists of his day, Sarasin was receptive to the waxing humanitarian critique of the dark undersides of European imperialism and its detrimental impact upon the indigenous societies drawn into the reach of "civilization." "Like in the animal kingdom," Sarasin summed up in 1913, "the white man has wreaked havoc among whole tribes of humans in a mad lust to kill. Not only was aboriginal man extinguished in streams of blood, but there was such an amount of agony and suffering inflicted upon the weak that anyone reading reports about it will be haunted by the sheer imagination."[111]

Sarasin pursued and constantly refined his project of *Weltnaturschutz* until his death in 1929. It was a scathing moral indictment of the detrimental interaction of European imperialism and capitalist trade. Despite obvious parallels in the proposed methods, such as the creation of reserves and the regulation of hunting and trade, his program was a radical departure from the imperial internationalism of the hunters as discussed above. By framing migratory birds or the wild animals of Africa as a "global common" beyond the exclusive competence of the colonial powers, his international commission posed a direct challenge to the sovereignty of these states and envisioned an alternative world order of organizing the relationships between humans, animals, and nature. By introducing a commission with the purpose and potential to monitor and report the misdoings and shortcomings of empires in the field of conservation, this order went beyond the institutional framework of empires despite retaining many elements of imperial culture. The breadth of his agenda had the potential to attract nature protection a far broader social constituency than the lobbying hunters. The degree to which *Weltnaturschutz* transcended the agenda of the hunter-conservationists can be gleaned from the applause Sarasin's motion received from animal rights activists, who themselves had forged transnational links since the turn of the century. For example, a resolution presented by the German animal rights activist Magnus Schwantje to the International Congress for the Protection of Animals in Copenhagen in 1911 expressed the "admiration and sympathy" to all movements trying to prevent "by international convention the extirpation of wild animals, including beasts of prey". Nature preservationists, Schwantje demanded, should join hands with the activism for the protection of animals.[112] Also the inclusion of "endangered peoples" among the concern of nature conservationists might have opened up a chance to forge alliances between nature conservationists and humanitarian philanthropists. In any case, it would have ascribed the function of a watchdog monitoring the rights of indigenous people to the proposed international commission. Even if furnished with no power, any activity of the commission in that direction would have provoked and embarrassed the colonial powers.

The zoologists gathered in Graz in 1910 consented to establish the provisional committee proposed by Sarasin.[113] As the Swiss conservationist had managed to convince his country's government to lend institutional and diplomatic support to the cause, the global protection of nature became part of the Swiss strategies to gain diplomatic leverage by governmental internationalism.[114] Lacking both colonies and access to the seas, the country indeed appeared to be well suited as disinterested broker for Sarasin's program. Within an astonishingly short span of time, the Swiss *Bundesrat* managed to convene representatives of seventeen states (mainly from Europe plus Argentina and the United States) for a conference that should constitute a consultative commission for the global protection of nature. The Conférence internationale pour la protection mondiale de la Nature convened in Berne in November 1913, where Sarasin's agenda was gradually dismantled.[115] Nongovernmental participants, although interested, were not admitted, and both Britain and Germany categorically objected to address issues that might interfere with the sovereign governance of their colonial empires. The imperial powers also had the most sensitive and controversial issues removed from the agenda, such as the preservation of *Naturvölker*.[116] Significantly, Africa's mammalian fauna was not even included among the list of topics to be pursued at further meetings since Germany and Britain only deemed the preservation of wildlife an international issue in stateless areas.[117] Although participants agreed to create the scheduled consultative committee, its formation was stymied by World War I and could not be revitalized after. The attempt to frame Africa's fauna, like other threatened species, as a "global common" was sacrificed to eagerly guarded national sovereignties.

The importance of this prewar activism for *Weltnaturschutz* did not lie with its practical consequences. Rather, it offered an alternative and critique to the internationalism of empires. Sarasin's internationalism reflected all the asymmetries and the racist paternalism of prewar European imperial culture, yet his concept of *Weltnaturschutz* provided an alternative for wildlife conservationists discontented with the mechanics of imperial decision-making.[118] The term put their concern with wildlife preservation both in a nutshell and into the widest possible framework: *Weltnaturschutz* implicated the globe, not just nations, empires, or colonies.[119] The concept provided a comprehensive framework to address grievances that, in the eyes of conservationists, should not be left to imperial trusteeship only. Those who found their initiatives blocked by their national governments, like Carl Georg Schillings, subscribed to *Weltnaturschutz* as a vision for "an international organisation for the preservation of the natural treasures of the world, similar to the Hague Peace Conference."[120] The Swiss-born internationalism of *Weltnaturschutz* presented an alternative to the internationalism of the imperial powers under British guidance, who struggled to avoid interference of nonimperial powers or a commission of independent experts. The series of conferences on wildlife preservation in Africa, all held in London in 1900, 1914, and later in 1933, were not only venues where the circle of stakeholders was deliberately kept "as small as possible"[121] to confine the regulation of wildlife conservation to those powers possessing colonies in Africa. They were also British initiatives to retain agenda-setting in the face of outside attempts to treat wildlife conservation in other venues. In 1900, Wissmann had attempted to hold the conference in Brussels; in 1914, the preservation of elephants and rhinoceroses was discussed among representatives of the imperial powers after the topic was effectively crossed from the agenda of the Berne conference the year before. In 1933, Britain reasserted initiative after an international conference on nature protection had been held in Paris in 1931. They also used their "home conference" to prevent the Belgian Office International pour le protection de la nature from achieving an official mandate for the dissemination of information on nature conservation and thereby gain leverage over the internal policies of empires.[122] Indeed, the British did everything to "avoid international control" and prevent the establishment of "an international organisation which will take upon itself to do in relation to the protection of game what the International Labour Office does in relation to forced labour."[123] In the field of African wildlife conservation, the integration of imperial internationalism and *Weltnaturschutz* was only achieved during the "postwar conservation boom" after World War II, when the retreat of empires enabled international organizations like UNESCO or the International Union for the Protection of Nature (IUPN) to influence the conservation agenda in the decolonizing East African states.[124]

Notes

1. BAB R 1001/7769, fol. 32: Sir Clement Hill to Hermann von Wissmann, London, 15 March 1901. Sir Clement Lloyd Hill (1845–1913) entered the British Foreign Service in 1867 and worked as superintendent of the African Protectorates in the foreign office from 1900 until his retirement 1905, cf. *British Biographical Archive*, Fiche 0551, 413–415, Fiche 1546, 124 (Sir Clement Lloyd Hill).
2. BAB R 1001/7768, fol. 29: AA KA to Wissmann, 11 July 1900.
3. BAB R 1001/7768, fol. 40–41: Wissmann to AA KA, 7 September 1900; and fol. 46–47, Wissmann to AA KA, 13 October 1900.
4. BAB R 1001/7769, fol. 32: Hill to Wissmann, London, 15 March 1901.
5. BAB R 1001/7769, fol. 49–54: Protocol of the Meeting, 13 April 1901.
6. KNA PC/CP/4/2/1: Annual Report Ukamba Province, 1910/11, 3; KNA DC MKS 1/4/2: Machakos District Political Record Book, 31 March 1911, 177; *Further Correspondence relating to the Preservation of Wild Animals in Africa*. London 1911 (= Parliamentary Papers LII. 521), no. 14: EPC Girouard to the Colonial Office, 18 January 1911.

7. PRO CO 885/20/230: Report of the Game Warden, 25 March 1911, 65. For German discussions about joint reserves see for example BAB R 8023/1000, fol. 79: Bericht über die Sitzung des Ausschusses am Freitag, den 12. Mai 1911, im Sitzungssaal der Deutschen Kolonialgesellschaft, 11; Fritz Bley, "Schutz unseres afrikanischen Großwildes!," *Deutsche Jägerzeitung* 54 (1909–10): 746.
8. Staatsarchiv Freiburg U 101/1: Böcklin Papers, no. 11, Notebook and receipts of Hotel Kaiserhof in Dar es Salaam for 8–11 February 1911; PRO CO 885/20/230: Report of the Game Warden, 25 March 1911, 65.
9. The most pervasive analysis of the international dimension of early African conservation from a British perspective is given by MacKenzie, *The Empire of Nature*, especially 200–24.
10. See MacKenzie, "European Imperialism: A Zone of Co-operation Rather than Competition?"; MacKenzie, "'Mutual Goodwill and Admiration"; Blackbourn, "As Dependent on Each Other as Man and Wife"; cf. Michael Fröhlich, *Von Konfrontation zur Koexistenz. Die deutsch-englischen Kolonialbeziehungen in Afrika zwischen 1884 und 1914* (Bochum, 1990), 327, who even argued that Anglo-German colonial relations developed "inversely proportional compared to the general Anglo-German antagonism."
11. For a broad and contextualized discussion of Anglo-German entanglements, various fields of imperial administration, and policies beyond wildlife see Lindner, *Koloniale Begegnungen*; see also Volker Barth and Roland Cvetkovski, eds., *Imperial Co-operation and Transfer, 1870-1930. Empires and Encounters* (London, 2015), and Jeremy Adelman, "Mimesis and Rivalry: European Empires and Global Regimes," *Journal of Global History* 10, no. 1 (2015): 77–98.
12. PRO FO 881/7395 D: Return showing approximately the amount of ivory exported from Africa from 1891 to 1899, 15–16: Imports into Zanzibar (including ivory and hippopotamus teeth), 1: Statement showing the value of ivory exported from the British East Africa Protectorate (by sea), £23,436 in 1896–97, £19,138 in 1897–98; p. 18: Exports of ivory from German East African possessions. See also PRO FO 881/7420, Report on the German Colonies for the year beginning July 1, 1898 and ending June 30, 1899, 14.
13. Frederick Dealtry Lugard, *The Rise of Our East African Empire. Early Efforts in Nyasaland and Uganda. Vol. 1: Nyasaland and Eastern Africa, with Chapters on Commerce, Slave-Trade and Sport* (London, 1968), 386, 449–54.
14. MacKenzie, *The Empire of Nature*, 151–57; Steinhart, *Black Poachers*, 69–77; Marion Johnson, "Elephants and Imperialists," in *The Exploitation of Animals in Africa. Proceedings of a Colloquium at the University of Aberdeen, March 1987*, ed. Jeffrey C Stone (Aberdeen, 1988), 157–91.
15. BAB R 1001/7776, fol. 2: Wissmann to AA, 28 April 1890; BAB R 1001/7776, fol. 21 and 22: Soden to AA, 5 May 1892 and 28 December 1892; TNA G 1/10, fol. 153–54: Gov DOA to Count von Götzen, 14 July 1893.
16. William M Adams, *Against Extinction. The Story of Conservation* (London, 2004), 19–20, 22–23.
17. "Zanzibar Ivory Trade," *The Gazette for Zanzibar and East Africa* 4, no. 191 (1895), 25 September.
18. *Correspondence relating to the Preservation of Wild Animals in Africa* (1906), no. 1: Salisbury to Hardinge and Berkeley, 27 May 1896.

19. MacKenzie, *The Empire of Nature*, 207. For South Africa see Carruthers, *Game Protection in the Transvaal 1846 to 1926*; Karen Brown, "Cultural Constructions of the Wild: The Rhetoric and Practice of Wildlife Conservation in the Cape Colony at the Turn of the Twentieth Century," *South African Historical Journal* 47 (2002): 75-95; William Beinart, *The Rise of Conservation in South Africa: Settlers, Livestock, and the Environment 1770-1950* (Oxford, 2003), and Van Sittert, "Bringing in the Wild."
20. The collected evidence of the foreign office revealed that game reserves had been in existence in Zululand since 1895, whereas the Cape Colony featured two elephant reserves in Knysna and Addo forests, see PRO FO 403/302 no. 10: Colonial Office to Foreign Office, 8 October 1896, transmitting a Memorandum on the Game Laws of Zululand; no. 28: Richard Crawshay to Foreign Office, 7 August 1897. Also the Boer Republic of Transvaal had established the Pongola Game Reserve in 1894, apparently bearing no influence on the discussions in East Africa, see Jane Carruthers, *The Kruger National Park. A Social and Political History* (Pietermaritzburg, 1995), 17-23.
21. *Correspondence relating to the Preservation of Wild Animals in Africa* (1906), no. 7: Sharpe to Salisbury, 9 September 1896 (Game Regulations British Central Africa), no. 9: Berkeley to Salisbury, 25 November 1896 (Game Regulations Uganda), no. 36: Craufurd to Salisbury, 11 August 1899 (Game Regulation East Africa Protectorate).
22. BAB R 1001/7776, fol. 53: Liebert to Count Hatzfeldt, 6 April 1898.
23. PRO FO 403/302, no. 31: Hardinge to Salisbury, Zanzibar, 27 August 1897; see also FOCP Vol. 6964: Further Correspondence respecting East Africa, April to June 1897, no. 87: Hardinge to Salisbury, Mombasa, 26 April 1897.
24. The files in BAB R 1001/7792-7802 contain the hunting regulations of other European colonies in Africa.
25. PRO FO 2/819, fol. 179: Eliot to Lansdowne, Mombasa, 19 October 1903.
26. *Correspondence relating to the Preservation of Wild Animals in Africa* (1906), Enclosure in no. 36: East Africa Protectorate Game Regulations 1899; Enclosure in no. 38: Uganda Protectorate Game Regulations 1899; Enclosure in no. 39: Game Preservation Ordinance 1899 (Southern Rhodesia). In Kenya, only two elephants were then allowed to be shot under a sportsman's, respectively, public officer's license. A sportsman's license cost 375 rupees (compared with the general fee of 10 rupees introduced in German East Africa in 1903).
27. BAB R 1001/7777, fol. 155-63: Memorandum of Carl Georg Schillings, July 1908.
28. Heinrich Brode, *British and German East Africa. Their Economic and Commercial Relations* (London, 1911), 144.
29. *Proceedings of the First International Conference on the Sleeping Sickness, Held at London in June 1907*. London, 1908, 7: Opening address 17 June 1907; Bernhard Dernburg, "Germany and England in Africa," *The Journal of the Royal African Society* 9 (1910): 117.
30. Franz Doflein, "Tiere als Krankheitsquellen," *Süddeutsche Monatshefte* 11, no. 1 (1913-14): 218.
31. Gradmann, *Krankheit im Labor*, 268-97.
32. Paul F Cranefield, *Science and Empire: East Coast Fever in Rhodesia and the Transvaal* (Cambridge, 1991), 87-120; Brown, "Tropical Medicine and Animal Diseases."

33. PRO FO 881/9226, no. 38: Memorandum communicated by German Embassy, 22 October 1907.
34. Brown, "Tropical Medicine and Animal Diseases," 515.
35. Robert von Ostertag, *Das Veterinärwesen und Fragen der Tierzucht in Deutsch-Südwestafrika* (Berlin, 1912), 150–54. In 1910, the German East African veterinary Georg Lichtenheld researched in Onderstepoort, see PRO FO 367/182, no. 5929: Germany Embassy London to FO, 18 February 1910.
36. BAL R 1001/6071, fol. 128: Gov DOA to RKA, 4 May 1912.
37. Brown, "Tropical Medicine and Animal Diseases," 515.
38. See the *Proceedings of the First International Conference on the Sleeping Sickness*, held at London in June 1907. London 1908.
39. PRO FO 881/9254, no. 17: Memorandum of Lord Fitzmaurice, FO, 9 January 1908, PRO FO 881/9226, no. 44: Grey to Metternich, 29 October 1907.
40. PRO FO 881/9254, no. 52: Metternich to Grey, 25 May 1908; no. 56: Grey to Metternich, 11 July 1908.
41. PRO FO 367/181, no. 3142: Rechenberg to the Acting Governor of Uganda, 28 November 1909.
42. Höring, "Die Rolle des Großwildes bei der Verbreitung der Schlafkrankheit," *Deutsches Kolonialblatt* 24, no. 18 (1913), 15 September: 801; BAB R 1001/6071, fol 71: Sommerfeld to Gov DOA, 24 August 1911; PRO FO 367/136, no. 30724: British Embassy Berlin to British FO, 13 August 1909; FK Kleine and W Fischer, "Schlafkrankheit und Tsetsefliegen," *Deutsch-Ostafrikanische Zeitung* 15, no. 20 (1913), 8 March.
43. Max Taute, "Untersuchungen über die Bedeutung des Großwildes und der Haustiere für die Verbreitung der Schlafkrankheit," *Arbeiten aus dem Kaiserlichen Gesundheitsamte* 45 (1913): 112; *Minutes of Evidence Taken by the Departmental Committee on Sleeping Sickness* [Cd. 7350, XLVIII.29], 256–58: Dr. H Hardy (German Colonial Office): The Extermination of Wild Animals in order to prevent the Spread of Infectious Diseases in German Colonies.
44. See Ulrike Lindner, "Colonialism as a European Project in Africa before 1914? British and German Concepts of Colonial Rule in Sub-Saharan Africa," *Comparativ* 19 (2009): 88–106.
45. Brode, *British and German East Africa*, 156–57.
46. See Lindner, *Koloniale Begegnungen*, chapter 4.
47. PRO FO 367/136, no. 40857: Speech of Colonial Secretary Bernhard Dernburg to the Royal African Society, 1909. The speech has been reprinted under the title "Germany and England in Africa," *The Journal of the Royal African Society* 9 (1910): 113–19.
48. See for example Arthur Blayney Percival, "Notes on the Game of British East Africa," *Journal of the Society for the Preservation of the Wild Fauna of the Empire* 3 (1907): 40–41; KNA PC 1/6/136: CW Woodhouse to Game Warden, Taveta, 28 November 1912; 27 and 28 December 1912.
49. Missionaries belong to this group, too, but they hardly featured in the records consulted for this study. Their attitude toward wildlife conservation awaits further investigation, see Jason Bruner, "Fishers of Men and Hunters of Lion: British Missionaries and Big Game Hunting in Colonial Africa," in *A Cultural History of Firearms in the Age of Empire*, ed. Karen Jones, Giacomo Macola, and David Welch (Farnham, 2013), 57–72.

50. Martin H Geyer and Johannes Paulmann, "Introduction. The Mechanics of Internationalism," in *Mechanics of Internationalism*, ed. Martin H Geyer and Johannes Paulmann (Oxford, 2001), 2–3.
51. Akira Iriye, *Global Community: The Role of International Organizations in the Making of the Contemporary World* (Berkeley, CA, 2002), 18; Akira Iriye, "Beyond Imperialism: The New Internationalism," *Daedalus* 134, no. 2 (2005): 108–16.
52. Jürgen Osterhammel, "'The Great Work of Uplifting Mankind.' Zivilisierungsmission und Moderne," in *Zivilisierungsmissionen: Imperiale Weltverbesserung seit dem 18. Jahrhundert*, ed. Boris Barth and Jürgen Osterhammel (Konstanz, 2005), 363–427.
53. Frederick Cooper, *Colonialism in Question. Theory, Knowledge, History* (Berkeley, CA, 2005), 104.
54. See for example Hermann Wissmann, "Wildschutz in Afrika," *Deutsche Jägerzeitung* 35 (1900): 443.
55. "Pan-African Conference," *The Times* (1900, 24 July): 7.
56. Alexander Walters et al., "To the Nations of the World (1900)," in *An ABC of Color. Selections Chosen by the Author from over Half a Century of Writings*, ed. WEB Du Bois (New York, 1969), 19–23.
57. See Daniel Laqua, "The Tensions of Internationalism. Transnational Anti-Slavery in the 1880s and 1890s," *International History Review* 33 (2011): 705–26.
58. See for example, "An Age of Extermination," *Quarterly Review* 191 (1900, April): 316.
59. *Correspondence relating to the Preservation of Wild Animals in Africa* (1906), no. 55: Convention signed at London, 19 May 1900.
60. BAB R 1001/7766, fol. 7: Wissmann to Chancellor Hohenlohe-Schillingsfürst, 29 October 1895.
61. *Correspondence relating to the Preservation of Wild Animals in Africa* (1906), no. 7: Sharpe to Salisbury, 9 September 1896.
62. PRO FO 403/302, no. 4: Martin Gosselin to the Marquess of Salisbury, 15 July 1896, and BAB R 1001/7766, fol. 14: Frank C Lascelles to Baron von Marschall, 28 August 1896.
63. For the reverse assessment based on published British sources only see Sherman Strong Hayden, *The International Protection of Wild Life. Examination of Treaties and Other Agreements for the Preservation of Birds and Mammals* (New York, 1942), 36–37.
64. BAB R 1001/7766, fol. 39–43: Wissmann to Colonial Department, 2 April 1897; PRO FO 403/302, enclosure 2 in no. 22: Gough to Salisbury, 1 Mai 1897.
65. Madeleine Herren, *Hintertüren zur Macht. Internationalismus und modernisierungsorientierte Außenpolitik in Belgien, der Schweiz und den USA 1865-1914* (Munich, 2000), 95–96; Daniel Laqua, *The Age of Internationalism and Belgium, 1880-1930. Peace, Progress and Prestige* (Manchester, 2013). chapter 2.
66. PRO FO 403/302, no. 30: Foreign Office to Colonial Office, 8 September 1897.
67. See for example JH Patterson, "Travel and Sport in East Africa," *United Empire* 3 (1912): 314–15; CW Hobley, "National Sanctuaries. The Key of the Wild Life Position," *The Journal of the Royal African Society* 32 (1933): 171; CW Hobley, "The Preservation of Wild Life in the Empire," *The Journal of the Royal African Society* 34 (1935): 403.

68. See PRO FO 403/302, no. 30: Foreign Office to Colonial Office, 8 September 1897.
69. PRO FO 403/302, no. 59: Colonial Office to Foreign Office, 13 March 1899.
70. Hans Wagner, "Wildschutz in Afrika," *Der Weidmann* 31 (1900): 449–50.
71. Cf. Henri Brunschwig, "Louis Gustave Binger (1856–1944)," in *African Proconsuls. European Governors in Africa*, ed. Lewis Gann and Peter Duignan (New York, 1978), 109–26.
72. *Morning Post*, 3 May 1900 (Clipping in Archives Ministère des Affaires Etrangères, du Commerce extérieur et de la Coopération au Développement, Bruxelles [AMDAE] AE 322 Carton 68/3, Dossier 4).
73. AMDAE AE 322 Carton 68/3, Dossier 4/1: Secrétariat general to Fuchs, 20 April 1900; PRO FO 403/302, enclosure in no. 79b: De Cuvelier to the British Embassy Brussels, 5 December 1899; no. 86*: French Embassy London to Salisbury, 29 December 1899.
74. *Morning Post*, 3 May 1900 (Clipping in AMDAE AE 322 Carton 68/3, Dossier 4).
75. PRO FO 881/7395 B, Meeting of the Commission on 26 April 1900, appendix: List of animals compiled by Edwin Ray Lankester. The list was previously published in HA Bryden, ed., *Great and Small Game of Africa* (London, 1899).
76. FO 881/7395 B: Protocols of the 3rd session, 27 April 1900, 4th session, 30 April 1900, 5th session, 1 May 1900, 6th session, 14 May 1900, 7th session, 15 May 1900.
77. "Convention for the Preservation of Wild Animals, Birds and Fish in Africa, 19th May 1900," in *Correspondence relating to the Preservation of Wild Animals in Africa* (1906), no. 55, especially Article II, paragraphs 3 and 5 concerning the hunting of females and the establishment of reserves.
78. PRO FO 367/79, no. 5617: Memorandum by Edward Parkes, concerning the Game Convention, 20 February 1908; BAB R 1001/7771, fol. 181: Promemorial of the English Embassy, 29 November 1911; BAB R 1001/7772, fol. 61: British Embassy London to AA, 2 August 1912; BAB R 1001/7779, fol. 200: AA to RKA, 10 August 1912.
79. Mark Cioc, *The Game of Conservation. International Treaties to Protect the World's Migratory Animals* (Athens, OH, 2009), chapter 1.
80. Rachelle Adam, *Elephant Treaties. The Colonial Legacy of the Biodiversity Crisis* (Lebanon, NH, 2014), 18.
81. Cioc, *The Game of Conservation*; Lynton Keith Caldwell, *International Environmental Policy. From the Twentieth to the Twenty-First Century* (Durham, NC, 1996), 38.
82. PRO FO 881/7395 B: Fourth Session of the Commission, 30 April 1900, 7.
83. PRO FO 881/7395 A, Protocols: Preservation of Game Conference, Protocol 1, 7.
84. The constellation was similar in the campaigns to prohibit the transcontinental trade in feathers endangering bird species like the egret or the birds of paradise in New Guinea, cf. Gissibl, "Paradiesvögel."
85. The conference proceedings can be found under PRO FO 881/10461.
86. Ramachandra Guha, *Environmentalism. A Global History* (Oxford, 2000), 45; Karl Jacoby, "Conservation," in *Encyclopedia of World Environmental History*, vol. 1, ed. Shepard Krech, John Robert McNeill, and Carolyn Merchant (London, 2004), 267.

87. John McCormick, *Reclaiming Paradise. The Global Environmental Movement* (Bloomington, IN, 1989), 18; Adams, "Nature and the Colonial Mind," 32. Cf. Adams, *Against Extinction*, 24–25; Roderick Neumann, "The Postwar Conservation Boom in British Colonial Africa," *Environmental History* 7 (2002): 22; Roderick Nash, *Wilderness and the American Mind*, 4th ed. (New Haven, CT, 2001), 355; Martin Holdgate, *The Green Web. A Union for World Conservation* (London, 1999), 10; Jepson and Whittaker, "Histories of Protected Areas," 138.
88. John W Meyer et al., "The Structuring of a World Environmental Regime, 1870–1990," *International Organization* 51 (1997): 630.
89. PRO FO 881/7935 B: 4th session, 30th April 1900.
90. See Jane Carruthers, "Conservation and Wildlife Management in South African National Parks 1930s–1960s," *Journal of the History of Biology* 41, no. 2 (2007): 203–36.
91. Martha Honey, *Ecotourism and Sustainable Development. Who Owns Paradise?*, 2nd ed. (Washington, DC, 2008), 218.
92. *The Times*, 24 April 1900.
93. Garland, "The Elephant in the Room."
94. See also Cioc, *The Game of Conservation*, chapter 1; MacKenzie, *The Empire of Nature*, 207–9; Maddox, *Sub-Saharan Africa*, 145; Adams and McShane, *The Myth of Wild Africa*, 45–46.
95. PRO Ministry of Agriculture, Fisheries and Food (MAF) 48/247B: International Congress on the Protection of Nature. Paris 1931, Minutes April 14 1932, 2; see also CW Hobley, "The London Convention of 1900," *Journal of the Society for the Preservation of the Wild Fauna of the Empire* 20 (1933): 33–49.
96. Carruthers, *Game Protection in the Transvaal 1846 to 1926*, 93–94.
97. AMDAE AE 322 Carton 68/3, Dossier 4: Département de l'Interieur a Affaires Etrangères, 21 August 1900; Decret du Souverain de l'État Indépendant du Congo, concernant la Protection des animaux vivant à l'état sauvage, Bruxelles, le 29 Avril, 1901. See also Patricia van Schuylenbergh, "De l'appropriation à la conservation de la faune sauvage. Pratiques d'une colonisation: le cas du Congo belge, 1885–1960," (PhD diss., Université catholique de Louvain, 2006).
98. Ross, "Tropical Nature as Global *Patrimoine*," 222.
99. For media coverage see for example Wagner, "Wildschutz in Afrika," *Der Weidmann* 31 (1900): 449–50. (The article had been printed in the *Tägliche Rundschau* before); Fritz Bley, "Wildschutz in Afrika," *Der Weidmann* 31 (1900): 669–70; Wissmann, "Wildschutz in Afrika," *Deutsche Jägerzeitung* 35 (1900), no. 28, 5 July: 442–43; "Schutzmaßregeln für das afrikanische Hochwild," *Geographische Zeitschrift* 6 (1900): 341.
100. *Journal of the Society for the Preservation of the Wild Fauna of the Empire* 1 (1904): 5, 9–10. See David Prendergast and William M. Adams, "Colonial Wildlife Conservation and the Origins of the Society for the Preservation of the Wild Fauna of the Empire (1903–1914)," *Oryx* 37 (2003): 251–60; Adams, *Against Extinction*, is in many aspects a history of the society.
101. Fritz Bley, "Besseren Wildschutz in unseren Kolonien!," *Monatshefte des Allgemeinen Deutschen Jagdschutzvereins und der Deutschen Versuchsanstalt für Handfeuerwaffen* 12 (1907): 119–22, 132–36. See also Fritz Bley, "Zum Wildschutz in Deutsch-Ostafrika," *Deutsch-Ostafrikanische Zeitung* 9, no. 38 (1907), 3 August.

102. Bericht über die Arbeiten der Wildschutz-Kommission, 4–5.
103. See for example BAB R 1001/7772, fol. 69: Schillings to Solf, 18 November 1912; "England als Vorbild," in *Blätter für Naturschutz* 5, no. 6 (1914): 13–15.
104. See Kupper, *Creating Wilderness*, chapter 2; Anna-Katharina Wöbse, *Weltnaturschutz. Umweltdiplomatie in Völkerbund und Vereinten Nationen 1920-1950* (Frankfurt, 2012), 36–45; Raf de Bont, "Dieren zonder grenzen. Over wetenschap en internationale natuurbescherming, 1890–1940," *Tijdschrift voor Geschiedenis* 125, no. 4 (2012): 520–35.
105. See in detail Bernhard C Schär, *Tropenliebe. Schweizer Naturforscher und niederländischer Imperialismus in Südostasien um 1900* (Frankfurt, 2015).
106. The following according to Sarasin, *Weltnaturschutz*; Sarasin, *Über nationalen und internationalen Vogelschutz*; Sarasin, *Ueber die Aufgaben des Weltnaturschutzes*.
107. Sarasin, *Weltnaturschutz*, 9.
108. Sarasin, *Ueber die Aufgaben des Weltnaturschutzes*, 39.
109. Ibid., 18; Raf de Bont, "'Primitives' and Protected Areas: International Conservation and the 'Naturalization' of Indigenous People, ca. 1910–1975".
110. Sarasin, *Weltnaturschutz*, 18 (italics removed).
111. Sarasin, *Ueber die Aufgaben des Weltnaturschutzes*, 55.
112. Cf. Resolution moved by Magnus Schwantje at the International Congress for the Protection of animals, held at Kopenhagen from the 1 to the 5 of August 1911 (Pamphlet); Magnus Schwantje, *Ueber die Verwerflichkeit des Jagdvergnügens, insbesondere der Hetzjagden. Rede zur Begründung einer die Reform des Jagdbetriebs betreffenden Resolution gehalten am 5. August 1911 auf dem Internationalen Tierschutz-Kongreß in Kopenhagen* (Berlin, 1911), 23–25.
113. Rudolf Ritter von Stummer-Traunfels, ed., *Verhandlungen des VIII. Internationalen Zoologen-Kongresses zu Graz, 15–20 August 1910* (Jena, 1912), 254–56, 338–39.
114. Herren, *Hintertüren zur Macht*, 351–62.
115. See ibid.; Wöbse, *Weltnaturschutz*, 51–54.
116. See BayHStA MA 92394, unfol.: Royal Bavarian Delegation to Bavarian Foreign Office, 20 November 1913.
117. Cf. PRO FO 881/10351, Report by NC Rothschild to Sir E Grey, 27 November 1913.
118. For approving reception see for example "Welt-Tierschutz," *Blätter für Naturschutz* 5, no. 3 (1914): 4.
119. BAB R 8023/1000, fol. 59ff.: Bericht über die Hauptversammlung der Deutschen Kolonialgesellschaft, 75–76; Hans Paasche, "Die deutschen Jäger," *Der Vortrupp* 1 (1912): 609–17.
120. Schillings, "Hagenbeck als Erzieher," 290.
121. PRO MAF 48/247B, Economic Advisory Council: Conclusions of a Meeting held at 2, Whitehall Gardens, S.W.1, on Thursday, 14 April 1932.
122. The *Office International* had been founded by the Dutch ornithologist Pieter van Tienhoven and the Belgian zoologist Jean-Marie Derscheid in 1927 to breathe new life into Sarasin's international monitoring commission. Its attempt to achieve recognition as the official clearing house for information relating to game protection worldwide was part of a renewed Belgian effort to draw the conservation-related internationalism to Brussels.

123. PRO CO 323/1234/11, fol. 28: Note on the First Draft, Second Report of the Preparatory Committee, paragraphs 69–73 [February 1933].
124. Neumann, "The Postwar Conservation Boom in British Colonial Africa"; Herren, *Hintertüren zur Macht,* 362; Holdgate, *The Green Web,* 17–38.

 CHAPTER 8

A Sense of Place
Representations of Africa and Environmental Identities in Germany

> Ein Land von der Geschichte Deutschlands
> kann keine reine Naturlandschaft haben
> —Friedrich Ratzel, *Die deutsche Landschaft* (1896)

Imagined geographies have real consequences. As historian of science David Livingstone has argued, the way "we imagine distant people and places, and how we choose to represent them to ourselves and to others, is of immense moral and political significance."[1] This chapter seeks to analyze the imperial imaginations that were mediated through Africa's wildlife and contextualizes them within the broader exchanges, mutual engagements, and the co-constitution of social and cultural practices "between metropole and colony."[2] What impact did the nature of German imperialism have on German society? The colonial encounter with wild animals was in a variety of ways and forms transferred back to Germany: physical bodies, body parts, texts, paintings, photographs, and other forms of representations of the African fauna shaped German ideas about the African continent, and at the same time about the nature of home. During the German *Kaiserreich*, no one did more to entrench the equation of "Africa" with a spectacular fauna than Carl Georg Schillings. His activities to popularize East Africa as a threatened paradise of primeval wildlife illustrate the diverse cultural realms in which the colonial encounter with Africa's fauna reverberated in German society. The spoils of his hunting were but a small part of the gigantic influx of animals mutilated into bones, skins, skulls, furs, horns, or tusks as a consequence of the colonial onslaught upon Africa's wildlife. As spectacular displays in trophy shows and hunting exhibitions, they were part of Schillings's public fashioning as Germany's foremost big game hunter.[3] Mounted in life-like posture, the prey to his rifle became part of taxonomic, evolutionist, or colonialist displays in Natural History Museums. Even more influential were Schillings's virtual representations of East Africa in texts, photographs, and public lectures, which conjured up images and fantasies of an endangered wilderness in the minds of his audience. Finally, Schillings was the foremost activist to translate the concern for the preservation of Africa's wildlife into German debates about nature protection.

Of course, it did not need Schillings to render Africa wild. The continent had, in various forms, served as Europe's "wild other" for centuries, and landscape, flora, and fauna had played a powerful role in this.[4] Still, there are good reasons to regard the colonial period as a decisive watershed in the formation and popularization of the stereotype of Africa as a pristine wilderness and Edenic paradise of wildlife. The amount of publications dealing with Africa experienced a marked increase, be it in the form of individual travelogues as well as in subject-related publications. There were media specializing in colonial matters. Attention also shifted toward the German colonies in hunting periodicals. Above all, there was a surge of publications popularizing nature and the natural sciences, a development closely related to the transformation of scientific institutions like natural history museums, which adapted their displays to the tastes of a broader public.[5] The emergence of a mass popular culture in the last quarter of the nineteenth century spawned new forms of leisure entertainment and consumption in which images of the "exotic," including the German colonies, reached a mass audience. Zoos, exhibitions, panoramas, cinema and slide shows, postcards, and the notorious *Völkerschauen* were all engaged in representing far-away places as "themed environments" (Eric Ames), in which nature and wildlife played a critical role.[6] These often spectacular representations also influenced the way how animals were represented as "scientific" in natural history museums.[7] Despite continuities to earlier representations, the stereotype of Africa as primeval wilderness found a completely different resonance in an increasingly urbanized and industrialized society, which came to project its desires of recourse to "pristine" and unspoilt landscapes not only onto idyllic rural landscapes of home, but also onto extra-European natures.[8] Another important factor that effected a change in the representations of wild Africa was the reception of Darwin's evolutionary theory. His rendering of nature as history temporalized flora and fauna as embodiments of primeval originality. And finally, from around the turn of the century onward, the image of Africa as a paradise of wildlife was transmitted through the new media of photography and film. These media bestowed a visual immediacy and the fiction of authenticity upon these images that earlier representations in text, paintings, and drawings were missing.

In what follows, I am less concerned with zoos, exhibitions, and natural history museums as the main spaces assigned to African animals in Europe but with the impact the wild fauna of East Africa had on environmental identities and conservationist discourse in early twentieth-century

Germany. The first section analyzes the production and reception of Carl Georg Schillings's photographs as the inception of the modern visuality of East Africa's wildlife across continents. It asks how the latest technology in photography was implicated in the production of anachronistic space and primeval wilderness and what meanings stay-at-home Germans derived from the vicarious encounter with African game in its native habitat. Afterward, it examines how the colonial encounter with Africa's megafauna was entangled with debates and developments in the field of nature protection in Germany. The fate of Africa's fauna not only served to legitimize colonial intervention on behalf of their preservation in Africa. It also provided a global context for the perception of nature in Germany and disclosed an emotional blank in the mentalities of German conservationists. The richness of Africa's mammalian fauna, whose equivalents had already been driven to extinction in German territory, evoked a sense of lost rootedness, originality, and naturalness among male conservationists that resulted in attempts to restore an imaginary "German" wilderness of the past.

Authentic, Noble, and Doomed: Carl Georg Schillings's Pictures from Paradise

An enthusiastic reviewer called them "the most sensational that ever an explorer brought home from his expeditions." Another spoke of "a unique contribution to our knowledge of African wild life" and the "most wonderful series of photographs of the great animals of Africa in their native haunts that the world has seen." Others again wondered if they were not "one of the greatest photographic achievements ever" or at least an "epoch-making contribution to the study of Zoology." By any means, the pictures brought the German public "into a completely different relationship to the creatures of the wild."[9]

The pictures that received this welter of accolades from both sides of the Atlantic were contained in Carl Georg Schillings's first book entitled *Mit Blitzlicht und Büchse*. It was published shortly before Christmas in 1904 and immediately became one of Germany's best-selling publications in the field of colonial literature. The first imprint sold out within four weeks. A pirated American translation appeared within a year; the authorized English version made it on the front page of the *Daily Mirror*.[10] As late as 1923, the book was translated into Dutch.[11] In order to capitalize on this enormous success, a second book under the title *Der Zauber des Elelescho* followed in 1906 and found an equally enthusiastic reception.[12] In Britain and the United States, the book sold under the title *In Wildest Africa,* an obvious variation of Stanley's famous travelogue *In Darkest Africa*.[13] In

France, the wildlife photographs contained in the book were published by the popular weekly *L'Illustration*.[14] In 1910, a German popular edition combined chapters of both books and saw twenty editions. It was in print as late as 1958.[15] For about half a century, German boys thrilled to Schillings's books as an enticing read that tickled fantasies of male bravery, adventure, wild animals, and the exotic,[16] including publications derived from Schillings's, such as Christian Morgenstern's illustrated children's book *Klaus Burrmann, der Tierweltphotograph*.[17] Sophisticated marketing strategies by Schillings's publisher Voigtländer exploited the photographs commercially, for example, by offering poster-size reprints of Schillings's pictures as *Natururkunden* for the living room wall. For decades, the phrase "Blitzlicht und Büchse" and variations of it popped up in a variety of contexts and publications.[18]

Several elements in Schillings's publications combined to thrill contemporary audiences. The titles were rife with exotic allure. *Mit Blitzlicht und Büchse* in particular had everything to be expected of a nineteenth-century account of hunting in the wild: dangerous beasts and hairbreadth escapes, cumbersome stalks and cunning opponents, safari romance, and a masculine white hero bravely mastering the wild. If these themes and topics justified the "rifle" in the title, the aspects disclosed by the "flashlight" added a melancholic tinge to Schillings's hunting heroism. Interspersed in the narratives of the brave hunter are desperate calls for wildlife preservation and a melancholic regret of wilderness and primeval originality passing away under the march of civilization. The first chapter, entitled *Die Tragödie der Kultur* ("The Tragedy of Civilization") was a scathing indictment of early twentieth-century globalization: "Far from the smoky centres of civilization, with their rush and turmoil and the unceasing throb and rattle of their machinery," there "disappears a rich and splendid fauna, which for thousands of years has made existence possible for the natives, but which now in a few years is recklessly slaughtered."[19] Schillings's valuation of wild animals was not only grounded in the hunters' concern about his prey, but was thoroughly shaped by contemporary debates about animal intelligence and *Tierseelenkunde* (animal psychology).[20] *Mit Blitzlicht und Büchse* contained a whole chapter on the "mind of animals." Schillings was convinced about the mental faculties and "intelligence" of wild animals and their capacity of spiritual bonding with humans. His books were indebted to Darwin's relativism of the human–animal divide in that they acknowledged the "animality" of the human as embodied by man the hunter, and the "humanity" of animals through the emphasis of their mental faculties and capacity for "ethical" behavior. Indeed, Schillings's observations of elephant behavior in the field were acknowledged as "careful" and still valuable when ethologists and behavioral ecologists embarked upon systematic field observations of this species over half a century later.²¹

Schillings portrayed East Africa as a primeval paradise of wildlife that was threatened in its existence, yet a challenge still to the hunter. This melancholic theme was continued in *Der Zauber des Elelescho*. Here, the melancholy of a disappearing evolutionary past was interwoven with Schillings's personal insecurity if he would ever be able to return to East Africa (he should not). Reminiscences and loss prevailed, and the calls for immediate measures of wildlife preservation became ever more urgent. The books can be regarded as the first self-reflexive accounts of big game hunting in German language that were at the same time manifestos for game conservation in the name of future generations. Yet, what made Schillings's books most outstanding were the lavish illustrations with original photographs that in the eyes of contemporaries conveyed an authenticity of nature "how it really is."²² What African explorers so far had only painted with words and supplementary drawings, Schillings documented in the visual language of photography. From his second expedition in 1898 onward, Schillings had supplemented rifle with camera in order to document a wilderness he believed to be irretrievably doomed. The result was a visual archive of roughly 2,000 photographs, many of which showing live animals in their natural surroundings, some of them taken at night with the help of flashlight and cunning trapping devices. Photography in tropical regions was by no means new and had been practiced at least since the 1870s. Rowland Ward's *Sportsman's Handbook* recommended hunters as early as 1882 to take a camera on their expeditions.²³ But few before Schillings had attempted to photograph animals in movement, even fewer had done so with animals in their natural surroundings, hardly anyone under conditions of tropical heat.²⁴ Capturing potentially dangerous animals in motion with the camera was still a ground-breaking novelty in the late 1890s and early 1900s, above all in Germany.²⁵

The reception of Schillings's wildlife photography was by no means restricted to his published books. In 1904, his photographs were part of the German pavilion at the St Louis World Exhibition. From the turn of the century onward, he traveled through Germany, Denmark, and Austria to present his pictures as colored lantern slides. Audiences were as diverse as scientific congresses, hunting associations, colonial societies, charity gatherings, and even the Kaiser and his entourage.²⁶ Contemporaries described Schillings as enthusiastic speaker. Wherever he turned up with his pictures, lecture halls were packed. In Copenhagen, for example, his presentations drew an audience of 1,500 each day, selling out the concert hall on three consecutive evenings in May 1908.²⁷ In Hamburg, his lectures were must-go events for the middle and upper classes,²⁸ while in Berlin, slides of Schillings's photographs were presented regularly for two years by the Urania, a society promoting the popularization of scientific knowledge. Allegedly, it was the Urania's most successful presentation in these years, and a separate lecturer had to be hired merely for repeating Schillings's explanations on each occasion.[29]

The widespread enthusiasm for Schillings's pictures was not restricted to mere reception. It influenced practices, too. Already before World War I, Schillings's visual translation of African wildlife to German audiences found a host of imitators and emulators. Among them were adventuring hunter-travelers like Hans Paasche, Arthur Berger, and Hans Schomburgk, all of whom forged the more than metaphoric symbiosis of gun and camera for "shooting" and "capturing" the wild.[30] The Duke Adolf Friedrich zu Mecklenburg and the safari entrepreneur Konrad Schauer made their photographs of African wildlife available for purposes of colonial propaganda after 1918, while the Swiss hunter-zoologist Adam David and the forester-turned-cinematographer Robert Schumann would advance the cinematic study of wild animals that Schillings only experimented with on his last journey.[31] Both, however, produced highly popular, yet rather sensationalist hunting films, which abandoned Schillings's conservatonist agenda and were chastized as fake, prearranged, and ethically objectionable by the wildlife photographer.[32]

Schillings's popularization of equatorial Africa as a threatened wilderness hit the nerve of popular taste in imperial Germany and beyond. His books and the 600 pictures within them appealed to such a broad range of audiences and interest groups because they could be interpreted in a variety of ways. Colonial and hunting circles in Germany saw the tangible results of his expeditions as proof of German imperial achievement in a domain that had previously been dominated by the British. The German translators of the Boy Scout idea, at pains to "Germanize" the concept, found Schillings a perfect example of a scouting pioneer.[33] British and American reviewers welcomed Schillings's pictures as an admirable novelty in a field that was "becoming wearied of books most of which bear the strongest family resemblance in their main features."[34] To be sure, the photographs still functioned as trophies, and the emphasis Schillings put on the danger and cunning involved in their capture made sure that the prowess of the hunter was not lost to the beholder.[35] At the same time, his hunting with the camera was widely hailed as the sportsmanship of the future and resonated well with the self-civilizing debates among penitent big game hunters across empires,[36] although some Anglo-American commentators had to include condescending remarks that Schillings's photographs came at the cost of "greater depredations on African game than the reasonable humane sportsman can approve of."[37] Of course, also his self-acclaimed accolade of pioneering the photography of wild animals did not remain uncontested; the reviewers of the science magazine *Nature,* for example, relegated him to an "unconscious disciple" of similar photographies procured by contemporaneous U.S. and British hunter-naturalists.[38] Photographers were fascinated by his technical equipment that would command people's respect for the capacities of human inventiveness and technology.[39] Above all, contemporary recipients emphasized the photographs' novelty, scientific value, and their authenticity in conveying the impression of pure "nature." Indeed, the degree of confidence audiences and reviewers were willing to invest into the authenticity of photography was astonishing. This confidence set the new medium apart from the earlier depictions of animals in sketches or paintings, where the element of artistic inspiration, if not modification of the depicted was part of the contract between artist and beholder. The camera, on the other hand, appeared to be a device that secured "biological facts" clinically and unhampered by human intervention.[40] Schillings was at pains to corroborate this impression by asserting that not a single picture was in any way retouched or modified. The quality of the images ranked from poor to outstanding, but only one reviewer dared to remark that some of the animals actually looked more akin to an "illuminated ghost in front of a black screen."[41] The foreword by the Berlin Zoo director Ludwig Heck left no doubt that naturalists assigned outstanding scientific and conservationist value to the photographs: in analogy to the *Naturdenkmäler* (natural monuments) that German nature protectionists strove to preserve, Heck assigned the pictures the status and function of *Natururkunden*.[42] Just as a document testified to a past legal transaction, Schillings's visual archive documented the presence of a fauna that was already consigned to the past. But they were still more than melancholy documents of seemingly inevitable extinction. Schillings introduced German audiences for the first time to that "absurdly intimate filmic reality" of animals enabled by the technological developments of late nineteenth and early twentieth century.[43] Indeed, he can be counted among the pioneers of camera-trapping as a tool for procuring "ecological" knowledge.[44] Naturalists, zoologists, and museum curators in Germany acclaimed the photographs for showing the animals in their natural habitat, documenting, for example, the phenomenon of animal mimicry as adaptation in the much-quoted struggle for survival.[45] Dissenting voices accused Schillings of a too generous understanding of symbiosis and mimicry, but such criticism shows that his scientific ambitions were taken serious.[46] Schillings's pictures helped to ground his activism in a claim to science. They were included as illustrative *Natururkunden* in popular zoological works such as the third edition of *Brehms Tierleben*,[47] and they served as "true to life" depictions, which allowed the modeling of biological or habitat groups in natural history museums.[48] Indeed, a diorama entitled *Deutschostafrikanisches Tierleben*, which the Senckenberg Museum of Natural History in Frankfurt opened in 1908, translated the photographs taken from Schillings's *Zauber des Elelescho* into a three-dimensional display.[49] Like-minded wildlife protectionists, finally, regarded Schillings's second book in particular as "a monument to the virgin Africa yet unaffected by the tragedy of culture" and "a wake-up call in the final hour for all those lovers of nature to engage in the preservation of natural monuments."[50] In what was the first conservationist campaign that transcended the country's borders, his photographs were an indispensible means to visualize what actually was at stake, to mobilize, and to stir affection for wild nature.

In his analysis of the role of photography in British imperialism, James Ryan has argued that photographs not only enabled stay-at-home Britons to symbolically travel through and even possess the colonial space, but that the physical space thus captured reveals "as much about the imaginative landscape of imperial culture."[51] Similarly, the allure of Schillings's picturing of wildlife must be ascribed to the meaning European urban and bourgeois audiences could derive from the pictures as well as the desires they could project onto them. Schillings's pictures were the technical yet nostalgic equivalent to the salvage documentation of anthropological and zoological material in ethnographic and natural history museums. Wilhelm Bölsche, who heard Schillings lecture at the Berlin war academy in 1904, described the enchantment achieved by the seeming disenchantment of animal life through the lantern slide: "There we sat, comfortably leaning back on a chair in the North-West of Berlin, to see for the very first time a hippopotamus on its nocturnal wanderings projected onto the wall."[52] Elisabeth von Heyking, herself a writer and imperialist-minded wife of a Prussian diplomat, complimented Schillings that his books and pictures would evoke "homesickness—not for a certain place, but more generally for space and loneliness, perhaps also for long forgotten pasts."[53] Schillings's photographic representations of Africa's wild animals were not only "ecologist" in the sense that they depicted animals in their natural surroundings and revealed heretofore unknown relationships and symbioses between them. Eternalizing the copresence of various species of ungulates on the African savanna as "paradise" testified to the existence of a natural balance and harmony from which (European) man had excluded himself in the civilizing process. Indeed, there were hardly people visible in Schillings's pictures. One photograph depicted two African women and a child in front of banana trees. It was subtitled "mimicry of humans," blending the members of a *Naturvolk* into nature and rendering them a product of their environment.[54] Depictions of a nature free from human impact reigned supreme. Schillings's pictures also resonated with contemporary antiurbanism and drew upon the noble savage-tradition of cultural criticism that depicted the extra-European world as allegedly unspoilt and a countersite to the "over-civilized" and morally deprived Europe.[55] The presentation of Africa's fauna as the tertiary past of Europe enabled his audience a temporary flight from civilization into the dawn of mammals in the tertiary age.

Just like the steamships and railways that brought the hunter to the game, the means to record primeval wilderness in the moment of its vanishing were provided by the latest technological achievements. The wild was a product of the very modernity and its techniques that threatened its existence. At the same time, the wild and potentially dangerous animal was effectively tamed by the virtuality of its medial representation. Coexisting with the hunters' narratives and iconography of human mastery over dangerous beasts was the framing of wild animals as embodiments of primeval originality and a paradise yet undisturbed by humans, culture, and history. It has been argued that the technologies of film and photography increasingly provided "virtual shelters for displaced animals."[56] Indeed, it was this medial taming of the wild that triggered and "authenticated" the virtual familiarity with Africa's wild fauna despite long distances. Schillings's pictures were the visual corollary to the detachment of conservationist debates in 1911. As the remarks of Bölsche and von Heyking suggest, the photographs enabled German city dwellers to temporarily inhabit the East African savanna from afar. They allowed Africa's wildlife to become what Annu Jalais has termed "cosmopolitan"[57]: a peculiar representation of certain charismatic species that corresponded with the needs and desires of Western urbanites. This representation made these species belong to "the world" and bestowed a feeling of cosmopolitan responsibility upon those who cared for them. To be sure, Schillings did not yet use his pictures to rally mass support and elicit funding for conservation. Because he expected crucial decisions for Africa's wildlife only from the centres of political power, he used his pictures to alert the target group of political decision-makers to the plight of Africa's wildlife. The Kaiser's court was treated to Schillings' pictures, and so was former US-President Theodore Roosevelt when he visited Berlin on his homeward journey from East Africa back to the United States in May 1910.[58] But certainly, his lantern-slide shows created a far broader social awareness. Therefore, they can be regarded as the beginning of a media-induced cosmopolitan conservationism that acted upon virtual and decontextualized representations of Africa's wildlife and was unquestionably regarded as morally good in Europe. The tangible consequences for the social relationships with nature in the countries that actually provided the habitat to this charismatic fauna remain the blind spot of this conservationist virtualism to this day.

Occasional critics condemned the public craze about Schillings's photographs exactly because of such cosmopolitanizing effects. They appeared to make Germans more acquainted with the ways of African game than with the habits of the animals of the German *Heimat*.[59] Therefore, his publisher Voigtländer put up a competition to propagate "hunting with the camera" as a new sport in the service of the sciences.[60] All amateur photographs in Germany were invited to venture out and create a similar visual archive of the natural monuments of home as Schillings had done for Equatorial East Africa. By 1908, Voigtländer had received some 1,200 pictures. The competition had not only made German nature lovers swarm to the countryside on the quest for motifs, but also turned out as an ideal advertising campaign for Hermann Meerwarth's multi-volume *Lebensbilder aus der Tierwelt*, which applied the principle of *Natururkunden* to the nature of the *Heimat*.[61] At the same time Franz Goerke, the director of the Urania in Berlin, started to popularize photography as a tool for *Heimatschutz*.[62] Picturing nature "alive" by photography was sensationalized in the tropics and then applied to the discovery and preservation of the nature of home. It was only slightly exaggerated when the popular scientific magazine *Kosmos* judged in 1910 that "it was Schillings who has given us nature photography."[63]

The fascination with the "liveness" of Schillings's photographs should, however, not mislead us to presume too straightforward and sudden a change from violent to nonviolent appropriation of wild animals. As Susan Sontag has observed, the metamorphosis of gun into camera was indicative of a deeper shift from threatening to threatened nature, from fear to nostalgia.[64] This nostalgia notwithstanding, hunting remained the prime mode of appropriating the wild until well after World War II, when big game hunting lost moral acceptability and the staggering extension of national parks was linked to the rise of mass wildlife tourism as a form of practiced development aid. Moreover, there was an interdependence between gun and camera that was both concrete and metaphorical: both were about capturing and ultimately domesticating the wild, and Schillings could photograph many wild animals only by intruding so close upon them as to cause either escape or aggression. In the latter case, the shot with the camera inevitably necessitated the lethal shot for the animal. Death was also implicated in the pictures where Schillings used a donkey as bait to attract predators in order to photograph the very moment of a lion's attack. While contemporaries waxed enthusiastic about Schillings's pictures showing African wildlife *alive*, the photographs are actually a very palpable illustration of Roland Barthes's observation that any picture inevitably bears the traces of a future and often calculated death.[65]

The particular colonial representation of Africa, which Schillings transmitted to German audiences with the visual technology of his day, was continued in later decades by wildlife films like Hans Schomburgk's *Das letzte Paradies* (1932), *Die Wildnis stirbt* (1936), and Bernhard Grzimek's *Serengeti Shall Not Die* (1959).[66] The pivotal role of Schillings in initiating the visual construction of Africa as an endangered paradise and in sensitizing the German public to the conservation of its wildlife must be emphasized, especially as this is so often and quite erroneously credited to the documentary films of the Frankfurt zoo director Bernhard Grzimek half a century later. Schillings literally reached hundreds of thousands of people, and it can be said without exaggeration that he, like few other authors, stamped German perceptions of Africa over the first half of the twentieth century. Grzimek himself saw his engagement for the preservation of Africa's charismatic animals in the footsteps of Schillings's photographs.[67] In doing so, he found himself in the company of many other latter-day hunters, adventurers, and conservationists who quoted Schillings's work as an initiating reading experience, source of inspiration, and reference to create a German tradition of concern for Africa's vanishing wildlife.[68] It was Schillings, judged the sculptor Fritz Behn in his reminiscences in 1918, "who made African nature and wildlife really popular in Germany."[69]

Wildlife Conservation between Colony and Metropole

When Robert Koch's proposal to counter the spread of tsetse by the regional extermination of game catapulted the question of game conservation in the German colonies on the agenda of public debate in Germany, the *Deutsche Jägerzeitung* published a fanfare to

> preserve the homeland and its natural monuments! This, however, needs to be interpreted generously insofar as we regard "that whole little planet" as our homeland, whose fruits, products, creations, characteristic animals and plants, mountains, waterfalls etc. belong to us all ... We can afford such cosmopolitanism for it does not diminish the value of the single nation. We have a shared interest to protect the products of the earth.[70]

This cosmopolitan extension of the German program of *Heimatschutz* to East Africa and the entire globe is remarkable for it draws attention to aspects of early German conservationism that have, although not entirely neglected, remained rather blind spots in the existing historiography. Among these are the significant participation of hunters in the movement for nature conservation; the global outlook of a social group that is commonly associated with provincialism rather than cosmopolitanism; and the role of the colonial encounter with wild nature for the development of the movement for nature protection before World War I.

When dealing with the *Kaiserreich,* environmental historians have focussed first and foremost on the movement for *Heimatschutz,* the emergence of landscape preservation, the care for natural monuments, and the state-centered beginnings of conservation in Prussia and Bavaria. A recurrent set of outstanding individuals, such as Ernst Rudorff, Wilhelm Wetekamp, Hugo Conwentz, and Paul Schultze-Naumburg, dominated these narratives. Although Friedemann Schmoll has made a powerful argument for the breadth of the movement, the diversity of its concerns, its ambivalent attitudes toward progress, and its orientation toward an alternative modernity,[71] the underlying assumption remained unquestioned that nature conservation in Germany was equivalent to a concern with German nature.

Putting the colonial experience back into the history of nature conservationism in Germany restores the global framework of environmental degradation in which the concern about the fauna and flora of home was embedded.[72] Indeed, a considerable part of German nature lovers was aware to this and perceived the transformation of the landscape and the vanishing of wild animals and birds as a consequence of technical and industrial progress, imperialist expansion, and the spread of capitalist trade. In an understanding of progress that was both diffusionist and declensionist, the blame was put on either the "advance of culture" or the "march of civilization" that had colonized away the big fauna of Europe and now continued its work on the other continents. The overseas colonies became spaces where the destructive impact of progress could be observed in fast motion. However, the awareness to species destruction beyond the German borders predated the acquisition of colonies. The various societies for bird protection that formed since the 1870s were, for example, forced to cast their gaze beyond the German borders by the very nature of their concern with migratory birds.[73] The foundation of zoological gardens in the 1860s and 1870s had obvious global ramifications through the animal trade, and recent research has shown the degree to which wild and "exotic" animals were commoditized during the second half of the nineteenth century to furnish the growing demand of traveling menageries, zoological gardens, circuses, and aristocratic estate owners with a taste for the exquisite.[74] The challenge to miniaturize the natural world within the confines of a zoological garden also spawned debates among zoo directors about species extinction and habitat loss in the non-European world. These latter concerns were put in a nutshell by Philipp Leopold Martin, a taxidermist of Silesian origin and a key figure in the reform of natural history and its popularization in museums.[75] Martin published a multi-volume *Praxis der Naturgeschichte* over the 1870s and early 1880s that, among many other topics, also addressed the issue of nature conservation at large and in general (*Allgemeiner Naturschutz*).[76] In this essay, published in 1882, he unfolded the whole panorama of late nineteenth-century anxieties about worldwide environmental degradation: following the frontiers of trade and colonial rule, he addressed the loss of forest cover in North America, the simplification of landscapes through rational forestry and agriculture in the German-speaking lands, and the extinction of marine, terrestrial, and avian fauna worldwide through the ravages of whaling and the ivory, fur, and plumage trades. For Martin, these developments had their origins in unfettered free trade, moral deprivation, and profit-seeking, but also a fatal Roman-Christian tradition of mastery over nature.[77]

Martin's global perspective on the environmental consequences of industrialization, capitalist agriculture, rational forestry, and commercial expansion could equally be found in popular natural histories like *Brehm's Tierleben*, the popular science series edited by *Kosmos*, hunting periodicals, museum bulletins, and the proceedings of learned scientific associations, not to mention the journals of the organized nature conservation movement after the turn of the century. All these publications were characterized by frequent reference and awareness to the state of nature in other countries and on other continents. The "vanishing of the colossal forms" and the "extinction of the giant fauna"[78] in the polar regions, the Western frontier of North America, as well as Southern and Eastern Africa gained foremost attention. This was not only because the giant species exerted a powerful allure to the European mind, but also because their size and habitat demands made them perfect indicators of landscape change or rapacious human exploitation through hunting.[79] The late nineteenth- and early twentieth-century catalogue of threatened species repetitively featured whales, the American bison, the big game of Africa, the polar bear and other arctic fauna, and birds with decorative plumage. While these species, with varying emphasis, dominated conservationist concern over extinction across Europe and North America,[80] German authors saw the demise of large species abroad as continuation of those predators and large mammals that had already vanished from the German landscape. This sample usually contained the European bison, brown bear, lynx, and wolf, while beaver, elk, and golden eagle were feared to be on the verge of extinction.[81] Wildlife degradation was a global yet localized process that affected the African elephant as well as the American bison and the elk in Eastern Prussia. Unsurprisingly, the advocates of such a global perspective on conservation shared a background of professional or amateur concern with animals, be it as zoo directors, museum curators, naturalists, explorers, or hunters. A global outlook on conservation did not necessarily involve personal mobility: There were a considerable number of armchair conservationists who derived their knowledge about nature degradation abroad through vicarious participation in European expansion, enabled by the flurry of travelogues, scientific journals, and a flourishing market of popular natural science.[82] A shared conviction, however, did neither automatically generate the cohesion that defines a social movement, nor translate into organized forms or action. Nor did all those who developed a global environmental consciousness necessarily reflect on strategies how species loss could be averted. A fatalist cultural criticism was pervasive, and there were many who deplored the loss of the large fauna as inevitable. There was no consensus which of the environmental grievances was the most urgent to address, and those who proposed measures to avert species extinction did so from differing vantage points. Some advocated conservation through utilization or domestication; some argued for trade bans in the commodified body parts of threatened animals; some addressed the problem within the logic and with the instruments of game management and sustainable hunting (*Hege*), while others advocated a comprehensive *Weltnaturschutz*.

The declensionist outlook on the globality of species degradation attained an entire new quality with the acquisition of colonies in the 1880s. Germany's overseas colonies, and in particular East Africa with its reputation as a Pleistocene zoological garden, became a focal point for conservation. Species degradation appeared to happen in fastest motion, and the colony's political status as dependent territory made it possible to frame wildlife conservation as a moral obligation that came with the status of being empire. Colonial rule entailed a greater and steadier flow of information, and it enabled more men to exchange a mere theoretical concern with game degradation for eyewitnessing and personal experience. A brief comparison between the above mentioned essay by Philipp Leopold Martin and Paul Sarasin's *Weltnaturschutz* illustrates the difference that colonies made. Martin anticipated many of the grievances addressed in Sarasin's *Weltnaturschutz* by three decades. Both drew upon personal experience in the tropics, and their observations were in many respects similar. Yet, the attention they received, and the methods they proposed in 1882 and 1911 respectively varied significantly. Martin's calls upon voluntary associations to raise people's awareness to these issues were hidden in a multivolume natural history publication and went largely unnoticed. Three decades later, the scientific observer had turned activist[83]: Sarasin addressed scientists, lobbied state authorities, and organized a fledgling international commission. The public mobilization of shame by Sarasin, Schillings, and Paasche could resonate because Germany had a direct stake in the stewardship for the wild, and there were colonial authorities that could be held accountable.

The nature of imperialism thus provided conservationists with a concrete arena for action. The diffuse workings of "civilization" and "culture" had become manifest in the tangible agency of state authorities, and unlike many of the local or regional conflicts about the utilization or preservation of certain landscapes or river sections in the German states, the East African game was an object of national and international concern. The framing of its conservation as an imperial obligation and a question of national pride was immediately plausible.

As much as wildlife degradation in the East African colony was to attain a focussing role for global conservationist concern in Germany, awareness to what was going on in the colonies was different in 1911 than it was in 1900 or in 1890. Attention to colonial game conservation and its social constiuency in Germany ebbed and waned. Initially, the colonies were a separate sphere where conservationist sensibilities emerged in response to local circumstances. The first wave of mobilization, roughly between the acquisition of colonies and the middle of the 1890s, was stirred by the *Vernichtungskrieg* against elephants.[84] There was little optimism that extinction could be halted, apart from hopes to draw the elephant over to the side of "culture" by domestication. The elephant scare of the 1880s resonated largely among a limited number of colonial enthusiasts, zoologists, and explorers with a global outlook on species loss who published in the specialized public sphere of zoology, hunting, the colonial press plus the occasional family magazine.[85] The emphasis on taming in Wissmann's game ordinance 1896 was surely an echo of these debates, but otherwise, the connections with the practice of conservation in the colony were rather weak, as Wissmann's measures largely sprang from the rationalities of hunting. There were also no discernible links to debates about nature protection in Germany. Discussions were compartmentalized in fragmented public spheres and their respective media, and little could be known about the practices of colonial conservation unless one was a regular and very attentive reader of the colonial and hunting press. When Wilhelm Wetekamp made his famous bid for the establishment of "state parks" to preserve the "monuments of nature's evolutionary history" in the Prussian Parliament in March 1898,[86] he referred to the American national parks, but not to Wissmann's putting the very idea into practice in East Africa two years earlier. Hugo Conwentz, the trained palaeobotanist, director of the Provincial Museum in Danzig (Gdansk) and mastermind behind the German approach of *Naturdenkmalpflege* (conservation of natural monuments), contacted Wissmann in 1901 to learn more about his measures at game conservation in East Africa. At the time, Conwentz was gathering material for his memorandum on the conservation of natural monuments. But whatever Wissmann told him in reply must not have exerted a lasting impression. The published memorandum included but a meager mention of "regulations concerning the conservation of the elephant and other species in East Africa."[87]

Unsurprisingly, the main transmitter of conservationist concepts and terminologies between metropole and colony was Carl Georg Schillings. It was him who applied the terminology of the *Naturdenkmal* to East Africa's game in order to sensitize larger segments of the German public to the issue of conservation in the German colonies.[88] When the Prussian State Agency for the Conservation of Natural Monuments (Staatliche Stelle für Naturdenkmalpflege) was founded under Conwentz's directorship in 1906, Schillings immediately demanded similar state custody for the protection of Africa's wildlife in his second book that was published the very year.[89] His lectures, pictures, and publications, the controversy sparked by Robert Koch in 1908 and the game clearance ordered by Rechenberg two years later, reverberated in the daily press and turned passive regret into active concern. Colonial conservation spawned its own lobbyist organizations, and the wildlife issue increased in prominence at the annual general meetings of the DKG. While a motion for enhanced game protection had still met with widespread disinterest when the society convened in Bremen in 1908, the opinion had completely changed at the meetings in Stuttgart and Hamburg in 1911 and 1912.[90] The medical scientist Hugo Salomon, another prominent advocate of colonial conservation, took this development as an indicator "for the extraordinary progress that the idea of nature conservation has recently made in the German nation."[91]

Toward the end of the first decade of the 1900s, the issue of colonial wildlife conservation reverberated in reformist circles and publications, and it was equally embraced by the organized movement for nature protection in Germany. There existed personal as well as conceptual links with colonial conservation. Its main advocates, like Fritz Bley, Wilhelm Bölsche, Franz Doflein, Kurt Floericke, Konrad Günther, Ludwig Heck, Wilhelm Kuhnert, Hugo Salomon, Georg Schweinfurth, Alexander Sokolowsky, Paul Sarasin, and Schillings all featured on the membership list of the Verein Naturschutzpark (VNP), an association founded in 1909 to promote the creation of national park-style reserves in Germany and Austria.[92] There were close links between the local members of the VNP and the DKG-branches in Magdeburg and the East Prussian Lyck who introduced the issue of a colonial *Naturschutzpark* at the annual general meeting of the DKG in 1911. However, despite the early reception of the national park idea in the East African colony, the VNP only drew attention to the colonies as a site for a *Naturschutzpark* in the wake of the Rechenberg scandal. The explanation that "the same fatal consequences of an inexorably advancing culture" were visible in the colony as at home suggests that the colonies were seen as an extension of conservationist concern at home.[93] In its publications, the VNP referred to the national parks in the United States, Switzerland, Sweden, and Canada, but there is no evidence that the VNP drew any inspiration from conservation in the colonies.

The VNP was not the only preservationist association that embraced the nature of the German colonies. The Bund zur Erhaltung der Naturdenkmäler aus dem Tier- und Pflanzenreiche, like the VNP an association formed in 1909 out of discontent with the narrow approach of the Bund Heimatschutz, explicitly incorporated the campaign against the "useless extinction of the big game in Africa" into its program. However, its activities in this matter appear to have been restricted to the submission of a five-point program to the colonial office in 1910 in order to halt the extinction of Africa's megafauna.[94] The less than half-hearted engagement of the VNP to donate money for the purchase of Ngorongoro as a permanent *Naturschutzpark* shows that these associations clearly prioritized the concern with the nature of home over the distant wildlife overseas. At a time when the VNP had just started to purchase the first parcels of land in the Lüneburg Heath, there was little interest in spending the earnings of a lottery on a territory that a majority of the VNP's members had never even heard of before.

Although the early reception of the national park idea in the East African colony might suggest otherwise, the colony did not serve as a "laboratory of modernity"[95] in the sense of an experimental space where practices and models of biopolitics and environmental governance were tested and developed under less restrained and regulated conditions than in Europe. Such an interpretation inadequately captures the awkward and messy realities of the colonial situation and misrepresents the identifiable directions of transfer. The metaphor of the laboratory conveys an intentionality of deliberate engineering and testing that is missing in the motivations of contemporaries. None of the key figures of wildlife conservation in East Africa went to the colony with a premeditated pattern or idea of conservation in mind. Wissmann, Schillings, and Paasche all came as hunters and went as conservationists. Conservation in East Africa was neither a deliberate attempt to apply allegedly German concepts of *Naturschutz* on colonial nature, nor an extension of the "pragmatic environmental concern associated with the ideal of *Heimat.*"[96] Among the various currents that altogether constituted the German movement for nature protection around 1900, the encounter with African nature was a source of conservationist thinking in its own right.

Indeed, wildlife conservation in East Africa was a variety of "green imperialism" in that it had its roots not in a preoccupation with *Naturschutz* imported from Germany, but in a transimperial concern with game and the regional economics of the ivory trade. The initial response sprang from the hunters' concern with *Hege,* and only gradually did the emphasis on *Jagdschutz* give way to *Wildschutz.* Rechenberg's *Wildmord* functioned as the ultimate catalyst for framing African game in terms of *Naturschutz,* which, in the colonial context, consisted largely of a change in language and justifications. It was more discourse than practice, and the colonial conservationists adopted the terminology of nature protection at home to gain publicity and lend relevance to their cause. They reframed game as *Naturdenkmal,* replaced the *Jagd-* or *Wildreservate* by the term *Naturschutzpark,* and occasionally, even calls for *Heimatschutz* in the colonies were heard. While the latter may partially testify to an increasing acceptance of the colonies as extended *Heimat* and constitutive part of a "Greater Germany,"[97] one should not overestimate the terminological consistency of such demands. *Heimatschutz* in the colonies could denote the preservation of indigenous customs and "natural peoples,"[98] but, as the introductory example of the *Jägerzeitung*'s claim to *Heimatschutz* indicated, also the preservation of untrammelled nature. Both were united in their criticism of European civilization, but the preservation of primeval nature was quite the opposite of the cultural landscape that *Heimatschutz* was supposed to preserve at home.

The change of terminology allowed the conservationists to conceal the self-interest of the hunter and present their claims in a language associated with a social and cultural concern that was understood as "good" and "modern." On a practical level, the modernity of *Naturschutz* in the colonies, as understood by its proponents at the time and as opposed to the earlier politics of game conservation, consisted in the demand to render reserves permanent and in the suspense of the distinction between "useful" animals and "vermin." The replacement of this distinction by a static ecology of paradise—a natural balance in which all animals were worthy of protection and any human interference constituted a violation—was, however, a disputed issue and perhaps the main dividing line between hunter-conservationists and nature protectionists, respectively preservationists. None of these demands was included into the practice of colonial conservation prior to World War I. The German East African colony globalized the concern of conservationists, but it did not serve as a laboratory for German conservationism as far as concepts and terminology of conservation were concerned.

Africa's Wildlife and German Environmental Identities

This said, Africa's unique wildlife did shape German cultures of nature as well as the environmental identities of conservation's masculine and hunting constituency in other ways. The pivotal role of large mammals in the colonial debates about nature conservation and their perceived deterioration in fast motion made the colonies a perfect mirror to reflect upon the state of nature in Germany.[99] This resulted, first, in a preservationist critique of a merely utilitarian rationale for game management and its underlying distinction into "noxious" and "useful." This criticism was not invented in the colonies, but developments at the frontiers of European expansion made the problem of a utilitarian take on flora and fauna obvious. For years, the deterioration of wildlife in the colony was spurred on by game laws whose economic rationale included the payment of bounties for the killing of predators. However, "noxious" animals in the context of East Africa involved species with an enormous emotional appeal to Europeans, such as lions and leopards. In the colony, the preying cats were only appreciated by hunters, but otherwise regarded as a threat to people's life, limb, and livestock. Seen from the safe distance of Germany, lions in particular were deemed charismatic and quintessentially African, a symbol of majesty, power and masculinity, and the undisputed "ruler in the realm of mammals."[100] Global conservationists portrayed the colonies as a last chance to avoid the mistakes of European industrialism and its driving *Nützlichkeitsfanatismus* (obsession with profitability) that destroyed anything that could not be commoditized into cash value. This included scathing criticism of capitalism, but also of the practices and the ethical foundations of game management in both colony and metropole. It was subject to controversial discussion if hunting was applied conservation without which no wild animals would be left in Germany, or if hunting, with its focus merely on game, in fact contributed to the comparative poverty of wild animals in the German landscape.[101]

Second, the colonial encounter with the species diversity and originality of the "continent of large mammals"—in nature as well as in its textual, visual, and corporeal representations—exposed a glaring deficit of German nature that lacked both large animals and "wildness." According to Schillings, the rigid application of utilitarian rationales to hunting in Germany had resulted in a completely managed and organized landscape that has come to resemble "the ideal of extensive, well-kept gardens" with "no touch of wild nature."[102] Assessments like this and the general fascination with the originality and vitality of the African game not only expose an emotional blank and a deeply felt lack of the wild in German environmental identities.[103] They also resulted in a quest to reverse the global division of landscapes of "civilized" nature here and "wild" nature there. The German landscape should be restored to its former species diversity and primeval originality. This took the pragmatic form of biotic transfer and acclimatization as well as the ideologically charged form of restoring a deep, "Germanic" landscape. German hunters and estate owners in particular were involved in countering deterioration of both the diversity of species as well as the overall population sizes of game animals in Germany by filling "the gaps in our fauna and avifauna ... through the acclimatisation of foreign species."[104] The decades since the 1880s witnessed more or less successful attempts to introduce Australian wallabies on an estate in the Prussian Rhine Province, Scottish grouse in the mountainous Eifel, or the mouflon (*Ovis orientalis musimon*), a species of wild sheep originally native to Sardinia and Corsica. The latter was introduced successfully in various low mountain regions between 1903 and World War I.[105] In the majority of cases, these species should add diversity to hunting, although occasionally, transfer was also rationalized by possible extinction abroad.[106] These efforts to add to the faunal diversity of the German countryside were too small and localized altogether to spawn a major discussion if these newcomers actually fit into the German landscape. Yet, they formed part of the very discourses of a global decline of wildlife, conservation, and the "improvement" of regional natures that were characteristic features of European imperialism.[107]

The other answer to the lack of wildness in the German landscape resulted in an ecology of rootedness and attempts to restore an allegedly original German landscape by the reintroduction of species already extinct in Germany. The vanishing of the authentic originality embodied in the big game of North America and the African savanna drew attention to the equivalent species of big game that had once existed in central Europe. The popularized notions of two contemporary scientific debates were important here. One was the political geography of the characteristic animal, an epistemic configuration that conflated space and species as well as habitat and time. The assumption that certain animals had been shaped in their evolution by their habitat and vice versa and therefore embodied its characteristics in more or less pure form had its scientific origins in the zoogeographic ordering of the world's fauna especially by Alfred Russel Wallace.[108] Originally a relational category that was to be established by careful comparison, hunters and popular scientists tagged the label "characteristic" to the more spectacular species associated with certain regions. Conspicuous large vertebrates, like elephants, rhinoceroses, or the varieties of bison on both sides of the Atlantic, figured as signifiers of their *Lebensraum* (living space), as remnants of deep time and a bygone world, and as living natural monuments. The survival of Africa's Pleistocene fauna into the present underwrote the colonial ideology that Africans were seemingly unable to master the nature of their continent. Large game thus embodied the powerful originality of a nature that Europeans had already domesticated in the process of settling and colonizing their own continent and that was just being conquered in the colonization of frontier territories of Africa. However, German conservationists did not only perceive the last giants of the animal kingdom as remnants of an earlier age but, by implication, African landscapes also as akin to the past landscapes of Europe. Indeed, a major issue among geographers around 1900 was the question how Germany's *Urlandschaft* (primeval landscape) might have looked like before it became transformed into the contemporaneous cultural landscape through centuries of settlement, agriculture, and industry.[109] Did central Europe feature a steppe, and if so, was this steppe akin to the contemporaneous steppes in central Asia or tropical Africa, or rather a park-like landscape? Or has the central European landscape been densely forested and only cleared by the first human settlers?[110] A key issue in this debate was the interpretation of fossilized mammals and their potential habitat in either forest or steppe. Because this was impossible without reference to related species in contemporaneous landscapes beyond Germany and Europe, one strand of the debate was closely linked with questions about the past distribution of Africa's mammalian fauna. Paleontologists like Ernst Stromer von Reichenbach, for example, believed "that animals today regarded as typically African, like hippopotami, lions, hyenas and monkeys, had still been common in the Europe of the diluvian age."[111] Wilhelm Bölsche continued along the same vein in his imaginary archaeology of the central European landscape through the millennia. The German landscape of the tertiary age, Bölsche believed, was best imagined as analogous to the "Kilimanjaro landscape so masterfully depicted by Schillings," for the "entirely tropical German *Urwald* and the hot German grasslands" then had featured a mammalian fauna similar to the East African fauna of the day.[112]

Of course, no one followed Bölsche's imagined German landscape of the past and suggested the restoration of Central Europe's Pleistocene fauna. Yet, many shared his desire for the primitive, the authentic, the natural, and the wild embodied in charismatic megafauna. It was more than mere coincidence that German hunting and conservationist periodicals dedicated constant attention to the fate of the last remaining herds of the European bison as a corollary to the fate of the so-called transatlantic bison in Yellowstone. The European bison, extinguished in German forests as early as 1755, was to become the one animal characteristic of a true and original Germanic nature by the late nineteenth century.[113] Popular wildlife painters of the day, like Wilhelm Kuhnert or Richard Friese, were renowned for their heroic paintings of the big game of Africa, but even more so for their depictions of the "Germanic" game like elk, bison, or bear. Friese gained a reputation as the "painter of the free and fighting beast," and for Kuhnert, these species bore the "stamp of original power and untameable vitality," strength, and the "wildest vigour."[114] These animals embodied the very values of masculinity and a precivilized, "natural" simplicity that the hunters claimed to have experienced in Africa and sought to reclaim in "overcivilized" Europe. However, the leftovers of Germany's big game featured little more than a few elk populations in Eastern Prussia, and the occasional bison that had survived on managed game estates. Otherwise, the wild and vigorous fauna of central Europe could only be retrieved by digging back into a premodern, if not Germanic or even prehistoric past. And that is what some conservationists did. The first attempts to restore an "original German landscape" by the reintroduction of big game were already made before World War I. It was Hermann Löns, a journalist, hunter, and writer for whom *Naturschutz* was equivalent to the "preservation of the race" and the protection of animals vital for the *Volksseele* (people's soul),[115] who suggested in 1912 to create a *Heimatpark* in the Harz mountains. Another patron behind the *Heimatpark* in the Harz was Johann Albrecht von Mecklenburg, the regent of the duchy of Brunswick in which the park was to be situated. Mecklenburg was also the long-time president of the German Colonial Society and therefore well familiarized with the issue of wildlife conservation in the colonies. In the Harz, an area of approximately eleven square kilometers south of Bad Harzburg should be restored to its original state not only by preservation of the remnants of its threatened flora and fauna, but also by reintroducing those species for whom the Harz mountains had once provided a habitat, such as lynxes, bears, elks, and bison. These animals were to be presented as in Hagenbeck's *Tierpark* in Hamburg, where fences and ditches were hidden to allow visitors the illusion of an immediate encounter with the animal in the wild.[116] The plan did not materialize for various reasons, including resistance from the side of local *Heimatschützer* who, ironically, accused the planned originality of the *Heimatpark* to be artificial.

Yet, as a product of the imperial mind-set, the restoration of the German *Urnatur* (primeval nature) was continued in and after World War I, within and beyond the country's shifting borders, thus reflecting Germany's changing geographies of empire. The conflation of space and species can, for example, be traced in the mental and practical reclamation of the east as the "actual frontier" and *Lebensraum* of the German people.[117] Anchored in a mythology of German eastward settlement since the Middle Ages and predicated upon the basic opposition between the cultural landscape of Germany and a Slavic "wilderness," the projection of wilderness onto the east supplemented the geopolitical ideology of the "people without space" (*Volk ohne Raum*) with a space seemingly without people. Once more, the bodily presence of large animals such as elk and bison was taken to "naturalize" the fiction of a wild, undeveloped, and underused emptiness. The one site where the ideology of an allegedly Germanic *Urnatur* and the conflation of space, race, time, and species in the bodies of charismatic game should play out most forcefully was the forest of Białowieża with its remaining herds of bison on the Polish-Lithuanian border. Occupied by German forces during both World Wars, Białowieża was reclaimed as a sanctuary of primeval Germanic game and forest. Its status as wilderness was forged by the erasure of its human population in the Eastern campaigns of World War II, perhaps a unique case of the intentional application of genocidal warfare in the making of a protected area.[118] Yet, the identification of certain charismatic animals with the nation and its alleged characteristics, and the associated attempts to restore a particularly "German" landscape through the reintroduction of these species, was not confined to the age of racialized geopolitics. Also, the discussions about the establishment of Germany's first national park in the Bavarian Forest from the middle of the 1960s were marked by similar longings of the restoration of a primeval German landscape through the reintroduction of its allegedly characteristic wildlife.[119] Once again influenced by contemporary debates about wildlife conservation in East Africa, they show that the close relationship between wildlife and environmental identities was rooted in deeper anxieties about "civilization," progress, and national identity that continued to influence conservationist thinking in the second half of the twentieth century.

Notes

1. David N Livingstone, *Putting Science in Its Place. Geographies of Scientific Knowledge* (Chicago, 2003), 8; Edward Said, *Culture and Imperialism* (London, 1994).
2. The quote is, of course, lifted from Stoler and Cooper's programmatic essay "Between Metropole and Colony."
3. See for example HUB MfN, Zool. Museum S III Schillings: Deutsch-Ostafrikanische Sonder-Ausstellung CG Schillings (2. Reise 1899/1900).
4. See Matthias Fiedler, *Zwischen Abenteuer, Wissenschaft und Kolonialismus. Der deutsche Afrikadiskurs im 18. und 19. Jahrhundert* (Cologne, 2005); Adams and McShane, *The Myth of Wild Africa*, 3–23; David Anderson and Richard Grove, *Conservation in Africa. People, Policies and Practice* (Cambridge, 1987); Philip D Curtin, *The Image of Africa. British Ideas and Action, 1780–1850* (Madison, WI 1973).
5. Andreas W Daum, *Wissenschaftspopularisierung im 19. Jahrhundert. Bürgerliche Kultur, naturwissenschaftliche Bildung und die deutsche Öffentlichkeit 1848–1914*, 2nd ed. (Munich, 2002); Köstering, *Natur zum Anschauen*; Carsten Kretschmann, *Räume öffnen sich. Naturhistorische Museen im Deutschland des 19. Jahrhunderts* (Berlin, 2006).
6. Stefanie Wolter, *Die Vermarktung des Fremden. Exotismus und die Anfänge des Massenkonsums* (Frankfurt, 2005); Anne Dreesbach, *Gezähmte Wilde. Die Zurschaustellung "exotischer" Menschen in Deutschland 1870–1940* (Frankfurt, 2005);

Eric Ames, *Carl Hagenbeck's Empire of Entertainments* (Seattle, 2008); Rothfels, *Savages and Beasts*; Assenka Oksiloff, *Picturing the Primitive. Visual Culture, Ethnography, and early German Cinema* (New York, 2001).
7. Nyhart, *Modern Nature*; Köstering, *Natur zum Anschauen*.
8. Kundrus, *Moderne Imperialisten*, 138–62; Ute Luig and Achim von Oppen, "Landscape in Africa. Process and Vision. An Introductory Essay," *Paideuma* 43 (1997): 7–45.
9. M Dankler, "Nacht- und Fernphotographie," *Der Weidmann* 36 (1905): 194–96; "Photographing Wild Animals," *Bulletin of the American Geographical Society* 37 (1905): 588; "Flashlights from the Jungle," *The National Geographic Magazine* 18 (1907): 534; "Aufnahmen wilder Tiere in der freien Natur," *Jahrbuch für Photographie und Reproduktionstechnik* 18 (1904): 431–32; "With Flashlight and Rifle," *The Spectator*, 9 December 1905; HH Johnston, "East Africa and Its Animal Life," *The Geographical Journal* 25 (1905): 557; "African Beasts," *New York Times*, 20 January 1906: BR 31; Stadtarchiv Düren (SAD), Schillings Papers, Miscellaneous Reviews: *Der Zauber des Elelescho*; Folder B: no. 24: Urteile über CG Schillings; Curt Thesing, "Der Photograph als Naturforscher!," *Aus der Natur* 1 (1905–6): 631.
10. Hauptschule Düren-Gürzenich, Documenta Schillingsi, Folder 3, Newspaper Clippings: "With Flashlight and Rifle in East Africa," *Daily Mirror*, 15 December 1905.
11. Carl Georg Schillings, *Met flitslicht en buks. Nieuwe waarnemingen en avonturen in de wildernis te midden van de dierenwereld van aequatoriaal-oost-Afrika* (Arnhem, 1923).
12. The *Elelescho* in the title refers to *ol-leleshwa*, the Maa term denoting the campher bush *Tarchonanthus camphoratus*.
13. Carl Georg Schillings, *In Wildest Africa* (New York, 1907).
14. Roland Cosandey, "Wahrheit und Machenschaften. Adam David und Alfred Machin mit Kinematograph und Büchse im afrikanischen Busch," *KINtop* 10 (2002): 111, fn. 9.
15. Schillings, *Mit Blitzlicht und Büchse im Zauber des Elelescho* (Leipzig, 1910); *Dürener Zeitung*, no. 281 (1965), 4 December.
16. See for example Hauptschule Düren-Gürzenich, Schillings Papers, Documenta Schillingsi I: Albert Schulte to Schillings, 18 April 1907; Wolfgang Hoffmann to Schillings, 7 June 1906.
17. Christian Morgenstern, *Klaus Burrmann, der Tierweltphotograph* (Oldenburg, 1941).
18. See for example Peter Scher, "Mit Blitzlicht und Büchse durchs dunkelste Bayern," *Das Tage-Buch* 7 (1926): 1945–47; Günther Anders, *Philosophische Stenogramme* (Munich, 1965), 71.
19. Carl Georg Schillings, *With Flashlight and Rifle: A Record of Hunting Adventures and of Studies in Wild Life in Equatorial East Africa,* trans. Frederic Whyte (London, 1906), 1–2.
20. Schillings was one of the foremost believers in the capacities of the "clever Hans," a horse whose "intelligence" was much debated between 1904 and 1907, see Oskar Pfungst, *Das Pferd des Herrn von Osten (Der kluge Hans). Ein Beitrag zur experimentellen Tier- und Menschenpsychologie* (Leipzig, 1907), 7–8; Karl Krall, *Denkende Tiere. Beiträge zur Tierseelenkunde aufgrund eigener Versuche. Der Kluge Hans und meine Pferde Muhamed und Zarif* (Leipzig, 1912), 22–25,

280–83. Among the horse's admirers were other key proponents of wildlife conservation in Africa, such as Paul Matschie and Ludwig Heck.
21. See for example Hubert Hendrichs, *Freinlandbeobachtungen zum Sozialsystem des Afrikanischen Elefanten, Loxodonta Africana* (Blumenbach, 1797), in Hubert Hendrichs and Ursula Hendrichs, *Dikdik und Elefanten. Ökologie und Soziologie zweier afrikanischer Huftiere* (Munich, 1971), 80.
22. SAD Schillings Papers, Folder B: Karl Möbius to Schillings, 12 October 1906.
23. Ryan, *Picturing Empire*, 115; cf. Jens Jäger, "Bilder aus Afrika vor 1918. Zur visuellen Konstruktion Afrikas im europäischen Kolonialismus," in *Visual History. Ein Studienbuch*, ed. Gerhard Paul (Göttingen, 2006), 134–48.
24. "Photographien wilder Tiere," *Illustrirte Jagd-Zeitung* 15 (1887–88): 600; Deac Rossell, *Faszination der Bewegung. Ottomar Anschütz zwischen Photographie und Kino* (Basel, 2001); Paul Hill, *Eadweard Muybridge* (Berlin, 2001). See for example Richard and Cherry Kearton, *Wild Life at Home. How to Study and Photograph It* (London, 1897); Richard and Cherry Kearton, *With Nature and a Camera. Being the Adventures and Observations of a Field Naturalist and an Animal Photographer* (London, 1897).
25. See for Britain Edward North Buxton, *Two African Trips with Notes and Suggestions on Big Game Preservation in Africa* (London, 1902); for the United States, George Shiras, "Photographing Wild Game with Flashlight and Camera," *National Geographic Magazine* 17 (1906): 367–423; Matthew Brower, *Developing Animals. Wildlife and Early American Photography* (Minneapolis, MN, 2011), chapter 2.
26. *Weltausstellung in St. Louis 1904. Amtlicher Katalog Ausstellung des Deutschen Reichs* (Berlin, 1904), 421, 499; *Verhandlungen der Gesellschaft deutscher Naturforscher und Ärzte, 77. Versammlung zu Meran. 24.–30. September 1905*, 2nd part (Leipzig, 1906), 216; Carl Georg Schillings, "Über die Biologie des deutsch-ostafrikanischen Wildes," *Sitzungsberichte der Gesellschaft naturforschender Freunde zu Berlin* (1900): 153–55.
27. SAD Schillings Papers, Folder B, no. 33: Telegraph *Politiken* to Schillings, 14 May 1908; *Politiken*, 9 May 1908, front page.
28. Percy Ernst Schramm, *Neun Generationen. Dreihundert Jahre deutscher "Kulturgeschichte" im Lichte der Schicksale einer Hamburger Bürgerfamilie*, vol. 2 (Göttingen, 1964), 439–40.
29. Ludwig Heck, *Heiter-ernste Lebensbeichte. Erinnerungen eines alten Tiergärtners* (Berlin, 1938), 238; Lutz Heck, *Auf Tiersuche in weiter Welt* (Berlin, 1941), 5–6; cf. Daum, *Wissenschaftspopularisierung im 19. Jahrhundert*, 178–82.
30. Paasche, *Im Morgenlicht*; Berger, *In Afrikas Wildkammern als Forscher und Jäger*, VII; Schomburgk, *Wild und Wilde im Herzen Afrikas*, 10; Arthur Radclyffe Dugmore, *Wild, Wald, Steppe: Waidmannsfahrten mit Kamera und Flinte in Britisch-Ostafrika*, 2nd ed. (Berlin, 1928), 14; Heck, *Auf Tiersuche in weiter Welt*, 5–6.
31. Konrad Schauer, ed., *Kolonial-Ausstellung, veranstaltet vom Ausschuß für Deutsche Kolonial-Propaganda* (s.l. 1918), 65–69; Adam David, "Mit Kinematograph und Büchse in der afrikanischen Wildnis [1908]," *KINtop* 10 (2001): 119–50. On Schillings's experiments with cinematography, which appear to have included scenes of African dances and camp life on safari, see "Der Kinematograph auf

wissenschaftlichen Reisen," *Jahrbuch für Photographie und Reproduktionstechnik* 21 (1907): 317–18. None of the films seems to have survived.
32. See for example Schillings, "Giraffenschlachten in Deutschostafrika," 151–56; Wolfgang Fuhrmann, "Propaganda, Science and Entertainment. Early Colonial Cinematography: A Case Study in the History of Early Nonfiction Cinema" (PhD diss., University of Utrecht, 2003), 225–27.
33. Alexander Lion and Maximilian Bayer, *Jungdeutschlands Pfadfinderbuch* (Leipzig, 1909), 11.
34. "Three African Books," *Country Life*, 2 November 1907 (Clipping in SAD Schillings Papers, Folder B, no. 9).
35. See for example Hauptmann Schöbl, "Die Jagd mit der photographischen Kamera," *Deutsche Jägerzeitung* 55 (1909–10): 401–5.
36. Karen Jones, "'Hunting with the Camera': Photography, Animals and the Technology of the Chase in the Rocky Mountains," in *Wild Things. Nature and the Social Imagination,* ed. William Beinart, Karen Middleton, and Simon Pooley (Stroud, 2013), 24–43; Dunaway, "Hunting with the Camera," 207–30; Ryan, *Picturing Empire,* chapter 4.
37. Henry Seton-Karr, "The Preservation of Big Game," *Journal of the Society for the Preservation of the Wild Fauna of the Empire* 4 (1908): 27.
38. RL, "Flashlight Photographs of Wild Animals," *Nature* (1906), 13 September: 489–90; Harry H Johnston, "Big Game Preservation," *Nature* (1907), 9 May: 34.
39. SAD Schillings Papers, Folder B, fol. 24: Urteile über CG Schillings: "Die Geheimnisse der Steppe," *Berliner Morgenpost* [undated clipping]; "Künstliches Licht," *Jahrbuch für Photographie und Reproduktionstechnik* 21 (1907): 330–32; "Anwendung der Photographie in der Wissenschaft," *Jahrbuch für Photographie und Reproduktionstechnik* 22 (1908): 483–84.
40. On such "visual facts," see Ina Heumann and Axel C Hüntelmann, "Bildtatsachen. Visuelle Praktiken der Wissenschaften," *Berichte zur Wissenschaftsgeschichte* 36 (2013): 283–93.
41. Quoted according to WW Lynkeus, "Über die Bedeutung der Naturphotographie," *Kosmos* 7 (1910): 352.
42. Ludwig Heck, "CG Schillings und sein Erstlingswerk," in Schillings, *Mit Blitzlicht und Büchse,* 4; cf. Richard Neuhauss, "Aufnahmen der afrikanischen Tierwelt," *Photographische Rundschau und photographisches Centralblatt* 18 (1904): 319–23.
43. Donna Haraway, *Primate Visions. Gender, Race, and Nature in the World of Modern Science* (New York, 1989), 42.
44. For a most recent, systematic, and long-term use of camera-trapping to address questions of wildlife ecology see Alexandra Swanson et al., "Snapshot Serengeti, High-Frequency Annotated Camera Trap Images of 40 Mammalian Species in an African Savanna," *Scientific Data* 2 (2015), Article number: 150026.
45. HUB MfN, Zool. Museum S III Schillings, fol. 230: Letter of reference of August Brauer for CG Schillings, 10 August 1906; Otto Schmeil, "Über die Färbung einiger afrikanischer Säugetiere," *Aus der Natur* 1 (1905–6): 24–28; Sokolowsky, *Gesammelte Aufsätze zoologischen Inhalts,* 80–85, 208–12; Konrad Günther, *Vom Tierleben in den Tropen. Für 12–15jährige Schüler aller Schulgattungen* (Leipzig, 1914); Heinrich Fonck, *Wildsteppen und Steppenwild in Ostafrika* (Berlin, 1924), 114.

46. See for example Franz Werner, "Das Ende der Mimikryhypothese?," *Biologisches Centralblatt* 27 (1907): 179.
47. *Brehms Tierleben. Allgemeine Kunde des Tierreichs. Vol. 3: Säugetiere*, 4th ed., ed. Otto zur Strassen (Leipzig, 1915), plate following 642.
48. Gottlieb von Koch, "Über die Modellierung künstlicher Körper für die dermatoplastische Darstellung von Wirbeltieren," *Museumskunde* 1 (1905): 45; Hugo Weigold, "Moderne Dermoplastik. Das Aufstellen von Säugetieren," *Kosmos* 7 (1910): 333; SAD Schillings Papers, Folder C: Letter of recommendation by August Brauer, 16 April 1910.
49. *Berichte der Senckenbergischen Naturforschenden Gesellschaft in Frankfurt am Main* 40 (1909): 31.
50. Theodor Knottnerus-Meyer, "Review of Schillings' Der Zauber des Elelescho," *Der zoologische Garten* 48 (1907): 221.
51. Ryan, *Picturing Empire*, 13, 19.
52. Wilhelm Bölsche, *Weltblick. Gedanken zu Natur und Kunst* (Dresden, 1904), 200-1. See also Dankler, "Nacht- und Fernphotographie," *Der Weidmann* 36 (1905): 195.
53. SAD Schillings Papers, Folder B, Letters: Elisabeth Heyking to Schillings, 6 November 1906.
54. Schillings, *Der Zauber des Elelescho*, 115.
55. See Andrew Lees, *Cities, Sin and Social Reform in Imperial Germany* (Ann Arbor, MI, 2002), 23-48; Georg Bollenbeck, *Eine Geschichte der Kulturkritik. Von Rousseau bis Günther Anders* (Munich, 2007), 206-15.
56. Akira Mizuta Lippit, *Electric Animal. Toward a Rhetoric of Wildlife* (Minneapolis, MN, 2000), 187.
57. Annu Jalais, "Unmasking the Cosmopolitan Tiger," *Nature and Culture* 3, no. 1 (2008): 25-40.
58. "Hunters and Zoo amuse Roosevelt", *New York Times*, 15 May 1910; "Roosevelt to meet Hunters", *New York Times*, 2 April 1910.
59. Thesing, "Der Photograph als Naturforscher!," 631; W Neumärker, "Die Verödung unserer Tierwelt," *Deutsche Jägerzeitung* 56 (1910-11): 359-61.
60. SAD Schillings Papers, Folder B, no. 43: Voigtländer, *Die Jagd mit der Camera. Ein neuer Sport im Dienste der Wissenschaft* (Leipzig, undated); Martin Kiesling, *Anleitung zum Photographieren freilebender Tiere* (Leipzig, 1905); Max Auerbach, "Über Tierphotographien," *Verhandlungen des Naturwissenschaftlichen Vereins in Karlsruhe* 21 (1907-8): 16-17.
61. Hermann Meerwarth, *Lebensbilder aus der Tierwelt* (Leipzig, 1908-12); Georg EF Schulz, *Natur-Urkunden. Biologisch erläuterte photographische Aufnahmen frei lebender Tiere und Pflanzen* (Berlin, 1908-9); Rudolf Zimmermann, *Die Naturphotographie. Eine kurzgefaßte Anleitung zur Pflanzen- und Tierphotografie* (Stuttgart, 1909); Carl Otto Bartels, *Auf frischer Tat. Beobachtungen aus der niederen Tierwelt in Bilderserien nach Natur-Aufnahmen* (Stuttgart, 1910).
62. "Anwendung der Photographie in der Wissenschaft," *Jahrbuch für Photographie und Reproduktionstechnik* 22 (1908): 482.
63. WW Lynkeus, "Über die Bedeutung der Naturphotographie," *Kosmos* 7 (1910): 349-52.
64. Susan Sontag, *On Photography* (Harmondsworth, 1977), 15.
65. Roland Barthes, *La chambre claire. Note sur la photographie* (Paris, 1980).

66. Gerlinde Waz, "Auf der Suche nach dem letzten Paradies. Der Afrikaforscher und Regisseur Hans Schomburgk," in *Triviale Tropen. Exotische Reise- und Abenteuerfilme aus Deutschland 1919–1939*, ed. Jörg Schöning (Munich, 1997), 95–110; Oksiloff, *Picturing the Primitive*, 79–84.
67. Johannes Paulmann, "Jenseits von Eden. Kolonialismus, Zeitkritik und wissenschaftlicher Naturschutz in Bernhard Grzimeks Tierfilmen der 1950er-Jahre," *Zeitschrift für Geschichtswissenschaft* 56 (2008): 544.
68. Heck, *Auf Tiersuche in weiter Welt*, 5–6; Arthur Lindgens, *Wild, Bild und Kugel. Mit 202 Natururkunden des Verfassers aus der Wildbahn* (Stuttgart, 1949), 10; Hardy Krüger, *Eine Farm in Afrika* (Bergisch Gladbach, 2008), 35.
69. Fritz Behn, *"Haizuru ..." Ein Bildhauer in Afrika*, 2nd ed. (Munich, 1918), 21.
70. J Müller, "Wildschutz in Deutsch-Ostafrika," *Deutsche Jägerzeitung* 51 (1908): 166.
71. Schmoll, *Erinnerung an die Natur*.
72. Uekötter, *The Greenest Nation*, 13–14.
73. Schmoll, *Erinnerung an die Natur*, 263–70, 298–99; Raf de Bont, "Poetry and Precision: Johannes Thienemann, the Bird Observatory in Rossitten and Civic Ornithology, 1900–1930," *Journal of the History of Biology* 44 (2011): 174.
74. Rothfels, *Savages and Beasts*, 53–59; Ames, *Carl Hagenbeck's Empire of Entertainments*, 27–31; Annelore Rieke-Müller and Lothar Dittrich, *Der Löwe brüllt nebenan. Die Gründung Zoologischer Gärten im deutschsprachigen Raum 1833–1869* (Cologne, 1998), 201–10.
75. On his biography and role in reforming Germany's natural history museums, see Nyhart, *Modern Nature*, 31, 35–78.
76. Philipp Leopold Martin, *Die Praxis der Naturgeschichte. Ein vollständiges Lehrbuch über das Sammeln lebender und todter Naturkörper; deren Beobachtung, Erhaltung und Pflege im freien und gefangenen Zustand; Konservation, Präparation und Aufstellung in Sammlungen etc.* Vol. 3.2: *Allgemeiner Naturschutz* (Weimar, 1882), 1–53.
77. Nyhart, *Modern Nature*, 107–117.
78. Quotes from A Bütow, "Die Riesen in der Tierwelt und ihr Schicksal," *Blätter für Naturschutz* 5 (1914): 6; Schillings, *Der Zauber des Elelescho*, 336.
79. Karl Sajo, "Ueber aussterbende Tiere," *Prometheus. Illustrirte Wochenschrift über die Fortschritte in Gewerbe, Industrie und Wissenschaft* 7 (1896): 229–33, 246–51, 262–66, 277–80; Paul Matschie, "Deutschlands Säugetierwelt einst und jetzt," *Natur und Haus* 5 (1897): 267; Ernst Schäff, "Das Schicksal der höheren Tierwelt," *Der Weidmann* 31 (1900): 300–1; Schillings, *Mit Blitzlicht und Büchse*, 7–16; O von Linstow, "Ausgestorbne [!] und aussterbende Tiere," *Die Grenzboten* 65 (1906): 313–20; Zell, *Riesen der Tierwelt*; Friedrich Knauer, *Der Niedergang unserer Tier- und Pflanzenwelt. Eine Mahn- und Werbeschrift im Sinne moderner Naturschutzbestrebung* (Leipzig, 1912).
80. Cf. Mark V Barrow Jr, *Nature's Ghosts. Confronting Extinction from the Age of Jefferson to the Age of Ecology* (Chicago, 2009).
81. Schmoll, *Erinnerung an die Natur*, 243–48.
82. Daum, *Wissenschaftspopularisierung im 19. Jahrhundert*, 337–76.
83. Raf de Bont and Geert Vanpaemel, "The Scientist as Activist: Biology and the Nature Protection Movement, 1900–1950," *Environment and History* 18 (2012): 203–8.

84. Baumann, *Usambara und seine Nachbargebiete* (Berlin, 1891), 300.
85. See for example Heinrich Bolau, *Der Elephant in Krieg und Frieden und seine Verwendung in unsern Afrikanischen Kolonien* (Hamburg, 1887); Josef Menges, "Die Verwendbarkeit des Elefanten zur Erschließung Afrikas," *Dr. A. Petermann's geographische Mitteilungen aus Justus Perthes' Geographischer Anstalt* 34 (1888): 276; Heinrich Bokemeyer, *Die Zähmung des Afrikanischen Elefanten. Ergebnisse der bisherigen Erörterung der Frage* (Berlin, 1891), Paul Staudinger, "Die Zähmung des Elefanten," *Deutsche Kolonialzeitung* 8 (1895): 139; Karl Müller, "Der afrikanische Elephant als Lastthier," *Die Natur* 14 (1895): 159–62.
86. Schmoll, *Erinnerung an die Natur*, 115–16.
87. Staatsbibliothek Berlin, Conwentz Papers Box 10, folder 2: Conwentz to Wissmann, 22 November 1901 (draft); Hugo Conwentz, *The Care of Natural Monuments with Special Reference to Great Britain and Germany* (Cambridge, 1909), 33–34, 155.
88. See also Coates, "Creatures Enshrined."
89. Schillings, *Der Zauber des Elelescho*, 117, 492–94. Cf. Michael Wettengel, "Staat und Naturschutz 1906–1945. Zur Geschichte der Staatlichen Stelle für Naturdenkmalpflege in Preußen und der Reichsstelle für Naturschutz," *Historische Zeitschrift* 257 (1993): 355–99.
90. Hugo Salomon, "Sorgen und Forderungen des Naturschutzes," in *La Protección de la Naturaleza en el Mundo. In Memoriam Doctoris Hugo Salomon*, ed. Georges Dennler de la Tour (Buenos Aires, 1957), 27–30, 29.
91. Hugo Salomon, "Bemerkungen zu den Wildschutzverhandlungen auf der Hauptversammlung der Deutschen Kolonialgesellschaft in Hamburg am 3. Juni 1912," *Blätter für Naturschutz* 3, no. 21 (1912): 11–14.
92. Verein Naturschutzpark, *Naturschutzparke in Deutschland und Österreich*, appendix: Aufruf zur Gründung von Naturschutzparken; see Schmoll, *Erinnerung an die Natur*, 212–30, 249–92. By 1913, the VNP had around 16,000 individual members plus 600 corporations; the Bund zur Erhaltung der Naturdenkmäler featured around 2,000 members in the same year.
93. Regensberg and Schillings, "Naturschutzparke in den Kolonien," 54; Kurt Floericke, "Entwicklung, Stand und Aussichten der Naturschutzparkbewegung," in Verein Naturschutzpark, *Naturschutzparke* (1911), 25; Fritz Bley, "Ein deutscher Naturschutzpark," *Tägliche Rundschau* (1910), 10 January: 26–27; Schmoll, *Erinnerung an die Natur*, 228.
94. BAB R 1001/7771, fol. 58: Note on the question raised by the Social Democrats in Parliament, 3 September 1910; BAB R 1001/7771, fol. 25: Bund zur Erhaltung der Naturdenkmäler to RKA, 4 April 1910; fol. 29–30. Arnold Schultze to RKA, 1 February 1910; "Schonung des Großwildes in den Kolonien," *Blätter für Naturschutz* 2 (1911): 35–36.
95. Stoler and Cooper, "Between Metropole and Colony," 5.
96. Wächter, *Naturschutz in den deutschen Kolonien in Afrika*; Rollins, "Imperial Shades of Green," 194 (quote).
97. Rollins, "Imperial Shades of Green"; see also Jens Jäger, "Colony as Heimat? The Formation of Colonial Identity in Germany around 1900," *German History* 27 (2009): 467–89.
98. Elisabeth Krämer-Bannow, *Heimatschutz in den deutschen Kolonien* (Munich, 1913) [Pamphlet of the *Dürerbund*].

99. On the function of the colonies as a mirror see Kundrus, *Moderne Imperialisten.*
100. See for example Alexander Sokolowsky, "Aus dem Leben des Königs der Tiere", in *Gesammelte Aufsätze zoologischen Inhalts,* 120–24; Zell, *Riesen der Tierwelt,* 1–32; Bronsart von Schellendorff, *Novellen aus der afrikanischen Tierwelt* (Leipzig, 1912); Günther, *Vom Tierleben in den Tropen,* 20–21, 28–29; *Brehms Tierleben. Allgemeine Kunde des Tierreichs,* Vol. 3: Säugetiere, 56 (quote).
101. Paasche, "Der Massenmord in Ostafrika"; Paasche, "Deutscher Naturschutz"; Knauer, *Der Niedergang unserer Tier- und Pflanzenwelt,* 69–73; Reinberger, "Tierschutzvereine, Vogelschutz und Jagd," *Deutsche Jägerzeitung* 60 (1912–13): 23–24; Reinberger, "Naturschutz," *Deutsche Jägerzeitung* 60 (1912–13): 629–30; Reinberger, "Jagd und Naturschutz," *Deutsche Jägerzeitung* 61 (1913): 773. For partial vindications of hunting, see Müller-Liebenwalde, "Tierschützler und Jagd," *Deutsche Jägerzeitung* 44 (1904–5): 353–56; Hans Ehrlich, "Die Bewegung für die Erhaltung und Gründung von Naturdenkmälern, beleuchtet vom weidmännischen Standpunkt," *Wild und Hund* 16 (1910): 457–60, 478–81.
102. Schillings, *In Wildest Africa* (1907), 193–94.
103. For a general conceptualization of environmental identity, see Susan Clayton, "Environmental Identity: A Conceptual and Operational Definition," in *Identity and the Natural Environment. The Psychological Significance of Nature,* ed. Susan Clayton and Susan Opotow (Cambridge, MA, 2003), 45–66.
104. Philipp Freiherr von Böselager, "Ueber Akklimatisirung [!]," *Der Weidmann* 22 (1891): 205–6, 213–14. See also Konrad Günther, *Der Naturschutz* (Freiburg, 1910), 232.
105. Wilhelm Schuster, "Deutsche Känguruhs," *Deutsche Jägerzeitung* 43 (1904): 545–46, 672; Hermann Löns, "Die Moorhühner in der Provinz Hannover," *Deutsche Jägerzeitung* 44 (1904–5): 662; Nikolaus Schiller-Tietz, "Die Einbürgerung fremder Vogelarten in Deutschland," *Der Weidmann* 37 (1906): 932–34; M Hübner, "Mufflons im Unterharz," *Deutsche Jägerzeitung* 52 (1908–9): 723–24; "Einbürgerungsversuche," *Der Weidmann* 40 (1909): 278–79; Freiherr von Loewenstern, "Erstes Muffelwild im Taunus," *Deutsche Jägerzeitung* 60 (1912–13): 385–89; Oskar Tesdorpf, "Die Ausbreitung des Muffelwildes in Deutschland," *Deutsche Jägerzeitung* 63 (1914): 703–4.
106. Wilhelm Bölsche, "Die deutsche Landschaft", in *Von Sonnen und Sonnenstäubchen. Kosmische Wanderungen* (Berlin, 1903), 69.
107. Iris Borowy, "The Other Side of Bio-Invasion. The Acclimatisation Movement in Germany," in *Invasive and Introduced Plants and Animals: Human Perceptions, Attitudes and Approaches to Management,* eds. Ian D Rotherham and Rob Lambert (London, 2011), 153–66.
108. Wallace, *The Geographical Distribution of Animals.* The volume was translated into German in the very year of its publication in 1876.
109. Most participants in the debate referred to "Germany's" original landscape.
110. The controversy focused, amongst others, on the capacity of large herbivores to maintain an open landscape. Therefore, references to the contemporary spread and behavior of African megafauna were an important aspect of the debate. See Alfred Nehring, *Ueber Tundren und Steppen der Jetzt- und Vorzeit, mit besonderer Berücksichtigung ihrer Fauna* (Berlin, 1890), 137–38; August Wollemann, "Über die Diluvialsteppe," *Verhandlungen des Naturhistorischen Vereins der*

Preussischen Rheinlande, Westfalens und des Reg.-Bezirks Osnabrück 45 (1888): 239–91; Robert Gradmann, "Das mitteleuropäische Landschaftsbild nach seiner geschichtlichen Entwicklung," *Geographische Zeitschrift* 7 (1901): 361–77, 435–47; Ratzel, "Die deutsche Landschaft."

111. Stromer von Reichenbach, "Die einstige Verbreitung afrikanischer Säugetiere," 816. Matschie, "Deutschlands Säugetierwelt einst und jetzt," 261–67; Kurt Lampert, "Deutschlands Tierwelt im Wechsel historischer Zeiten," *Berichte der Senckenbergischen Naturforschenden Gesellschaft* (1918): 59.
112. Wilhelm Bölsche, *Die deutsche Landschaft in Vergangenheit und Gegenwart* (Berlin, 1915), 65.
113. See Jawad Daheur, "Les usages identitaires de l'élan et du bison en Allemagne, en Pologne et à Kaliningrad: Étude de six sculptures monumentales de la fin du XIXe siècle à nos jours," *Trajectoires* 7 (2013). http://trajectoires.revues.org/1111.
114. Wilhelm Kuhnert, *Im Lande meiner Modelle* (Leipzig, 1918), 3; Emil Friese, *Richard Friese. Ein deutsches Künstlerleben* (Berlin, 1930), 20, 46.
115. Quoted according to Schmoll, *Erinnerung an die Natur*, 228; Hermann Löns, *Die Erhaltung unserer Tierwelt* (Munich, 1913), 1.
116. "Ein großer Naturschutzpark im Harz," *Blätter für Naturschutz* 3, no. 18 (1912): 23; Susanne Ude-Koeller, *Auf gebahnten Wegen. Zum Naturdiskurs am Beispiel des Harzklubs e.V.* (Münster, 2004), 227–29.
117. On Eastern Europe as continental German frontier, see Robert L Nelson, ed., *Germans, Poland, and Colonial Expansion to the East, 1850 through the Present* (New York, 2009); David Blackbourn, *The Conquest of Nature. Water, Landscape, and the Making of Modern Germany* (London, 2006), chapter 5; Jeffrey K Wilson, "Environmental Chauvinism in the Prussian East: Forestry as a Civilizing Mission on the Ethnic Frontier, 1871–1914," *Central European History* 41 (2008): 27–70.
118. See Bernhard Gissibl, "Frevert und die großen Tiere. Jagd, Herrschaft und der Schutz von 'Urnatur' zwischen 'deutschem Osten', Schwarzwald und Ostafrika," in *Kontinuitäten im Naturschutz Deutschlands nach 1945*, ed. Nils M. Franke and Uwe Pfenning (Baden-Baden, 2014), 107-131; Thaddeus Sunseri, "Exploiting the *Urwald*. German Post-Colonial Forestry in Poland and Central Africa, 1900–1960," *Past & Present* 214 (2012): 305–42.
119. Bernhard Gissibl, "A Bavarian Serengeti. Space, Race and Time in the Entangled History of Nature Conservation in East Africa and Germany," in *Civilizing Nature. National Parks in Global Historical Perspective*, ed. Bernhard Gissibl, Sabine Höhler, and Patrick Kupper (Oxford, 2012), 102–19.

Epilogue
Germany's African Wildlife and the Presence of the Past

"Over the last decades, all civilized nations of the world have introduced zones of nature protection and game reserves, both in the motherlands and in the colonies. Germany, for example, had identified the giant crater Ngorongoro in former German East Africa as a *Naturschutzgebiet*. With its 300 square kilometres and around 50,000 heads of game … it is the greatest natural zoo."[1] This bold conversion of the conservationist failure of 1914 into retrospective achievement was the message of a huge relief representation of the Ngorongoro crater that formed part of the section on nature conservation at the International Hunting Exhibition held in Berlin in November 1937. Under the auspices of the Nazi's chief hunter and forester Hermann Göring, the exhibition convened hunters from all over the world to showcase the Nazi state as pioneer in the stewardship and management of the wild, shortly after the enactment of new game and nature conservation laws in 1934 and 1935.[2] An entire section of the trophy show was dedicated to the former colonies to remind visitors of Germany's continuing claim to the restoration of its former overseas empire.[3] So should the relief of Ngorongoro, and visitors to the exhibition were unaware of the irony that it was in fact the loss of the colonies after World War I that had allowed for Ngorongoro's survival as nature's largest zoo.

The propagandistic utilization of Ngorongoro testifies to the continued engagement of German hunters and nature protectionists with Africa's wildlife after 1918. Germany's forced decolonization at the hands of the Allies in 1918–19 had little impact upon the ongoing allure of the mediatized as well as the embodied encounter with Africa's wild fauna. Tanganyika remained a preferred site for Germans willing to engage with African nature and wildlife. From the mid 1920s, German settlers were allowed to return to the colony. By 1939, they even outnumbered the British.[4] Among those returning were Friedrich Wilhelm Siedentopf, Konrad Schauer, and Margarete Trappe, whose safari enterprises were popular especially among visiting German hunters.[5] While Kenya remained more easily accessible, the Germans in Tanganyika now provided the contact points for those desirous of combining their safari with the support of the German colonial diaspora abroad.[6] Particularly Trappe's farm Momella afoot the Mount Meru developed into the center of attraction for German big game hunters between the wars. After her death in 1957, big game hunters of wealth and reputation, among them Eugen Gerstenmaier, then president of the West German Parliament and head of the German branch of the World Wildlife Fund (WWF), tried to retain this *lieu de mémoire* of German big game hunting in Tanganyika in German hands. In 1963, the actor Hardy Krüger, of *Hatari* fame, took over Momella Game Lodge and romanticized Momella as the German equivalent to Karen Blixen's "farm in Africa."[7] As late as 2007, a German TV production entitled *Momella* continued the vein of Karen Blixen–style mystification by presenting white huntress Margarete Trappe as Germany's forgotten colonial heroine who braved the wilds of Africa. The film showed no interest whatsoever in the enabling structures of colonial rule, the context of Maasai displacement or the colonial politics of wilderness and big game hunting.[8]

In the various forms of cultural productions that dealt with the former German colonies in Africa in the 1920s and 1930s, the established stereotypes of a wildlife paradise became charged with revisionist agendas. Although numbering but a few thousands, settlers, soldiers, and colonial officials returning from the colonies filled the pages of the hunting and colonial press. A flurry of book-length melancholic hunting memories fostered the German bond with wild nature at the same time as they bewailed the former colony as a lost and locked paradise.[9] Older travelogues were edited anew, and in 1921, the newly established *Safari-Verlag* dedicated its program to the popularization of the colonies, adventure, travel, and zoology, thereby becoming one of the leading publishers in popular nonfiction in Germany.[10] However, it was the screen that attained a pivotal role in perpetuating the colonial myth of the African game paradise. As mentioned above, Schillings's visualization of Africa as a threatened paradise of wildlife was continued in films like Hans Schomburgk's *Das letzte Paradies* (1932), *Die Wildnis stirbt* (1936), or Bernhard Grzimek's *Kein Platz für wilde Tiere* (1956) and *Serengeti shall not die* (1959). The seemingly unchanging constellation of a primeval paradise endangered by the forces of "civilization" should, however, not obliterate important shifts in their appeal to German audiences. In Schillings's pictures, the threatened wildlife of the savanna embodied an original harmony of the wild that was threatened by German colonialism itself. The lost paradise in the films of Schomburgk stood as a proxy for Germany's lost colonial empire, a subtext that was still present in Grzimek's wildlife films of the 1950s. But after World War II, it was exactly the early loss of this colonial empire that enabled Grzimek to intervene as an allegedly disinterested advocate of wildlife. After the experience of another war, the innocence of African wilderness as seen through the lens of Grzimek's camera embodied the eternal good and noble of nonhuman nature in opposition to the destructive potential of human civilization.[11]

The propagandistic reinterpretation of Ngorongoro by the Nazi hunter conservationists in 1937 also shows that Germans continued to actively engage with the conservation of East Africa's wildlife. Of course, this engagement was greatly diminished in scope, and for decades, largely virtual. World War I and the loss of the colonies had provided a setback in several respects. The deaths of Hans Paasche and Carl Georg Schillings in 1920 and 1921 silenced the most knowledgeable and outspoken advocates of conservation and dealt an enormous blow to Germany's global environmental conscience. Hugo Salomon, another dedicated champion of colonial conservation, emigrated to Argentina in 1921 where he became an important figure in South American nature protection until his death in 1954.[12] There was no one to follow in their footsteps until Bernhard Grzimek appeared on the scene in the middle of the 1950s. The country's political isolation after World War I also affected the networks of Paul Sarasin and severed many of the transnational ties among the movement for *Weltnaturschutz*.[13] Germany was neither represented at the international conferences on nature conservation in Paris in 1923 and 1931, nor at the successor conference that updated the London Convention in 1933. This said, concern for wildlife conservation also found new platforms for discussion, such as the *Gesellschaft für Säugetierkunde* (Society for Mammalian Zoology) founded in Berlin in 1926. Among its members were a considerable number of the zoologists and colonial officials who had been engaged in colonial conservation before the war.[14] German conservation periodicals continued to monitor developments in African conservation, using the slightest opportunity to criticize British policies in Tanganyika.[15] Unsullied by direct responsibility, a new generation of hunter-conservationists convinced itself that Germany had not only been "among the first, but also the nation that took more comprehensive measures than all the other colonial powers to conserve the game. Also on the Black Continent, we had not forgotten that nature is entrusted to man for protection."[16]

Such myths of Germans pioneering the field of game conservation in colonial Africa underwrote aspirations of Nazi conservationists to reestablish Germany in the arena of international conservation.[17] One of the driving forces behind these efforts was Walther Schoenichen, a trained biologist who had taken over from Conwentz as director of the Prussian State Agency in 1922.[18] The agency was turned into the Reichsstelle für Naturschutz in 1936 and held, among others, responsibility for international conservation. For Schoenichen, colonies represented the territorialized entitlement to participate in international conservation. Addressing the fourth national convention of German conservationists in Berlin in 1931, Schoenichen regretted that Germany, deprived of its colonies, could not participate in the grand project of large-scale nature preservation in foreign continents, however, only "for the time being."[19] It was his Reichsstelle that reclaimed Ngorongoro as a German *Naturschutzgebiet* at the International Hunting Exhibition in Berlin, and anticipating the second coming of German rule in the former colonies, Schoenichen proposed to form a commission for colonial nature conservation and the establishment of national parks in 1937. Because all powers holding territory in Africa and South East Asia had embraced the idea of the national park, Germany should equally articulate its willingness and qualification to contribute to colonial preservation. His efforts to bring Germany back into the civilizing mission of conservation culminated in concrete plans for an international conference on nature conservation, to be held in Berlin in 1939. The protection of the tropical megafauna featured prominently on the agenda.

However, neither did the conference materialize, nor did Schoenichen's comprehensive motion find support among the higher echelons of Nazi conservation.[20] Schoenichen found his Reichsstelle increasingly marginalized by the Reichsforstamt, the imperial ministry created by Hermann Göring in 1934 to monopolize responsibility for game, forestry, and nature protection. Still, several of Schoenichen's propositions resurfaced when conservationists staked their claim in the economic planning for the future takeover of Germany's former African colonies. In February 1940, the Ministry of Economy urged the association of German colonial enterprises (*Gruppe Deutscher Kolonialwirtschaftlicher Unternehmungen, Deko*) to submit comprehensive plans about the current economic potential of the former German colonies, including methods at its realization and improvement under a future German administration.[21] These plans, labeled "instant programs" (*Sofortprogramme*), were classified as top secret and consisted of one part that outlined the current state and another that contained the future plans for administration and development.

Eager to emphasize that conservation needed to take space and that colonies consisted of more than exploitable resources,[22] the task to elaborate on "Forestry, hunting and fishery in German East Africa" was assigned to Hermann Eidmann and Christoph Graf Dönhoff. Eidmann was an entomologist of standing and head of the department for colonial zoology in the scientific branch of the Reichsforschungsrat; Dönhoff, the brother of the renowned postwar publisher Marion Gräfin Dönhoff, had a prehistory as settler in Kenya and held a post in the colonial department of the Nazi party's foreign branch (Auslandsorganisation) in 1940.[23] During 1940 and 1941, he was also associated as a consultant in matters of colonial hunting and game conservation to the Reichsforstamt. Relatively unknown in the literature on Nazi conservation, the Reichsforstamt temporarily featured a colonial department. There, Dönhoff elaborated on the "future obligations of the German people towards African nature" and conceived of a comprehensive framework legislation for hunting and conservation in all former German colonies in Africa, together with the Austrian big game hunter Ernst Alexander Zwilling.[24]

This framework legislation was crafted parallel to the system of colonial conservation Eidmann and Dönhoff elaborated for the Deko. In their detail and in their comprehensiveness, they were most impressive pieces of imaginary planning and racialized environmentalism.[25] Yet, exactly because they were imaginary, the schemes are so significant because they reveal the allure of dictatorial regimes for authoritarian conservationism, or in Dönhoff's words, a conservation regime in which all the "tedious procedures" associated with parliamentary deliberations were replaced by the stroke of a pen of "centralized responsibility."[26] Dönhoff and Eidmann's scheme was predicated upon the assumption that the regulations currently in force under the British in East Africa were basically sound, but inadequately applied. Future hunting regulations would have to come down on indigenous hunting as the main threat to the game and establish as a principle that hunting was the sole prerogative of the "master race" (*Herrenvolk*). With a view to conservation, the draft took the reserves established by the British as the "natural nucleus" for the protected areas to be established. Combining concepts from the German conservationist tradition and the categories established by the conference on African wildlife conservation held in London in 1933, Eidmann and Dönhoff envisioned a differentiated system that included game reserves, nature reserves, national parks, preserved landscapes, and natural monuments. While the game reserves took up the idea of producing overflow for the surrounding country, nature reserves afforded stricter protection of all fauna and flora within them. While all reserves established under British rule were to be retained, and as in the case of the Serengeti, considerably extended in size, further reserves on Lake Manyara, along River Sassawara and the coast should be added. The Serengeti, Lake Manyara, the Selous, and Lake Rukwa were to be developed into national parks accessible to the public, while a wildlife research institute with smaller dependencies should use the national parks as laboratories for zoological fieldwork.[27] In addition, the framework regulation for hunting explicitly entitled the future governor to remove indigenous residents from protected areas without compensation.[28] Obviously, the program never faced the test of practice, including all the likely conflicts with other imperial agendas such as the development of agriculture. But it anticipated many of the institutions and practices that the transnational elite of conservationists around Bernhard Grzimek would introduce with the financial support of international conservationist organizations in postindependence Tanzania twenty years later.[29]

Germans laid the basis of Tanzania's environmental conservation complex before 1914 and engaged in impressive exercises at imaginary conservation during the 1930s and 1940s. The internationalization of East African conservation since the middle of the 1950s, then, paved the way for their active return. The colonial powers' gradual retreat from accountability at the eve of Tanzanian independence not only meant that Western-dominated international conservationist organizations like IUCN, UNESCO, and WWF increasingly took over stewardship for East African wildlife since the late 1950s.[30] This transfer of imperial responsibility also allowed German conservationists to reappear actively on the scene as "honest brokers,"[31] seemingly untainted by colonial baggage or other obvious stakes in East African conservation. Bernhard Grzimek's books and films came too late to intervene directly in the late colonial debates over the boundaries of the Serengeti National Park so that he failed to achieve the demarcation of the national park's boundaries according to the seasonal migration patterns of the wildebeest that the Grzimeks had established by aerial survey.[32] However, the film turned Grzimek into a conservation celebrity and bestowed him with expert status, which, together with well-orchestrated publicity campaigns and a weekly series in West German TV, provided the Frankfurt Zoo director and his zoological society with other means to wield influence on the future management of wildlife conservation in Tanzania. Apart from his informal counseling of Tanzanian Prime Minister Julius Nyerere in matters of wildlife conservation, he coordinated Western NGOs, including the fledgling German branch of the WWF, in funding the rapid growth of protected areas in Tanzania during the 1960s. Moreover, he solicited German development aid to contribute to the founding of the College of African Wildlife Management in Mweka in 1963.[33] Not only did Mweka's teaching staff feature several adventuring German game managers in the initial decades, but grants and stipends from German development funds also enabled the future education of wardens. Above all, Grzimek became the single most important campaigner to raise public awareness in Germany to the plight of wildlife worldwide and in East Africa in particular. Unlike Schillings half a century earlier, Grzimek tapped the visual media's potential for fundraising. In 1961, he set off a fundraising campaign to "help the endangered wildlife" (*Hilfe für die bedrohte Tierwelt*) that transformed the heretofore vicarious conservationist concern of his TV audience into direct cosmopolitan engagement through donations. The money thus collected enabled Grzimek and the Frankfurt Zoological Society (ZGF) to funnel funds into the management, personnel, and antipoaching campaigns not only, but especially in the Serengeti

National Park, which expanded gradually at the cost of the Maasai since the 1960s. At least parts of the money that German schoolchildren or animal-loving elderly ladies donated to Grzimek for the preservation of Africa's wildlife financed the rifles of an antipoaching patrol or the village settlement officer supervising the removal of homesteads that threatened the ecological integrity of the park. The ZGF further invested into wildlife education campaigns in Tanzanian schools as well as in villages all over the country. ZGF-sponsored posters tried to inculcate the country's wildlife and national parks as a national heritage that should be valued by the modern Tanzanian citizen—because this wildlife was cherished by people all over the world, because it brought revenue into the country, and because it was "civilized" to do so. Finally, ZGF funds and money solicited from the German Fritz Thyssen Foundation contributed significantly to the foundation of another multidonor project, the Serengeti Research Institute (SRI) at Seronera.[34] Among the international researchers flocking to Seronera during the 1960s and early 1970s were a considerable number of ethologists from Konrad Lorenz's Max-Planck-Institute for Behavioral Physiology in Seewiesen, who studied the sociology and behavior of wild dogs, elephants, lions, or hyraxes.[35] West German science and funding, thus, helped turning the Serengeti into an ecological and ethological laboratory of international significance for research into savanna ecosystems, and the SRI bolstered the conservation fortress through the production of scientific knowledge that helped eclipse the human ecology of the area.[36]

The Grzimek approach to wildlife conservation in the 1960s and 1970s was marked by the path dependencies of colonial conservation. Empire was replaced by humankind as the legitimizing moral instance of conservation, but otherwise, wildlife was preserved for the consumption of first and foremost Euro-American tourists capable of affording the necessary expenses of time and travel. Western funding and scientific expertise supported the centralized state in its appropriation of the coercive potential of protected areas as well as in its utilization of wildlife as a source of revenue—another strategy of "extraversion" at the cost of the local population. In the critical climate of decolonization, Grzimek scorned big game hunting as an ideologically tainted form of utilizing game, which he deemed untenable if the mission of teaching Africans the value of wildlife preservation was to be successful. Regarded also as economically dispensable, hunting was in fact banned in Tanzania between 1973 and 1978. The photo safari carried the day, promoted since the late 1950s by Grzimek as a civilized, peaceful, and seemingly noninterventive form of encountering Africa's charismatic wildlife. Like other ecologists at the time, Grzimek believed the merely visual embodied encounter from a safari car to be compatible with both mass tourism and the ecological balance within national parks.

By the middle of the 1980s, the ivory crisis and the economic failure of Tanzania's socialist Ujamaa policies, rampant poaching, human-wildlife conflicts, rural poverty on the borders of protected areas and unexpected ecological dynamics within parks had exposed the flaws of the fortress and hands off-approach to conservation.[37] The temporary ban of tourist hunting had turned out to exacerbate the problem as it removed the presence of tourist hunters and safari outfitters as an at least informal check on poaching. These developments corresponded with a shift toward sustainability in international conservationist discourse, which envisioned parks no longer merely as spaces where wild nature was "set aside," but strove to integrate protected areas and development in an attempt to render conservation both ecologically and socially sustainable.[38] One consequence was the emergence of community-based resource management (CBRM) as a paradigm that promised to allow for more flexible, market-led, and participatory forms of sustainable conservation.[39] Again, German conservationist organizations were crucially involved in the implementation of this paradigm in Tanzania. Hesitantly and partially forced by the emergence of vociferous pastoralist NGOs in Maasailand, the ZGF included community-based conservation schemes into its management practices in the Serengeti-Ngorongoro area by the late 1990s. Earlier, the NGO was already involved in the measures to secure the survival of the Selous Game Reserve through CBRM since the middle of the 1980s. Elevated to the status of a World Natural Heritage by UNESCO in 1982 for its enormous extent, variety of vegetation zones, and "the world's largest protected populations of elephants, crocodiles, hippos, and black rhinos,"[40] a survey conducted by the ZGF in 1986 found the stocks of elephants and rhinoceroses alarmingly depleted. Poverty induced by evictions and resettlement from the reserve during the Ujamaa villagization programs as well as world market demands for ivory had stimulated illegal hunting, and elephant numbers in the Selous slumped from 110,000 in 1976 to 55,000 in 1986 and around 32,000 in 1989. The government's response was twofold and consisted of policing first, participation later: in June 1989 it launched Operation *Uhai* ("Life"), a nationwide campaign to come down on illegal elephant hunting. Within two years, more than 2,000 people were arrested in ill-documented operations that involved the military, police, and the staff of wildlife authorities.[41] While the exertion of state violence brought "poaching" to a short-range halt, but entrenched the hostilities between communities and reserve management, the introduction of community-based wildlife management was expected to reduce illegal hunting in the medium term by allowing villages in the vicinity of the Selous to share in the reserve's revenue. The ZGF survey had formed the basis of a report submitted to the Tanzanian government in 1987, which proposed a multidonor emergency program for the rehabilitation of the reserve. Personal networks and an initiative by the German Embassy in Dar es Salaam achieved that the Tanzanian government entered into the joint Selous Conservation Programme (SCP) with the official agency for German Development Cooperation, the Gesellschaft für technische Zusammenarbeit (GTZ) in 1987.[42] Initially conceived of as a one-year emergency program cofinanced by the German organizations GTZ and ZGF, the U.S.-based African Wildlife Foundation, and WWF International, the SCP evolved into an official commitment of the German Ministry of Development to assist in the sustainable management of the Selous. Altogether, it consumed well over twenty million euros, more than half of which was German taxpayers' money, until the cooperation was halted after sixteen years in 2003.

The SCP was among the first community-based conservation programs in Tanzania. At its inception, it was an equally novel approach for the GTZ. The organization had had little experience with wildlife management before. The SCP was an opportunity to learn, broaden its portfolio, and flag its engagement in the burgeoning field of sustainable development. Significantly, if management expertise for Africa's wildlife was assumed by hunter-naturalists before 1914 and by ecologists in the 1960s, now the economists took over. The project evolved in stages. After the foremost target to curb illegal hunting was achieved—also with the help of Operation *Uhai*—the next step was to restore managerial and financial sustainability to the reserve. The Selous had the status of a game reserve, also because it lacked the infrastructure for game viewing on a mass basis. Therefore, strictly monitored commercial hunting had always been admitted, but still suffered from the hunting ban in the 1970s and a lack of capitalist enterprise. The SCP helped to boost and privatize the hunting industry, and a high-profile tourist hunting was to become the financial mainstay of the reserve. If in 1991, just over one hundred tourist hunters flocked to the Selous, their number had more than quadrupled by 2001. Revenue generated from the return of the white hunters contributed up to 90 percent of the Selous Game Reserve's income and filled the coffers of the wildlife division in the Ministry of Natural Resources and Tourism. The GTZ achieved to negotiate a retention scheme by 1994 that allowed the Selous Game Reserve management to retain 50 percent of the revenue gained from photographic and safari tourism for the reserve's management.[43]

Although some of the income from the retention scheme was shared voluntarily with communities, it was never intended to base the management of the Selous Game Reserve on a joint or at least more equal footing. Rather, the third step of the SCP foresaw to invest communities located in the buffer zones around the Selous Game Reserve with management and utilization rights of wildlife on their own lands. After decades of bearing the costs of conservation, this was a gesture of compensation for the loss of crops and human life at the hands of wildlife. Granting participatory management was also an attempt to elicit support for conservation and an effort to diversify rural livelihood strategies and make wildlife a valued part of them. Communities were encouraged to set up land use plans and to form local wildlife committees to decide how the allocated wildlife quota were to be used and what should be done with the fees realized from sustainable wildlife utilization. To this end, the Wildlife Management Area (WMA) was introduced as a new category of protected area that implicated the devolution of management rights to so-called authorized associations at the communal level. However, although the new Tanzanian Wildlife policy drafted in 1998 included a pledge to devolution and the introduction of WMAs, the practical implementation of such policies were deferred time and again to frustrate the GTZ into phasing out its commitment to the SCP in 2003. After sixteen years, the community-based development scheme had never reached a stage beyond the pilot status of roughly 80 participating villages waiting to establish WMAs. Looking back on the project, its practitioners had to admit that, while the conservationist side of stopping wildlife loss had been fully achieved, its attempts at devolution and community participation remained extremely wanting.[44]

The German engagement in the SCP emphasizes the lasting and profound nature of the country's involvement in wildlife conservation in its former East African colony over the twentieth century. Since the colonial period, the fate of Tanzania's wildlife has also depended on decisions and actions taken in Berlin, Frankfurt, or for that matter, Eschborn, where the offices of the GTZ are located. The German-Tanzanian development cooperation to safeguard the Selous is also a vivid reminder of the ongoing presence of the colonial past in today's conservation. From the outset, the SCP confronted the enormous task of redressing the legacy of almost a century of conservation against the people in South Central Tanzania. This legacy comprised the transformation of indigenous hunting into illegitimate poaching through colonial legislation, one of the measures that triggered Maji Maji. It continued with the depopulations of Maji Maji and the East African Campaign of World War I, which enabled the further extension of the Mahenge reserve, the Matandu River Reserve northeast of Liwale, and the Upper Rufiji Reserve, respectively, their integration into one enormous reserve in 1922. Named the Selous Game Reserve, the area not only became the largest game sanctuary on the African continent, but also a memorial dedicated to the memory of a notorious British imperialist, big game hunter, and "penitent butcher"—Frederick Courteney Selous, who had died in the northern part of the later reserve during the East African campaign in 1917.[45] Resettlement schemes related to British measures against sleeping sickness between the 1920s and 1940s, and the Ujamaa villagizations of the 1970s, continued the process of removing human habitation to make way for wilderness.[46] Operation *Uhai* was but the last instance of violent state intervention in order to protect wildlife as a resource for the gain of the central state and rent-seeking elites in its ministries. Although the SCP partnership helped to bring about a new wildlife policy that contained a pledge to devolution, the fate of community conservation in the Selous and the gradual abandonment of the retention scheme since 2003 suggest that governmental elites ultimately had little interest in sharing benefits and rights with local communities. Some observers ascribed this reluctance to corruption and a deliberate lack of transparency in the running of the lucrative hunting sector,[47] others discern a general "pattern of nominal decentralization followed by the re-assertion of bureaucratic control" that has been characteristic also of other policy fields in Tanzania in the last decade.[48] These developments, together with plans of dam construction and uranium ore mining within the borders of the reserve, have spurred the UNESCO to issue a serious warning to the Tanzanian government to guarantee the integrity of the World Heritage Site. Since 2012, the Frankfurt Zoological Society has taken up where the GTZ has left and engages in a ten-year development scheme, the foremost aim of which being once more to safeguard the integrity of Africa's largest protected area.[49]

Seen in a long-term perspective, the defiance of effective devolution in the SCP means nothing else than the continuation of a century of wildlife ownership by the centralized state. The structural inequalities and governance constellations that characterized East African conservation since its colonialist origins—a strong central state responsible less to the people it governs but to foreign donors that finance its functioning, the political impact of outside experts and conservationist organizations, and a marginalized local population still bearing the main cost of conservation—appear equally persistent. So is the link between tourism and conservation to render the natural capital of wildlife productive, and so, too, is the appropriation of wildlife value for the state: In the decades of direct colonial rule, the Germans first exploited, later conserved elephants to support their state-building. Fifty years later under the counseling of Bernhard Grzimek, the revenue from the capitalist-conservationist appropriation of wildlife contributed to the functioning of Tanzania as a "state of nature" (Elizabeth Garland) after independence. The most recent instance of deferred devolution shows just how closely wildlife and Tanzanian statehood have been entwined. To be sure, the GTZ's pressure for "good governance" and community participation was serious and more than lip service to the latest development speak. But as much as it shows that the alliance between Tanzanian state and some Western donors has not remained unquestioned, one should not expect too much in terms of democratization via conservation. As revolutionary as the discursive twinning of conservation and community rights has been after almost a century of exclusion, there is no community development project without official approval. And when it comes to the crunch between communities and state, conservationist NGOs usually know what side to take. Ultimately, their agenda is the benefit of wildlife and protected areas, not the promotion of human rights.

Finally, also the reinvention of big game hunting as a form of sustainable utilization and pro-poor development in CBRM discourse is only a departure of sorts. Drawing attention away from protected areas to the necessity of wildlife management beyond their borders is surely a step forward, and if based on scientifically grounded quota, the limited off-take of trophy hunting can be arranged without negative long-term effects for the overall population of the respective species. However, selling big game hunting as a form of responsible ecotourism glosses over the questionable ethics and history of trophy hunting, and it reinforces the old paternalism of the white hunter who distributes the spoil of his hunting among hapless villagers, albeit now in the form of money rather than meat. Above all, it mobilizes once more the well-established ideological imaginaries in the related tourist industries. One safari camp in the reserve advertises that no other safari in Tanzania would "evoke the romance, mystique and spiritual delight of the African bush as one in the Selous Game Reserve." Another outfitter promises that only there "visitors can experience the pristine splendour and beauty—as well as the sense of adventure in Africa—that those like Selous enjoyed."[50] Such a marketing blend of imperial nostalgia with myths of originality is not innocent. When we deny, Roderick Neumann argued, "the role of the human hand in shaping landscape, we contribute to the validation of a particular historical narrative of European imperialism."[51] To this day, the images deployed by a thriving and competitive tourist industry perpetuate the mental colonization of Africa as a "pristine" and heterotopian wildlife paradise.

In 2010, the German Delegation of the International Council of Game and Wildlife Conservation (CIC), a high-profile transnational lobby organization of hunters, and the Tanzanian Wildlife Division unveiled a plaque at the entrance gate of the Selous Game Reserve in Mtemere.[52] It reminds visitors that it was Imperial Governor Hermann von Wissmann who established a first reserve along the Upper Rufiji in 1896. In theory, such markers of human history in an area otherwise traded as wilderness have the potential to attract a different kind of cultural tourism to the Selous, if contextualized and supplemented with other memorials, for example, to the core sites of Maji Maji. Currently, however, the memorial panel lacks any historical context of conquest and oppression, so that it forges a one-sided myth of a progressive German colonial policy that bestowed Africa with one of its oldest protected areas.

Just a few months earlier in 2009, the practitioners of the SCP published *The Wild Heart of Africa*, a lavishly illustrated coffee-table book that digested their experiences of one and a half decades of conservationist engagement in Tanzania's largest game reserve.[53] Published with Rowland Ward, the world's authoritative publisher in the field of big game hunting and wildlife since imperial times, the book is a melancholic memorial to the lifework and dedication of these development experts. It also provides insight into the sometimes dangerous and often frustrating day-to-day practicalities of running a protected area that is about five times the size of Switzerland. The book's 268 pages are a plea for a pragmatic approach to conservation that includes trophy hunting as a form of sustainable utilization and an urgent call to continue the path of community-based conservation. Reviews in hunting and wildlife-related periodicals oscillated between benevolent and enthusiastic and suggest that the book succeeded in drawing the attention of the international hunting and conservation community to the current state of affairs in the Selous.

At the same time, *The Wild Heart of Africa* is a traditional, if not revisionist, German book about Africa. Colonial nostalgia and antipoaching heroism loom large; the chapters relish in outdoor adventure, rifles, big game, and helicopter patrols. Descriptions of the various species of the Selous are juxtaposed with uncritical and incomplete accounts of colonial wars and policies, heroic stories of the area's European exploration, excerpts of colonial period hunting tales, and a detailed investigation of Frederick Courtney Selous's rifles. The book's visual program is equally ambivalent. Wilhelm Kuhnert's ideologically charged depictions of majestic African game from the years of the Maji Maji War are placed, without contextualizing comment, alongside photographs of animals, convicted "poachers," or armed and uniformed game rangers in action. One particularly noteworthy picture of a helicopter, probably on antipoaching patrol, is subtitled "Ride of the Valkyrie," alluding, of course, to the iconic scene of the helicopter attack in Francis Ford Coppola's Vietnam saga *Apocalypse Now*.[54] Probably the editors themselves were unaware to the cynical truth behind applying the visual language of asymmetrical imperial warfare to recent practices of wildlife conservation. Such pictures, as well as a chapter on the eternal war between hunters and poachers, sensationalize the harsh realities of the struggles over the legitimate access to wildlife at the same time as they trivialize them. Little is done to make readers understand the social and political realities and economies behind "poaching." A dedication to Mzee Madogo, a poacher turned trustworthy warden, notwithstanding, few chapters are written by Tanzanians, and if so, they are comparatively short, written by people affiliated to the reserve and its administration, and largely reciprocate Western conservationist discourse. There are virtually no voices from the villages that the SCP was supposed to integrate, also, because no contributor could be identified. Still, this omission is not accidental but structural. *The Wild Heart of Africa* is not their book, as little as the Selous has been their reserve. Instead, the volume is marked by an unreflected glorification of colonial conservation and the imaginary ownership of "our" African wildlife. *The Wild Heart of Africa* leaves the uncomfortable feeling that the nature of German imperialism not only stood at the beginning of Tanzanian wildlife conservation. Its key elements have retained an unbecoming presence to this day.

Notes

1. Erich Schoennagel, "Die Abteilung 'Naturschutz' auf der Internationalen Jagdausstellung 1937 in Berlin," *Naturschutz* 18 (1937): 261; see also "Internationale Jagdausstellung Berlin 1937," *Deutsche Kolonialzeitung* 49 (1937): 350; Fr Luchs, "Die Internationale Jagdausstellung Berlin 1937," *Wild und Hund* 43 (1937): 589–93.
2. On Nazi conservation and the *Reichsnaturschutzgesetz*, see Joachim Radkau and Frank Uekötter, eds, *Naturschutz und Nationalsozialismus* (Frankfurt, 2003); Franz-Josef Brüggemeier, Mark Cioc, and Thomas Zeller, eds, *How Green Were the Nazis? Nature, Environment, and the Nation in the Third Reich* (Athens, OH, 2005); Frank Uekötter, *The Green and the Brown. A History of Conservation in Nazi Germany* (Cambridge, 2006).
3. Reichsbund Deutsche Jägerschaft, ed., *Internationale Jagdausstellung 1937. Amtlicher Katalog* (Berlin, 1937), 381.
4. Iliffe, *A Modern History of Tanganyika*, 303.
5. During World War II, Schauer was employed in the department for colonial conservation in the Imperial Forestry Office to compose a manual on the animal life of the German colonies for the use of future colonial hunters and administrators. The manuscript never went into print, see BAB R 3701/501, Tätigkeitsbericht des Referates "Jagd- und Naturschutz in den deutschen Kolonien," Dönhoff, December 1941, 8.
6. Gustav von Hochwächter, *Afrika ruft den Jäger. Praktisches aus der Praxis* (Berlin, 1931); Schaber, "Deutsche Jäger jagt in Ostafrika!," *Wild und Hund* 39 (1933): 92; Hans Waldner, "Die weitere Entwicklung der Jagd im früheren Deutsch-Ostafrika," *Wild und Hund* 39 (1933): 419; Otto Martens and Oskar Karstedt, *Afrika. Ein Handbuch für Wirtschaft und Reisende*, 2nd ed. (Berlin, 1931), 18, 929, 947.
7. Maximilian von Rogister, *Momella. Abseits vom Wege im afrikanischen Jagdparadies* (Hamburg, 1954); Gerd von Lettow-Vorbeck, *Am Fusse des Meru. Das Leben von Margarete Trappe, Afrikas großer Jägerin* (Hamburg, 1957); Krüger, *Eine Farm in Afrika*. See also Gissibl, "Die Mythen der Serengeti. Naturbilder, Naturpolitik und die Ambivalenz westlicher Um-Weltbürgerschaft in Ostafrika," *Denkanstöße* 10 (2013): 64.

8. Wolfgang Struck, "Reenacting Colonialism. Germany and Its Former Colonies in Recent TV Productions," in *German Colonialism, Visual Culture, and Modern Memory*, ed. Volker M Langbehn (New York, 2010), 260–77.
9. See for example Kuhnert, *Im Lande meiner Modelle*; Behn, "*Haizuru* ..."; Arthur Berger, *Aus einem verschlossenen Paradiese* (Berlin, 1920); Neckschies, *Safarizauber*; Robert Unterwelz, *In Tropensonne und Urwaldnacht. Wanderungen und Erlebnisse in Deutsch-Ostafrika* (Stuttgart, 1923); Konrad Schauer, *Afrikanisches Wanderleben* (Friedeberg, 1923); Fonck, *Wildsteppen und Steppenwild in Ostafrika*; Hans Behrends, *Steppenwanderer. Aus meinem Pflanzer- und Jägerleben in Ostafrika* (Berlin, 1928); Wilhelm Köhler, *Unter Afrikas Sonne. Eine Sammlung der interessantesten Erlebnisse, Reiseberichte und Abenteuer aus unseren ehemaligen Kolonien* (Minden, 1925); Vageler, *Afrikanisches Mosaik*.
10. Wolfgang Schwerbrock and Dieter Jaspert, eds, *Die Wandlung unseres Bildungsgutes in 40 Jahren: Safari Verlag Berlin 1921–1961* (Würzburg, 1961).
11. Paulmann, "Jenseits von Eden"; Lekan, "Serengeti Shall Not Die"; Waz, "Auf der Suche nach dem letzten Paradies," 106.
12. Dennler de la Tour, *La Protección de la Naturaleza en el Mundo*.
13. Wöbse, "Naturschutz global," 639–45.
14. The minutes and membership list for 1927 features, amongst others, the names of Kurt Floericke, Ludwig and Lutz Heck, Oscar Neumann, Jesco von Puttkamer, Paul Sarasin, Hans Schomburgk, Hermann Schubotz, Alexander Sokolowsky, Ernst Stromer von Reichenbach, Eduard Paul Tratz, and the sons of Carl Hagenbeck; see *Zeitschrift für Säugetierkunde* 2 (1927), and Hermann Pohle, "Der Anfang der Deutschen Gesellschaft für Säugetierkunde," *Zeitschrift für Säugetierkunde* 42 (1977): 129–32.
15. See for example Rudolf Hermann, "Die Elefanten in Nord-Rhodesia und Portugiesisch-Afrika," *Naturschutz* 9 (1928): 304–5; Rudolf Hermann, "Tiervernichtung in Afrika," *Naturschutz* 13 (1932): 259–60; "Das Serengeti-Paradies," *Deutsche Kolonialzeitung* 47 (1935): 86–87; Leo von Boxberger, "Koloniale Zukunft und Wildschutz," *Der deutsche Jäger* 62 (1940): 103–5.
16. Adolf von Duisburg, "Wildschutz und Schongebiete in Afrika," *Deutsche Kolonialzeitung* 48 (1936): 87–88, 122–23.
17. See for example BAB R 3701/501, Christoph Graf Dönhoff: *Die Aufgaben des Reiches gegenüber der afrikanischen Natur* [1941]; Walther Schoenichen, "Fragen des kolonialen Naturschutzes," *Biologia generalis. Internationale Zeitschrift für allgemeine Biologie* 16 (1942): 138–39; Schoenichen, *Naturschutz als völkische und internationale Kulturaufgabe. Eine Übersicht über die allgemeinen, die geologischen, botanischen, zoologischen und anthropologischen Probleme des heimatlichen wie des Weltnaturschutzes* (Jena, 1942).
18. A biographical sketch is provided by Hans-Werner Frohn and Friedemann Schmoll, eds, *Natur und Staat. Staatlicher Naturschutz in Deutschland 1906–2006* (Bonn, 2006), 177.
19. Schoenichen, "Fünfundzwanzig Jahre preußischer Naturschutz," *Beiträge zur Naturdenkmalpflege* 9 (1931): 78; see further Wöbse, "Naturschutz global," 648–49, 652.
20. BAK B 245/196, fol. 444: note Schoenichen, 28 December 1937; BAK B 245/196, fol. 392–93: Invitation to the International Congress on Nature Conser-

vation, Berlin, September 1939 (undated draft). See further Wöbse, "Naturschutz global," 653-61.

21. The Deko was formed in 1936 under Kurt Weigelt, director of the Deutsche Bank and head of the economic department in the colonial office (Kolonialpolitisches Amt) of the Nazi party NSDAP, see Karsten Linne, "Afrika als 'wirtschaftlicher Ergänzungsraum': Kurt Weigelt und die kolonialwirtschaftlichen Planungen im 'Dritten Reich,'" *Jahrbuch für Wirtschaftsgeschichte* (2006): 141-62; Karsten Linne, *Deutschland jenseits des Äquators? Die NS-Kolonialplanungen für Afrika* (Berlin, 2008), 72-75, 114-17.

22. BAB R 3701/501, Ch. Dönhoff, "Tätigkeitsbericht des Referates 'Jagd- und Naturschutz in den Kolonien,'" December 1941, 3-4. The draft game regulations can be found in BAB R 3701/502.

23. Biographical information on Dönhoff (1906-92) is provided in BAB PK B 0340. See also Wöbse, "Naturschutz global," 678-83.

24. Zwilling had been responsible for drafting the game law for Cameroon where he had worked as big game hunter and safari entrepreneur during the 1930s. The law was revised in cooperation with the jurist Adolf Vollbach, a former colonial official in East Africa and one of the architects of the German hunting and conservation laws enacted in 1934 and 1935. It found the full approval of the chief Nazi conservationists Ulrich Scherping and Lutz Heck, see BAB R 3701/501, Ch. Dönhoff, "Tätigkeitsbericht des Referates 'Jagd- und Naturschutz in den Kolonien,'" December 1941, 2.

25. Dirk van Laak, "'Ist je ein Reich, das es nicht gab, so gut verwaltet worden?' Der imaginäre Ausbau der imperialen Infrastruktur in Deutschland nach 1918," in *Phantasiereiche. Zur Kulturgeschichte des deutschen Kolonialismus*, ed. Birthe Kundrus (Frankfurt, 2003), 71-90.

26. BAB R 3701/479, Dönhoff: "Jagd- und Naturschutz im Belgisch Kongo," Paris, 8 September 1942.

27. DITSL, Gruppe Deutscher Kolonialwirtschaftlicher Unternehmungen, *Sofort-Programm Deutsch-Ostafrika*. Teil II: Soll Programm, Part VI: Forst, Jagd und Fischerei in Deutsch-Ostafrika (1942), 10, 12-20.

28. BAB R 3701/502, Draft Ordinance § 69; BAB R 3701/501, Die Aufgaben des Reiches gegenüber der afrikanischen Natur, Appendix: Deutsch-Ostafrika, 7.

29. See Elizabeth Garland, "State of Nature: Colonial Power, Neoliberal Capital, and Wildlife Management in Tanzania" (PhD diss., University of Chicago, 2006).

30. See Neumann, "The Postwar Conservation Boom in British Colonial Africa."

31. Lekan, "Serengeti Shall Not Die," 230, 244.

32. Summaries of the Serengeti debate are provided by Shetler, *Imagining Serengeti*, 201-37; Neumann, *Imposing Wilderness*, 122-56; Lekan, "Serengeti Shall Not Die," and Gissibl, "Die Mythen der Serengeti."

33. On Mweka, see Garland, "State of Nature."

34. See Arbeitsgemeinschaft deutscher Stiftungen, ed., *Die Fritz Thyssen Stiftung 1960-1970* (Tübingen, 1970), 127-32.

35. Wolfgang Wickler, "Science on Safari: Research in the Serengeti," *Afrika* 12 (1971): 35-37.

36. See Charles E Kay, "Two Views of the Serengeti: One True, One Myth," *Conservation and Society* 7, no. 2 (2009): 145-47.

37. See Brockington, Sachedina, and Scholfield, "Preserving the New Tanzania: Conservation and Land Use Change."
38. See IUCN's World Conservation Strategy of 1980 and the theme of the World Congress on National Parks in Bali, Indonesia, in October 1982; Jeffrey A McNeely and Kenton R Miller, eds, *National Parks, Conservation, and Development. The Role of Protected Areas in Sustaining Society* (Washington, DC, 1982).
39. For recent critical assessments of this paradigm in Tanzania, see Fred Nelson, ed., *Community Rights, Conservation and Contested Land. The Politics of Natural Resource Governance in Africa* (London, 2010) and Tor A Benjaminsen and Ian Bryceson, "Conservation, Green/Blue Grabbing and Accumulation by Dispossession in Tanzania," *The Journal of Peasant Studies* 39, no. 2 (2012), 335–55.
40. UNESCO World Heritage Nomination, IUCN Technical Review, 15 April 1982, http://whc.unesco.org/archive/advisory_body_evaluation/199bis.pdf.
41. Roderick P Neumann, "Moral and Discursive Geographies in the War for Biodiversity in Africa," *Political Geography* 23 (2004): 813–37; Roderick P Neumann, "Disciplining Peasants in Tanzania: From State Violence to Self-Surveillance in Wildlife Conservation," in *Violent Environments,* ed. Nancy Lee Peluso and Michael Watts (Ithaca, NY, 2001), 305–27.
42. The GTZ was founded in 1975 as the prime agency for the development cooperation projects mandated by the Federal German Ministry of Development. Since 2011, the GTZ merged with other German development organizations to form the *Gesellschaft für internationale Zusammenarbeit.*
43. Rolf Baldus, Benson Kibonde, and Ludwig Siege, "Seeking Conservation Partnerships in the Selous Game Reserve, Tanzania," *Parks* 13, no. 1 (2003): 53–54.
44. Rolf D Baldus, *The Crucial Role of Governance in Ecosystem Management— Results and Conclusions of the Selous Conservation Programme/Tanzania 1987–2003* (26 June 2006), http://www.wildlife-baldus.com/download/Governance%20 in%20Tanzania%20Wildlife%20Conservation.pdf. The best developed CBRM project by the end of the SCP was the so-called Jukumu-cooperation of around twenty villages in the northern buffer zone of the Selous, which had already started to realize substantial income from the sale of hunting concessions. For a critical discussion, see Fred Nelson et al., "Community-Based Conservation and Maasai Livelihoods in Tanzania," in *Staying Maasai. Livelihoods, Conservation and Development in East African Rangelands,* ed. K Homewood, P Kristjanson, and P Chenevix Trench (New York, 2009), 229–334; Sarah Gillingham and Phyllis Lee, "People and Protected Areas: A Study of Local Perceptions of Wildlife Crop-Damage Conflict in an Area Bordering the Selous Game Reserve, Tanzania," *Oryx* 37 (2003): 316–25; Caroline Ashley, Ntengua Mdoe, and Lou Reynolds, *Rethinking Wildlife for Livelihoods and Diversification in Rural Tanzania: A Case Study from Northern Selous* (LADDER Working Paper no. 15, Overseas Development Group University of East Anglia Norwich 2002); and Hajo Junge, *Democratic Decentralisation of Natural Resources in Tanzania. The Case of Local Governance and Community-Based Conservation in Districts around the Selous Game Reserve* (Eschborn, 2004).
45. Selous had also been a member of the Society for the Preservation of the Wild Fauna of the Empire, see *Journal of the Society for the Preservation of the Wild Fauna of the Empire* 2 (1905), 9; see also Stephen Taylor, *The Mighty Nimrod:*

A Life of Frederick Courteney Selous, African Hunter and Adventurer, 1851–1917 (London, 1989).
46. Gordon Matzke, *Wildlife in Tanzanian Settlement Policy. The Case of the Selous* (Syracuse, NY, 1977); Gordon Matzke, "The Development of the Selous Game Reserve," *Tanganyika (Tanzania) Notes and Records* 79/80 (1976): 37–48.
47. Nigel Leader-Williams, Rolf D Baldus, and RJ Smith, "The Influence of Corruption on the Conduct of Recreational Hunting," in *Recreational Hunting, Conservation and Rural Livelihoods: Science and Practice,* ed. Barney Dickson, Jon Hutton, and William M Adams (Chichester, 2009), 296–316.
48. Fred Nelson and Tom Blomley, "Peasants' Forests and the King's Game? Institutional Divergence and Convergence in Tanzania's Forestry and Wildlife Sectors," in *Community Rights, Conservation and Contested Land. The Politics of Natural Resource Governance in Africa,* ed. Fred Nelson (London, 2010), 94.
49. André Baumgarten, "Wildnis so weit das Auge reicht ...," *ZGF-Gorilla* 4/2012, 6–9.
50. See Selous Riverside Safari Camp, http://www.selousriversidecamp.com/selous-game-reserve.html; and http://www.privateluxurytravel.com/safaris/safaris_africa/south_tanzania.htm.
51. Neumann, *Imposing Wilderness,* 29.
52. "CIC German delegation donates plaque in Tanzania," *CIC Newsletter* 2010/1, 19.
53. Rolf D Baldus, ed., *The Wild Heart of Africa. The Selous Game Reserve in Tanzania* (Johannesburg, 2009). A German edition was published in 2011 under the title *Wildes Herz von Afrika. Der Selous—traumhaftes Wildschutzgebiet* (Stuttgart, 2011).
54. Baldus, *Wildes Herz von Afrika,* 235.

Appendix

*Synopsis of Game Ordinances in
German East Africa, 1891–1914*

This survey charts the main development of hunting regulations and licenses. Not included are regional hunting bans of individual species. Ordinances since 1896 were gazetted and can be retrieved in: *DKB* 7 (1896): 340; *AA DOA* 4 (1903), no. 14, 13 June 1903; *AA DOA* 9 (1908), no. 23, 11 Nov 1908; *AA DOA* 12 (1911), no. 49, 19 Nov 1911; *Gesetz und Recht für Deutsch-Ostafrika* 1 (1912), no. 1, 3 January 1912. The game ordinances never used the scientific names of species classified as game.

Date	Ordinance type	License needed	Game affected
23 February 1891	Local regulation for the district of Moshi (Kilimanjaro)	Mandatory license of 500 rupees for elephant hunting	Regulation of elephant hunting
7 May 1896	Game ordinance	Obligatory license for sport or commercial hunting, especially of elephants (500 rupees per year)	Regulation of elephant hunting
		Shooting fees for the first (100 rupees) and any further elephant (250 rupees)	Prohibition of the hunting of Zebra (Moshi District), eland, giraffe, buffalo, ostrich, and secretary bird
		Obligatory license of 20 rupees for Europeans hunting any other game (except vermin)	
		Native license, 5 rupees	
17 January 1898	Revision of the game ordinance	Obligatory license for sport or commercial hunting of elephants (500 rupees per year, European and native)	Regulation of elephant hunting
		Shooting fee of 100 rupees per elephant	
		800 rupees per European participant of sport hunting expeditions	
		Obligatory license of 10 rupees (European), and 5 rupees (native) for the hunting of all other game (except the hunting of vermin)	

Synopsis of Game Ordinances in German East Africa, 1891–1914   319

Date	Ordinance type	License needed	Game affected
1 June 1903	Game ordinance (*Jagdschutzverordnung*)	Obligatory license of 10 rupees for all hunters, European and native	Regulation of elephant hunting
		Shooting fees for nonnative hunters: 100 rupees or one tusk per elephant, 30 rupees per rhinoceros, 20 rupees per hippopotamus or buffalo; 3 rupees per wildebeest, hartebeest, sable antelope, waterbuck, koodoo, oryx, colobus, or marabou	Complete prohibition of the hunting of giraffe, eland, chimpanzee, ostrich, secretary bird, all owls, vulture, oxpecker, and cattle egret
		Native hunting restricted to districts, no hunting with breech-loading rifles	Bounty of 20 rupees for an adult lion, 10 rupees for leopard
		Native elephant hunting only with permission of district stations, no more than six hunters, no poisoned arrows, fire, nets, or pits	
		Shooting fee of 100 rupees or one tusk per elephant	
5 November 1908	Game ordinance	*Großer Jagdschein*: 750 rupees, hunting of any classified game	Introduction of two categories of game:
		Kleiner Jagdschein: 50 rupees, hunting of game category I	I: All antelopes (including wildebeest, excluding eland); all gazelles, buffalo, colobus, and marabou
		Bezirks-Jagdschein: district license, 25 rupees, hunting of game category I	II: Elephant, eland, giraffe, rhinoceros, and zebra
		Tages-Jagdschein: 5 rupees, game category I	Prohibition of the hunting of chimpanzee, ostrich, vultures, secretary bird, and smaller owls
		Vorderlader-/Schrofflinten-Jagdschein: 3 rupees, muzzle-loaders, district only	
		Additional shooting fee of 150 rupees per elephant (or a tusk with a minimum weight of 10 kilograms)	

320 *Appendix*

Date	Ordinance type	License needed	Game affected
5 November 1911	Amendment of the game ordinance issued November 1908	*Großer Eingeborenen-Jagdschein*: 50 rupees, muzzle-loaders, game categories I and II	Introduction of three categories of game:
		Kleiner Eingeborenen-Jagdschein: 3 rupees, muzzle-loaders, game category I	I: All antelopes (including wildebeest, excluding kudu and oryx); all gazelles (excluding gerenuk), buffalo, colobus, marabou, probab., and great egret (*Edelreiher*)
		Bezirks-Jagdschein: 25 rupees, breech-loaders, game category I, district only	II: Rhinoceros, giraffe, zebra, kudu, oryx, and gerenuk
		Kleiner Jagdschein: 50 rupees, breech-loaders, game category I	III: Elephant
		Großer Jagdschein: 450 rupees, breech-loaders, game categories I and II	Prohibition of the hunting of chimpanzee, ostrich, vultures, secretary bird, and smaller owls
		Tages-Jagdschein: 5 rupees, breech-loaders, game category I, one day	
		Special license for the hunting of game category III: First elephant 150 rupees, second elephant 450 rupees, in combination with a *große Jagdschein* only	

Synopsis of Game Ordinances in German East Africa, 1891–1914   321

Date	Ordinance type	License needed	Game affected
30 December 1911	Additional amendment to the amendment of the game ordinance issued November 1908	*Großer Eingeborenen-Jagdschein*: 50 rupees, game categories I and II	Introduction of four categories of game:
		Kleiner Eingeborenen-Jagdschein: 10 rupees, game category I	I: All species commonly understood as game, excluding those listed in the further categories
		Bezirks-Jagdschein: 10 rupees, game category I, district only	II: Rhinoceros, giraffe, zebra, kudu, oryx, and gerenuk
		Kleiner Jagdschein: 50 rupees (200 rupees nonresident), game category I	III: Elephant
		Großer Jagdschein: 450 rupees (750 rupees nonresident), game categories I and II	IV: All predators, wild pig, warthog, porcupine, all other monkeys, reptiles, and preying birds
		Tages-Jagdschein: 5 rupees, game category I, one day	Additional prohibition of the hunting of gorillas
		Special license for the hunting of game category III: First elephant 150 rupees, second elephant 400 rupees, in combination with a *große Jagdschein* only	Confiscation of elephant tusks below a weight of 15 kilograms
		No more than two specimens allowed of rhinoceros, buffalo, giraffe, or eland	
		No more than four specimens of zebra, kudu, oryx, gerenuk, colobus, or marabou	
		No license necessary for the hunting of game category IV	

Select Bibliography

Unpublished Material (up to 1945)

Archiv der Erzabtei St Ottilien

von Hassel, Theodor. *Der Militairbezirk Mahenge im Aufstand 1905*. Unpublished manuscript, Mahenge, 1929.

Archives Ministère des Affaires Etrangères, du Commerce extérieur et de la Coopération au Développement, Bruxelles (AMDAE)

Archives Africaines
AE 322 (Traités, Conventions, Conférences internationaux)

Bayerisches Hauptstaatsarchiv Munich (BayHStA)

Dep. II: *Neuere Bestände*
Außenministerium MA 92394
Dep. IV: *Militärarchiv*
Papers Rudolf von Hirsch

Oxford, Bodleian Library, Commonwealth and African Manuscripts (OBL)

Micr. Afr. 446: Theodor Gunzert, *Service in German East Africa & German Foreign Service, 1902–33* (Extracts)
MSS. Afr. r. 703: Letters and Documents concerning the life of Sir Clement Hill, 1867–1905.
Mss. Afr. s. 1237a: H. St. J. Grant, *Masai History and Mode of Life. A Summary Prepared for the Committee of Enquiry into the Serengeti National Park*, 1957.
Mss. Afr. s. 1237b, Oltimbau ole Masiaya on behalf of the Masai of the Serengeti National Park, *Memorandum on the Serengeti National Park*, 1957.
MSS. Afr. s. 1455: R.F.P. Huebner, *Es fuhr ein Mann nach Kenya. Erinnerungen eines alten Afrika-Pioniers an die Gründung und Aufbauzeit der Kenya Kolonie*.

Bundesarchiv Berlin-Lichterfelde (BAB)

Files of the Reichskolonialamt (R 1001)
25, 222, 224, 234, 237–240, 244, 259, 266, 278, 286-293, 295, 298–300, 461, 644/1, 698–701, 726, 740, 768, 775, 812–814, 4812, 4990, 4999, 6059–6071, 6229-1, 6467, 6621, 6632, 6726/1, 7766–7802, 8381, 8390, 8529, 8531, 8533, 8534, 8540, 8541, 9055, 9057, 9065, 9077, 9078

Files of the Deutsche Kolonialgesellschaft (R 8023)
1000

Files of the NS-Reichsforstamt (R 3701)
479, 501, 502

Berlin Document Center
PK B 0340: Christoph Graf Dönhoff

Bundesarchiv Koblenz (BAK)

Papers Wilhelm Solf
B 245 Reichsstelle für Naturschutz

Bundesarchiv-Militärarchiv, Freiburg (BAM)

N 85/3: Oskar Pusch, *Ostafrikanische Briefe des Leutnants der Kaiserlichen Schutztruppe Harald Pfeiffer und sein mysteriöser Tod* (Oberhausen, 1962)
Papers Harald Pfeiffer

Deutsches Institut für tropische und subtropische Landwirtschaft (DITSL), Witzenhausen

von Hassel, Theodor. *Ein Tagebuch aus Ostafrika*. Unpublished manuscript (undated).
Gruppe Deutscher Kolonialwirtschaftlicher Unternehmungen, Sofort-Programm Deutsch-Ostafrika, Part I: Ist-Zustand 1939 (1941)
Gruppe Deutscher Kolonialwirtschaftlicher Unternehmungen, Sofort-Programm Deutsch-Ostafrika, Part II: Soll Programm, Part VI: Forst, Jagd und Fischerei in Deutsch-Ostafrika (1942)

Hauptschule Düren-Gürzenich

Papers Carl Georg Schillings

Kenya National Archives Nairobi (KNA)

DC MKS 1/4/2
PC/CP/4/2/1
PC 1/6/136
PC Coast 1/1/286

Landesarchiv Baden-Württemberg—Staatsarchiv Freiburg

U 101/1: Papers Ruprecht Böcklin von Böcklinsau

Leibniz-Institut für Länderkunde, Leipzig (LIL)

Papers Georg Robert Wilhelm von Prittwitz und Gaffron
Papers Carl Uhlig

Museum für Naturkunde der Humboldt-Universität zu Berlin, Historische Bild- und Schriftgutsammlungen (HUB MfN)

Zoologisches Museum
S III, Mecklenburg, Hrzg. A.Fr.v.
S III, Niedieck, Paul
S III, Fromm, P
S III, Schillings, CG

Private Collections Angelika Grettmann-Werner, Bremen

Papers Wilhelm Kuhnert: Diary of his second East African expedition 1905–6

Public Record Office, The National Archives, London (PRO)

Records of the Colonial Office (CO)
323/1234/11, 691/16, 735/1, 885/20/230, 885/22/287

Records of the Foreign Office (FO)
2/819, 367/79, 367/136, 367/181, 367/182, 403/302, 881/7395, 881/7420, 881/7935, 881/9226, 881/9254, 881/10351, 881/10461

Records of the Ministry of Agriculture, Fisheries and Food (MAF)
48/247B

Reiß-Engelhorn-Museen Mannheim (REM)

Papers Theodor Bumiller

Staatsarchiv Hamburg

621-1 Wm. O'Swald & Co. Papers

Staatsbibliothek zu Berlin

Papers Hugo Conwentz

Stadtarchiv Düren (SAD)

Papers Carl Georg Schillings

Tanzania National Archives, Dar es Salaam (TNA)

German Records
1/5, 1/6, 1/8, 1/10, 1/30, 3/39, 3/54, 8/54, 8/55, 8/99–103, 8/143, 8/144, 8/193, 8/908, 8/909, 8/910, 8/912, 21/148, 21/247, 21/411, 21/539, 31/1, 31/5, 31/32, 31/170, 50/9, 50/12, 55/8, 55/27, 58/40, 58/41, 59/2

Tanganyika Territory Files
TT AB 145, TT AB 150, TT AB 151, TT AB 729, TT AB 1132

Tierpark Hagenbeck, Hamburg

Folder Kilimanjaro-Handels- und Landwirtschaftsgesellschaft

Newspapers and Periodicals (selected volumes)

Amtlicher Anzeiger für Deutsch-Ostafrika
Berichte über Land- und Forstwirtschaft in Deutsch-Ostafrika
Blätter für Naturschutz
Denkschrift über die Entwickelung der Schutzgebiete in Afrika und der Südsee
Deutsches Kolonialblatt
Deutsche Kolonialzeitung
Deutsche Jägerzeitung
Deutsch-Ostafrikanische Zeitung
Die deutschen Schutzgebiete in Afrika und der Südsee; Amtliche Jahresberichte
Dürener Volkszeitung
Foreign Office Confidential Prints
The Geographical Journal
Gesetz und Recht für Deutsch-Ostafrika
Illustrirte Jagd-Zeitung. Organ für Jagd, Fischerei, Naturkunde
Jahrbuch für Photographie und Reproduktionstechnik
The Journal of the Royal Anthropological Institute of Great Britain and Ireland
Journal of the Royal Geographical Society of London
Journal of the Society for the Preservation of the (Wild) Fauna of the Empire
Kilimandjaro- und Meru-Zeitung
Kosmos. Handweiser für Naturfreunde
Missions-Blätter. Illustrierte Zeitschrift für das katholische Volk
Mittheilungen der Afrikanischen Gesellschaft in Deutschland
Mitteilungen von Forschungsreisenden und Gelehrten aus den Deutschen Schutzgebieten
Museumskunde
Naturwissenschaftliche Wochenschrift
Ostafrikanisches Weidwerk

Petermanns geographische Mitteilungen
Proceedings of the Royal Geographical Society and Monthly Record of Geography
Sitzungsberichte der Gesellschaft naturforschender Freunde zu Berlin
Süddeutsche Monatshefte
Usambara-Post
Verhandlungen der Deutschen Kolonialkongresse 1902, 1905, 1910
Der Vortrupp
Das Waidwerk in Wort und Bild. Illustrierte jagdliche Unterhaltungsblätter
Der Weidmann. Blätter für Jäger und Jagdfreunde
Wild und Hund
Zeitschrift für Kolonialpolitik, Kolonialrecht und Kolonialwirtschaft
Zeitschrift für Säugetierkunde

British Parliamentary Papers

Agreement and Protocol between the United Kingdom and Germany with Regard to Sleeping Sickness. Signed at London, 27 October 1908 (= PP Cd. 4319, 1908 CXXV.393).
Correspondence relating to the Preservation of Wild Animals in Africa. London 1906 (= PP Cd. 3189, 1906 LXXIX. 25).
Further Correspondence relating to the Preservation of Wild Animals in Africa. London (= PP Cd. 4472, 1909 LIX. 635; PP Cd. 5775, 1911 LII. 521; PP Cd. 6671, 1913, XLV).
Minutes of Evidence taken by the Departmental Committee on Sleeping Sickness (= PP Cd. 7350, 1914 XLVIII.29).
Proceedings of the First International Conference on the Sleeping Sickness, Held at London in June 1907. London, 1908 (= PP Cd. 3778, LXXXVIII.523).

Primary Sources (including literature and ethnographies published before 1945)

Articles in colonial newspapers, hunting, or scientific periodicals have only been included in this bibliography when cited more than once or when comprising five pages or more.

Abdallah bin Hemedi bin Ali Liajjemi. "The Story of Mbega." *Tanganyika Notes and Records* (1936), no. 1: 38–51 and no. 2: 80–91.
Adams, Alfons. *Lindi und sein Hinterland*. Berlin, 1903.
Austen, Ernest Edward. *A Monograph of the Tsetse-Flies (Genus Glossina, Westwood) Based on the Collection in the British Museum*. London, 1903.
"Auszug aus der Rede von Prof. CG Schillings auf der Hauptversammlung der Deutschen Kolonialgesellschaft am 10. Juni 1911 in Stuttgart." *Zeitschrift des Allgemeinen Deutschen Jagdschutzvereins* 16 (1911): 361–64, 375–78.
Bartels, Carl Otto. *Auf frischer Tat. Beobachtungen aus der niederen Tierwelt in Bilderserien nach Natur-Aufnahmen*. Stuttgart, 1910.

Baumann, Oscar. *Durch Massailand zur Nilquelle. Reisen und Forschungen der Massai-Expedition des Deutschen Antisklaverei-Komite in den Jahren 1891–1893.* Berlin, 1894.
Becker, Alexander. *Aus Deutsch-Ostafrikas Sturm- und Drangperiode. Erinnerungen eines Alten Afrikaners.* Halle, 1911.
Becker, Alexander, Conradin von Perbandt, Georg Richelmann, Rochus Schmidt, Werner Steuber. *Hermann von Wissmann. Deutschlands größter Afrikaner.* 5th ed. Berlin, 1914.
Behn, Fritz. *"Haizuru ..." Ein Bildhauer in Afrika.* 2nd ed. Munich, 1918.
———. "Naturerhaltung und Wildmord in Deutsch-Ostafrika—ein Kulturskandal," *Naturwissenschaftliche Wochenschrift* 10 (1911): 801–07.
Behrends, Hans. *Steppenwanderer. Aus meinem Pflanzer- und Jägerleben in Ostafrika.* Berlin, 1928.
Bell, WDM. *The Wanderings of an Elephant Hunter.* London, 1923.
Berger, Arthur. *Aus einem verschlossenen Paradiese.* Berlin, 1920.
———. *In Afrikas Wildkammern als Forscher und Jäger.* Berlin, 1910.
Bericht über die Arbeiten der Wildschutz-Kommission der Deutschen Kolonialgesellschaft. Berlin, 1912.
Besser, Hans. *Raubwild und Dickhäuter in Deutsch-Ostafrika.* Stuttgart, 1915.
Bley, Fritz. "Besseren Wildschutz in unseren Kolonien!", *Monatshefte des Allgemeinen Deutschen Jagdschutzvereins und der Deutschen Versuchsanstalt für Handfeuerwaffen* 12 (1907), 119–22, 132–36.
Blohm, Wilhelm. *Die Nyamwezi. Land und Wirtschaft.* 3 vols. Hamburg, 1931.
Böhm, Richard. *Von Sansibar zum Tanganjika. Briefe aus Ostafrika.* Edited by Herman Schalow. Leipzig, 1888.
Bölsche, Wilhelm. *Die deutsche Landschaft in Vergangenheit und Gegenwart.* Berlin, 1915.
———. *Weltblick. Gedanken zu Natur und Kunst.* Dresden, 1904.
———, ed. *Von Sonnen und Sonnenstäubchen. Kosmische Wanderungen.* Berlin, 1903.
Bokemeyer, Heinrich. *Die Zähmung des Afrikanischen Elefanten. Ergebnisse der bisherigen Erörterung der Frage.* Berlin, 1891.
Bolau, Heinrich. *Der Elephant in Krieg und Frieden und seine Verwendung in unsern Afrikanischen Kolonien.* Hamburg, 1887.
Bongard, Oskar. *Die Studienreise des Staatssekretärs Dernburg nach Deutsch-Ostafrika.* Berlin, 1908.
Brandis, Louis von. *Deutsche Jagd am Victoria Nyanza.* Berlin, 1907.
Braun, Hanns. *Die Reise nach Ostafrika.* Berlin, 1939.
Brehms Tierleben. Allgemeine Kunde des Tierreichs. Vol. 3: Säugetiere. 4th rev. ed. Edited by Otto zur Strassen. Leipzig, 1915.
Brode, Heinrich. *British and German East Africa. Their Economic and Commercial Relations.* London, 1911.
Bronsart von Schellendorff, Fritz. *Thierbeobachtungen und Jagdgeschichten aus Ostafrika.* Berlin, 1900.
Burton, Richard. "The Lake Regions of Central Equatorial Africa, with Notices of the Lunar Mountains of the White Nile; Being the Results of an Expedition Undertaken under the Patronage of Her Majesty's Government and the Royal Geographical Society of London, in the Years 1857–1859." *Journal of the Royal Geographical Society of London* 29 (1859): 1–454.

Busse, Joseph. *Die Nyakyusa. Wirtschaft und Gesellschaft.* Münster, 1995.
Buxton, Edward North. *Two African Trips with Notes and Suggestions on Big Game Preservation in Africa.* London, 1902.
Conwentz, Hugo. *The Care of Natural Monuments with Special Reference to Great Britain and Germany.* Cambridge, 1909.
Culwick, Arthur Theodore, and Geraldine Mary. *Ubena of the Rivers.* London, 1935.
Dale, Godfrey. "An Account of the Principal Customs and Habits of the Natives Inhabiting the Bondei Country." *The Journal of the Anthropological Institute of Great Britain and Ireland* 25 (1896): 181–239.
Darwin, Charles. *The Origin of Species.* Oxford, 1996. First published 1859.
Dernburg, Bernhard. "Germany and England in Africa." *The Journal of the Royal African Society* 9 (1910): 113–19.
———. *Zielpunkte des deutschen Kolonialwesens. Zwei Vorträge.* Berlin, 1907.
Doflein, Franz. *Ostasienfahrt. Erlebnisse und Beobachtungen eines Naturforschers in China, Japan und Ceylon.* Leipzig, 1906.
———. "Wildschutz und Wissenschaft in den deutschen Kolonien." *Naturwissenschaftliche Wochenschrift* (1911): 817–20.
Dugmore, Arthur Radclyffe. *Wild, Wald, Steppe: Waidmannsfahrten mit Kamera und Flinte in Britisch-Ostafrika.* 2nd ed. Berlin, 1928.
Elton, Frederic J. *Travels and Researches among the Lakes and Mountains of Eastern and Central Africa.* Edited and compiled by HB Cotterill. London, 1879.
Falz-Fein, Woldemar von. *Askania Nova. Das Tierparadies. Ein Buch des Gedenkens und der Gedanken.* Neudamm, 1930.
Fischer, Gustav. *Mehr Licht im dunklen Weltteil. Betrachtungen über die Kolonisation des tropischen Afrika unter besonderer Berücksichtigung des Sansibar-Gebiets.* Hamburg, 1885.
Fonck, Heinrich. *Deutsch-Ostafrika. Eine Schilderung deutscher Tropen nach 10 Wanderjahren.* Berlin, 1910.
———. *Wildsteppen und Steppenwild in Ostafrika.* Berlin, 1924.
Fülleborn, Friedrich. *Das Deutsche Njassa- und Ruwuma-Gebiet, Land und Leute, nebst Bemerkungen über die Schire-Länder.* Berlin, 1906.
Gottberg, Achim, ed. *Unyamwesi. Quellensammlung und Geschichte.* Berlin, 1971.
Götzen, Gustav Adolf Graf von. *Durch Afrika von Ost nach West. Resultate und Begebenheiten einer Reise von der Deutsch-Ostafrikanischen Küste bis zur Kongomündung in den Jahren 1893/94.* Berlin, 1895.
Grzimek, Bernhard, and Michael Grzimek. *Serengeti darf nicht sterben. 367000 Tiere suchen einen Staat.* Berlin, 1959.
Günther, Konrad. *Vom Tierleben in den Tropen. Für 12-15jährige Schüler aller Schulgattungen.* Leipzig, 1914.
———. *Der Naturschutz.* Freiburg, 1910.
Hayden, Sherman Strong. *The International Protection of Wild Life. Examination of Treaties and Other Agreements for the Preservation of Birds and Mammals.* New York, 1942.
Heck, Ludwig. *Heiter-ernste Lebensbeichte. Erinnerungen eines alten Tiergärtners.* Berlin, 1938.
Heck, Lutz. *Auf Tiersuche in weiter Welt.* Berlin, 1941.
Hendle, Innozenz. *Die Sprache der Wapogoro (Deutsch-Ostafrika) nebst einem deutsch-chipogoro und chipogoro-deutschen Wörterbuche.* Berlin, 1907.

Hennig, Edwin. *Am Tendaguru. Leben und Wirken einer deutschen Forschungs-Expedition zur Ausgrabung vorweltlicher Riesensaurier in Deutsch-Ostafrika.* Stuttgart, 1912.

Hennings, Curt. "Heimatschutz und Naturdenkmalpflege." *Verhandlungen des Naturwissenschaftlichen Vereins Karlsruhe* 22 (1908–9): 101–21.

Hochwächter, Gustav von. *Afrika ruft den Jäger. Praktisches aus der Praxis.* Berlin, 1931.

Hodgson, AGO. "Some Notes on the Hunting Customs of the Wandamba of the Ulanga Valley, Tanganyika Territory, and Other East African Tribes." *The Journal of the Royal Anthropological Institute of Great Britain and Ireland* 56 (1926): 59–70.

Hoffmann, Hermann Edler von. *Einführung in das deutsche Kolonialrecht.* Leipzig, 1911.

Hornaday, William Temple. *The Extermination of the American Bison, with a Sketch of Its Discovery and Life History.* Washington, DC, 1889.

Jaeger, Fritz. "Der Gegensatz von Kulturland und Wildnis und die allgemeinen Züge ihrer Verteilung in Ost-Afrika. Eine anthropogeographische Skizze." *Geographische Zeitschrift* 16 (1910): 121–33.

Jagdhandbuch für Deutsch-Ostafrika. Auf Grund amtlicher Quellen bearbeitet. Dar es Saalam, 1912.

Karstedt, Oskar. "Betrachtungen zur Sozialpolitik in Ostafrika." *Koloniale Rundschau* 12 (1914): 133–41.

———. *Deutsch-Ostafrika und seine Nachbargebiete. Ein Handbuch für Reisende.* Berlin, 1914.

Kearton, Richard, and Cherry Kearton. *With Nature and A Camera. Being the Adventures and Observations of a Field Naturalist and an Animal Photographer.* London, 1897.

———. *Wild Life at Home. How to Study and Photograph It.* London, 1897.

Knauer, Friedrich. *Der Niedergang unserer Tier- und Pflanzenwelt. Eine Mahn- und Werbeschrift im Sinne moderner Naturschutzbestrebung.* Leipzig, 1912.

Knochenhauer, August. "Aus dem Tagebuch eines Elefantenjägers." In *Eine Jagdfahrt nach Ostafrika. Mit dem Tagebuch eines Elefantenjägers,* edited by Oberländer (i.e., Karl Rehfus), 243–383. Berlin, 1903.

Koch, Robert. *Gesammelte Werke,* edited by Julius Schwalbe, Georg Gaffky, and Eduard Pfuhl. 2 vol. Leipzig, 1912.

———. "Remarks on Trypanosome Diseases." *British Medical Journal* no. 26, 19 November 1904: 1445–49.

———. "Ueber die Trypanosomenkrankheiten." *Deutsche medizinische Wochenschrift* 30, no. 47 (1904), 17 November: 1705–11.

Kootz-Kretschmer, Elise. *Die Safwa. Ein ostafrikanischer Volksstamm in seinem Leben und Denken.* 2 vols. Berlin, 1926.

Krall, Karl. *Denkende Tiere. Beiträge zur Tierseelenkunde aufgrund eigener Versuche. Der Kluge Hans und meine Pferde Muhamed und Zarif.* Leipzig, 1912.

Krüger, Hardy. *Eine Farm in Afrika.* Bergisch Gladbach, 2008. First published 1970.

Kuhnert, Wilhelm. *Im Lande meiner Modelle.* Leipzig, 1918.

Kunz, George Frederick. *Ivory and the Elephant in Art, in Archaeology, and in Science.* Garden City, 1916.

Langheld, Wilhelm. *Zwanzig Jahre in deutschen Kolonien.* Berlin, 1909.

Lettow-Vorbeck, Gerd von. *Am Fusse des Meru. Das Leben von Margarete Trappe, Afrikas großer Jägerin.* Hamburg, 1957.

Lichtenheld, Georg. "Beobachtungen über Nagana und Glossinen in Deutsch-Ostafrika." *Archiv für wissenschaftliche und praktische Tierheilkunde* 36 (1910): 272–82.

Liebert, Eduard von. *Neunzig Tage im Zelt. Meine Reise nach Uhehe, Juni bis September 1897*. Berlin, 1898.

Lindgens, Arthur. *Wild, Bild und Kugel. Mit 202 Natururkunden des Verfassers aus der Wildbahn*. Stuttgart, 1949.

Lion, Alexander, and Maximilian Bayer. *Jungdeutschlands Pfadfinderbuch*. Leipzig, 1909.

Lippe, Bernhard Graf zur. *In den Jagdgründen Deutsch-Ostafrikas. Erinnerungen aus meinem Tagebuch mit einem kurzen Vorwort über das ostafrikanische Schutzgebiet*. Berlin, 1904.

Löns, Hermann. *Die Erhaltung unserer Tierwelt*. Munich, 1913.

Lüders, Ewald. *Das Jagdrecht der deutschen Schutzgebiete*. Hamburg, 1913.

Ludwig, Emil. *Die Reise nach Afrika*. 2nd ed. Berlin, 1913.

Lugard, Frederick Dealtry. *The Rise of Our East African Empire. Early Efforts in Nyasaland and Uganda. Vol. 1: Nyasaland and Eastern Africa, with Chapters on Commerce, Slave-Trade and Sport*. London, 1968. First published 1893.

Maji Maji Research Project, *Collected Papers*, Department of History, University College of Dar es Salaam 1968.

Martin, Philipp Leopold. *Die Praxis der Naturgeschichte. Ein vollständiges Lehrbuch über das Sammeln lebender und todter Naturkörper; deren Beobachtung, Erhaltung und Pflege im freien und gefangenen Zustand; Konservation, Präparation und Aufstellung in Sammlungen etc. Vol. 3.2: Allgemeiner Naturschutz*. Weimar, 1882

Matschie, Paul. "Deutschlands Säugetierwelt einst und jetzt." *Natur und Haus* 5 (1897): 261–67.

———. *Die Säugethiere Deutsch-Ostafrikas*. Berlin, 1895.

Mecklenburg, Adolf Friedrich Herzog zu. *Ins innerste Afrika. Bericht über den Verlauf der Deutschen Wissenschaftlichen Zentral-Afrika-Expedition 1907–1908*. Leipzig, 1909.

Meerwarth, Hermann. *Lebensbilder aus der Tierwelt*. Leipzig, 1908–1912.

Meyer, Heinrich Adolf. *Erinnerungen an Heinrich Christian Meyer—Stockmeyer*. Hamburg, 1900.

Meyer, Oskar Erich. *Afrikanische Briefe. Erinnerungen an Deutsch-Ost-Afrika*. Munich-Pullach, 1923.

Merker, Moritz. *Die Masai. Ethnographische Monographie eines ostafrikanischen Semitenvolkes*. Berlin, 1904.

Methner, Wilhelm. *Unter drei Gouverneuren. 16 Jahre Dienst in deutschen Tropen*. Breslau, 1938.

Neckschies, David. *Safarizauber. Jagdabenteuer in afrikanischer Wildnis*. Braunschweig, 1923.

Niedieck, Paul. *Mit der Büchse in fünf Weltteilen*. Berlin, 1905. English translation: *With Rifle in Five Continents*. London, 1908.

Nigmann, Ernst. *Die Wahehe. Ihre Geschichte, Kult-, Rechts-, Kriegs- und Jagdgebräuche*. Berlin, 1908.

———. *Felddienstübungen für farbige (ostafrikanische) Truppen*. Dar es Salaam, 1910.

———. *Geschichte der kaiserlichen Schutztruppe für Deutsch-Ostafrika*. Berlin, 1911.

Oberländer (i.e., Karl Rehfus). *Eine Jagdfahrt nach Ostafrika. Mit dem Tagebuch eines Elefantenjägers*. Berlin, 1903.

Obst, Erich. "Von Mkalama ins Land der Wakindiga (Deutsch-Ostafrika). Vorläufiger Bericht der Ostafrika-Expedition der Hamburger Geographischen Gesellschaft." *Mitteilungen der geographischen Gesellschaft in Hamburg* 26 (1912): 1–45.

Orwell, George. "Shooting an Elephant." In *The Collected Essays, Journalism and Letters of George Orwell. Vol. 1: An Age Like This, 1920–1940,* edited by Sara Orwell and Ian Angus, 265–72. Harmondsworth, 1970.

von Ostertag, Robert. "Über Rinderpest. Ein Beitrag zum Stande und zur Bekämpfung der Tierseuchen in Deutsch-Ostafrika." *Zeitschrift für Infektionskrankheiten, parasitäre Krankheiten und Hygiene der Haustiere* 18 (1916): 1–48.

Paasche, Hans. "Deutsch-Afrikanische Naturschutzparke." *Der Tag* no. 198 (1911), 24 August.

———. "Der Massenmord in Ostafrika." *Deutsch-Ostafrikanische Zeitung* 13, no. 38 (1911), 13 May.

———. "Deutscher Naturschutz." *Der Vortrupp* 1, no. 1 (1912): 609–17, 641–45.

———. *Im Morgenlicht. Kriegs-, Jagd- und Reiseerlebnisse in Ostafrika.* Berlin, 1907.

Pfungst, Oskar. *Das Pferd des Herrn von Osten (Der kluge Hans). Ein Beitrag zur experimentellen Tier- und Menschenpsychologie.* Leipzig, 1907.

Picarda, Cado. "Autour de Mandéra. Notes sur l'Ouzigoua, l'Oukwéré et l'Oudoé." *Les Missions catholiques. Bulletin hebdomadaire illustre de l'oeuvre de la propagation de la foi* 18 (1886): 258–61.

Pink, Louis, and Georg Hirschberg. *Das Liegenschaftsrecht in den deutschen Schutzgebieten.* Vol. 1. Berlin, 1912.

Ratzel, Friedrich. "Die deutsche Landschaft." In *Kleine Schriften von Friedrich Ratzel,* vol. 1, edited by Hans Helmholt, 127–50. Munich, 1906.

Reck, Hans. *Oldoway, die Schlucht des Urmenschen. Die Entdeckung des altsteinzeitlichen Menschen in Deutsch-Ostafrika.* Leipzig, 1933.

Regensberg, Friedrich, and Carl Georg Schillings, "Naturschutzparke in den Kolonien." In *Naturschutzparke in Deutschland und Österreich. Ein Mahnwort an das deutsche und österreichische Volk,* 2nd edition, edited by Verein Naturschutzpark, 54–57. Stuttgart, 1911.

Reichard, Paul. "Das afrikanische Elfenbein und sein Handel." *Deutsche geographische Blätter* 12 (1889): 132–68.

———. "Die Wanjamuesi." *Zeitschrift der Gesellschaft für Erdkunde zu Berlin* 24 (1889): 246–59; 304–31.

———. *Deutsch-Ostafrika. Das Land und seine Bewohner, seine politische und wirtschaftliche Entwickelung.* Leipzig, 1892.

Reichskolonialamt, ed. *Jagd und Wildschutz in den deutschen Kolonien.* Jena, 1913.

Richards, Audrey I. *Land, Labour and Diet in Northern Rhodesia. An Economic Study of the Bemba Tribe.* Oxford, 1939.

Rogister, Maximilian von. *Momella. Abseits vom Wege im afrikanischen Jagdparadies.* Hamburg, 1954.

Roosevelt, Theodore. *Jagden in amerikanischer Wildnis. Eine Schilderung des Wildes der Vereinigten Staaten und seiner Jagd.* Berlin, 1905.

Sajo, Karl. "Ueber aussterbende Tiere." *Prometheus. Illustrirte Wochenschrift über die Fortschritte in Gewerbe, Industrie und Wissenschaft* 7 (1896): 229–33, 246–51, 262–66, 277–80.

Sander, Karl Ludwig. "Die Viehseuchen in Afrika und Mittel zu ihrer Bekämpfung." *Verhandlungen der Gesellschaft deutscher Naturforscher und Ärzte* 65 (1893): 515–26.
Sarasin, Paul. *Ueber die Aufgaben des Weltnaturschutzes. Denkschrift gelesen an der Delegiertenversammlung zur Weltnaturschutzkommission in Bern am 18. November 1913.* Basel, 1914.
———. *Über nationalen und internationalen Vogelschutz, sowie einige anschliessende Fragen des Weltnaturschutzes.* Vortrag, gehalten am 12. Mai 1911 am zweiten deutschen Vogelschutztag in Stuttgart und in dessen Auftrag in Druck gegeben. Basel, 1911.
———. *Weltnaturschutz. Global Protection of Nature.* Bern, 1910.
Schauer, Konrad. *Afrikanisches Wanderleben.* Friedeberg, 1923.
———. *Höhenkurort "Kijabe-Hill." Handbuch für Jagd- und wissenschaftliche Expeditionen sowie Vergnügungsreisen nach Ost-Afrika.* Kijabe-Hill s.a.
Schillings, Carl Georg. "Die Arche Noah," *Süddeutsche Monatshefte* 11/2 (1914): 147–54.
———. "Giraffenschlachten in Deutschostafrika." *Süddeutsche Monatshefte* 10 (1912–13): 151–56.
———. "Hagenbeck als Erzieher." *Süddeutsche Monatshefte* 8 (1911): 275–90.
———. *In Wildest Africa.* New York, 1907.
———. *Met flitslicht en buks. Nieuwe waarnemingen en avonturen in de wildernis te midden van de dierenwereld van aequatoriaal-oost-Afrika.* Arnhem, 1923.
———. *Mit Blitzlicht und Büchse. Neue Beobachtungen und Erlebnisse in der Wildnis inmitten der Tierwelt von Äquatorial-Ostafrika.* Leipzig, 1905.
———. *Mit Blitzlicht und Büchse im Zauber des Elelescho.* Leipzig, 1910.
———. *With Flashlight and Rifle: A Record of Hunting Adventures and of Studies in Wild Life in Equatorial East Africa.* 2 vols. Translated by Frederic Whyte. London, 1906.
———. "Zur Frage des Naturschutzes in den deutschen Kolonien, namentlich in Deutsch-Ostafrika." *Naturwissenschaftliche Wochenschrift* 10 (1911): 807–16.
———. *Der Zauber des Elelescho.* Leipzig, 1906.
Schoeller, Max. *Mitteilungen über meine Reise nach Äquatorial-Ost-Afrika und Uganda 1896–1897.* 2 vols. Berlin, 1901 and 1904).
Schoenichen, Walther. "Fragen des kolonialen Naturschutzes." *Biologia generalis. Internationale Zeitschrift für allgemeine Biologie* 16 (1942): 122–48.
Schomburgk, Hans. *Wild und Wilde im Herzen Afrikas. Zwölf Jahre Jagd- und Forschungsreisen.* Berlin, 1926. First published 1910.
Schulz, Christoph. *Auf Großtierfang für Hagenbeck. Selbsterlebtes aus afrikanischer Wildnis.* Dresden, 1921.
———. *Jagd- und Filmabenteuer in Afrika. Streifzüge in das Innere des dunklen Erdteils.* Dresden, 1922.
Schulz, Georg EF. *Natur-Urkunden. Biologisch erläuterte photographische Aufnahmen frei lebender Tiere und Pflanzen.* Berlin, 1908–9.
Schwappach, Adam. *Forstpolitik, Jagd- und Fischereipolitik.* Leipzig, 1894.
Schweinitz, Hans Hermann Graf von. *Deutsch-Ost-Afrika in Krieg und Frieden.* Berlin, 1894.
Shiras, George. "Photographing Wild Game with Flashlight and Camera." *National Geographic Magazine* 17 (1906): 367–423.

Sokolowsky, Alexander, ed. *Gesammelte Aufsätze zoologischen Inhalts. Für Zoologen, Landwirte, Tierzüchter und Kolonialfreunde.* Leipzig, 1909.
Stentzler, Julius. *Deutsch-Ostafrika. Kriegs- und Friedensbilder.* 2nd ed. Berlin, 1910.
Stromer von Reichenbach, Ernst. "Die einstige Verbreitung afrikanischer Säugetiere." *Naturwissenschaftliche Wochenschrift* 10 (1911): 814–16.
Stuhlmann, Franz. "Elfenbein." In *Deutsches Kolonial-Lexikon,* Vol. 1, edited by Heinrich Schnee, 556–59. Leipzig, 1920.
———. *Mit Emin Pascha ins Herz von Afrika.* Berlin, 1894.
Sutherland, James. *The Adventures of an Elephant Hunter.* Long Beach, CA, 2002. First published 1912.
Thomson, Joseph. *To the Central African Lakes and Back. The Narrative of the Royal Geographical Society's East Central African Expedition, 1878–80.* 2 vols. London, 1881.
Unterwelz, Robert. *In Tropensonne und Urwaldnacht. Wanderungen und Erlebnisse in Deutsch-Ostafrika.* Stuttgart, 1923.
Vageler, Paul. *Afrikanisches Mosaik. Fünfundzwanzig Jahre Wanderungen durch die afrikanische Wirklichkeit.* Berlin, 1941.
Verein Naturschutzpark, ed. *Naturschutzparke in Deutschland und Österreich. Ein Mahnwort an das deutsche und österreichische Volk.* 2nd ed. Stuttgart, 1911.
von der Decken, Carl Claus. *Baron Carl Claus von der Decken's Reisen in Ost-Afrika in den Jahren 1862 bis 1865. Nebst Darstellung von R. Brenner's und Th. Kinzelbach's Reisen zur Feststellung des Schicksals der Verschollenen.* Edited by Otto Kersten. Leipzig, 1871.
von Hassel, Gertrud. *Meine Kindheit in Afrika.* Heide, 1994.
Wallace, Alfred Russel. *The Geographical Distribution of Animals. With a Study of the Relations of Living and Extinct Faunas as Elucidating the Past Changes of the Earth's Surface.* 2 vols. London, 1876.
Werner, Alice. *Myths and Legends of the Bantu.* London, 1968. First published 1933.
Werther, Waldemar. *Die mittleren Hochländer des nördlichen Deutsch-Ost-Afrika. Wissenschaftliche Ergebnisse der Irangi-Expedition 1896–1897.* Berlin, 1898.
Westendarp, Wilhelm. "Das Gebiet der Elephanten und der Elfenbein-Reichthum Indiens und Afrikas." *Mitteilungen der geographischen Gesellschaft in Hamburg* 3 (1878–79): 201–13.
———. "Der Elfenbein-Reichtum Afrikas." In *Verhandlungen des fünften deutschen Geographentages zu Hamburg,* edited by Heinrich Michow, 80–91. Berlin, 1885.
Weule, Karl. *Negerleben in Ostafrika. Ergebnisse einer ethnologischen Forschungsreise.* Leipzig, 1908.
———. *Wissenschaftliche Ergebnisse meiner ethnographischen Forschungsreise in den Südosten Deutsch-Ostafrikas.* Berlin, 1908.
White, Edward Stewart. *The Rediscovered Country.* London, 1915.
Widenmann, A. *Die Kilimandscharo-Bevölkerung. Anthropologisches und Ethnographisches aus dem Dschaggalande.* Gotha, 1899.
Wissmann, Hermann. *Afrika. Schilderungen und Rathschläge zur Vorbereitung für den Aufenthalt und Dienst in den Deutschen Schutzgebieten.* Berlin, 1894.
———. "Afrikanische Jagd." *Militär-Wochenblatt* no. 99 (1894): 2629–34.
———. *In den Wildnissen Afrikas und Asiens. Jagderlebnisse.* Berlin, 1901.

———. *Unter deutscher Flagge quer durch Afrika von West nach Ost. Von 1880 bis 1883 ausgeführt von Paul Pogge und Hermann Wissmann*. Berlin, 1889.
Wissmann, Hermann, Ludwig Wolf, Curt von François und Hans Mueller. *Im Innern Afrikas. Die Erforschung des Kassai während der Jahre 1883, 1884 und 1885*. 3rd ed. Leipzig, 1891.
Zell, Theodor. *Riesen der Tierwelt. Jagdabenteuer und Lebensbilder*. Berlin, 1911.
Zimmermann, Rudolf. *Die Naturphotographie. Eine kurzgefaßte Anleitung zur Pflanzen- und Tierphotografie*. Stuttgart, 1909.

Books and articles after 1945

Please note: Essays, books, and articles that are referred to only once in the endnotes have not been included in this bibliography.

Adams, Jonathan S, and Thomas O McShane. *The Myth of Wild Africa. Conservation without Illusion*. Berkeley, CA. 1992.
Adams, William M. *Against Extinction. The Story of Conservation*. London, 2004.
———. "Nature and the Colonial Mind." In *Decolonizing Nature. Strategies for Conservation in a Post-colonial Era,* edited by William M Adams and Martin Mulligan, 16–50. London, 2003.
Allsen, Thomas T. *The Royal Hunt in Eurasian History*. Philadelphia, PA, 2006.
Alpers, Edward A. *Ivory and Slaves. Changing Patterns of International Trade in East Central Africa to the Later Nineteenth Century*. Berkeley, CA, 1975.
———. "The Ivory Trade in Africa. An Historical Overview." In *Elephant. The Animal and Its Ivory in African Culture,* edited by Doran H Ross, 349–63. Los Angeles, 1992.
Ames, Eric. *Carl Hagenbeck's Empire of Entertainments*. Seattle, 2008.
Anderson, David, and Richard Grove, eds. *Conservation in Africa. People, Policies and Practice*. Cambridge, 1987.
———. "Introduction: The Scramble for Eden: Past, Present and Future in African Conservation." In *Conservation in Africa. People, Policies and Practice,* edited by David Anderson and Richard Grove, 1–12. Cambridge, 1987.
Anderson, Virginia DeJohn. *Creatures of Empire. How Domestic Animals Transformed Early America*. Oxford, 2004.
Baldus, Rolf D, ed. *Wildes Herz von Afrika. Der Selous—traumhaftes Wildschutzgebiet*. Stuttgart, 2011 (English edition *The Wild Heart of Africa. The Selous Game Reserve in Tanzania*. Johannesburg, 2009).
Baldus, Rolf D, Benson Kibonde, and Ludwig Siege. "Seeking Conservation Partnerships in the Selous Game Reserve, Tanzania." *Parks* 13 (2003): 50–61.
Bayart, Jean-François. "Africa in the World. A History of Extraversion." *African Affairs* 99 (2000): 217–67.
Beachey, Raymond W. "The Arms Trade in East Africa." *Journal of African History* 3 (1962): 451–67.
———. "The East African Ivory Trade in the Nineteenth Century." *Journal of African History* 8 (1967): 269–90.
Becker, Felicitas. *Becoming Muslim in Mainland Tanzania 1890–2000*. Oxford, 2008.

Becker, Felicitas. "Traders, 'Big Men' and Prophets: Political Continuity and Crisis in the Maji Maji Rebellion in Southeast Tanzania." *Journal of African History* 45 (2004): 1–22.
Beinart, William. "Beyond the Colonial Paradigm: African History and Environmental History in Large-Scale Perspective." In *The Environment and World History*, edited by Edmund Burke III and Kenneth Pomeranz, 211–28. Berkeley, CA, 2009.
———. *The Rise of Conservation in South Africa: Settlers, Livestock, and the Environment 1770–1950*. Oxford, 2003.
Beinart, William, and Lotte Hughes. *Environment and Empire*. Oxford, 2007.
Berman, Russell A. "Der ewige Zweite. Deutschlands Sekundärkolonialismus." In *Phantasiereiche. Zur Kulturgeschichte des deutschen Kolonialismus*, edited by Birthe Kundrus, 19–32. Frankfurt, 2003.
Bhabha, Homi K. *The Location of Culture*. London, 2004. First published 1994.
Blackbourn, David. "'As Dependent on Each Other as Man and Wife': Cultural Contacts and Transfers." In *Wilhelmine Germany and Edwardian Britain. Essays on Cultural Affinity*, edited by Dominik Geppert and Robert Gerwarth, 15–37. Oxford, 2008.
Blaikie, Piers M, and Harold Brookfield. *Land Degradation and Society*. London, 1987.
Bont, Raf de. "'Primitives' and Protected Areas: International Conservation and the 'Naturalization' of Indigenous People, ca. 1910–1975," *Journal of the History of Ideas* 76, no. 2 (2015): 215–36.
Bridges, Roy. "Elephants, Ivory and the History of the Ivory Trade in East Africa." In *The Exploitation of Animals in Africa. Proceedings of a Colloquium at the University of Aberdeen, March 1987*, edited by Jeffrey C Stone, 193–220. Aberdeen, 1988.
Brockington, Dan. *Fortress Conservation. The Preservation of the Mkomazi Game Reserve, Tanzania*. Oxford, 2002.
———. "The Politics and Ethnography of Environmentalisms in Tanzania." *African Affairs* 105 (2006): 97–116.
Brown, Karen. "Political Entomology: The Insectile Challenge to Agricultural Development in the Cape Colony, 1895–1910." *Journal of Southern African Studies* 29 (2003): 529–49.
———. "Tropical Medicine and Animal Diseases: Onderstepoort and the Development of Veterinary Science in South Africa 1908–1950." *Journal of Southern African Studies* 31 (2005): 513–29.
Brown, Karen, and Daniel Gilfoyle, eds. *Healing the Herds. Disease, Livestock Economies, and the Globalization of Veterinary Medicine*. Athens, OH, 2010.
Carruthers, EJ. *Game Protection in the Transvaal 1846 to 1926*. Pretoria, 1995.
Carruthers, Jane. *The Kruger National Park. A Social and Political History*. Pietermaritzburg, 1995.
Cartmill, Matt. *A View to a Death in the Morning: Hunting and Nature through History*. Cambridge, MA, 1993.
Cioc, Mark. *The Game of Conservation. International Treaties to Protect the World's Migratory Animals*. Athens, OH, 2009.
Clayton, Susan. "Environmental Identity: A Conceptual and Operational Definition." In *Identity and the Natural Environment. The Psychological Significance of Nature*, edited by Susan Clayton and Susan Opotow, 45–66. Cambridge, MA, 2003.
Coates, Peter. "Creatures Enshrined: Wild Animals as Bearers of Heritage." *Past & Present, Supplement* 10 (2015): 272–98.

Conrad, Sebastian. *Globalisation and the Nation in Imperial Germany.* Cambridge, 2010.
———. "Globalization Effects: Mobility and Nation in Imperial Germany, 1880–1914." *Journal of Global History* 3 (2008): 43–66.
———. "Rethinking German Colonialism in a Global Age." *Journal of Imperial and Commonwealth History* 41 (2013): 543–66.
Conte, Christopher A. *Highland Sanctuary. Environmental History in Tanzania's Usambara Mountains.* Athens, OH, 2004.
Cooper, Frederick. *Colonialism in Question. Theory, Knowledge, History.* Berkeley, CA, 2005.
———. "Conflict and Connection. Rethinking Colonial African History." *American Historical Review* 99 (1994): 1516–45.
Cox, James. "Nineteenth Century Diplomacy on Mt. Kilimanjaro: Rindi of Moshi Reconsidered." In *Personality and Political Culture in Modern Africa. Studies Presented to Professor Harold G Marcus,* edited by Melvin E Page, Stephanie Beswick, Tim Carmichael, and Jay Spaulding, 107–18. Boston, 1998.
Daum, Andreas W. *Wissenschaftspopularisierung im 19. Jahrhundert. Bürgerliche Kultur, naturwissenschaftliche Bildung und die deutsche Öffentlichkeit 1848–1914.* 2nd ed. Munich, 2002.
Dennler de la Tour, Georges, ed. *La Protección de la Naturaleza en el Mundo. In Memoriam Doctoris Hugo Salomon.* Buenos Aires 1957.
Denoon, Donald, and Adam Kuper. "Nationalist Historians in Search of a Nation. The 'New Historiography' in Dar es Salaam." *African Affairs* 69 (1970): 329–49.
Deutsch, Jan-Georg. "Celebrating Power in Everyday Life: The Administration of Law and the Public Sphere in Colonial Tanzania, 1890–1914." *Journal of African Cultural Studies* 15 (2002): 93–103.
———. *Emancipation without Abolition in German East Africa c. 1884–1914.* Oxford, 2006.
Deutsch, Jan-Georg, Peter Probst, and Heike Schmidt, eds. *African Modernities. Entangled Meanings in Current Debate.* Portsmouth, NH, 2002.
Dominick, Raymond. *The Environmental Movement in Germany. Prophets & Pioneers, 1871–1971.* Bloomington, IN, 1992.
Douglas, Mary. *Implicit Meanings.* London, 1975.
Dunaway, Finis. "Hunting with the Camera: Nature Photography, Manliness, and Modern Memory, 1890–1930." *Journal of American Studies* 34 (2000): 207–30.
Eckert, Andreas. *Herrschen und Verwalten. Afrikanische Bürokraten, staatliche Ordnung und Politik in Tanzania, 1920–1970.* Munich, 2007.
Ehlers, Sarah. "Europeanising Impacts from the Colonies: European Campaigns against Sleeping Sickness 1900–1914." In *Pour une lecture historique de l'europeanisation au XXe siecle / Europeanisation in the 20th century: The Historical Lens,* edited by Matthieu Osmont, Émilia Robin-Hivert, Katja Seidel, Mark Spoerer, and Christian Wenkel, 111–26. Brussels, 2012.
Ekemode, Gabriel. "Fundi: Trader and Akida in Kilimanjaro, c. 1860–1898." *Tanzania Notes and Records* 77/78 (1976): 95–101.
Elkins, Caroline, and Susan Pedersen. "Introduction: Settler Colonialism: A Concept and Its Uses." In *Settler Colonialism in the Twentieth Century. Projects, Practices, Legacies,* edited by Caroline Elkins and Susan Pedersen, 1–20. New York, 2005.
Fabian, Johannes. *Time and the Other. How Anthropology Makes Its Object.* New York, 2002. First published 1983.

Feierman, Steven. *The Shambaa Kingdom. A History*. Madison, WI, 1974.
Fiedler, Matthias. *Zwischen Abenteuer, Wissenschaft und Kolonialismus. Der deutsche Afrikadiskurs im 18. und 19. Jahrhundert*. Cologne, 2005.
Fischer-Tiné, Harald. *Low and Licentious Europeans. Race, Class and "White Subalternity" in Colonial India*. New Delhi, 2009.
Ford, John. *The Role of the Trypanosomiases in African Ecology*. Oxford, 1971.
Foucault, Michel. "Of Other Spaces." *Diacritics* (1986, Spring): 22–27.
Fröhlich, Michael. *Von Konfrontation zur Koexistenz: Die deutsch-englischen Kolonialbeziehungen in Afrika zwischen 1884 und 1914*. Bochum, 1990.
Frohn, Hans-Werner, and Friedemann Schmoll, eds. *Natur und Staat. Staatlicher Naturschutz in Deutschland 1906–2006*. Bonn, 2006.
Garland, Elizabeth. "The Elephant in the Room. Confronting the Colonial Character of Wildlife Conservation in Africa." *African Studies Review* 51 (2008): 51–74.
Giblin, James L. "East Coast Fever in Socio-Historical Context: A Case Study from Tanzania." *The International Journal of African Historical Studies* 23 (1990): 401–21.
———. *The Politics of Environmental Control in Northeastern Tanzania, 1840–1940*. Philadelphia, PA, 1992.
———. "Trypanosomiasis Control in African History. An Evaded Issue?" *Journal of African History* 31 (1990): 59–80.
Giblin, James L, and Gregory Maddox. "Introduction: Custodians of the Land. Ecology and Culture in the History of Tanzania." In *Custodians of the Land. Ecology and Culture in the History of Tanzania*, edited by Gregory Maddox, James Giblin, and Isaria N Kimambo, 1–14. London, 1996.
Giblin, James, and Jamie Monson, eds. *Maji Maji. Lifting the Fog of War*. Leiden, 2010.
Giles, Linda L. "Spirit Possession and the Symbolic Construction of Swahili Society." In *Spirit Possession, Modernity, and Power*, edited by Heike Behrend and Ute Luig, 142–64. London, 1999.
Gilfoyle, Daniel. "Veterinary Research and the African Rinderpest Epizootic: The Cape Colony 1896–1898." *Journal of Southern African Studies* 29 (2003): 133–54.
Gissibl, Bernhard. "A Bavarian Serengeti. Space, Race and Time in the Entangled History of Nature Conservation in East Africa and Germany." In *Civilizing Nature. National Parks in Global Historical Perspective*, edited by Bernhard Gissibl, Sabine Höhler, and Patrick Kupper, 102–19. Oxford, 2012.
———. "Das kolonisierte Tier. Zur Ökologie der Kontaktzonen des deutschen Kolonialismus." *Werkstatt Geschichte* 56 (2010): 7–28.
———. "Die Mythen der Serengeti. Naturbilder, Naturpolitik und die Ambivalenz westlicher Um-Weltbürgerschaft in Ostafrika." *Denkanstöße* 10 (2013): 48–75.
———. "Paradiesvögel: Kolonialer Naturschutz und die Mode der deutschen Frau am Anfang des 20. Jahrhunderts." In *Ritual-Macht-Natur. Europäisch-ozeanische Beziehungswelten in der Neuzeit*, edited by Johannes Paulmann, Daniel Leese, and Philippa Söldenwagner, 131–54. Bremen, 2005.
Gissibl, Bernhard, and Johannes Paulmann. "Serengeti darf nicht sterben." In *Kein Platz an der Sonne. Erinnerungsorte der deutschen Kolonialgeschichte*, edited by Jürgen Zimmerer, 96–108. Frankfurt, 2013.
Gissibl, Bernhard, Sabine Höhler, and Patrick Kupper, eds. *Civilizing Nature. National Parks in Global Historical Perspective*. Oxford, 2012.

Glassman, Jonathon. *Feasts and Riot. Revelry, Rebellion, and Popular Consciousness on the Swahili Coast, 1856–1888.* Portsmouth, NH, 1994.
Gradmann, Christoph. *Krankheit im Labor. Robert Koch und die medizinische Bakteriologie.* Göttingen, 2005.
Grettmann-Werner, Angelika. *Wilhelm Kuhnert. 1865–1926. Tierdarstellung zwischen Wissenschaft und Kunst.* Hamburg, 1981.
Griffin, Emma. *Blood Sport. Hunting in Britain since 1066.* Yale, 2007.
Grove, Richard H. *Green Imperialism. Colonial Expansion, Tropical Island Edens and the Origins of Environmentalism, 1600–1860.* Cambridge, 1995.
Guha, Ramachandra. *Environmentalism. A Global History.* Oxford, 2000.
Gunderson, Frank. *Sukuma Labor Songs from Western Tanzania. "We Never Sleep, We Dream of Farming."* Leiden, 2010.
Gwassa, Gilbert Clement Kamana. *The Outbreak and Development of the Maji Maji War 1905–1907.* Cologne, 2005.
Gwassa, Gilbert Clement Kamana, and John Iliffe, eds. *Records of the Maji Maji-Rising. Part One.* Dar es Salaam, 1967.
Hahner-Herzog, Iris. *Tippu Tip und der Elfenbeinhandel in Ost- und Zentralafrika im 19. Jahrhundert.* Munich, 1990.
Håkansson, N Thomas. "The Human Ecology of World Systems in East Africa: The Impact of the Ivory Trade." *Human Ecology* 32 (2004): 561–91.
———. "Rulers and Rainmakers in Precolonial South Pare, Tanzania: Exchange and Ritual Experts in Political Centralization." *Ethnology* 37 (1998): 263–83.
Håkansson, N Thomas, Mats Widgren, and Lowe Börjeson. "Introduction: Historical and Regional Perspectives on Landscape Transformations in Northeastern Tanzania, 1850–2000." *International Journal of African Historical Studies* 41, no. 3 (2008): 369–82.
Hall, C Michael, and John Shultis. "Railways, Tourism and Worthless Lands: The Establishment of National Parks in Australia, Canada, New Zealand and the United States." *Australian-Canadian Studies* 8, no. 2 (1991): 57–74.
Haraway, Donna. *Primate Visions. Gender, Race, and Nature in the World of Modern Science.* New York, 1989.
Hartwig, Gerald W. *The Art of Survival in East Africa. The Kerebe and Long-Distance Trade, 1800–1895.* New York, 1976.
Herren, Madeleine. *Hintertüren zur Macht. Internationalismus und modernisierungsorientierte Außenpolitik in Belgien, der Schweiz und den USA 1865–1914.* Munich, 2000.
Heywood, Linda M. "Towards an Understanding of Modern Political Ideology in Africa: The Case of the Ovimbundu in Angola." *The Journal of Modern African Studies* 36 (1998): 139–67.
Hiller, Hubertus. *Jäger und Jagd. Zur Entwicklung des Jagdwesens in Deutschland zwischen 1848 und 1914.* Münster, 2003.
Hinz, Manfred O. "'Waidgerechtigkeit' versus afrikanische Tradition. Deutsches Jagdrecht in Namibia?" In *Kolonialisierung des Rechts. Zur kolonialen Rechts- und Verwaltungsordnung,* edited by Rüdiger Voigt and Peter Sack, 336–48. Baden-Baden, 2001.
Holdgate, Martin. *The Green Web. A Union for World Conservation.* London, 1999.
Homewood, Katherine, Patti Kristjanson, and Pippa Chenevix Trench. "Changing Land Use, Livelihoods and Wildlife Conservation in Maasailand." In *Staying*

Maasai? Livelihoods, Conservation and Development in East African Rangelands, edited by K Homewood, P Kristjanson, and P Chenevix Trench, 1–41. New York, 2009.
Hoppe, Kirk Arden. *Lords of the Fly. Sleeping Sickness Control in British East Africa, 1900–1960*. London, 2003.
Hughes, Lotte. *Moving the Maasai. A Colonial Misadventure*. Houndmills, 2006.
Iliffe, John. *A Modern History of Tanganyika*. Cambridge, 1979.
———. *Tanganyika under German Rule 1905–1912*. Cambridge, 1969.
Ingold, Tim. "From Trust to Domination. An Alternative History of Human-Animal Relations." In *Animals and Human History. Changing Perspectives*, edited by Aubrey Manning, 1–22. London, 1994.
———. *The Perception of the Environment. Essays on Livelihood, Dwelling and Skill*. Abingdon, 2000.
Iriye, Akira. *Global Community: The Role of International Organizations in the Making of the Contemporary World*. Berkeley, CA, 2002.
Isaacman, Allen F, and Barbara S Isaacman. *Slavery and Beyond. The Making of Men and Chikunda Ethnic Identities in the Unstable World of South-Central Africa, 1750–1920*. Portsmouth, NH, 2005.
Jacoby, Karl. "Conservation." In *Encyclopedia of World Environmental History*, edited by Shepard Krech, John Robert McNeill, and Carolyn Merchant, 262–68. London, 2004.
Jalais, Annu. "Unmasking the Cosmopolitan Tiger." *Nature and Culture* 3, no. 1 (2008): 25–40.
Jepson, Paul, and Robert J Whittaker. "Histories of Protected Areas: Internationalisation of Conservationist Values and Their Adoption in the Netherlands Indies (Indonesia)." *Environment and History* 8 (2002): 129–72.
Jones, Karen. "Unpacking Yellowstone. The American National Park in Global Perspective." In *Civilizing Nature. National Parks in Global Historical Perspective*, edited by Bernhard Gissibl, Sabine Höhler, and Patrick Kupper, 31–49. Oxford, 2012.
Kimambo, Isaria N. *Penetration and Protest in Tanzania. The Impact of the World Economy on the Pare 1860–1960*. London, 1991.
Kirchberger, Ulrike. "Wie entsteht eine imperiale Infrastruktur? Zum Aufbau der Naturschutzbürokratie in Deutsch-Ostafrika." *Historische Zeitschrift* 291 (2010): 41–69.
Kjekshus, Helge. *Ecology Control and Economic Development in East African History. The Case of Tanganyika 1850–1950*. London, 1977.
Köhler, Axel. "Half-Man, Half-Elephant. Shapeshifting among the Baka of Congo." In *Natural Enemies. People-Wildlife Conflicts in Anthropological Perspective*, edited by John Knight, 50–77. London, 2000.
Köstering, Susanne. *Natur zum Anschauen. Das Naturkundemuseum des deutschen Kaiserreichs 1871–1914*. Cologne, 2003.
Koponen, Juhani. *Development for Exploitation. German Colonial Policies in Mainland Tanzania, 1884–1914*. Helsinki, 1995.
———. *People and Production in Late Precolonial Tanzania. History and Structures*. Helsinki, 1988.
Kundrus, Birthe. *Moderne Imperialisten. Das Kaiserreich im Spiegel seiner Kolonien*. Cologne, 2003.

———, ed. *Phantasiereiche. Zur Kulturgeschichte des deutschen Kolonialismus*. Frankfurt, 2003.

———. "Von der Peripherie ins Zentrum. Zur Bedeutung des Kolonialismus für das Deutsche Kaiserreich." In *Das Deutsche Kaiserreich in der Kontroverse*, edited by Sven Oliver Müller and Cornelius Torp, 359–73. Göttingen, 2009.

Kupper, Patrick. *Creating Wilderness. A Transnational History of the Swiss National Park*. Oxford, 2014.

Langbehn, Volker. "Introduction. Picturing Race: Visuality and German Colonialism." In *German Colonialism, Visual Culture, and Modern Memory*, edited by Volker Langbehn, 1–33. New York, 2010.

Laqua, Daniel. "The Tensions of Internationalism. Transnational Anti-Slavery in the 1880s and 1890s." *International History Review* 33 (2011): 705–26.

Lawrance, Benjamin N, Emily Lynn Osborn, and Richard L Roberts. "Introduction. African Intermediaries and the 'Bargain' of Collaboration." In *Intermediaries, Interpreters and Clerks. African Employees and the Making of Colonial Africa*, edited by Benjamin N Lawrance, Emily Lynn Osborn, and Richard L Roberts, 3–34. Madison, WI, 2006.

Legros, Hugues. *Chasseurs d'Ivoire. Une histoire du royaume yeke du Shaba (Zaïre)*. Brussels, 1996.

Lehmann, Philipp N. "Between Waterberg and Sandveld: An Environmental Perspective on the German-Herero War of 1904." *German History* 32, no. 4 (2014): 533–58.

Lekan, Thomas. *Imagining the Nation in Nature. Landscape Preservation and German Identity, 1885–1945*. Cambridge, MA, 2004.

———. "Serengeti Shall Not Die: Bernhard Grzimek, Wildlife Film, and the Making of a Tourist Landscape in East Africa." *German History* 29 (2011): 224–64.

Lindner, Ulrike. "Colonialism as a European Project in Africa before 1914? British and German Concepts of Colonial Rule in Sub-Saharan Africa." *Comparativ* 19 (2009): 88–106.

———. *Koloniale Begegnungen. Deutschland und Großbritannien als Imperialmächte in Afrika 1880–1914*. Frankfurt, 2011.

Livingstone, David N. *Putting Science in Its Place. Geographies of Scientific Knowledge*. Chicago, 2003.

Loo, Tina. "Of Moose and Men. Hunting for Masculinities in British Columbia, 1880–1939." *Western Historical Quarterly* 32 (2001): 296–319.

Lorimer, Jamie. "Nonhuman Charisma." *Environment and Planning D: Society and Space* 25 (2007): 911–32.

MacKenzie, John M. *The Empire of Nature. Hunting, Conservation and British Imperialism*. Manchester, 1988.

———. "European Imperialism: A Zone of Co-operation Rather than Competition?" In *Imperial Co-operation and Transfer, 1870–1930. Empires and Encounters*, edited by Volker Barth and Roland Cvetkovski, 35–53. London, 2015.

———. "'Mutual Goodwill and Admiration' or 'Jealous Ill-Will'? Empire and Popular Culture." In *Wilhelmine Germany and Edwardian Britain. Essays on Cultural Affinity*, edited by Dominik Geppert and Robert Gerwarth, 91–114. Oxford, 2008.

Maddox, Gregory H. "Networks and Frontiers in Colonial Tanzania." *Environmental History* 3 (1998): 436–59.

———. *Sub-Saharan Africa. An Environmental History*. Santa Barbara, CA, 2006.

Marks, Stuart. *Large Mammals and a Brave People. Subsistence Hunters in Zambia*. New Brunswick, 2005.
Matzke, Gordon. *Wildlife in Tanzanian Settlement Policy: The Case of the Selous*. Syracuse, NY, 1977.
Médard, Jean-François. "Le 'Big Man' en Afrique: Esquisse d'Analyse du Politicien Entrepreneur." *L'Année sociologique* 49 (1992): 167–92.
Meredith, Martin. *Africa's Elephant. A Biography*. London, 2001.
Meyer, John W, David John Frank, Ann Hironaka, Evan Schofer, and Nancy Brandon Tuma. "The Structuring of a World Environmental Regime, 1870–1990." *International Organization* 51 (1997): 623–51.
Mitchell, WJT. "Imperial Landscape." In *Landscape and Power*, edited by WJT Mitchell, 5–34. Chicago, 2002.
Möllers, Bernhard. *Robert Koch. Persönlichkeit und Lebenswerk 1843–1910*. Hannover, 1950.
Monson, Jamie. "Relocating Maji Maji: The Politics of Alliance and Authority in the Southern Highlands of Tanzania, 1870–1918." *Journal of African History* 39 (1998): 95–120.
Morris, Brian. *Animals and Ancestors. An Ethnography*. Oxford, 2000.
———. *The Power of Animals. An Ethnography*. Oxford, 1998.
Munson, Robert B. *The Nature of Christianity in Northern Tanzania. Environmental and Social Change, 1890–1916*. Lanham, MD, 2013.
Naranch, Bradley D. "'Colonized Body,' 'Oriental Machine': Debating Race, Railroads, and the Politics of Reconstruction in Germany and East Africa, 1906–1910." *Central European History* 33 (2000): 299–338.
Nash, Roderick. *Wilderness and the American Mind*. 4th ed. New Haven, CT, 2001. First published 1967.
Neill, Deborah J. *Networks in Tropical Medicine. Internationalism, Colonialism, and the Rise of a Medical Specialty, 1890–1930*. Stanford, CA, 2012.
Nelson, Fred, ed. *Community Rights, Conservation and Contested Land. The Politics of Natural Resource Governance in Africa*. London, 2010.
Neumann, Roderick P. "Africa's Last Wilderness. Reordering Space for Political and Economic Control in Colonial Tanzania." *Africa* 71 (2001): 641–65.
———. "Dukes, Earls and Ersatz Edens: Aristocratic Nature Preservationists in Colonial Africa." *Environment and Planning D: Society and Space* 14 (1996): 79–98.
———. *Imposing Wilderness. Struggles over Livelihood and Nature Preservation in Africa*. Berkeley, CA, 1998.
———. *Making Political Ecology*. London, 2005.
———. "The Postwar Conservation Boom in British Colonial Africa." *Environmental History* 7 (2002): 22–47.
Nyagava, Seth I. "Were the Bena Traitors? Maji Maji in Njombe and the Context of Local Alliances Made by the Germans." In *Maji Maji. Lifting the Fog of War*, edited by James Giblin and Jamie Monson, 241–57. Leiden, 2010.
Nyhart, Lynn K. *Modern Nature. The Rise of the Biological Perspective in Germany*. Chicago, 2009.
Ofcansky, Thomas P. *Paradise Lost. A History of Game Preservation in East Africa*. Morgantown, 2002.
Oksiloff, Assenka. *Picturing the Primitive. Visual Culture, Ethnography, and Early German Cinema*. New York, 2001.
Osterhammel, Jürgen. *Colonialism. A Theoretical Overview*. Princeton, NJ, 2005.

———. "'The Great Work of Uplifting Mankind.' Zivilisierungsmission und Moderne." In *Zivilisierungsmissionen: Imperiale Weltverbesserung seit dem 18. Jahrhundert*, edited by Boris Barth and Jürgen Osterhammel, 363–427. Konstanz, 2005.
Pandian, Anand S. "Predatory Care: The Imperial Hunt in Mughal and British India." *Journal of Historical Sociology* 14 (2001): 79–107.
Paulmann, Johannes. "Jenseits von Eden. Kolonialismus, Zeitkritik und wissenschaftlicher Naturschutz in Bernhard Grzimeks Tierfilmen der 1950er-Jahre." *Zeitschrift für Geschichtswissenschaft* 56 (2008): 541–60.
Pels, Peter. "The Anthropology of Colonialism. Culture, History, and the Emergence of Western Governmentality." *Annual Review of Anthropology* 26 (1997): 163–83.
Pesek, Michael. *Koloniale Herrschaft in Deutsch-Ostafrika. Expeditionen, Militär und Verwaltung seit 1880*. Frankfurt, 2005.
Pratt, Mary Louise. *Imperial Eyes. Travel Writing and Transculturation*. London, 1992.
Prendergast, David K, and William M Adams. "Colonial Wildlife Conservation and the Origins of the Society for the Preservation of the Wild Fauna of the Empire (1903–1914)." *Oryx* 37 (2003): 251–60.
Prestholdt, Jeremy. *Domesticating the World. African Consumerism and the Genealogies of Globalization*. Berkeley, CA, 2008.
———. "On the Global Repercussions of East African Consumerism." *American Historical Review* 109 (2004): 755–81.
Rempel, Ruth. "Trade and Transformation: Participation in the Ivory Trade in Late 19th-Century East and Central Africa." *Canadian Journal of Development Studies* 19 (1998): 529–52.
Richards, John F. *The Unending Frontier. An Environmental History of the Early Modern World*. Berkeley, CA, 2003.
Rockel, Stephen J. *Carriers of Culture. Labor on the Road in Nineteenth Century East Africa*. Portsmouth, NH, 2006.
———. "Decentering Exploration in East Africa." In *Reinterpreting Exploration. The West in the World*, edited by Dane Kennedy, 172–94. Oxford, 2014.
Rollins, William H. "Imperial Shades of Green: Conservation and Environmental Chauvinism in the German Colonial Project." *German Studies Review* 22 (1999): 187–213.
Ross, Corey. "Tropical Nature as Global *Patrimoine*. Imperialism and International Nature Protection in the Early Twentieth Century." *Past & Present Supplement* 10 (2015): 214–39.
Rothfels, Nigel. *Savages and Beasts. The Birth of the Modern Zoo*. Baltimore, MD, 2002.
Russell, Edmund. *Evolutionary History. Uniting History and Biology to Understand Life on Earth*. Cambridge, 2011.
Ryan, James R. *Picturing Empire. Photography and the Visualization of the British Empire*. Chicago, 1997.
Sahlins, Marshall D. "Poor Man, Rich Man, Big-Man, Chief: Political Types in Melanesia and Polynesia." *Comparative Studies in Society and History* 5 (1963): 285–303.
Salazar, Noel. *Envisioning Eden. Mobilizing Imaginaries in Tourism and Beyond*. New York, 2011.
Schabel, Hans G. "Tanganyika Forestry under German Colonial Administration, 1891–1919." *Forest & Conservation History* 34 (1990): 130–41.
Schiefel, Werner. *Bernhard Dernburg, 1865–1937: Kolonialpolitiker und Bankier im wilhelminischen Deutschland*. Zürich, 1974.

Schmidt, Heike I. "Colonial Intimacy. The Rechenberg Scandal and Homosexuality in German East Africa." *Journal of the History of Sexuality* 17 (2008): 25–59.
Schmoll, Friedemann. *Erinnerung an die Natur. Die Geschichte des Naturschutzes im deutschen Kaiserreich.* Frankfurt, 2004.
Scott, James C. *Seeing Like a State. How Certain Schemes to Improve the Human Condition Have Failed.* New Haven, CT, 1998.
Sheail, John. *Nature's Spectacle. The World's First National Parks and Protected Areas.* London, 2010.
Sheriff, Abdul. *Slaves, Spices and Ivory in Zanzibar. Integration of an East African Commercial Empire into the World Economy, 1770–1873.* London, 1987.
Shetler, Jan Bender. *Imagining Serengeti. A History of Landscape Memory in Tanzania from Earliest Times to the Present.* Athens, OH, 2007.
———. *Telling Our Own Stories. Local Histories from South Mara, Tanzania.* Leiden, 2003.
Short, John Philip. *Magic Lantern Empire. Colonialism and Society in Germany.* Ithaca, NY, 2012.
Shorter, Aylward. *Chiefship in Western Tanzania. A Political History of the Kimbu.* Oxford, 1972.
Sinclair, Anthony RE. *The Serengeti Story. Life and Science in the World's Greatest Wildlife Region.* Oxford, 2012.
Singleton, M. "Dawa: Beyond Science and Superstition." *Anthropos* 74 (1979): 817–63.
Sippel, Harald. "Aspects of Colonial Land Law in German East Africa: German East Africa Company, Crown Land Ordinance, European Plantations and Reserved Areas for Africans." In *Land Law and Land Ownership in Africa. Case Studies from Colonial and Contemporary Cameroon and Tanzania,* edited by Robert Debusmann and Stefan Arnold, 3–38. Bayreuth, 1996.
Smith Kipp, Rita, and Edward M Shortman. "The Political Impact of Trade in Chiefdoms." *American Anthropologist* 91 (1989): 370–85.
Söldenwagner, Philippa. *Spaces of Negotiation. European Settlement and Settlers in German East Africa, 1900–1914.* Munich, 2006.
Spear, Thomas. *Mountain Farmers. Moral Economies of Land & Agricultural Development in Arusha & Meru.* Oxford, 1997.
Spinage, Clive A. *African Ecology. Benchmark and Historical Perspectives.* Berlin, 2012.
———. *Cattle Plague. A History.* New York, 2003.
Steinbach, Daniel Rouven. "Carved Out of Nature: Identity and Environment in German Colonial Africa." In *Cultivating the Colonies. Colonial States and Their Environmental Legacies,* edited by Christina Folke Ax, Niels Brimnes, Niklas Thode Jensen, and Karen Oslund, 47–77. Athens, OH, 2011.
Steinhart, Edward I. *Black Poachers, White Hunters. A Social History of Hunting in Colonial Kenya.* Oxford, 2006.
———. "Elephant Hunting in 19th-Century Kenya: Kamba Society and Ecology in Transformation." *The International Journal of African Historical Studies* 33 (2001): 335–49.
Steinmetz, George. *The Devil's Handwriting. Precoloniality and the German Colonial State in Qingdao, Samoa, and Southwest Africa.* Chicago, 2007.
Stoler, Ann Laura. *Along the Archival Grain. Epistemic Anxieties and Colonial Common Sense.* Princeton, NJ, 2009.

Stoler, Ann Laura, and Frederick Cooper. "Between Metropole and Colony: Rethinking a Research Agenda." In *Tensions of Empire. Colonial Cultures in a Bourgeois World*, edited by Frederick Cooper and Ann Laura Stoler, 1–56. Berkeley, CA, 1997.

Struck, Wolfgang. "Reenacting Colonialism. Germany and Its Former Colonies in Recent TV Productions." In *German Colonialism, Visual Culture, and Modern Memory*, edited by Volker M Langbehn, 260–77. New York, 2010.

Sukumar, Raman. *The Living Elephants. Evolutionary Ecology, Behavior, and Conservation*. Oxford, 2003.

Sunseri, Thaddeus. "The *Baumwollfrage*. Cotton Colonialism in German East Africa." *Central European History* 34 (2001): 31–51.

———. "The Entangled History of *Sadoka* (Rinderpest) and Veterinary Science in Tanzania and the Wider World, 1891–1901." *Bulletin of the History of Medicine* 89, no. 1 (2015): 92–121.

———. "Exploiting the *Urwald*. German Post-Colonial Forestry in Poland and Central Africa, 1900–1960." *Past & Present* 214 (2012): 305–42.

———. "Famine and Wild Pigs: Gender Struggles and the Outbreak of the Maji-Maji War in Uzaramo." *Journal of African History* 38 (1997): 235–59.

———. "Reinterpreting a Colonial Rebellion: Forestry and Social Control in German East Africa, 1874–1915." *Environmental History* 8 (2003): 430–51.

———. *Vilimani. Labor Migration and Rural Change in Early Colonial Tanzania*. Portsmouth, NH, 2002.

———. "The War of the Hunters: Maji Maji and the Decline of the Ivory Trade." In *Maji Maji. Lifting the Fog of War*, edited by James Giblin and Jamie Monson, 117–48. Leiden, 2010.

———. *Wielding the Ax. State Forestry and Social Conflict in Tanzania, 1820–2000*. Athens, OH, 2009.

Tetzlaff, Rainer. *Koloniale Entwicklung und Ausbeutung. Wirtschafts- und Sozialgeschichte Deutsch-Ostafrikas 1885–1914*. Berlin, 1970.

Tilley, Helen. *Africa as a Living Laboratory. Empire, Development and the Problem of Scientific Knowledge 1870–1950*. Chicago, 2011.

Tyrrell, Ian. "America's National Parks: The Transnational Creation of National Space in the Progressive Era." *Journal of American Studies* 46, no. 1 (2012): 1–21.

Uekötter, Frank. *The Greenest Nation? A New History of German Environmentalism*. London 2014.

Umbach, Maiken, Lora Wildenthal, Jürgen Zimmerer, Russel A. Berman, Jan Rüger, Bradley Naranch, and Birthe Kundrus."Forum: The German Colonial Imagination." *German History* 26 (2008): 251–71.

van Laak, Dirk. *Imperiale Infrastruktur. Deutsche Planungen für eine Erschließung Afrikas 1880 bis 1960*. Paderborn, 2004.

———. "Kolonien als 'Laboratorien der Moderne'?" In *Das Kaiserreich transnational. Deutschland in der Welt 1871–1914*, edited by Sebastian Conrad and Jürgen Osterhammel, 257–79. Göttingen, 2004.

van Sittert, Lance. "Bringing in the Wild: The Commodification of Wild Animals in the Cape Colony/Province c. 1850–1950." *Journal of African History* 46 (2005): 269–91.

Vansina, Jan. *Paths in the Rainforest. Toward a History of Political Tradition in Equatorial Africa*. Madison, WI, 1990.

Von Oppen, Achim. "Matuta. Landkonflikte, Ökologie und Entwicklung in der Geschichte Tanzanias." In *Tanzania. Koloniale Vergangenheit und neuer Aufbruch*, edited by Ulrich van der Heyden and Achim von Oppen, 47–84. Münster, 1996.

Wächter, H Jürgen. *Naturschutz in den deutschen Kolonien in Afrika (1884–1918)*. Münster, 2008.

Walker, John Frederick. *Ivory's Ghosts. The White Gold of History and the Fate of Elephants*. New York, 2009.

Waller, Richard. "'Clean' and 'Dirty': Cattle Disease and Control Policy in Colonial Kenya, 1900–1940." *Journal of African History* 45 (2004): 45–80.

———. "Ecology, Migration, and Expansion in East Africa." *African Affairs* 84 (1985): 347–70.

———. "Emutai: Crisis and Response in Maasailand 1883–1902." In *The Ecology of Survival. Case Studies from Northeast African History*, edited by Douglas H Johnson and David M Anderson, 73–112. London, 1988.

Warde, Paul. *Ecology, Economy and State Formation in Early Modern Germany*. Cambridge, 2006.

Waz, Gerlinde. "Auf der Suche nach dem letzten Paradies. Der Afrikaforscher und Regisseur Hans Schomburgk." In *Triviale Tropen. Exotische Reise- und Abenteuerfilme aus Deutschland 1919–1939*, edited by Jörg Schöning, 95–110. Munich, 1997.

White, Richard. *The Middle Ground. Indians, Empires, and Republics in the Great Lakes Region, 1650–1815*. Cambridge, 1991.

Wimmelbücker, Ludger. *Kilimanjaro—A Regional History. Vol. 1: Production and Living Conditions, c. 1800–1920*. Münster, 2003.

Wöbse, Anna-Katharina. "Naturschutz global—oder: Hilfe von außen. Internationale Beziehungen des amtlichen Naturschutzes im 20. Jahrhundert." In *Natur und Staat. Staatlicher Naturschutz in Deutschland 1906–2006*, edited by Hans-Werner Frohn and Friedemann Schmoll, 625–727. Bonn, 2006.

———. *Weltnaturschutz. Umweltdiplomatie in Völkerbund und Vereinten Nationen 1920–1950*. Frankfurt, 2012.

Wright, Marcia. "Local Roots of Policy in German East Africa." *Journal of African History* 9 (1968): 621–30.

———. "Maji Maji: Prophecy and Historiography." In *Revealing Prophets. Prophecy in Eastern African History*, edited by David Anderson and Douglas H Johnson, 124–42. London, 1995.

Zimmerman, Andrew. "Africa in Imperial and Transnational History: Multi-Sited Historiography and the Necessity of Theory." *Journal of African History* 54 (2013): 331–40.

———. *Anthropology and Antihumanism in Imperial Germany*. Chicago, 2001.

Unpublished Theses and Papers

Becker, Felicitas. "A Social History of Southeast Tanzania, Ca. 1890–1950." PhD diss., University of Cambridge, 2001.

Ekemode, Gabriel. "German Rule in North-East Tanzania, 1885–1914." PhD diss., University of London, 1973.

Evers, Karl. "Das Hamburger Zanzibarhandelshaus Wm. O'swald & Co. 1847–1890. Zur Geschichte des Hamburger Handels mit Ostafrika." PhD diss., University of Hamburg, 1986.

Fisher, Eleanor. "What Future for the Shamba la Bibi? Livelihoods and Local Resource Use in a Tanzanian Game Reserve." PhD diss., University of Hull, 1997.

Fuhrmann, Wolfgang. "Propaganda, Science and Entertainment. Early Colonial Cinematography: A Case Study in the History of Early Nonfiction Cinema." PhD diss., University of Utrecht, 2003.

Garland, Elizabeth. "State of Nature: Colonial Power, Neoliberal Capital, and Wildlife Management in Tanzania." PhD diss., University of Chicago, 2006.

Larson, Lorne E. "A History of the Mahenge (Ulanga) District, ca. 1860–1957." PhD diss., University of Dar es Salaam, 1976.

Nyagava, Seth Ismael. "A History of the Bena to 1908." PhD diss., University of Dar es Salaam, 1988.

van Schuylenbergh, Patricia. "De l'appropriation à la conservation de la faune sauvage. Pratiques d'une colonisation: le cas du Congo belge (1885–1960)." PhD diss., Université catholique de Louvain, 2006.

Index

Persons

Abdallah Mapanda, 55, 130
Adams, Alfons, 58
Alpers, Edward, 52
Barthes, Roland, 277
Baumann, Oskar, 46, 52
Behn, Fritz, 185, 195n26, 278
Berman, Russell A., 15
Bley, Fritz, 157–58, 255, 283
Blohm, Wilhelm, 57
Böcklin von Böcklinsau, Ruprecht, 233–34
Böhm, Richard, 47, 67
Bölsche, Wilhelm, 275, 276, 283, 288
Bronsart von Schellendorf, Fritz, 210, 214, 227n38
Brown, Karen, 240
Bülow, Bernhard von, 159, 175n81
Bumiller, Theodor, 83
Burton, Antoinette, 15
Burton, Richard, 38, 56–57, 67, 151
Conwentz, Hugo, 279, 282–83, 301
Cooper, Frederick, 79, 245
Coudenhove, Richard, 193
Decken, Carl Claus von der, 7, 74, 102n80
Dernburg, Bernhard, 142, 150, 159–62, 163, 175n81, 179, 182, 242
Dönhoff, Christoph Graf, 302–3
Doflein, Franz, 210, 283
Eidmann, Hermann, 302–3
Eliot, Sir Charles, 233
Elton, Frederic, 52
Falz-Fein, Friedrich, 210
Farler, John Prediger, 48
Floericke, Kurt, 216, 283, 313n14

Ford, John, 151–52
Friese, Richard, 288–89
Fromm, Paul, 131
Fundi (trader), 84–85, 90, 102n80, 114
Garland, Elizabeth, 309
Giblin, James, 151–52
Girouard, Percy, 233
Göring, Hermann, 299, 302
Goerke, Franz, 277
Götzen, Gustav Adolf Graf von, 115–19, 120, 125, 128, 131, 135n26, 139n110
Goldschmidt-Rothschild, Rudolf von, 193
Grzimek, Bernhard, 1, 7, 8–9, 215, 278, 300–301, 303–5
Grzimek, Michael, 1
Günther, Konrad, 283
Hagenbeck, Carl, 155, 189, 210, 289, 313n14
Håkansson, N. Thomas, 12
Hardinge, Sir Arthur, 237
Hassel, Gertrud von, 111, 126
Hassel, Theodor von, 109–12, 125–27, 133–34, 134n2, 134n6
Heck, Ludwig, 155, 210, 274, 283, 292n20, 313n14
Heck, Lutz, 313n14, 314n24
Hennings, Curt, 158
Heyking, Elisabeth von, 275, 276
Heywood, Linda, 54
Hill, Sir Clement, 232–34, 238, 243, 249, 259n1
Hohenlohe-Langenburg, Hermann von, 67
Hohenlohe-Schillingsfürst, Chlodwig zu, 211

Hornaday, William, 212
Huebner, Richard, 193
Ingold, Tim, 58
Isike, 56, 69
Jalais, Annu, 276
Kibasira, 130
Kiwanga, 93, 124, 125, 130, 131
Koch, Robert, 16, 153–55, 157–58, 179, 181, 186, 239–40, 278, 283
Köhler, Axel, 133
Königsmarck, Hans von, 233, 234
Konrad, Prince of Bavaria, 193
Kopa-Kopa, 130
Krüger, Hardy, 300
Kuhnert, Wilhelm, 126, 185, 283, 288–89, 311
Langheld, Wilhelm, 83
Leopold, Prince of Bavaria, 207–8
Leopold II, King of Belgium, 88, 103n90, 173n55
Liebert, Eduard von, 91–92, 115, 148, 203
Lippe, Bernhard zur, 78, 156
Livingstone, David, 44, 67
Löns, Hermann, 289
Lorenz, Konrad, 305
MacKenzie, John M., 81, 237
Magewa, 130
Mangula, 109–11, 122, 123, 126, 133–34, 134n5, 224
Martin, Philipp Leopold, 279–80, 281
Matschie, Paul, 158, 174n66, 174n67, 210, 292n20
May, Karl, 212
Mbegha, 49
Mboga, 48
Mecklenburg, Adolf Friedrich von, 157, 189, 273
Mecklenburg, Johann Albrecht von, 157, 173n55, 289
Meerwarth, Hermann, 277
Merere, 52, 83, 93, 124
Meyer, Adolf, 41, 61n27, 67
Mirambo, 56, 97n12
Mkwawa, 48, 56, 93–94, 104n113, 124
Monson, Jamie, 84

M'siri, 49–50
Mtinginya, 84
Mujinga, 48
Neumann, Roderick, 310
Nyerere, Julius, 304
Nyungu-ya-Mawe, 56, 97n12
Omari Kinjala, 130
Orwell, George, 110
Paasche, Hans, 126, 141, 166, 169n1, 184, 185, 186, 187, 188, 214, 255, 273, 281, 284, 301
Pogge, Paul, 88
Prestholdt, Jeremy, 40
Prince, Tom von, 93–94, 95, 219, 222
Rashid bin Masoud, 55, 93, 130, 131
Rechenberg, Albrecht von, 22, 142, 148, 150, 159–166, 178, 179–83, 185, 186, 188–90, 203, 204, 210, 213, 219, 233, 255, 283, 285
Rehfus, Karl, 75
Reichard, Paul, 45, 67, 83
Richards, John F., 202
Rindi, 37, 59n9
Roosevelt, Theodore, 189, 212, 276
Ross, Corey, 254
Rudorff, Ernst, 279
Ryan, James, 275
Salazar, Noel, 2
Salomon, Hugo, 283, 301
Sander, Karl Ludwig, 158, 174n67
Sarasin, Paul, 186–87, 255–58, 283, 301, 313n14
Schauer, Konrad, 193, 273, 299, 312n5
Schillings, Carl Georg, 9, 17, 18, 113–15, 116, 117, 142, 156, 161–62, 175n81, 179, 184–86, 188, 189–90, 191, 202, 210, 213, 214–15, 243, 248, 249, 255, 258, 269, 270–278, 281, 283, 284, 286, 288, 292n20, 293n31, 300, 301, 304
Schmoll, Friedemann, 279
Schoeller, Max, 113
Schoenichen, Walther, 301–2
Schomburgk, Hans, 78, 232, 273, 278, 300, 313n14
Schultze-Naumburg, Paul, 279
Schwantje, Magnus, 257

Schweinfurth, Georg, 44, 283
Selous, Frederick Courteney, 308, 310, 311, 315n45
Sharpe, Alfred, 247
Simba, 56
Simmel, Georg, 76
Speke, John Hanning, 47
Sokolowsky, Alexander, 283, 313n14
Solf, Wilhelm, 178, 189–90, 204, 213
Sontag, Susan, 277
Stanley, Henry Morton, 67, 88, 270
Stolz, Adolf Ferdinand, 77–78, 99n48
Sunseri, Thaddeus, 11–12, 112, 131, 222
Theiler, Arnold, 239–40
Thomson, Joseph, 44, 123
Trappe, Margarete, 299–300
Victor II, Duke of Ratibor, 157, 174n64
Wetekamp, Wilhelm, 279, 282
Weule, Karl, 57
White, Richard, 79
Wilhelm II, German Emperor, 154, 157, 161, 178, 189–90, 204, 207, 247
Wissmann, Hermann (von), 25n15, 69, 72, 82, 83, 84–85, 85–90, 91, 94, 103n90, 112–14, 117, 142,148, 157, 201, 203, 204, 205, 207, 211–12, 218, 221, 232–33, 234, 236, 237–38, 243, 246, 247, 248, 253, 259, 282–83, 284, 310
Woosnam, Richard B, 233
Zache, Hans, 155
Zwillling, Ernst Alexander, 303, 314n24

Places

Amsterdam, 41
Angola, 54
Antwerp, 41
Arusha, 65n93, 69, 180
Askania Nova, 210
Bagamoyo, 40, 43, 92, 97n7, 97n18, 221, 225, 230n89
Bavarian Forest, 290
Białowieża, 290
British East Africa, 22, 114, 117, 192, 201, 233, 235–39, 240–43, 245, 260n12. *See also* Kenya
Buitenzorg, 210, 240
Cadinen, 189
Congo
    basin, 46, 72, 88, 133, 157, 235, 236
    free state, 69, 70, 242, 247, 248, 249, 253
    French, 249
    Upper, 86
Dar-es-Salaam, 3, 6, 7, 17, 18, 20, 46, 70, 71, 82, 85, 86, 88, 90, 91, 92, 97n18, 118, 120, 125, 128, 129, 131, 144, 148, 159, 160, 168, 188, 190, 206, 207, 209, 218, 219, 238, 240, 307
German South-West Africa (Namibia), 182
Hamburg, 41, 155, 173n55, 193, 272, 283, 289
Harz, 289
India, 16, 23, 40, 41, 43, 74, 76, 88, 153, 166, 192, 234, 237, 239, 240
Indian Ocean, 40, 42
Kakoma, 47
Katanga, 49, 50
Kenya, 114, 141, 142, 147, 159, 161, 162, 178, 179, 180, 181, 188, 190, 191–93, 208, 211, 213, 233–34, 235–39, 261n26, 299, 302. *See also* British East Africa
Kibwezi, 193
Kilimanjaro, Mt., 5, 10, 37, 43, 82, 83, 84–85, 86, 87, 89, 90, 95, 113, 114, 115, 117, 121, 143, 144, 156, 158, 163, 164, 166, 180, 192, 201, 206, 208, 214, 225, 227n38, 232, 243, 288, 318
Kilombero, 93, 109, 123, 124, 219
Kilwa, 40, 42, 43, 81, 123, 125, 132, 167, 168, 222
Kimweri, 48–9
Lake Manyara, 232, 303
Lake Nyasa, 42
Lake Rukwa, 303
Lake Tanganyika, 43, 49, 243

Lake Victoria, 3, 43, 84, 154, 179, 180, 204, 208, 215, 232, 239
Langenburg, 83, 92
Lindi, 42, 47, 81, 90, 93, 110, 121, 122, 129, 130, 131, 168
Liwale, 47, 55, 130, 308
London, 18, 41, 85, 112, 117, 218, 232, 238, 240, 246, 259, 303. *See also* Conference on the Preservation of Wild Animals, Birds, and Fish in Africa (London 1900); Conference on the Protection of African Fauna and Flora (London 1933); Convention for the Preservation of Wild Animals, Birds and Fish in Africa (1900)
Lüneburg heath, 4, 184, 284
Lupembe, 125, 183, 190, 224
Lyck, 186, 283
Maasailand, 4, 43, 232–33, 306
Maasai reserve
  in German East Africa, 5, 206, 209
  in Kenya, 179–80
Maasai Steppe, 4, 10, 80, 113, 141, 156, 185, 202
Magdeburg, 186, 283
Mahenge, 21, 46, 109–11, 121, 122, 123–27, 131, 132, 133–34, 134n6, 168, 183, 204
Malawi, 181
Mara, 48
Masasi, 47
Matandu, 130, 308
Mbwemkuru (river), 47, 90, 130, 167, 225
Mbeya, 77
Meru, Mt., 115, 143, 146, 166, 180, 201, 206, 300
Mikindani, 47, 90
Mkalinzo, 132
Mkata, 208, 215
Mombasa, 40, 179, 191, 192, 235, 239, 241
Momella, 300
Moshi, 5, 37, 43, 69, 84–85, 90, 152, 163, 164, 179, 180, 223, 318
Mpwapwa, 69, 90, 92, 93
Mumbai (Bombay), 41

Mweka, 304
Namibia, 182
New York, 41
Ngorongoro, 1–8, 24n1, 26n22, 193, 204, 209, 215, 217, 284, 299, 301, 302, 306
Onderstepoort, 240, 262n35
Pangani, 37, 43, 84, 85, 90
Pangani rapids, 209
Pare, 45, 208, 218, 221
reserves
  Aruwimi (Congo), 253
  Lake Natron, 206, 207–8, 218, 223, 233
  Liwale, 125
  Lupembe ('Kisiwani'), 125, 183, 190, 224
  Mahenge, 132, 204, 209, 213, 219, 225, 308
  Matandu, 130, 308
  Ngorongoro, 1–8, 204, 209, 217, 284, 299, 301, 302, 306
  Northern Railway (Pare), 208, 218, 221
  Ruaha, 125, 126, 132
  Rufiji, 22, 87, 128, 129, 132, 163, 164, 201, 206, 207, 218, 219, 224, 225, 308, 310
  Selous, 1, 132, 303, 306–12
  Southern Reserve (Kenya), 208, 233
  transboundary 232–34, 256
Rhodesia, 153, 154, 181, 238, 239
Rominten, 207
Rovuma, 47, 51, 90, 93, 130, 167
Ruaha (river), 123, 125, 132, 165
Rufiji 120, 123, 125, 126, 129, 141, 209, 214. *See also* reserves, Rufiji
Rutenganyo, 77
Schorfheide, 22, 207
Selous Game Reserve, 1, 132, 303, 306–12
Senckenberg Museum of Natural History Frankfurt, 275
Serengeti, 1, 220–21, 303, 304
Serengeti Research Institute, 305
Southern Reserve (Kenya), 208, 233

Sukuma, 3, 4, 46, 152, 192
Tabora, 43, 47, 69, 84, 163, 167, 168, 172n36, 222, 223
Tanga, 43, 148, 159, 180
Uhehe, 43, 46, 48, 56, 93, 95, 129, 219
Ukambani, 43
Ukimbu, 48, 56
Ukonongo, 56
Ulanga, 51, 81, 123, 125, 215
Unyamwezi, 43, 48, 50, 52, 55, 56, 83, 97n12, 167–8, 192
Unyanyembe, 84
Urania (Berlin), 273, 277
Usagara, 48

Usambara, 116, 120, 143, 144, 148, 155, 239
Ussangu, 52, 83, 93, 124
Uzigua, 49, 85, 152
Vuga, 48–49
Wembere, 46, 215, 218, 219
Yellowstone
    as a game reserve, 212, 288
    national park, 6, 22, 211–12
    translation to East Africa, 211–14
Zambezi, 46, 51
Zanzibar, 21, 24, 40, 42–43, 46, 47, 50, 51, 53, 67, 70, 85, 124, 125, 159, 236, 241, 243, 260n12

General

A

adventure, 76
Afrikaner, 4, 143, 145, 147. *See also* Boers
agency
    animal, 11, 47, 58
    indigenous, 19
    nonhuman, 152
    and trust, 58
akida (Pl. *maakida*), 80, 104n109, 163, 167, 222
Allgemeiner Deutscher Jagdschutz-Verein, 157
Anglo-Boer War, 4, 246, 248
animal
    agency, 11, 47, 58
    characteristic animal, 17, 30n71, 212, 278, 287, 290
    charismatic animal, 13, 74, 76, 184, 212, 215, 250, 276, 278, 286, 288, 290, 305
    commodification, 4, 21, 279, 281
    domestication 86, 87, 155–56, 247, 281, 282
    habituation, 218, 225
    migration, 239–40, 251, 257
    trapping of, 36, 38, 40, 166, 223, 272, 274
anti-Americanism, 212

antipoaching, 223, 304–5, 306, 311
armchair conservationist, 281
askari, 25n15, 81, 82, 110, 115, 166, 180, 182, 183, 218, 222

B

Baka, 133
bear (European brown), 280, 289
Bena, 48, 51, 123, 124
big game hunting, 20, 73–79, 80–85, 116, 145–46, 162, 174n67, 192–93, 236, 246, 272, 277, 300, 305, 310–11. *See also* commercial hunting, elephant hunting, hunting
big man/men, 14, 21, 36–37, 50–56, 84, 86, 88, 93, 95, 96, 112, 119, 121, 129, 130, 131, 219
billiards, 42
biocoenosis, 213
biological groups, 274–75. *See also* diorama
Bisa, 42
bison
    European, 280, 287, 288–89, 290
    North American, 202, 212, 236, 280, 287, 288
Blue Book (Correspondence relating to the Preservation of Wild Animals in Africa, 1906), 161, 254–55

Boers, 4, 143, 146, 147, 148, 164, 166, 185, 243
Brehms Tierleben, 274
Bund Heimatschutz, 284
Bund zur Erhaltung der Naturdenkmäler aus dem Tier- und Pflanzenreiche, 284
bushmeat. *See* game meat, meat

C
cash crops, 120, 208. *See also* cotton, rubber, tobacco
cattle, 2–5, 36, 48, 149–55, 179–82, 239–40
    and colonial economy, 149–50, 179–181
    ranching, 3, 180–81
    trade, 4, 150, 179–80
    as tribute, 82, 83
    stock, 172n39, 194n7
    See also livestock, rinderpest
Chagga, 37, 84, 85, 147
charismatic megafauna, 13, 184, 215, 288. *See also* animal, charismatic
College of African Wildlife Management, 304
colonial rule, 7–8, 10, 12, 19, 90–96, 205, 281–82
    categories, 23
    and hunting, 76, 90–96
    and local allliances, 79, 84, 118, 124
    local roots, 14, 68, 87
    and race, 23, 223, 242, 245–46
colonial state
    as ivory trader, 71, 73, 94, 121–22
    local intermediaries, 80, 163, 167, 222–23 (*see also jumbe, akida*)
    representatives, 76, 81, 82, 85, 95, 96, 121, 131, 164, 168, 204, 206, 218, 222
colonization, 10–11, 36, 76, 143, 153, 160, 216, 253, 288, 310
Committee for the Taming of the African Elephant, 155–56
community-based resource management, 306

Conference on the Preservation of Wild Animals, Birds, and Fish in Africa (London 1900), 18, 112–13, 117, 156, 157, 204, 218, 232, 234, 235, 237–38, 245–53, 259
Conference on the Protection of African Fauna and Flora (London 1933), 259, 301, 303
Convention for the Preservation of Wild Animals, Birds and Fish in Africa (London 1900), 113, 114, 115, 117, 122, 157, 160, 161, 162, 204, 207, 233, 235, 246, 249, 251–53, 254, 255, 303
Convention on International Trade in Endangered Species of Wild Fauna and Flora (CITES), 252
connections
    transcontinental, 9, 16, 50
    transimperial, 14–16, 235–45
conservation
    and dictatorial regimes, 303
    forest, 120–21, 234
    imaginary, 304
    and National Socialism 289–90, 299, 301–4
    and preservation, 23
conspicuous consumption, 14, 42, 159, 187
consumerism
    African, 40–41
contact zone, 11, 14, 19, 27n40, 40, 52, 79, 94, 131
    ship as, 74, 242
cosmopolitan animal, 276
cotton, 3, 120, 150, 208, 215
Crown Land Declaration, 120, 205–6, 214
cultural landscape, 206, 214, 285, 288, 289

D
Das letzte Paradies (1932), 278, 300
dawa, 57, 78
demography
    colonial, 143, 145
    precolonial, 36
    See also population development

denial of coevalness, 16, 214
depopulation, 132, 152, 163, 308
Deutsche Kolonial-Gesellschaft (DKG), 68, 183, 186, 188, 255, 283
Deutscher Landwirtschaftsrat, 154, 155, 157
Deutsch-Ostafrikanische Gesellschaft (DOAG), 69, 88, 125
development, 141, 142, 160
Die Wildnis stirbt (1936), 278, 300
diorama, 76, 275
Dorobo, 37, 80, 147, 166

E
east coast fever, 150, 151, 153, 172n37, 239, 240
ecology
    moral, 21, 56–58
    political, 9, 10–11, 20, 21, 50, 68, 79, 112, 119, 168
    social, 21, 50–54
    of restoration, 286–89
    of rootedness, 22–23, 287
elephant
    agency, 47–48
    fear of extinction, 13, 44–45, 48, 155–56, 202
    forest elephant, 42
    Committee for the Taming of, 155–56
    mòkìlà, 133
    savanna elephant (*Loxodonta Africana Africana*), 42, 72
    tusklessness, 72
elephant hunting, 39, 40–48, 49–50, 56–57, 68, 77–78, 84, 123, 127–31, 166, 178, 238, 306
    ban of, 72, 92, 117, 130, 163, 164
    commercial, 147, 165, 204, 238
    professional, 84, 86, 91–92
    and rituals, 56–57, 77–78, 129
    and weaponry, 51, 52, 118
    See also hunting, ivory
elk, 280, 289, 290
emutai, 5. *See also* rinderpest

entomology, 153
environmental consciousness, 281, 301
Equus quagga, 202
extinction, 13, 44–45, 46, 48, 89, 114, 116, 155–56, 162, 185, 188, 191, 202, 217, 251, 253, 270, 274, 279, 280, 281, 282, 284, 287

F
fire
    environmental management by, 172n36, 221
firearms, 37, 43, 50–51, 52, 54, 56, 114, 115, 118, 119, 167, 190, 191, 243
fiscal ivory, 71, 72–73, 94, 121, 122
foraging, 37
forest conservation, 120–21, 237
forest reserves, 120–21, 125, 210
forestry, 11, 120, 211, 280, 302
framing, 8, 15, 23, 88, 147, 148, 158, 183, 186, 213, 243–44, 254, 255, 257, 276, 282, 285,
frasila, xi, 42, 69
Fritz-Thyssen-Foundation, 305
frontier
    ivory, 46–48, 68
    imperial, 74, 114, 236, 280
fundi (pl. *mafundi*), 51, 57, 84, 85, 91, 92, 122

G
game
    as *res nullius*, 148
    as biopolitical category, 87, 251
game laws
    of Belgian Congo, 253
    in Germany, 148–49
game reserves
    as heterotopias, 213–17, 310
    as landscapes of production, 120, 208, 216
    and national park effect, 225
    as *shamba ya bibi*, 224
    and wilderness, 213–17
    See also reserve
genocide, 12, 290

Germanic
    landscape, 287
    species, 287–8
Gesellschaft für Säugetierkunde, 301
Gesellschaft für technische Zusammenarbeit, 307–309
global history, 16
globality, 15, 281
global protection of nature. See *Weltnaturschutz*
globalization, 22, 35, 41, 244, 277
glossinae, 11, 151, 154, 172n36, 173n47, 181, 240
Gogo, 93
going native, 147, 159
governance, 8, 14, 16, 18, 21, 22, 112, 203, 204, 223, 238, 241, 246, 258, 284, 309
ground tusk, 54
    principle, 54–55, 91, 95
Gruppe Deutscher Kolonialwirtschaftlicher Unternehmungen, 302, 303

H
Habari za Wakilindi, 49
Hadzabe, 37
Hege, 157, 281, 285
Hehe, 69, 93, 124
Heimat, 17, 185, 277, 284, 285
Heimatpark, 289
Heimatschutz, 277, 278–79, 285, 289
Hemba, 48
heritage, 1, 8, 114, 183, 305, 306, 309
Hippotragus leucophaeus (bluebuck), 202
hongo, 55
hunter entrepreneur, 14, 51, 52, 55, 84, 85, 86, 93, 94, 192. *See also* Makua
hunter-gatherer societies, 35, 37, 118, 166, 206
hunter magician, 49, 51
hunter principle, 20, 21, 54, 90–96
hunting
    African hunting rituals, 38, 39, 51, 55, 56–58, 78
    African meanings, 56–58, 78
    and ancestral spirits, 39
    commercial hunting, 131, 147, 164, 165, 204, 238
    communal hunting, 38–39, 51, 222
    ethics 14, 23, 38, 39, 56–58, 75, 79, 88, 131, 146–47, 156, 157, 159, 310 (*see also Weidgerechtigkeit*)
    and gender, 14, 38, 39, 74–76, 77, 79, 144, 215, 243, 286, 289
    imperial ritual, 74–78, 191, 192, 206, 223, 310
    licenses, 71, 81, 84–86, 90–94, 114–115, 117, 118, 121, 125, 130, 141, 143–145, 147, 149, 159, 161–67, 188, 190, 193, 218, 238, 248, 252, 261n26, 317–21
    masculinity, 14, 74–76, 77, 79, 144, 215, 243, 286, 289
    as performance of power, 38, 40, 48–50, 74, 75, 77, 82, 96, 111, 145
    and property in land, 148–49, 170n19
    and sexual restrictions, 39
    and spiritual order, 39
    with the camera, 270–78, 301
    with nets, 38, 118, 128, 129, 168, 223, 250, 319
    with pitfalls, 118, 119, 168, 223, 250

I
identity
    environmental, 269, 286–90
    occupational, 37, 51
    settler, 146
    traveling identity, 52
Ikizu, 48
Ikoma, 48
imperial cosmopolitans, 243
imperialism
    and internationalism, 15, 244–45, 245–53, 254–59
    transimperial cooperation, 14–16, 235–45, 245–53
    See also metropole

intermediary, 14, 19, 84–86, 95, 104n109, 104n112, 218, 222–23. *See also* Fundi
International Hunting Exhibition (Berlin, 1937), 299, 302
internationalism
    antislavery, 70, 246
    environmental, 16, 245–53
    and imperialism, 15, 244–45, 245–53, 254–59
    scientific, 240
    veterinary, 239–41
International Union for the Conservation of Nature (IUCN), 251, 304
Iraqw, 3
ivory
    as currency, 21, 73, 82–83, 91
    commodification, 4, 21, 35, 40–43, 50, 56, 121, 123, 150
    commodity chain, 40–43
    dead ivory, 62n50
    export, 40, 41, 260n12 (*see also* ivory, weight)
    fiscal, 71, 72–73, 94, 121, 122
    fresh ivory, 71
    frontier, 46–48, 68
    revolution, 41
    statistics, 46, 67, 69–73, 91, 94, 121–122
    weight, 41, 71–73, 92, 113, 115, 117, 121–122, 163, 188, 190, 239, 243, 247–48, 250, 251, 253, 319
    See also ground tusk principle
ivory trade
    decline, 68–70, 71, 121
    development, 40–48, 68–73, 131–32
    networks, 21, 38, 40–44, 50, 69, 84, 92, 112, 120, 131
    value of, 68, 70, 82–83, 136n51

J
jumbe (pl. *majumbe*), 80, 104n112, 109–10, 120, 126, 128, 129, 130, 163, 167, 203, 218, 222. *See also akida*

K
Kamba, 37, 43, 53, 118
Kein Platz für wilde Tiere (1956), 300
Komitee zur Zähmung des Afrikanischen Elefanten, 155–56
Kommission zur Besserung des Wildschutzes in Deutsch-Afrika, 155–59, 235, 238, 254

L
labor market, 182, 192, 208
landscape
    cultural, 206, 214, 285, 288, 289
    German/Germanic, 287–90
    natural, 7, 268
    primeval, 214, 288
    of production, 120, 208, 216
    way of seeing, 216
Lebensraum, 287, 289
lion
    as vermin, 87
    predation on humans, 90, 128
livestock, 3, 4, 5, 6, 11, 37, 87, 89, 115, 141, 149–155, 160, 161, 179–82, 183, 184, 185, 188, 205, 219, 286. *See also* cattle
Livwelelo, 57
liwali, 70, 93, 97n11
lynx, 280, 289
London convention (1900), 113, 114, 115, 117, 122, 157, 160, 161, 162, 204, 207, 233, 235, 246, 249, 251–253, 254, 255, 303
Loxodonta Africana Africana. *See* elephant

M
Maasai, 2, 3–5, 7, 26n22, 37, 166, 180, 206, 209, 243, 300, 305
mafundi. *See* fundi
maji, 129
Maji Maji, 11, 12, 20, 21–22, 79, 109–134, 141, 142, 143, 159, 160, 161, 163, 167, 169n1, 179, 190, 192, 204, 212, 214, 217, 219, 221, 224, 308, 310, 311

Makua, 42, 50, 51–52, 57, 80, 93, 114, 118, 166
Max-Planck-Institute for Behavioral Physiology, Seewiesen, 305
meat, 37, 40, 49, 76, 78, 80, 81–82, 133, 148, 160, 180, 310
metropole, 12, 13, 16, 112, 142, 143, 148, 155, 159, 183, 210, 240, 241, 244, 268, 278, 283, 286
mganga, 57
middle ground, 20, 67, 68, 73, 79, 82, 83, 94, 131
mimicry
    by animals, 274
    as postcolonial concept, 94–95
mnyampara, 80
museums of natural history, 18, 76, 85, 113, 115, 158, 249, 268, 269, 274–75

N
nagana, 150–155, 181
Nata, 48
national park
    Bavarian Forest, 290
    as game reserve, 212, 288
    and respectability, 211–12
    and scientific research, 213
    Swiss, 210
    transfer of, 211–14, 283, 284
    typical or sublime nature, 212
    Yellowstone, 6, 22, 211–12
natural monument, 156, 157, 209, 287, 303. See also Naturdenkmal
Naturdenkmal, 156, 274, 282, 283, 285
Naturdenkmalpflege, 282–83
Naturschutz, 13, 23, 156–57, 185, 280, 284–85, 289, 301–2
    movement, 13, 17, 20, 156, 204, 257, 278–90, 299–304
    role of hunters, 13
    See also Weltnaturschutz
Naturschutzpark, 6, 7, 185–86, 188, 208–9, 212–13, 214, 216, 283–85. See also Heimatpark, national park
Naturvolk, 255, 258, 275
Natururkunden, 271, 274, 277

Ndamba, 51, 125
Ngindo, 42
Ngoni, 43, 55, 93, 124, 130
noble savage, 56, 276
Nyamwezi, 43, 48, 50, 52, 53, 56, 57, 69, 84, 93, 118, 168, 192

O
Office International pour le protection de la nature (Brussels), 259, 267n122
Operation Uhai, 306, 307
oral tradition, 48–50, 54, 129, 133

P
paradise, 156, 185, 189, 210, 214–15, 216–17, 229n67, 268, 269, 272, 275, 276, 278, 285, 300, 310
pastoralism, 4, 37, 206
piano, 41–42
Pleistocene, 78, 216–17, 281, 287, 288
poaching, 117, 223, 251, 304, 306, 308, 311
political ecology, 9, 10–11, 20, 21, 50, 68, 79, 112, 119, 168
population development, 36, 143, 145
porterage, 19, 43, 76, 80–82, 85, 126, 192
predators, 74, 76, 87, 111, 112, 119, 125, 128, 221, 250, 280, 286, 321
primeval landscape, 214, 288

R
Reichsforstamt, 302, 303
Reichstag (German Parliament), 67, 157, 222
reintroduction of species, 287–90
res nullius, 148
Rhipicephalus, 151
rifle
    breech-loading, 114, 118, 130, 139n105, 162, 166, 319, 320
    muzzle-loading, 38, 51, 52, 84, 117, 118, 162, 163, 166, 319, 320
rinderpest, 5, 22, 89, 149–155, 178, 179–182, 188, 202, 239, 251
Rowland Ward, 272, 311
rubber, 55, 70, 120, 121, 123

S

sadoka. See rinderpest
safari, 6, 7, 79, 80, 81, 100n54, 131, 156, 161, 163, 191–93, 233, 235, 239, 271, 273, 299, 305, 306, 307, 310
safari tourism, 191–93, 235, 307
Safari-Verlag, 300
Sandawe, 37
savanna, 2, 10, 38, 42, 184–85, 202, 209, 214–15, 216, 221, 275, 276, 287, 300, 305
    as garden Eden, 229n67
    and ideas of time, 214
    management by burning, 221
    and struggle for life, 215
    and wildlife, 161, 214, 216
Selous Conservation Programme, 307
Serengeti shall not die (film/book, 1959), 2, 278, 300
Shambaa, 37, 48–49
shape-shifting, 133
shauri, 95, 221, 223
shetani, 109, 140n118
shikar, 233
Shooting an Elephant (George Orwell, 1936), 110
slave trade, 70, 84, 88
Society for the Preservation of the Wild Fauna of the Empire, 157, 235, 238, 254–55
South Africa
    as reference, 154, 237, 239, 261n20
    tsetse policies, 181
sportsmanship, 23, 146, 273
Staatliche Stelle für Naturdenkmalpflege, 283, 301
strategy of extraversion, 41, 54, 305
Swahili, 14, 19, 37, 40, 42, 43, 47, 51, 52, 54, 69, 70, 79, 80, 86, 94, 114, 123, 124, 151, 235, 236

T

tax labor, 119
theileriosis, 151
threatened species, 113, 131, 162, 191, 211, 250, 251, 256, 258, 280, 281, 289

Tierschutz (protection of animals), 23, 161
Tindiga, 166, 219
transfer, 12, 15, 16, 18, 94, 120, 150–51, 208, 210, 211–12, 237, 239–40, 241–42, 287
    of hunting rituals, 51
    of the national park idea, 211–14, 283, 284
    transimperial, 14–16, 235–45
trapping, 36, 38, 40, 223, 272, 274
trophy, 77–78, 238, 268, 273, 310, 311
trust, 14, 58
trypanosomiasis
    animal, 37, 150–54, 239 (*see also* nagana)
    human, 150–52, 239
    See also tsetse
tsetse, 4, 11, 36, 37, 132, 151–155, 157, 158, 168, 180, 241, 278
    controversy, 151–55, 157–59, 174n67, 186, 204, 208, 213
    fly, 36, 151–55, 168, 181
    See also glossinae
tusklessness, 72
tusks. *See* ivory

U

Ujamaa, 306
uwuyege, 50

V

vaccination, 153, 179, 182
Verein Hirschmann, 157
Verein Naturschutzpark, 6, 283
Vernichtungskrieg (against elephants), 44, 282
veterinary science, 15, 76, 142, 239, 240, 244
    as transimperial project, 239–41
Voigtländer (publishing house), 271, 277
vulnerability, 39, 128, 129, 167–68, 224

W

wage labor, 119, 160, 205
Wakilindi, 49

Weidgerechtigkeit, 23, 75, 79, 88, 131, 146–47, 156, 157, 159
    as self-civilization, 159
Weltnaturschutz, 178, 235, 254–59, 281, 301
whiteness, 242
wilderness, 1, 7, 11, 16–17, 22, 36, 58, 75, 132, 161, 185, 193, 202, 206, 207, 212, 213–17, 220, 221, 224, 268–70, 270–76, 289, 290, 300, 301, 309, 310. *See also* savanna
wildlife
    control of, 37, 149
    diseases (*see* nagana, rinderpest, tsetse)
    damage, 5, 115, 129, 132, 149, 163, 164, 167–68, 183, 205, 219, 224
    and game (terminology), 26n23
    as a Pleistocene remnant, 78, 216–17, 281, 287, 288
    transcontinental governance, 8, 9–10, 252–53
wild pigs, 49, 74, 87, 125, 128–29, 132, 152, 154, 167, 168
Wild und Hund (German hunting periodical), 20, 75
World Heritage (UNESCO), 1, 306
World Wildlife Fund (WWF), 300, 304, 307

Y

Yao, 42, 51, 58
Yeke, 49–50

Z

Zaramo, 128, 129–30
zoogeography, 17, 76, 174n66, 202, 287

www.ingramcontent.com/pod-product-compliance
Lightning Source LLC
Chambersburg PA
CBHW072142100526
44589CB00015B/2052